U0904401

Regulation of Investment Management

Cases and Materials for Study of the U.S. 40 Acts

美国投资管理经典案例研究

姚承曦（Chengxi Yao） 著

中国金融出版社

责任编辑：曹亚豪
责任校对：刘　明
责任印制：赵燕红

图书在版编目（CIP）数据

美国投资管理经典案例研究/姚承曦著. —北京：中国金融出版社，2018.11
ISBN 978 - 7 - 5049 - 9792 - 0

Ⅰ. ①美…　Ⅱ. ①姚…　Ⅲ. ①投资管理—案例—美国　Ⅳ. ①F837.124.8

中国版本图书馆CIP数据核字（2018）第232115号

出版发行　中国金融出版社
社址　北京市丰台区益泽路2号
市场开发部　（010）63266347，63805472，63439533（传真）
网上书店　http://www.chinafph.com
（010）63286832，63365686（传真）
读者服务部　（010）66070833，62568380
邮编　100071
经销　新华书店
印刷　北京市松源印刷有限公司
尺寸　187毫米×252毫米
印张　46
字数　990千
版次　2018年11月第1版
印次　2018年11月第1次印刷
定价　89.00元
ISBN 978 - 7 - 5049 - 9792 - 0
如出现印装错误本社负责调换　联系电话（010）63263947

序言

1998年3月，国泰基金、南方基金二家基金公司成立，作为国内首批规范的基金管理公司，开启了"新基金时代"。我国从此有了真正意义上的专业机构投资者。

机构投资者的市场规模是资本市场成熟的重要标志。截至2018年3月底，我国境内共有基金管理公司116家，公募基金资产合计12.37万亿元，基金数量5085只。值得一提的是，公募基金持有人总户数已经超过6亿户，其中，绝大部分基金账户的资产规模在5万元以下，公募基金成为普惠金融的典型代表，为投资人创造了可观的回报。二十年来公募基金累计实现利润、为投资者分红均超过2万亿元。在这个过程中，公募基金逐步建立了先进的管理制度，具体体现在强制托管、公允估值、组合投资、公开披露、独立运作等制度安排上。并且，公募基金已经发展成为落实信托关系到位、运作模式透明、对持有人利益保护充分的资产管理行业典范。

自2013年6月《证券投资基金法》正式将私募基金纳入监管范围后，私募基金也已成为大资管行业的新兴重要组成部分，私募基金在阳光化、规范化运作中实现了跨越式发展。截至2018年6月底，中国证券投资基金业协会（中基协）已登记私募证券投资基金管理人8776家，已备案基金35983只，基金规模达2.54万亿元。此外，还有相当规模的保险资金、养老基金等集合投资的专业机构投资者入市。随着资本市场的不断开放，截至2018年6月底，累计有287家QFII机构合计获得994.59亿美元、196家RQFII机构合计获得6158.52亿元人民币投资额度，境外机构和个人持股规模达1855亿美元（约1.28万亿元人民币），占A股流通股市值的比例为3.18%。有147只保险公司产品投资于513只A股，合计持有市值1.37

万亿元，全国社保基金共通过 41 个投资主体持有 555 只 A 股，合计持仓 2436.22 亿元。有 35 家信托公司投资于 82 只 A 股，合计持仓 532.23 亿元。

基金业的发展离不开行业规范的保驾护航：2003 年 10 月，《证券投资基金法》发布，明确了公募基金的法律地位，奠定了行业发展的基石；2009 年《刑法修正案（七）》增加了“利用未公开信息交易罪”、修订“内幕交易、泄露内幕信息罪”部分规定，确立了基金“老鼠仓”和利益输送行为的刑事责任，是基金行业法律规制的重大突破；2012 年 6 月，中国证券投资基金业协会成立，为基金行业自律监管奠定了组织基础；2013 年 6 月，新修订的《证券投资基金法》开始实施；2016 年 2 月，由中国证监会与中国人民银行联合颁布了《货币市场基金监督管理办法》；2017 年 6 月，财政部、中国人民银行和中国证监会联合发布《关于规范开展政府和社会资本合作项目资产证券化有关事宜的通知》；2017 年 8 月，国务院法制办公室发布了《私募投资基金管理暂行条例(征求意见稿)》。我们可以看到，我国基金业在贯彻执行《中共中央关于制定国民经济和社会发展第十三个五年规划的建议》中提出的“健全符合我国国情和国际标准的监管规则，实现金融风险监管全覆盖”方面取得了重要成果，不断完善的制度建设保证了基金业的可持续发展。

当然，与西方发达国家相比，我国的基金业仍然还有很长的路要走。学习和借鉴发达国家资本市场机构投资者监管机制、监管标准和监管理念，对于我国的基金行业的进一步发展，有着重要的理论意义与实践价值。尽管证券投资基金行业在我国得到了蓬勃发展，但近年来尤其是在私募基金领域出现了涉嫌非法集资、高管跑路等问题，甚至引发了群体性事件。私募基金管理公司向非合格投资者推介基金、未按规定办理基金备案手续、未按合同约定向投资者披露基金定期报告、未对投资者风险识别能力和风险承担能力进行评估等问题相当普遍。这一系列现实问题都反映了我们加强私募基金监管的迫切需求，无论是从立法还是从具体监管经验方面都有提升的空间。

由汕头大学商学院金融监管学教授姚承曦撰写的“REGULATION OF INVESTMENT MANAGEMENT—CASES AND MATERIALS FOR STUDY OF THE U.S. 40 ACTS”（《美国投资管理经典案例研究》）是我国第一部全面和权威地研究美国证券投资基金及机构投资者监管的专著，填补了资本市场机构投资者规制的空白。

该书以普惠金融的代表——共同基金的规制为研究重点，同时对从事集合理财的其他类型的机构，例如：保险资产管理公司、银行集合信托基金、养老与退休基金、资产证券化集合投资基金、私募基金的特殊监管机制进行了阐析。既有对美国《投资基金法》和《投资顾问法》主要监管理念与法规的系统分析，又深入研究了在美国基金监管史上产生重大影响和代表性的经典案例。作者以通俗易懂的英文风格行文，将抽象的理论与具体的案例融合，进行了深入而广泛的理论研究与文献综述，尤其是书中大量的代表性案例，详细地阐述了相关规则的历史背景及其借鉴。

姚承曦教授在美国生活了 30 年，有着很强的法学与金融学背景和丰富的监管与实践经验。我相信，该书的出版对我国证券投资基金以及其他机构投资者的监管有着重要的指导意义。

国务院参事室金融研究中心研究员
民革中央经济委员会副主任
何杰
二○一八年八月

Foreword

As of the end of 2017, the aggregate value of assets managed by United States registered investment companies, comprised of mutual funds, exchange-traded funds, closed-end funds, and unit investment trusts, totaled $22.5 trillion. Mutual funds are the dominant format, accounting for $18.7 trillion of this amount. Approximately 45.4% of all U.S. households own investment company shares (figures from Investment Company Institute's 2018 Fact Book (58th ed.). Registered funds serve as investment vehicles through which ordinary citizens save for retirement, education of their children and other financial goals. Investment companies make available to investors of modest means diversification and professional management. Through the financial markets, professional fund managers allocate the savings of millions of individuals to businesses and governments. This allocation of capital, in turn, stimulates economic growth and job creation, as businesses that rely on financial markets use this capital to fund their enterprises, develop new technologies and hire employees. Over the 78 years since enactment of the Investment Company Act of 1940 (1940 Act), this virtuous cycle has continued to operate, albeit with occasional slowdowns.

The bulk of investment company investors are individuals of limited wealth and little experience with financial institutions. Laws, and confidence that those laws will be enforced, are necessary if these investors are to trust their savings to anonymous institutions. The 1940 Act is largely the result of a report produced between 1938 and 1940 by the U.S. Securities and Exchange Commission (SEC) documenting excesses and abuses in the investment company industry. Industry leaders recognized that responsible regulation would contribute greatly to regaining public confidence and cooperated in crafting the new law. The SEC's report documented numerous instances of self-dealing and overreaching by fund insiders, and insiders' use of pyramid ownership structures to control funds while risking a disproportionately small amount of capital. In the 1920's, few mutual funds existed; closed-end funds dominated the market. Many of these funds were controlled by large financial institutions that also earned revenue from underwriting and brokerage businesses. To earn underwriting fees, these firms caused the funds that they controlled to purchase securities of dubious value. The contents of fund portfolios were not disclosed to investors. Thus, this abuse was not readily detectable. Firms caused controlled funds to engage in excessive securities trading to generate commissions for affiliated brokers. Funds diluted the value of fund shares sold to the public by issuing shares to insiders as compensation or at discounted prices. If share prices fell, funds would sometimes repurchase shares selectively from insiders or affiliates. Closed-end funds used substantial amounts of leverage, and that leverage magnified the profits from a generally rising stock market. Partly due to this, closed-end fund shares traded at double digit premiums to the value of the securities that they held. With the precipitous fall of stock prices in late 1929 and subsequent depression, debt servicing requirements left little or no income for distribution to shareholders. As losses mounted, and investors needed cash, sellers outnumbered buyers, and closed-end fund share prices fell from steep premiums to discounts. Losses were less severe among the few mutual funds available at that time. Because of the need to meet redemption requests, these funds used little or no leverage. Nevertheless, the entire investment company industry's image was tarnished.

The provisions of the 1940 Act were designed to address specific, recently experienced, and not just theoretical, excesses and abuses. First, the 1940 Act severely limits leverage by closed-end funds by requiring at least 300% asset coverage for borrowings and 200% asset coverage for preferred stock. (An exception was later made for "business development companies" (BDCs), *i.e.*, public venture capital companies regulated as a specialized type of closed-end funds, for which asset coverage must be at least 150%.) Mutual funds are limited to bank borrowings, and these must have asset coverage of at least 300%. Next, the 1940 prohibits a fund adviser or its affiliates from issuing securities to, or buying assets from the fund that it manages. Moreover, a fund may not purchase a security from an underwriting syndicate if its adviser or an affiliate of the adviser is a member of that syndicate. In addition, a fund may not engage in a joint enterprise or transaction if its adviser, principal underwriter, promoter or any of their affiliated persons participates in the transaction as principal. This last provision is particularly expansive. Determining exactly what conduct constitutes a prohibited joint transaction has frustrated fund lawyers for decades. In this regard, Professor Yao's discussion does not provide an answer, but she identifies the important cases and commentaries.

The 1940 Act's many specific and detailed prohibitions and requirements might have stifled innovation but for provisions that give the SEC broad authority to grant exemptions from its restrictions by means of orders applicable to specific transactions or funds or by rules more generally applicable to the fund industry. This authority is supplemented by SEC staff no-action letters that do not have the force of law but provide useful guidance on a somewhat expedited basis. Professor Yao's discussion of these ancillary developments is particularly thorough. Included are both the exemptive orders that made exchange traded funds possible, and interval fund experiment under rule 23c-3, a rule that permits a closed-end fund to redeem a limited percentage of its securities at specified, fixed intervals (*e.g.*, each quarter or each year) as an experiment intended, in part, to address the discount at which closed-end fund shares often trade. Also included is a no-action letter issued to Eaton Vance Management during the recent financial crisis to facilitate financing of certain closed-end funds. This letter was issued in coordination with the Internal Revenue Service of the U.S. Department of the Treasury and is an example of regulatory flexibility when circumstances demand it.

Today, as China's gross domestic product (GDP) is poised to surpass that of the United States, its regulated fund market is much smaller both in absolute terms and as a percentage of GDP. This is unsurprising in view of the relatively short time capital markets have had to develop. The potential benefits of a well-regulated investment company industry both to individual investors and the nation are great. Professor Yao provides a well-organized, comprehensive and up to date survey of U.S. fund regulation. She appears to have read and digested not only every case involving the 1940 Act but every important commentary on those cases.

James M. Curtis
Branch Chief, Division of Investment Management
U.S. Securities and Exchange Commission (1991 – 2017)
United States
August 2018

美国证券与交易委员会
投资管理司前任官员（一九九一至二〇一七年）

Acknowledgements

致谢

本书撰写过程中受到多位领导和同事的支持与帮助，在此难以一一尽表，仅选择其中代表致以诚挚的谢意：汕头大学副校长林丹明教授、汕头大学商学院前院长徐宗玲教授，自我从美国金融业界到中国教学以来，始终是我的教育事业的良师益友和为人之师的楷模。美国 Skadden, Arps, Slate, Meagher & Flom LLP 律师公司投资管理部主任 Michael K. Hoffman，中国金融出版社金融文化研训院院长刘钊博士，给我的作品提出了宝贵的专业意见。汕头大学研究生院副院长、商学院金融专业王建华教授，汕头大学商学院院长徐二明教授，党总支书记高见副教授，汕头大学国际处处长廖学全博士等全方位热心支持我的科研工作。

勤奋与多才多智的图书馆文献与索引工作人员为这本书的研究过程做出了重大贡献，其中包括：汕头大学图书馆学科馆员谢芦青老师、曾昭鸿老师、万庐山老师，美国麻省法院图书馆数位馆员，美国麻省波士顿学院法学院法学文献研究员兼讲师 Karen Breda 老师等。此外，也一并感谢中国清华大学图书馆、中国图书进出口（集团）总公司等单位的大力支持。他们是我的研究工作不可缺少的宝贵资源。

姚承曦
二〇一八年七月
于中国广东汕头大学

Convention Used in Case Editing

Footnote numbering used in edited and excerpted case studies generally consecutively follows the footnote numbering used in the original documents. Where a footnote appearing in an original document is omitted in the edited/excerpted case study, the footnote number sequence of the edited/excerpted case study may differ from the sequence of the original document.

本书获汕头大学研究出版基金资助

This Book was supported by a research grant from Shantou University.

Statement of President Roosevelt
On Signing Two Statutes to Protect Investors

August 23, 1940
http://www.presidency.ucsb.edu/ws/?pid=15993

"I have just signed the Investment Company Act of 1940 and the Investment Advisers' Act of 1940; . . . They mark another milestone in this Administration's vigorous program—begun in 1933 and supplemented in 1934, . . .—to protect the investor. . . . I have great hopes that the Act which I have signed today will enable the investment trust industry to fulfill its basic purpose as a vehicle to diversify the small investors' risk and to provide a valuable source of equity capital for deserving small and new business enterprises which the investment bankers have been unable to finance."

SUMMARY OF CONTENTS

TABLE OF CONTENTS

Chapter 1 Concept of Investment Company

> "... investment companies are affected with a national public interest in that, ... (2) the principal activities of such companies—investing, reinvesting, and trading in securities—are conducted by use of the mails and means and instrumentalities of interstate commerce, . . . ; (3) such companies customarily invest and trade in securities issued by, and may dominate and control or otherwise affect the policies and management of, companies engaged in business in interstate commerce; (4) such companies are media for the investment in the national economy..."
>
> ----Investment Company Act of 1940, § 1(a)

Section 1.1 Primary Engagement: Managing Investments *vs* Operating Business

Laws & Rules Highlight:

"Investment Company": Statutory Definitions & Selected Exclusions

IC Act (15 USC 80a-1 *et seq.*)

- § 3(a)(1) (***primarily investment business***: *three alternative tests of ICs*)
  - § 3(a)(1)(A) (***classic/orthodox IC:*** *issuer is or holds out as being "engaged* ***primarily*** *in" investment company business*)
  - § 3(a)(1)(B) (*archaic IC: issuer of face-amount certificates of installment type*)
  - § 3(a)(1)(C) (***presumptive/prima facie IC:*** *issuer "****engaged*** *in" investment company business and having over* ***40%*** *of its total assets on an unconsolidated basis in "****investment securities****"*)
- § 3(b) (***primarily non-investment business***: *exclusions from* ***§ 3(a)(1)(C)***)
  - § 3(b)(1) (*self-operating exclusion: excludes an* ***issuer*** *"****primarily*** *engaged in"* ***non****-investment company business, directly or through* ***wholly-owned*** *subsidiaries*)
  - § 3(b)(2) (*SEC exemptive order exclusion: excludes an* ***issuer*** *"****primarily*** *engaged in"* ***non****-investment company business, directly, or through* ***majority-owned*** *subsidiaries, or through* ***controlled*** *companies conducting* ***similar*** *types of businesses*)
  - § 3(b)(3) (*excludes* ***wholly-owned subsidiaries*** *of industrial corporate parent: where both parent and subsidiaries are presumptive ICs solely due to § 3(a)(1)(C), and parent company is excluded from IC by § 3(b)(1) or § 3(b)(2)—requirements designed to prevent a parent company from circumventing § 3(a)(1)(C) by downstreaming all its*

investments into a wholly-owned subsidiary)

- § 3(c) (***specific types of issuers***: *exclusions from* ***§ 3(a)***)
  - §§ 3(c)(1) & 3(c)(7) (*exclusions for private investment funds*)
  - § 3(c)(2) (*exclusions for brokers, dealers, and underwriters*)
  - § 3(c)(3) (*exclusions for banks, bank common trust funds, and insurance companies*)
  - §§ 3(c)(5)(A)-(B)-(C) (*exclusions for commercial finance (factoring & sales financing) companies, and mortgage banking issuers*)
  - § 3(c)(11) (*exclusions for qualified pension and profit-sharing plans, bank collective investment funds and insurance company separate accounts consisting solely of assets of such qualified plans*)

Laws & Rules Highlight:
"Investment Company": Selected SEC Safe Harbor Exemptions*

17 CFR §§ 270.0-1 *et seq.*

*Safe harbor rules obviate the need for case-by-case SEC exemptive order process under § 3(b)(2). [IC-10937, 44 FR 66608 (1979)]. "A determination under either § 3(b)(2) or § 3(b)(1) that an issuer primarily is engaged in a noninvestment business also means that it is not an investment company under § 3(a)(1)." [IC-19566, 58 FR 38095, 38096 n.10 (1993)]

Rule 3a-1 Certain Prima Facie Investment Companies

*Rule 3a-1 deems certain "**prima facie**" ICs under § 3(a)(1)(C) "**not to be in fact**" ICs **if** the issuer **(1)** is a prima facie IC solely by virtue of § 3(a)(1)(C); **(2)** consolidating with its wholly-owned subsidiaries, has no more than 45% of assets invested in and no more than 45% of net income derived from investment securities; and **(3)** is not a special situation investment company; and it has primary control over controlled companies, which are not ICs and through which the issuer engages in non-investment business.*

[Certain Prima Facie Investment Companies, IC-10937, 44 FR 66608 (1979); IC-11551, 46 FR 6879 (1981)]

Rule 3a-2 Transient Investment Companies

*Rule 3a-2 excludes "**transient ICs**" from §§ 3(a)(1)(A) and 3(a)(1)(C), **if** the issuer **(1)** does not hold itself out as being engaged primarily in investment business; **(2)** has a bona fide intent to be primarily engaged in a noninvestment business within the safe harbor period; and **(3)** is subject to a maximum safe harbor period of one year and one reliance on the safe harbor rule in any three-year period—to both accommodate temporary investment needs of transient ICs and prevent circumvention of IC Act by non-transient ICs.*

[Transient Investment Companies, IC-10943, 44 FR 67152 (1979); IC-11552, 46 FR 6882 (1981)]

Rule 3a-3 Certain Investment Companies Owned by Companies Which Are Not Investment Companies

*Rule 3a-3 **extends § 3(b)(3)** statutory exclusion for **wholly-owned subsidiaries** of corporate parent, and deems certain subsidiaries not to be IC, where **(1)** such **subsidiaries** solely due to specified technical reasons do not meet § 3(b)(3) statutory exclusion; **(2) corporate parent** is not an IC under § 3(a), or is excluded from IC by § 3(b)(1) or § 3(b)(2), or is deemed not to be an IC under Rule 3a-1; and **(3) corporate parent and wholly-owned subsidiaries** on a consolidated basis have no more than 45% of assets in and no more than 45% of net income from investment securities, as a safeguard to prevent use of corporate structural arrangement to circumvent IC Act. Notwithstanding Rule 3a-3 exclusion for the subsidiaries, the parent and subsidiary relationships can be collapsed and the totality of the corporate arrangement be deemed an IC under § 3(a)(1)(A).*

[Certain Investment Companies Owned by Companies Which Are Not Investment Companies, IC-10944, 44 FR 67150 (1979); IC-11553, 46 FR 6884 (1981)

Rule 3a-5 Exemption for Subsidiaries Organized to Finance the Operations of Domestic or Foreign Companies

The ***primary purpose*** *of a "****finance subsidiary****" of an industrial parent is to finance the business operations of the parent (or other subsidiaries of the parent which are not ICs), by issuing debt or nonvoting preferred securities to the public, remitting the proceeds to its parent company, and receiving securities of the parent as consideration. By thus issuing its own securities and investing in or holding securities of its parent, a finance subsidiary could be an IC under § 3(a)(1)(A) or § 3(a)(1)(C). Rule 3a-5 exempts finance subsidiaries of industrial parents from IC, subject to* ***conditions*** *including parent's unconditional guarantee of payment on finance subsidiary's securities issued to or held by the public, and based on the* ***rationale*** *that such a finance subsidiary is* ***essentially a conduit*** *for the industrial parent to raise capital for its business operations (or those of its other subsidiaries).*

[Exemption from the Definition of Investment Company for Certain Finance Subsidiaries of United States and Foreign Private Issuers, IC-14275, 49 FR 49441 (1984); IC-5330, 33 FR 5294 (1968)]

Rule 3a-8 Certain Research and Development Companies

Rule 3a-8 is designed to exclude ***bona fide R&D companies*** *from IC status under § 3(a)(1)(A) and § 3(a)(1)(C), applying a "****use,****" instead of a "****composition,****" of assets and income test:* ***(1)*** *R&D expenses substantial, and investment-related expenses insignificant, of total expenses;* ***(2)*** *R&D expenses consuming sufficient burn rate on investments; and* ***(3)*** *investments in securities to conserve capital and liquidity until R&D uses, allowing limited "strategic investments" pursuant to collaborative R&D arrangements.*

[Certain Research and Development Companies, IC-19566, 58 FR 38095 (1993); IC-25835, 67 FR 71915 (2002); IC-26077, 68 FR 37046 (2003)]

Topic 1 Operating Company *vs* Investment Company

Laws & Rules Highlight

IC Act (15 USC 80a-1 *et seq.*)

Section 3. Definition of Investment Company

(a)(1) When used in this title, "investment company" means any issuer which—

(A) is or holds itself out as being engaged primarily, or proposes to engage primarily, in the business of investing, reinvesting, or trading in securities;

(B) * * * ; or

(C) is engaged or proposes to engage in the business of investing, reinvesting, owning, holding, or trading in securities, and owns or proposes to acquire investment securities having a value exceeding 40 per centum of the value of such issuer's total assets (exclusive of Government securities and cash items) on an unconsolidated basis.

Case Study 1: The Tonopah "Investment Company" Story

Organized as a conventional mining company in 1901, The Tonopah Mining Company of Nevada was primarily engaged in the mining business, operating mining properties both directly and through majority owned subsidiaries. Over time, Tonopah's subsidiaries became largely inactive and its mining operations mostly discontinued. On the other hand, Tonopah acquired a large portfolio of mining securities, which comprised over 90% of its total assets and were the source of most of its income.

The SEC applied a five-factor test for "primary" engagement, which has since become the standard approach to primary engagement determination: ***"engaged primarily" in investment business*** under § 3(a)(1)(A), or, ***"primarily engaged" in non-investment business*** under § 3(b)* *[Certain Prima Facie Investment Companies, IC-10937, 44 FR 66608, 66610 n.24 (1979)]. The **Tonopah Five Factors** are the following: (1) the company's historical development; (2) its public representations of policy; (3) the activities of its officers and directors; (4) the nature of its present assets; (5) the sources of its present income.

Noting that the nature of the ***assets*** (invested in investment securities) and sources of the ***income*** (derived from investment securities) of Tonopah was such as to "***lead***

investors to believe" that the principal activity of the company was trading and investing in securities, the SEC found Tonopah's primary engagement had become one of investment business, and Tonopah an investment company.

In *re* The Tonopah Mining Co. of Nevada
IC-1084, 26 SEC 426 (1947)

Case Study 2: The Presto "Operating Company" Story

Founded in 1905, National Presto designed, manufactured, and marketed small appliances and housewares sold by retailers. In 2002, alleging that since at least 1994, Presto's holdings of investment securities had exceeded 40% of its total assets thus failing the 40% statistical test in § 3(a)(1)(C) and it had derived more than 45% of its net income from securities, the SEC sought a court order to require Presto either to register as an investment company, or to restructure its business to comply with the IC Act. The District Court ruled against Presto.

In reversing, the Seventh Circuit described the "***model inadvertent investment company***" as "*one in which the firm has sold all or almost all of its assets, reduced its operations to a skeleton staff, and purports to be looking for acquisitions but never seems to find them*." In contrast, tested against the **Tonopah Five Factors**: (1) Presto maintained active business operations in product markets; (2) Presto presented itself to the public and to investors as an operating company, whose net income and stock price could increase or decrease as a result of operating profits; (3) 95% of Presto managers' time was devoted to running the firm's products and businesses, instead of managing investment portfolio; (5) Presto's operating profits exceeded investment profits for the decade as a whole, demonstrating Presto was "primarily" an operating business.

Tested against Tonopah Factor (4), nature of assets: more than 60% of Presto's book assets were investment securities. Yet determination of investment company status simply by using GAAP asset figures "has a potential to mislead," as substantial assets such as patents and trademarks do not show up on a company's balance sheet as assets.

The Seventh Circuit concluded: "***Reasonable investors*** would treat Presto as an operating company rather than a competitor with a closed-end mutual fund.... It follows that Presto is not an investment company."

SEC v. Nat'l Presto Indus., Inc.

486 F.3d 305 (7th Cir. 2007)

[***Procedural history***: SEC v. Nat'l Presto Indus., Inc., Civil Action No. 02 C 5027 (ND Ill., E. Div. July 25, 2002); 397 F. Supp.2d 943 (ND Ill., E. Div. 2005), *rev'd*, 486 F.3d 305 (7th Cir. 2007)]

Post-*Tonopah* Note:[Biblio]

R&D Companies: Factors Determining "Primary Engagement"

For **operating companies**, traditionally two factors of the Tonopah test most significantly determine whether a company is "*primarily engaged*" in investment business under § 3(a) or is "*primarily engaged*" in non-investment business under § 3(b): the company's ***asset composition***, as evidenced by the percentage of the company's assets invested in investment securities; and the company's ***sources of income***, as evidenced by the percentage of the company's income derived from investment securities.[1; 2]

R&D companies, as the term is defined in financial accounting standards, typically have a lengthy, distinct life cycle. At the "start-up phase," the company raises capital and acquires personnel and facilities. At the "product development phase," the company raises additional capital and conducts R&D activities. At the "mature product sales phase," the company begins to realize significant revenues from the sale of products it has developed.[3a] ***Development-phase R&D companies*** may have few assets other than investment securities. Long before reaching the mature product phase, R&D companies must raise capital; must *invest the proceeds in securities*, many of which "investment securities," pending use of the principal and return on the investments to fund their lengthy period of product development. To jointly conduct R&D activities under strategic alliance, one R&D company may *purchase a non-controlling equity stake*, a type of "investment securities," in another R&D company. Such *securities investment* and *strategic investment* activities may cause an R&D company to fall within the statutory definition of IC and to fail to qualify for an exclusion from IC status, if the "primary" business of an R&D company is determined by application of the ***traditional "assets-and-income composition" test***.[3b]

Modifying the traditional Tonopah test,[4] R&D company safe harbor Rule 3a-8 adopts an ***"assets-and-income use" test***, to ensure that bona fide R&D companies are not incompatibly regulated as ICs and that companies engaged primarily in the investment business are regulated under the IC Act.[3b] For an R&D company to establish that it is ***primarily engaged in a noninvestment business*** thus qualifying for the safe harbor:[3c]

- its ***R&D expenses*** must constitute a "*substantial*" percentage, and its ***investment-related expenses*** must be an "*insignificant*" percentage, of its total expenses for the specified period;
- each of its investments in securities must be a "***capital preservation***" investment until needed to fund its R&D operations, except *limited* "strategic investments made pursuant to collaborative R&D arrangements" and *de minimis* "non-capital preservation" investments;
- its investments in securities must meet a ***minimum*** "***burn rate***" to fund R&D activities, negating the running of a perpetual investment program.

Bibliography

1. Certain Prima Facie Investment Companies, IC-10937, 44 FR 66608 (1979)
2. ICOS Corp.; Order Granting Exemption, IC-19334, 58 FR 15392 (1993)
3. Certain Research and Development Companies: **3a.** IC-19566, 58 FR 38095 (1993); **3b.** IC-25835, 67 FR 71915 (2002); **3c.** IC-26077, 68 FR 37046 (2003)
4. Lybecker & Chambers, *Definition of Investment Company: A Riddle Wrapped in a Mystery Within an Enigma*, 10 INVEST. LAW. 1 (2003)

In *re* The Tonopah Mining Co. of Nevada

IC-1084, 26 SEC 426 (1947)

The Tonopah Mining Company of Nevada has applied for an order under Section 3 (b) (2) of the Investment Company Act of 1940, declaring it not to be an investment company within the meaning of the Act on the ground that it is primarily engaged in the business of metal mining. * * * Our findings are based upon an independent review of the record.

It is not disputed that over 40% of applicant's assets, exclusive of cash and Government securities, are investment securities. Applicant therefore falls within the definition contained in § 3(a)(3) of the Act, which defines an investment company to include any issuer which

> "is engaged or proposes to engage in the business of investing, reinvesting, owning, holding, or trading in securities, and owns or proposes to acquire investment securities having a value exceeding 40 per centum of the value of such issuer's total assets (exclusive of Government securities and cash items) on an unconsolidated basis."

However, notwithstanding the quoted provisions of § 3(a)(3), if the Commission finds that an applicant is "primarily engaged in a business or businesses other than that of investing, reinvesting, owning, holding or trading in securities," such applicant may obtain an order declaring it not to be an investment company under the provisions of § 3(b)(2).[1] The issue raised by a § 3(b)(2) application is one of fact, and must be resolved by a review of the special circumstances applicable to the particular case. The principal relevant considerations are 1) the company's historical development; 2) its public representations of policy; 3) the activities of its officers and directors; and, most important, 4) the nature of its present assets; and 5) the sources of its present income. We will consider each of these in turn.

---

[1] Section 3 (b) provides in part:

"Notwithstanding paragraph (3) of subsection (a), none of the following persons is an investment company within the meaning of this title: * * * *

"(2) Any issuer which the Commission, upon application by such issuer, finds and by order declares to be primarily engaged in a business or businesses other than that of investing, reinvesting, owning, holding, or trading in securities either directly or (A) through majority-owned subsidiaries or (B) through controlled companies conducting similar types of businesses. . . ."

Historical Development of the Company

Applicant was incorporated in Delaware in 1901. In its early years of existence the company was undoubtedly primarily engaged in the mining business directly and through majority-owned subsidiaries. It regarded its portfolio of investments as a so-called exploration fund for the purpose of exploring and developing mining properties. However, nearly all of the majority-owned mining subsidiaries have now become inactive. The result has been that for a number of years, and as of the present time, the only active mining property in the enterprise has been the gold-silver mine at Tonopah, Nevada. The company has granted leases to miners for exploitation of this property on a royalty basis and supplies certain equipment and services to the lessees.

It has been argued that applicant is also engaged in the mining business through LaLuz Mines, Ltd. in Nicaragua. Applicant explored this property in 1936 at a cost of over $175,000, and had rights to acquire a one-third interest in the corporation to be formed to develop the mine. However, it was not in a position in 1938 to invest the required capital, but reduced its participation to 10%. The remaining 90% of the stock was acquired by Ventures, Ltd., an affiliate of the applicant.[2] In its brief, applicant points to the fact that Ventures and itself have a common president and executive vice president, and claims that "as a matter of economic fact" applicant is an operator of the La Luz mining property. The evidence does not support this claim. On the contrary, applicant's secretary-treasurer testified that Ventures and La Luz Mines, Ltd. were not controlled by Tonopah; that La Luz was controlled by Ventures and that Tonopah's interest in La Luz was a stock interest.

This witness further testified that the La Luz and various other investments in mining properties were made because "Mr. Lindsley [applicant's president] as head of Ventures naturally is very closely informed on them, and is advised that those companies have very good possibilities of developing into active mining ventures, and in that way any investment on our part should have more possibility . . . for the future than merely investing a small amount in Kennecott or something like that, which is an already

[2] Ventures, Ltd. owns over 5% of the stock of the applicant. According to its annual report for 1945 the applicant owns 10,000 shares of Ventures, Ltd., but the record does not show what percentage of voting power the block represents. In the annual reports filed with the Commission pursuant to § 13 of the Securities Exchange Act of 1934, applicant's holdings in Ventures are listed under marketable securities rather than as an investment in securities of an affiliate.

developed mine." This testimony appears to indicate that applicant is not investing in these enterprises for the purpose of gaining control or operating the businesses of the companies involved, but rather that its primary interest is that of an investor. As is shown below, applicant's portfolio consists in large part of mining securities, but this circumstance is entirely consistent with a policy of investment rather than engaging in the business of mining. It merely indicates that the company, because of historical reasons and because of the expert knowledge of some of the members of its management, favors concentrating most of its investments in a particular type of industry. This is a well recognized form of investment company activity.

Representations of Policy

The company's charter, as drafted in 1901, stated its principal purpose to be:

"To acquire and own and operate mines of gold, silver, copper, coal and other minerals and to conduct any mercantile business in connection with the same."

The purpose clause also provided that "in furtherance and not in limitation of the general powers conferred by the laws of the State of Delaware, and the objects and purposes herein set forth" the company might, among other things, buy, sell, mortgage or lease real property, manufacture and deal in goods and merchandise of every description, acquire other businesses and pay for the same in securities of the company, acquire or grant licenses, and purchase, hold or sell securities created by any other corporation.

In 1935, the company filed with the Commission an application for registration of its 1,000,000 shares of common stock, par value $1 per share, on the Philadelphia Stock Exchange.[3] In the application for registration the general character of the business done by the registrant was described as follows:

"Mining property at Tonopah, Nevada, being operated by leasers on a royalty basis; principal metals gold and silver. Its milling plant and tailings at Millers, Nevada, being operated by an outside company—General Metals Recovery Corporation—on a rental and royalty basis. Company maintains a small staff of engineers in field in search for new properties."

---

[3] Registration is still in effect. At the present time there are outstanding 870,000 shares in the hands of about 3,250 shareholders.

The registration statement listed nine majority-owned subsidiaries engaged in mining or related businesses; but of these five were said to be inactive. As to the remaining four, two were stated to be engaged, inter alia, in making "outside investments" in stocks and bonds of industrial, public utility, railroad and mining companies; one was stated to be engaged in the distribution of electric power to various mining companies; and one was stated to be engaged in hauling supplies and ore to and from various mines in the vicinity of Tonopah. In a report to stockholders dated April 15, 1935 the management stated:

> "Your Board has adopted a policy of liquidating securities whenever prices seem to warrant such a course, and not making further investments in other securities, excepting stocks of mining companies which have been investigated and show reasonable prospect of substantial appreciation.
>
> "Your Company for some years has operated somewhat in the nature of a holding company, new properties as acquired being operated and financed as independent companies. The proposed legislation regarding holding companies, now before Congress, is being considered by your Board, and when the outcome of this legislation is definitely known, it is quite likely that certain recommendations must be made by the directors as to the future financing of the company, in the event of any large properties being acquired by us."

The subsequent annual reports to stockholders contain few or no direct representations as to the nature of the company with the exception of a report for 1943, dated March 24, 1944, in which it is stated: "There is attached a list of the securities owned by the company, for your information, showing the manner in which the company invests its surplus funds until such time as they may be required for mining purposes."

While the evidence of direct representation is not unequivocal, it does indicate that as nearly as 1935 the management regarded the enterprise as being "somewhat in the nature of a holding company" and gave notice to stockholders that the proposed legislation regarding "holding companies" might affect it.[4] More important, however, as appears below, the nature of the assets and income of the company, disclosed in the annual reports filed with the Commission and in reports sent to stockholders, was such as to lead

---

[4] The reference was apparently to § 30 of the Public Utility Holding Company Act of 1935 which directed the Commission to "make a study of the functions and activities of investment trusts and investment companies" and to report the results of its study to Congress on or before January 4, 1937.

investors to believe that the principal activity of the company was trading and investing in securities.[5]

Activities of Officers and Directors

The principal offices of the company are in Philadelphia. Applicant asserts that none of the members of its management have ever been engaged in banking, brokerage or the investment business. However, it is stated that the individual directors have had wide experience in investing in mining securities and in mining operations, *i.e.*, that they are experts in the business of mining and are qualified to pass upon the merits of investments in mining stocks in which they may be interested.

Lindsley, applicant's president, is not very active, keeps in contact with company activities through means of reports and copies of minutes of board meetings, and attends such meetings whenever possible. As already stated he is also president of Ventures, Ltd. The superintendent at Tonopah is neither an officer nor a director of applicant. The record does not show that any members of the corporate management spend any considerable part of their time in connection with the company's mining operations.

Nature of Assets

As of September 30, 1946, the date of the latest available data, the company's total assets per books were $1,426,345, of which $248,150 represented cash and U.S. Government bonds. Of the remaining $1,178,195, "marketable securities" and "other investment securities" (neither of which items includes securities of controlled subsidiaries) accounted for $1,104,895, or about 94%. The portfolio (aside from U.S. Government bonds) contained 21 items of mining and smelting securities carried on the books at $695,526 and representing about 63% of total investment securities. The balance consisted of 35 items including public utility, railroad, aviation, banking, insurance, foreign government, and miscellaneous industrial securities. In addition, 130,000 shares of treasury stock, which had been reacquired at a cost of $177,950, were carried as a deduction from the capital stock and surplus accounts. Investments in subsidiaries are not carried on the books at all or at only nominal amounts.

A review of the company's balance sheets since December 31, 1934, shows that

---

[5] In addition to a balance sheet and profit and loss statement, an itemized list of the security holdings was attached to each of the annual reports sent to stockholders.

investment securities have constituted similarly large percentages of assets during the past thirteen years, that mining securities at all times constituted a large portion thereof, and that other securities have been diversified. In short, there has been no substantial change in the general character of the portfolio in recent years.

Sources of Income

The following table shows the company's major sources of income and its exploration expenditures by years for the period 1934-1945:

Year	Income from Interest and Dividends	Profit or (Loss) from Sales of Securities	Exploration Expenditures	Profit or (Loss) from Mining or Leasing
1934	$293	$1,344	$13,315	$69,201
1935	210		29,302	94,538
1936	15,829		16,588	109,587
1937	9,777		26,625	114,533
1938	10,415	(12,370)	5,359	67,551
1939	9,277	(8,251)	7,309	39,661
1940	16,594	(27,775)	13,641	41,947
1941	19,479	(28,565)	551	36,061
1942	32,474	(236,570)	441	18,336
1943	48,082	3,421	3,676	2,649
1944	58,276	12,285	769	(9,799)
1945	56,293	56,498	12	(13,214)

It will be noted that mining income and exploration expenditures have been decreasing very substantially while income from securities has materially increased. Applicant contends that these trends represent an abnormal condition due to the war. However, the table shows that income from mining and exploration expenditures began to drop sharply in 1938. In addition, there is testimony by witnesses for the applicant that the quality of the ore at Tonopah is depreciating and that the possibilities of continued production cannot be projected for any considerable period. It also appears that there has been a substantial reduction in the number of leases under which ore is being extracted. There can be no question that as of the present time the company's only source of net income consists of interest, dividends and profits on the sale of securities; and we find nothing to indicate that this situation will be changed substantially in the foreseeable future.

Conclusions

At organization the applicant was undoubtedly primarily engaged in the mining business. It has since changed its character and it has become in large part a company engaged in the business of holding and trading in securities. In recent years its holdings of investment securities have been such as to bring it within the definition of an investment company contained in § 3(a)(3) of the Act. While it has specialized in the securities of mining enterprises, it has not done so with a view to exercising control or engaging in the business of mining; on the contrary it has assumed the position of an investor. Approximately 94% of its total assets (exclusive of cash and U.S. Government bonds) are represented by investment securities and all of its net income is derived from interest, dividends or trading profits in such securities.

While it may be true that the management hopes some day to acquire controlling interests and exercise control in existing or new mining enterprises in which it is interested, we cannot find that applicant is at present primarily engaged in the business of metal mining. Accordingly the application must be denied.[6] An appropriate order will issue.

---

[6] Applicant has not attempted to show that any undue burden would be imposed on its mining operations by reason of registration under the Act; if such a showing were to be made, our action herein would not, of course, preclude applicant from requesting exemption from the provisions asserted to create such burdens.

SEC, Plaintiff-Appellee v. Nat'l Presto Indus., Inc., Defendant-Appellant

486 F.3d 305 (7th Cir. 2007)

Before EASTERBROOK, Chief Judge, and POSNER and EVANS, Circuit Judges.

OPINION

EASTERBROOK, Chief Judge:

Most mutual funds and other investment companies come within the scope of the Investment Company Act of 1940 because they hold themselves out "as being engaged primarily, or propos[ing] to engage primarily, in the business of investing, reinvesting, or trading in securities";15 USC § 80a-3(a)(1)(A). But firms can be dragged within the Act's coverage kicking and screaming, even though they depict themselves as operating businesses rather than as managing other people's money. Any issuer that owns "investment securities" worth 40% of its total assets is an investment company under § 80a-3(a)(1)(C) unless some other provision of the Act takes it outside the definition. For this purpose, however, "Government securities and cash items" are omitted from both the numerator and the denominator.

National Presto Industries, a seller of both consumer goods (cookware, diapers, and other household items) and munitions, used to make everything it sold. During the 1970s it began to divest its manufacturing facilities and to contract production to third parties. In 1993 the Department of Defense closed a facility that Presto had used to make artillery shells. Presto was left with a pile of cash, most of which it retained with a long-term plan to acquire other businesses, and a shrunken book value of operating assets. Financial instruments were 86% of its total assets by 1994 and 92% in 1998. Since 2000 Presto has purchased two manufacturers of military supplies and two makers of diapers and puppy pads. But in 2003 financial instruments still represented 62% of its physical and financial assets. Intellectual property, although of considerable value to Presto, is not carried on corporate books at its full economic value, so this ratio overstates the significance of its portfolio of securities, but Presto does not argue that it could come under the 40% ratio by marking its patents and trademarks to current market value.

All of Presto's consumer products other than absorbent products are made by subcontractors, so although it has a substantial operating *income* it does not have operating *assets* to match—and the Investment Company Act's main test is asset-based. The SEC concluded that Presto was well past the 40% trigger. When the firm refused to register as an investment company—and make the changes to its corporate structure, management, and financial reporting required of investment companies—or request an administrative exemption, the SEC filed this suit to seek an injunction that would require compliance. After preliminary maneuvering vindicated the SEC's choice of forum, see 347 F.3d 662 (7th Cir. 2003), the district court granted summary judgment in the agency's favor, 397 F. Supp.2d 943 (ND Ill. 2005), and issued an injunction requiring Presto to register under the 1940 Act. The firm has complied pending appeal.

After suffering defeat on the merits, Presto replaced enough of its existing portfolio with "Government securities and cash items" to bring investment securities under the 40% threshold. The SEC had proposed an injunction that would have allowed Presto the opportunity to do this (or to seek an administrative exemption) in lieu of registration; the firm thought to avail itself of the opportunity even before the injunction was entered.

Without inviting comment from the parties, however, the district judge deleted these options from the SEC's draft and entered an injunction unconditionally requiring Presto to register as an investment company. The judge did not explain why. The result was a regulatory mismatch: a firm that is today required (by statute) to be organized and to report its financial position as an operating company is required (by injunction) to be organized and report its financial position as an investment company. Instead of doing this, the district court would have been well advised to craft an injunction commanding registration only if Presto should revert to its old portfolio design; obliging it to register as an investment company even when its investments do not require this is hard to fathom except as a form of punishment for Presto's conduct in past years, and civil injunctions are not supposed to punish litigants.

The unconditional injunction has caused considerable trouble. Investment companies are subject to many governance requirements that do not apply to operating companies; see, *e.g.*, 15 USC §§80a-16, -17, -18, -19, -29, -55, -56 (and the corresponding regulations). Presto's auditor, Grant Thornton, resigned because the SEC questioned its certification of Presto's financial statements as those of an operating company. Now that Presto is officially an investment company, Grant Thornton has refused to allow the statements it certified to be used for any purpose. This has disabled Presto from complying fully with *either* the Investment Company Act or the Securities Exchange Act of 1934. Without the financial statements, it is unable to file quarterly and annual reports. It has hired another auditor, but recreating and re-certifying financial statements for many past years is expensive and time consuming. Meanwhile stock exchanges have threatened to delist its stock because Presto is out of compliance with both statutory and exchange-based financial reporting requirements.

At oral argument we inquired whether Presto's financial rearrangement has made the case moot. Now that it has complied with the injunction by registering as an investment company, can't it deregister and go back to its preferred status as an operating company, subject to registration under the Securities Exchange Act, no matter what happens on appeal? Deregistration requires the consent of the SEC, however, and although Presto filed the appropriate papers with the agency in January 2006 the SEC has failed to act on them.

One senses from this prolonged silence, and the tenor of the SEC's brief and oral argument, that the agency (or its senior staff) is in a snit because Presto declined to do what many other firms with excess liquid assets have done—apply to the agency for an exemption; see 15 USC § 80a-3(b)(2); (Microsoft, for example, holds more than 40% of its assets in the form of investment securities but received permission to operate outside the 1940 Act.) The agency's counsel implied at oral argument that an exemption would have been forthcoming if sought. Yet a firm's refusal to kowtow to an agency is not a good reason to force its investors to bear unnecessary costs—for it is the investors who must pay to recreate the financial statements, though *they* did not contribute to this imbroglio—and keep a firm inappropriately registered, as Presto now is. Why is the SEC bent on grinding down a corporation that it appears to acknowledge would not mislead or otherwise injure investors by using the governance and reporting devices appropriate to an operating company?

Because Presto remains registered as an investment company while the SEC sits on its hands, there is a live case or controversy, because a remedy is possible: we could end its registration forthwith. Moreover, if we hold that Presto's former portfolio does not bring it within the Investment Company Act, it will be free to rejigger its investments; the old investments likely had a higher rate of return, which is why Presto switched only after the district court's opinion.

Let us begin, then, with Presto's argument that even before the recent changes to its portfolio, enough of its investments were "Government securities and cash items" to keep its "investment securities" under the 40% trigger.

"Government securities" is a defined term. The phrase "means any security issued or guaranteed as to principal or interest by the United States, or by a person controlled or supervised by and acting as an instrumentality of the Government of the United States pursuant to authority granted by the Congress of the United States; or any certificate of deposit for any of the foregoing." 15 USC § 80a-2(a)(16). According to Presto, pre-refunded municipal bonds ("refunded bonds" for short) fit this definition. Presto held these instruments in quantity.

A refunded bond is a bond backed by U.S. securities as well as the credit of the issuer. Suppose that a municipality issues long-term bonds for a project (say, an airport) and that the market rate of interest later falls. The issuer would like to take advantage of the lower rate, but the bonds lack a call feature. The municipality can issue new bonds at the current lower rate and use the proceeds to buy Treasury bonds with the same maturity as the original issue of municipal bonds. The Treasury securities are held in trust to pay interest and principal on the original issue. The municipality pays the interest on the new issue; the Treasury securities may cover the old issue, and if not the municipality can chip in the difference. Refinancing in this way works because municipal bonds are not subject to federal taxes, so they often pay lower interest rates than Treasury securities. Bonds that can be bought with the proceeds of the new municipal issue may produce enough interest by themselves to cover the interest on the old issue.

The Treasury bonds held in trust lead Presto to call the refunded bonds themselves "Government securities." It should be apparent, however, that they do not fit the statutory definition. Refunded municipal bonds are still municipal bonds, exactly as they were before the refunding transaction. Municipal bonds are neither issued nor guaranteed by the national government or any federal instrumentality. If the municipality defaults, or a local employee reaches into the till and makes off with the Treasury securities, the national government will not cover the loss. The bonds in trust make the municipal bonds safer, but 15 USC § 80a-2(a)(16) does not include in the category of "Government securities" everything that a company deems "almost as safe as" Treasury securities.

The argument "X has the same economic attributes as Y, so X must have the same legal attributes as Y" has a history in securities law. It was the basis of the sale-of-business doctrine that many courts accepted before *Landreth Timber Co. v. Landreth*, 471 US 681 (1985). The idea was that someone who bought all of the stock in a closely-held corporation was buying the corporation's assets, as an economic matter, so the transaction should not be governed by the securities laws. *Landreth Timber* held, however, that someone who wants the legal treatment of an asset acquisition must buy the assets rather than the stock; people may choose between transacting in securities and transacting in assets, and the law follows the form—not only because that is what the statute says, but also because trying to determine, one case at a time, when a transaction "really" has the economic attributes of a different form would lead to a great deal of uncertainty for little purpose. *Landreth Timber* represents the norm in securities law. Stock or bonds in a company that invests the proceeds in land, or gold, or art, are still regulated as securities rather than as land, or gold, or art. Pooled interests in orange groves are regulated as investment contracts rather than as oranges; see *SEC v. W.J. Howey Co.*, 328 US 293 (1946). And municipal bonds issued by a city that plans to repay using U.S. bonds are still municipal bonds.

Securities laws regulate the form of financial transactions, rather than looking through form to substance; see *Reves v. Ernst & Young*, 494 US 56 (1990) (demand notes are regulated as securities even though they have many economic attributes of exempt instruments). True enough, § 80a-2 begins, as several other definitional clauses in the securities laws do, with the phrase, "unless the context otherwise requires". The Supreme Court used this in *Marine Bank v. Weaver*, 455 US 551 (1982), to hold that a one-off transaction—a 50% interest in a neighbor's farm in exchange for a short-term loan, the sort of investment that could not even in principle be traded among anonymous investors—should not be treated as a security.

We know from *Rowland v. California Men's Colony*, 506 U.S. 194 (1993), however, as well as from *Landreth Timber*, that this use of the context clause cannot be generalized into a norm that substance trumps form. Rowland holds that context clauses refer to *linguistic* rather than *economic* contexts, and even as so limited should be employed—as they say—only when the context of a phrase elsewhere in a statute "requires" a departure from the definitional clause. Neither the interest in the neighbor's farm nor the bank account involved in *Marine Bank* was a "security" under the Securities Exchange Act because neither fit the model of homogenous instruments that (at least potentially) could be traded among anonymous investors. The context clause prevented a need to jam a square peg into a round hole; see Scott FitzGibbon, *What is a Security?—A Redefinition Based on Eligibility to Participate in the Financial Markets*, 64 MINN. L. REV. 893 (1980).

But nothing in § 80a-3(a)(1)(C) similarly "requires" a departure from the definition in § 80a-2(a)(16). The definition of the phrase "Government securities" in the latter makes perfect sense when plugged into the former.

Judge Friendly once remarked, with respect to the definition of the term "note" in the securities laws: "So long as the statutes remain as they have been for over forty years, courts had better not depart from their words without strong support for the conviction that, under the authority vested in them by the 'context' clause, they are doing what Congress wanted when they refuse to do what it said"; *Exchange Nat'l Bank of Chicago v. Touche Ross & Co.*, 544 F.2d 1126 (2d Cir. 1976). That high standard has not been met here. The Investment Company Act has been with us for 67 years without giving problems through the definition of "Government securities." And even if there were some wriggle room via the context clause, Presto has not established that refunded bonds are the economic equivalent of Treasury bonds. A report in the record from Morgan Stanley shows that the yield for Treasury bonds maturing in 2006 was 4.95%, while the taxable equivalent yield for refunded bonds was 6.1% for taxpayers in the 38% bracket. That's a 23% premium over Treasuries, which must reflect extra risk. (The nominal interest rate for refunded bonds is below that for Treasury bonds, because of the tax subsidy for municipal securities; an adjustment must be made to find real returns and implicit risks.)

Mutual funds may treat refunded bonds as if they were "Government securities" for the purpose of 15 USC § 80a-5, which says how an investment company's portfolio must be structured if it calls itself "diversified"; 17 CFR § 270.5b-3(b). How can refunded bonds be "Government securities" for one purpose but not the other?, Presto asks. Yet treating A as if it were B for one purpose does not imply that A *is* B for every purpose. The regulation on which Presto relies governs how investment companies describe their portfolios; that's a very different subject from whether something is an investment company in the first place. Equating refunded bonds with Treasury securities for the purpose of diversification allows mutual funds to offer tax advantages (which refunded bonds supply) without any change in the covariance of risk across a fund's assets. Denying investors that opportunity would injure them; it's sensible for the SEC to look at the economic attributes of instruments when determining what counts as diversification (another economic inquiry) while insisting that the statutory definition be used to determine what entities are covered by the statute in the first place.

"Cash items" also are excluded when calculating the 40% ratio, and Presto maintains that "variable-rate demand notes" should be treated as "cash items." A variable-rate demand note is an instrument (usually a bond or debenture) whose rate of interest is updated weekly (if not more often) based on some index, such as the London Interbank Offering Rate. Whenever the interest rate changes, the note's holder is entitled to redeem at par. Usually this transaction is handled by a remarketing agent, who buys the note from the holder and resells it in the secondary market to another investor; the note's issuer is involved only if the note is trading for less than par.

In contrast to the detailed statutory definition of "Government securities," the Investment Company Act does not define "cash items." Presto maintains that variable-rate demand notes are equivalent to cash because of the weekly opportunity to sell the instruments at par for cash. If liquidity were enough, however, one would treat all shares of stock in large issuers, and many bonds, as "cash items" because they can be sold on liquid markets in a matter of minutes. The reason that such investments are not treated as cash or its equivalent, however, is that the market price the instrument will fetch when sold is variable. Presto thinks that the "redeem at par" feature of the variable-rate demand note insulates them from that sort of risk, but that's not true. The investor is entitled to *demand* redemption at par, but whether the issuer will comply depends on its financial health. A business reverse (or, for a municipal issuer, a shortfall of taxes) will mean no redemption, or redemption at a discount. That's a kind of risk an investor takes with any stock or bond—but does not take with cash.

Although the statute does not define "cash item," the SEC gave this definition when adopting a safe-harbor rule (17 CFR § 270.3a-1):

> For purposes of determining compliance with the proposed rule, cash, coins, paper currency, demand deposits with banks, timely checks of others (which are orders on banks to immediately supply funds), cashier checks, certified checks, bank drafts, money orders, traveler's checks and letters of credit generally would be considered cash items. Certificates of deposit and time deposits typically would not be considered cash items absent convincing evidence of no investment intent. *Certain Prima Facie Investment Companies*, IC-10937 (1979), at n.29; regulation adopted in final form 46 FR 6879 (1981).

This definition applies only to Rule 3a-1, but Presto does not contend that we should ignore it—or that it is arbitrary or capricious. Agencies are entitled to add detail to the statutes they administer, and their resolution of ambiguities is entitled to respect; see *Chevron U.S.A. Inc. v. Natural Resources Defense Council, Inc.*, 467 US 837 (1984).

A variable-rate demand note does not fit this definition. Presto chose to invest in variable-rate demand notes rather than, say, money-market funds (which are diversified portfolios of safe and liquid investments) because the notes have higher rates of return. The higher return stems from higher risk, which explains why the notes differ from "cash items." (Presto does observe that many variable-rate demand notes are backed by letters of credit, which the SEC is willing to treat as "cash items," but that's a replay of the argument that refunded bonds are "Government securities" because they are secured by Treasury bonds.) Presto was making an investment in these notes, along the lines of "time deposits" (which are "cash items" only with "convincing evidence of no investment intent"), rather than holding them for liquidity.

Presto therefore comes within the 40% test and is an investment company unless one of the (many) statutory exceptions applies. The one on which Presto relies is § 80a-3(b)(1): "Any issuer primarily engaged, directly or through a wholly-owned subsidiary or subsidiaries, in a business or businesses other than that of investing, reinvesting, owning, holding, or trading in securities." Presto is actively engaged in several businesses. A visitor to its web site for consumers (http://www.gopresto.com) will find sales promotions, warranty information, and instruction manuals for pizza ovens and coffee makers but nary a hint that someone would want to buy Presto's stock as a means to own a derivative interest in refunded municipal bonds or variable-rate demand notes. But is Presto "primarily" engaged in selling pressure cookers, deep fryers, popcorn poppers, diapers, and ordnance rather than the business of holding securities? The statute is unhelpful; "primarily" is not a defined term. No regulation fills the gap.

Sixty years ago the SEC announced that it would consider five factors to decide whether a firm that sold off its operating assets and chose not to distribute the proceeds to its stockholders had become what people today call an "inadvertent investment company"; *In re Tonopah Mining Co.*, 26 SEC 426 (1947); see also Mendelsohn, Goldfus & Mackey, *Status Seeking: Resolving the Status of Inadvertent Investment Companies*, 38 BUS. LAW. 193 (1982); Kerr, *The Inadvertent Investment Company: Section 3(a)(3) of the Investment Company Act*, 12 STAN. L. REV. 29 (1959).

According to Tonopah, what matter are the company's history, the way the company represents itself to the investing public today, the activities of its officers and directors, the nature of its assets, and the sources of its income. Of these, all but the fourth favor Presto. Founded in 1905, Presto was an active manufacturer of industrial, consumer, and military products until the 1980s, when it started to subcontract manufacturing activities. It remains an active manufacturer of absorbent goods and military ordnance and sells a line of kitchen goods under its own trademarks.

As far as we can see, this is the first time that the SEC has argued that a firm with such a substantial ongoing presence in product markets is an inadvertent investment company. The model inadvertent investment company—of which Tonopah Mining is the initial exemplar and Fifth Avenue Coach Lines is perhaps the best-known, see *SEC v. Fifth Avenue Coach Lines, Inc.*, 289 F. Supp. 3 (SDNY 1968), *affirmed*, 435 F.2d 510 (2d Cir. 1970)—is one in which the firm has sold all or almost all of its assets, reduced its operations to a skeleton staff (Tonopah Mining was down to one unprofitable mine and Fifth Avenue Coach Lines to no busses at all), and purports to be looking for acquisitions but never seems to find them. Perhaps one could have applied the "purports to be looking for acquisitions" label to Presto in the 1980s and 1990s, but one could *not* say that Presto had withdrawn from active business operations in the meantime. It continued selling both consumer and military products. It changed from a manufacturer to a firm that was (principally) a designer and marketer of products assembled by others, but this did not make Presto less an operating enterprise. Many other firms have made a similar transition (Apple comes to mind) without being thought to have evolved into mutual funds.

Presto presents itself to the public (and to investors) as an operating company. That's how its web site, its annual reports, and its publicity all depict it. The contrast with Tonopah Mining and Fifth Avenue Coach Lines is stark. An investor in the market for a mutual fund, a hedge fund, or any other investment pool would not dream of turning to Presto, whose net income can increase or decrease substantially as a result of business successes or reverses. The price of Presto's stock moves in response to changes in its operating profits rather than the slight annual changes in its investment income. The SEC has not identified even one confused investor who bought stock in Presto thinking that he was making an investment in a closed-end mutual fund whose assets were the securities that Presto holds.

"Activities of Officers and Directors," the third factor in Tonopah, likewise favors Presto. Directors and senior managers at Tonopah Mining and Fifth Avenue Coach Lines spent most of their time managing the firms' investment portfolios. Presto estimates that

95% of its managers' time is devoted to running its consumer-products and military-ordnance businesses. The SEC has not offered any contrary evidence.

As for the fifth factor, income, *Tonopah* looked at both gross and net figures, as well as at the firm's expenditures to produce income. (Looking at both gross and net is essential; otherwise an operating loss, with negative net income, would turn a firm into an "investment company".) Gross income at Presto is dominated by receipts from its consumer and military sales. More than 90% of Presto's gross receipts for every year covered by the record (1994 through 2003) comes from its sales of products. In 2003, for example, Presto recorded about $125 million in sales, yielding a net profit of $18.9 million; total receipts from investment securities that year were $ 4.2 million.

Only net income helps the SEC's position: the agency calculates that, over the decade covered by the record, 50.22% of Presto's net profits were derived from investments in securities. Presto's calculations show that operating profits exceed investment profits for the decade as a whole. The SEC acknowledges that, in each of the three years immediately preceding the district court's injunction requiring Presto to register as an investment company, investments produced less than 40% of Presto's net profit. So even if we take the view most favorable to the SEC, that a firm is "primarily" engaged in a business other than investment management only if more than half of its net profits come from non-investment sources, Presto was "primarily" an operating business when the injunction issued. Whatever classification may have been appropriate in the 1990s (when more than half of net profits came from investments) cannot support an injunction issued in 2005, when at least 60% of net profit was coming from consumer and military sales. In *Tonopah*, by contrast, "the company's only source of net income consists of interest, dividends and profits on the sale of securities; and we find nothing to indicate that this situation will be changed substantially in the foreseeable future."

This leaves the fourth *Tonopah* factor, the nature of Presto's assets. Here the picture at last favors the SEC, for more than 60% of Presto's assets were investment securities during every year covered by the record. In full flight from the Commission's multi-factor approach in *Tonopah*, the SEC's lawyer in this court urges us to give little weight to any consideration other than Presto's asset structure. Yet looking primarily at accounting assets has a potential to mislead. Imagine a firm that owns substantial assets such as patents and trademarks that do not show up on its balance sheet as assets, and that operates a business from a leased headquarters where it designs, contracts for, and sells products. Such a firm could have annual sales exceeding $100 million, and profits exceeding $10 million as Presto does, with book-value assets of only $1 million in office furniture. If that firm stored even 10% of two years' profits in refunded bonds, as a hedge against business reverses (or to finance expansion), instead of distributing all profits to investors in dividends, it would become an investment company under the approach the SEC urges in this litigation. Yet no investor would perceive such a firm as a substitute for a closed-end mutual fund; its stock returns would continue to depend on its operating profits and losses.

According to the SEC's brief, *Tonopah* deemed assets the "most important" of the five considerations. It would be surprising if that were so, because it would make the exclusion in § 80a-3(b)(1) unavailable as a practical matter. The only reason one turns to this exclusion is that the 40% asset test has been satisfied. If subsection (b)(2) does nothing except raise the 40% test to 50% as a definition of the firm's "primary" engagement, it is an odd statutory provision indeed. What sense would it make to enact a law using 40% as the threshold in subsection (a)(1)(C), and convert the "real" rule to 50% in subsection (b)(1) by using words rather than numbers? Subsection (b)(1) has to be about considerations other than assets (or at least in addition to assets). And that's what the SEC said in *Tonopah*:

> More important . . . [is] the nature of the assets and income of the company, disclosed in the annual reports filed with the Commission and in reports sent to stockholders, was such as *to lead investors to believe* that the principal *activity* of the company was trading and investing in securities; 26 SEC at 430 (emphasis added).

In other words, the Commission thought in *Tonopah* that what principally matters is the beliefs the company is likely to induce in investors. Will its portfolio and activities lead investors to treat a firm as an investment vehicle or as an operating enterprise? The Commission has never issued an opinion or rule taking a different view, and its lawyers cannot adopt a new approach by filing briefs. Only the Commission's members may change established norms, and they must do so by rulemaking or administrative adjudication; see *SEC v. Chenery Corp.*, 318 US 80 (1943); *SEC v. Chenery Corp.*, 332 US 194 (1947).

Reasonable investors would treat Presto as an operating company rather than a competitor with a closed-end mutual fund. The SEC has not tried to demonstrate anything different about investors' perceptions or behavior. It follows that Presto is not an investment company.

The judgment of the district court is reversed. Presto, which registered as an investment company only under judicial compulsion, now is free to drop that registration and operate under the Securities Exchange Act of 1934 whether or not the SEC gives its formal approach to that step.

Topic 2 Industrial Holding Company *vs* Special Situation Investment Company

Laws & Rules Highlight:

IC Act (15 USC 80a-1 *et seq.*) & Rules (17 CFR §§ 270.0-1 *et seq.*)

- § 3(a)(1)(C) (***presumptive/prima facie IC:*** *issuer "**engaged** in" investment business and having over **40%** of its total assets on an unconsolidated basis in "**investment securities**"*)
  - § 2(a)(22) (*def. "issuer"*); § 2(a)(28) (*def. "person"*); § 2(a)(8) (*def. "company"*)
  - § 2(a)(41)(A) (*def. "value" for purposes of § 3*)
  - IC Rule 3a-1(a) (*"**total assets**" exclusive of Government securities and cash items*)
  - § 2(a)(36) (*def. "security"*); § 3(a)(2) (*def. "**investment securities**," to include all securities **except** §§ 3(a)(2)(A), (B), (C) securities*):
    - ✓ § 3(a)(2)(A) (***Government securities***); § 2(a)(16) (*def. "Government security"*)
    - ✓ § 3(a)(2)(B) (***securities issued by employees' securities companies***); § 2(a)(13) (*def. "employees' securities company"*)
    - ✓ § 3(a)(2)(C) (***securities issued by majority-owned subsidiaries** which are neither ICs nor §§ 3(c)(1) & (c)(7) private funds—a requirement designed to prevent the issuer from circumventing § 3(a)(1)(C) by carrying on its investment company activities through a majority-owned subsidiary*)
- § 3(b)(1) (***self-operating exclusion:*** *excludes an **issuer** "**primarily** engaged in" **non**-investment business, directly or through **wholly-owned** subsidiaries*)
  - § 2(a)(43) (*def. "wholly-owned subsidiary"—**95% threshold** voting securities ownership test*)
- § 3(b)(2) (***SEC exemptive order exclusion:*** *excludes an **issuer** "**primarily** engaged in" **non**-investment business, directly, or through **majority-owned** subsidiaries, or through **controlled** companies conducting **similar** types of businesses*)
  - § 2(a)(24) (*def. "majority-owned subsidiary"—**50% threshold** voting securities ownership test*)
  - § 2(a)(9) (*def. "control"—**more than 25%** voting securities ownership test*)

§ 3(a)(1)(C) Statistical Test of Prima Facie Investment Company:

$$\frac{\text{"investment securities"}}{\text{"total assets"} - A - \textit{cash items}} = \frac{\text{all "securities"} - A - B - C}{\text{"total assets"} - A - \textit{cash items}} > 40\% \text{ (on an unconsolidated basis)}$$

where

A = § 3(a)(2)(A) Government securities

B = § 3(a)(2)(B) securities issued by employees' securities companies

C = § 3(a)(2)(C) securities issued by 50% majority-owned subsidiaries which are neither investment companies nor private funds

Holding Company Outside of § 3(a)(1)(C) Prima Facie Investment Company:

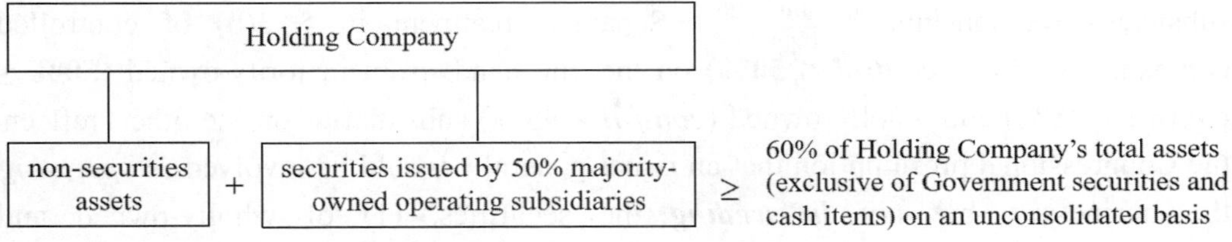

Pre-Case Background Note:[Biblio]

Industrial Holding Company *vs* Special Situation Investment Company: Operating *vs* Investing in Portfolio Companies

An **industrial holding company** will hit **§ 3(a)(1)(C)**'s statistical criteria for "*prima facie*" investment company "engaged" in investment business when it holds "*investment securities*" having a value exceeding 40% of its "*total assets*," computed on an unconsolidated basis so as not to distort the 40% standard. For the purposes of the 40% statistical test, "investment securities" do not include securities issued by *majority-owned subsidiaries* which are themselves neither statutory "investment companies" nor private funds. "Investment securities" include securities issued by *non-majority owned, controlled companies*. The design of § 3(a)(1)(C) is thus to exclude industrial holding companies from the coverage of the IC Act, but not to exclude all holding companies, such as those doing business through non-majority owned, controlled companies.[1 (p.66609 nn.5-6, 10)]

Even where an industrial holding company meets the "***prima facie***" investment company test under § 3(a)(1)(C), § 3(b) excludes it from the IC Act if it is "primarily engaged" in non-investment business directly or "through" subsidiary and certain controlled companies, where "*through*" means the issuer's control of such companies and active exercise of that control.[1 (p.66610 n.19)] Section **3(b)(1)** automatically excludes from statutory "investment company" status a holding company "primarily engaged" in a non-investment business directly or through "*wholly-owned*" subsidiaries. Section **3(b)(2)**, through SEC exemptive order process for "borderline companies,"[1 (p.66610 n.11)] excludes a holding company determined by the SEC to be "primarily engaged" in a non-investment business directly, through "*majority-owned*" subsidiaries, or through 25% "*controlled companies conducting similar types of businesses*." The controlled companies are subject to an additional business similarity requirement, to counterbalance the holding company's "more tenuous business engagement" under such a control relationship than under a parent-wholly owned or parent-majority owned subsidiary relationship.[1 (p.66610 n.15)] Separate treatment in § 3(b) of controlled companies (**25% < *control* < 50%**) on the one hand, from majority-owned (**50% ≤ *control* < 95%**) and wholly-owned (***control* ≥ 95%**) subsidiaries on the other, reflects the Congressional presumption that an issuer generally would be involved ***in operating*** the businesses, but not ***in trading*** the securities, (1) of wholly-owned and majority-owned subsidiaries regardless of whether or not such subsidiaries engage in similar businesses, and (2) of controlled companies engaged in similar businesses. Conversely, an issuer with interests in a number of controlled companies in unrelated businesses would present the same concerns as traditional investment companies.[2 (§6.4.3)] Separate treatment of controlled companies is important to ensure that "*special situation investment companies*" are not excluded from the statutory definition of "investment company."[1 (p.66610 n.18)]

A "**special situation investment company**," while not defined in the IC Act, is characterized by the SEC as a company which secures control of portfolio companies primarily for the purpose of making a profit in the sale of the portfolio securities, in contrast to an industrial holding company which secures control of portfolio companies in order to primarily engage in the non-investment businesses through such companies. Thus, ***primary investment purpose***[3 (pp.197-98 n.17)] differentiates an industrial holding company from a special situation investment company: an industrial holding company is *engaged primarily in operating* its portfolio companies, and looks to its portfolio companies as a source of *operating profits*; a special situation investment company is *engaged primarily in investing* in its portfolio companies, and looks to its portfolio companies as a source of *investment gain*.[1 (p.66610 nn.19-20)] Venture capital and other private equity investment firms are examples of "special situation investment company"—being in the business of periodically acquiring majority interests in several companies, operating the subsidiaries, and selling the interests when it is profitable to do so.[4 (§3.02[2])] Then, it buys into a new "situation."[5 (p.365)] Because such acquisitions are made primarily for investment purposes, "special situation companies" are investment companies for purposes of the IC Act.[1 (p.66610)] Since registration as investment company under the IC Act would subject such companies to restrictions inconsistent with their business strategies, special situation ICs typically rely on § 3(c)(1) or § 3(c)(7) private fund exclusion to avoid registration under the IC Act.[4 (§3.02[2]); 6]

Two specific investing characteristics of a "special situation" investment company are:[4 (§3.02[2])]

- a pattern of activities of acquiring a diversified portfolio of securities for investment with a view to increasing their value and disposing of them within a short period of time for capital gains; and
- a policy of shifting from one investment to another.

Critically, a company may be actively managing its portfolio companies and thus superficially appears to be an industrial holding company. However, its history of buying and selling securities, whether of 25% controlled companies, majority-owned subsidiaries, or wholly-owned subsidiaries may disclose that it is a special situation investment company.[1 (p.66610 n.20)]

Bibliography

1. Certain Prima Facie Investment Companies, IC-10937, 44 FR 66608 (1979)
2. ROSENBLUM, INVESTMENT COMPANY DETERMINATION UNDER THE 1940 ACT—EXEMPTIONS AND EXCEPTIONS (2nd ed. 2003)
3. Mendelsohn *et al.*, *Status Seeking: Resolving the Status of Inadvertent Investment Companies*, 38 BUS. LAW. 193 (1982)
4. LEMKE, LINS & SMITH, REGULATION OF INVESTMENT COMPANIES (Lexis 2017)
5. Garrett, *When Is An Investment Company?*, 37 U. DET. L.J. 355 (1960)
6. Brown *et al.*, *Internet Incubators: How to Invest in the New Economy Without Becoming an Investment Company*, 56 BUS. LAW. 273 (2000)

Case Study: Bankers "Special Situation Investment Company" Story

Organized in 1928—predating the enactment of the Investment Company Act of 1940—**Bankers Securities Corporation** in its corporate charter described its business as "*purchasing, owning, using, selling, investing and dealing in, for its own account or for the account of others, securities, obligations and investments*."

From the very beginning, Bankers' assets had consisted principally of corporate securities: its portfolio included diverse types of securities of department store, newspaper, hotel, apartment house, and office building; insurance companies; banks; theaters and other amusement centers; a candy company; a drug company; and a department store holding company. Often, Bankers bought controlling interests with a view to later block resale; in some cases, Bankers actively managed to rehabilitate the going businesses, so as to enhance the selling value of its holdings. The history of Bankers' operations showed a pattern of general investment, acquisition, rehabilitation, and disposition of investments—a well-recognized form of investment company business, known as ***dealing in "special situations."***

The Investment Company Act became law on August 22, 1940 and became effective on November 1, while Bankers' declared policy "*to engage primarily in trading in securities*" continued unchanged since the IC Act's passage. The SEC found that Bankers both affirmatively demonstrated that it was organized and had always been operated as an *investment enterprise*, and failed to demonstrate that it was primarily engaged in *mercantile enterprise*. In affirming the SEC's decision, the U.S. Court of Appeals stated: "the Court does not know of any way of describing it any more accurately" than the SEC's description of Bankers Securities Corporation as a ***"special situation" investment company***.

In *re* Bankers Sec. Corp.

IC-639, 15 SEC 695 (1944)

[***Procedural history:*** In *re* Bankers Sec. Corp., IC-639, 15 SEC 695 (1944), *aff'd*, Bankers Sec. Corp. v. SEC, 146 F.2d 88 (3d Cir. 1944)]

In *re* Bankers Sec. Corp.

IC-639, 15 SEC 695 (1944)

FINDINGS AND OPINION OF THE COMMISSION

Bankers Securities Corporation has applied for an order under § 3(b)(2) of the Investment Company Act of 1940 declaring it not to be an investment company. It has also requested such an order under § 3(a) and it has requested an order excepting it from the definition of "investment company" under § 3(c). An application for exemption under § 6(c) was made, but later abandoned.

Section 3(a) defines an investment company as any issuer which—

> (1) is or holds itself out as being engaged primarily, or proposes to engage primarily, in the business of investing, reinvesting, or trading in securities;
>
> (2) is engaged or proposes to engage in the business of issuing face amount certificates of the installment type, or has been engaged in such business and has any such certificates outstanding; or
>
> (3) is engaged or proposes to engage in the business of investing, reinvesting, owning, holding, or trading in securities, and owns or proposes to acquire investment securities having a value exceeding 40 per centum of the value of such issuer's total assets (exclusive of Government securities and cash items) on an unconsolidated basis.

As used in this section, "investment securities" includes all securities except (A) Government securities, (B) securities issued by employees' securities companies, and (C) securities issued by majority-owned subsidiaries of the owner which are not investment companies.

Section 3(c) contains certain exceptions to these definitions. We are not empowered to issue declaratory orders under either of these provisions of the Act and for that reason the application must be dismissed insofar as it requests orders under § § 3(a) and 3(c).

Section 3(b)(2) provides in pertinent part as follows:

> Notwithstanding paragraph (3) of subsection (a), none of the following persons is an investment company within the meaning of this title:
>
> * * * *
>
> (2) Any issuer which the Commission, upon application by such issuer, finds and by order declares to be primarily engaged in a business or businesses other than that of investing, reinvesting, owning, holding, or trading in securities either directly or (A)

through majority-owned subsidiaries or (B) through controlled companies conducting similar types of businesses. . . .

APPLICANT'S HISTORY AND BUSINESS

Applicant was incorporated in 1928 under Pennsylvania law. It has outstanding $13,000,000 par value of preferred and common stock. Although a majority of both classes is held by members of the board of directors, applicant has over 1,100 stockholders. The stock is listed and registered on the Philadelphia Stock Exchange. The articles of incorporation state the purpose of the company to be that of:

> . . . purchasing, acquiring, subscribing for, guaranteeing, owning, holding, using, selling, mortgaging, pledging, investing and dealing in, for its own account or for the account of others, government, state, municipal, township, corporate, association, partnership and individual loans, bonds, notes, debentures, contracts, concessions, mortgages, leases, evidence of indebtedness and cognate securities, obligations and investments, both domestic and foreign, and to make loans and advances of money thereon, and to secure such loans and advances by purchase, acquisition, hypothecation, pledge or other use or disposition of the same, and the investing on behalf of itself or others, of any part of its capital, and such additional funds as it may obtain in any real or personal property, or any interest therein, either as tenant in common or otherwise, and selling or otherwise disposing of the same or any part thereof or interest therein.

From its inception applicant has held itself out as an investment company. In a prospectus issued in 1928 the company stated:

> Bankers Securities Corporation is organized to buy and hold, underwrite, acquire, sell and generally deal in corporate stocks, bonds, mortgages and mortgage bonds and securities, including those of banks, insurance companies and other financial institutions, and deal, finance, invest in or refinance, reorganize and rehabilitate enterprises whether for its own account or the account of others, and generally engage in business similar to that done by the securities companies closely allied to the larger banks and trust companies of New York, Chicago and elsewhere.

Annual and intermediate reports to stockholders, although brief and uninformative, confirmed the impression created by the charter and prospectus. * * * * In 1935 applicant registered its securities under the Securities Exchange Act of 1934 for listing on the Philadelphia Stock Exchange. The Commission's rule for the use of Form 15 "For Incorporated Investment Companies" provided as follows:

> This form shall be used for applications . . . of any corporation which is *engaged*, either directly or through subsidiaries, *primarily* in the business of investing and reinvesting, or trading in securities, for the purpose of revenue and for profit, and not in general for the purpose, or with the effect, of exercising control . . . (emphasis supplied)

The applicant filed on this form on August 14, 1935. Items 11, 13, and 15, under the heading "Business and Property" and the answers of the applicant (as later amended) were as follows:

11. Describe briefly the general character of the investments of the registrant and the subsidiaries; and state whether the policy of the registrant and its subsidiaries is to engage primarily in trading of securities or in holding for investment:

> The general character of investments of the registrant consists of bonds (generally corporate obligations of all types), stocks, first mortgages, loans and real estate. The general character of the investments of its subsidiary, Bansecor Corporation, consists of stocks and loans. The general character of the investments of its subsidiary, City Stores Co. consists of stocks of its subsidiaries. The general character of the assets of the subsidiaries of City Stores Co. consists of merchanidse, real estate, accounts receivable and other items usually connected with the department store business. The policy of the registrant is to engage primarily in trading in securities. The policy of its subsidiary, Bansecor Corp. is to engage primarily in holding for investment. The policy of City Stores Co. is to act as a holding company. The subsidiaries of City Stores Co. conduct general department store businesses or hold and operate real estate incidental thereto.

13. Describe briefly the general development of the business of the registrant and its subsidiaries during the past five years [After noting its purchases of real estate bonds and real estate, the acquisition of some of its own shares, and the acquisition of City Stores Company stock, applicant stated]:

> Otherwise, there has been no materially important change in the policy of the corporation and its subsidiary [Bansecor Corporation] as to the character of its investments or trading in securities. There has been no materially important development affecting the character of the corporation and its subsidiary as an investment company.

15. Outline briefly any provisions contained in the charter or by-laws of the registrant with respect to the following:

> (a) Any limitations upon the kind of investments which may be made by the registrant: NONE
>
> (b) Any limitations upon the amount, or proportion, of assets which may be invested in any one security, class of securities or group of securities: NONE
>
> (c) Any geographical limitations upon investments: NONE

Subsequent annual reports filed by the applicant with this Commission for the years 1935 through 1939, were similarly filed on Form 15-K "For Incorporated Investment Companies." * * * The last of these reports on Form 15-K was filed on June 1, 1940, for the year 1939.

The Investment Company Act became law on August 22, 1940, and the effective date thereof was November 1. Thereafter the applicant ceased to file annual reports on Form 15-K and instead filed on Form 10-K "For Corporations." However, in its annual reports filed in 1941 and 1942 (for the years 1940 and 1941), in replying to Item 7 on Form 10-K, which requires a brief description of "the material changes . . . in the general character of the business done" by the reporting company and its subsidiaries, the applicant reported "*no changes*." Thus, the declared policy of the applicant "to engage primarily in trading in securities," initially reported in 1935, continued unchanged after the passage of the Investment Company Act, notwithstanding the use of a different form for its reports.

In its reply to the questionnaire circulated by the Commission in connection with the Investment Trust Study, calling for lists of portfolio securities shown yearly from December 31, 1928 to December 31, 1935, the applicant stated as follows [in response to Item 19, Part IV, of the questionnaire]:

(a) Original activities of declarant. Outline briefly the scope and extent of the business and activities of declarant during the first year after the commencement of business operations.

> During the first year after the commencement of business, the declarant employed its capital in making unsecured loans and loans secured by collateral, traded in securities and bought securities for investment consisting of stocks, bonds and first mortgages. Declarant did not regularly furnish investment advisory services to anybody on securities issued by declarant. Declarant participated in underwriting or distribution of securities issued by others. Declarant participated in trading or syndicate accounts in securities issued by others . . .

(b) Development of activities of declarant. Outline briefly the general development of the business of declarant during the period from January 1, 1927 to December 31, 1934, particularly referring to any changes in the business or activities of declarant enumerated in Item 19(a) hereof.

> During the period to December 31, 1934 the declarant has not changed its activities as recited above in (a).

(c) Present activities of declarant. Outline briefly the business and activities of declarant during the calendar year 1935, particularly referring to the activities enumerated in 19(a) and (b) hereof.

> During the calendar year 1935 declarant has not changed its activities as recited above in (a). * * * *

The public representations of the applicant from its origin to the present are those of an investment company. That evidence is more than sufficient to necessitate a conclusion that applicant holds itself out as being primarily engaged in investing and reinvesting and trading in securities within the meaning of § 3(a)(1). The evidence does more—it illuminates certain evidence of applicant's activities claimed to show that it is primarily engaged in other businesses.

The assets of the company have, from the very beginning, consisted principally of corporate securities. The portfolio presently includes (among miscellaneous holdings in utility and industrial companies) securities of department store, newspaper, hotel, apartment house, office building and insurance companies, banks, theaters and other amusement centers, a candy company, a drug company and a department store holding company.

The applicant has traded actively in securities since its organization. In the years 1928 to 1941 inclusive it bought and sold about $160,000,000 of securities. [These figures include government securities, the total purchases of which amounted to $20,270,925. The government securities were all sold during the calendar years in which they were purchased. Transactions for a 4-year period—mortgages and mortgage participations excluded—were as follows:]

Year	Issues at hand at beginning of year	Issues at hand at end of year	Transaction during year	
			Acquisitions	Dispositions
1939	251	232	203	140
1940	232	217	153	98
1941	217	210	134	64
1942	210	199	91	32

In its early days, in addition to investing and trading in corporate stocks and bonds, the applicant made large loans involving major portions of its capital. For example, in 1928 it purchased $1,200,000 of debentures of Philadelphia Record Company; it made a collateral loan to City Stores Company of $8,000,000; it lent $7,600,000 in call loans. In 1929 the company purchased $2,000,000 of the debentures of Albert M. Greenfield & Co.; it lent $10,000,000 to Fox Theatres Corporation.

From the very beginning applicant concentrated chiefly (but not exclusively) on a limited number of issues, and it often bought securities with the object of obtaining a controlling interest in the issuer with a view to block resales. In some cases applicant has actively endeavored to use its control to rehabilitate going businesses by management reforms so as to enhance the selling value of its holdings. This type of activity has brought the management into contact with various miscellaneous businesses. At present it is active in the management of department stores, a candy manufacturing and distribution business, radio stations, real estate properties, and other businesses. With respect to many of these it was testified that resale of the holdings of securities blocks was intended when an acceptable price could be obtained. [A recent example is the completion of the acquisition of a controlling interest in the Girard Life Insurance Company. It was testified that a resale of these securities as a block is intended.] The applicant, however, now claims that it is interested in the operation of department stores as a permanent engagement, and that it does not contemplate selling its interest in City Stores Company and other direct or indirect interests in department stores.

Prior to 1932 the applicant held collateral notes of City Stores Company (a department store holding company) which were defaulted in that year. Thereupon the applicant obtained representation on the board of the defaulting company which, in 1935, was reorganized under § 77B of the Bankruptcy Act. As a result of the reorganization the applicant obtained a controlling interest in the capital stock of the debtor, and at least by that time it was active in the management of the Cities Stores business.

Perhaps the largest part of this record concerns the operations of City Stores and its subsidiaries and the management functions of applicant in City Stores. The two enterprises have interlocking managements. There is no doubt (1) that applicant's representatives in City Stores spend almost all of their time on City Stores business and (2) that applicant's management (especially Albert M. Creenfield, chairman of applicant's board) spend some time in considering management problems of City Stores. The block of holdings (debt and stock) in City Stores represents the largest single item in the portfolio and, although no current income is being drawn up through City Stores stock, City Stores yield income through interest on its debt, it is amortizing that debt, and it is claimed by applicant that City Stores is in a present position to yield dividends on its stock should applicant wish to withdraw them.

Counsel for applicant claims that the investment in City Stores has become so important, and the extent of applicant's management thereof so pervasive, the any recourse to applicant's history to clarify its status is "academic." We cannot agree. Notwithstanding the importance of the interest in City Stores the applicant, as such, retains its character as a vehicle for extensive and diversified investment. There is no evidence nor is there any claim of change in the general policy, manifest from this record, of seeking profitable investment wherever it can be found. This company's portfolio contains 200 issues of securities (excluding mortgages) of the most diverse types in which it owns from nominal to majority participations and which afford it a range from no participation to control in the enterprise. It has held some issues for short periods and others for long periods. In many instances its management interlocks with that of the issuer. It has obtained its holdings in a variety of ways and it has disposed of them similarly—some as initially acquired, others as built up through a series of acquisitions, some after a basic rehabilitation of the enterprise.

The management of this applicant cannot be characterized in any adequate terms except as businessmen in a general sense. Many of the members of the management have a general financial background. Although there has been an attempt to weight the record toward the conclusion that they are primarily operating business managers and real estate men, the diversity and the nature of their activities stamps them as versatile handlers of money—investment specialists to begin with, and dedicated to the idea that their supervision ought to follow their investments when possible. This explains the diversity of their interests and the extent to which they have concerned themselves with issuers' operations. It explains why Albert M. Greenfield, the chairman of its board, was able to testify on the one hand that he spends 60 percent of his time in the management of City Stores, a primary concern of applicant, and on the other that he manages a company which is "as pure an investment house as any corporation can be," which "does a general investment banking business," which "will ultimately become the principal central city real estate owners," which knows "more about that [real estate] than . . . about most things, because that is our business—real estate," which not only invests in the Loft Candy Company but gives the operations of that company "daily attention," which not only invests in legitimate theaters in New York but manages them ("jointly" with the Schuberts) even to the extent of actually participating in the selection of shows, which participates "in everything in connection with" the operations of the company owning the so-called "Million Dollar" pier in Atlantic City and which is not loath to take on control and active operations of other businesses, including The Media drug chain in and around Philadelphia.

While all this is taking place, general investment, the acquisition, rehabilitation and disposition of investments goes on all the time. Nevertheless we are asked to believe that a transformation has come: that the applicant is now primarily engaged in retail merchandising and real estate, and that it solemnly intends to stay in those fields.

As examples of the type of supervision exercised by applicant we are told that it, through the chairman of its board, took over the letting of contracts for the installation of elevators and air-conditioning for City Stores subsidiaries, assumed the major functions in building a great warehouse, adjusting fire losses, switching operating personnel, negotiating insurance and credits, financial rearrangements, and the like. Significantly, many of these things were being done at times when applicant publicly declared itself an investment company, and many of them are of the type which any controlling person—whatever his intentions—might undertake as part of the emoluments of control. They bespeak an active concern for the investment, they do not compel a finding that the investment is merely a vehicle for engagement in a mercantile business rather than a primary concern, in itself.

Two alternative inferences may be drawn. Either the applicant holds City Stores stock as a medium for controlling a department store business—and thus in a sense for the purpose of itself engaging in the department store business; or the applicant finds itself the owner of a large investment in City Stores and actively participates in the management thereof incidentally and in order to enhance the value of and return on such investment. The whole history of the applicant, as well as the manner of its original acquisition of the controlling interest in City Stores, gives support to the latter inference.

In the course of its history applicant has obtained large and controlling interests in various businesses, disposed of some, and retained others. Its officers have actively managed controlled businesses for the purpose of rehabilitating important investments in the portfolio. This is a well-recognized form of investment company business, known as dealing in "special situations." As far as the active management of City Stores is concerned, the contemporaneous construction put upon that activity by the applicant itself, consistently adhered to throughout the years (as shown by its filings with this Commission) established it as part and parcel of applicant's originally announced business. Even assuming that the management has no present intention of disposing of the investment in City Stores does not establish the applicant as a mercantile enterprise, or indicate a change in the nature of its investment company business. Only recently, in the light of the Investment Company Act and these proceedings, has the applicant endeavored to read such significance into its managerial activities and repudiate the import of its earlier public assertions.

Not only does this record fall short of sustaining applicant's claim that it is primarily engaged in noninvestment company business, but it demonstrates affirmatively that Bankers Securities Corporation was organized, and has always been operated, as an investment enterprise. Public investment in the company was invited and has been maintained on representations which meant, in essence, that the company was diversifying stockholders' risk by a varied investment program. Stockholders were not asked to rely on the skill of applicant's management in the merchandising, or in any other specific mercantile or commercial business. They were given to understand that the management was alert always to find profitable repositories of invested funds, and the history of the company bears out the understanding, created in stockholders, that the company was not committing itself primarily to any specific business.

The application will be denied. An appropriate order will issue.

Section 1.2 Types of Registered Investment Companies

Laws & Rules Highlight:

IC Act (15 USC 80a-1 *et seq.*) & Rules (17 CFR §§ 270.0-1 *et seq.*)

Three Classes of Registered Investment Companies

§ 4 Classification of Investment Companies

- § **4(1)** (*def. "**face-amount certificate company**"*)
- § **4(2)** (*def. "**unit investment trust**"*)
- § **4(3)** (*def. "**management company**"*)
  - § 5(a)(1) (*def. "open-end company"*); § 5(a)(2) (*def. "closed-end company"*)
  - § 5(b)(1) (*def. "diversified company"*); § 5(b)(2) (*def. "non-diversified company"*)

Management Companies

§ 5 Subclassification of Management Companies

open-end management company (*aka* mutual fund)

- § 5(a)(1) (*def. "**open-end company**"*); § 2(a)(32) (*def. "**redeemable security**"*)
- § 22 Distribution, Redemption, and Repurchase of Redeemable Securities
  - Rule 22c-1 Pricing of Redeemable Securities for Distribution, Redemption and Repurchase (*regulates **pricing** of redemption: **daily computed, forward-priced NAV** requirement for mutual fund **sales and redemptions***); § 22(c) (*authorizes the SEC to issue rules relating to redeemable securities issued by open-end companies*)
    - ✓ Rule 2a-4 Definition of "Current Net Asset Value" for Use in Computing Periodically the Current Price of Redeemable Security; § (2)(a)(41)(B) (*def "value"*)
  - § 22(e) (*regulates **timing** of redemption payment: mutual fund **may not suspend** the right of redemption and must pay redemption proceeds within **seven calendar days**, except in certain emergencies or as the SEC by rule may permit—designed to prevent funds and their advisers from interfering with shareholders' redemption rights for improper purposes, such as preservation of management fees*)
    - ✓ Rule 22e-4 Liquidity Risk Management Programs (*applicable to open-end funds excluding money market funds: limits fund's illiquid investments to not more than **15%** of fund's net assets, designed to **reduce liquidity risk**, i.e., risk that funds may be unable to meet their redemption obligations without diluting the interests of remaining fund shareholders*)
  - § 22(g) (*limits types of consideration for open-end company securities to **cash or securities**—designed to prevent insider overreaching*)

- § 18 Capital Structure
  - § 18(f)(1) (***prohibits** mutual fund from issuing "**senior security**," except bank borrowings with 300% asset coverage*); § 18(g) (*def. "senior security"*)

closed-end management company (*aka* closed-end fund)

- § 5(a)(2) (*def. "**closed-end company**"*)
- § 23 Distribution and Repurchase of Securities: Closed-End Companies
  - § 23(a) (*limits types of consideration for closed-end company securities to **cash and securities**—designed to prevent insider overreaching*)
  - § 23(b) (*generally prohibits closed-end fund from **selling** its common stock in an offering at a price **below** the stock's "**current net asset value**"*); § 30(e) (*closed-end fund must report its NAV to fund shareholders **semi-annually***)
- § 18 Capital Structure
  - §§ 18(a)-(e) (***permit** closed-end fund to issue **senior securities**, limited to: one class of debt and one class of preferred stock; 300% asset coverage for debt; 200% asset coverage for preferred stock*); § 18(h) (*def. "asset coverage" applicable to senior securities*)

Basic Structural Features of Open-End Fund, Closed-End Fund, and UIT

<table>
<tr><th>Three Classes of Registered IC;
IC Act</th><th colspan="2">Statutory Definition</th><th>Governance: Board of Directors</th><th>Active Management by Investment Adviser</th><th>Issuing Redeemable Securities</th><th>Secondary Market Trading</th></tr>
<tr><td>Unit Investment Trust (UIT)</td><td colspan="2">§ 4(2)</td><td>No § 4(2)(B)</td><td>No (being a fixed portfolio with a fixed duration) § 4(2)</td><td>Yes §§ 2(a)(32), 4(2)(C)</td><td>Yes (where UIT sponsor acts as market maker in the units to reduce redemption pressure on UIT)</td></tr>
<tr><td colspan="7"><u>Cast of Players:</u> Sponsor/Depositor: creating UIT and assembling trust portfolio; depositing portfolio with trustee; offering UIT units; maintaining secondary market in units. Trustee/Custodian: role assumed by a qualified bank, holding legal title to and safekeeping UIT's assets, and performing day-to-day trust administration. Evaluator: valuing UIT's portfolio for purposes of redemption and the secondary market. Principal Underwriter: role assumed by the UIT sponsor solely or with an underwriting group.</td></tr>
<tr><td rowspan="2">Management Company</td><td colspan="2">Open-end (aka mutual fund)
§§ 4(3), 5(a)(1)</td><td>Yes §§ 10, 15, 16</td><td>Yes (continuous public offering) §§ 4(3), 5(a)(1)</td><td>Yes (continuous redeeming) §§ 2(a)(32), 5(a)(1), 22</td><td>No § 22(d)</td></tr>
<tr><td colspan="2">Closed-end
§§ 4(3), 5(a)(2)</td><td>Yes §§ 10, 15, 16</td><td>Yes (no continuous offering after the initial public offering) §§ 4(3), 5(a)(2)</td><td>No §§ 5(a)(2), 23</td><td>Yes (on stock exchange or in OTC) § 23(c)</td></tr>
<tr><td colspan="7"><u>Cast of Players:</u> Investment Adviser (also as Sponsor and Administrator): organizing and promoting the fund; performing investment counselor and portfolio manager functions; providing extra-advisory administrative services. Board of Directors/Committee of Trustees: approving investment advisory and underwriting contracts; oversight of investment adviser and fund investments. Advisory Board (of mutual fund): performing advisory functions with respect to fund investments but no power to determine purchase or sale of any security. Principal Underwriter: role usually assumed by the Investment Adviser or an affiliate controlled by the Adviser. Custodian: retaining custody of fund assets and computing fund NAV. Transfer Agent: providing services to fund shareholders.</td></tr>
</table>

Basic Structural Features of Open-End Fund, Closed-End Fund, and UIT

Three Classes of Registered IC; IC Act	**Statutory Definition**	**Governance: Board of Directors**	**Active Management by Investment Adviser**	**Issuing Redeemable Securities**	**Secondary Market Trading**
Face-amount certificate company	§ 4(1)	[Treatment omitted due to its obsolescence]			

Bibliography

1. Gould & Lins, *Unit Investment Trusts: Structure and Regulation Under the Federal Securities Laws*, 43 BUS. LAW. 1177 (1987-1988)
2. Close, *Investment Companies: Closed-End versus Open-End*, 29 HARVARD BUS. REV. 79 (1952)
3. Schonfeld & Kerwin, *Organization of a Mutual Fund*, 49 BUS. LAW. 107 (1993)
4. ICI, 2017 INVESTMENT COMPANY FACT BOOK (57th ed.), Appendix A pp.243-47: The Organization of a Mutual Fund

Topic 1 "Redeemable Security": Open-End/Closed-End Dichotomy

Laws & Rules Highlight

IC Act (15 USC 80a-1 *et seq.*)

Section 2 General Definitions

(a) When used in this title, unless the context otherwise requires—

(1) * * *

(32) "***Redeemable security***" means any security, other than short-term paper, under the terms of which the holder, upon its presentation to the issuer or to a person designated by the issuer, is entitled (whether absolutely or only out of surplus) to receive approximately his proportionate share of the issuer's current net assets, or the cash equivalent thereof.

Pre-Case Background Note:[Biblio]

"Redeemable Security" and Its Implications for Open-End and Closed-End Structures

Under the Investment Company Act, there are two structures of management companies: open-end company (popularly known as *mutual fund*), and closed-end company (popularly known as *closed-end fund*), each receiving different regulatory treatment unique for its structure, while both being subject to the many core provisions under the IC Act. The ***distinguishing feature*** of an "open-end" fund from a "closed-end" fund is implied by their names: An open-end fund by law must issue redeemable securities, whereas a closed-end fund by law may not issue any redeemable security.[1 (§§5(a)(1)-(2)); 2; 3; 4 (II.A); 5 (II.A, IV.C.3)]

Under an **open-end fund structure**, the "***redeemable security***" by definition "*entitles*" the investor to tender his shares to the mutual fund for repurchase at any time, receiving in return from the fund "*approximately his proportionate share of the issuer's current net assets, or the cash equivalent thereof.*"[1 (§2(a)(32))] The fund's sale price and redemption price by law must both be based upon the pro rata ownership interest in the fund's net assets that a share represents, "*next computed after receipt of a tender of such security for redemption or of an order to purchase or sell such security,*"[6] known as the fund's forward-priced NAV. As mutual funds regularly repurchase their shares in response to investors' exercise of their redemption rights, mutual funds must also engage in a continuous public offering of shares to new investors, to avoid fund contraction and eventual self-liquidation.[4 (II.A)]

Being under the legal obligation to honor redemption requests within *seven calendar days*, mutual funds are subject to extensive liquidity regulation with respect to their portfolio investments. A mutual fund is required to classify each of its portfolio investments as a highly liquid investment, moderately liquid investment, less liquid investment, or illiquid investment. A mutual fund's "illiquid investments," *i.e.*, any investment that the fund reasonably expects cannot be sold or disposed of in current market conditions in *seven calendar days or less* without the sale or disposition significantly changing the market value of the investment, may not exceed 15% of the fund's net assets.[1 (§22(e)); 7] The capital structure of mutual funds is marked by simplicity: being allowed to issue a single class of common stock, and prohibited from issuing any "senior security" except bank borrowings subject to 300% asset coverage.[1 (§18(f)(1)); 5 (IV.C.2)] The prohibition against open-end fund issuing senior security is explained by the nature of the funds' common stock being "redeemable security": any senior security would be inherently unsound when a fund's common stock, *i.e.*, the equity cushion otherwise supporting the senior security, could be redeemed away at any time.[2]

Under a **closed-end fund structure**, fund investors—much like shareholders in ordinary operating companies—have ***no redemption rights*** and must rely on secondary market trading, such as stock exchanges or the OTC market, for liquidity.[4 (II.A)] A closed-end fund by law generally may not sell its common stock in an offering "*at a price below the current net asset value of such stock, exclusive of any distribution commission or discount*"[1 (§23(b))]—a prohibition designed to prevent insider overreaching with the resulting dilutive effect on the fund's assets.[8] After the initial offering, closed-end fund shares trade in the secondary market at prices determined by the forces of supply and demand, almost always deviating from the fund's NAV: often at a discount, and at times at a premium. Having ***no redemption obligations***, closed-end funds do not engage in a continuous public offering of their shares. Similar to ordinary operating companies, they raise capital through an initial public offering; and only infrequently do they engage in subsequent public offerings.[4 (II.A)]

Having no redemption obligations also allows closed-end funds to invest in less liquid securities and in specialized markets.[8] Research examining the link between portfolio composition and the choice of open-end versus closed-end fund form has found that:[9]

- *foreign funds* are more likely to be closed-end than *domestic funds*;
- *debt funds* are more likely to be closed-end than *equity funds*;
- equity funds investing in *less liquid equities* are more likely to be closed-end than equity funds investing in *more liquid equities*;
- *long-term* debt funds are more likely to be closed-end than *short-term* debt funds;
- long-term *municipal* debt funds are more likely to be closed-end than long-term *Treasury or agency* debt funds; and
- funds that invest in *restricted securities* are more likely to be closed-end than funds that do not invest in restricted securities.

Their common stock being a non-redeemable security, closed-end funds' capital structure is allowed more leverage than that of open-end funds. Closed-end funds are allowed to issue senior securities representing one class of preferred stock and one class of debt, subject to 200% asset coverage for preferred stock and 300% asset coverage for debt.[1 (§18); 2]

Bibliography

1. Investment Company Act of 1940, 15 USC 80a-1 *et seq.* (2012)
2. DIV. OF INV. MGMT, SEC. & EXCH. COMM'N, PROTECTING INVESTORS: A HALF CENTURY OF INVESTMENT COMPANY REGULATION, Ch. 11 Repurchases and Redemptions of Investment Company Shares (1992)
3. Smith, *Closed-End Interval Funds: Combining the Qualities of Open-End and Closed-End Funds*, PERS. FIN. PLAN. 26, (1995)
4. Roiter, *Disentangling Mutual Fund Governance from Corporate Governance*, 6 HARV. BUS. L. REV. 1 (2016)
5. Morley, *Collective Branding and the Origins of Mutual Fund Regulation*, 6 VA. L. & BUS. REV. 341 (2012)
6. Rule 270.22c-1 Pricing of Redeemable Securities for Distribution, Redemption and Repurchase
7. Rule 270.22e-4 Liquidity Risk Management Programs; Investment Company Liquidity Risk Management Programs, 33-10233, IC-32315, 81 FR 82142 (2016)
8. LEMKE ET AL., REGULATION OF INVESTMENT COMPANIES, § 4.04 Management Companies: Section 4(3) (Lexis 2017)
9. Deli & Varma, *Closed-end Versus Open-end: The Choice of Organizational Form*, 8 J. CORP. FIN. 1 (2001)

Case Study: Meaning of "Redeemable Security"

Liquidity arrangement for ***Liquidity Protected Preferred shares*** (LPPs) to be issued by Eaton Vance closed-end funds: Each Fund would enter into a *Liquidity Agreement* with a Liquidity Provider. If LPP purchase orders are insufficient to match LPP sell orders (a ***Liquidity Event***), the Liquidity Provider will unconditionally purchase all LPPs of such unfilled sell orders, paying the LPP sellers not from the Fund's "current net assets" but from the Liquidity Provider's assets. The Liquidity Provider may enter into a *Put Agreement* with the parent company of the Funds' investment adviser, Eaton Vance Corporation (***EVC Put***), or with the issuing Fund (***Fund Put***). In the case of an EVC Put, payment will be made to the Liquidity Provider not from the Fund's "current net assets" but from EVC's assets. In the case of a Fund Put, although payment will be made to the Liquidity Provider from the Fund's current net assets, the payment is subject to significant restrictions. The SEC agreed with Eaton Vance Management that the *Liquidity Event* feature, the *EVC Put* feature, and the *Fund Put* feature would not cause the LPP to be a "redeemable security" under IC Act § 2(a)(32).

Eaton Vance Mgmt.; Closed-End Fund LPP Shares

IC Act § 2(a)(32) etc; 2008 SEC No-Act. LEXIS 484 (June 13, 2008)

Eaton Vance Mgmt.; Closed-End Fund LPP Shares

SEC No-Action Letter; File No. 801-15930 (June 13, 2008)

Securities and Exchange Commission
Response of the Office of Chief Counsel, Division of Investment Management
Response of the Office of Mergers and Acquisitions, Division of Corporation Finance

Your letter dated June 12, 2008 requests our assurance that we would not recommend enforcement action to the Securities and Exchange Commission under §§ 34(b) or 35(d) of the Investment Company Act of 1940 or Rule 22c-1 thereunder against open-end investment companies that hold themselves out as money market funds in reliance on Rule 2a-7 under the Act if they purchase liquidity protected preferred shares (**LPP**), a new type of preferred stock described in your letter, to be issued by closed-end investment companies (**Funds**) advised by Eaton Vance Management (**Eaton Vance**).[1]

Your letter also requests that we concur with your view that the LPP would not be redeemable securities, as defined in § 2(a)(32) of the Investment Company Act, if: (a) the Funds issue LPP that is subject to purchase in certain circumstances by a third-party liquidity provider (**Liquidity Provider**); and (b) the Liquidity Provider has the right to sell any such LPP to an affiliate of the Funds or to the Funds themselves in certain circumstances, as described in your letter. * * * *

I. Facts

As described in your letter, a number of Funds have outstanding one or more series of auction rate preferred shares (**ARP**), and the current disruption in the auction rate securities market imposes significant hardship on ARP holders that need access to liquidity. You state that it is highly unlikely that the existing auction markets for ARP will resume normal functioning in the near term. In light of these events, and in an effort to

---

[1] Money market funds that fail to meet certain conditions of Rule 2a-7 may violate §§ 34(b) and 35(d) of the Investment Company Act.... Section 34(b), in relevant part, makes it unlawful for any person to make an untrue statement of material fact in a registration statement or other document filed pursuant to the Investment Company Act. Section 35(d) makes it unlawful for any registered investment company to adopt as part of its name any word or words that the Commission finds materially deceptive or misleading, and authorizes the Commission to adopt rules to define such names as are materially deceptive or misleading. Money Market Funds that do not satisfy Rule 2a-7's conditions may also violate Rule 22c-1 under the Investment Company Act, which requires open-end funds to sell and redeem their shares at a price based on current net asset value, if they use the amortized cost method, as defined in Rule 2a-7(a)(2), to value their portfolio securities....

create a more stable long-term market for preferred shares issued by closed-end funds, Eaton Vance is developing LPP as a permissible investment for Money Market Funds.

You state that the Funds propose to offer LPP to supplement or replace their existing ARP. The LPP will pay a dividend that will be reset every seven days in a remarketing process administered by one or more financial institutions acting as remarketing agent(s). After providing a preliminary notice of the likely dividend rate, the remarketing agent(s) will solicit existing holders and potential buyers for indications of interest. The remarketing agent(s) will then match buyers and sellers at the lowest possible dividend rate. Under normal circumstances, the dividend rate in each remarketing will be set as the lowest possible rate at which all of the LPP would be either held or bought after matching up sell, bid and buy orders. All orders to buy and sell LPP in any remarketing will be subject to a cap rate (the *Boundary Rate*).[2] The LPP will be sold only at a price equal to their $25,000 per share liquidation preference plus accumulated and unpaid dividends. Within three days of the remarketing, proceeds from the sales of the LPP will be remitted to holders of the LPP participating in the remarketing.[3]

You state that each Fund will enter into an agreement (the *Liquidity Agreement*) with a Liquidity Provider. Under the Liquidity Agreement, the Liquidity Provider will have a contractual obligation (the *Liquidity Event Feature*) to purchase unconditionally all LPP subject to sell orders in a remarketing that have not been matched with purchase orders (a *Liquidity Event*). You represent that, before entering into the Liquidity Agreement, the Liquidity Provider will have received a short-term rating in one of the two highest short-term rating categories from the Requisite Nationally Recognized Statistical Rating Organizations (**NRSROs**) with respect to a class of debt obligations that is comparable in priority and security to the Liquidity Event Feature.[4]

---

[2] You state that the Boundary Rate will be set as either (a) a specified interest rate (*e.g.*, two-month LIBOR) plus a specified number of basis points, or (b) a specified percentage of a specified interest rate (*e.g.*, a percentage times two-month LIBOR).

[3] You state that the same considerations, analysis and conclusions would apply to preferred stock with liquidity protection features substantially the same as the LPP but that trades in an auction process similar to that in which ARP trade.

[4] Rule 2a-7 limits a Money Market Fund's portfolio investments to securities that have received credit ratings from the Requisite NRSROs in one of the two highest short-term rating categories or comparable unrated securities (*i.e.*, "Eligible Securities"). A security that is subject to a Guarantee, as defined in Rule 2a-7(a)(15), may be determined to be an Eligible Security based solely on the rating assigned to the Guarantee, under paragraph (c)(3)(iii) of Rule

You represent that, as a result of the Liquidity Agreement, any LPP holder (including any Money Market Fund) that seeks to sell its holdings will be able to do so.[5] Like all other LPP sold in a remarketing, the LPP purchased by the Liquidity Provider will be bought at a price equal to the $25,000 per share liquidation preference plus accumulated but unpaid dividends. In the event that a Liquidity Agreement will not be renewed, will otherwise be terminated, or a new Liquidity Agreement with a replacement Liquidity Provider will be entered into, holders of the LPP will be notified at least two remarketings in advance of such event and given the opportunity to sell their LPP in these remarketings. Thus, you state that LPP holders will always have the opportunity to sell their LPP pursuant to the Liquidity Agreement, if necessary, on at least two occasions subsequent to the receipt of notice of a change in or termination of the Liquidity Agreement.

You state that after a Liquidity Event has occurred, additional terms may take effect. These include: (a) escalating dividend rates;[6] and (b) additional fees that Funds will pay to the Liquidity Provider.[7] In addition, there may be an agreement under which the Liquidity Provider would have rights to sell (or *put*) any of the LPP that it had purchased to the parent company of the Funds' investment adviser, Eaton Vance Corp. (**EVC** and the *EVC Put*),[8] or to the issuing Fund (the *Fund Put*), at a price per share equal to the liquidation preference.

You state that the precise terms of the EVC Put are subject to negotiation with a

---

2a-7. The term "Requisite NRSROs" is defined in Rule 2a-7(a)(21).

[5] Upon completion of the remarketing, the Liquidity Provider will be required to purchase automatically all LPP subject to sell orders that have not been fulfilled with purchase orders.

[6] If upon any given Liquidity Event the Liquidity Provider is required to purchase LPP in an amount less than 50% (or some other agreed-upon percentage) (the *Trigger Percent*) of the shares in the remarketing, the dividend rate for the next dividend period will be the Boundary Rate. If, however, the Liquidity Provider is required to purchase more than the Trigger Percent of the shares in a particular remarketing, the dividend rate will be the last Boundary Rate plus an additional pre-determined percentage (the *Raised Boundary Rate*). If upon subsequent consecutive remarketings the Liquidity Provider must continue to purchase greater than the Trigger Percent of the shares, then the dividend rate will be the Raised Boundary Rate plus an increasing pre-determined percentage up to a specified maximum.

[7] You state that the Funds will pay a bifurcated fee to the Liquidity Provider; one fee on the committed amount of the liquidity facility and a second fee for amounts drawn to purchase LPP pursuant to a Liquidity Event. Accordingly, the Liquidity Provider will receive an overall higher fee to the extent that the liquidity facility is used.

[8] You state that the EVC Put is not expected to be an ongoing feature of the LPP arrangements and will be offered only to the Liquidity Provider for the LPP issued in the first LPP offering by a Fund.

particular Liquidity Provider. You expect, however, that for the nine-month period ending on the first anniversary of the effectiveness of the Liquidity Agreement (the *Anniversary Date*), if the Liquidity Provider owns all outstanding LPP, the Liquidity Provider may exercise the EVC Put with respect to all LPP that it owns. On the Anniversary Date, if the Liquidity Provider owns any outstanding LPP, the Liquidity Provider may exercise the EVC Put with respect to all LPP that it owns.[9]

You state that a Fund may provide a Liquidity Provider with a Fund Put as an inducement to potential Liquidity Providers, both initially (in lieu of the EVC Put) and on an ongoing basis. The Fund Put would be exercisable only (a) upon the expiration of not less than one year from the effective date of the Liquidity Agreement, and (b) with respect to any LPP that the Liquidity Provider has held for no less than three consecutive months and unsuccessfully attempted to sell in remarketings. You state that the Liquidity Provider would be able to exercise a Fund Put only following written notice. You also state that a Fund will provide a Fund Put only if the Internal Revenue Service issues new guidance clarifying with a high degree of certainty that such a feature would not cause the LPP to become taxable as debt rather than equity for federal income tax purposes.

II. Analysis

A. Money Market Funds

As we noted above, the LPP are designed to be purchased by Money Market Funds. The instruments that Money Market Funds may purchase must meet Rule 2a-7's maturity and quality requirements.[10] You acknowledge that a Money Market Fund's investment in preferred stock, including auction rate preferred stock, would not meet these requirements. You assert, however, that the LPP, together with the Liquidity Event Feature, is functionally equivalent to securities that meet Rule 2a-7's maturity and quality conditions. * * * *

B. Redeemable Securities

Section 2(a)(32) of the Investment Company Act defines "redeemable security" as "any security, other than short-term paper, under the terms of which the holder, upon its

---

[9] You state that the exercise of the EVC Put would create no obligation for a Fund to redeem its LPP.

[10] Rule 2a-7's portfolio maturity conditions appear in paragraphs (c)(2) and (d) and the portfolio quality conditions appear in paragraph (c)(3). Rule 2a-7 contains conditions that apply to each investment a Money Market Fund proposes to make, as well as conditions that apply to a Money Market Fund's entire portfolio.

presentation to the issuer or to a person designated by the issuer, is entitled … to receive approximately his proportionate share of the issuer's current net assets, or the cash equivalent thereof." Under § 5(a) of the Investment Company Act, an open-end company is defined as a management company that is "offering for sale or has outstanding any redeemable security of which it is the issuer," and a closed-end company is defined as "any management company other than an open-end company." Thus, if the LPP were redeemable securities, then any Fund issuing LPP would be an open-end company and not a closed-end company.

You assert that the LPP should not be considered redeemable securities based on the plain wording of § 2(a)(32) because of the Liquidity Event Feature or the EVC Put. The Liquidity Provider is required to purchase LPP in a remarketing if there are insufficient purchase orders to fill sell orders. Although the Liquidity Provider could be considered a "person designated by the issuer" within the meaning of § 2(a)(32) for purposes of paying liquidation amounts to an investor selling its LPP, the amounts are not paid from a Fund's "current net assets" but rather from the Liquidity Provider's assets. You also assert that, as with the Liquidity Event Feature, exercise of the EVC Put entails payment from EVC's assets rather than from a Fund's "current net assets."

You concede that exercise of the Fund Put would result in a payment from a Fund's current net assets of a proportionate share of such assets to the Liquidity Provider. You argue, however, that a Fund Put would not make the LPP a redeemable security because it involves substantial restrictions on transfer. This put right can be exercised only if a Liquidity Event has occurred and only if the Liquidity Provider has been unable, after a period of at least three months, to sell LPP it has been required to purchase as a result of a Liquidity Event. In support of your argument, you cite to two no-action letters: *Nebraska Higher Education Loan Program, Inc.*, SEC Staff No-Action Letter (Apr. 3, 1998) and *California Dentists' Guild Real Estate Mortgage Fund II*, SEC Staff No-Action Letter (Jan. 4, 1990). In these letters, the staff considered whether a security is a redeemable security in the context of the exception in Rule 3a-7 and the exclusion in § 3(c)(5)(C), respectively, from the definition of investment company under the Investment Company Act.[11]

---

[11] Rule 3a-7 conditionally excepts from the definition of investment company an issuer that "does not issue redeemable securities" and that "is engaged in the business of purchasing, or otherwise acquiring, and holding" financial assets that by their terms convert into cash within a finite time period. Section 3(c)(5)(C) of the Investment Company Act provides an exclusion from the definition of investment company for an issuer that is not

You explain that in *Nebraska*, the loan program issued three series of variable rate demand bonds to finance the purchase of student loans from originating lenders. Bondholders were permitted to tender the bonds weekly to a paying agent unaffiliated with the issuer that would pay for the tendered bonds using the proceeds from remarketing the tendered bonds or, if the remarketing was unsuccessful, from the sale of the tendered bonds to Sallie Mae. For the first series, the issuer was required to purchase the bonds acquired by Sallie Mae as the liquidity provider if Sallie Mae had held such bonds for no less than three years and failed to sell them in a remarketing during that period. For the second series, the issuer was required to purchase the bonds acquired by Sallie Mae if Sallie Mae had held such bonds for no less than two weeks and failed to sell them in a remarketing during that period. For the third series, the required holding period was thirty days. The staff took the position that the bonds subject to the three-year holding period requirement were not redeemable securities for purposes of § 2(a)(32) and Rule 3a-7 because the holding period was sufficiently restrictive. The staff, however, was unable to conclude that the bonds subject to a two-week or thirty-day holding period were not redeemable securities. You indicate that in *California Dentists* the staff used a similar approach in concluding that the restrictions on investor withdrawal rights would not cause the securities to be considered redeemable securities for purposes of § § 2(a)(32) and 3(c)(5)(C).

You conclude that the LPP is not a redeemable security because of the Liquidity Event Feature or the EVC Put under the plain wording of § 2(a)(32). You also conclude that the LPP is not a redeemable security because the exercise of the Fund Put is subject to significant restrictions similar to those in *Nebraska*. We agree.

C. Tender Offer [omitted]

III. Conclusions

Based on the facts and representations set forth in your letter, the Division of Investment Management would not recommend that the Commission take any enforcement action under § § 34(b) or 35(d) of the Investment Company Act or Rule 22c-1 thereunder against Money Market Funds if they purchase the LPP, as described in your letter, provided that such Money Market Funds otherwise comply with the conditions

---

engaged in the business of, among other things, "issuing redeemable securities" and that is primarily engaged in "purchasing or otherwise acquiring mortgages and other liens on and interest in real estate."

of Rule 2a-7. This response expresses our views on enforcement action only and does not express any legal or interpretive conclusion on the issues presented.

Further, based on the facts and representations set forth in your letter, and without necessarily agreeing with your analysis, the Division of Investment Management concurs that the Liquidity Event Feature, EVC Put and Fund Put features of the LPP will not cause the LPP to be redeemable securities under § 2(a)(32) of the Investment Company Act. * * * *

Topic 2 Interval Funds: Periodic Repurchasability *vs* Limited Redeemability

Laws & Rules Highlight:

IC Act (15 USC 80a-1 *et seq.*) & Rules (17 CFR §§ 270.0-1 *et seq.*)

§ 23 Distribution and Repurchase of Securities: Closed-End Companies

- § 23(a) (*limits types of consideration for closed-end company securities to* ***cash and securities****—designed to prevent insider overreaching*)
- § 23(b) (*generally prohibits closed-end fund from* ***selling*** *its common stock in an offering at a price* ***below*** *the stock's* ***current net asset value****—designed to protect existing shareholders from equity dilution due to issuance of common stock to favored persons at below NAV*)
- § 23(c) (*prohibits closed-end fund from* ***repurchasing*** *its securities, with* ***three exceptions****— designed to protect existing shareholders from dilution in favor of insiders*):

◆ § 23(c)(1) (*permits a closed-end fund to conduct* ***open-market repurchases*** *on national securities exchanges and other open markets designated by the SEC, subject to "written notice" to all shareholders to prevent insiders' secret sales*)

- ✓ Rule 23c-1 Repurchase of Securities by Closed-End Companies (*permits closed-end fund repurchases for cash in the* ***over-the-counter market****, subject to additional conditions including: maintenance of prescribed asset coverage for senior securities; repurchase price not exceeding the lower of the market value and the net asset value of the security*)
- ✓ Rule 23c-2 Call and Redemption of Securities Issued by Registered Closed-End Companies (*permits a closed-end fund to* ***call or redeem,*** *solely at the issuer's option and without any choice on the part of the shareholder, its securities according to their terms*)

◆ § 23(c)(2) (*permits a closed-end fund to make* ***periodic tender offers****, subject to "reasonable opportunity" to tender given to all shareholders of the class to prevent discrimination, and subject to Exchange Act tender offer rules*)

◆ **§ 23(c)(3)** (***authorizes the SEC to permit****, by rule or order, other means of closed-end fund repurchases that do "****not unfairly discriminate****" against any shareholders of the class to be repurchased*)

- ✓ **Rule 23c-3** Repurchase Offers by Closed-End Companies (*exempts "****closed-end interval fund****" from the definition of being issuer of "redeemable securities"; conditions: repurchase offers to all shareholders,* ***at current net asset value****, either at* ***periodic intervals*** *pursuant to a fundamental policy, or on a* ***discretionary*** *basis not more frequently than once every two years*)
- ✓ § 8(b)(3) (*requires registration statement of a registered IC to contain a recital of matters of "fundamental policy"*)

Pre-Case Background Note:[Biblio]

Charting New Territory Between Two Extremes:[1] Closed-End Interval Fund

The Investment Company Act of 1940 established a rigid classification system, dividing management companies into open-end and closed-end. In 1992, the SEC concluded:[1]

> The rigidity of the Act's classification system has become a limitation on sponsors' ability to offer innovative products.... It would be appropriate to provide the opportunity for investment companies to ***chart new territory between the two extremes*** of the open-end and closed-end forms, consistent with investor protection.... It is appropriate to modernize the existing regulatory structure to permit the development of new investment companies that, while having characteristics of the current open-end and closed-end forms, would offer ***a degree of redeemability or "repurchase-ability" between*** the two traditional extremes.

Accords an academic study (Deli & Varma 2001):[2] There is a tradeoff between asset liquidity and portfolio efficiency. Open-end and closed-end represent two ends of a spectrum with respect to the "fixity" of claims on the fund. Expanding the feasible set of organizational forms could lead to real wealth gains for fund investors.

Closed-end funds possess certain portfolio management advantages over open-end funds, not being subject to redemption obligations as open-end funds are. On the other hand, the very lack of established procedures for shareholders to resell shares to the funds in conjunction with the funds' tendency of trading at a discount to net asset value caused closed-end funds to attract much less investment than open-end funds. IC Rule 23c-3 was designed to both provide investors with greater investment choices of closed-end funds with less liquid portfolios, and offer shareholders an "intermediate degree of liquidity" between the traditional open-end and closed-end procedures as well as a mechanism to bypass the secondary market trading discount.[3a] By exempting "*repurchase offers*" of closed-end funds of their common stock at "*periodic intervals*" from the definition of "*redeemable securities*," Rule 23c-3 authorizes a non-traditional type of closed-end funds—the "***close-end interval funds***."[3b; 4]

A closed-end interval fund making **periodic repurchase offers** pursuant to Rule 23c-3 must:[3; 4]

- Adopt a ***fundamental policy*** changeable only by a vote of a majority of the outstanding voting securities, specifying key terms of the fund's repurchase offers:

the ***interval*** (*i.e.*, frequency of repurchase offers, uniformly set at every three, six, or twelve months) between two repurchase request deadlines, and ***schedule*** of repurchase request deadline, repurchase pricing date, and repurchase payment deadline.

- Extend the repurchase offers ***to all holders*** of the security that is the subject of the repurchase offer—consistent with the current "all holders, best price" tender offer rule under the Securities Exchange Act,[5] to protect against unfair discrimination.
- Set the ***repurchase price at net asset value***, subject to a repurchase fee not exceeding 2% of the proceeds—intended to *avoid dilution* to either the tendering or the remaining shareholders, and to *preclude recurrence of abuses* which predated the 1940 IC Act, wherein some funds repurchased in the market at discounts from the NAV, and other funds repurchased from insiders at premiums to the NAV.
- Limit the size of ***each repurchase offer*** to not less than ***5%*** and not more than ***25%*** of the amount of common stock outstanding on the repurchase request deadline date, such a min-max mechanism being designed to both *assure* shareholders of certainty of minimum size of repurchase offers and *sufficiently distinguish* redeemable from non-redeemable securities.
- Satisfy the ***closed-end interval fund liquidity standard*** designed to ensure that funds can complete repurchase offers, *i.e.*, *from* the time of the repurchase offer notification *until* the repurchase pricing date, *individual assets* of the fund's portfolio, equal to the repurchase offer amount, can be sold or disposed of in the ordinary course of business, at approximately the price at which the fund has valued the investment, and within the time period within which the fund pays repurchase proceeds[3b (p.19339 n.77)]—in contrast to the ***open-end company "seven day liquidity standard,"*** *i.e., at all times, at least 85% of the fund's portfolio* be assets that can be sold in seven days at approximately the price used in determining the fund's net asset value.[3a (p.34704 n.35)]

As they make periodic repurchases, closed-end interval funds have different **offering needs** from both traditional closed-end and open-end funds. ***Traditional closed-end funds*** offer their shares through an underwritten offering of a *fixed* number of shares in their initial public offering, and do not engage in continuous offering; their shares are generally offered and sold at the current NAV, as required by IC Act § 23(b). ***Traditional open-end funds*** generally offer and sell new shares to the public on a *continuous* basis, to offset the effect of continuous redemption of shares on fund capital; both sales and redemptions are at the current NAV daily computed, as required by IC

Rule 22c-1. To offset the effect of periodic repurchases of their common stock on fund capital, ***closed-end interval funds*** may need to offer their shares on an ongoing basis; both repurchases and sales must be at the current NAV computed in connection with each repurchase offer and each offering, as required by Rule 23c-3 and § 23(b). Thus, ongoing offerings by closed-end interval funds may be a *continuous* offering, *intermittent* offerings coinciding with periodic repurchases, or *delayed and suspended* when fund shares are available at a discount to net asset value in a secondary market. To complement and coordinate with IC Rule 23c-3 governing repurchase operations, rules have been adopted under the Securities Act governing offering operations: Rule 415(a)(1)(xi) allows closed-end interval funds to utilize *both continuous and delayed* shelf offering procedures. Rule 486 provides a mechanism for closed-end interval funds to maintain *continuously effective registration statements* patterned after the mechanism for open-end funds in Rule 485.[6]

Schedule of Rule 23c-3 Repurchase by Closed-End Interval Fund:

Notification of Repurchase Offer — |-42| ≥ Day ≥ |-21|

Repurchase Request Deadline — **Day 0**

Repurchase Pricing Date — Day 14

Repurchase Payment Deadline — Day 21

Rule 23c-3 Repurchase Periodic Interval:

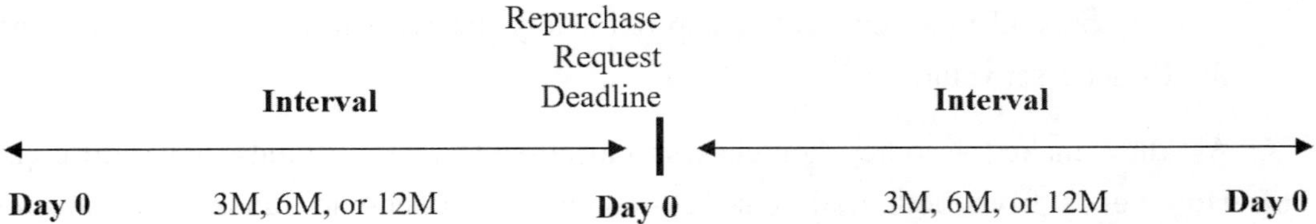

Bibliography

1. DIV. OF INV. MGMT, SEC. & EXCH. COMM'N, PROTECTING INVESTORS: A HALF CENTURY OF INVESTMENT COMPANY REGULATION, Ch. 11 Repurchases and Redemptions of Investment Company Shares (1992)
2. Deli & Varma, *Closed-end Versus Open-end: The Choice of Organizational Form*, 8 J. CORP. FIN. 1 (2001)

3. Rule 23c-3 Rels.: **3a.** Periodic Repurchases by Closed-End Management Investment Companies; Redemptions by Open-End Management Investment Companies and Registered Separate Accounts at Periodic Intervals or with Extended Payment, IC-18869, 57 FR 34701 (1992); **3b.** Repurchase Offers by Closed-End Management Investment Companies, IC-19399, 58 FR 19330 (1993)
4. 270.23c-3 Repurchase Offers by Closed-End Companies; 270.23c-3(d) Exemption from the Definition of Redeemable Security (2017)
5. 240.13e-4 Tender Offers by Issuers; 13e-4(f)(8) (2017)
6. Rule 415(a)(1)(xi) & Rule 486 Rels.: **6a.** Continuous or Delayed Offerings by Certain Closed-End Management Companies; Automatic Effectiveness of Certain Registration Statements and Post-Effective Amendments, 33-6989, IC-19391, 58 FR 19361 (1993); **6b.** Post-Effective Amendments to Investment Company Registration Statements, 33-7015, IC-19722, 58 FR 50291 (1993); **6c.** Continuous or Delayed Offerings by Certain Closed-End Management Investment Companies, 33-7084, IC-20487, 59 FR 43469 (1994); **6d.** Post-Effective Amendments to Investment Company Registration Statements, 33-7083, IC-20486, 59 FR 43460 (1994)

Case Study: Charting New Territory Between Two Extremes: Limited Redemption Fund*

Closed-end companies making periodic repurchases pursuant to Rule 23c-3 are "***closed-end interval funds***." Their "periodic repurchase offers" are not "redeemable securities" since significant regulatory restrictions apply to such repurchases, and *control over most aspects of the repurchase process remains with the company and not the tendering shareholders*. Conversely, **open-end** companies issuing redeemable securities subject to certain redemption limits which are tightly controlled by regulation to assure *some* degree of *real* redeemability do not become "closed-end," since the security is *redeemable at the option of the holder rather than the issuer*. To avoid investor confusion and ensure investor protection, however, such "***limited redemption fund***" may not hold itself out as a "***mutual fund***"—the traditional open-end management company.

*_Ref._ [DIV. OF INV. MGMT, SEC. & EXCH. COMM'N, PROTECTING INVESTORS: A HALF CENTURY OF INVESTMENT COMPANY REGULATION, § 11-III (1992); Periodic Repurchases by Closed-End Management Investment Companies; Redemptions by Open-End Management Investment Companies and Registered Separate Accounts at Periodic Intervals or with Extended Payment, IC-18869, 57 FR 34701 (1992)]

Emerging Markets Growth Fund, Inc.

IC-23433, 63 FR 49717 (1998)

[***Procedural history:*** Emerging Markets Growth Fund, Inc., IC-23433, 63 FR 49717 (1998) (Application); In *re* Emerging Markets Growth Fund, Inc., IC-23481 (1998) (Order)]

Emerging Markets Growth Fund, Inc.

Notice of Application; IC-23433, 63 FR 49717 (1998)

Summary of Application:

The order would permit applicant Emerging Markets Growth Fund, Inc. (**EMGF**) to operate as a registered open-end investment company that would redeem its shares at monthly intervals.

Applicant's Representations:

1. EMGF, a Maryland corporation, is a closed-end management investment company registered under the Act. EMGF's shares are registered under the Securities Act of 1933. Capital International, Inc. (**Adviser**), registered under the Investment Advisers Act of 1940, serves as EMGF's investment adviser. EMGF's investment objective is to seek long-term capital growth by investing in equity securities of issuers in developing countries.

2. EMGF's shares are not listed on any securities exchange (except for a nominal listing on the Luxembourg Stock Exchange). EMGF offers new shares for sale on a limited basis to investors that meet certain suitability criteria prescribed by EMGF. EMGF's current investor suitability criteria provide that a prospective investor that is a "company" (as defined in § 2(a)(8) of the Act) must have total assets in excess of $5 million and that each prospective investor that is a natural person must be an "accredited investor" within the meaning of Regulation D under the 1933 Act. Under EMGF's articles of incorporation, outstanding shares of EMGF may be transferred only to persons who meet this suitability criteria. Because of these restrictions on transferability, and EMGF's concern that its shares, if listed on a securities exchange, might trade at a discount to their net asset value (**NAV**), a secondary market in EMGF's shares has not developed.

3. EMGF would like to be able to offer its shareholders an opportunity to dispose of their shares at NAV should they wish to do so, without unduly disrupting EMGF's portfolio or interfering with EMGF's investment objectives. EMGF states that it considered making periodic tender offers to its shareholders, but believes that the process is cumbersome, expensive and of limited benefit to the shareholders. EMGF also considered relying on rule 23c-3 under the Act, the "closed-end interval fund" rule, that permits closed-end funds to make periodic repurchase offers to their shareholders as an alternative to periodic tender offers. EMGF concluded that this alternative was undesirable because of the rule's restrictions on the frequency and amount of repurchase offers. EMGF also states that its

portfolio, which consists primarily of equity securities of issuers in emerging markets, is not sufficiently liquid to enable EMGF to operate as a traditional open-end fund that redeems its shares daily.

4. EMGF thus proposes to convert into a registered open-end investment company. EMGF would redeem its shares monthly, as further described in this notice (**Redemption Policy**). The Redemption Policy would be a fundamental policy of EMGF, changeable only by vote of a majority of the outstanding voting securities of EMGF, as defined in the Act. EMGF's existing shareholders have approved the Redemption Policy. EMGF's board of directors (**Board**), including a majority of directors who are not "interested persons," as defined in § 2(a)(19) of the Act, also has approved the Redemption Policy.

5. Under EMGF's proposal, EMGF's new investors will be limited to "qualified purchasers," within the meaning of § 2(a)(51) of the Act and the rules and SEC interpretive positions under the Act.[1] Existing shareholders who are not qualified purchasers will be permitted to remain shareholders of EMGF and to purchase additional shares. Prior to relying on the requested order, EMGF will implement procedures to assure that shares are not transferred by shareholders to third parties that are not qualified purchasers. EMGF's current articles of incorporation provide that transfers of EMGF's shares may be made only to those investors that satisfy EMGF's suitability criteria specified by the Board. As provided for in EMGF's article of incorporation, the Board will amend the current share transfer restrictions to provide that no shareholder may transfer shares to any other person or entity that is not a qualified purchaser. EMGF would seek to enforce the transfer restriction against any shareholder who attempted to transfer shares in violation of the restriction. The Board may not further amend the share transfer restrictions to permit transfers to persons or entities other than qualified purchasers without the prior approval of the Commission.

6. Under the Redemption Policy, EMGF would accept redemption requests on or before the close of business on the first business day of each month (**Redemption Request Deadline**). (The first Redemption Request Deadline will occur no sooner than 45 days after EMGF's prospectus is mailed to the shareholders. The prospectus will include disclosure of the change in share transfer restrictions discussed above.) Any redemption

---

[1] Section 2(a)(51) of the Act generally defines qualified purchasers as natural persons who own $5 million of investments and institutions that own or manage on a discretionary basis $25 million of investments.

request received during the course of any calendar month would be effective as of the next Redemption Request Deadline. Redemption requests received prior to a Redemption Request Deadline would be revocable until the Redemption Request Deadline. On the Redemption Request Deadline, redemption requests would become irrevocable.[2] EMGF will price the shares for redemption at the close of business on the last business day of that month (**Redemption Pricing Date**). EMGF would pay the proceeds of redemption requests within seven calendar days after the Redemption Pricing Date (**Redemption Payment Date**).

7. The Board will have the right to suspend the Redemption Pricing Date and the Redemption Payment Date only in accordance with § 22(e) of the Act.[3] The Board will have the right to accelerate the Redemption Pricing Date and the Redemption Payment Date only if doing so would be in the best interests of EMGF's shareholders and only upon the following conditions: (a) the Redemption Payment Date will occur within seven days of the accelerated Redemption Pricing Date; and (b) the Board finds that the accelerated Redemption Pricing Date is not likely to result in any significant dilution of interests of the redeeming or the remaining shareholders.[4]

8. EMGF states that at least 85% of its assets must either (a) mature by the next Redemption Payment Date; or (b) be capable of being sold between the Redemption Request Deadline and the Redemption Payment Date at approximately the price used in computing EMGF's NAV (**Liquidity Standard**). The Liquidity Standard would be a fundamental policy of EMGF, changeable only by vote of a majority of the outstanding voting securities of EMGF, as defined in the Act.

9. EMGF will accept orders to purchase its shares on the last business day of each week and month. The purchase price will be the NAV next determined following receipt of

---

[2] EMGF states that the irrevocability of redemption requests after the Redemption Request Deadline is necessary to permit the Adviser to make arrangements to meet redemption requests made as of that date with the least disruption to EMGF's portfolio.

[3] Section 22(e) generally provides that the right of redemption may not be suspended and the date of payment may not be postponed except for a period during which the New York Stock Exchange is closed or trading on the NYSE is restricted, during certain emergencies, or for periods as permitted by Commission order. Section 22(e) also provides that the Commission shall by rules and regulations determine the conditions under which (i) trading will be deemed to be restricted and (ii) an emergency will be deemed to exist.

[4] The Board may not suspend the Redemption Request Deadline or the right to make redemption requests.

the purchase order.[5] To protect investors, purchase payments received by EMGF before the last business day of the week or month will be placed in a segregated account for the benefit of the purchaser.

10. EMGF states that any change in the Redemption Policy, the Liquidity Standard, or the operation of EMGF as described in the application that is not otherwise permitted by the Act and the rules under the Act will require approval by the SEC.

Applicant's Legal Analysis:

1. Section 22(e) of the Act provides that a registered investment company may not suspend the right of redemption, or postpone the date of payment or satisfaction upon redemption of any redeemable security in accordance with its terms for more than seven days after the tender of the security to the company. EMGF requests an exemption from § 22(e) to permit EMGF to redeem its shares on a monthly cycle.

2. EMGF states that the primary purpose of § 22(e) was to address the following abuses: (a) the lack of provisions in a fund's governing documents concerning redemption rights; (b) the ability of fund management to restrict redemptions without shareholder approval; and (c) inadequate or misleading disclosure in fund documents and marketing materials concerning redemption rights. EMGF states that the Redemption Policy will not raise the possibility of any of these abuses. EMGF states that its existing shareholders have approved the Redemption Policy, and that the Redemption Policy will be changeable only by a majority vote of its shareholders and only upon approval by the SEC or its staff. EMGF further states that the Redemption Policy will be stated on the cover of its prospectus and in any marketing materials and that EMGF will not hold itself out as a "mutual fund." EMGF also states that its new investors will be limited to qualified purchasers, who EMGF asserts are unlikely to misunderstand their limited redemption opportunity. EMGF notes that Congress has determined that qualified purchasers are sophisticated investors who do not need the protections of the Act. Finally, as noted above, EMGF states that it would suspend the Redemption Pricing Date and the Redemption Payment Date only in accordance with § 22(e) of the Act.

3. EMGF asserts that the Liquidity Standard will enable EMGF to meet redemptions

---

[5] EMGF will maintain an "800" telephone number (or will use an equivalent method) to provide shareholders with ready access to updated information on the NAV of EMGF's shares.

without unduly disrupting its portfolio. Any change in EMGF's Liquidity Standard will require approval by a majority of EMGF's shareholders and the SEC. In addition, EMGF states that it will comply with rule 2a-4 under the Act, which concerns the valuation of the portfolio securities of an open-end investment company, and any related SEC or staff interpretations or releases (except to the extent that EMGF may have its assets invested according to the Liquidity Standard).

4. Rule 22c-1 under the Act generally requires an open-end investment company to calculate its NAV each day on which an order to purchase or redeem its shares is received, and to price its shares for sale or redemption at a price next determined after receipt of a redemption request. EMGF requests relief from rule 22c-1 to postpone pricing its shares tendered for redemption on or before a Redemption Request Deadline until the next Redemption Pricing Date.

5. EMGF asserts that rule 22c-1 was designed primarily to prevent the practice of "backward pricing" of fund shares. EMGF argues that its proposal does not raise this concern because shares would be priced after a redemption request is received. EMGF also asserts that its proposed pricing timeline is consistent with the Act because it is designed to treat all investors in EMGF equally and avoid any dilution of non-redeeming shareholders' interests. EMGF further asserts that its Redemption Policy will provide its existing shareholders with a greater opportunity to dispose of their shares than they have had in the past. In addition, EMGF states that since new investors will be qualified purchasers, they will be in a position to understand any risks associated with EMGF's pricing timeline.

6. EMGF also requests relief from rule 22c-1 to permit it to calculate its NAV and price shares for purchase only on the days on which EMGF actually will accept requests to purchase its shares (*i.e.*, on the last business day of each week and month). To protect investors, funds received prior to the date on which they will be invested in EMGF will be placed in a segregated account for the benefit of the purchaser.

7. Section 6(c) under the Act permits the SEC to exempt any person or transaction from any provision of the Act, if such exemption is necessary or appropriate in the public interest and consistent with the protection of investors and the purposes fairly intended by the policies of the Act. For the reasons discussed above, EMGF submits that the requested order meets these standards. EMGF states that its proposal will enable it to offer its shareholders an opportunity to dispose of their shares at NAV should they wish to

do so, without unduly disrupting EMGF's portfolio or interfering with EMGF's investment objectives.

Applicant's Conditions:

EMGF agrees that any order of the SEC granting the requested relief will be subject to the following conditions:

1. EMGF's shareholders will have approved the Redemption Policy prior to EMGF's relying on the requested order (**Reliance Date**).

2. Any new investor purchasing EMGF's shares on or after the Reliance Date will be a "qualified purchaser" within the meaning of § 2(a)(51) of the Act and the rules and SEC or staff interpretive positions under the Act.

3. Prior to the Reliance Date, the Board, including a majority of the disinterested directors, will have adopted procedures designed to assure that EMGF will comply with the terms and conditions of the requested order. The Board will review these procedures at least annually and approve such changes as it deems necessary.

4. EMGF will not hold itself out as a "mutual fund" and will disclose its Redemption Policy on the cover page of its prospectus and in any marketing materials.

Topic 3　Exchange-Traded Fund: Open-End/Closed-End Hybrid

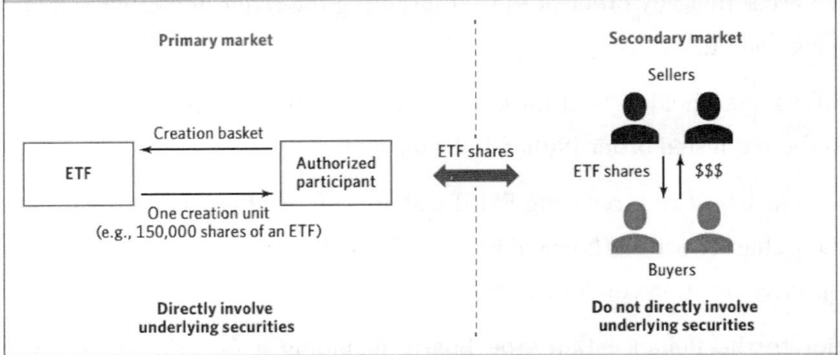

FIGURE 3.3
Creation of ETF Shares

Note: The creation basket represents a specific list of securities, cash, and/or other assets.

Source of graph: ICI, 2017 INVESTMENT COMPANY FACT BOOK 61 (57th ed.)

Research Note:[Biblio]

ETFs: An Evolving Segment of the Mutual Fund Marketplace

The concept of exchange-traded funds (ETFs) was introduced in a 1976 Financial Analysts Journal article by ***Nils Hakansson***, a professor at the University of California, Berkeley. Hakansson presented the concept of a "*purchasing power fund*" issuing "*supershares*," which provides payoffs only for a predetermined level of market return.[1a; 1b (p.12)]

For purposes of the Investment Company Act, there are two types of ETFs: ***investment company ETFs*** and ***commodity ETFs***. The former issue securities and invest primarily in securities. Such ETFs are "investment companies" within the meaning of and are registered under the IC Act, and trade on the securities exchanges. The latter invest primarily in commodities or commodity-based instruments. Commodity ETFs trade on a securities exchange, as investment company ETFs do, but they are not investment companies under the IC Act.[2b (p.14618 n.4)] This research note discusses investment company ETFs.

Spiders (*aka* the SPDR Trust; **S**tandard & **P**oor's **D**epository **R**eceipts)—the first

ETF—appeared in 1993. **Formed as a UIT**, the SPDR has a portfolio which by definition is relatively fixed and not actively managed. The SPDR tracks the Standard & Poor's 500 Composite Stock Price Index by holding weighted positions of all the securities in the S&P Index, and trades on the American Stock Exchange.[2a (p.57615); 3] Subsequent index-based ETFs formed as UITs include ***Diamonds*** (the Diamonds Trust), which tracks the Dow Jones Industrial Average and trades on the NYSE;[4] and ***QQQQ*** (the NASDAQ-100 Trust) (renamed ***PowerShares QQQ*** in March 2007), which tracks the NASDAQ-100 Index and trades on Nasdaq.[5]

In 1996, the American Stock Exchange complemented its UIT-form, domestic equity index-based ETF (the Spiders) with the first international equity index-based ETF, **formed as an open-end investment company**—***WEBS*** ("World Equity Benchmark Shares"). WEBS tracks the MSCI Indices (the international stock market indices developed by Morgan Stanley Capital International).[6; 7; 2b (p.14619 n.14); 2a (p.57615)] Since May 2000, WEBS has been renamed ***iShares***.[8]

Starting 2008, the SEC has granted exemptive orders to ***non-index-based, fully transparent, actively managed ETFs***. Actively managed ETFs do not seek to track the return of a particular index—unlike the index-based ETFs; but seek to create a unique mix of investments to meet a particular investment objective and policy—much like traditional actively managed mutual funds. All the actively managed ETFs adopt the open-end fund structure which allows greater investment flexibility, rather than the fixed portfolio UIT structure which limits an index-based ETF to replicating or sampling a particular index.[2b (p.14620 n.20, pp.14623-24 n.66); 9]

Compared with ***mutual funds***—which issue redeemable securities but do not trade in the secondary market, ***closed-end funds***—which do not issue redeemable securities but trade in the secondary market, and ***UITs***—which like mutual funds issue redeemable securities and like closed-end funds trade in the secondary market, ***ETFs*** are a hybrid of the three. All ETFs—whether index based or actively managed, whether formed as a UIT or as an open-end fund—have similar trading and pricing mechanisms.

In the **primary market**, ETF shares are created when a qualified broker-dealer acting as "authorized participant" (**AP**) transfers a "***creation basket***" of specified securities to the ETF in return for the ETF's delivery of a "***creation unit***" (*i.e.*, standard block) of ETF shares to the AP. The value of the creation basket equals the value of the creation unit based on the ETF's NAV on the creation day. The redemption process works reversely: An AP returns the creation unit to the ETF for redemption and receives the "***redemption basket***" of the underlying portfolio securities in return. The value of the redemption basket equals the value of the creation unit based on the ETF's NAV on the redemption day. The in-kind purchases and redemptions of creation units between APs and an ETF distinguish ETFs from traditional mutual funds: the latter sell and redeem fund's *individual shares* generally in *cash transactions* and with both *institutional and retail investors* alike. On the other hand, an ETF is required to post the mark-to-market NAV of its portfolio at the end of each trading day; creations and redemptions of ETF creation units are aggregated and executed only once a day at NAV—two features that make ETFs look like traditional mutual funds.[2b (p.14629); 9]

In the **secondary market**, all investors can participate—in contrast to the primary market where only APs participate by interacting directly with the ETFs. Trading takes place in existing, individual ETF shares each of which represents an undivided interest in the portfolio of assets held by the ETF, rather than in block-size creation units. ETF shares are not individually redeemable from the ETF at its NAV; trading is between investors and at the current market prices—two features that make ETFs look like closed-end funds and unlike traditional mutual funds.[2b (pp.14624-25); 9]

The **pricing** of ETFs—both index based and actively managed—differs from both mutual funds and closed-end funds. Mutual funds are "***forward priced***": Investors placing buy or sell orders throughout the day will receive the same price, *i.e.*, the NAV the *next* time it is computed, typically daily at 4:00 p.m. EST when the U.S. stock exchanges close.[9] Closed-end funds trade in the secondary market for the most part at a ***discount*** and at times at a substantial discount.[10] An ETF trades at market prices approximating its underlying value, *i.e.*, the ***market value of its portfolio***. Two features in the ETF structure promote pricing efficiency:[7; 9]

- ***ETF portfolio transparency***. The ETF's underlying value is calculated and disseminated throughout the trading day at about *15 second interval* (or in *real time* by the use of proprietary data feeds). This transparency enables investors to spot and exploit any arbitrage opportunity existing between an ETF's share price and the ETF's underlying value throughout the trading day.
- ***APs' ability to create and redeem ETF units***. Where an ETF is trading at a *discount* to its NAV, an AP may buy the ETF shares and simultaneously sell short the underlying securities during the trading day; at the end of the day the AP redeems the creation unit for the redemption basket of the underlying securities to

cover its securities short position. Where an ETF is trading at a *premium* to its NAV, an AP may sell the ETF shares short and simultaneously buy the underlying securities during the trading day; at the end of the day the AP delivers the creation basket of the underlying securities to the ETF for the creation unit to cover its ETF short position.

Based on the 2015 median figure, ETF-owning households in the U.S. demonstrate the following characteristics:

Characteristics of ETF-Owning Households (Median, 2015)*

*Data compiled from: ICI, 2016 INVESTMENT COMPANY FACT BOOK, 2015 Facts at a Glance; Part 1 Ch.3 Figures 3.12, 3.13 (56th ed.)

Parameters	Household Owning **ETFs**	Household Owning **Individual Stocks**	Household Owning **Mutual Funds**
Household Income	**$110,000**	$100,000	$87,500
Household Financial Assets	**$375,000**	$300,000	$200,000
Percentages of Households Willing to Take "*substantial or above-average investment risk for substantial or above-average gain*"	**53%**		31%
Total Mutual Fund Assets (U.S. 2015)	$15.7 trillion		
Total ETF Assets (U.S. 2015)	$2.1 trillion		

The ICI's 2015 data appear to have borne out the observations of an academic paper (Poterba & Shoven 2002),[11] comparing before-and-after-tax returns on an *S&P 500 Index-tracking ETF* (SPDR) with those of an *S&P 500 Index-tracking mutual fund* (Vanguard Index 500) during the 1994-2000 sample period. The paper predicted: ETFs may be part of an emerging trend toward ***segmentation of the mutual fund marketplace***. ETFs may be appropriate for investors who demand short-term liquidity and trade in large lots, whereas traditional equity mutual funds are for investors who place less value on liquidity and make small purchases or sales. The low rate of taxable distributions of ETFs thanks to their in-kind creation and redemption feature may make them more attractive for non-tax deferred accounts, whereas the tax attributes of traditional mutual funds may make them more attractive for tax-advantaged retirement accounts. Eventually, high-turnover investors will be segregated into funds offering them the ability to trade frequently and charging substantial expense ratios and management fees associated with high-turnover, leaving low-turnover investors to continue to invest in traditional equity mutual funds with a reduced turnover rate.

While there have been regulatory enforcement actions based on unsuitable sales of leveraged ETFs to retail investors who suffered losses from holding the investments for extended periods of time,[12] and there are regulatory educational materials concerning ETFs,[13] this research note has found little legal scholarship addressing ETF-related suitability and retail investor protection issues, as similarly observed by Birdthistle (2008).[14 (p.75 n.24)] As this book is being sent to the printer, the SEC has proposed IC Rule 6c-11 [83 FR 37332 (July 31, 2018)] to "***modernize*** the regulatory framework for ETFs" supplanting the ETF regulation by individual exemptive orders used in the past 26 years, to establish "a ***consistent*** regulatory framework" governing ETFs, and "to facilitate greater ***competition and innovation*** among ETFs."[2c]

Bibliography

1. **1a.** Hakansson, *The Purchasing Power Fund: A New Kind of Financial Intermediary*, 32 FIN. ANALYSTS J. 49 (1976); **1b.** CLOSED-END FUNDS, EXCHANGE-TRADED FUNDS, AND HEDGE FUNDS—ORIGINS, FUNCTIONS, AND LITERATURE 12 (Anderson et al. eds. Springer 2010)
2. ETF Rels: **2a.** Actively Managed Exchange-Traded Funds; Concept Release, IC-25258, 66 FR 57614 (2001); **2b.** Exchange-Traded Funds, 33-8901, IC-28193, 73 FR 14618 (2008); **2c.** Exchange-Traded Funds, 33-10515, IC-33140, 83 FR 37332 (2018)
3. SPDR Trust, Series 1, et at.: IC-18959, 57 FR 43996 (1992) (notice); IC-19055 (1992) (order)
4. Diamonds Trust, Series 1, et al.: IC-22927, 62 FR 65453 (1997) (notice); IC-22979 (1997) (order)
5. **5a.** Nasdaq-100 Trust, Series 1, *et al.*: IC-23668, 64 FR 5082 (1999) (notice); IC-23702 (1999) (order); **5b.** QQQQ prospectus, http://www.powershares.com/pdf/P-QQQ-PRO-1.pdf
6. The Foreign Fund, Inc., *et al.*: IC-21737 (1996) (notice); IC-21803 (1996) (order)
7. Olienyk, Schweback & Zumwalt, *WEBS, SPDRs, and Country Funds: An Analysis of International Cointegration*, 9 J. MULTINAT'L FIN. MGMT. 217 (1999)
8. iShares, Inc.: **8a.** SROs; Notice of Filing of Proposed Rule Change ... Relating to ... iShares MSCI Index Funds, SR-Amex-00-26, 65 FR 50249 (2000); **8b.** SROs; Notice of Filing and Order Granting Accelerated Approval ... Relating to ... iShares, Inc. Based on Foreign Stock Indexes, SR-Amex-2001-45, 66 FR 55712 (2001)
9. INVESTMENT COMPANY INSTITUTE, 2016 INVESTMENT COMPANY FACT BOOK PART 1 CH. 3 (56th ed.)
10. Pratt, *Myths Associated With Closed-End Investment Company Discounts*, 22 FIN. ANALYSTS J. 79 (1966)
11. Poterba & Shoven, *Exchange-Traded Funds: A New Investment Option for Taxable Investors*, 92 AM. ECON. REV. 422 (2002)
12. FINRA: **12a.** FINRA Orders Stifel, Nicolaus and Century Securities to Pay Fines and Restitution Totaling More Than $ 1 Million for Unsuitable Sales of Leveraged and Inverse ETFs, and Related Supervisory Deficiencies (Jan. 9, 2014); **12b.** Press Release: FINRA Sanctions Four Firms $9.1 Million for Sales of Leveraged and Inverse Exchange-Traded Funds (May 1, 2012)
13. SEC Office of Investor Education and Advocacy, Mutual Funds and ETFs—A Guide for Investors, SEC Pub. 182 (12/16)

14. Birdthistle, *The Fortunes and Foibles of Exchange-Traded Funds: A Positive Market Response to the Problems of Mutual Funds*, 33 DEL. J. CORP. L. 69 (2008)

Case Study: A Hybrid of ETF and Mutual Fund—ETMF*

ETMF—***exchange-traded mutual fund***—is a hybrid of traditional mutual fund and ETF. ***Like an ETF***, an ETMF has shares listed and traded on a national securities exchange; directly issues and redeems shares in creation units only; imposes fees on creation units issued to and redeemed by authorized participants, to offset the related costs to the ETMF; and primarily utilizes in-kind transfers of portfolio deposits in issuing and redeeming creation units. ***Like a mutual fund***, an ETMF is bought and sold at prices linked to NAV; and seeks to maintain the confidentiality of its current portfolio positions. ETMFs were first approved by the SEC in 2014; and Eaton Vance Management launched its first ETMF—***the Eaton Vance Stock NextShares***—on Friday, Feb. 26, 2016 [Nasdaq: EVSTC]

*[*Ref.* Investment Company Liquidity Risk Management Programs, 33-10233, IC-32315, 81 FR 82142, 82145 n.31 (Nov. 18, 2016); Murphy, *Eaton Vance's ETMF Finally Debuts*, www.etf.com (Feb. 25, 2016)]

Eaton Vance Mgmt.; ETMF Application

IC-31333, 79 FR 67471 (2014)

[***Procedural history:*** Eaton Vance Mgmt., *et al.*, IC-31333, 79 FR 67471 (2014) (Application); In *re* Eaton Vance Mgmt., *et al.*, IC-31361 (2014) (Order)]

Eaton Vance Mgmt.; Exchange-Traded Managed Fund (ETMF)

Notice of Application; IC-31333, 79 FR 67471 (2014)

Summary of Application:

Applicants request an order that permits: (a) actively managed series of certain open-end management investment companies to issue shares (**Shares**) redeemable in large aggregations only (**Creation Units**); (b) secondary market transactions in Shares to occur at the next-determined net asset value (**NAV**) plus or minus a market-determined premium or discount (**premium/discount**) that may vary during the trading day (**NAV-based Trading**); (c) certain series to pay redemption proceeds, under certain circumstances, more than seven days from the tender of Shares for redemption; (d) certain affiliated persons of the series to deposit securities into, and receive securities from, the series in connection with the purchase and redemption of Creation Units; (e) certain registered management investment companies and unit investment trusts outside of the same group of investment companies as the series to acquire Shares; and (f) certain series to create and redeem Shares in kind in a master-feeder structure. * * * *

Applicants' Proposal:

3. Applicants seek an exemptive order that would permit them to offer exchange-traded managed funds, a new kind of registered investment company that is a hybrid between traditional mutual funds and exchange-traded funds (*exchange-traded managed funds* or **ETMFs**, as defined below).[1]

Like exchange-traded funds (**ETFs**), ETMFs would: list and trade on a national securities exchange; directly issue and redeem Shares only in Creation Units; impose fees on Creation Units issued and redeemed to Authorized Participants (as defined below) to offset the related costs to the ETMFs; and primarily utilize in-kind transfers of Portfolio Positions in issuing and redeeming Creation Units. Like mutual funds, ETMFs would be bought and sold at prices linked to NAV and would seek to maintain the confidentiality of their current Portfolio Positions. Applicants have structured the product in this manner to provide certain cost and tax efficiencies of ETFs to investors, while maintaining the

---

[1] In accordance with the conditions to the requested relief, neither the Trusts nor any ETMF would be marketed or otherwise held out as an "open-end investment company," a "mutual fund" or "exchange-traded fund." Instead, each ETMF would be marketed as an "exchange-traded managed fund" or "ETMF."

confidentiality of current Portfolio Positions.[2] * * * *

A. Exchange Trading and NAV-Based Trading

5. Shares would be listed and traded on an Exchange (**Listing Exchange**).[3] Shares would trade throughout the day at NAV[4] plus or minus a premium/ discount that may vary during the trading day.[5] This premium/discount (solely by way of example, +$0.20/Share, -$0.30/Share) would be quoted by Market Makers in Shares.[6] Although Share prices would be quoted throughout the trading day relative to NAV (solely by way of

---

[2] Through in-kind redemptions (as described below), ETMFs would seek to achieve tax efficiencies for its shareholders by avoiding the tax consequences of selling portfolio positions to meet redemption requests in cash. ETMFs could also limit the costs associated with managing inflows and outflows (*e.g.*, trading costs and "cash drag"). By trading on an Exchange, ETMFs would greatly reduce their expenses for transfer agency services. (ETMF shareholders would still be able to receive comparable services through their brokers and would pay only for those services that they elect to receive.) Finally, applicants represent that ETMFs will not charge sales loads or pay any asset-based distribution or service fees.

[3] Applicants currently expect that The NASDAQ Stock Market LLC (**Nasdaq**) will be the Listing Exchange for the Initial ETMFs. One or more member firms of the Listing Exchange will act as market maker (**Market Maker**) and maintain a market for Shares trading on the Listing Exchange.

[4] An ETMF's NAV will be determined at the end of each Business Day. A "Business Day" is any day the ETMF is open, including any day when it satisfies redemption requests as required by § 22(e) of the Act. ETMFs may compute their NAV more than once each Business Day or once daily at times other than 4:00 p.m. ET, consistent with rule 22c-1 under the Act.

[5] Unlike other exchange-traded securities, there would not be an absolute dollar amount per Share until the end of the day. Accordingly, prior to the initial operations of ETMFs, the Exchanges and brokers would install systems for the entry of orders to buy and sell shares using NAV-based Trading. Applicants have been working with intermediaries and Nasdaq to ensure they are implementing appropriate operational arrangements to accommodate the unique pricing mechanism of ETMFs (e.g., the convention for reporting the intraday pricing of Shares on the consolidated tape). Applicants have also represented that they would establish and support a robust education program to ensure that investors and the marketplace understand, among other things, how to buy and sell Shares. Applicants would also provide related information in the ETMFs' registration statements, website and advertising and marketing materials.

[6] The amount of the premium/discount would depend on market factors, including the balance of supply and demand for Shares among investors, the Transaction Fees (as defined below) and other costs associated with creating and redeeming Creation Units, competition among Market Makers, Share inventory positions, inventory strategies of Market Makers, and the volume of Share trading. Premiums/discounts on market transactions in Shares are not sales charges, and therefore would not be subject to the limitation applicable to sales charges under NASD Conduct Rule 2830 or any other set limitation. Any reference to NASD Conduct Rule 2830 includes any successor or replacement rule that may be adopted by the Financial Industry Regulatory Authority.

example, NAV + $0.20/share, NAV - $0.30/share), there would not be a fixed relationship between Share trading prices and their NAVs. For each trade, the premium/discount (which may be zero) would be locked in at trade execution and the final transaction price (*i.e.*, NAV plus or minus the premium/discount) would be determined at the end of the Business Day when the ETMF's NAV is calculated.[7]

6. Accordingly, unlike ETFs, NAV-based Trading would not offer investors the opportunity to transact intraday at prices based on current (versus end-of-day) determinations of the Shares' value. Instead, like intraday orders to buy or sell shares of mutual funds, an ETMF investor would not know the NAV at the time the order is placed, but the levels of premium/discount would be fully transparent allowing investors to see the execution costs of buying or selling Shares.[8] Market Makers and other dealers, in turn, would compete for transactions in Shares at a profitable premium/discount level.

B. Issuance and Redemption of Creation Units

7. Shares would not be individually redeemable and owners of Shares may acquire those Shares from an ETMF, or tender such shares for redemption to the ETMF, in Creation Units only.[9] Like ETFs, all orders to purchase Creation Units must be placed with a distributor (**Distributor**) that is a broker-dealer registered under the Securities Exchange Act of 1934 by or through a party (an **Authorized Participant**) that has entered into a participant agreement with the Distributor with respect to the creation and redemption of Creation Units.[10]

---

[7] Transactions involving the purchases and sales of Shares on the Exchange would also be subject to customary brokerage commissions and charges.

[8] Trading prices of Shares would be available intraday through market data services and on the ETMFs' website. Quotations, however, would be expressed relative to NAV (solely by way of example, NAV + $0.20/Share, NAV - $0.20/Share) rather than as absolute dollar prices like ETF prices. Historical information regarding levels of premiums/discounts also would be available on the ETMFs' website.

[9] In any advertising material that describes the purchase or sale of Creation Units or refers to redeemability there would be an appropriate statement to the effect that Shares are not individually redeemable. The Adviser also would maintain a public website disclosing current ETMF information and containing links to the current prospectus and other ETMF documents. The website also would include the disclosure required by condition 3 under ETMF Relief.

[10] An Authorized Participant would be either: (a) a Broker (as defined below) or other participant in the Continuous Net Settlement System of the National Securities Clearing Corporation (**NSCC**), a clearing agency registered with the Commission; or (b) a participant in The Depository Trust Company (**DTC**) (**DTC Participant**).

8. Like ETFs, and to keep trading costs low and permit each ETMF to be as fully invested as possible, Shares would be purchased and redeemed in Creation Units and primarily on an in-kind basis. Authorized Participants would be required to purchase Creation Units by making an in-kind deposit of specified instruments (these instruments are referred to, in the case of either a purchase or redemption, as the "**Basket Instruments**," and, together as the "**Basket**"), specified by the ETMF at the beginning of each Business Day and Authorized Participants redeeming their Shares would receive an in-kind transfer of Basket Instruments.[11] The Basket would not necessarily include all Portfolio Positions of the applicable ETMF in order to protect the confidentiality of current Portfolio Positions.

9. Each ETMF would process purchases and redemptions of Creation Units in a manner that would protect the ETMF from any investor who might seek advantageous treatment vis-à-vis other investors. Therefore, each Business Day, the Basket would be constructed in accordance with policies and procedures that: (a) have been approved by the relevant ETMF's Board based on a determination that such policies and procedures are in the best interests of the ETMF; and (b) are administered in accordance with rule 38a-1 under the Act by the chief compliance officer designated by the ETMF under that rule. Moreover, the names and quantities of the instruments that constitute the Basket Instruments on a given Business Day would be identical for all purchasers and redeemers of an ETMF's Creation Units that day, except in certain limited circumstances.[12]

---

[11] ETMFs must comply with the federal securities laws in accepting Basket Instruments and satisfying redemptions with Basket Instruments, including that the Basket Instruments would be sold in transactions that would be exempt from registration under the Securities Act of 1933. In accepting Basket Instruments and satisfying redemptions with Basket Instruments that are restricted securities eligible for resale pursuant to Rule 144A under the Securities Act, ETMFs would comply with the conditions of Rule 144A.

[12] An ETMF's Basket could vary if the required policies and procedures of the ETMF allowed such differences by permitting an Authorized Participant to deposit cash in lieu of some or all of the Basket Instruments solely because: (a) such Basket Instruments, in the case of a purchase of a Creation Unit, are not available in sufficient quantity; (b) such Basket Instruments are not eligible for trading by the Authorized Participant or the investor on whose behalf the Authorized Participant is acting; or (c) a holder of Shares of an ETMF investing in foreign instruments would be subject to unfavorable income tax treatment if the holder received redemption proceeds in kind. A "custom order" is any purchase or redemption of Shares made in whole or in part on a cash basis in reliance on clause (a) or (b). An ETMF may also determine, upon receiving a purchase or redemption order from an Authorized Participant, to require the purchase or redemption, as applicable, to be made entirely in cash.

10. To preserve the confidentiality of an ETMF's trading activities, the Basket would normally not be a pro rata slice of the Portfolio Positions. Instruments being acquired by the ETMF would generally be excluded from the Basket until their purchase is completed and Basket Instruments being sold may not be removed from the Basket until the sale program is substantially completed. Further, when deemed by the Adviser to be in the best interests of an ETMF and its shareholders, other Portfolio Positions would be excluded from the Basket. Whenever Portfolio Positions are excluded from the Basket, the Basket may include proportionately more cash than is in the portfolio. Furthermore, if there is a difference between the NAV attributable to a Creation Unit and the aggregate market value of the Basket exchanged for the Creation Unit, the party conveying a Basket with the lower value would also pay to the other an amount in cash equal to that difference (the **Balancing Amount**).

11. Each Business Day, before the open of trading on the Listing Exchange, the Adviser would cause to be published through the NSCC the names and quantities of the Basket Instruments, as well as the estimated Balancing Amount (if any), for that day. The published Basket would apply until a new Basket is announced on the following Business Day, and there would be no intraday changes to the Basket except to correct errors in the published Basket.[13]

12. Any purchasers or redeemers of Creation Units are expected to incur a transaction fee (**Transaction Fee**) to cover the estimated cost to the ETMF of processing the transaction, including the costs of clearance and settlement charged to it by NSCC or DTC, and the estimated trading costs incurred in converting the Basket to the desired Portfolio Positions. The Transaction Fee would be borne only by purchasers and redeemers of Creation Units and would be limited to amounts that have been authorized by the Board and determined appropriate by the Adviser to defray the transaction expenses that would

[13] ETMFs would arrange for an independent third party to disseminate every 15 minutes an amount representing, on a per Share basis, the intraday indicative value (*IIV*) of the ETMFs' Shares throughout the regular trading session of the Listing Exchange each Business Day. An investor may use the IIV to estimate the number of Shares to buy or sell based on the dollar amount the investor wants to transact in. Applicants note that unlike for ETFs, IIVs for ETMFs would not provide pricing signals for market intermediaries or other buyers or sellers of Shares seeking to estimate the difference between the current value of the ETMF's portfolio and the price at which Shares are currently trading. With ETMF's NAV-based Trading, market intermediaries and other buyers or sellers of Shares assume no intraday market risk in their Share inventory positions and therefore would not need to estimate any such difference.

be incurred by an ETMF when an investor purchases or redeems Creation Units.[14] With respect to ETMFs operating in a master-feeder structure (as discussed below), the Transaction Fee may be paid to the Master Fund as a Master Fund Transaction Fee.[15]

C. The Role of Market Intermediaries and Portfolio Transparency

13. Applicants assert that in light of NAV-based Trading, daily portfolio transparency is not necessary for ETMFs. Applicants recognize that contemporaneous portfolio holdings disclosure has been viewed as necessary for effective arbitrage and efficient secondary market trading of ETFs. In particular, applicants note that in ETF trading, tight bid-ask spreads and narrow premiums/discounts cannot be assured unless Market Makers have sufficient knowledge of portfolio holdings to enable them to effectively arbitrage differences between an ETF's market price and its underlying portfolio value and to hedge the intraday market risk they assume as they take inventory positions in connection with their market-making activities. According to applicants, in NAV-based Trading, by contrast, Market Makers do not engage in arbitrage and assume no intraday market risk in their Share inventory positions because all trading prices are linked to NAV.[16] Applicants

---

[14] Where an ETMF permits an in-kind purchaser to deposit cash in lieu of depositing one or more Basket Instruments, the purchaser may be assessed a higher Transaction Fee to offset the cost to the ETMF of buying those particular Basket Instruments. In all cases, the Transaction Fee and the Master Fund Transaction Fee (as defined below) will be limited in accordance with the requirements of the Commission applicable to open-end management investment companies offering redeemable securities.

[15] Applicants believe that, to treat investors fairly and consistently, a Master Fund with two or more Feeder Funds should transact with each Feeder Fund on a basis that protects the Master Fund (and, indirectly, other Feeder Funds) against the costs of accommodating the Feeder Fund's inflows and outflows. In the proposed structure, the Master Fund would accomplish this by imposing a fee (**Master Fund Transaction Fee**) on Feeder Fund inflows and outflows, sized to cover the estimated cost to the Master Fund of, in connection with a sale of its interests, converting the cash and/or other instruments it receives to the desired Portfolio Positions and, in connection with a redemption of its interests, converting Portfolio Positions to cash and/or other instruments to be distributed. The Master Fund Transaction Fee would be applied to all Feeder Funds in the same manner so as to avoid discrimination by the Master Fund among Feeder Funds.

[16] Applicants state that Market Makers would realize a profit to the extent the premium/ discount exceeded their cost in entering into these transactions. Applicants assert that these costs would include, indirectly if the Market Maker is not an Authorized Participant, the Transaction Fees paid to an ETMF and the cost of purchasing or selling the Basket Instruments exchanged with the ETMF. According to applicants, these costs would not include a cost of hedging an intraday position in Shares. Applicants assert that the cost of intermediation would be lower with respect to ETMFs than for ETFs and profits would be relatively more predictable, which should foster intermediary participation in the market for Shares and therefore the competition necessary to limit the levels of the

state that no intraday market risk means no need for Market Makers to engage in intraday hedging activity, and therefore no associated requirement for current portfolio holdings disclosure to maintain a tight relationship between Share trading prices and NAV.[17] Accordingly, applicants maintain that because Share transaction prices would be based on end-of-day NAV, ETMFs can be expected to trade at consistently narrow premiums/discounts to NAV and tight bid-ask spreads even in the absence of full portfolio holdings disclosure.

14. Applicants claim that ETMFs, not being required to provide daily portfolio transparency, have the potential for providing investors with access to a broad range of active strategies in a structure that provides the cost and tax efficiencies and shareholder protections of an ETF.

Requested Exemptive Relief:

* * * *

16. Applicants' request for relief is novel only under § 22(d) and rule 22c-1 under the Act with respect to NAV-based Trading. In all other respects, applicants are seeking the same relief that the Commission has previously granted to permit the operation of ETFs. * * * *

A. Novel Relief Under § 22(d) and Rule 22c-1

18. Section 22(d) of the Act, among other things, prohibits a dealer from selling a redeemable security that is currently being offered to the public by or through a principal underwriter other than at a current public offering price described in the fund's prospectus. Rule 22c-1 under the Act requires open-end funds, their principal underwriters, and dealers in fund shares (and certain others) to sell and redeem fund shares at a price based on the current NAV next computed after receipt of an order to buy

---

premium/discount.

[17] Applicants believe that Market Makers will generally seek to minimize their exposure to price risk in Shares by holding little or no overnight inventory. ETMFs also will have smaller creation unit sizes than ETFs. Applicants also believe that these smaller creation unit sizes will support secondary market trading efficiency by facilitating tighter market maker inventory management because it facilitates closing out positions at the end of each trading day. To the extent that Market Makers hold small positions in Shares overnight, applicants expect them to aggregate such holdings with any other risk positions that they are holding and transact at or near the market close to buy or sell offsetting positions in appropriate, broad-based hedging instruments, such as S&P 500 and other index futures and ETFs.

or redeem. Together, these provisions are designed to prevent dilution caused by riskless trading schemes, require that shareholders are treated equitably when buying and selling fund shares, and assure an orderly distribution system of investment company shares.

19. Applicants request relief from these provisions to permit NAV-based Trading of Shares. Because of ETMFs' NAV-based Trading, the need for exemptive relief from § 22(d) and rule 22c-1 for ETMFs arises due to the portion of the trading price that is the negotiated amount (*i.e.*, premium/discount).

20. * * * Applicants maintain that while there is little legislative history regarding § 22(d), its provisions, as well as those of rule 22c-1, appear to have been designed to (a) prevent dilution caused by certain riskless-trading schemes by principal underwriters and contract dealers, (b) prevent unjust discrimination or preferential treatment among buyers resulting from sales at different prices, and (c) assure an orderly distribution system of investment company shares by eliminating price competition from brokers offering shares at less than the published sales price and repurchasing shares at more than the published redemption price.

21. Applicants believe that none of these purposes would be thwarted by permitting NAV-based Trading of Shares. * * * *

24. ETMF trading prices, as discussed above, would be directly tied to NAV. Unlike ETFs, ETMFs' need for relief arises because their trading price deviate from NAV only with respect to the execution costs of buying and selling ETMF Shares (*i.e.*, the premium/discount). In contrast, ETFs need relief because of differences related to the value of the underlying portfolio positions. Therefore, because ETMF Shares' trading prices are directly tied to NAV, an arbitrage mechanism that would keep market price close to or at NAV is not necessary.

B. Other Relief*

*[This other relief is the same relief that the Commission has previously granted to permit the operation of ETFs]

Applicants' Conditions:

Applicants agree that any order of the Commission granting the requested relief will be subject to the following conditions:

A. ETMF Relief

1. As long as an ETMF operates in reliance on the requested order, its Shares will be listed on an Exchange.

2. Neither the Trusts nor any ETMF will be advertised or marketed as an open-end investment company, a mutual fund or an ETF. Any advertising material that describes the purchase or sale of Creation Units or refers to redeemability will prominently disclose that Shares are not individually redeemable and that owners of Shares may acquire those Shares from an ETMF and tender those Shares for redemption to the ETMF in Creation Units only.

3. The website for the ETMFs, which will be publicly accessible at no charge, will contain, on a per Share basis, for each ETMF, the prior Business Day's NAV; intraday high, low, average and closing trading prices (expressed as premiums/discounts to NAV); the midpoint of the highest bid and lowest offer prices as of the close of Exchange trading (**Closing Bid/Ask Midpoint**) (expressed as a premium/discount to NAV); and the spread between the highest bid and lowest offer prices as of the close of Exchange trading (**Closing Bid/Ask Spread**). The website for the ETMFs also will contain charts showing the frequency distribution and range of values of trading prices, Closing Bid/Ask Midpoints and Closing Bid/Ask Spreads over time.

4. The Adviser or any Subadviser, directly or indirectly, will not cause any Authorized Participant (or any investor on whose behalf an Authorized Participant may transact with the ETMF) to acquire any Basket Instrument for the ETMF through a transaction in which the ETMF could not engage directly. * * * *

Topic 4 Money Market Fund: A Type of Open-End Investment Company

Laws & Rules Highlight:

IC Act (15 USC 80a-1 *et seq.*) & Rules (17 CFR §§ 270.0-1 *et seq.*)

Money Market Funds (Rule 2a-7)

two-tier system: stable & floating NAVs

- Rule 2a-7**(c)(1)(i)** (***permits*** *government money market funds and retail money market funds to compute the current price per share using* ***"amortized cost method"*** *and/or* ***"penny-rounding method"***)
  - 2a-7(a)(14) (*def.* ***"government money market fund"***); 2a-7(a)(21) (*def.* ***"retail money market fund"***)
  - 2a-7(a)(2) (*def.* ***"amortized cost method of valuation"***); 2a-7(a)(19) (*def.* ***"penny-rounding method of pricing"***)
  - 2a-7(g)(1) (***amortized cost method:*** *required procedures reasonably designed to* ***stabilize*** *MMF's NAV per share at a* ***single value***); 2a-7(g)(2) (***penny-rounding method:*** *required procedures reasonably designed to* ***assure*** *MMF's price per share as rounded to the nearest 1% not deviate from the intended* ***single price***)
- Rule 2a-7**(c)(1)(ii)** (***requires*** *all MMFs other than government and retail MMFs to compute their current price per share using fund's* ***current NAV*** *per share and applying* ***"basis point" rounding,*** *e.g.,* ***$1.0000***)

portfolio risk-limiting conditions

- Rule 2a-7(d)(1) Portfolio Maturity
  - 2a-7(d)(1)(i) (*maximum portfolio* ***instrument*** *remaining maturity:* ***397*** *days*)
  - 2a-7(d)(1)(ii) (*maximum* **WAM** *dollar-weighted average portfolio maturity:* ***60*** *days*)
  - 2a-7(d)(1)(iii) (*maximum* **WAL** *dollar-weighted average life to maturity:* ***120*** *days*)
- Rule 2a-7(d)(2) Portfolio Quality
  - 2a-7(a)(11) (*def. "eligible security": minimal credit risk standard*)
- Rule 2a-7(d)(3) Portfolio Diversification
  - 2a-7(d)(3)(i)-(ii) (*issuer diversification*)
  - 2a-7(d)(3)(iii)-(iv) (*demand feature and guarantee diversification*)
- Rule 2a-7(d)(4) Portfolio Liquidity
  - 2a-7(d)(4)(i) (*maximum* ***"illiquid securities"***: ***5%*** *of MMF's total assets*)
  - 2a-7(d)(4)(ii) (*minimum* ***"daily liquid assets"***: ***10%*** *of taxable MMF's total assets*)

- ◆ 2a-7(d)(4)(iii) (*minimum "**weekly liquid assets**": **30%** of MMF's total assets*)

redemption fees & gates; affiliate support; fund liquidation

- Rule 2a-7(c)(2) Liquidity Fees and Temporary Suspensions of Redemptions
  - ◆ 2a-7**(c)(2)(i)** (***discretionary** liquidity fees & redemption gates; **threshold:** "weekly liquid assets" fall below **30%** of MMF's total assets*)
  - ◆ 2a-7**(c)(2)(ii)** (***mandatory** liquidity fees; **threshold:** "weekly liquid assets" fall below **10%** of MMF's total assets*)
- Rule 17a-9 Purchase of Certain Securities from a Money Market Fund by an Affiliate, or an Affiliate of an Affiliate (*permits affiliated persons of MMF to purchase distressed portfolio securities from the fund, subject to pricing requirement and reporting on Form N-CR*)
- Rule 22e-3 Exemption for Liquidation of Money Market Funds (*exempts MMF from § 22(e): permitting **permanent suspension** of redemptions to allow for **orderly liquidation** of fund assets if: **(1)** the fund's level of "weekly liquid assets" falls below **10%** of its total assets; or **(2)** the fund board determines that the **extent of deviation** between amortized cost price per share and market-based NAV per share may result in material dilution or other results unfair to investors or to existing shareholders*)

transparency of portfolio risks

- Rule 2a-7(h)(10)(ii)-(iii) (***daily web site disclosure**: percentages of daily liquid assets, weekly liquid assets, and fund's net inflows/outflows; fund's shadow NAV price per share with 10-basis point rounding, e.g., **$1.000***)
- Form N-MFP: Monthly Schedule of Portfolio Holdings of Money Market Funds
- Form N-CR: Current Report—Money Market Fund Material Events

A Two-Tier System of MMF Regulation

<table>
<tr><th>Types of MMFs Based on “Investor Types”</th><th colspan="3">Types of MMFs Based on “Asset Types”</th></tr>
<tr><td>• Retail MMF
A money market fund that has policies and procedures reasonably designed to limit all beneficial owners of the fund to natural persons. [2a-7(a)(21)]
• Institutional MMF (i.e., non-Retail MMF)</td><td>Government MMF
A money market fund that invests 99.5% or more of its total assets in cash, government securities, and/or repurchase agreements that are “collateralized fully” (i.e. collateralized by cash or government securities) [2a-7(a)(14); IC-31166 n.627]</td><td>Tax-Exempt MMF
Tax-exempt MMFs (aka “Municipal MMFs”) primarily hold obligations of state and local governments and their instrumentalities, and pay interest that is generally exempt from federal income tax [2a-7(a)(23); IC-31166 nn.22, 737, 1990]</td><td>Prime MMFs
MMFs which invest substantially in private debt markets, generally holding: taxable short-term obligations issued by corporations and banks; repurchase agreements; asset-backed commercial paper [IC-31166 nn.21-22]</td></tr>
<tr><td rowspan="2">Valuation & Pricing Methods
• “amortized cost method of valuation”: stable NAV per share [2a-7(a)(2)]
• “penny-rounding method of pricing”: stable price per share [2a-7(a)(19)]
• floating NAV with “basis point” rounding [2a-7(c)(1)(ii)]</td><td rowspan="2">Permitted:
• amortized cost valuation;
• penny rounding pricing (e.g., $1.00)</td><td>Tax Exempt Retail—Permitted:
• amortized cost valuation;
• penny rounding pricing (e.g., $1.00)</td><td>Prime Retail—Permitted:
• amortized cost valuation;
• penny rounding pricing (e.g., $1.00)</td></tr>
<tr><td>Tax Exempt Institutional—Required:
floating NAV applying basis point rounding (e.g., $1.0000)</td><td>Prime Institutional—Required:
floating NAV applying basis point rounding (e.g., $1.0000)</td></tr>
</table>

Ref. 1. Rule 2a-7 Money Market Funds (2017); 2. Money Market Reform; Amendments to Form PF, IC-31166, 79 FR 47736 (2014)

A Two-Tier System of MMF Regulation (continued)

Types of MMFs Based on "Investor Types"	**Types of MMFs Based on "Asset Types"**		
• **Retail MMF** A money market fund that has policies and procedures reasonably designed to limit all beneficial owners of the fund to natural persons. [2a-7(a)(21)] • **Institutional MMF (*i.e.*, non-Retail MMF)**	**Government MMF** A money market fund that invests 99.5% or more of its total assets in cash, government securities, and/or repurchase agreements that are "collateralized fully" (i.e. collateralized by cash or government securities) [2a-7(a)(14); IC-31166 n.627]	**Tax-Exempt MMF** Tax-exempt MMFs (*aka* "Municipal MMFs") primarily hold obligations of state and local governments and their instrumentalities, and pay interest that is generally exempt from federal income tax [2a-7(a)(23); IC-31166 nn.22, 737, 1990]	**Prime MMFs** MMFs which invest substantially in private debt markets, generally holding: taxable short-term obligations issued by corporations and banks; repurchase agreements; asset-backed commercial paper [IC-31166 nn.21-22]
Liquidity Fees & Redemption Gates • ***discretionary fees & gates:*** *threshold:* "weekly liquid assets" fall below ***30%*** of MMF's total assets; *maximum fee:* 2%; *maximum gate:* 10 business days in a rolling 90-calendar day period [2a-7(c)(2)(i)] • ***mandatory fees:*** *threshold:* "weekly liquid assets" fall below ***10%*** of MMF's total assets; *default liquidity fee:* 1%, subject to maximum fee of 2% [2a-7(c)(2)(ii)]	***Not subject to:*** Liquidity Fees & Redemption Gates; ***May choose to apply:*** Liquidity and redemption requirements consistent with the requirements of 2a-7(c)(2)(i)-(ii) [2a-7(c)(2)(iii)]	**Subject to:** Liquidity Fees & Redemption Gates	**Subject to:** Liquidity Fees & Redemption Gates

Pre-Case Background Note[Biblio]

Pricing Conventions of Money Market Funds: A Type of Mutual Funds and An Alternative to Bank Deposit and Checking Accounts

Money market funds (MMFs) are a type of open-end investment companies having as their investment objectives generation of income and preservation of capital and liquidity. MMFs offer two advantages: (1) through ***pooling***, MMFs provide a vehicle to permit individual small investors, a well as institutional investors, to take advantage of the higher short-term interest rates earned on larger-denomination instruments; and (2) through portfolios composed of ***short-term, high-quality securities*** (typically, U.S. government and government agency issues, certificates of deposit, banker's acceptances, and commercial paper), MMFs are efficient and popular cash management vehicles for both retail and institutional investors.[1a; 1e (IC-21837)] As of year end 2016:[2 (Figure 2.3; Table 65)]

- The total net assets of **mutual funds** (MFs) in the United States stood at $16.3 trillion, of which about $2.7 trillion or 17% were **MMFs**;
- Of the total **U.S. MMF assets**: about 60% were held by households, and about 40% were held by institutional investors;
- The worldwide total net assets of regulated open-end funds stood at about $40.4 trillion, of which about $18.9 trillion or 47% were in the **U.S. market**, and about $1.2 trillion or 3% were in the **Chinese market**.

Pricing Convention of Non-MMF Mutual Funds

Compared to non-MMF mutual funds, MMFs most prominently differ in the determination of net asset value per share or ***NAV***, for purposes of distribution, redemption and repurchase of fund shares.[3; 1g(IC-28807 n.299; IC-29132 n.22); 1h(IC-31166 §II.B.3)] Non-MMF mutual funds are generally required to calculate their current NAV per share by:[1h (IC-31166 nn.5, 9, §III.B)]

- valuing those portfolio securities with respect to which market quotations are readily available at ***current market value***;
- valuing other portfolio securities and assets at their ***fair value*** as determined in good faith by the board of directors.

Non-MMF mutual fund shares must be transacted at the NAV of the fund's portfolio next calculated using such daily mark-to-market or fair value accounting, or ***floating***

NAV, applying ***"10 basis point" rounding***: *e.g.*, **$1.000**; **$10.00**. [*See* § 2(a)(41) definition of "*value*" of fund assets; Rule 2a-4 "*Definition of 'Current Net Asset Value' for Use in Computing Periodically the Current Price of Redeemable Security*"; Rule 22c-1 "*Pricing of Redeemable Securities for Distribution, Redemption and Repurchase*"].

Amortized Cost Method of Valuation; Penny Rounding Method of Pricing

From 1978 to 1983, via exemptive order procedure the SEC exempted MMFs from the mutual fund pricing requirements and permitted MMFs to employ ***amortized cost method of valuation of portfolio securities*** and ***penny-rounding method of pricing fund shares***, to facilitate MMFs' ability to:[1b (IC-12206)]

- provide a steady flow of investment income (in the form of dividends) at rates comparable to the interest rates available by direct investment in money market instruments; and
- maintain a $1.00 stable NAV per share without regard to small variations in the value of the fund portfolio securities—one of the "trademark" features of MMFs.

In 1983, codifying its prior exemptive positions, the SEC adopted Rule 2a-7 "Money Market Funds"—the principal rule governing MMFs.[1a; 1b (IC-13380); 1g (IC-28807 §III.A)]

Under the "**amortized cost method of valuation**" as defined in Rule 2a-7(a)(2), the portfolio securities of an MMF—regardless of whether their market quotations are readily available—are valued ***at acquisition cost***. Then, the interest earned on each portfolio security, plus any discount received or less any premium paid upon purchase, is ***accrued*** ratably over the remaining maturity of the security. By declaring these accruals to its shareholders as a daily dividend, the MMF is able to set a fixed price per share, typically **$1.00**.[1c (IC-14983 n.2); 1d (IC-18005 n.4); 1e (IC-21837 n.6)] In the case of government MMFs and retail MMFs, the amortized cost method of valuation may be applied to the entire portfolios; in the case of non-government institutional MMFs, the amortized cost method may only be applied to the specific individual portfolio securities whose remaining maturities do not exceed 60 days and where the amortized cost value of an individual security *is approximately the fair value* of the security determined using market-based factors.[1h (IC-31166 §III.D)] A basic premise justifying the use of the amortized cost valuation method is the fact that high-quality, short-term debt securities held until maturity will eventually yield a value equivalent to the amortized cost value, regardless of the current disparity between amortized cost value and market value.[1b (IC-13380 n.6); 1g (IC-29132 n.6)] However, if a portfolio security defaults, or if a portfolio security's sale results in a realized capital gain or loss, the temporary disparity between the fund's amortized cost value and its market value becomes permanent.[1h (IC-31166 §II.B.3)]

For an MMF using the amortized cost valuation method, the fund's board of directors has a responsibility to establish procedures reasonably designed to ***stabilize*** the fund's NAV per share at a single value and to ensure that the stable price represents ***fairly*** the fund's market-based NAV. For this purpose, the fund board must periodically monitor the ***deviation*** of the current market-based NAV per share ("***shadow NAV***") from the amortized cost price per share—a process referred to as "***shadow pricing***" [*see* Rule 2a-7(g)(1)]. If the deviation *exceeds 0.5%* of the fund's $1 stable share price (*i.e.*, 50 basis points), or if the amount of deviation may result in *material dilution or other unfair results* to investors or current shareholders, Rule 2a-7 imposes specific obligations on the board of directors to eliminate or reduce the dilution or unfair results, such as by ***re-pricing*** the securities below (or above) $1.00, *i.e.*, "***breaking the buck***."[1b (IC-13380 n.44); 1d (IC-18005 n.9); 1g (IC-29132 nn.7-10); 1h (IC-31166 n.20)]

<table>
<tr><td colspan="2">Amortized cost method of valuation: calculating "50 basis point" deviation
(1) Assuming amortized cost price per share = $1.00; (2) Shadow NAV: market-based NAV carries 4 decimals with no rounding [Ref. IC-13380, 48 FR 32555, 32564 n.47 (1983)]</td></tr>
<tr><td>Example 1: market-based NAV per share = $0.9950;
Deviation not exceeding 0.5% benchmark:
($1 - $0.9950)/$1 = 0.5%</td><td>Example 2: market-based NAV per share = $0.99499;
Deviation exceeding 0.5% benchmark:
($1- $0.9949)/$1 = 0.51%</td></tr>
</table>

Under the "**penny-rounding method of computation**" as defined in Rule 2a-7(a)(19), the *current net asset value* of an MMF is calculated by:

- valuing portfolio securities for which market quotations are readily available at ***current market value***, pursuant to Rule 2a-4;
- valuing other securities and assets at ***fair value*** as determined in good faith by the board of directors, pursuant to Rule 2a-4; and
- valuing portfolio securities with remaining maturities of 60 days of less by ***amortized cost*** method, if the amortized cost value of the individual portfolio security is ***approximately the same as the fair value*** of the security determined without the use of amortized cost valuation.

Then, the current NAV per share value is rounded to the nearest 1%, *i.e.*,

penny-rounding, to allow the fund to maintain the $1.00 fixed price per share.[1a (IC-9786); 1b (IC-12206 n.5; IC-13380 nn. 44, 53); 1c (IC-14983 n3); 1e (IC-21837 n.7); 1g (IC-28807 n.296); 1h (IC-31166 §III.D)] The penny rounding method of pricing is only available to government MMFs and retail MMFs, and is not available to non-government institutional MMFs.[1h (IC-31166 §III.B)]

For an MMF using the penny-rounding method, the fund's board of directors has a responsibility to assure, to the extent reasonably practicable, that the fund's price per share remains ***stabilized*** at the single NAV value determined. If the NAV per share begins to deviate from the single price, the board should consider actions (such as maintaining appropriate average portfolio maturity; permitting fund investment only in securities of minimal credit risk and high quality; disposing of securities whose quality falls below high quality), in order to stabilize the current price per share at the selected NAV value.[1b (IC-13380 n.40)] For purposes of calculating the ***deviation***, *all* of the fund's portfolio securities—including those with remaining maturities of 60 days or less—must be valued based on current market factors. Further, for a penny-rounding fund having a material portion of its portfolio consisting of securities with remaining maturities of 60 days or less which are valued by the amortized cost method, ***monitoring*** of actual market values may be necessary particularly in a volatile market, in order for the fund board to determine the ***current fairness*** of price obtained under the penny-rounding method.[1b (IC-13380 nn.44-46)]

<table>
<tr><td colspan="2">Penny-rounding method of computation: calculating “50 basis point” deviation
(1) Assuming penny-rounding single price per share = $1.00; (2) Market-based NAV carries 4 decimals with no rounding [Ref. IC-13380, 48 FR 32555, 32565 n.53 (1983)]</td></tr>
<tr><td>Example 1:
market-based NAV per share without rounding fell below $0.99500: ($1-$0.99500)/$1 = 0.5%
<u>Fund needs to:</u>
(1) change its price per share to: $0.99; or
(2) cease using the penny-rounding method, and calculate the price with the accuracy of at least $0.001</td><td>Example 2:
market-based NAV per share without rounding rose above $1.00500: ($1-$1.00500)/$1 = -0.5%
<u>Fund needs to:</u>
(1) change its price per share to: $1.01; or
(2) cease using the penny-rounding method, and calculate the price with the accuracy of at least $0.001</td></tr>
</table>

Two-Tier System of MMFs: Stable NAV and Floating NAV

In light of the run on MMFs during the 2008 financial crisis, the 2010 *Report of the*

President's Working Group on Financial Markets—Money Market Fund Reform Options recommended, inter alia, a two-tier system of MMFs: stable NAV funds and floating NAV funds.[4] In 2014, effecting a structural change to the ***stable NAV system*** in place since 1983 which was applicable to all types of MMFs regardless of differences in their investment strategy or investor base, the SEC instituted a ***floating NAV system*** governing non-government institutional MMFs, while reserving the ***stable NAV system*** for government MMFs and retail MMFs. The SEC cited the following as part of its rationale:[1h (IC-31166 §III.B)]

- Stable NAV valuation and pricing methods have an inherent "first-mover advantage," providing a structural incentive to redeem when an MMF's shadow price falls below the fund's stable price.
- Institutional shareholders, as compared to retail shareholders, are more likely to be such first mover due to their sophistication and large investments at stake, exposing non-government institutional MMFs to risk of runs with resulting wealth transfers from remaining shareholders to redeeming shareholders.
- Floating NAV pricing will disincentivize portfolio loss-induced first mover incentive to redeem, since redeeming shareholders will receive market value rather than a stable price for their shares.

As a result, non-government institutional MMF shares must now be transacted at ***floating NAV***, similar to non-MMF mutual funds. Unlike non-MMF mutual funds, however, whose pricing applies ***"10 basis point" rounding*** (*e.g.*, $1.000; $10.00), non-government institutional MMFs' pricing must apply ***"basis point" rounding*** (*e.g.*, $1.0000; $10.000; $100.00)—a greater precision to accentuate the visibility of credit market risks which non-government institutional MMFs are exposed to. For economic literature studying use of the amortized cost method of valuation, arbitrage, and dilution in the context of institutional MMFs, see, for example, Lyon (1984).[5]

Stable NAV MMFs: An Alternative to Bank Accounts and "Special Purpose Bank" Regulation?

Money market funds were first introduced in 1971.[2 (p.265)] In the early 1980's, inflation and interest rates skyrocketed. When interest rates in money markets exceeded 15%, banks remained subject to the Regulation Q rate ceiling of 5.25% for interest on savings accounts, and the statutory prohibition of any interest on checking accounts. Investors flocked to MMFs—which offered both market interest rates and checking account features. Thus during a period when many depository institutions were having difficulty attracting savings, MMFs were experiencing dramatic growth.[6; 7; 8] MMFs' stable share price enables investors to easily ascertain their account balances, by simply knowing the number of shares in their accounts. Many MMFs also offer bank-like transaction services such as check writing for redemption. These features lead to MMFs being used by many investors as an alternative to bank deposit and checking accounts, although critical distinctions exist between MMFs and bank accounts. MMF shares represent equity interest in the MMFs, whereas bank deposits are debt liability of the banks. Bank accounts have federal deposit insurance, whereas MMFs do not.[1d (IC-17589 nn.6-7; IC-18005 n.3); 1e (IC-19959 n.6; IC-21837 n.5); 6; 7]

Empirical research studying the risk-taking behavior of MMFs during the 2007-2010 financial crisis concludes that, because fund inflows are highly responsive to fund yields, MMFs have strong incentives to chase yield and thus risk and are vulnerable to runs.[9] Debate on whether stable NAV MMFs should be regulated as "special purpose banks" (**SPBs**) or otherwise be subject to bank-type regulation has continued from the time of the MMF innovation in 1971 to the present day.[4; 7; 10]

Literature **opposing** SPB treatment of MMFs includes:

- U.S. Securities and Exchange Commission (1981)[7] (*stating: "The Commission does not share this view" that "investors in money market funds might be better protected if those funds were subject to bank-type regulation"*); SEC (2014)[1h] (*noting SEC's lack of regulatory authority to transform MMFs into SPBs, stating: MMFs have some features similar to banks but also other features quite different from banks that do not lend themselves to applying substantial parts of the bank regulatory regime to MMFs not tailored to the specific structure and risks of MMFs*);
- Macey (2011)[3] (arguing: *too much homogeneity* among risk-management strategies of financial institutions can *increase systemic risk*; subjecting MMFs to a *bank-like regulatory structure* would increase systemic risk);
- Hawke & Freeman (2009)[11] (commenting on Group Thirty's recommendation of reorganizing stable NAV MMFs into special-purpose banks: "*A 'death sentence' is fundamentally a bad idea.*").

Literature **supporting** SPB treatment of MMFs includes:

- Roe (2012)[12] (advocating imposing "*bank-style rules on capital and reserves*" on MMFs);

- Gordon (2010)[13a] (proposing "*narrow savings banks*" concept to regulate stable NAV MMFs); Gordon (1993)[13b] (arguing: investors' MMF accounts "*resemble bank demand deposit accounts*");
- Working Group on Financial Reform, Group of Thirty (a private international body of financial experts) (2009)[14] (proposing treating stable NAV MMFs which offer bank-like services as *special purpose banks*, and subjecting such MMFs to prudential regulation and supervision, government insurance, and access to central bank lender-of-last-resort facilities).

Literature **supporting** a weaker form of bank-type regulation of MMFs includes:

- Committee on Capital Markets Regulation (a private research organization with membership from financial sector and academic community) (2012)[15] (arguing: MMFs are "*the best candidates for insurance*"; insuring MMF investments is "*the narrowest way*" to reduce the spread of contagion during a financial crisis).

Bibliography

1. Rule 2a-7 Rels.: **1a.** Valuation of Debt Instruments by Money Market Funds and Certain Other Open-End Investment Companies; Rule Interpretation, IC-9786, 42 FR 28999 (1977); **1b.** Valuation of Debt Instruments and Computation of Current Price Per Share by Certain Open-End Investment Companies (Money Market Funds), IC-12206, 47 FR 5428 (1982); IC-13380, 48 FR 32555 (1983); **1c.** Acquisition and Valuation of Certain Portfolio Instruments by Registered Investment Companies, IC-14983, 51 FR 9773 (1986); **1d.** Revisions to Rules Regulating Money Market Funds, IC-17589, 55 FR 30239 (1990); IC-18005, 56 FR 8113 (1991); **1e.** Revisions to Rules Regulating Money Market Funds, IC-19959, 58 FR 68585 (1993); IC-21837, 61 FR 13956 (1996); **1f.** Technical Revisions to the Rules and Forms Regulating Money Market Funds, IC-22383, 61 FR 66621 (1996); IC-22921, 62 FR 64968 (1997); **1g.** Money Market Fund Reform, IC-28807, 74 FR 32688 (2009); IC-29132, 75 FR 10060 (2010); **1h.** Money Market Fund Reform; Amendments to Form PF, IC-30551, 78 FR 36834 (2013); IC-31166, 79 FR 47736 (2014); **1i.** Removal of Certain References to Credit Ratings and Amendment to the Issuer Diversification Requirement in the Money Market Fund Rule, IC-31828, 80 FR 58124 (2015)
2. ICI, 2017 INVESTMENT COMPANY FACT BOOK (57th ed.)
3. Macey, *Reducing Systemic Risk: The Role of Money Market Mutual Funds as Substitutes for Federally Insured Bank Deposits*, 17 STAN. J.L. BUS. & FIN. 131 (2011)
4. REPORT OF THE PRESIDENT'S WORKING GROUP ON FINANCIAL MARKETS—MONEY MARKET FUND REFORM OPTIONS (2010)
5. Lyon, *Money Market Funds and Shareholder Dilution*, 39 J. FIN. 1101 (1984)
6. MISHKIN & EAKINS, FINANCIAL MARKETS AND INSTITUTIONS, CH. 20 (8th ed. 2015)
7. Stmt. of the Hon. John R. Evans, Comm'ner of the SEC, Before the United State Sen. Comm. on Banking, Housing and Urban Affairs, Concerning the Regulation of Money Market Funds (May 13, 1981), *referencing* Report of the Staff of the Div. Inv. Mgmt. of the Sec. Exch. Comm'n on the Regulation of Money Market Funds, Before the Business, Labor & Econ. Develop. Comm. of the Utah State Senate (Feb 13, 1981)
8. FEIN, MUTUAL FUND ACTIVITIES OF BANKS, § 1.02 Growth of Mutual Funds (2004)
9. Kacperczyk & Schnabl, *How Safe are Money Market Funds?*, 128 Q.J. ECON. 1017 (2013)
10. FINANCIAL STABILITY OVERSIGHT COUNCIL, PROPOSED RECOMMENDATIONS REGARDING MONEY

MARKET MUTUAL FUND REFORM (2012)

11. Hawke & Freeman, *Money Market Funds Have No Place on Banking Sheets*, 174 AM. BANKER 8 (2009)
12. Roe, *Money-Market Resistance*, PROJECT SYNDICATE (2012)
13. Gorton: **12a.** Gorton & Metrick, *Regulating the Shadow Banking System* (Brookings Institution Press 2010); **12b.** Gorton & Pennacchi, *Money Market Funds and Finance Companies: Are They the Banks of the Future?* STRUCTURAL CHANGE IN BANKING CH.3 (Klausner & White eds. 1993)
14. WORKING GRP. ON FIN. REFORM, GRP. OF THIRTY, FINANCIAL REFORM: A FRAMEWORK FOR FINANCIAL STABILITY, PART 2(3) (2009)
15. COMM. OF CAPITAL MKT. REGULATION, INTERCONNECTEDNESS AND CONTAGION 239 (2012)

Case Study: The Reserve Primary Fund "Breaking the Buck" and Run on MMFs*

Significance of the Reserve Primary Fund's Breaking the Buck.[1] In the 25 years since the adoption of Rule 2a-7 in 1983 as of 2008, only two MMFs had broken the buck. In 1994, a small government MMF with less than $100 million in assets, having a narrow group of investors principally of small community bankers, and investing 27.5% of its assets in an idiosyncratic portfolio—the **Community Bankers U.S. Government Money Market Fund**—broke the buck because of exposures to interest rate derivatives. The event passed without significant repercussions.[2] When the **Reserve Primary Fund**—the very first MMF in the United States which began public offering of its shares in 1972 and one of the largest MMFs with assets under management of $62 billion[3; 4]—broke the buck on September 16, 2008 amid the broader financial crisis, it triggered heavy redemptions from The Reserve's other MMFs, and from institutional prime MMFs in general. The September 2008 run on prime MMFs contributed to severe dislocations in the short-term credit markets, affected the entire financial system, and threatened the broader economy.

Events in the Week of September 15, 2008.[1; 5; 6] On September 15, 2008, **Lehman Brothers Holdings Inc.** filed for bankruptcy, leading to heavy redemptions from money market funds that held Lehman Brothers debt securities. On the same day, the **Reserve Primary Fund**—a $62 billion MMF and holding $785 million in Lehman Brothers debt—immediately began experiencing a run, with shareholder redemption requests totaling approximately $40 billion in just the two days of September 15-16. On September 16, 2008, **The Reserve** announced that as of that afternoon, its Reserve Primary Fund would ***break the buck*** and re-price its securities at ***$0.9667*** per share. As of September 17, 2008, the Reserve Primary Fund suspended redemptions. On September 22, 2008, the SEC issued an emergency order, permitting the Primary Fund's suspension of redemption and postponement of redemption payment, in order to enable the Fund to liquidate portfolio securities without impairing its net asset value and for the protection of the Fund security holders. The emergency order was retroactive from September 17, 2008, the day the Primary Fund suspended redemptions [IC-28386, 73 FR 55572 (Sept. 25, 2008)].

The run on The Reserve's Primary Fund quickly spread to the other **Reserve funds**, which rapidly depleted their cash in order to satisfy redemptions and began offering to sell the funds' portfolio securities into the market, further depressing the funds' valuations. On October 24, 2008, the SEC issued an emergency order permitting the other Reserve funds to suspend redemptions and postpone payment, to allow the funds the ability to orderly liquidate their portfolio securities and for the protection of all shareholders in the process. The emergency order was retroactive from October 8, 2008, the day the Reserve funds' boards determined to liquidate the Reserve funds in an orderly manner, in view of the unprecedented illiquidity of the markets existing at the time and the extraordinary levels of redemptions the Reserve funds had experienced, and with the goal to ensure that the shareholders of each Reserve fund be treated appropriately [IC-28466, 73 FR 64993 (Oct. 31, 2008)].

During the four-week period ending October 8, 2008, the run from MMFs was primarily a flight by institutional investors. Prime institutional funds experienced 30% net outflows, compared to 4.6% outflows experienced by prime retail funds; institutional investors withdrew substantial sums from prime MMFs even before the Reserve Primary Fund broke the buck. Managers of MMFs, fearing further redemptions, retained cash rather than invest it in short-term instruments. Short-term financing markets froze.

Market Intervention Programs of the Federal Government.[1; 5] On September 19, 2008, the Board of Governors of the Federal Reserve System and the U.S. Department of the Treasury announced an unprecedented market intervention to provide liquidity to the short-term markets and to provide support for the MMF industry: The Fed announced the creation of its "Asset-Backed Commercial Paper Money Market Mutual Fund Liquidity Facility," extending credit to U.S. banks and bank-holding companies to finance their purchases of certain commercial paper from MMFs; the Treasury Department announced its "Temporary Guarantee Program for Money Market Funds," guaranteeing that each shareholder in a participating MMF would receive the $1 stable share price for each share held in the fund, up to the number of shares held as of the close of business on September 19, 2008.[1 (n.23)] The Temporary Guarantee Program represented the first time that the federal government had provided any "insurance or guarantee to money market funds," and "placed certain money market fund holdings on par with federally insured bank deposits."[3] On November 26, 2008, the SEC adopted Rule 22e-3T as "an interim final temporary rule," exempting MMFs participating in the Treasury's Guarantee Program from IC Act § 22(e), and permitting any participating MMF that "breaks the buck" to temporarily suspend redemption of shares and postpone payment of redemption proceeds for the orderly liquidation of fund assets. In 2010, the SEC adopted on a permanent basis Rule 22e-3 replacing Rule 22e-3T, designed to facilitate an MMF's orderly liquidation. [IC-28487, 73 FR 71919 (2008); IC-29132, 75 FR 10060 (2010)].

The SEC Enforcement Action. In May 2009, the SEC filed civil fraud charges against the investment adviser and certain officers operating The Reserve Primary Fund, for ***failing to*** provide key material facts to the Fund's investors, board of trustees, and ratings agencies after Lehman Brothers filed bankruptcy on September 15, 2008, and for ***misrepresenting*** that the Fund's investment adviser would provide credit support necessary to protect the Fund's NAV at $1.00 when in fact the adviser had no such intention. The SEC also sought to expedite the distribution of the Fund's remaining assets to investors.

**Ref.* [1. Report of the President's Working Group on Financial Markets—Money Market Fund Reform Options (2010); 2. In *re* Craig S. Vanucci and Brian K. Andrew, Respondents, Adm. Proc. 3-9804, IC-23638, IA-1782 (1999); 3. Fuller *et al.*, *2008—Developments in Fund Regulation*, 16 INV. LAW. 1 (2009); 4. Bent, *Sorting Out the Money Market Funds*, 115 TRUSTS & EST. 408 (1976); 5. Money Market Fund Reform, IC-28807, 74 FR 32688 (2009) & IC-29132, 75 FR 10060 (2010); 6. Money Market Reform; Amendments to Form PF, IC-31166, 79 FR 47736 (2014)]

SEC v. Reserve Mgmt. Co., Inc.

09-CV-4346 (SEC Compl., SDNY May 5, 2009)

[***Procedural history and related materials***: SEC, *Spotlight on Information for Reserve Primary Fund Investors* (Modified: Jan. 28, 2010); SEC v. Reserve Mgmt. Co., Inc., 09-CV-4346: Dk#1 SEC Complaint (SDNY May 5, 2009); Dk#272 Memorandum Opinion & Order (SDNY Feb. 24, 2010); Dk#648 Memorandum Opinion & Order (SDNY Sept. 30, 2010); Dk#650 Amended Judgment (SDNY Sept. 30, 2013); Dk#652 Amended Judgment (SDNY Jan 13, 2014); Dk#654 Stipulation (SDNY Jan 21, 2014)]

Research Topic:

Development and regulation of money market funds in China.

SEC v. Reserve Mgmt. Co., Inc., *et al.*

09-CV-4346 (SEC Compl., SDNY May 5, 2009)

Plaintiff Securities and Exchange Commission brings this action against Defendants Reserve Management Company, Inc. (**RMCI**), Resrv Partners, Inc., Bruce Bent Sr., and Bruce Bent II (collectively, **Defendants**) and Relief Defendant The Reserve Primary Fund (**Primary Fund** or the **Fund**). The Commission alleges the following:

SUMMARY OF ALLEGATIONS

1. Over a two day period in September 2008, after the news of Lehman Brothers' bankruptcy filing roiled the US financial markets, Defendants engaged in a systematic campaign to deceive the investing public into believing that the Primary Fund—their flagship money market fund—was safe and secure despite its substantial Lehman holdings. That campaign involved both the knowing dissemination of false information to the Primary Fund's Board of Trustees, investors, and rating agencies and, in the case of certain Defendants, the knowing concealment of the true effect of the Lehman holdings on the Fund.

2. The Primary Fund is a money market fund that historically provided shareholders with a $1.00 per share NAV. Like most investors in money market funds, investors in the Primary Fund viewed it as a safe and stable option for preservation of capital. For many investors seeking preservation of capital and virtually immediate access to their funds, money market funds are an attractive regulated alternative to bank deposits.

3. On September 15, 2008—the day Lehman Brothers filed for bankruptcy protection—the Fund held $785 million in Lehman debt securities. RMCI, the Primary Fund's adviser, was immediately besieged by shareholders seeking to redeem their shares based on fears that a decline in the value in the Fund's Lehman holdings could compromise the Fund's $1.00 NAV.

4. In order to persuade investors to refrain from redeeming shares, and to induce new purchases of shares, Defendants systematically violated the antifraud provisions of the federal securities laws by, *inter alia*, misrepresenting material facts concerning the Primary Fund's status, most notably by falsely assuring shareholders, the Fund's Board of Trustees and the rating agencies that RMCI had agreed to provide the Fund with sufficient capital to maintain its NAV at $1.00. In the case of RMCI, Bent Sr. and Bent II, rather than comply with their fiduciary obligations as investment advisers, they placed their own

financial and reputational interests ahead of the Fund and its shareholders.

5. Defendants' campaign of misinformation came to an end at 4:00 p.m. EST on September 16, 2008, when RMCI disclosed that the Primary Fund had broken the buck, *i.e.*, its shares had declined in value below $0.995, the lowest point at which they could permissibly be rounded to $1.00.

6. Defendants' misconduct on September 15 and 16 arose from a simple reality: unless RMCI could persuade shareholders that the $1.00 NAV of the Fund was absolutely safe despite the Fund's Lehman exposure, shareholders would continue to redeem shares in massive and unsustainable amounts. Defendants also know that Moody's and Standard & Poor's—both of which had assigned the Primary Fund their highest ratings—would likely initiate crippling ratings downgrades absent evidence of a plan to protect the $1.00 NAV, a scenario which would accelerate the pace of redemptions and increase the likelihood that the Fund would break the buck.

7. In order to falsely assure shareholders, the Board, and the rating agencies that the Fund's $1.00 NAV would remain intact, and that the Fund remained a safe and liquid investment, Defendants published, or authorized the dissemination of, numerous materially false statements, including that:

a. RMCI "intended to protect" the $1.00 NAV of the Primary Fund to "whatever degree is required";

b. RMCI and the Bents had sufficient capital available to maintain the Fund's NAV at $1.00 in the event it fell below that level;

c. RMCI was in the process of executing a credit support agreement whereby it would provide capital to the Primary Fund to allow it to maintain a per share NAV of $1.00;

d. RMCI had submitted a request for "no-action" relief to the Commission to implement a credit support agreement to protect the $1.00 NAV of the Fund, and expected such relief to be granted within hours; and

e. The Primary Fund was liquid and was timely honoring shareholder redemptions.

8. All of these statements of material fact were false. RMCI and the Bents did not intend to provide the levels of credit support necessary to maintain the NAV of the Primary Fund at $1.00 per share and, in fact, knew on September 15 that they would not do so even as they told shareholders, the Board and the rating agencies otherwise. Moreover,

contrary to Defendant Resrv Partners' September 15,2008 press release claiming that RMCI *already* had credit support agreements in place that would "ensure the integrity of a $1.00 NAV" for the Primary Fund and was submitting "appropriate documentation to the SEC," RMCI never implemented *any* such agreements or submitted *any* documents to the Commission.

9. On September 15, RMCI and the Bents also knew that the skyrocketing levels of redemptions by Fund shareholders had outstripped the Fund's ability to generate liquidity to pay those requests, a disastrous state of affairs for a money market fund. By approximately 10:10 a.m. on September 15, the Fund's custodian bank, State Street Bank, had suspended the Fund's overdraft privileges because of massive redemption outflows. Therefore, by approximately 10:10 a.m. on September 15, although the Fund was no longer in a position to pay investors, redeeming shareholders had no knowledge of this critically important fact and continued to believe that they would timely be paid at the NAV of S1.00 per share.

10. Public knowledge of the fact that the Primary Fund was illiquid would have irreparably damaged the Fund's and RMCI's reputation, prompted a downgrade in the Fund's ratings, and frustrated Defendants' ongoing efforts to falsely persuade investors that the $1.00 NAV was safe. As a result, RMCI and the Bents omitted or misrepresented material facts concerning redemption activity and the Fund's liquidity to the Fund's Board, shareholders, and Moody's.

11. The misinformation imparted by RMCI and the Bents on September 15, 2008 was intended to, and did in fact, prevent the Primary Fund's Board of Trustees from acting in an informed manner in setting the Fund's NAV. As a result, the process the Board used to strike the NAV of the Fund up until 4:00 p.m. on September 16, when RMCI disclosed the Fund had broken the buck, was hopelessly flawed, to the advantage of some investors who were the beneficiaries of redemption confirmations at an artificially derived $1.00 NAV and the disadvantage of others who were not. * * * *

DEFENDANTS AND RELIEF DEFENDANT

19. **Defendant RMCI**, which carries out its business under the name "The Reserve," is a privately held corporation owned and controlled by Bruce Bent Sr. and his family, including Defendant Bruce Bent II, with its headquarters and principal place of business in New York, New York. RMCI bas been registered with the Commission as an investment

adviser since 1984. In 2008, RMCI provided investment advisory services to five registered, open-end, investment companies set up as trusts, offering a total of 22 open-end investment portfolios (collectively, **Reserve Funds**). RMCI had approximately $120 billion in assets under management as of September 12, 2008.

20. **Defendant Resrv Partners** is a broker-dealer registered with the Commission and a member of FINRA. Resrv Partners is the distributor for the funds managed by RMCI. The Bents collectively own and control Resrv Partners. Resrv Partners has its headquarters and principal place of business in New York, NewYork.

21. **Defendant Bruce Bent Sr.**, age 71, is Chairman of RMCI, and Chairman, President, Treasurer and Trustee of the Primary Fund. Bent Sr. has been employed by The Reserve family of companies since 1971. Bent Sr. resides in Manhasset, New York.

22. **Defendant Bruce Bent II**, age 42, is Vice Chairman and President of RMCI. Bent II is Co-Chief Executive Officer, Senior Vice President and Assistant Treasurer of the Primary Fund. Bent II has been employed by RMCI since 1991. Bent II resides in Manhasset, New York.

23. **Relief Defendant The Reserve Primary Fund** is a series of the Reserve Fund, a Massachusetts business trust registered with the Commission under the Investment Company Act as an open-end investment company. * * * *

DEFENDANTS' FRAUDULENT CONDUCT

Overview of Relevant Reserve Entities

26. Defendant Bruce Bent Sr. is the public face of the Reserve, and a longtime advocate of the safety and stability of money market funds. Bent Sr. and his family own and control Defendants RMCI and Resrv Partners. According to RMCI, as of September 2008:

> The Reserve is the world's most experienced money fund manager and the largest asset management company dedicated solely to cash and liquidity management. With over $125 billion in assets, representing the trust of hundreds of institutions and millions of individuals, The Reserve is recognized as the fastest growing money fund complex in 2005, 2006 and 2007 according to *iMoneyNet*.

27. Defendant Bruce Bent II is Bent Sr.'s son and, in his capacity as co-Vice Chairman of RMCI, had substantial responsibility for overseeing RMCI's business operations, including on September 15 and 16, 2008. * * * *

30. At the time of the transactions and events alleged in this Complaint, and as a result of the control and influence alleged further herein, Bent Sr. and Bent II each were investment advisers for purposes of the violations of the Investment Advisers Act alleged herein, and controlling persons of RMCI for the purposes of Section 20(a) of the Exchange Act.

The Primary Fund's Redemption Procedures

* * * *

33. Until September 15, 2008, the Primary Fund's hourly NAV calculation was mechanical in nature, as the Fund's holdings were all carried at amortized cost (as permitted under Rule 2a-7), meaning the Fund's hourly per share NAV remained constant at $1.00. If, however, the Board determined that a given security should no longer be valued at amortized cost, and should be assigned a "fair value"—as it did with the Lehman holdings following Lehman's bankruptcy—the Board would rely upon RMCI to provide it with timely and accurate information to ensure that the assigned fair value remained accurate in light of available market data.

The Primary Fund's Increasingly Risky Investment Profile

34. From its inception in 1971, the Primary Fund historically invested in very conservative assets such as government securities and bank certificates of deposit. The Fund also carried the highest possible ratings from Moody's and Standard & Poor's denoting safety and liquidity, a fact which RMCI highlighted in its promotional materials.

35. In 2007 and 2008, however, the Fund began to purchase riskier commercial paper issued by financial institutions, including Lehman, Merrill Lynch, and Washington Mutual. The higher yields paid by these securities generated attractive returns for Fund shareholders, and helped the Fund attract billions of new dollars in investments, which in turn bolstered the management and advisory fees earned by RMCI.

36. The Primary Fund's shifting investment strategy, and substantial increase in assets under management, had significant implications given RMCI's status as a private family-owned company. Unlike many other large mutual fund complexes, RMCI, and the funds it advises, are not owned, or otherwise affiliated with, a large public company or commercial bank with the resources to provide financial support in the event a portfolio security were to become impaired. To the contrary, in the event a Primary Fund holding declined in value to the point where it threatened the Fund's $1.00 NAV, the Fund's ability

to maintain a stable $1.00 NAV depended exclusively on the Bent family's ability and willingness to provide or secure capital—either personal resources, those of RMCI, or from some third party—to support the NAV.

37. While an investment adviser such as RMCI is under no legal obligation to provide financial support to maintain the $1.00 NAV of a distressed money market fund, breaking the buck is a catastrophic development for a money market fund and its shareholders. Although agreements to protect a fund's $1.00 NAV can be implemented in a variety of ways, they generally require a fund adviser or other third party to commit financial resources to protect a fund's $1.00 per share NAV, *e.g.*, by providing the fund with capital to maintain the $1.00 NAV, by providing capital to offset the decline in value in the impaired security, or by purchasing the impaired security out of the portfolio.

38. The Bents were fully aware prior to September 15, 2008 of the devastating reputational and business damage that would arise if a fund managed by RMCI broke the buck....

RMCI Ignores Issues Raised By Moody's

39. Beginning in the summer of 2007, as economic conditions worsened, some money market funds began to experience declines in the value of securities held in their portfolios. Many of the funds implemented credit support agreements that allowed the funds to maintain a $1.00 per share NAV to avoid breaking the buck. * * * *

42. RMCI did not develop or even discuss internally the type of contingency plan discussed with Moody's or investigate the credit support agreements that had been utilized by other money market funds even though the agreements were often publicly available.

RMCI Ignores Lehman's Potential Impact on The Reserve Funds

43. Throughout the summer and first half of September 2008, RMCI maintained that Lehman's financial condition—which the financial press and rating agencies had described as increasingly troubled—did not pose a risk to the three Reserve funds with Lehman exposure. * * * *

51. Shortly after midnight, in the early morning of September 15, 2008, Lehman Brothers Holdings, Inc. announced that it was filing for bankruptcy protection pursuant to Chapter 11 of the United States Bankruptcy Code. * * * *

62. As a result, while shareholders could and did continue to place redemption requests with RMCI—which they believed would entitle them to redemption at $1.00 per share based on a purportedly accurate hourly NAV strike—the Primary Fund lacked liquidity from State Street or any other source to fund those redemptions.... At no point on September 15, however, did RMCI and Bent II disclose this material fact to the Board; instead, they actively fostered the impression that the situation was under control. * * * *

RMCI Continues to Deceive Investors During the Evening of September 15

107. By approximately 5:00 p.m. on September 15, redemption requests had climbed to over $20 billion, nearly half of which were unfunded. RMCI had also failed in its efforts to persuade State Street, or any other third parties, to provide it with additional liquidity to meet the large and growing backlog of investor redemptions.

108. Despite knowledge of these facts, as part of a last-ditch effort to salvage the Primary Fund's viability as a money market fund, Bent II continued to authorize false statements by RMCI during the evening of September 15 to reassure investors that RMCI would—without reservation—support the $1.00 NAV of the Primary Fund. * * * *

RMCI Failed to Timely Disclose That The Primary Fund Had Broken the Buck

119. Based on the valuation of the Lehman debt at $0.80 and the redemption figures available to RMCI, the Primary Fund's NAV declined below $0.995 at some point prior to 11:00 a.m. on September 16. * * * *

121. On September 16 at approximately 4:00 p.m. ... RMCI issued a press release announcing that the "value of the debt securities issued by Lehman Brothers Holdings, Inc. ... and held by the Primary Fund has been valued at zero effective 4:00PM New York time today. As a result, the NAV of the Primary Fund, effective as of 4:00PM, is $0.97 per share."

Chapter 2 Mutual Fund Structural Conflicts; Governance; Overreaching Risk

> " . . . the national public interest and the interest of investors are adversely affected . . . (2) when investment companies are organized, operated, managed, or their portfolio securities are selected, in the interest of directors, officers, investment advisers, depositors, or other affiliated persons thereof, in the interest of underwriters, brokers, or dealers, in the interest of special classes of their security holders, or in the interest of other investment companies or persons engaged in other lines of business, rather than in the interest of all classes of such companies' security holders; . . . "
>
> ----Investment Company Act of 1940, § 1(b)(2)

Section 2.1 Fiduciary Nature of Adviser-Fund Investors Relationship

Topic 1 Structure of the Investment Company Industry

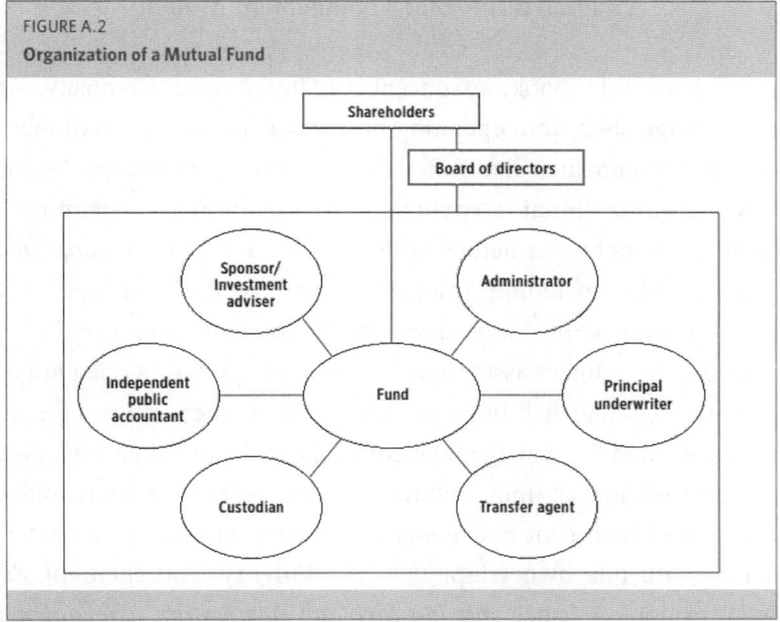

Source of Figure: ICI, 2017 INVESTMENT COMPANY FACT BOOK 245 (57th ed.)

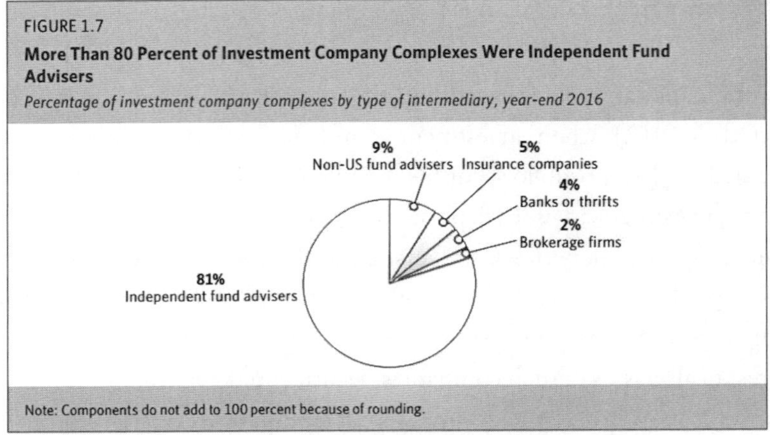

Source of Figure: ICI, 2017 INVESTMENT COMPANY FACT BOOK 15 (57th ed.)

Research Note:[Biblio]

Manager-Fund Structure in the U.S. Mutual Fund Industry:
Fidelity External Management Model *versus*
Vanguard Internal Management Model

In Chapter I of this book, "Concept of Investment Company," investment companies are distinguished from operating businesses, by the nature of their respective **assets**. Investment companies also differ from operating businesses by the nature of their respective **organizational structures**. While ordinary operating companies adopt a one-entity corporate structure with "*separation of ownership and control*," investment companies including mutual funds typically adopt a two-entity organizational structure with "*separation of funds and managers*." Under this two-entity structure, investment assets and liabilities are placed in one entity—the fund; and management assets and liabilities are placed in another entity—the management company. The fund and the management company each have their own distinct sets of owners, and each seek to maximize returns for their respective shareholders. Under such a structure, the investment management company is said to be "external" to the fund and to have "outside ownership."[1a; 2; 3; 4] **Fidelity Management & Research Company** is an example of such ***outside (private) ownership, external management model***.[5]

In contrast to the two-entity structure with two disparate sets of owners, the fund and the adviser may vertically integrate under a single ownership structure, with one set of owners. Such an integrated mutual fund company is run just like an ordinary operating business: to maximize profits for its owners—the fund shareholders. Under such a structure, the investment management company is said to be "internal" to the fund and to have "mutual ownership."[1a; 2; 3] **The Vanguard Group, Inc.** is an example of such ***mutual ownership, internal management model***. The Vanguard Group is owned directly and jointly by the Vanguard funds, and indirectly by all Vanguard funds' shareholders. The Vanguard Group internalizes administration, portfolio management, and share distribution all within Vanguard, and provides services to the Vanguard funds on an at-cost basis—in contrast to the profit component in management fees for owners of an external management company.[1a; 6] As to Vanguard's actively managed equity funds which are sub-advised by external managers, Vanguard funds' boards negotiate management fees with such external managers at arm's length, to minimize shareholder costs and maximize shareholder returns.[2; 3] In this sense, Vanguard is a "truly '*mutual*' mutual fund complex."[1a]

According to John Bogle, founder and former chairman of Vanguard: the ***mutual ownership*** structure views mutual funds as ***trust accounts***, managed pursuant to fiduciary duty and trusteeship; the ***outside ownership*** structure views investment funds as ***products***, manufactured and distributed by management companies to earn a profit for themselves.[1a] Given the uniqueness of Vanguard's "*mutual*" structure in the U.S. mutual fund industry, Bogle lamented: the U.S. fund management industry has mutated from a profession to a business, and devolved from ***owners' capitalism*** to ***managers' capitalism***.[1b] Bogle recommends:[1c]

- If advisory firms are owned by responsible managers who put the interests of their fund shareholders first, mutualization may not be required.
- When a fund complex reaches a certain size and becomes more a business than a profession, mutualization should be considered by the fund board.
- Improving fund governance structure is a major step towards the ideal *Alpha* structure—the original *mutual* structure of America's first mutual fund (the Massachusetts Investors Trust).

Empirical finance literature has attested to Bogle's "***fiduciary principle: no man can serve two masters***."[1d] Golez & Marin (2015)[7] studying the **Spanish mutual fund industry**, specifically mutual funds advised by asset management firms that are fully owned or controlled by publicly traded Spanish financial conglomerates or banks in which the funds invest, concludes: "Ownership of asset management firms matters because it can distort the allocation of capital and impact asset prices and fund performance." As "double agents," fund managers are supposed to "serve both fund investors and owners of management firms"; but "the controlling company's management and shareholders could influence managers of affiliated funds to invest in the controlling company in their interests rather than the interests of fund investors."

The emergence of the "fund complex" or indeed the "investment complex" as the dominant form of organization in the mutual fund industry, in which investment funds of a group or family are managed by a common external adviser and sold by a common external distributor, has added a new dimension to the manager's outside ownership structure. Each fund in a complex must be concerned not only with its relationship with the external manager, but also with the manager's dealings with other funds and a variety of other investment vehicles in the complex, including the adviser's own portfolio. Regardless of whether the manager-fund relationship is one of outside ownership or mutual ownership, and regardless of whether the fund is formed as a corporation or a trust and the adviser formed as a public or private corporation or a partnership, the Investment Company Act requires a fund governance system reflecting the standard corporate democracy: a ***fund board of directors*** to, *inter alia*, police the adviser's operational conflicts of interest; and ***shareholder voting*** to, *inter alia*, approve management fees, changes in fundamental investment policies, and any assignment of the advisory contract.[8; 9]

Bibliography

1. Bogle: **1a.** Bogle, *A New Order of Things: Bringing Mutuality to the "Mutual" Fund*, 43 WAKE FOREST L. REV. 1089 (2008); **1b.** BOGLE, THE BATTLE FOR THE SOUL OF CAPITALISM (2005); **1c.** Bogle, *Re-Mutualizing the Mutual Fund Industry—The Alpha and the Omega*, 45 B.C. L. REV. 391 (2004); **1d.** Bogle, *The Fiduciary Principle: No Man Can Serve Two Masters*, J. PORTFOLIO MGMT. 15 (2009)
2. Freeman & Brown, *Mutual Fund Advisory Fees: The Cost of Conflicts of Interest*, 26 J. CORP. L. 609, §§ II-B, IV-D (2001)
3. HUBBARD ET AL., THE MUTUAL FUND INDUSTRY: COMPETITION AND INVESTOR WELFARE, Ch.7 Mutual Funds' Organizational Form and Conflicts of Interest (2010)
4. Morley, *The Separation of Funds and Managers: A Theory of Investment Fund Structure and Regulation*, 123 YALE L. J. 1228 (2014)
5. FIDELITY MANAGEMENT & RESEARCH COMPANY FORM ADV PART 2A; SCHEDULE A; SCHEDULE B (2017)
6. VANGUARD 500 INDEX FUND PROSPECTUS, 12-13 (April 27, 2016); VANGUARD® INDEX FUNDS STATEMENT OF ADDITIONAL INFORMATION, B22-B30 (April 27, 2016); THE VANGUARD GROUP, INC. FORM ADV: SCHEDULE A; SCHEDULE B (2017)
7. Golez & Marin, *Price Support by Bank-Affiliated Mutual Funds*, 115 J. FIN. ECON. 614 (2015)
8. Glazer, *A Study of Mutual Fund Complexes*, 119 U. PENN. L. REV. 205 (1970)
9. DIV. OF INV. MGMT, SEC. & EXCH. COMM'N, PROTECTING INVESTORS: A HALF CENTURY OF INVESTMENT

COMPANY REGULATION, Ch. 7. Investment Company Governance (1992)

Research Topics:

Structure of the Chinese Mutual Fund Industry (*e.g.*, external *vs* internal management structure; public *vs* private ownership of fund management companies; mutual fund governance regulation; impact of fund governance structure on fund investment performance).

Topic 2 Fiduciary Duty in Respect of Management Fees

Laws & Rules Highlight:

IC Act (15 USC 80a-1 *et seq.*)

- § 2(a)(20) (*def. "investment adviser of an investment company"*)
- § 36 Breach of Fiduciary Duty
  - ◆ § 36(a) (***general fiduciary duties:*** *authorizes* ***SEC court action*** *against fund directors, IA, principal underwriter, and other specified persons for* ***"breach of fiduciary duty*** *involving* ***personal misconduct****" in respect of registered IC*)
  - ◆ § 36(b) (***fiduciary duty with respect to fees paid by fund:*** *subjects adviser of registered IC to* ***fiduciary duty*** *with respect to IA and its affiliates' receipt of compensation and material fees paid by IC or fund shareholders; authorizes* ***SEC action*** *and* ***fund investor private action*** *in a judicial forum against adviser and its affiliates for receiving* ***excessive*** *advisory compensation or non-advisory fees (other than sales load);* ***plaintiff's burden of proving*** *breach of fiduciary duty*)

Pre-Case Background Note:[Biblio]

Management Fees:

Gartenberg **Factors;** ***Jones*** **Market Approach; § 36(b) Fiduciary Duty Standard**

In ***Gartenberg I*** (1982),[1] a suit brought by money market fund individual shareholders against the fund investment adviser and its affiliates claiming "unreasonably high" advisory compensation, the **Second Circuit** rejected the notion that "market price" should be the principal factor determining fairness of the management fee. It explained an adviser's § 36(b) fiduciary duty as follows ("***Gartenberg Standard***"):

> Reliance on prevailing industry advisory fees will not satisfy § 36(b). * * * To be guilty of a violation of § 36(b), ... the adviser-manager must charge a fee that is so disproportionately large that it bears no reasonable relationship to the services rendered and could not have been the product of arm's-length bargaining.

The Second Circuit then identified six factors ("***Gartenberg factors***") bearing on whether a management fee is so excessive as to constitute an IA's breach of fiduciary duty under § 36(b):

- the nature and quality of the adviser's services to investment company shareholders;

- the adviser's compensation and profitability;
- the indirect costs and benefits of providing the advisory services;
- the extent to which economies of scale are shared with the fund shareholders;
- a comparison of fees with those paid by other similar investment companies; and
- the role played by the fund's independent directors.

In ***Gartenberg II*** (1984),[2] the **Second Circuit** again applied the *Gartenberg factors* to a similar claim by the *Gartenberg I* fund shareholders challenging a different year's management fee.

In ***Jones*** (2008),[3] a suit brought by mutual fund shareholders against the fund investment adviser claiming "disproportionately large" advisory fees, the **Seventh Circuit** "disapprove[s] the *Gartenberg* approach" for "*it relies too little on markets*." Pointing to competitive processes in several industries, including the mutual fund industry where "*investors can and do 'fire' advisers cheaply and easily by moving their money elsewhere*," the Seventh Circuit theorized:

- Section 36(b) "fiduciary duty" concept does not equate with judicially created "reasonable fee" standard; "§ 36(b) does not make the federal judiciary a rate regulator," and "judicial price-setting does not accompany fiduciary duties."
- Section 36(b) "fiduciary duty" concept points to trust law. Both trust law principle and the Investment Company Act work by "requiring disclosure and then allowing price to be set by competition in which investors make their own choices."

Dissenting from the *Jones* Panel's rejection of "a cap on compensation," ***Judge Posner*** pointed to the growing literature studying excessive executive compensation in large, publicly traded firms, and to the "same structure of incentives" or conflicts of interest operating on large corporations and mutual funds alike. Posner concluded: "Competition in product and capital markets can't be counted on to solve the problem."

To resolve the split between the Courts of Appeals over the proper standard under § 36(b), the **U.S. Supreme Court** granted a writ of certiorari to review ***Jones*** (2010).[3] In vacating and remanding *Jones*, the Supreme Court formulates its theory of "fiduciary duty" under § 36(b):

- "Fiduciary duty" standard in § 36(b) represents a "*delicate compromise*": neither requiring plaintiff shareholders to meet "common-law standards of corporate waste," nor permitting a court to review adviser compensation for "reasonableness."

- "Fiduciary duty" has a shared meaning under trust law and § 36(b): "*whether or not under all the circumstances the transaction carries the earmarks of an arm's length bargain*." Significantly different from trust law, however, § 36(b) shifts the burden of proof from the defendant fiduciary adviser to the plaintiff shareholders, to show that the advisory fee is outside the range that arm's-length bargaining would produce. "*Gartenberg* was correct in its basic formulation of what § 36(b) requires."

Concurring and writing separately, ***Justice Thomas*** points out that the *Jones* Court and other courts "have wisely eschewed" a "free-ranging judicial 'fairness' review of fees" which *Gartenberg* could be read to authorize. Thus, he "would not shortchange the Court's effort by describing it as affirmation of [or endorsing] the '*Gartenberg* standard.' "

Bibliography:

1. Gartenberg v. Merrill Lynch Asset Mgmt., Inc., 528 F. Supp. 1038 (SDNY 1981), *aff'd*, 694 F.2d 923 (2d Cir. 1982) ("***Gartenberg I***," *setting forth* "***Gartenberg factors***"), *cert. denied sub nom.* Andre v. Merrill Lynch Ready Assets Trust, 461 US 906 (1983)
2. Gartenberg v. Merrill Lynch Asset Mgmt., Inc., 573 F. Supp. 1293 (SDNY 1983), *aff'd*, 740 F.2d 190 (2d Cir. 1984) ("***Gartenberg II***")
3. Jones v. Harris Assocs. L.P., 2007 U.S. Dist. LEXIS 13352 (ND Ill. 2007), *aff'd*, 527 F.3d 627 (7th Cir. 2008) (*rejecting Gartenberg I approach*), *reh'g en banc denied*, 537 F.3d 728 (7th Cir. 2008) (Posner, J., dissenting), *vacated and remanded*, 559 U.S. 335 (2010) (Thomas, J., concurring)

Case Study 1:

Interpreting § 36(b) fiduciary duty with respect to adviser compensation: the ***Gartenberg standard*** and the ***six Gartenberg factors***.

Gartenberg v. Merrill Lynch Asset Mgmt., Inc.
694 F.2d 923 (2d Cir. 1982)

[***Procedural history:*** Gartenberg v. Merrill Lynch Asset Mgmt., Inc., 528 F. Supp. 1038 (SDNY 1981), *aff'd*, 694 F.2d 923 (2d Cir. 1982) ("*Gartenberg I*"), *cert. denied sub nom.* Andre v. Merrill Lynch Ready Assets Trust, 461 U.S. 906 (1983)]

Case Study 2:

The U.S. Supreme Court's construction of ***meaning of "fiduciary duty" under § 36(b)*** with respect to management fee. *In terms of traditional fiduciary standard*: "the essence of the test is whether or not under all the circumstances the transaction carries the earmarks of an arm's-length bargain." *In terms of burden of proof allocated by §*

36(b): for plaintiff shareholders to show breach of fiduciary duty, rather than for defendant fiduciary to show good faith and inherent fairness of the transaction as under the traditional law of trusts.

Jones v. Harris Assocs. L.P.

559 U.S. 335 (2010)

[***Procedural history***: Jones v. Harris Assocs. L.P., 2007 U.S. Dist. LEXIS 13352 (ND Ill. 2007), *aff'd*, 527 F.3d 627 (7th Cir. 2008), *reh'g en banc denied*, 537 F.3d 728 (7th Cir. 2008) (Posner, J., dissenting), *vacated and remanded*, 559 U.S. 335 (2010) (Thomas, J., concurring), *aff'd on remand*, 611 Fed. Appx. 359 (7th Cir. 2015)]

Post-Case Research Note:[Biblio]

Mutual Fund Management Fee Debate: Competition for Advisory Contracts and Competition for Investor Assets

In the *Jones* case, the U.S. Supreme Court stated: "The debate ... regarding today's mutual fund market [competition] is a matter for Congress, not the courts." Thus, pursuant to *Jones*, lower courts will not be able to dismiss fund shareholders' § 36(b) excessive fee claims solely on the ground that a given management fee is within industry norms.[1] Legal and finance literatures have debated the competitiveness of the U.S. mutual fund industry, including competition among advisers for advisory contracts, and competition among funds for investor assets.

Literature finding ***sufficiently strong market forces*** in constraining advisory fees includes:

- Coates & Hubbard (2007)[2] (*arguing* that redeemability of mutual fund shares allows fund shareholders to rapidly and cheaply "fire" advisers, such pressure making it largely unnecessary for competition among funds in the selection of advisers to exist; *finding* competition among funds and fund complexes for assets to be "strong," "robust," and "exerting a strong disciplinary force on funds and fees"; *advocating* "an appropriate consideration of price competition in cases brought under § 36(b).").
- Wahal & Wang (2011)[3] (*empirical study* testing the effects of new mutual funds' entry on the incumbent funds' prices, revenues, costs, performance, and survival; *findings*: incumbents reduce management fees and experience lower flows, but distribution costs rise so that benefits to consumers are not as large;

entrant-incumbent overlap is related to the future survival rates, confirming Darwinian notions embedded in the idea of competitive markets; *concluding*: on the whole, the picture that emerges is one of a competitive market.).

Literature finding ***inadequate price competition*** in the mutual fund industry includes:

- Freeman & Brown (2001)[4a] (*stating*: fund managers compete aggressively for new sales but refuse to compete with each other for advisory business; *finding* "no proof" that fee ranges within the fund industry, where arm's-length dealing is lacking, tend to be within hailing distance of the fee rates that the same advisory firms charge elsewhere when selling investment advisory services in the free market, and *finding* rather "the opposite" that funds truly are prisoners: their captor-advisers have little incentive to invade other advisers' turfs thereby inviting retaliatory price-cutting; *calling for* public, standardized disclosure of advisory fees, costs, and profitability data, to spur price competition and to enable fund shareholders in § 36(b) excessive fee suits to sustain the burden of proof).
- Freeman (2008)[4b] (existence of *competition for investors* says next to nothing about *competition for advisory services*; throughout the fund industry, there is *virtually no competition for advisory services*; the lack of price competition in the fund industry is *attributable* to fiduciary duty breaches stemming from the conflict of interest created when the external adviser negotiates price with a fund board the adviser dominates and controls.).
- Freeman, Brown & Pomerantz (2008)[4c] (recommending a *"most favored nation" concept*: captive mutual funds pay management fees no higher than the adviser's non-captive funds for similar investment advisory services).

Other economics and finance literature studying ***advisory fee excessiveness*** includes:

- Deli (2002)[5] (*empirical study* investigating *how fund characteristics affect adviser compensation*, *finding*: (a) equity and foreign fund advisers receive higher marginal compensation than debt and domestic fund advisers, (b) advisers of funds with greater turnover receive higher marginal compensation, (c) closed-end fund advisers receive higher marginal compensation than open-end fund advisers, and (d) marginal compensation is lower for advisers of large funds and members of large fund families; *arguing*: differences in marginal compensation reflect differences in adviser marginal product, differences in difficulty of monitoring adviser performance, differences in control environments, and scale economies; *suggesting*: regulatory focus on fund average costs, *i.e.*, expense ratios, rather than on fund marginal costs is misguided and may lead to incorrect inferences about management fees.).

- Curtis & Morley (2014)[6] (*empirical study*, positing that there are ***two ways of thinking*** about fee excessiveness: (1) an ***adviser's profit-centered*** way of thinking, *i.e.*, a fee might be excessive if it generates revenue for an adviser that greatly exceeds the adviser's costs of running the fund; (2) ***investor-centered*** way of thinking, *i.e.*, given two funds that provide similar risks and returns, investors should always prefer the fund with the lowest fees, regardless of which fund's advisers are more profitable; concluding: the *Gartenberg Six Factors* suggest both an interest in the investor-centered way of thinking and in the adviser-centered way of thinking.).

Bibliography:

1. Coates, *The Downside of Judicial Restraint: The (Non-)Effect of Jones v. Harris*, 6 DUKE J. CONST. L. & PUB. POL'Y 58 (2011)
2. Coates & Hubbard, *Competition in the Mutual Fund Industry: Evidence and Implications for Policy*, 33 J. CORP. L. 151 (2007)
3. Wahal & Wang, *Competition Among Mutual Funds*, 99 J. FIN. ECON. 40 (2011)
4. **4a.** Freeman & Brown, *Mutual Fund Advisory Fees: The Cost of Conflicts of Interest*, 26 J. CORP. L. 609 (2001); **4b.** Freeman, *Working Paper Responding to Coates & Hubbard* (2008); **4c.** Freeman, Brown & Pomerantz, *Mutual Fund Advisory Fees: New Evidence and a Fair Fiduciary Test*, 61 OKLA. L. REV. 83 (2008)
5. Deli, *Mutual Fund Advisory Contracts: An Empirical Investigation*, 57 J. FIN. 109 (2002)
6. Curtis & Morley, *An Empirical Study of Mutual Fund Excessive Fee Litigation: Do the Merits Matter?*, 30 J.L. ECON. & ORG. 275, 287-88 (2014)

Gartenberg v. Merrill Lynch Asset Mgmt., Inc.

694 F.2d 923 (2d Cir. 1982)

JUDGES: Mansfield, Van Graafeiland and Newman, Circuit Judges.

OPINION

MANSFIELD, Circuit Judge:

Irving L. Gartenberg and Simone C. Andre, two shareholders of the Merrill Lynch Ready Assets Trust, a money market fund (the "Fund"), appeal from a judgment of the Southern District of New York, Milton Pollack, *Judge*, entered after a non-jury trial, dismissing their consolidated derivative actions against the Fund and its affiliates, Merrill Lynch Asset Management, Inc., the adviser and manager of the Fund (the "Manager") and Merrill Lynch, Pierce, Fenner & Smith, Inc. (the "Broker"). The plaintiffs claimed violations of § 36(b) of the Investment Company Act of 1940.[1] 528 F. Supp. 1038. The principal claim is that the fees paid by the Fund to the Manager for various services, including investment advice and processing of daily orders of the Fund's shareholders, were so disproportionately large as to constitute a breach of fiduciary duty in violation of § 36(b). We affirm the judgment dismissing the complaint.

Since the facts are fully set forth in detail in Judge Pollack's opinion, 528 F.Supp. 1038,

---

[1] Section 36(b) provides in pertinent part:

(b) For the purposes of this sub-section, the investment adviser of a registered investment company shall be deemed to have a fiduciary duty with respect to the receipt of compensation for services, or of payments of a material nature, paid by such registered investment company, or by the security holders thereof, to such investment adviser or any affiliated person of such investment adviser. An action may be brought under this subsection by the Commission, or by a security holder of such registered investment company on behalf of such company, against such investment adviser, or any affiliated person of such investment adviser, or any other person enumerated in subsection (a) of this section who has a fiduciary duty concerning such compensation or payments, for breach of fiduciary duty in respect of such compensation or payments paid by such registered investment company or by the security holders thereof to such investment adviser or person. With respect to any such action the following provisions shall apply:

"(1) It shall not be necessary to allege or prove that any defendant engaged in personal misconduct, and the plaintiff shall have the burden of proving a breach of fiduciary duty.

"(2) In any such action approval by the board of directors of such investment company of such compensation or payments, or of contracts or other arrangements providing for such compensation or payments, and ratification or approval of such compensation or payments, or of contracts or other arrangements providing for such compensation or payments, by the shareholders of such investment company, shall be given such consideration by the court as is deemed appropriate under all the circumstances.

only a brief summary here is necessary. The Fund, organized in 1975 as a no-load, diversified, open-end investment company, invests in short-term money market securities expected to pay the highest current income consistent with preservation of capital and maintenance of liquidity, such as short-term securities of the U.S. Government or its agencies, bank certificates of deposit, and commercial paper. An investor may purchase and redeem shares of the Fund without any charges or penalties. There is a daily declaration of dividends, reflecting the net income of the Fund's portfolio. As the district court noted, the purchaser's investment in the Fund is more like a bank account than the traditional investment in securities. Idle money can be invested in the Fund for as little as a day and put to work earning interest. The ease of entrance and egress for the investor, coupled with the ability to share in high yields which the modest investor could not obtain through a bank deposit and might not be able to realize alone, has with the rise (until recently) of interest rates attracted an increasing number of investors. As a result the size of the Fund increased enormously over a few years, from $288 million in April 1977 to over $19 billion as of September 1981.

The Fund has an 8-person Board of Trustees, of whom 2 are interested and 6 are independent and unaffiliated. The operations of the Fund are conducted by the Manager, which provides the Fund with office space and facilities, administrative staff, equipment, portfolio management, compliance with SEC and state record-keeping and reporting requirements, and services to Fund shareholders. For the processing of approximately 80% of the purchases and redemptions of shares of the Fund the Manager uses the Broker, another Merrill Lynch affiliate, which is the largest registered broker-dealer in the United States, with 408 domestic offices located in numerous cities and towns, in which more than 7,000 account executives are located. In addition, the Manager uses the vast facilities of the Merrill Lynch organization and its affiliates to render special services to the Fund. For example, Merrill Lynch Economics, Inc. provides economic research and forecasting services while Merrill Lynch Government Securities, Inc. provides expertise with respect to U.S. government and agency securities. A customer located anywhere in the United States can call the nearest office of the Broker or the Bank of New York, the Fund's custodian and transfer agent, order the purchase or redemption without charge of shares of the Fund, and through use of wires and computers the transaction will be carried out immediately. An average of 30,000 such orders are processed daily by the Broker's large organization.

Under the foregoing management the Fund has performed reasonably well in terms of average percentage yields for its shareholders. Its average percentage yields from 1978 through 1980 were slightly above the average for all similar funds. In 1980 it ranked 37th out of 76 money funds in terms of yield.

For all of these services the Manager charges the Fund an advisory fee based on a percentage of the average daily value of the Fund's net assets. The fee rate is graduated downward as the Fund's total assets increase in value. Since 1979 the schedule called for payment of 0.50% (1/2 of 1%) of the Fund's average daily value of net assets under $500 million and for various intermediate percentages as the value of the net assets increases down to 0.275% for assets in excess of $2.5 billion, resulting in an effective rate of 0.288%. This schedule is the product of a series of negotiations by the 6 independent Fund Trustees with the Manager over the period from 1977 to 1979, which resulted in reductions in the effective rate as the Fund grew in size.

Three studies were made at the Fund's instance to determine the estimated cost of the processing services provided by the Broker through the Manager to the Fund, two by the Merrill Lynch organization's internal accounting staff and one by the independent accounting firm of Peat, Marwick, Mitchell & Co. ("PMM"). The estimates ranged from $2.02 to $7.50 per Fund order. The earlier internal study which produced the lowest figure did so mainly because it used a modified "incremental" cost method of accounting, based on the assumption that most costs would have been incurred by the Broker even if it had processed no Fund orders. By the time the PMM study was conducted in late 1979, however, modified full cost accounting methods were used for the reason that Fund orders represented a sizeable proportion of all business processed by the Broker; indeed, by April 1981 Fund orders accounted for 37% of all Broker business, necessitating the hiring by the Broker of close to 3,000 non-sales personnel. Had the Manager been required to reimburse the Broker for these costs instead of their being absorbed by the Broker as another Merrill Lynch affiliate, the Broker's net profit after taxes would have been greatly reduced, resulting in a figure ranging from a 38.4% profit to a substantial loss depending on which cost accounting study was used. In 1980, for instance, the last calendar year for which full figures are available, the Manager's fee was slightly over $33 million on the Fund's average net assets of $11.16 billion. Based on the volume of orders generated by 675,324 purchasers, the Broker's processing costs, estimated according to the PMM study, were so large that the Manager suffered a loss during 1980. 528 F. Supp. at 1053-54.

Judge Pollack, construing the legislative history of the Act, decided that the standard for determining whether the Manager had been guilty of a breach of fiduciary duty in violation of § 36(b) was not whether its fees were "reasonable" as urged by plaintiffs but whether they were unfair to the Fund and shareholders, which was to be determined by reference to the nature, quality and extent of the manager's services to the Fund, the money market fund industry practice and level of management fees, and to a lesser extent the Manager's net earnings as a result of providing the services. After reviewing the evidence and appraising the live witnesses who testified, he concluded that the compensation paid to the Manager was fair. *Id.* at 1055. The package of services described above was found to be extensive and valuable, providing Fund customers with the vast facilities of the Merrill Lynch organization, which were not available to non-Merrill Lynch funds.

The Manager's fee schedule was found by Judge Pollack to "bear a fair relation to the subject matter from which they are derived." *Id.* at 1068. He further found that "the total fee was fair to the Fund" after taking into consideration the nature and extent of the services, the fees charged by other advisers to other money market funds, the overall cost to the Merrill Lynch organization of providing the services, and the fee schedule's allowance for economies of scale by reducing the rate as the Fund's net assets increased. *Id.* at 1055. Judge Pollack also gave weight to the process by which the 6 noninterested trustees of the Fund approved of its management agreement with the Manager. The trustees, who were represented by capable independent counsel, were found to be competent, independent and conscientious in the performance of their duties. They were furnished with sufficient information to evaluate the contract. They thoroughly reviewed and weighed all facts pertinent to the fee, many of which are now part of the record, before approving the Manager's fee after negotiations.

The district court rejected plaintiffs' argument that in determining the fairness of the Manager's compensation the court must take into account as an offset to the Manager's fee the value to the Merrill Lynch organization of "fall-out" business generated by Fund customers who, after opening up a no-charge Fund account, transact other financial business with the Merrill Lynch Broker, such as purchases of stocks and bonds, for which the customer is charged a fee or commission. Thirty-eight percent of new Fund customers for the third quarter of 1979 transacted some non-Fund business through the Broker by January 1980. The fall-out benefit argument was rejected on the ground that any such offset could not be measured since it could not be established with certainty and without heavy expense what portion of the increase in brokerage business would have gone to the Broker without regard to the Fund. Judge Pollack further reasoned that the idea of an offset lacked logic since the customer would in any event have to pay a brokerage fee on non-Fund business. The possible benefit to the Merrill Lynch organization from a "float" resulting from its having the use of redemption funds before paying them to the redeeming Fund customer was found unpersuasive since it was obvious to all concerned. Plaintiffs' claim that there was unnecessary duplication in the Manager's services based on the Bank of New York's obligation to perform them was rejected for lack of proof.

The district court further found that an adequate disclosure of the pertinent facts needed to determine the fairness of the Manager's fee had been made to the Fund's trustees and shareholders.

DISCUSSION

Section 36(b) of the Investment Act of 1940, which governs this case, provides that "the investment adviser of a registered investment company shall be deemed to have a fiduciary duty with respect to the receipt of compensation for services" paid by the investment company or its security holders and that in an action by a security holder on behalf of the investment company against the adviser or affiliate "it shall not be necessary to allege or prove that any defendant engaged in personal misconduct" but "the plaintiff shall have the burden of proving a breach of fiduciary duty."

Appellants contend that the district court erred in rejecting a "reasonableness" standard for determining whether the Manager performed its "fiduciary duty" in compliance with § 36(b). They further urge that the district court erred in relying primarily, in determining whether there was a breach of fiduciary duty, on other money market funds' level of management fees and on the Broker's costs. They argue that since each investment company fund is a captive of its manager, from which it cannot as a practical matter divorce itself, and since there is no possibility that a competitor will take the fund's business from its manager by offering a lower rate, the manager sets its own fee and the fund has no practical alternative but to pay it. It is contended that the test should therefore be what rate would have resulted from arm's-length negotiations in light of the services to be rendered. Appellants further contend that under this standard the fee in this case would have been substantially lower because of economies of scale, the Fund's massive bargaining power as the largest fund in history, and the Broker's duplication of services which the Bank of New York was already required to render. In short it is argued that a fee percentage which may have been reasonable when the Fund was freshly-launched became unreasonable when the Fund grew to its present huge size. See, *e.g., Fogel v. Chestnutt*, 668 F.2d 100 (2d Cir. 1981), *cert. denied*, 459 U.S. 828 (1982).

In support of their advocacy of a "reasonableness" standard as the test by which a fiduciary's conduct under § 36(b) should be governed, appellants point to excerpts from the Act's tortuous legislative history, just as the district court relied on other portions of the same history apparently rejecting that criterion in favor of a "breach of fiduciary duty" standard. The legislative history contains statements of legislators and legislative reports pointing in both directions. Bills introduced in 1967 and 1968, which would have imposed a "reasonableness" test, failed of passage. See H.R. 9510, H.R. 9511, and S. 1659, 90th Cong., 1st Sess. (1967) and S. 3724, 90th Cong., 2d Sess. (1968). When the mutual fund industry objected to this standard, a bill (S. 2224) was introduced in 1969 containing § 36(b) in its present form, which was enacted in 1970. The Senate Report on the bill and the House Committee Report accompanying the companion bill do not define the term "fiduciary duty" as used in the bill or how it was to be distinguished from the term "reasonable" that had been used in predecessor bills. See Investment Company Amendments Act of 1970, S. Rep. No. 91-184, 91st Cong., 2d Sess. (1970), and Investment Company Amendments Act of 1970, H.R. Rep. No. 91-1382, 91st Cong., 2d Sess. (1970). The Senate Report does state that an adviser-manager would not be precluded from earning a profit on services provided by it to a fund, that a "cost-plus" type of contract is not required, and that the court is not authorized "to substitute its business judgment for that of a mutual fund's board of directors in the area of management fees," *id.* On the other hand, the same Report states that a "corporate waste" standard would be "unduly restrictive," and Congressman Moss, Chairman of the Committee on Interstate and Foreign Commerce, who was one of the chief sponsors of § 36(b), explained to the House that "this [bill], by imposition of the fiduciary duty, would in effect require a standard of reasonableness in the charges." Thus there was no attempt to set forth a definitive test by which observance or breach of fiduciary duty was to be determined.

In short, the legislative history of § 36(b) indicates that the substitution of the term "fiduciary duty" for "reasonable," while possibly intended to modify the standard somewhat, was a more semantical than substantive compromise, shifting the focus slightly from the fund directors to the conduct of the investment adviser-manager. As the district court and all parties seem to recognize, the test is essentially whether the fee schedule represents a charge within the range of what would have been negotiated at arm's-length in the light of all of the surrounding circumstances. The Senate recognized that as a practical matter the usual arm's length bargaining between strangers does not occur between an adviser and the fund, stating:

> "Since a typical fund is organized by its investment adviser which provides it with almost all management services and because its shares are bought by investors who rely on that service, a mutual fund cannot, as a practical matter sever its relationship with the adviser. Therefore, the forces of arm's-length bargaining do not work in the mutual fund industry in the same manner as they do in other sectors of the American economy." S. Rep. No.91-184, *supra*.

To be guilty of a violation of § 36(b), therefore, the adviser-manager must charge a fee that is so disproportionately large that it bears no reasonable relationship to the services rendered and could not have been the product of arm's-length bargaining. To make this determination all pertinent facts must be weighed.

We disagree with the district court's suggestions that the principal factor to be considered in evaluating a fee's fairness is the price charged by other similar advisers to funds managed by them, that the "price charged by advisers to those funds establishes the free and open market level for fiduciary compensation," that the "market price ... serves as a standard to test the fairness of the investment advisory fee," and that a fee is fair if it "is in harmony with the broad and prevailing market choice available to the investor." Competition between money market funds for shareholder business does not support an inference that competition must therefore also exist between adviser-managers for fund business. The former may be vigorous even though the latter is virtually non-existent. Each is governed by different forces. Reliance on prevailing industry advisory fees will not satisfy § 36(b).

We do not suggest that rates charged by other adviser-managers to other similar funds are not a factor to be taken into account. Indeed, to the extent that other managers have tended "to reduce their effective charges as the fund grows in size," the Senate Committee noted that such a reduction represents "the best industry practice [which] will provide a guide," S. Rep. No. 91-184, *supra*. However, the existence in most cases of an unseverable relationship between the adviser-manager and the fund it services tends to weaken the weight to be given to rates charged by advisers of other similar funds. Report of the Securities and Exchange Commission on the Public Policy Implications of Investment Company Growth, H.R. Rep. No. 2337, 89th Cong., 2d Sess. (1966).[2] A fund cannot move easily from one adviser-manager to another. Therefore "investment advisers seldom, if ever, compete with each other for advisory contracts with mutual funds." *Id.*

One reason why fund competition for shareholder business does not lead to competition between adviser-managers for fund business is the relative insignificance of the adviser's fee to each shareholder. The fund customer's shares of the advisory fee is usually too small a factor to lead him to invest in one fund rather than in another or to monitor adviser-manager's fees. "Cost reductions in the form of lower advisory fees ... do not figure significantly in the battle for investor favor." *Id.* Hence money market funds do not generally advertise that their advisory fees may be lower than those charged by advisers to other funds. The disparity is competitively insignificant. In the present case, for instance, the alleged excessive Manager's fee amounts to $2.88 *a year* for each $1,000 invested. If rates charged by the many other advisers were an affirmative competitive

---

[2] The following statement in the REPORT OF THE SECURITIES AND EXCHANGE COMMISSION ON THE PUBLIC POLICY IMPLICATIONS OF INVESTMENT COMPANY GROWTH, while directed to mutual funds, is pertinent to money market funds:

"It has been the Commission's experience in the administration of the Act that in general the unaffiliated directors have not been in a position to secure changes in the level of advisory fee rates in the mutual fund industry. In most instances the adviser serves as, or is closely affiliated with, the fund's principal underwriter which maintains a distributing organization for the fund's shares. The organization that has developed over a period of years to manage the fund's portfolio and to furnish it with some, and in certain cases virtually all, of the nonadvisory services necessary to its operation belongs to the adviser and not to the fund. Indeed, in some cases all of the fund's records are maintained by the fund's adviser. Although the unaffiliated directors under State law have an unqualified right of access to these records, the adviser, as a practical matter, is in a position to seriously hamper any employment of that right which might interfere with or threaten the adviser's operation of or control over the fund.

"Thus, negotiations between the unaffiliated directors and fund advisers over advisory fees would lack an essential element of arm's-length bargaining—the freedom to terminate the negotiations and to bargain with other parties for the same services. In view of the fund's dependence on its existing adviser and the fact that many shareholders may have invested in the fund on the strength of the adviser's reputation, few unaffiliated directors would feel justified in replacing the adviser with a new and untested organization simply because of difficulty in obtaining a reduction in long-established fee rates which are customary in the industry." H.R. Rep. No. 2337, 89th Cong., 2d Sess. 131 (1966).

criterion, there would be little purpose in § 36(b). Congress, however, recognized that because of the potentially incestuous relationships between many advisers and their funds, other factors may be more important in determining whether a fee is so excessive as to constitute a "breach of fiduciary duty." These include the adviser-manager's cost in providing the service, the nature and quality of the service, the extent to which the adviser-manager realizes economies of scale as the fund grows larger, and the volume of orders which must be processed by the manager. The legislative history of § 36(b) makes clear that Congress

> "intended that the court look at all the facts in connection with the determination and receipt of such compensation, including all services rendered to the fund or its shareholders and all compensation and payments received, in order to reach a decision as to whether the adviser has properly acted as a fiduciary in relation to such compensation." S. Rep. No.91-184, *supra*.

As the district court recognized, the expertise of the independent trustees of a fund, whether they are fully informed about all facts bearing on the adviser-manager's service and fee, and the extent of care and conscientiousness with which they perform their duties are important factors to be considered in deciding whether they and the adviser-manager are guilty of a breach of fiduciary duty in violation of § 36(b). But even if the trustees of a fund endeavored to act in a responsible fashion, an adviser-manager's fee could be so disproportionately large as to amount to a breach of fiduciary duty in violation of § 36(b). Moreover, an intent to defraud need not be proved to establish a violation. Section 36(b)(1) expressly relieves the plaintiffs of the necessity of alleging or proving that any defendant engaged in personal misconduct.

Nor do we subscribe to the district court's suggestion that because § 36(b) was adopted in response to public concern over fees charged to investors in front-end load equity funds, the standard for determining whether there has been a breach of duty in avoiding excessive fees should be different or lower for managers of no-load money market funds, which are a recent, post-statute phenomenon. A potential for abuse of fiduciary relationship regarding fees charged for management and advisory services exists with respect to both types of fund since the adviser-manager's fee remains insignificant to each shareholder, whether or not a load factor inhibits redemption of shares.[3]

---

[3] Appellants' argument that the lower fees charged by investment advisers to large pension funds should be used

Application of the foregoing standards to this case confirms that plaintiffs have failed to meet their burden of proving that the fees charged by the Manager to the Fund were so excessive or unfair as to amount to a breach of fiduciary duty within the meaning of § 36(b). There is no evidence that the services rendered by the Manager have not been of the highest quality, bringing to bear the expertise and facilities of the huge, far-flung Merrill Lynch organization. The average investor in the Fund, while not realizing the highest possible yield for his investment, has enjoyed a better-than-average return. * * * *

A more serious problem is posed by appellants' claim that in negotiating the Manager's fee the Merrill Lynch Fund and Manager failed to take into account that the Merrill Lynch Broker has gained large "fall-out" financial benefits annually in the form of commissions on non-Fund securities business generated by Fund customers and interest income on funds (known as the "float") held by the Broker from the date when a redemption check is issued by the Fund to its customer until the date it clears. If these benefits were taken into consideration, the argument goes, they would constitute a very substantial offset calling for a lower fee to the Manager than that paid by the Fund. Therefore, appellants contend, the Manager and the Fund, by failing to offset these benefits, were guilty of a breach of fiduciary duty in violation of § 36(b).

The record reveals that a large percentage of persons who opened accounts with the Broker as Fund customers, *e.g.*, some 38% of those who opened such accounts in the third quarter of 1979, later did some non-Fund business with Merrill Lynch, generating commissions for the Broker. Robert Diemer, the Broker's Director of Financial Services, testified that processing of Fund accounts helped to attract new equity security business which increased the Broker's commission revenue. These benefits to an affiliate in the Merrill Lynch organization, to the extent quantifiable, should be taken into account in determining whether the Manager's fee meets the standard of § 36(b). Although the independent trustees may have been aware of these benefits, we are unpersuaded by the district court's suggestion that they cannot be measured or quantified because of inability to determine "whether customers who normally did an above-average level of brokerage business also tended to have Fund accounts" or to ascertain "what portion of the

---

as a criterion for determining fair advisory fees for money market funds must also be rejected. The nature and extent of the services required by each type of fund differ sharply. As the district court recognized, the pension fund does not face the myriad of daily purchases and redemptions throughout the nation which must be handled by the Fund, in which a purchaser may invest for only a few days.

[increased brokerage business] would ... have gone to Merrill Lynch in any event." It would not seem impossible, through use of today's sophisticated computer equipment and statistical techniques, to obtain estimates of such "fall-out" and "float benefits" which, while not precise, could be a factor of sufficient substance to give the Funds' trustees a sound basis for negotiating a lower Manager's fee. However, the burden was on appellants, not the defendants, to adduce evidence demonstrating that the benefits were so substantial that they rendered the Manager's fee so disproportionately large as to label its negotiation a "breach of fiduciary duty" within the meaning of § 36(b). Since appellants failed to offer such evidence, the dismissal of their contention must be affirmed. * * * *

Our affirmance is not a holding that the fee contract between the Fund and the Manager is fair and reasonable. We merely conclude that on this record appellants failed to prove by a preponderance of the evidence a breach of fiduciary duty. Whether a violation of § 36(b) might be established through more probative evidence of (1) the Broker's processing costs, (2) the offsetting commission benefits realized by the Broker from non-Fund securities business generated by Fund accounts, and (3) the "float" interest income gained by the Broker from its method of handling payment on Fund redemptions, must therefore remain a matter of speculation. Indeed, the independent trustees of the Fund might well be advised, in the interests of Fund investors, to initiate such studies. * * * * The judgment of the district court is affirmed.

Jones v. Harris Assocs. L.P.

559 U.S. 335 (2010)

JUDGES: Alito, J., delivered the opinion for a unanimous Court. Thomas, J., filed a concurring opinion.

OPINION

Justice Alito delivered the opinion of the Court.

We consider in this case what a mutual fund shareholder must prove in order to show that a mutual fund investment adviser breached the "fiduciary duty with respect to the receipt of compensation for services" that is imposed by § 36(b) of the Investment Company Act of 1940.

I-A.

The Investment Company Act of 1940 regulates investment companies, including mutual funds. "A mutual fund is a pool of assets, consisting primarily of [a] portfolio [of] securities, and belonging to the individual investors holding shares in the fund." The following arrangements are typical. A separate entity called an investment adviser creates the mutual fund, which may have no employees of its own. The adviser selects the fund's directors, manages the fund's investments, and provides other services. Because of the relationship between a mutual fund and its investment adviser, the fund often " 'cannot, as a practical matter sever its relationship with the adviser. Therefore, the forces of arm's-length bargaining do not work in the mutual fund industry in the same manner as they do in other sectors of the American economy.' "

"Congress adopted the [Investment Company Act of 1940] because of its concern with the potential for abuse inherent in the structure of investment companies." Recognizing that the relationship between a fund and its investment adviser was "fraught with potential conflicts of interest," the Act created protections for mutual fund shareholders. Among other things, the Act required that no more than 60 percent of a fund's directors could be affiliated with the adviser and that fees for investment advisers be approved by the directors and the shareholders of the fund. See § § 10, 15(c).

The growth of mutual funds in the 1950's and 1960's prompted studies of the 1940 Act's effectiveness in protecting investors. Studies commissioned or authored by the Securities and Exchange Commission identified problems relating to the independence of investment company boards and the compensation received by investment advisers. In response to such concerns, Congress amended the Act in 1970 and bolstered shareholder protection in two primary ways.

First, the amendments strengthened the "cornerstone" of the Act's efforts to check conflicts of interest, the independence of mutual fund boards of directors, which negotiate and scrutinize adviser compensation. The amendments required that no more than 60 percent of a fund's directors be "persons who are interested persons," *e.g.*, that they have no interest in or affiliation with the investment adviser.[1] 15 USC §80a-10(a); §80a-2(a)(19). These board members are given "a host of special responsibilities." In particular, they must "review and approve the contracts of the investment adviser" annually, and a majority of these directors must approve an adviser's compensation, 15 USC §80a-15(c). Second, §36(b) of the Act imposed upon investment advisers a "fiduciary duty" with respect to compensation received from a mutual fund, and granted individual investors a private right of action for breach of that duty.

The "fiduciary duty" standard contained in §36(b) represented a delicate compromise. Prior to the adoption of the 1970 amendments, shareholders challenging investment adviser fees under state law were required to meet "common-law standards of corporate waste, under which an unreasonable or unfair fee might be approved unless the court deemed it 'unconscionable' or 'shocking,' " and "security holders challenging adviser fees under the [Investment Company Act] itself had been required to prove gross abuse of trust." Aiming to give shareholders a stronger remedy, the SEC proposed a provision that would have empowered the Commission to bring actions to challenge a fee that was not "reasonable" and to intervene in any similar action brought by or on behalf of an investment company. This approach was included in a bill that passed the House. Industry representatives, however, objected to this proposal, fearing that it "might in

[1] An "affiliated person" includes (1) a person who owns, controls, or holds the power to vote 5 percent or more of the securities of the investment adviser; (2) an entity which the investment adviser owns, controls, or in which it holds the power to vote more than 5 percent of the securities; (3) any person directly or indirectly controlling, controlled by, or under common control with the investment adviser; (4) an officer, director, partner, copartner, or employee of the investment adviser; (5) an investment adviser or a member of the investment adviser's board of directors; or (6) the depositor of an unincorporated investment adviser. §80a-2(a)(3). The Act defines "interested person" to include not only all affiliated persons but also a wider swath of people such as the immediate family of affiliated persons, interested persons of an underwriter or investment adviser, legal counsel for the company, and interested broker-dealers. §80a-2(a)(19).

essence provide the Commission with ratemaking authority."

The provision that was ultimately enacted adopted "a different method of testing management compensation," that was more favorable to shareholders than the previously available remedies but that did not permit a compensation agreement to be reviewed in court for "reasonableness." This is the fiduciary duty standard in § 36(b).

I-B.

Petitioners are shareholders in three different mutual funds managed by respondent Harris Associates L. P., an investment adviser. Petitioners filed this action in the Northern District of Illinois pursuant to § 36(b) seeking damages, an injunction, and rescission of advisory agreements between Harris Associates and the mutual funds. The complaint alleged that Harris Associates had violated § 36(b) by charging fees that were "disproportionate to the services rendered" and "not within the range of what would have been negotiated at arm's length in light of all the surrounding circumstances."

The District Court granted summary judgment for Harris Associates. Applying the standard adopted in *Gartenberg v. Merrill Lynch Asset Management, Inc.*, 694 F.2d 923 (CA2 1982), the court concluded that petitioners had failed to raise a triable issue of fact as to "whether the fees charged ... were so disproportionately large that they could not have been the result of arm's-length bargaining." The District Court assumed that it was relevant to compare the challenged fees with those that Harris Associates charged its other clients. But in light of those comparisons as well as comparisons with fees charged by other investment advisers to similar mutual funds, the court held that it could not reasonably be found that the challenged fees were outside the range that could have been the product of arm's-length bargaining.

A panel of the Seventh Circuit affirmed based on different reasoning, explicitly "disapprov[ing] the *Gartenberg* approach." 527 F.3d 627 (2008). Looking to trust law, the panel noted that, while a trustee "owes an obligation of candor in negotiation," a trustee, at the time of the creation of a trust, "may negotiate in his own interest and accept what the settlor or governance institution agrees to pay" (citing Restatement (Second) of Trusts § 242, and Comment *f*). The panel thus reasoned that "[a] fiduciary duty differs from rate regulation. A fiduciary must make full disclosure and play no tricks but is not subject to a cap on compensation." In the panel's view, the amount of an adviser's compensation would be relevant only if the compensation were "so unusual" as to give rise to an inference "that deceit must have occurred, or that the persons responsible for decision have abdicated."

The panel argued that this understanding of § 36(b) is consistent with the forces operating in the contemporary mutual fund market. Noting that "[t]oday thousands of mutual funds compete," the panel concluded that "sophisticated investors" shop for the funds that produce the best overall results, "mov[e] their money elsewhere" when fees are "excessive in relation to the results," and thus "create a competitive pressure" that generally keeps fees low. The panel faulted *Gartenberg* on the ground that it "relies too little on markets." And the panel firmly rejected a comparison between the fees that Harris Associates charged to the funds and the fees that Harris Associates charged other types of clients, observing that "[d]ifferent clients call for different commitments of time" and that costs, such as research, that may benefit several categories of clients "make it hard to draw inferences from fee levels."

The Seventh Circuit denied rehearing en banc by an equally divided vote. 537 F.3d 728 (2008) (per curiam). The dissent from the denial of rehearing argued that the panel's rejection of Gartenberg was based "mainly on an economic analysis that is ripe for reexamination" (opinion of Posner, J.). Among other things, the dissent expressed concern that Harris Associates charged "its captive funds more than twice what it charges independent funds," and the dissent questioned whether high adviser fees actually drive investors away.

We granted certiorari to resolve a split among the Courts of Appeals over the proper standard under § 36(b).

II-A.

Since Congress amended the Investment Company Act in 1970, the mutual fund industry has experienced exponential growth. Assets under management increased from $38.2 billion in 1966 to over $9.6 trillion in 2008. The number of mutual fund investors grew from 3.5 million in 1965 to 92 million in 2008, and there are now more than 9,000 open- and closed-end funds.

During this time, the standard for an investment adviser's fiduciary duty has remained an open question in our Court, but, until the Seventh Circuit's decision below, something of a consensus had developed regarding the standard set forth over 25 years ago in *Gartenberg*, 694 F.2d 923. The [*Gartenberg* standard] has been adopted by other federal courts,[2] and "[t]he SEC's regulations have recognized, and formalized, *Gartenberg*-like factors." In the present case, both petitioners and respondent generally endorse the *Gartenberg* approach, although they disagree in some respects about its meaning.

In *Gartenberg*, the Second Circuit noted that Congress had not defined what it meant by a "fiduciary duty" with respect to compensation but concluded that "the test is essentially whether the fee schedule represents a charge within the range of what would have been negotiated at arm's-length in the light of all of the surrounding circumstances." The Second Circuit elaborated that, "[t]o be guilty of a violation of § 36(b), ... the adviser-manager must charge a fee that is so disproportionately large that it bears no reasonable relationship to the services rendered and could not have been the product of arm's-length bargaining." "To make this determination," the court stated, "all pertinent facts must be weighed," and the court specifically mentioned "the adviser-manager's cost in providing the service, ... the extent to which the adviser-manager realizes economies of scale as the fund grows larger, and the volume of orders which must be processed by the manager."[3] Observing that competition among advisers for the business of managing a fund may be "virtually non-existent," the court rejected the suggestion that "the principal factor to be considered in evaluating a fee's fairness is the price charged by other similar advisers to funds managed by them," although the court did not suggest that this factor could not be "taken into account." The court likewise rejected the "argument that the lower fees charged by investment advisers to large pension funds should be used as a criterion for determining fair advisory fees for money market funds," since a "pension fund does not face the myriad of daily purchases and redemptions throughout the nation which must be handled by [a money market fund]."[4]

---

[2] See, *e.g., Gallus* v. *Ameriprise Financial, Inc.*, 561 F.3d 816 (CA8 2009); *Krantz* v. *Prudential Invs. Fund Management LLC*, 305 F.3d 140 (CA3 2002) (per curiam); *In re Franklin Mut. Funds Fee Litigation*, 478 F. Supp.2d 677 (NJ 2007); *Yameen v. Eaton Vance Distributors, Inc.*, 394 F. Supp.2d 350 (Mass. 2005); *Hunt v. Invesco Funds Group, Inc.*, 2006 U.S. Dist. LEXIS 40944 (SD Tex. 2006); *Siemers v. Wells Fargo & Co.*, 2006 U.S. Dist. LEXIS 60858 (ND Cal. 2006); see also *Amron v. Morgan Stanley Inv. Advisors Inc.*, 464 F.3d 338 (CA2 2006).

[3] Other factors cited by the *Gartenberg* court include (1) the nature and quality of the services provided to the fund and shareholders; (2) the profitability of the fund to the adviser; (3) any "fall-out financial benefits," those collateral benefits that accrue to the adviser because of its relationship with the mutual fund; (4) comparative fee structure (meaning a comparison of the fees with those paid by similar funds); and (5) the independence, expertise, care, and conscientiousness of the board in evaluating adviser compensation.

[4] A money market fund differs from a mutual fund in both the types of investments and the frequency of

II-B.

The meaning of § 36(b)'s reference to "a fiduciary duty with respect to the receipt of compensation for services"[5] is hardly pellucid, but based on the terms of that provision and the role that a shareholder action for breach of that duty plays in the overall structure of the Act, we conclude that Gartenberg was correct in its basic formulation of what § 36(b) requires: To face liability under § 36(b), an investment adviser must charge a fee that is so disproportionately large that it bears no reasonable relationship to the services rendered and could not have been the product of arm's-length bargaining.

II-B-1.

We begin with the language of § 36(b). As noted, the Seventh Circuit panel thought that the phrase "fiduciary duty" incorporates a standard taken from the law of trusts. Petitioners agree but maintain that the panel identified the wrong trust-law standard. Instead of the standard that applies when a trustee and a settlor negotiate the trustee's fee at the time of the creation of a trust, petitioners invoke the standard that applies when a trustee seeks compensation after the trust is created. A compensation agreement reached at that time, they point out, " 'will not bind the beneficiary' if either 'the trustee failed to make a full disclosure of all circumstances affecting the agreement' " which he knew or should have known or if the agreement is unfair to the beneficiary (quoting Restatement (Second) of Trusts § 242, Comment *i*). Respondent, on the other hand, contends that the term "fiduciary" is not exclusive to the law of trusts, that the phrase means different things in different contexts, and that there is no reason to believe that § 36(b) incorporates the specific meaning of the term in the law of trusts.

We find it unnecessary to take sides in this dispute. In *Pepper v. Litton*, 308 U.S. 295 (1939), we discussed the meaning of the concept of fiduciary duty in a context that is analogous to that presented here, and we also looked to trust law. At issue in *Pepper* was

---

redemptions. A money market fund often invests in short-term money market securities, such as short-term securities of the United States Government or its agencies, bank certificates of deposit, and commercial paper. Investors can invest in such a fund for as little as a day, so, from the investor's perspective, the fund resembles an investment "more like a bank account than [a] traditional investment in securities."

[5] Section 36(b) provides as follows: "[T]he investment adviser of a registered investment company shall be deemed to have a fiduciary duty with respect to the receipt of compensation for services, or of payments of a material nature, paid by such registered investment company, or by the security holders thereof, to such investment adviser."

whether a bankruptcy court could disallow a dominant or controlling shareholder's claim for compensation against a bankrupt corporation. Dominant or controlling shareholders, we held, are "fiduciar[ies]" whose "powers are powers [held] in trust." We then explained:

> "Their dealings with the corporation are subjected to rigorous scrutiny and where any of their contracts or engagements with the corporation is challenged the burden is on the director or stockholder not only to prove the good faith of the transaction but also to show its inherent fairness from the viewpoint of the corporation and those interested therein.... *The essence of the test is whether or not under all the circumstances the transaction carries the earmarks of an arm's length bargain.* If it does not, equity will set it aside." See also *Geddes* v. *Anaconda Copper Mining Co.*, 254 U.S. 590 (1921) (standard of fiduciary duty for interested directors).

We believe that this formulation expresses the meaning of the phrase "fiduciary duty" in § 36(b). The Investment Company Act modifies this duty in a significant way: It shifts the burden of proof from the fiduciary to the party claiming breach, to show that the fee is outside the range that arm's-length bargaining would produce.

The *Gartenberg* approach fully incorporates this understanding of the fiduciary duty as set out in *Pepper* and reflects § 36(b)(1)'s imposition of the burden on the plaintiff. As noted, *Gartenberg* insists that all relevant circumstances be taken into account, as does § 36(b)(2) ("[A]pproval by the board of directors ... shall be given such consideration by the court as is deemed appropriate under *all the circumstances*" (emphasis added)). And *Gartenberg* uses the range of fees that might result from arm's-length bargaining as the benchmark for reviewing challenged fees.

II-B-2.

Gartenberg's approach also reflects § 36(b)'s place in the statutory scheme and, in particular, its relationship to the other protections that the Act affords investors.

Under the Act, scrutiny of investment-adviser compensation by a fully informed mutual fund board is the "cornerstone of the ... effort to control conflicts of interest within mutual funds." The Act interposes disinterested directors as "independent watchdogs" of the relationship between a mutual fund and its adviser. To provide these directors with the information needed to judge whether an adviser's compensation is excessive, the Act requires advisers to furnish all information "reasonably ... necessary to evaluate the terms" of the adviser's contract, 15 USC § 80a-15(c), and gives the SEC the authority to enforce that requirement. See § 80a-41. Board scrutiny of adviser compensation and shareholder suits under § 36(b) are mutually reinforcing but independent mechanisms for controlling conflicts. See *Daily Income Fund, Inc. v. Fox*, 464 U.S. 523 (1984) (Congress intended for § 36(b) suits and directorial approval of adviser contracts to act as "independent checks on excessive fees"); *Kamen v. Kemper Financial Services, Inc.*, 500 U.S. 90 (1991) ("Congress added § 36(b) to the [Act] in 1970 because it concluded that the shareholders should not have to rely solely on the fund's directors to assure reasonable adviser fees, notwithstanding the increased disinterestedness of the board").

In recognition of the role of the disinterested directors, the Act instructs courts to give board approval of an adviser's compensation "such consideration ... as is deemed appropriate under all the circumstances." § 80a-35(b)(2). Cf. *Burks v. Lasker*, 441 U.S. 471 (1979) ("[I]t would have been paradoxical for Congress to have been willing to rely largely upon [boards of directors as] 'watchdogs' to protect shareholder interests and yet, where the 'watchdogs' have done precisely that, require that they be totally muzzled").

From this formulation, two inferences may be drawn. First, a measure of deference to a board's judgment may be appropriate in some instances. Second, the appropriate measure of deference varies depending on the circumstances. *Gartenberg* heeds these precepts. *Gartenberg* advises that "the expertise of the independent trustees of a fund, whether they are fully informed about all facts bearing on the [investment adviser's] service and fee, and the extent of care and conscientiousness with which they perform their duties are important factors to be considered in deciding whether they and the [investment adviser] are guilty of a breach of fiduciary duty in violation of § 36(b).

III.

While both parties in this case endorse the basic *Gartenberg* approach, they disagree on several important questions that warrant discussion.

The first concerns comparisons between the fees that an adviser charges a captive mutual fund and the fees that it charges its independent clients. As noted, the *Gartenberg* court rejected a comparison between the fees that the adviser in that case charged a money market fund and the fees that it charged a pension fund (noting that "[t]he nature and extent of the services required by each type of fund differ sharply"). Petitioners contend that such a comparison is appropriate, but respondent disagrees. Since the Act requires consideration of all relevant factors, 15 USC § 80a-35(b)(2), § 80a-15(c), we do not think that there can be any categorical rule regarding the comparisons of the fees charged different types of clients. See *Daily Income Fund, supra* (discussing concern with investment advisers' practice of charging higher fees to mutual funds than to their other clients). Instead, courts may give such comparisons the weight that they merit in light of the similarities and differences between the services that the clients in question require, but courts must be wary of inapt comparisons. As the panel below noted, there may be significant differences between the services provided by an investment adviser to a mutual fund and those it provides to a pension fund which are attributable to the greater frequency of shareholder redemptions in a mutual fund, the higher turnover of mutual fund assets, the more burdensome regulatory and legal obligations, and higher marketing costs. 527 F.3d, at 634 ("Different clients call for different commitments of time"). If the services rendered are sufficiently different that a comparison is not probative, then courts must reject such a comparison. Even if the services provided and fees charged to an independent fund are relevant, courts should be mindful that the Act does not necessarily ensure fee parity between mutual funds and institutional clients, contrary to petitioners' contentions. See *id.*, at 631 ("Plaintiffs maintain that a fiduciary may charge its controlled clients no more than its independent clients").[6]

By the same token, courts should not rely too heavily on comparisons with fees charged to mutual funds by other advisers. These comparisons are problematic because these fees, like those challenged, may not be the product of negotiations conducted at arm's length. See 537 F.3d, at 731-732 (opinion dissenting from denial of rehearing en banc); *Gartenberg, supra* ("Competition between money market funds for shareholder business does not support an inference that competition must therefore also exist between [investment advisers] for fund business. The former may be vigorous even though the latter is virtually non-existent").

---

[6] Comparisons with fees charged to institutional clients, therefore, will not "doo[m] [a]ny [f]und to [t]rial." Brief for Respondent 49; see also *Strougo v. BEA Assocs.*, 188 F. Supp.2d 373 (SDNY 2002) (suggesting that fee comparisons, where permitted, might produce a triable issue). First, plaintiffs bear the burden in showing that fees are beyond the range of arm's-length bargaining. § 80a-35(b)(1). Second, a showing of relevance requires courts to assess any disparity in fees in light of the different markets for advisory services. Only where plaintiffs have shown a large disparity in fees that cannot be explained by the different services in addition to other evidence that the fee is outside the arm's-length range will trial be appropriate. See also *In re Alliance Bernstein Mut. Fund Excessive Fee Litigation*, 2006 U.S. Dist. LEXIS 34853 (SDNY, May 31, 2006) (citing report finding that fee differential resulted from different services and different liabilities assumed).

Finally, a court's evaluation of an investment adviser's fiduciary duty must take into account both procedure and substance. See 15 USC §80a-35(b)(2) (requiring deference to board's consideration "as is deemed appropriate under all the circumstances"); cf. *Daily Income Fund, supra* ("Congress intended security holder and SEC actions under §36(b), on the one hand, and directorial approval of adviser contracts, on the other, to act as independent checks on excessive fees"). Where a board's process for negotiating and reviewing investment-adviser compensation is robust, a reviewing court should afford commensurate deference to the outcome of the bargaining process. See *Burks, supra* (unaffiliated directors serve as independent watchdogs). Thus, if the disinterested directors considered the relevant factors, their decision to approve a particular fee agreement is entitled to considerable weight, even if a court might weigh the factors differently. This is not to deny that a fee may be excessive even if it was negotiated by a board in possession of all relevant information, but such a determination must be based on evidence that the fee "is so disproportionately large that it bears no reasonable relationship to the services rendered and could not have been the product of arm's-length bargaining." *Gartenberg, supra.*

In contrast, where the board's process was deficient or the adviser withheld important information, the court must take a more rigorous look at the outcome. When an investment adviser fails to disclose material information to the board, greater scrutiny is justified because the withheld information might have hampered the board's ability to function as "an independent check on management." *Burks, supra.* "Section 36(b) is sharply focused on the question of whether the fees themselves were excessive." *Migdal v. Rowe Price-Fleming Int'l, Inc.*, 248 F.3d 321 (CA4 2001); see also 15 USC §80a-35(b) (imposing a "fiduciary duty with respect to the receipt of compensation for services, or of payments of a material nature"). But an adviser's compliance or noncompliance with its disclosure obligations is a factor that must be considered in calibrating the degree of deference that is due a board's decision to approve an adviser's fees.

It is also important to note that the standard for fiduciary breach under §36(b) does not call for judicial second-guessing of informed board decisions. See *Daily Income Fund, supra*; see also *Burks, supra* ("Congress consciously chose to address the conflict-of-interest problem through the Act's independent-directors section, rather than through more drastic remedies"). "[P]otential conflicts [of interests] may justify some restraints upon the unfettered discretion of even disinterested mutual fund directors, particularly in their transactions with the investment adviser," but they do not suggest that a court may supplant the judgment of disinterested directors apprised of all relevant information, without additional evidence that the fee exceeds the arm's-length range. In reviewing compensation under § 36(b), the Act does not require courts to engage in a precise calculation of fees representative of arm's-length bargaining. See 527 F.3d, at 633 ("Judicial price-setting does not accompany fiduciary duties"). As recounted above, Congress rejected a "reasonableness" requirement that was criticized as charging the courts with rate-setting responsibilities. See *Daily Income Fund, supra.* Congress' approach recognizes that courts are not well suited to make such precise calculations. Cf. *GMC v. Tracy*, 519 U.S. 278 (1997) ("[T]he Court is institutionally unsuited to gather the facts upon which economic predictions can be made, and professionally untrained to make them"); *Verizon Communs., Inc. v. FCC*, 535 U.S. 467 (2002); see also *Concord v. Boston Edison Co.*, 915 F.2d 17 (CA1 1990) (opinion for the court by Breyer, C. J.) ("[H]ow is a judge or jury to determine a 'fair price' "). *Gartenberg*'s "so disproportionately large" standard reflects this congressional choice to "rely largely upon [independent director] 'watchdogs' to protect shareholders interests." *Burks, supra.*

By focusing almost entirely on the element of disclosure, the Seventh Circuit panel erred. See 527 F.3d, at 632 (An investment adviser "must make full disclosure and play no tricks but is not subject to a cap on compensation"). The [*Gartenberg* standard], which the panel rejected, may lack sharp analytical clarity, but we believe that it accurately reflects the compromise that is embodied in § 36(b), and it has provided a workable standard for nearly three decades. The debate between the Seventh Circuit panel and the dissent from the denial of rehearing regarding today's mutual fund market is a matter for Congress, not the courts.

IV.

For the foregoing reasons, the judgment of the Court of Appeals is vacated, and the case is remanded for further proceedings consistent with this opinion.

It is so ordered.

CONCUR

Justice Thomas, concurring.

The Court rightly affirms the careful approach to § 36(b) cases, that courts have applied since (and in certain respects in spite of) *Gartenberg v. Merrill Lynch Asset Management, Inc.*, 694 F.2d 923 (CA2 1982). I write separately because I would not shortchange the Court's effort by describing it as affirmation of the "*Gartenberg* standard."

The District Court and Court of Appeals in *Gartenberg* created that standard, which emphasizes fee "fairness" and proportionality, in a manner that could be read to permit the equivalent of the judicial rate regulation the *Gartenberg* opinions disclaim, based on the Investment Company Act of 1940's "tortuous" legislative history and a handful of extrastatutory policy and market considerations. Although virtually all subsequent § 36(b) cases cite *Gartenberg*, most courts have correctly declined its invitation to stray beyond statutory bounds. Instead, they have followed an approach (principally in deciding which cases may proceed past summary judgment) that defers to the informed conclusions of disinterested boards and holds plaintiffs to their heavy burden of proof in the manner the Act, and now the Court's opinion, requires. See, *e.g.*, *ante* (underscoring that the Act "modifies" the governing fiduciary duty standard "in a significant way: It shifts the burden of proof from the fiduciary to the party claiming breach, to show that the fee is outside the range that arm's-length bargaining would produce"); *ante* (citing the "degree of deference that is due a board's decision to approve an adviser's fees" and admonishing that "the standard for fiduciary breach under § 36(b) does not call for judicial second-guessing of informed board decisions").

I concur in the Court's decision to affirm this approach based upon the Investment Company Act's text and our longstanding fiduciary duty precedents. But I would not say that in doing so we endorse the "*Gartenberg* standard." Whatever else might be said about today's decision, it does not countenance the free-ranging judicial "fairness" review of fees that *Gartenberg* could be read to authorize, and that virtually all courts deciding § 36(b) cases since *Gartenberg* (including the Court of Appeals in this case) have wisely eschewed in the post-*Gartenberg* precedents we approve.

Topic 3 Fiduciary Restrictions on Profitable Transfer of Advisory Contract

Laws & Rules Highlight:

IC Act (15 USC 80a-1 *et seq.*) & Rules (17 CFR §§ 270.0-1 *et seq.*)

- § 1 Findings and Declaration of Policy
  - § 1(b)(6) ("… the national public interest and the interest of investors are adversely affected … when the control or management [of investment companies] is transferred, without the consent of their security holders")
- § 15 Investment Advisory and Underwriting Contracts
  - § 15(a) (*makes it unlawful for any person to serve as an IA except pursuant to a* ***written contract*** *approved by a majority vote of the outstanding voting securities of the IC, the board of the IC, and a majority of disinterested directors*); § 2(a)(42) (*def. "voting security"*)
  - § 15(a)(3) (*advisory contract* ***terminable*** *by the board or by vote of a majority of the outstanding voting securities of IC, on not more than 60 days' notice without penalty*)
  - § 15(a)(4) (*advisory contract* ***automatically terminates*** *upon assignment—designed to inhibit trafficking of investment advisory contracts*)
    - ✓ § 2(a)(4) (*def. "****assignment****" to include transfer of a contract, or of a controlling block of the assignor's outstanding voting securities*); § 2(a)(9) (*def. "****control****"*)
    - ✓ Rule 2a-6 Certain Transactions Not Deemed Assignments (*safe harbor for intra-corporate reorganizations: transaction that does not result in a* ***change of actual control*** *of an adviser is not an* ***assignment*** *of the advisory contract*)
  - § 15(f)(1) (*non-exclusive* ***safe harbor*** *for sale or assignment of advisory contract with a registered IC for profit if* ***two conditions*** *are met*):
    - ✓ **§ 15(f)(1)(A)** (*for at least* ***three years*** *following the advisory contract assignment, directors independent of both selling and purchasing advisers constitute at least 75% of the fund board*); § 15(f)(2)(A) (*meaning of "interested person"*)
    - ✓ **§ 15(f)(1)(B)** (***no unfair burden*** *is imposed on the fund as a result of the transaction*); § 15(f)(2)(B) (*meaning of "unfair burden" on a registered IC*)

Pre-Case Background Note:[Biblio]

Manager Stewardship; Manager Entrepreneurship: Prohibition of Profiteering from Fiduciary Office *versus* Market Reward for Entrepreneurship

On the conflict of an investment adviser ***as fiduciary*** and ***as entrepreneur***,

Professor Frankel commented:[1a (§12.04[D]); *cf.* 1b (§§3.F-G) & 1c]

> Fiduciaries do not have property rights in the relationship. This principle conflicts with another principle, that persons have property rights in their businesses. The conflict arises when the businesses are fiduciary businesses.
>
> Investment advisers can be viewed as fiduciaries hired by investor-shareholders to manage their funds. Advisers who serve as external advisers can also be viewed as entrepreneurs, who establish independent advisory businesses and invest in sponsorship and organization of investment vehicles for public investors. These adviser-entrepreneurs take the risk that their investment vehicles will not attract investors and that they will lose their investments. Because we assume that their activities are beneficial to society, such adviser-entrepreneurs should be compensated. One form of compensation is through fees they receive from serving the investment companies they created. These fees include not only their cost of rendering the services but also profits. Another potential form of compensation is through capital gains from the sale of their businesses."

John C. Bogle, founder and former chairman of The Vanguard Group of Investment Companies, commenting on case law's failure to treat the value of the advisory contract as representing an asset of the trust fund, and on "the age of conglomeration that has now overwhelmed" the investment management industry, stated: the industry is set "on a new course in which ***manager entrepreneurship*** in the search for personal profit would supersede ***manager stewardship*** in the search for prudent investment returns for fund shareholders."[2]

In *SEC v. Insurance Sec., Inc.* (***SIS*** **case, Ninth Circuit 1958**),[3] directors of a registered mutual fund held a controlling interest in the stock of the management company, a closely-held company and investment adviser to the fund, sold their stock for a profit of more than 25 times the stock's book value, and thereafter fees of the management company charged to the mutual fund more than doubled. In an enforcement action in the court, the SEC sought an accounting of the "*inequitable and wrongful profits*" realized by the fund directors from the sale of their management company stock. **The SEC's** action was based on its long-held position, stated in 1942, that IC Act § 15(a)'s prescription for automatic termination of advisory contract upon its assignment reflected a clear Congressional intention to prevent all trafficking in investment advisory contracts, and that an investment adviser of a registered investment company thus could not legally profit by selling its advisory contract.[4] The **Ninth Circuit**, while acknowledging the "general principle of equity" that "a personal trustee cannot sell his office," and that a large part of the value of the management company stock was attributable to the advisory contract the management company had with the fund, held nevertheless:

> [The fund directors'] sale of their stock in the service company cannot be said to represent compensation for the sale or transfer of a fiduciary office .... [T]he capitalized value of the contract between the service company and Trust Fund ... does not represent an asset of Trust Fund.

Commenting on the *SIS* case:

- Jaretzki (1959)[5a] (***agreeing with*** the Ninth Circuit that value of the expectancy of an advisory contract's renewal does not belong to the investment company, but rather belongs to the advisory company and its stockholders; ***disagreeing with*** the SEC's position that a sale of a controlling block of stock of an investment advisory company by a director of the investment company serviced by such advisory company would be unlawful if made at a price in excess of the net asset value of the stock sold.).
- Note (1958)[5b] (***finding*** the Ninth Circuit's determination that the "fiduciary office was not transferred through the sale of controlling shares" in the management company "untenable" and the court's reasoning "unsound"; ***noting*** the stock transferors and transferees' withholding from the fund shareholders knowledge of the amount paid for corporate control; ***arguing*** that the court should have ascertained that portion of the sales price constituting an unjust enrichment of the fiduciaries, and that portion fairly attributable to the anticipated earnings of an organization capable of performing valuable services.).
- Greene (1959)[5c] (***expressing concerns*** over the impact of the *SIS* case: the lucrative nature of the NAV-based management fees greatly in excess of the cost of the services rendered has attracted the attention of those seeking to profit from trading in the stock of service companies; it would be most unfortunate if there were a revival of the condemned practice of trafficking in service contracts, and if the pressure to assign such contracts to the highest but not necessarily the most scrupulous or most capable bidder as existed prior to the 1940 Act would reappear.).

In *Rosenfeld v. Black* (***Rosenfeld* case, Second Circuit 1971**),[6] the outgoing adviser to a mutual fund received compensation from the new adviser, for using its "practical control of the proxy machinery" to recommend approval of the new adviser, and for effectuating transfer of the advisory contract. The fund shareholders sued for an accounting of the compensation. The **Second Circuit** opined:

> A fiduciary endeavoring to influence the selection of a successor must do so with an eye single to the best interests of the beneficiaries.... If Lazard did not wish to continue as adviser and chose to recommend a successor and assist in the latter's installation, it was obliged to forego personal gain from the change of office, no matter how deeply or rightly it was convinced it had made the best possible choice. It is wholly immaterial that the prospect of receiving future management fees if it had continued as an adviser would have been an asset of Lazard rather than of the Fund; ... [While] under "the morals of the marketplace," Lazard should see no reason why, having selected a competent adviser willing to serve on the same terms Lazard had done, it should not receive what the new incumbent was willing to pay for the opportunity. But equity imposes a higher standard.

Commenting on the *Rosenfeld* case:

- Lipton (1971)[7a] (*criticizing Rosenfeld*'s "***absolute prophylactic rule***" as "too harsh and restrictive" but *admitting* "***unrestricted license***" of *SIS* "did not offer adequate protection to fund shareholders"; *stating*: "internalization of management ... perhaps will turn out to be the only long-run solution to the conflicts created by external management.").
- Sterrett (1973)[7b] (*stating* that reward for entrepreneurial risk is essential to promoting the continued establishment of new mutual funds; *analyzing* two chief means of rewarding mutual fund sponsor entrepreneurial risk: ***management fees*** and ***succession fees***; *agreeing* with *Rosenfeld* that succession fees inflict undisclosed costs on mutual fund shareholders, and *arguing* for entrepreneurial reward to be paid as a component of periodic management fees.).
- Markham (1973)[7c] (consistent with the purposes of § 15 of the IC Act, *Rosenfeld* should be applied ***only to deny*** an incumbent adviser profits paid on its assurance that the purchaser would succeed to the incumbent's advisory contract, ***but not to deny*** the incumbent adviser profits paid for its intrinsic worth and the entrepreneurial risk it assumed.).
- Frankel (2017)[1a (§12.04[C])] (*noting* the ***consensus*** that an adviser that uses influence and control over the proxy machinery to install a new adviser for compensation breaches fiduciary duties; and courts' ***disagreement*** on whether an "accounting" will be ordered rather than "damages" on a showing that the investment company

had been injured by the transfer in the case of a transfer that does not comply with § 15(f): certain jurisdictions may award an *injunction* to prevent the transfer, others may also award an *accounting*, and still others may award only *damages*.).

In response to the "***uncertainty***" about *Rosenfeld*'s application to the circumstances under which an adviser could receive a profit upon the transfer of its investment company advisory business, similar to the reward for entrepreneurial risk in American corporate enterprise,[7a] **Congress in 1975 added § 15(f)** to the Investment Company Act.[8; 7d; 1a (§12.04[D] n.735)] Section 15(f) provides a non-exclusive safe harbor permitting investment advisers of registered investment companies to sell their advisory businesses resulting in assignment of the advisory contract without incurring liability to their IC clients, if the statutory conditions are met; and the burden of proof lies with the selling adviser.

In *Meyer v. Oppenheimer Mgmt. Corp.* (***Oppenheimer* case, Second Circuit 1985, 1990**),[9] a money market fund shareholder sued the adviser, alleging that the adviser sold its controlling interest shortly after causing the fund to adopt a Rule 12b-1 Plan, which was designed to keep the fund's assets high thus making the investment adviser more valuable and to help obtain a higher sales price, but which imposed an "unfair burden" on the fund. The Second Circuit decided the case based on "***the combination***" of *Rosenfeld* and the 1975 addition of IC Act *§ 15(f)*.

Bibliography:

1. Frankel: **1a.** FRANKEL & LABY, THE REGULATION OF MONEY MANAGERS—MUTUAL FUNDS AND ADVISERS (3d ed. 2017); **1b.** Frankel, FIDUCIARY LAW (2010); **1c.** Frankel, *How Did We Get into This Mess?*, 1 J. BUS. & TECH. L. 133 (2006)
2. Bogle, *A New Order of Things: Bringing Mutuality to the "Mutual" Fund*, 43 WAKE FOREST L. REV. 1089 (2008)
3. *SEC v. Insurance Sec., Inc.*, 254 F.2d 642 (9th Cir. 1958) [Procedural history: SEC v. Ins. Sec., Inc., 146 F. Supp. 778 (ND Ca. 1956), *aff'd*, 254 F.2d 642 (9th Cir. 1958), *cert. denied*, 358 U.S. 823 (1958)]
4. Opinion of SEC's General Counsel Chester T. Lane, IC-354 (1942)
5. **5a.** Jaretzki, *The Investment Company Act: Problems Relating to Investment Advisory Contracts*, 45 VA. L. REV. 1023 (1959); **5b.** Note, *Protecting the Interests of Mutual-Fund Investors in Sales of Management-Corporation Control (Or, Policing the Traffic in Other People's Money)*, 68 YALE L.J. 113 (1958); **5c.** Greene, *Fiduciary Standards of Conduct Under The Investment Company Act of 1940*, 28 GEO. WASH. L. REV. 266 (1959)
6. *Rosenfeld v. Black*, 445 F.2d 1337 (2d Cir. 1971)
7. **7a.** Lipton, *Rosenfeld v. Black*, 4 REV. SEC. REG. 853 (1971); **7b.** Sterrett, *Reward for Mutual Fund Sponsor Entreprenurial Risk*, 58 CORNELL L. REV. 195 (1973); **7c.** Markham, *The Sale of Advisory Contracts—Rosenfeld v. Black*, 19 N.Y.L.F. 61 (1973); **7d.** Hazen, *Transfers of Corporate Control and Duties of Controlling Shareholders—Common Law, Tender Offers, Investment Companies—and a Proposal for Reform*, 125 U. PA. L. REV. 1023 (1977)

8. SECURITIES ACTS AMENDMENTS OF 1975, PL No. 94-29, 89 Stat. 97, § 28(1) (June 4, 1975); Hearings on S. 249 Before Subcomm. on Securities of Sen. Comm. on Banking, Housing and Urban Affairs, 94th Cong., 1st Sess. (1975)
9. *Meyer v. Oppenheimer Mgmt. Corp.*, 764 F.2d 76 (2d Cir. 1985); *Meyer v. Oppenheimer Mgmt. Corp.*, 895 F.2d 861 (2d Cir. 1990)

Case Study 1:

Outgoing adviser to a mutual fund received compensation from the successor adviser for using the former's "practical control of the proxy machinery" to effectuate the selection and appointment of the successor adviser and the transfer of the advisory contract. The outgoing adviser was found to have violated the fiduciary principle, based on a ***prophylactic rationale***: *The outgoing adviser* used its influence to recommend a successor adviser whose qualifications included a willingness to compensate the outgoing adviser for help; *the successor adviser* was less qualified or more expensive than other candidates and was on the lookout for ways to recoup his "succession fee" at the expense of the fund.

Rosenfeld v. Black

445 F.2d 1337 (2d Cir. 1971)

[***Procedural history***: Rosenfeld v. Black, 319 F. Supp. 891 (SDNY 1970), *rev'd*, 445 F.2d 1337 (2d Cir. 1971), *cert. dism'd sub nom.* Lazard Freres & Co. v. Rosenfeld, 409 U.S. 802 (1972), *settlement approved*, 336 F. Supp. 84 (SDNY 1972)]

Case Study 2:

Money market fund shareholder sued selling investment adviser under IC Act § 15(f), claiming adviser imposed "undue burden" on the fund in connection with the sale. Held: "by the combination of *Rosenfeld* and the addition of § 15(f)," fund shareholders have ***implied right of action**** under § 15(f). Although also designed to provide some relief for investment advisers, § 15(f) was patently enacted for the "***especial benefit***"* of fund stockholders.

**Cf.* [Subsequent case law on implied right of action under other provisions of the IC Act: Olmsted v. Pruco Life Ins. Co. of New Jersey, 283 F.3d 429 (2d Cir. 2002), denying implied private right of action under §§ 26(f) and 27(i) of the IC Act, quoting Alexander v. Sandoval, 532 U.S. 275 (2001) ("Statutes that focus on the person regulated rather than the individuals protected create 'no implication of an intent to confer rights on a particular class of persons.' "); but see *Olmsted*, *supra*, n.4 (citing *Meyer I* and other courts which have recognized a private right of action under various IC Act sections); n.5 (SEC declined to respond to the court's inquiry regarding §§ 26(f) and 27(i) of the IC Act on other grounds.)]

Meyer v. Oppenheimer Mgmt. Corp.

764 F.2d 76 (2d Cir. 1985)

[***Procedural history***: Meyer v. Oppenheimer Mgmt. Corp., 609 F. Supp. 380 (SDNY 1984), *rev'd and remanded*, 764 F.2d 76 (2d Cir. 1985) ("***Meyer I***"), *corrected on remand*, 707 F. Supp. 1394 (SDNY 1988) ("***Meyer II***"), 709 F. Supp. 67 (SDNY 1989) & 715 F. Supp. 574 (SDNY 1989), *aff'd*, 895 F.2d 861 (2d Cir. 1990) ("***Meyer III***")]

Research Topics:

Regulation of management fees and assignments of advisory contracts in respect of registered investment companies in China.

Rosenfeld *et al.*, Plaintiffs-Appellants v. Black *et al.*, Defendants-Appellees
445 F.2d 1337 (2d Cir. 1971)

JUDGES: Friendly, Chief Judge, and Waterman and Hays, Circuit Judges.

OPINION

FRIENDLY, Chief Judge:

The appeal here is by plaintiffs, stockholders in what was The Lazard Fund, Inc. ("the Fund"), a mutual fund organized in 1958 and registered under the Investment Company Act of 1940. Their complaints, brought in the District Court for the Southern District of New York, sought, *inter alia*, an accounting of profits allegedly realized by Lazard Freres ("Lazard"), the organizer and investment adviser of the Fund, when, in 1967, it ceased to be the adviser and was replaced by Moody's Advisors & Distributors, Inc. ("Moody's A & D"), a wholly-owned subsidiary of Moody's Investors Service, Inc., which in turn was a wholly-owned subsidiary of Dun & Bradstreet, Inc. ("D & B"). The district court granted defendants' motion for summary judgment. The appeal raises an important question with respect to the obligations of an investment adviser that wishes to terminate its services to an investment company.

I.

Lazard, a highly reputed investment banking firm, had organized the Fund in 1958. The initial offering was of 8,500,000 shares at a price to the public of $15 per share.[1] Although originally organized as a closed-end investment company, the terms of the initial public offering made the Fund "open end" within § 5(a)(1) of the Act in the sense that the shares were redeemable, at a charge of 1% of the net asset value of the shares tendered for redemption. The Fund employed Lazard as investment adviser. The advisory contract, which conformed to the requirements of § 15(a) of the Act and was renewed on one occasion with directors' and thereafter with stockholders' approval, provided for quarterly fees which, translated to an annual basis, amounted to 1/2 of 1% on the first $100,000,000 of the Fund's average daily net assets, 3/8 of 1% on the next $50,000,000, and 1/4 of 1% on any excess over $150,000,000. In return, Lazard was obligated not only to advise the Fund in respect of investments but also to provide necessary office

[1] The issue was underwritten, with the proceeds realized by the Fund being $13.875 per share. Lazard was the underwriter with respect to 4,500,000 shares. Apparently a considerable portion of these was placed with customers of the firm.

facilities and personnel including corporate officers; its compensation was to be reduced by any amounts up to $50,000 per year paid by the Fund to members of its board of directors, executive committee or consultants.

The principal moving affidavit, by a Lazard partner, set forth the following: In contrast to most open-end investment companies, the Fund did not engage in a continuous public offering of its shares. The shrinkage attendant upon redemptions unaccompanied by sales was expected to be counteracted by an additional offering. However, developments in the mutual fund industry accelerated the shrinkage to such an extent that it would not likely be offset by such an offering. By the time of the events here in question, the number of shares had decreased to 5,304,711 and net assets had declined to some $85,000,000. In light of this, Lazard concluded that the best interests of the Fund's stockholders would be served if the Fund were to engage in a continuous offering of its shares and institute various new investment plans and programs of the type provided by competing funds. However, it would have been contrary to Lazard's traditional policies and mode of operation to create the organization needed to that end. In 1966, when Lazard learned that Moody's Investors Service, Inc., which managed more than $4 billion worth of investments for customers as investment adviser, was considering the possibility of entering the mutual fund area, it felt that an ideal solution to the Fund's problem might be in sight.

With the knowledge and approval of the Fund's directors, Lazard approached D & B. The result was a series of agreements. One provided for the "merger" of the Fund into Moody's Capital Fund, which Moody's Investors Service would organize with a capital of $100,000 in cash and Government securities. Each share of the Lazard Fund was exchangeable for one share of the Capital Fund having the same net asset value as one share of the Lazard Fund, and the shares of the Capital Fund owned by Moody's Investors Service prior to merger would also be converted into shares of the surviving corporation having the same net asset value as the shares issued to Lazard Fund stockholders.[2] The Capital Fund would employ Moody's A & D both as investment adviser, on substantially the same terms previously provided with respect to Lazard, and as exclusive agent for the sale of Capital Fund stock at net asset value, plus a scale of sales charges payable to Moody's A

---

[2] One change clearly beneficial to the Fund's holders was the proposed elimination of the redemption charge of 1% of net asset value.

& D. Approval of the merger by the Fund's stockholders would constitute approval of the new advisory contract between Capital Fund and Moody's A & D. Thus, as a result of the proposed transactions, the Fund would evolve into an open-end company which offered special investment services and engaged in continuous offering of its shares through the Moody's A & D distributor.

The aspect of the Lazard-D & B negotiations most important for our purposes, was an agreement dated April 5, 1967 between Lazard and D & B, which was to become effective upon the effective date of the merger if the advisory contract between Capital Fund and Moody's A & D were approved at that time. The proxy statement sent to stockholders of the Fund described this as follows:

Agreement between Dun & Bradstreet, Inc. and Lazard Freres & Co.

> Dun & Bradstreet, Inc. of which Moody's Investors is a wholly-owned subsidiary has entered into an agreement with Lazard Freres & Co., investment adviser of the Corporation, to take effect upon the consummation of the merger, pursuant to which Lazard Freres & Co. has agreed for a period of five years from the effectiveness of the merger not (a) to become associated, either in a management or advisory capacity, with another investment company subject to registration under the Investment Company Act of 1940; (b) to permit the use of the name "Lazard," or any combination including such name, by any such investment company or investment company manager or adviser; and (c) to act as principal distributor for any open-end investment company making a continuous offering of its shares, and which is subject to registration under the Investment Company Act of 1940.
>
> Lazard Freres & Co. has also agreed for a period of five years from the effectiveness of the merger unless otherwise specified (a) to make available Mr. Hettinger (or others) for the purpose of [editor's note: providing listed services to Moody's Capital Fund and/or Moody's Fund, Inc.] * * * *
>
> As consideration for such agreements, Dun & Bradstreet, Inc. will deliver to Lazard Freres & Co. 75,000 shares of its common stock, par value $1 per share. The 75,000 shares will be placed in escrow by Lazard Freres & Co. to secure performance of its obligations set forth in the first paragraph of this subsection and, subject to such performance, will be released at the rate of 10,000 shares annually for the next four years with the remaining 35,000 shares to be released at the end of the fifth year. Cash dividends will not be paid on such shares as from time to time remain unreleased from escrow, but such shares may be voted by Lazard Freres & Co. while they are

subject to the escrow.

Plaintiffs allege, and defendants do not dispute, that D & B stock was selling over the counter at more than $37 per share at the time the contract was signed, although it had been selling at a lower price earlier during the negotiating period.[3]

On April 6, 1967, the Fund sent to stockholders a letter, a notice of special meeting of stockholders, a proxy and a proxy statement. The notice stated the chief business of the meeting to be approval of the merger of the Fund with Moody's Capital Fund and consequent adoption of the advisory contract between Capital Fund and Moody's A & D. While the stockholders were told of the agreement between Lazard and D & B in the manner already set forth, they were not asked to approve it. The letter, signed by Mr. Hettinger, a partner of Lazard and president of the Fund, informed the stockholders that the Fund's board of directors[4] recommended approval of the merger largely because it would cure the disadvantages which the Fund suffered by not engaging in continuous offering of its shares and by not making available special investment services. The proxy statement also recited that Lazard held of record 2,066,310 shares, constituting some 39% of the capital stock of the Fund, although none of these were owned beneficially.

Plaintiff Rosenfeld brought actions in the federal and state courts[5] on April 11 and 12,

---

[3] The stock issuable to Lazard would not have commanded its full free trading price, both because of the dividend restriction stated in the last sentence of the quoted material, and because Lazard represented it was acquiring the stock for its own account and not with a view to resale or other distribution, except for Lazard's right, during certain periods, to require D & B to file a registration statement permitting such sale. In some instances this was to be at D & B's expense, in others at Lazard's. D & B also made, subject to certain qualifications, the usual "piggy-back" agreement to include the shares issuable to Lazard in any registration statement it might file of its own volition.

[4] The Fund had eight directors. Two of them were Lazard partners; another was a senior partner in Lazard's counsel; all had been selected by Lazard. The meeting at which the merger was approved was attended by only five directors, including the three listed above. An outside director telephoned his approval during the meeting and still another had cabled his approval. The two Lazard partners abstained from voting.

[5] We unreservedly condemn this practice which, for reasons that are well understood, is so frequently utilized in stockholder actions in the Southern District of New York with respect to investment companies and in many other stockholder suits. A litigant is entitled to his day in one court, but not in two—a consideration of special moment in these times of serious delays in trials.... District judges should feel free to make use of their power to stay the federal action unless the state action is discontinued, when no good reason for simultaneous maintenance of the state suit can be shown. We would hope state judges would feel similarly free to take appropriate action to avoid this sort of imposition.

1967, for an injunction and an accounting, alleging that the transactions involved a sale of its advisory office by Lazard.... Later, other similar actions were brought in state and federal courts.

A motion to enjoin the merger was made in one of the state court actions but was withdrawn before the return day. At the meeting 4,269,346 shares were voted in favor of the merger, and only 38,545 against it. The transactions were thereupon consummated. The state actions were discontinued without prejudice, after a considerable number of motions unnecessary to recount, and defendants moved for summary judgment in the federal suits. That was granted, 319 F. Supp. 891 (1970), and this appeal followed.

Plaintiffs' case was predicated on a contention that the 75,000 shares of D & B ultimately deliverable to Lazard were not in fact issued solely in consideration of the four undertakings summarized in the quotation from the Proxy Statement but in large part for Lazard's assistance in bringing about the merger and the consequent appointment of Moody's A & D as investment adviser, with the profits anticipated therefrom. Defendants argued that plaintiffs had failed to adduce sufficient evidence on this to resist their motion for summary judgment. While regarding plaintiffs' contrary position as "so extremely thin, in the face of solid proof sustaining defendants' position, that upon a trial we would probably be forced to set aside a verdict in plaintiffs' favor,"[6] the judge did not place his decision on that ground. Rather, referring to the provision of § 15(a) of the Investment Company Act whereby any assignment of an advisory contract automatically terminates it, he held that "Where (as here) a majority of the stockholders approve a new advisory contract, as they are empowered to do by 15 USC § 80a-15(a), the management's conduct in arranging such a substitution does not violate the Act, regardless how it is labeled." In so holding the judge relied heavily on *SEC v. Insurance Securities, Inc.*, 254 F.2d 642 (9 Cir.), *cert. denied*, 358 U.S. 823 (1958), for the proposition that "the evil toward which the Act is directed is the transfer of control without consent of the shareholders ... not the

---

[6] We do not share the judge's views on this point. Whether the consideration be valued at a price representing its worth to D & B or its lower value to Lazard, see fn. 3, a trier of the facts could readily find that the value of the covenants in the second paragraph of the material quoted from the proxy statement would not have come anywhere near the lower figure, and that the importance of the non-compete agreement was questionable under the circumstances. The weight that should be given to these agreements in determining how much of the consideration would be subject to restitution is another matter.

money received by the assignors of service contracts."

II.

We start from one of the "well-established principles of equity," recognized in *Insurance Securities* itself, *supra*, "that a personal trustee, corporate officer or director, or other person standing in a fiduciary relationship with another, may not sell or transfer such office for personal gain." There are ample authorities to support this proposition: [citations omitted]. The reason for the rule is plain. A fiduciary endeavoring to influence the selection of a successor must do so with an eye single to the best interests of the beneficiaries. Experience has taught that, no matter how high-minded a particular fiduciary may be, the only certain way to insure full compliance with that duty is to eliminate any possibility of personal gain.

Postponing the question of the effect of specific provisions of the Investment Company Act, we see no reason to doubt that, on the facts of this case, Lazard in its position as investment adviser came within the scope of this principle. In describing the far less intimate role of the publisher of an investment advisory bulletin, the Supreme Court quoted with approval Professor Loss' reference to "the delicate fiduciary nature of an investment advisory relationship." *SEC v. Capital Gains Research Bureau*, 375 U.S. 180 (1963), citing 2 LOSS, SECURITIES REGULATION 1412 (2d ed. 1961). Lazard could hardly deny the existence of a fiduciary relationship if stockholders of the Fund had alleged, for example, that the firm had taken for its own account an opportunity that should have been made available to the Fund, even though § 17(e) does not specifically prohibit this. While "to say that a man is a fiduciary only begins analysis," *SEC v. Chenery Corp.*, 318 U.S. 80 (1943) (Frankfurter, J.), we would see no reason why the "well-established principle of equity" forbidding realization of profit for effecting the turn-over of corporate or other fiduciary office should not apply to the investment adviser of a mutual fund. See Note, *Protecting the Interests of Mutual-Fund Investors in Sales of Management-Corporation Control*, 68 YALE L.J. 113 (1958); Note, *Transfer of Management Company Control Upheld Despite Allegation of Domination over Mutual Fund Directors*, 63 COLUM. L. REV. 153 (1963). Lazard's influence with the Fund's stockholders can scarcely be questioned. Lazard had organized the Fund, and people had bought shares in it because of their trust and confidence in Lazard. All the Fund's personnel were furnished by Lazard. Unless the pattern differed from that of the industry, Lazard effectively managed the Fund's investments, despite the ultimate authority of the directors, quite as a trustee would do.

If Lazard did not wish to continue as adviser and chose to recommend a successor and assist in the latter's installation, it was obliged to forego personal gain from the change of office, no matter how deeply or rightly it was convinced it had made the best possible choice.[7] It is wholly immaterial that the prospect of receiving future management fees if it had continued as an adviser would have been an asset of Lazard rather than of the Fund; the same would be true of a trustee's right to receive future commissions or a corporate president's right to receive future salary and other benefits. Even ratification by the beneficiaries would not save a fiduciary from accountability for any amounts realized in dictating or influencing the choice of a successor unless this was secured with notice that the beneficiaries were entitled to the profit if they wished, cf. *United Hotels Co. of America v. Mealey*, 147 F.2d 816 (2 Cir. 1945), and it is questionable whether even such ratification by a majority of the beneficiaries could bind others or the Fund itself. Quite apart from the question hereafter discussed whether the proxy statement was misleading as to the terms of the Lazard-D & B agreement, it is clear in any event that the Fund's stockholders were never asked to—and did not—ratify it.

It is understandable that, under "the morals of the marketplace," Lazard should see no reason why, having selected a competent adviser willing to serve on the same terms Lazard had done, it should not receive what the new incumbent was willing to pay for the opportunity. But equity imposes a higher standard. It is fitting to repeat Chief Judge Cardozo's familiar words, "Many forms of conduct permissible in a workaday world for those acting at arm's length, are forbidden to those bound by fiduciary ties .... Not honesty alone, but the punctilio of an honor the most sensitive, is then the standard of behavior. As to this there has developed a tradition that is unbending and inveterate." *Meinhard v. Salmon*, 249 N.Y. 458 (1928).

---

[7] While the moving affidavit seeks to make the Moody transaction appear as a once in a lifetime opportunity, it is plain that the Fund had many other choices. It could have merged with a fund already being operated and engaging in continuous sales, possibly one whose advisory contract provided for a lower management fee. It could also have hired another adviser, perhaps on better terms, or performed its own management, very likely at less cost,... It might have become closed-end to avoid further shrinkage. The $4 billion of assets already being managed by Moody's Investors Service could be regarded as a detriment rather than an advantage.... There might also be concern lest D & B's issuance to Lazard of stock having a market value of some $3,000,000 might have a negative influence on any future negotiations to reduce the management fee. Even if an independent examination would reject all such possibilities in favor of the Moody merger, the prophylactic rationale behind the prohibition of fiduciary profit in this situation would remain.

III.

It is argued that, however all this might otherwise be, a different result is demanded because Lazard's advisory contract necessarily terminated under § 15(a)(4) of the Investment Company Act and that, pursuant to § 15(a), the stockholders of the Fund authorized a new contract with Moody's A & D, allegedly on full disclosure, an issue we will discuss below.

Insofar as the argument hinges merely on the statutory nonassignability of the contract with the consequent inference that there was no advisory office that Lazard could sell or transfer, it proves too much. The same could be said of an alleged sale of corporate office or directorship or, in the absence of appropriate provisions in the dispositive instrument, of an executor's or trustee's position.[8] The role of Lazard, an organizer of the Fund and its practical control of the proxy machinery used to recommend the approval of Moody's A & D as new adviser, made it quite as active and influential as a corporate president who recommends a successor to his board of directors, or a trustee who puts the name of a successor before a judge. Indeed, the very fact of nonassignability demonstrates that any payment made to the outgoing adviser by his successor in these circumstances over and above the value of any continuing services represents consideration not for lawful assignment of the contract—which is prohibited—but primarily for the use of influence in securing stockholder approval of the successor who expects to profit from the post. While it is true that the advisory contract is not conceptually an asset of the Fund, it is equally true that the expectation of profits under that contract is not an asset which, under the Act, the adviser can assign outright. Hence, if plaintiffs are correct in asserting that Lazard's few covenants were only a minor part of the consideration for D & B's payment to Lazard, Lazard and D & B must have assumed that the outgoing adviser was in a position to help effect the transfer of his office and that his efforts in so doing were worth valuable consideration.

The more serious contention is that § § 15(a), (c) and (d) constitute a policy determination by Congress that compliance with those provisions was to be the exclusive protection to an investment company when there is a change in advisory office. We cannot accept that view on the facts of this case. In § 1(b) of the Act, after noting abuses

---

[8] Indeed, Lazard's contract, being for personal services, could not have been assigned by it without at least the consent of the Fund's directors irrespective of § 15(a)(4). See 3 WILLISTON, CONTRACTS § 421 (3d ed. 1960).

that had been disclosed with respect to investment companies, including the management of such companies in the interest of investment advisers and the transfer of control or management without the consent of the security holders, Congress declared:

> that the policy and purposes of this title, in accordance with which the provisions of this title shall be interpreted, are to mitigate and, so far as is feasible, to eliminate the conditions enumerated in this section which adversely affect the national public interest and the interest of investors.

The purpose of § 15 was to furnish the added protection of approval of a new adviser by a majority of the stockholders,[9] not to withdraw safeguards already afforded by equity. As has been said, "Section 15(a)(4) is directed at transfers of control without shareholder consent, as distinct from profiteering on a transfer of fiduciary office. Hence, the section on its face hardly compels the conclusion that it is the exclusive antidote for such conduct." See Note, *supra*, 68 Yale L.J. at 131.

That alone might suffice to require reversal here, since any argument that simple failure of § 15 to supplant the rule of equity leaves plaintiffs with only a state-created claim would be answered by the fact that their contentions with respect to the inadequacy of the proxy statement, hereafter considered, afford a sufficient basis for pendent federal jurisdiction. However, we do not rest decision on that ground. We believe rather that the statute not merely did not withdraw safeguards equity had previously provided but impliedly incorporated them. We held in *Brown v. Bullock*, 294 F.2d 415 (2 Cir. 1961), that in requiring annual approval of investment advisory contracts by directors (or, alternatively, by stockholders) Congress meant to prescribe a uniform federal standard of directorial responsibility. It is wholly consistent with that view to say that when Congress required stockholder approval of a contract with a new investment adviser, it intended that the retiring adviser's use of the proxy machinery to procure appointment of the new

---

[9] When, as here, a new adviser is appointed, it is clear that § 15(a) requires stockholder approval. Although question has been raised whether the alternative of approval "by a majority of the directors who are not parties to such contract or agreement or affiliated persons of any such party," § 15(c), is sufficient for "reinstatement" of a contract terminated by a change in control of the advisor, § 2(a)(4), see Note, *Protecting the Interests of Mutual Fund Investors in Sales of Management-Corporation Control*, *supra*, we think a negative answer to be rather clearly dictated. Congress has decreed that a change in control terminates the contract, so that the fund would be dealing with a new party in fact even though not in form. The policy behind § 15(a) would thus seem to require that the new contract be approved by the fund's shareholders. See JENNINGS & MARSH, SECURITIES REGULATION 1246 (2d ed. 1968).

adviser must conform to the standards of abnegation of personal gain that equity had long imposed. When Congress, in § 15(a), required shareholder approval of any new advisory contract, it must have meant an approval uninfluenced by any improper motivations on the part of the outgoing adviser-fiduciary. If lured by the possibility of profit, the retiring adviser might recommend a successor who was less qualified or more expensive than other candidates, and who might be on the lookout for ways to recoup his "succession fee" at the expense of the Fund. See Note, *supra*, 68 Yale L.J. at 128. There is thus every reason for believing that Congress meant to adopt the established prophylactic rule. Just as it is unimaginable that, with respect to the responsibility of directors of investment companies, Congress would have been content "if a particular state of incorporation should be satisfied with lower standards of fiduciary responsibility for directors than those prevailing generally," see 294 F.2d at 421, it is similarly unthinkable that if a particular state had chosen not to recognize the rule of equity here in question Congress would have sanctioned an investment adviser's profiting from using his influence in securing stockholder approval of the appointment of a successor. Indeed, on defendants' view of the law, even disclosure would not be required in such a case, although they assert it was made here, since the profit acquired by the retiring adviser would not be material.

This brings us to the *Insurance Securities* case, *supra*. The SEC there unsuccessfully attacked a transaction whereby controlling stockholders of a service company which acted as sponsor, depositor, investment adviser and principal underwriter of an investment company sold their stock to a new controlling group at a price twenty-five times its net asset value, and the stockholders of the investment company then approved new contracts with the service company. The actual holding can be readily distinguished since the SEC was proceeding under § 36 of the Act. This authorized the Commission to bring suit for "gross misconduct or gross abuse of trust" and provided that if the court found the Commission's allegations to be established, it should enjoin the person found guilty from acting in its prior capacity either permanently or for such period as the court deemed appropriate. Words and remedies such as these were clearly addressed to highly reprehensible conduct, see *Los Angeles Trust Deed & Mortgage Exchange v. SEC*, 264 F.2d 199 (9 Cir. 1959), *cert. denied*, 366 U.S. 919 (1961); we would not dream of suggesting, much less holding, that Lazard's actions were so culpable. However, there are passages in the opinion suggesting that in the court's view none of the excess of the price received by the controlling stockholders over the book value of their stock would be recoverable under any circumstances by stockholders of the investment company. *Accord*, *Krieger v. Anderson*, 182 A.2d 907 (Del. Sup.Ct. 1962). While we do not find it necessary at this time to determine whether the difference between a transaction such as that here before us and the sale of a controlling block in a corporate adviser at a price reflecting the expectation of profits under a renewed contract with the corporation which the sellers were to aid in procuring, is sufficiently substantial to warrant a different result in this latter case, we should not wish to be understood as accepting these views.[10-11]

---

[10] Some difficulties in applying the principle prohibiting profit in the transfer of the advisory office to the sale of controlling stock in a corporate investment adviser are mentioned in Jaretzki, *The Investment Company Act: Problems Relating to Investment Advisory Contracts*, 45 VA. L. REV. 1023 (1959). Since our decision does not rest on § 36 of the Act, as it then stood, many of these criticisms would be inapposite even if we were dealing with the sale of stock situation. Similarly, to the extent that our decision rests on a prophylactic rationale—removing the temptation for the outgoing adviser to use his influence to recommend a successor, one of whose qualifications is willingness to compensate the retiring adviser for his help—most of the author's other criticisms also miss the mark. The *Insurance Securities* decision is criticized in Note, *supra*, 68 Yale L.J. at 121-33, which, however, argues that the amount of unjust enrichment may be less when the same adviser is expected to continue. *Krieger v. Anderson*, 182 A.2d 907 (Del. Sup.Ct. 1962), which followed *Insurance Securities*, is criticized in Note, *supra*, 63 Colum. L. Rev. 153 (1963).

[11] Appellees also argue that stock, perhaps even controlling stock, in banks or trust companies administering trusts is frequently sold at a profit, without any known case in which this has been held recoverable by beneficiaries of trusts being administered. The sale of stock not constituting control is readily distinguishable. Payment of premiums for control stock has generally been considered by the cases and commentators as raising a problem with respect to the duty of the controlling stockholders to the minority, see CARY, CORPORATIONS: CASES AND MATERIALS (4th ed. 1969), rather than in the context here considered. Usually, of course, commissions for acting as trustees or investment adviser will be only a fraction of the income of a bank or trust company, and the price realized for the control stock represents, in the main, an appraisal of the total. Furthermore, issuance or sale of a controlling block of stock in a bank or trust company acting as a trustee differs from the investment advisory context in important respects. A person who selects a bank or trust company as trustee must contemplate that a change in control of the corporate trustee may occur during the life of the trust. While trust instruments often confer advance sanction on mergers on the one hand, or provide an absolute right to terminate a trusteeship on the other, the settlor does not expect that he or the *cestuis* will have any voice in the timing or nature of a shift in control. There is thus no need to fear that the person who purchases the controlling interest will pay the seller for exerting his influence to have the purchase approved by the beneficiaries of the trusts. This contrasts with the provisions of the Act which specifically give a fund's shareholders a right to exercise their judgment in approving any new advisory contract. The prime vice in the realization of profit by an investment adviser or a controlling shareholder from a would-be successor lies in the danger that in return for this he may exert his influence to secure stockholder approval of the new or reinstated contract when that may not be the best possible course. It will be time to deal with the unlikely case where the adviser retires or the controlling stockholder sells his interest in the advisory company at a profit but scrupulously avoids any involvement with the required approval of the new

IV.

Appellees also rely on the history of the recent amendment to the Investment Company Act, 84 Stat. 1413 (1970). In the Investment Company Report, after stating that "the manager of a mutual fund is unquestionably in a fiduciary relationship to it," and that "consequently, the transfer of that relationship for a price has some elements of the sale of a fiduciary office [which was] strictly prohibited at common law because of the conflicts of interest which are involved," the Report added that "certain of the protective provisions of the Act have had the somewhat ironical, and presumably unintended, effect of diluting the protections provided by common law principles of fiduciary responsibility." The Report continued that "by reason of the automatic termination provisions in the event of assignment and the requirement that shareholders approve the new arrangements, it can be argued, as was successfully done in *SEC v. Insurance Securities, Inc.*, that there is no sale of the fiduciary office, since that office automatically terminates and a new one is created with stockholder approval." It went on to say that "however unrealistic this conclusion may appear in the light of the ability of the retiring management to use the proxy machinery to insure the installation of its self-chosen successors, application of the strict common-law principle might well be unfair insofar as it denies to the retiring management any compensation for the elements of value in the relationship which they may have built up over the years" and "could also be harmful to the Fund, since existing management might be reluctant to surrender that relationship and to provide the Fund with new and possibly more effective management."[12] Arguing that "there is presently no

---

contract, when it arises. Cf. *McClure v. Law*, 161 N.Y. 78 (1899).

[12] It is hard to accept the implication that it is solely up to the adviser to decide whether he will retire from that position in favor of a more effective manager. Section 15(a)(2) has long provided that an advisory contract must be approved annually by the fund's board of directors or stockholders, and § 15(a)(3) gives the fund's directors and stockholders the right to terminate the advisory contract without penalty upon sixty days' notice to the adviser. While, in a practical sense, the fact that the adviser ordinarily dominates the fund and its directors lessens the value of these provisions, still the fund's directors are amenable to suit if they discharge their annual approval function in a merely perfunctory fashion. See *Brown v. Bullock, supra*. And the 1970 amendment of § 15(c) makes more stringent the requirements of director approval. Annual advisory contract renewals now *must* receive approval of a majority of disinterested directors casting their votes in person at a meeting specially called for that purpose. Hence, the directors can no longer avoid responsibility for approving a disadvantageous advisory contract by leaving the approval to a majority of the outstanding shares. Moreover, the amended section enjoins upon the directors a duty "to request and evaluate ... such information as may reasonably be necessary to evaluate the terms of any contract whereby a person undertakes regularly to serve or act as investment adviser." Hence, in a situation like that at bar, if Lazard was convinced that its unwillingness to

adequate remedy in the Act" since the Commission "must rely primarily at present on its authority to seek an injunction under § 36 of the act upon the ground that, in arranging the succession, management or directors have been 'guilty' of 'gross misconduct or gross abuse of trust,' " a stigma which the courts "might be extremely reluctant" to place upon businessmen "merely because the terms of succession appear unfair," it urged Congress to amend the Act to prohibit a transfer of an advisory contract or the sale of a controlling block in an adviser, "if the sale, or any express or implied understanding in connection with the sale, is likely to impose additional burdens on the investment company or to limit its freedom of future action." The bill enacted by Congress did not carry out this recommendation.

Appellees would have us draw two inferences from this episode. One is that the SEC has acceded to the view that the prohibition against receiving compensation for the sale of a fiduciary office is inapplicable to a situation where the retiring adviser of an investment company profits from influencing the designation of a successor. The passages we have quoted demonstrate that if there was any such acceptance, it was a reluctant one, believed, erroneously in our view, to be compelled by the Ninth Circuit's decision in *Insurance Securities*. That case, as we have pointed out, dealt only with the Commission's powers under § 36 as it then stood. The SEC's belief that the unamended Act did not adequately protect fund shareholders against sales of the management organization rested upon a realistic assessment of its own power under § 36 but what we deem an unjustifiably defeatist view of private equitable actions, which the Report apparently did not consider. Although we respect the SEC's interpretation of the statutes it administers, the ultimate responsibility for construction lies with the courts.

The second and even more important inference we are asked to draw is that, by failing to adopt the SEC's proposal, Congress indicated an intention to exclude all remedies other than termination of the old contract and the need for stockholder approval of the new one, even if such approval was obtained by an adviser who was realizing a profit. We have been cited to nothing in the committee reports, in the floor debates, or even in the hearings that casts light on the failure to enact the proposal, or shows that the SEC seriously pressed it. As is well known, the SEC had other, and more important, fish to fry. Congress could well have thought it had handled the problem created by the *Insurance*

---

engage in continuous sales was detrimental to the Fund, and the independent directors believed this, they would have an affirmative responsibility to seek out a successor.

Securities decision by expanding the SEC's powers under § 36 so that, instead of having to allege that a defendant had been "guilty ... of gross misconduct or gross abuse or trust," the Commission need now allege only that he has engaged or is about to engage "in any act or practice constituting a breach of fiduciary duty involving personal misconduct."[13] While a new § 36(b) expressly declares that "the investment adviser of a registered investment company shall be deemed to have a fiduciary duty with respect to the receipt of compensation for services, or of payments of a material nature, paid by such registered investment company, or by the security holders thereof, to such investment adviser or any affiliated person of such investment advisor," the context makes plain that Congress did not mean this to be the only fiduciary duty of investment advisers.

We come finally to appellants' contention that, regardless of the issues thus far discussed, they were entitled to relief because the portion of the proxy statement quoted above did not fairly summarize the agreement between Lazard and D & B.[14] Two somewhat related criticisms are made. The first is a claim that in truth and fact the 75,000 shares of D & B referred to in the third paragraph were not being delivered to Lazard solely "as consideration for" the agreements of Lazard listed in the two preceding paragraphs but rather were to be given, at least in part, for Lazard's influencing the Fund's stockholders to assent to the merger and the consequent employment of Moody's A & D as investment adviser. Contrary to the district court's assumption, we do not believe that nothing more was involved here than an alleged misstatement of Lazard's "true motive." Lazard's motive—obtaining 75,000 D & B shares—was never contested. The disputed issue is what consideration Lazard was furnishing for that stock, only the various covenants recited in the proxy statement or also the use of its influence in securing stockholder approval. For reasons already indicated in another context, see fn. 6, we believe appellants' contentions here raised a factual issue which should not have been determined on a motion for summary judgment.

---

[13] The amendment also changed the remedial provision so that instead of being limited to enjoining a person from acting in his former capacity, the court might "award such injunctive or other relief against such person as may be reasonable and appropriate in the circumstances, having due regard to the protection of investors and to the effectuation of the policies declared in § 1(b) of this title." Congress recognized that "The highly punitive overtones of the existing section, together with the injunctive penalty, seriously impairs the ability of the courts to deal flexibly and adequately with wrongdoing by certain affiliated persons of investment companies." S. Rep. No. 91-184, 91st Cong. 2d Sess., p. 36 (1970).

[14] If this argument is sound, it would also negate any contention with respect to shareholder approval.

The second criticism is that the reference to 75,000 D & B shares "par value $1 per share" not only gave the stockholders no conception of how much Lazard was obtaining but tended to mislead them. While sophisticated investors could have ascertained the price at which D & B was selling over-the-counter from the New York Times or the Wall Street Journal or, for that matter, by calling their brokers, many would not know, or think, of these possibilities. Moreover, although a lawyer or a sophisticated investor would realize the lack of significance in a statement of $1 par value, which the Fund's shares themselves had, a court could find that not all shareholders would do so. Hence, despite the considerations mentioned in note 3, the failure to give the Fund's shareholders some notion that Lazard was obtaining a very substantial sum from D & B, as could so easily have been done, might well be considered to constitute an omission to state a material fact "necessary in order to make the statements therein not false or misleading," Rule 14a-9.... If summary judgment had not been granted here, the plaintiffs might have shown that in light of the character and distribution of the Fund's shareholders, the omission to give some indication of the true value of the D & B shares, after disclosing the nominal par value, was misleading. And we do not entertain the district court's substantial doubt as to the materiality of this information, for even though Lazard was receiving the payment from D & B, not from the Fund, the Fund's stockholders might have hesitated to approve the merger and advisory contract terms if they were told that D & B was willing to pay so large a sum to have the transactions consummated.

Lazard's argument that the Proxy Statement was made by the Fund and not by itself is unimpressive. All employees of the Fund were hired and paid for by Lazard, and discovery could well show that the statement, or at least the summary of the Lazard-D & B agreement, was prepared by Lazard or persons for whose acts it is legally responsible. It would surely come as a surprise to discover that Lazard did not control the Fund's proxy machinery. Finally, if the proxy statement should be held to have been misleading, plaintiffs' remedies are not limited to injunctions or rescission but could include an accounting for profits wrongfully obtained. *Mills v. Electric Auto-Lite Co.*, 396 U.S. 375 (1970). The devising of an appropriate remedy concerning this claim, as well as with respect to that earlier considered, if found to be warranted, is in the first instance for the district court.

The order granting defendants' motion for summary judgment is reversed and the cause is remanded for further proceedings not inconsistent with this opinion.

Meyer, Plaintiff-Appellant

v.

Oppenheimer Mgmt. Corp. *et al.*, Defendants-Appellees

764 F.2d 76 (2d Cir. 1985)

JUDGES: Feinberg, Chief Judge, Van Graafeiland and Newman, Circuit Judges. Van Graafeiland, Circuit Judge, concurring.

OPINION

FEINBERG, Chief Judge:

Plaintiff Richard Meyer, as custodian for Pamela Meyer, appeals from an order of the United States District Court for the Southern District of New York, Abraham D. Sofaer, J., dismissing plaintiff's amended complaint against the Daily Cash Accumulation Fund, Inc. (the Fund), the Fund's investment adviser, Centennial Capital Corporation (Centennial), and various securities dealers that together owned all of the stock in Centennial (the brokerage defendants). The amended complaint challenges on several grounds the legality of a decision by the Fund to adopt a plan of distribution (the Plan), pursuant to Rule 12b-1, of the Securities and Exchange Commission. The Plan authorizes the Fund to reimburse securities dealers, including the brokerage defendants, for "administrative and sales related costs in rendering distribution assistance to the Fund." For the reasons stated below, we reverse the order dismissing the complaint and remand for further proceedings.

I.

Taking plaintiff-appellant's allegations as true, as we must for the purpose of this appeal, the relevant facts are as follows. Appellant is a shareholder of the Fund, a money market mutual fund regulated by the Investment Company Act of 1940 (**ICA**). The Fund's shares are sold largely through the facilities and efforts of five brokerage firms, defendants-appellees Oppenheimer Management Corporation, Thomson McKinnon Securities, Inc., A.G. Edwards & Sons, Inc., Bateman Eichler, Hill Richards, Inc., and J.C. Bradford & Co.

At all relevant times, these five firms, either directly or in one case through a wholly owned subsidiary, owned all of the stock in the Fund's investment adviser, Centennial. Oppenheimer Management Corporation owned all of the stock of defendant-appellee Oppenheimer Asset Management Corporation, which in turn owned a majority of the stock in Centennial. The other four brokerage firms owned the remainder of Centennial's stock. The remaining two defendants were also closely related to their co-defendants: Oppenheimer & Co. owned almost all of the stock of Oppenheimer Management Corporation, one of the brokerage defendants.

Centennial provides the Fund with investment advisory services in exchange for a fee that prior to 1980 was set at one-half of one percent of the Fund's net assets. In 1980, the plaintiff-appellant in this suit filed an action against the Fund, the investment adviser (Centennial was then called The Management Group), the Oppenheimer defendants, A.G. Edwards and Thomson McKinnon. That suit, *Meyer v. Oppenheimer Management Corp.*, 609 F. Supp. 380 (SDNY 1984) (***Meyer I***), alleged that the fee charged by the investment adviser pursuant to its agreement with the Fund was excessive and therefore that the non-Fund defendants had violated § 36(b) of the ICA, which provides that an investment adviser of a mutual fund has a "fiduciary duty with respect to the receipt of compensation." *Meyer I* was settled in 1981 when the parties agreed to a reduction of the adviser's compensation so that the advisory fee rate, as a percentage of assets, decreases as the Fund's assets increase. In the Stipulation of Settlement, the parties also agreed that the new advisory fee could not be increased without court approval for five years, and that Centennial would "perform and offer to continue to perform all of the investment advisory services specified or required by the terms of the Advisory Agreement currently in effect between Centennial and the Fund." At the time, both sides acknowledged that the brokerage defendants, which owned Centennial, also performed significant services for the Fund without compensation. The settlement, however, nowhere expressly provided that the brokerage defendants must continue to perform these services.

Judge Sofaer approved the settlement in *Meyer I* in August 1981, concluding that the proposed settlement was "fair, reasonable and adequate." In the spring of 1982, the Fund proposed and its shareholders adopted a Rule 12b-1 plan of distribution, which authorized the Fund to reimburse the brokerage defendants, among others, for administrative and sales-related costs incurred in rendering distribution assistance to the Fund.

Shortly thereafter, the plaintiff in *Meyer I* filed the present action, in which he makes the following claims: (1) The Plan violates the *Meyer I* settlement by authorizing payment for services that were intended under the settlement to be covered by the advisory fee; (2) The Plan's administrative fee, when coupled with the settlement's advisory fee, violates § § 36(b) and 48 of the ICA, because it is excessive and therefore represents a breach of the non-Fund defendants' fiduciary duty. According to the amended complaint, at the Fund's then current size the advisory fee fixed by the settlement would be approximately $18.5 million per year and the Plan's administrative fee would be approximately $10 million; (3) The Fund violated § 14(a) of the Securities Exchange Act of 1934, and § 20 of the ICA, because the proxy statement proposing the Plan failed to state that the advisory fee paid by the Fund to Centennial was intended to cover the expenses for which the Plan would reimburse brokers; (4) The sale of two of the Oppenheimer defendants, which resulted in a change in the control of Centennial, violated § 15(f) of the ICA, by placing an "unfair burden" on the Fund.

After appellant complied with the district court's ruling that he present his demand to the Fund's directors, and the board rejected the demand, the district court granted defendants-appellees' motion to dismiss under Fed. R. Civ. P. 12(b)(6). This appeal followed.

II.

The overarching issue on this appeal is whether appellant's averments are sufficient to withstand appellees' motion to dismiss. Dismissal of a complaint for failure to state a claim is a "drastic step," which must not be taken "unless it appears beyond doubt that the plaintiff can prove no set of facts in support of his claim which would entitle him to relief." With this admonition in mind, we turn to consider appellant's claims.

II-A. Breach of Settlement Claim

Appellant's first claim is that implementation of the Plan, under which securities dealers are reimbursed for costs incurred in rendering administrative assistance to the Fund, deprived him of the benefits of the settlement in *Meyer I*. * * * *

Judge Sofaer, interpreting the settlement agreement "within its four corners," *United States v. Armour & Co.*, 402 U.S. 673 (1971), concluded that the services paid for under the Plan are not those that Centennial obligated itself to render under the settlement agreement. In doing so, he rejected appellant's argument that statements made by both sides in support of the settlement establish that the fee agreed to in the settlement was meant to include payment for the services now paid for under the Plan. As appellees emphasize, Judge Sofaer presided over the settlement hearing and approved the settlement in *Meyer I*; he is therefore in a particularly good position to interpret the agreement's terms. Nevertheless, we are persuaded by appellant's contention that discovery might reveal at least some overlap between the settlement's advisory services and the Plan's administrative services, and hence that the settlement was violated. Dismissal for failure to state a claim was not warranted. * * * *

We realize that appellant framed his complaint to allege that the charges for administrative services violate the settlement, but we decline to hold him to that strict a reading of the complaint. His basic point, on this cause of action, is that he has been denied the benefits of the settlement. That would be true if either (a) the Fund must now pay for services that Centennial had agreed to perform under the settlement, or (b) the settlement fee is no longer fair because it was predicated on the Fund's not having to pay for certain administrative services. Both aspects of the claim are substantial and should not have been rejected on the face of the complaint.[1]

II-B. Section 36(b) of the ICA

Section 36(b) of the ICA, added to the Act by the Investment Company Amendments Act of 1970, Pub. L. No. 91-547, § 20, 84 Stat. 1413, 1428-29, provides that "the investment adviser of a registered investment company shall be deemed to have a fiduciary duty with respect to the receipt of compensation for services" paid by the investment company or its security holders "to such investment adviser or any affiliated person of such investment adviser." The brokerage defendants, by virtue of their ownership of Centennial, are "affiliated persons" under the Act. See 15 USC § 80a-2(a)(3). An investment adviser violates § 36(b) when it, or an affiliated person, charges "a fee that is so disproportionately large that it bears no reasonable relationship to the services rendered and could not have been the product of arm's-length bargaining." *Gartenberg v. Merrill Lynch Asset Mgmt., Inc.*, 694 F.2d 923 (2d Cir. 1982), *cert. denied*, 461 U.S. 906 (1983).

The Fund's Plan was established pursuant to Rule 12b-1, issued by the SEC in 1980. Under the Rule's framework, an investment company such as the Fund may act "as a distributor of securities of which it is the issuer" only pursuant to a Rule 12b-1 plan. 17 CFR § 270.12b-1(b). A company acts as a distributor

---

[1] As indicated, appellant also claims that the 1982 proxy statement failed to reflect the true nature of Centennial's obligations under the settlement and therefore violated § 14(a) of the Securities Exchange Act of 1934 and § 20 of the ICA. In view of our disposition of the breach of settlement claim, this related claim must be reinstated as well.

> if it engages directly or indirectly in financing any activity which is primarily intended to result in the sale of shares issued by such company, including, but not necessarily limited to, advertising, compensation of underwriters, dealers, and sales personnel, the printing and mailing of prospectuses to other than current shareholders, and the printing and mailing of sales literature.

17 CFR § 270.12b-1(a)(2). The Rule further provides that a company may implement a distribution plan "only if the directors who vote to approve such implementation ... conclude, in the exercise of reasonable business judgment and ... their fiduciary duties under ... § § 36(a) and (b) [of the ICA], that there is a reasonable likelihood that the plan will benefit the company and its shareholders." 17 CFR § 270.12b-1(e).

Appellant offers three theories in support of his claim that implementation of the Rule 12b-1 Plan violates § 36(b). First, he repeats his contention that the advisory fee agreed to in the settlement was intended to include payment for costs incurred by the defendant brokerage firms that are now paid for under the Plan. Second, he claims that apart from a breach of the settlement the Plan's administrative fee, when added to the advisory fee paid under the settlement, is excessive. Third, he argues that the Plan violates Rule 12b-1 itself because it permits payment for services not "primarily" for the sale of new Fund shares.

Before turning to the individual claims, we are met by appellees' threshold argument, not addressed by the district court, that the fiduciary duty imposed by § 36(b) "has no application to payments made under a Rule 12b-1 plan," and that the dismissal of appellant's § 36(b) claim was proper "on this ground alone." Appellees' argument is based on the mistaken notion that because Rule 12b-1 sets the conditions under which mutual funds like the Fund may pay for distribution-related expenses, Rule 12b-1 plans may not be measured against standards other than those set out in the Rule itself. Section 36(b), the argument runs, deals only with compensation for advisory services. But § 36(b) expressly applies to payments made to "any affiliated person" of the investment adviser, and the brokerage defendants here are concededly affiliated persons. Moreover, in proposing what ultimately became § 36(b), the SEC made clear the broad scope of that provision:

> The statutory requirement ... would apply to *all* forms of compensation paid by all investment companies to their affiliated persons, principal underwriters, and affiliates of such persons. This would include *all* forms of compensation paid to officers,

> directors, advisory board members, trustees, sponsors, investment advisors, principal underwriters, and controlling persons of both externally and internally managed companies as well as persons or organizations with which such persons are affiliated. Although advisory fees are the principal form of managerial compensation in the investment company industry, externally managed companies frequently pay fees for various nonadvisory services to principal underwriters, trustees, business managers, and sponsors who, like investment advisers, are likely to have close and dominant relationships with such companies that preclude arm's-length bargaining.

SECURITIES AND EXCHANGE COMMISSION, PUBLIC POLICY IMPLICATIONS OF INVESTMENT COMPANY GROWTH, H.R. Rep. No. 2337, 89th Cong., 2d Sess. 144 (1966). Moreover, in proposing Rule 12b-1, the SEC emphasized that the Rule was not intended "to reduce or limit in any way" the fiduciary duties imposed by § 36(b). *Bearing of Distribution Expenses by Mutual Funds*, IC-10252 (1978). A claim that payments made under Rule 12b-1 are excessive when combined with advisory fees, where both payments are made to "affiliated persons" of an investment adviser, is cognizable under § 36(b).

The district court dismissed appellant's first § 36(b) claim on the ground that it "is identical to his [already rejected] claim that the Plan violates the *Meyer I* settlement agreement." We agree that resolution of this claim turns on resolution of appellant's breach of settlement claim. In view of our reinstatement of the latter, we conclude that this aspect of his § 36(b) cause of action states a claim on which relief can be granted and therefore must be reinstated as well.

Appellant's second claim, that independent of a settlement violation the aggregate payment made by the Fund (advisory fee plus administrative fee) is excessive, was also prematurely dismissed. The district court relied principally on the approval of the two fees by the Fund's board of directors, despite the suggestion in *Burks v. Lasker*, 441 U.S. 471 (1979), that board action may not cut off shareholder suits under § 36(b). Noting § 36(b)'s provision that "approval by the board of directors ... shall be given such consideration by the court as is deemed appropriate under all the circumstances," and emphasizing that Centennial's board is "unusually independent," the district court reached the following conclusion:

> The Board's determination, combined with plaintiff's failure to allege any facts (other than those already rejected in connection with the settlement argument) to suggest that the Board did not fulfill its responsibilities under Rule 12b-1, is sufficient for the

> court to conclude that plaintiff's complaint should be dismissed.

In addition, the court noted that at the time the board acted, 80 other funds had adopted plans of distribution pursuant to Rule 12b-1.

To the extent that the court relied on its rejection of the breach of settlement claim, our reinstatement of that claim mandates reinstatement here as well. Moreover, under *Gartenberg, supra*, in deciding whether a fee is so high as to constitute a breach of fiduciary duty, a court should examine all the facts surrounding a fee determination. Whether or not appellant prevails on this claim, or even reaches a trial on the merits, he has stated a claim on which relief can be granted and on which he is at least entitled to discovery.

Appellant's final § 36(b) claim, although not set out in the amended complaint, was presented in appellant's demand letter to the Fund's board of directors and was fully addressed by the district court. In the demand letter, appellant charged that

> the Plan is defective for the additional reason that it does not comply with Rule 12b-1. That Rule permits certain payments by a fund only for expenses that are "primarily" for the sale of new fund shares, whereas the stated purpose of the Fund's Plan is to maintain old, existing accounts.

The district court disagreed, apparently deciding that the Plan's payments were "primarily intended to result in the sale of shares" within the meaning of the Rule. Emphasizing the Plan's express statement that reimbursement be for costs incurred "in rendering distribution assistance," and noting that existing shareholders "may purchase new shares," the court concluded that "plaintiff has failed to allege a single fact that might show that the Plan as operated violates the restrictions of Rule 12b-1."

We cannot be certain at this stage of the litigation whether appellant's claim concerning Rule 12b-1 provides a distinct basis on which liability under § 36(b) may be predicated. Uncertainty arises both because of some ambiguity in the terms of the Rule, which has not yet been clarified by the SEC, and some ambiguity as to the nature of appellant's claim. Prior to promulgation of the Rule in 1980, the SEC had taken the position that a mutual fund may not act as a distributor of its own shares: "It is generally improper under the [ICA] for mutual funds to bear direct or indirect expenses related to the distribution of their shares." *Bearing of Distribution Expenses by Mutual Funds*, IC-11414 (1980); see generally 4 T. FRANKEL, THE REGULATION OF MONEY MANAGERS 111-19

(1978 and 1984 Supp.). The Rule reflected a sharp change in SEC policy by permitting mutual funds to bear distribution-related expenses under limited circumstances and provided certain conditions are met. The requirements of the Rule are triggered whenever a mutual fund engages in financing "any activity which is primarily intended to result in the sale of" its shares. 17 CFR § 270.12b-1(a)(2). A fund doing so is "deemed to be acting as a distributor." *Id.* The Rule requires that any payments made by a fund "in connection with" a distribution must be made pursuant to a written plan. *Id.* § 270.12b-1(b). The Rule specifies various requirements concerning information to be disclosed in the plan and necessary approvals by the fund's board, shareholders, and outside directors. *Id.*

In order to be entitled to pay distribution expenses, the Fund adopted a plan, purportedly under the authority of Rule 12b-1. The Plan authorizes the Fund to make monthly "distribution assistance payments" to any securities dealer or other organization "which has rendered assistance in the distribution of" Fund shares. The purpose of the payment is stated to be reimbursement of the recipient for "its administrative and sales related costs in rendering distribution assistance." The payment is limited to the lesser of (a) two-tenths of one percent of the average net asset value of the Fund's shares owned by the recipient or owned by customers of the recipient and held in accounts maintained by the recipient, or (b) the recipient's total cost during the month in rendering "distribution assistance." In the proxy statement seeking approval of the Plan, the Fund noted that the SEC has not determined whether dealers' expenses "in providing distribution related and administrative services to an investment company, which facilitate the sale of shares, are distribution expenses for purposes of Rule 12b-1." The proxy statement reported that the Fund's directors had therefore decided that all amounts to be paid under the Plan would be viewed as distribution expenses "regardless of whether or not certain expenses are subsequently determined not to be distribution expenses."

Appellant appears to claim that the Plan violates the Rule because the payments being made are not " 'primarily' for the sale of new fund shares" but instead "to maintain old, existing accounts." This aspect of the claim concerns the uses to which the payments are put by the recipient, or, more precisely, the uses to which the recipient has put its own money and for which it then seeks reimbursement from the Fund's "distribution assistance payments." Yet appellant also contends that the Plan violates the Rule because the payments are really being made "to pay the brokers (whose clients own over 90% of the

Fund's shares) not to move their business elsewhere." This contention does not concern the uses to which the payments are put but rather the Fund's motive for making them.

We see nothing in the Rule or in § 36(b) that prevents a mutual fund from deciding to pay distribution expenses to dealers in order to retain the interest of those dealers in selling fund shares to their customers.[2] To the extent that appellant's Rule 12b-1 claim assails the motive of the Fund, it fails to state a claim. However, to the extent that the claim challenges the uses to which the "distribution assistance payments" have been put, we decline to reject at this stage the possibility that liability under § 36(b) may be shown. It is arguable that any payments not devoted to costs of distribution are simply beyond the scope of the Rule and for that reason cannot violate it. On the other hand, since the Rule is triggered whenever a fund makes some payments that are primarily intended to result in the sale of its shares, it is also arguable that all payments purported to be made under the authority of a Rule 12b-1 plan must be devoted to distribution expenses. Even if payments under a plan are thus limited, it is not clear at this stage whether some portion of the payments made by the Fund fail to qualify as distribution payments. Appellant contends that the payments are used by the dealers to service their customers' accounts, a function appellant distinguishes from distribution of shares. The district court apparently viewed the payments as within the ambit of permissible distribution expenses simply because existing shareholders might purchase additional shares. We are not prepared to say at this point that the possibility of additional share purchases makes payments for all costs of shareholder servicing a distribution expense contemplated by the Rule. Yet we acknowledge that the Rule itself, in specifying the payments that might be made pursuant to a plan, refers not to "distribution expenses" but to any payments "in connection with" a distribution.

We are also in doubt as to appellant's theory of the legal basis for this aspect of the claim. If the claim purports to arise directly under Rule 12b-1, then a substantial question arises whether a private right of action exists for any violation of the Rule or for

[2] Appellees stoutly defend the Fund's right to pay brokers in order to retain the brokers' customers as shareholders of the Fund. They point out that, if the customers redeem Fund shares and purchase shares of other funds, expenses per share would increase both because the Fund's fixed costs would be borne by a reduced number of shares and because the per share cost of the investment advisory fee is higher at lower levels of net assets. Of course, to whatever extent Rule 12b-1 is ultimately determined to limit the permissible purposes for which any fund may pay brokers pursuant to a distribution plan, there will be no competitive disadvantage among funds.

any violation of a plan approved pursuant to the Rule. On the other hand, if, as appears likely, appellant claims only that liability arises under § 36(b), then the pertinent inquiry becomes whether any deviation from the Rule, or from the Plan, is so substantial as to constitute a breach of fiduciary obligations. We do not understand § 36(b) to be an enforcing mechanism for every SEC regulation or every action authorized thereunder.

Since appellant's first and second bases for claiming liability under § 36(b) suffice to withstand a motion to dismiss, we conclude, in light of all the uncertainties noted concerning the third basis, that it too should be returned for further consideration by the district court. This will afford appellant an opportunity to refine this aspect of the claim, and perhaps, subject to control of the district court, to detail the substance of the claim with at least some limited discovery. The remand will also provide an occasion for the district court to invite the SEC to submit its views on the Rule 12b-1 issues, once those issues have been clarified by refinement of appellant's claims. The SEC's views should be especially helpful in better understanding the scope and meaning of its recently adopted Rule.

II-C. Section 15(f) of the ICA

Section 15(f) of the ICA sets the conditions under which investment advisers (or affiliated persons) may realize a profit upon the sale or transfer of their business without incurring liability to the investment company or its shareholders. It permits the receipt by an investment adviser or affiliated person of "any amount or benefit in connection with a sale of securities of, or a sale of any other interest in, such investment adviser," provided that (1) the board of directors of the investment company is, and remains, sufficiently independent and (2) "there is not imposed an unfair burden on such company as a result of such transaction." 15 USC § 80a-15(f)(1). An "unfair burden" is defined to include

> any arrangement, during the two-year period after the date on which any such transaction occurs, whereby the investment adviser ... or any interested person of any such adviser ... receives or is entitled to receive any compensation directly or indirectly (i) from any person in connection with the purchase or sale of securities or other property to, from, or on behalf of such company, other than bona fide ordinary compensation as principal underwriter for such company, or (ii) from such company or its security holders for other than bona fide investment advisory or other services.

Id. § 80a-15(f)(2)(B).

Section 15(f) was added to the ICA in response to this court's decision in *Rosenfeld v. Black*, 445 F.2d 1337 (2d Cir. 1971), *cert. dismissed*, 409 U.S. 802 (1972), in which we held that profits realized by a retiring investment adviser of a fund from the successor it had caused to be installed were recoverable by the fund. In an effort to "clarify the law in light of" *Rosenfeld*, S. Rep. No. 75, 94th Cong., 1st Sess. 71, Congress enacted § 15(f) in 1975.[3] The Senate Report states:

> The bill would clarify the law in light of the 1971 decision of the Court of Appeals for the Second Circuit in *Rosenfeld v. Black*, 445 F.2d 1337 (2d Cir. 1971) by removing the uncertainty surrounding the circumstances in which an investment adviser of an investment company can receive any profit upon the transfer of its business without incurring liability to the company or its shareholders.
>
> The bill would make clear that an investment adviser can make profit on the sale of its business subject to two principal safeguards to protect the investment company and its shareholders. (Section 25 of the bill). The first safeguard would require that 75 percent of the investment company's directors be independent for a period of three years after the investment adviser sells its business or otherwise transfers the advisory relationship. The second safeguard would provide that such a transaction must not impose any unfair burden on the investment company.

Appellant's argument that § 15(f) was violated proceeds as follows: In the spring of 1982, shortly after the Rule 12b-1 Plan was adopted, the Oppenheimer defendants sold their controlling interest in the investment adviser (Centennial), thus implicating § 15(f); the sale was "inseparably linked" to the administrative fee imposed by the Plan in that the Plan was designed to keep the Fund's assets high, which in turn would make the investment adviser more valuable and therefore raise the sale price; the administrative fee, which was thus designed to increase the value of Centennial, imposed an "unfair burden" on the Fund, whether or not the fee is consistent with Rule 12b-1.

The district court, at a hearing in October 1982, expressed its intention to dismiss the § 15(f) claim on the theory, subsequently explained, that disposition of the breach of settlement and § 36(b) claims would "effectively render the § 15 claims nugatory." In its final Opinion and Order, the court did dismiss the § 15(f) claim stating that "since payments of distribution expenses do not impose an undue burden upon the Fund,

---

[3] As we noted in *Newman v. Stein*, 464 F.2d 689, 695 & n.14 (2d Cir. 1972), *cert. denied*, 409 U.S. 1039 (1972), our decision in *Rosenfeld* occasioned considerable comment in legal periodicals before § 15(f) was enacted.

Oppenheimer's sale of its interest in [Centennial] does not violate § 15 of the ICA."

Appellees' threshold response to this claim is that there is no implied private right of action under § 15(f). In *Merrill Lynch, Pierce, Fenner & Smith, Inc. v. Curran*, 456 U.S. 353 (1982), the Supreme Court stated:

> In determining whether a private cause of action is implicit in a federal statutory scheme when the statute by its terms is silent on that issue, the initial focus must be on the state of the law at the time the legislation was enacted. More precisely, we must examine Congress' perception of the law that it was shaping or reshaping. When Congress enacts new legislation, the question is whether Congress intended to create a private remedy as a supplement to the express enforcement provisions of the statute. When Congress acts in a statutory context in which an implied private remedy has already been recognized by the courts, however, the inquiry logically is different. Congress need not have intended to create a new remedy, since one already existed; the question is whether Congress intended to preserve the pre-existing remedy.

Id. at 378-79. The Court went on to find that since the lower courts had clearly recognized a private right of action under the Commodity Exchange Act, the failure of Congress to say anything about a private right of action in a comprehensive overhaul of the Act indicated an intent to retain that right of action. *Id.* at 381-82.

As we have already indicated, Congress enacted § 15(f) in response to this court's decision in *Rosenfeld*, *supra*, in which mutual fund stockholders sued the outgoing investment adviser. The unstated premise of *Rosenfeld*, and of the Congress that "clarified" it, is that a stockholder may bring such a suit. In response, appellees apparently contend that *Rosenfeld* was based on the common law prohibition against the sale of a fiduciary office for profit and that § 15 of the ICA was implicated only as a defense. But *Rosenfeld* plainly held that § 15 of the ICA was designed to incorporate that common law prohibition and impose a uniform national standard. Moreover, that Congress understood the stockholder's suit in *Rosenfeld* to be grounded in the ICA is evidenced not only by the addition of § 15(f) but also by a statement to that effect by the amendment's co-sponsor. See 119 Cong. Rec. 20028 (1973) (statement of Senator Williams) ("In [*Rosenfeld*], the court of appeals held that the general equitable principal that a fiduciary cannot sell his office is impliedly incorporated in § 15(a) of the [ICA].").

The situation here presents a stronger case for an implied private right of action than that in *Merrill Lynch*, *supra*, which turned on the failure to amend the provisions under which lower courts had found an implied right of action. Here, Congress specifically addressed *Rosenfeld* and did not question the propriety of a private suit. The inference that Congress intended to preserve the private right of action, and include within it the right to sue for violations of § 15(f), is compelling. Absent evidence to the contrary, we have no reason to think that Congress, in giving the industry some relief from the rigors of *Rosenfeld*, meant to abolish the implied cause of action for shareholders that had been there recognized. Appellees have failed to cite any such evidence in § 15(f)'s legislative history. Although also designed to provide some relief for investment advisers, § 15(f) was patently enacted for the "especial benefit" [sic] of fund stockholders, *Cort v. Ash*, 422 U.S. 66 (1975). Congress expressly conditioned the receipt of payment for the sale of an investment adviser's business on "two principal safeguards to protect the investment company and its shareholders." Senate Report, *supra*. And the existence of a remedy for shareholders is plainly "consistent with the underlying purpose of the legislative scheme." *Cort v. Ash, supra*. Indeed, the SEC expressly contemplated private enforcement of a provision it recommended to Congress in 1966, not enacted at the time, quite similar to the rule ultimately fashioned by the combination of Rosenfeld and the addition of § 15(f). See PUBLIC POLICY IMPLICATIONS, *supra*. We believe that "in view of our construction of the intent of the Legislature there is no need for us to [further] 'trudge through all four of the factors [for deciding whether there is an implied right of action] when the dispositive question of legislative intent has been resolved.' " *Merrill Lynch, supra* (quoting *California v. Sierra Club*, 451 U.S. 287 (1981) (Rehnquist, J., concurring)).

Citing *Nizin v. Bright*, 478 F. Supp. 713 (D. Mass. 1979), *aff'd mem.*, 618 F.2d 93 (1st Cir. 1980), appellees note that since § 15(f) was enacted at least one court has rejected the reasoning of *Rosenfeld*. *Nizin* held that Congress had not "originally intended to prohibit the sale of an investment adviser's office for profit" by incorporating common law principles into § 15 of the Act. *Nizin* did not address the question whether shareholders may sue to enforce the provision of § 15(f) that permits a sale of an investment adviser only if the sale does not impose an "unfair burden" on the fund. We hold that mutual fund stockholders do have such an implied right of action under § 15(f).

We now turn to consider whether appellant's § 15(f) claim was properly dismissed nonetheless. Here, too, we conclude that appellant has stated a claim that must survive a motion to dismiss. Appellees argue that because § 15(f) expressly excludes from its definition of "unfair burden" payment for "bona fide investment advisory or other services," 15 USC §80a-15(f)(2)(B), and because the amended complaint does not explicitly allege that the Rule 12b-1 Plan involved payment for other than such bona fide services, appellant's §15(f) claim was properly dismissed. But appellant alleges that the Plan was adopted to facilitate the sale of the controlling interest in Centennial. We do not suggest that appellant is likely to prove the truth of such an allegation, but if he is able to do so, it at least suggests that the services paid for are in some sense not "bona fide." Whether or not appellant prevails on his breach of settlement claim or his §36(b) claim, he has at least stated a claim under §15(f) upon which relief can be granted.

For the foregoing reasons, the judgment of the district court is reversed and the case is remanded for further proceedings consistent with this opinion.

Section 2.2 Independent Watchdog for Fund Investors

Topic 1 Role of Mutual Fund Board

Laws & Rules Highlight:

IC Act (15 USC 80a-1 *et seq.*) & Rules (17 CFR §§ 270.0-1 *et seq.*)

- Rule 0-1(a)(7) Fund Governance Standards (***Five Governance Standards*** *set forth in Rule 0-1(a)(7)(ii)-(iii), (v)-(vi)-(vii);* ***Ten Exemptive Rules*** *requiring the fund board to meet the Five Governance Standards*):
    - Rule 10f-3 Exemption for the Acquisition of Securities During the Existence of an Underwriting or Selling Syndicate
    - Rule 12b-1 Distribution of Shares by Registered Open-End Management Investment Company
    - Rule 15a-4 Temporary Exemption for Certain Investment Advisers
    - Rule 17a-7 Exemption of Certain Purchase or Sale Transactions Between an Investment Company and Certain Affiliated Persons Thereof
    - Rule 17a-8 Mergers of Affiliated Companies
    - Rule 17d-1 Applications Regarding Joint Enterprises or Arrangements and Certain Profit-Sharing Plans
    - Rule 17e-1 Brokerage Transactions on a Securities Exchange
    - Rule 17g-1 Bonding of Officers and Employees of Registered Management Investment Companies
    - Rule 18f-3 Multiple Class Companies
    - Rule 23c-3 Repurchase Offers by Closed-End Companies
- § 10 Affiliations of Directors
    - § 10(a) (*requires fund board to have at least* ***40%*** *disinterested/independent directors—designed to provide* ***an independent check*** *on management and* ***a vehicle for representation*** *of shareholder interests in investment company affairs*)
    - § 2(a)(12) (*def.* ***"director,"*** *referring to both directors of funds organized as corporations, and trustees of funds organized as business trusts*)
- Rule 12b-1 Distribution of Shares by Registered Open-End Management Investment Company (*12b-1 distribution plans must be* ***approved*** *by both full board and independent directors; independent directors also have authority to* ***terminate*** *12b-1 plans*)
- § 15 Investment Advisory and Underwriting Contracts
    - § 15(c) (***"15(c) process"****: terms of any advisory and underwriter contracts, and any renewal thereof, must be approved by a vote of a majority of disinterested directors*)

- § 16 Changes in Board of Directors; Provisions Relative to Strict Trusts (*permissible methods for selecting directors and independent directors*)
- § 17 Transactions of Certain Affiliated Persons and Underwriters
  - Rule 17e-1 Brokerage Transactions on a Securities Exchange (***safe harbor** rule specifying standard and procedures for affiliated broker's commission to be deemed "not exceeding usual and customary"; availability of safe harbor conditions on fund board satisfying **fund governance standards***)
- § 36 Breach of Fiduciary Duty
  - § 36(a) (***general fiduciary duties***)
  - § 36(b) (***fiduciary duty with respect to fees paid by fund***)

Case Study:*

Case addresses ***interaction of corporate law and regulatory law*** in mutual fund governance. Mutual funds are organized under state law either in the form of a corporation governed by a board of directors called an "investment company," or in the form of an unincorporated association governed by a board of trustees called a "business trust" or a "statutory trust." Fund management firms made the choices based on the attractiveness of the ***governing state law***. The three most popular forms of organization for mutual funds are "*Delaware statutory trusts*": 40%; "*Massachusetts business trusts*": 35%; and "*Maryland corporations*": 16%. Regardless of the form a fund takes under its organizational state law, and while each fund is also subject to the laws of its organizational state, the Investment Company Act makes identical fiduciary standards applicable to managers and directors of investment companies and to managers and trustees of investment trusts.[1]

The ***Investment Company Act*** does not purport to be the source of authority for managerial power; rather, the Act functions primarily to impose *controls and restrictions* on the internal management of investment companies. On the other hand, the *duties* imposed on directors by the Act are in addition to those imposed by state law. Under ***state law***, directors are bound by duties of loyalty and care: *duty of loyalty* generally prohibits a director from taking advantage of a corporation and its shareholders; *duty of care* generally requires that a director exercise the degree of skill, diligence, and care that a reasonably prudent person would exercise in the same circumstances or in the management of his own affairs.[2]

The structure and purpose of the IC Act indicate that Congress entrusted to the independent directors of investment companies the primary responsibility for looking after the interests of the fund's shareholders. Independent fund directors thus serve in a "***watchdog***" capacity on behalf of the fund and its shareholders, furnishing an "***independent check***" upon the management of investment companies. In an *amicus* brief filed with the U.S. Supreme Court, the SEC urged that courts should defer to fund directors' decision if "the directors are truly independent, are fully informed of the material facts, and render a business judgment that is reasonable under all the circumstances."

Ref.* [1a.** ICI, 2017 INVESTMENT COMPANY FACT BOOK (57th ed.), pp.243-44: The Organization of a Mutual Fund; **1b.** LEMKE ET AL., REGULATION OF INVESTMENT COMPANIES, § 6.01 Form of Organization (2017); **2.** DIV. OF INV. MGMT, SEC. & EXCH. COMM'N, PROTECTING INVESTORS: A HALF CENTURY OF INVESTMENT COMPANY REGULATION, § 7.II.A (1992)]

Burks v. Lasker

441 U.S. 471 (1979)

[***Procedural history & related materials***: Lasker v. Burks, 404 F. Supp. 1172 (SDNY 1975), *summary judgment granted*, 426 F. Supp. 844 (SDNY 1977), *rev'd & remanded*, 567 F.2d 1208 (2d Cir. 1978), *cert. granted*, Burks v. Lasker, 439 U.S. 816 (1978), Brief for the Securities and Exchange Commission as *Amicus Curiae* (1978), *rev'd & remanded*, 441 U.S. 471 (1979) (Blackmun, J., concurring; Stewart, J., concurring]

Burks v. Lasker

441 U.S. 471 (1979)

JUDGES: BRENNAN, J., delivered the opinion of the Court, in which BURGER, C. J., and WHITE, MARSHALL, BLACKMUN, and STEVENS, JJ., joined. BLACKMUN, J., filed a concurring opinion. STEWART, J., filed an opinion concurring in the judgment, in which POWELL, J., joined. REHNQUIST, J., took no part in the consideration or decision of the case.

OPINION

MR. JUSTICE BRENNAN delivered the opinion of the Court:

The question presented in this case is whether the disinterested directors of an investment company may terminate a stockholders' derivative suit brought against other directors under the Investment Company and Investment Advisers Acts of 1940. To decide that question, we must determine the appropriate roles of federal and state law in such a controversy.

Respondents, shareholders of Fundamental Investors, Inc., an investment company registered under the Investment Company Act, brought this derivative suit in February 1973 in the District Court for the Southern District of New York. The action was brought against several members of the company's board of directors and its registered investment adviser, Anchor Corp. The complaint alleged that the defendants had violated their duties under the Investment Company Act (ICA), the Investment Advisers Act (IAA), and the common law in connection with the 1969 purchase by the corporation of $ 20 million in Penn Central Transportation Co. commercial paper. [1] In response to the suit, Fundamental's board of directors determined that the five of its members who were neither affiliated with the investment adviser[2] nor defendants in the action would decide

---

[1] The complaint alleged, *inter alia*, that "Anchor breached its statutory, contractual and common law fiduciary duties by relying exclusively upon the representations of Goldman, Sachs & Co. (a seller of commercial paper), rather than independently investigating the quality and safety of the Penn Central 270-day notes purchased by the Fund. It is further alleged that the defendant directors knew or should have known of Anchor's failure to meet its responsibility; that they violated their ... duties as corporate fiduciaries by acquiescing in Anchor's omissions; that the financial condition of the Penn Central steadily worsened during the period from November 28, 1969 to June 21, 1970, the date that it filed for reorganization; and that during this period of decline all of the defendants failed to investigate and review the financial condition of the Penn Central and the quality and safety of its commercial paper."

[2] The five were "disinterested" within the meaning of the ICA which provides: "No registered investment company

what position the company should take in the case. On the basis of outside counsel's recommendation and their own investigation, the five, acting as a quorum pursuant to the company's bylaws, concluded that continuation of the litigation was contrary to the best interests of the company and its shareholders and moved the District Court to dismiss the action.

The District Court held that under the so-called "business judgment rule," a quorum of truly disinterested and independent directors has authority to terminate a derivative suit which they in good faith conclude is contrary to the company's best interests. 404 F. Supp. 1172 (1975). After permitting discovery on the question of the directors' independence, the District Court entered summary judgment against respondents, finding no evidence that the directors who voted to terminate the suit had acted other than independently and in good faith. 426 F. Supp. 844 (1977). The Court of Appeals for the Second Circuit reversed, 567 F.2d 1208 (1978), holding that as a consequence of the ICA, "disinterested directors of an investment company do not have the power to foreclose the continuation of non-frivolous litigation brought by shareholders against majority directors for breach of their fiduciary duties." We granted certiorari, 439 U.S. 816 (1978). We reverse.

I.

A fundamental issue in this case is which law—state or federal—governs the power of the corporation's disinterested directors to terminate this derivative suit. The first step in making that determination is to ascertain which law creates the cause of action alleged by the plaintiffs. Neither the ICA nor the IAA—the plaintiff's two federal claims—expressly creates a private cause of action for violation of the sections relevant here. However, on the basis of District and Circuit precedent, the courts below assumed that an implied private right of action existed under each Act. *Brown v. Bullock*, 194 F. Supp. 207 (SDNY), *aff'd*, 294 F.2d 415 (CA2 1961) (en banc) (ICA); *Abrahamson v. Fleschner*, 568 F.2d 862 (CA2 1977) (IAA); *Bolger v. Laventhol, Krekstein, Horwath & Horwath*, 381 F. Supp. 260 (SDNY 1974) (IAA). The two courts also sanctioned the bringing of the suit in derivative form, apparently assuming that, as we held in *J. I. Case Co. v. Borak*, 377 U.S. 426 (1964),

---

shall have a board of directors more than 60 per centum of the members of which are persons who are interested persons of such registered company." 15 USC § 80a-10(a). The definition of "interested person" is found at 15 USC § 80a-2(a)(19). Of the remaining six directors, five were defendants in the *Lasker* suit, and one was a director of the investment adviser.

“[to] hold that derivative actions are not within the sweep of the [right] would ... be tantamount to a denial of private relief.” As petitioners never disputed the existence of private, derivative causes of action under the Acts, and as in this Court all agree that the question has not been put in issue, we shall assume without deciding that respondents have implied, derivative causes of action under the ICA and IAA.[3]

Since we proceed on the premise of the existence of a federal cause of action, it is clear that “our decision is not controlled by *Erie R. Co. v. Tompkins*, 304 U.S. 64,” and state law does not operate of its own force. *Sola Electric Co. v. Jefferson Co.*, 317 U.S. 173 (1942). See *Board of Comm'rs v. United States*, 308 U.S. 343 (1939); *Deitrick v. Greaney*, 309 U.S. 190 (1940); WRIGHT, FEDERAL COURTS 284 (3d ed. 1976); Mishkin, *The Variousness of “Federal Law”: Competence and Discretion in the Choice of National and State Rules for Decision*, 105 U. PA. L. REV. 797 (1957); Hart, *The Relations Between State and Federal Law*, 54 COLUM. L. REV. 489 (1954); 2 LOSS, SECURITIES REGULATION 971 (2d ed. 1961). Rather, “[when] a federal statute condemns an act as unlawful, the extent and nature of the legal consequences of the condemnation, though left by the statute to judicial determination, are nevertheless federal questions, the answers to which are to be derived from the statute and the federal policy which it has adopted.” [citations omitted]. Legal rules which impact significantly upon the effectuation of federal rights must, therefore, be treated as raising federal questions. [citations omitted]. See generally Friendly, *In Praise of Erie—and of the New Federal Common Law*, 39 N.Y.U.L. REV. 383 (1964); Hill, *State Procedural Law in Federal Nondiversity Litigation*, 69 HARV. L. REV. 66 (1955). Thus, “the overriding federal law applicable here would, where the facts required, control the appropriateness of redress despite the provisions of state corporation law ....” *J. I. Case Co. v. Borak, supra.*

II.

The fact that “the scope of [respondents'] federal right is, of course, a federal question” does not, however, make state law irrelevant. *De Sylva v. Ballentine*, 351 U.S. 570 (1956). Cf. *United States v. Kimbell Foods, Inc.*, 440 U.S. 715(1979). It is true that in certain areas we have held that federal statutes authorize the federal courts to fashion a complete body

---

[3] The question whether a cause of action exists is not a question of jurisdiction, and therefore may be assumed without being decided. [citations omitted]. Other Courts of Appeals have agreed with the Second Circuit that the ICA and IAA create private causes of action. [citations omitted].

of federal law. See *Textile Workers v. Lincoln Mills*, 353 U.S. 448 (1957). Corporation law, however, is not such an area.

A derivative suit is brought by shareholders to enforce a claim on behalf of the corporation. See Note, *The Demand and Standing Requirements in Stockholder Derivative Actions*, 44 U. CHI. L. REV. 168 (1976). This case involves the question whether directors are authorized to determine that certain claims not be pursued on the corporation's behalf. As we have said in the past, the first place one must look to determine the powers of corporate directors is in the relevant State's corporation law. See *Santa Fe Industries, Inc. v. Green*, 430 U.S. 462 (1977); *Cort v. Ash*, 422 U.S. 66 (1975). "Corporations are creatures of state law," *ibid.*, and it is state law which is the font of corporate directors' powers. By contrast, federal law in this area is largely regulatory and prohibitory in nature—it often limits the exercise of directorial power, but only rarely creates it. Cf. *Price v. Gurney*, 324 U.S. 100 (1945). In short, in this field congressional legislation is generally enacted against the background of existing state law; Congress has never indicated that the entire corpus of state corporation law is to be replaced simply because a plaintiff's cause of action is based upon a federal statute. [citations omitted]. See ... ; BATOR *ET AL.*, THE FEDERAL COURTS AND THE FEDERAL SYSTEM 470-471 (1973 ed.).

Federal regulation of investment companies and advisers is not fundamentally different in this respect. Mutual funds, like other corporations, are incorporated pursuant to state, not federal, law. Although the Court of Appeals found it significant that "nothing in ... the legislation regulating investment companies and their advisers ... suggests that ... disinterested directors ... have the power to terminate litigation brought by mutual fund stockholders ...," 567 F.2d, at 1210, such silence was to be expected. The ICA does not purport to be the source of authority for managerial power; rather, the Act functions primarily to "[impose] controls and restrictions on the internal management of investment companies." *United States v. Nat'l Assn. of Securities Dealers*, 422 U.S. 694, 705 n. 13 (1975).

The ICA and IAA, therefore, do not require that federal law displace state laws governing the powers of directors unless the state laws permit action prohibited by the Acts, or unless "their application would be inconsistent with the federal policy underlying the cause of action ...." *Johnson v. Railway Express Agency*, 421 U.S. 454 (1975).[4] Cf.

---

[4] This is not a situation where federal policy requires uniformity and, therefore, where the very application of

[citations omitted]. Although "[a] state statute cannot be considered 'inconsistent' with federal law merely because the statute causes the plaintiff to lose the litigation," *Robertson v. Wegmann*, 436 U.S. 584 (1978), federal courts must be ever vigilant to insure that application of state law poses "no significant threat to any identifiable federal policy or interest ...." *Wallis v. Pan American Petroleum Corp.*, 384 U.S. 63 (1966). See [citations omitted]. And, of course, this means that "unreasonable," *Wallis v. Pan American Petroleum Corp.*, or "specific aberrant or hostile state rules," *United States v. Little Lake Misere Land Co.*, 412 U.S. 580 (1973), will not be applied. See, *e.g.*, *Levitt v. Johnson*, 334 F.2d 815 (CA1 1964). The "consistency" test guarantees that "[nothing] that the state can do will be allowed to destroy the federal right," *Board of Comm'rs v. United States, supra*, and yet relieves federal courts of the necessity to fashion an entire body of federal corporate law out of whole cloth.

III.

The foregoing indicates that the threshold inquiry for a federal court in this case should have been to determine whether state law permitted Fundamental's disinterested directors to terminate respondents' suit. If so, the next inquiry should have been whether such a state rule was consistent with the policy of the ICA and IAA. Neither the District Court nor the Court of Appeals decided the first question, apparently because neither considered state law particularly significant in determining the authority of the independent directors to terminate the action.[5] And in that circumstance, neither court addressed the question of inconsistency between state and federal law. At least implicitly, however, the Court of Appeals did make a related determination. Its holding that nonfrivolous derivative suits may never be terminated makes manifest its view that no other rule—whether state or federal—would be consistent with the ICA.[6] We disagree.

---

varying state laws would itself be inconsistent with federal interests. In enacting the ICA and IAA, Congress did declare that "the activities of such companies, extending over many States,... make difficult, if not impossible, effective State regulation of such companies ...." 15 USC § 80a-1(a)(5). But as long as private causes of action are available in federal courts for violation of the federal statutes, this enforcement problem is obviated. The real concern, therefore, is not that state laws be uniform, but rather that the laws applied in suits brought to enforce federal rights meet the standards necessary to insure that the "prohibition of [the] federal statute ... not be set at naught," *Sola Electric Co. v. Jefferson Co.*, 317 U.S. 173 (1942). The "consistency" requirement described in text guarantees that state laws failing to meet these standards will be precluded.

[5] See 567 F.2d 1208 (CA2 1978); 404 F. Supp. 1172 (SDNY 1975).

[6] The Court of Appeals did not undertake any separate analysis of the policy behind the ICA's companion statute,

The Court of Appeals correctly noted that Congress was concerned about the potential for abuse inherent in the structure of investment companies. A mutual fund is a pool of assets, consisting primarily of portfolio securities, and belonging to the individual investors holding shares in the fund. *Tannenbaum v. Zeller*, 552 F.2d 402 (CA2 1977). Congress was concerned because

> "[mutual] funds, with rare exception, are not operated by their own employees. Most funds are formed, sold, and managed by external organizations, [called 'investment advisers,'] that are separately owned and operated.... The advisers select the funds' investments and operate their businesses....
>
> "Since a typical fund is organized by its investment adviser which provides it with almost all management services ..., a mutual fund cannot, as a practical matter sever its relationship with the adviser. Therefore, the forces of arm's-length bargaining do not work in the mutual fund industry in the same manner as they do in other sectors of the American economy." S. Rep. No. 91-184, p. 5 (1969).

As a consequence, "[the] relationship between investment advisers and mutual funds is fraught with potential conflicts of interest," *Galfand v. Chestnutt Corp.*, 545 F.2d 807 (CA2 1976). See generally [citations to congressional materials omitted]; SECURITIES AND EXCHANGE COMMISSION, REPORT ON INVESTMENT TRUSTS AND INVESTMENT COMPANIES, pt.3, pp.1-49 (1940); 15 USC § 80a-1(b) (findings and declaration of policy).[7] Yet, while these potential conflicts may justify some restraints upon the unfettered discretion of even disinterested mutual fund directors, particularly in their transactions with the investment adviser,[8] they hardly justify a flat rule that directors may never terminate nonfrivolous derivative actions involving codirectors. In fact, the evidence is overwhelming that Congress did not intend to require any such absolute rule.

---

the IAA.

[7] See also *Tannenbaum v. Zeller*, 552 F.2d 402 (CA2 1977); Radmer, *Duties of the Directors of Investment Companies*, 3 J. CORP. L. 61 (1977); Note, *Mutual Fund Independent Directors: Putting a Leash on the Watchdogs*, 47 FORD. L. REV. 568 (1979).

[8] See, *e.g.*, § 36 of the ICA, as amended, and § 206 of the IAA, as amended, imposing minimum standards on the behavior of investment company directors and advisers which presumably apply as much to their decisions regarding litigation as to the other decisions they may be called upon to make. See *Santa Fe Industries, Inc. v. Green*, 430 U.S. 462 (1977) ("Congress intended the Investment Advisers Act to establish federal fiduciary standards for investment advisers"); *SEC v. Capital Gains Research Bureau*, 375 U.S. 180 (1963); *Cramer v. General Tel. & Electronics Corp.*, 582 F.2d 259 (CA3 1978); *Tannenbaum v. Zeller, supra*.

The cornerstone of the ICA's effort to control conflicts of interest within mutual funds is the requirement that at least 40% of a fund's board be composed of independent outside directors.[9] 15 USC § 80a-10(a). As originally enacted, § 10 of the Act required that these 40% not be officers or employees of the company or "affiliated persons" of its adviser. 54 Stat. 806. In 1970, Congress amended the Act to strengthen further the independence of these directors, adding the stricter requirement that the outside directors not be "interested persons." See 15 USC § § 80a-10(a), 80a-2(a)(19).[10] To these statutorily disinterested directors, the Act assigns a host of special responsibilities involving supervision of management and financial auditing. They have the duty to review and approve the contracts of the investment adviser and the principal underwriter, 15 USC § 80a-15(c); the responsibility to appoint other disinterested directors to fill vacancies resulting from the assignment of the advisory contracts, 15 USC § 80a-16(b);

---

[9] Under certain circumstances, independent directors must constitute a majority rather than 40% of the board. See 15 USC § 80a-10(b).

[10] Title 15 USC § 80a-2(a)(19) defines an " 'interested person' of another person ... when used with respect to an investment company," as

"**(i)** any affiliated person of such company, **(ii)** any member of the immediate family of any natural person who is an affiliated person of such company, **(iii)** any interested person of any investment adviser of or principal underwriter for such company, **(iv)** any person or partner or employee of any person who at any time since the beginning of the last two fiscal years of such company has acted as legal counsel for such company, **(v)** any broker or dealer registered under the Securities Exchange Act of 1934 or any affiliated person of such a broker or dealer, and **(vi)** any natural person whom the Commission by order shall have determined to be an interested person by reason of having had, at any time since the beginning of the last two fiscal years of such company, a material business or professional relationship with such company or with the principal executive officer of such company or with any other investment company having the same investment adviser or principal underwriter or with the principal executive officer of such other investment company."

Title 15 USC § 80a-2(a)(2) states that " '[affiliated] company' means a company which is an affiliated person," and 15 USC § 80a-2(a)(3) defines " 'affiliated person' of another person" as

"**(A)** any person directly or indirectly owning, controlling, or holding with power to vote, 5 per centum or more of the outstanding voting securities of such other person; **(B)** any person 5 per centum or more of whose outstanding voting securities are directly or indirectly owned, controlled, or held with power to vote, by such other person; **(C)** any person directly or indirectly controlling, controlled by, or under common control with, such other person; **(D)** any officer, director, partner, copartner, or employee of such other person; **(E)** if such other person is an investment company, any investment adviser thereof or any member of an advisory board thereof; and **(F)** if such other person is an unincorporated investment company not having a board of directors, the depositor thereof."

and are required to select the accountants who prepare the company's Securities and Exchange Commission financial filings, 15 USC § 80a-31(a).

Attention must be paid as well to what Congress did *not* do. Congress consciously chose to address the conflict-of-interest problem through the Act's independent-directors section, rather than through more drastic remedies such as complete disaffiliation of the companies from their advisers or compulsory internalization of the management function. See REPORT OF THE SEC ON THE PUBLIC POLICY IMPLICATIONS OF INVESTMENT COMPANY GROWTH, H.R. Rep. No. 2337, 89th Cong., 2d Sess. (1966). Congress also decided *not* to incorporate into the 1940 Act a provision, proposed by the SEC, that would have forced investment companies to seek court approval before settling claims against "insiders" that could be the target of derivative suits. See S. 3580, 76th Cong., 3d Sess., § 33(a) (1940); *Wolf v. Barkes*, 348 F.2d 994 (CA2 1965). And when Congress did intend to prevent board action from cutting off derivative suits, it said so expressly. Section 36 (b), added to the Act in 1970, performs precisely this function for derivative suits charging breach of fiduciary duty with respect to adviser's fees.[11] No similar provision exists for derivative suits of the kind involved in this case.

Congress' purpose in structuring the Act as it did is clear. It "was designed to place the unaffiliated directors in the role of 'independent watchdogs,' " *Tannenbaum v. Zeller*, 552 F.2d, at 406, who would "furnish an independent check upon the management" of investment companies, Hearings on H. R. 10065 before a Subcommittee of the House Committee on Interstate and Foreign Commerce, 76th Cong., 3d Sess. (1940). This "watchdog" control was chosen in preference to the more direct controls on behavior exemplified by the options not adopted. Indeed, when by 1970 it appeared that the "affiliated person" provision of the 1940 Act might not be adequately restraining conflicts of interest, Congress turned not to direct controls, but rather to stiffening the requirement of independence as the way to "remedy the act's deficiencies." S. Rep. No. 91-184 (1969). Without question, "[the] function of these provisions with respect to unaffiliated directors [was] to supply an independent check on management and to provide a means for the representation of shareholder interests in investment company affairs." *Id.*

---

[11] See also § 16(b) of the Securities Exchange Act of 1934, which authorizes shareholder suits to recover insider "short swing" profits on behalf of the company notwithstanding the decision of the board of directors not to sue.

In short, the structure and purpose of the ICA indicate that Congress entrusted to the independent directors of investment companies, exercising the authority granted to them by state law, the primary responsibility for looking after the interests of the funds' shareholders.[12] There may well be situations in which the independent directors could reasonably believe that the best interests of the shareholders call for a decision not to sue—as, for example, where the costs of litigation to the corporation outweigh any potential recovery. See Note, 47 FORD. L. REV. 568 (1979); Note, 44 U. CHI. L. REV., 168 (1976). See, *e.g., Tannenbaum v. Zeller, supra*; *Cramer v. General Tel. & Electronics Corp.*, 582 F.2d 259 (CA3 1978). In such cases, it would certainly be consistent with the Act to allow the independent directors to terminate a suit, even though not frivolous. Indeed, it would have been paradoxical for Congress to have been willing to rely largely upon "watchdogs" to protect shareholder interests and yet, where the "watchdogs" have done precisely that, require that they be totally muzzled.[13]

IV.

We hold today that federal courts should apply state law governing the authority of independent directors to discontinue derivative suits to the extent such law is consistent with the policies of the ICA and IAA. Moreover, we hold that Congress did not require

---

[12] As an adjunct to its main argument which rested upon the structure of the ICA, the Court of Appeals was also of the view that mutual fund directors can never be truly disinterested in suits involving their codirectors. 567 F.2d, at 1212. While lack of impartiality may or may not be true as a matter of fact in individual cases, it is not a conclusion of law required by the ICA. Congress surely would not have entrusted such critical functions as approval of advisory contracts and selection of accountants to the statutorily disinterested directors had it shared the Court of Appeals' view that such directors could never be "disinterested" where their codirectors or investment advisers were concerned. In fact, although it was speaking only of the statutory definition, Congress declared in the second section of the Act that "no person shall be deemed to be an interested person of an investment company solely by reason of ... his being a member of its board of directors or advisory board ...." 15 USC § 80a-2(a)(19). See also 15 USC § 80a-2(a)(9) ("A natural person shall be presumed not to be a controlled person within the meaning of this subchapter").

[13] As an alternative ground in support of the judgment below, respondents urge that Fed. Rule Civ. Proc. 23.1 prohibits termination of this derivative action. That Rule states that a derivative action "shall not be dismissed or compromised without the approval of the court ...." However, as Judge Friendly noted with respect to former Rule 23(c), those words apply only to voluntary settlements between derivative plaintiffs and defendants, and were intended to prevent plaintiffs from selling out their fellow shareholders. They do not apply where the plaintiffs' action is involuntarily dismissed by a court, as occurred in this case. *Wolf v. Barkes*, 348 F.2d 994 (CA2 1965). The same is true of the identically worded Rule 23.1. See WRIGHT & MILLER, FEDERAL PRACTICE AND PROCEDURE § 1839 (1972); 3B MOORE, FEDERAL PRACTICE (1978).

that States, or federal courts, absolutely forbid director termination of all nonfrivolous actions. However, since "[we] did not grant certiorari to decide [a question of state law]," *Butner v. United States*, 440 U.S. 48 (1979), and since neither the District Court nor the Court of Appeals decided the point,[14] the case is reversed and remanded for further proceedings consistent with this opinion. *Butner v. United States*; *Wallis v. Pan American Petroleum Corp., supra.*

Reversed and remanded.

[14] In this Court, the parties hotly dispute the content of the correct state rule. Compare Brief for Petitioners 36-38 with Brief for Respondents 35-39.

Topic 2 Fund's Independent Directors: Watchdogs and the Watched

Laws & Rules Highlight:

IC Act (15 USC 80a-1 *et seq.*) & Rules (17 CFR §§ 270.0-1 *et seq.*)

- Rule 0-1(a)(7) Fund Governance Standards (***Five Governance Standards*** *as condition for a fund to rely on any of the Ten Exemptive Rules*):
  - **(ii)** (*disinterested directors of the fund* ***select and nominate*** *any other disinterested director*)
  - **(iii)** (*legal counsel for the disinterested directors of the fund is an* ***independent legal counsel***)
  - **(v)** (*board's* ***annual evaluation*** *of performance and effectiveness of the board and committees of the board*)
  - **(vi)** (***quarterly sessions*** *of disinterested directors*)
  - **(vii)** (*disinterested directors being authorized to* ***hire employees and retain advisers and experts*** *to carry out their duties*)
- § 2(a)(3) (*def.* ***"affiliated person"***)
  - §§ 2(a)(3)**(A)-(F)** (*six categories of "affiliated person" of another person; reference to "control"*)
  - § 2(a)(9) (*def.* ***"control"***)
- § 2(a)(19) (*def.* ***"interested person,"*** *a* ***substantially wider concept*** *than "affiliated person"*):
  - §§ 2(a)(19)**(A)(i)-(vii)** (*seven categories of "interested person" of IC*)
  - §§ 2(a)(19)**(B)(i)-(vii)** (*seven categories of "interested person" of investment adviser of, or principal underwriter for, IC*)

> ***"Who picks the unaffiliated directors? The affiliated men pick the unaffiliated men. The men who need to be watched pick the watchdogs to watch them."***

—Statement of Abraham Pomerantz, "Conflicts of Interest in the Mutual Fund Structure," *in* Mundheim, *University of Pennsylvania Law School Conference on Mutual Funds*, 115 U. PA. L. REV. 726, 739 (1967)

Laws & Rules Highlight

IC Act § 2(a)(19) "***interested person***" of another person means:

[*edited from original statutory text*]

(A) when used with respect to an IC—	**(B) when used with respect to an IA of or principal underwriter for any IC**—
(i) any ***affiliated person*** of the IC, **(ii)** any ***member of the immediate family*** of any natural person who is an affiliated person of the IC, **(iii)** any ***interested person*** of IA of, or principal underwriter for, the IC, **(iv)** any person, partner, or employee of any person who, within the past two years, has acted as ***legal counsel*** for the IC, **(v)** any person or any affiliated person of a person (other than a registered IC) who, within the past 6-month period, has executed any ***portfolio transactions*** for, engaged in any principal transactions with, or distributed shares ***for*** the IC, ***for*** any other IC having the same IA or holding itself out as a related company, or ***for*** any account over which the IC's IA has brokerage placement discretion, **(vi)** any person or any affiliated person of a person (other than a registered IC) who, within the past 6-month period, ***has loaned money or property to*** the IC, ***to*** any other IC having the same IA or holding itself out as a related company, or ***to*** any account for which the IC's IA has borrowing authority,	**(i)** any ***affiliated person*** of such IA or principal underwriter, **(ii)** any ***member of the immediate family*** of any natural person who is an affiliated person of such IA or principal underwriter, **(iii)** any person who knowingly has any direct or indirect ***beneficial interest in***, or who is designated as trustee, executor, or guardian of any ***legal interest in***, any security issued either by such IA or principal underwriter or by a controlling person of such IA or principal underwriter, **(iv)** any person, partner, or employee of any person who, within the past two years, has acted as ***legal counsel*** for such IA or principal underwriter, **(v)** any person or any affiliated person of a person (other than a registered IC) who, during the past 6-month period, has executed any ***portfolio transactions*** for, engaged in any principal transactions with, or distributed shares ***for*** any IC for which the IA or principal underwriter serves as such, ***for*** any IC holding itself out as a company related to the IC for which the IA or principal underwriter serves as such, or ***for*** any account over which the IA has brokerage placement discretion,

<table>
<tr><th colspan="2">Laws & Rules Highlight
IC Act § 2(a)(19) “interested person” of another person means: (Continued)
[edited from original statutory text]</th></tr>
<tr><td>(vii) any natural person which the SEC by order shall have determined to be an interested person by reason of having had, within the past two years, a material business or professional relationship with the IC or its principal executive officer, or with any other IC having the same IA or principal underwriter or the principal executive officer of such other IC,

<u>PROVISO</u>: No person shall be deemed to be an “interested person” of an IC solely by reason of his (aa) being a member of the IC’s board or its advisory board, or being an owner of the IC’s securities, or (bb) being a member of the immediate family of any person specified in (aa).</td><td>(vi) any person or any affiliated person of a person (other than a registered IC) who, during the past 6-month period, has loaned money or other property to any IC for which the IA or principal underwriter serves as such, to any IC holding itself out as a company related to the IC for which the IA or principal underwriter serves as such, or to any account for which the IA has borrowing authority,

(vii) any natural person whom the SEC by order shall have determined to be an interested person by reason of having had, within the past two years, a material business or professional relationship with such IA or principal underwriter, or with the principal executive officer or any controlling person of such IA or principal underwriter.</td></tr>
</table>

Pre-Case Background Note[Biblio]

"Disinterested" Directors: Compensation and "Independence"

Mutual funds have a "*unique*" structure: they are owned by fund investors for whose benefit the funds must be operated. Practically, however, mutual funds are generally organized and operated by "external management" or "people whose primary loyalty and pecuniary interest lie outside the [funds]." To control such "inherent conflicts of interest and potential for abuses," Congress in the Investment Company Act § 10(a) requires that members of the fund board who are not "interested persons" of the fund constitute at least 40 percent of the fund board, and assigns a special role to the funds' independent directors: to supply a check on management and act as independent watchdogs for investors.[1a.]

The extent of dissociation from management required of independent directors of a fund has evolved over time. Prior to 1970, fund independent directors were merely required not to be an "***affiliated person***" of the fund, as the concept is defined in § 2(a)(3) of the IC Act. The Investment Company Amendments Act of 1970 added an expanded concept of "***interested person***," as defined in § 2(a)(19) of the IC Act; and requires that fund independent directors not to be an "interested person" of the fund, *i.e.*, they must be not only "unaffiliated" but also "disinterested."[2; 3 (§II.A)] The SEC refers to directors who are not "interested persons" of the fund as "***independent directors***."[1a (n.20)] The SEC has also taken the position that a director of a fund who is also a director of another fund managed by the same adviser generally would not be viewed as an "interested person" of the fund under § 2(a)(19) solely as a result of this relationship.[1b (n.40)] Legal commentators have criticized the SEC's assumption equating a "technically disinterested" director under § 2(a)(19) with an "in fact independent" director (Goldberg 1978);[4] pointed out the conflict between the status-based "disinterested director" concept under the IC Act and the specific decision-based "independent director" concept under state law, and the problems paradoxically resulted when states partially adopted the IC Act (Frankel 2000);[5] and proposed borrowing the doctrinal concept of "***genuine independence***" from corporate law, to replace the "***ostensible independence***" in the mutual fund governance parlance simplistically defined as a lack of interestedness (Johnson 2008).[6]

Some legal and empirical finance literatures studying independent directors' multiple board memberships and compensation, and their impact on independence have reached the following conclusions:

- Nutt (1971)[7 (§III)] (Unless the ***combined fees*** paid to an independent director become significant in relation to his total income, there is little reason to believe that increasing compensation to reflect added responsibilities impairs a director's independence. A different and difficult ***competitive problem*** arises when an independent director sits not only on multiple boards in a single fund complex but also on multiple boards in several complexes: the director may be placed in a potentially awkward position in which he must approve certain portfolio selections or investment strategies that he has been told are unwise by the adviser of another fund group which he serves.).
- Hanks (1999)[8] (***criticizing*** the *Strougo* decision: "The Act sets forth specific criteria for determining when a director will be deemed an 'interested person' of an investment company. Service on the boards of multiple funds with a common investment adviser and the receipt of 'substantial' compensation for this service are not among these criteria.").
- Tufano & Sevick (1997)[9] (empirical study examining the relation between board structure and fees charged by **mutual funds** to shareholders, found: (1) shareholder fees are lower when fund boards have a greater fraction of independent directors, and when directors sit on multiple boards in the same fund complex: but the ***concentration benefit*** does not arise from common board membership better solving agency conflicts between the fund sponsor and shareholders; rather, common board membership is closely associated with tougher negotiations and enhanced bargaining strength with outside vendors for lower service fees; (2) "some evidence" that funds whose independent directors are paid relatively ***higher directors' fees*** approve ***higher shareholder fees***.).
- Guercio *et al.* (2003)[10] (empirical study analyzing, *inter alia*, director compensation and independence in **closed-end funds**: found a *positive relation* between board's "***recurring decisions***" (such as fund expense ratios) and director compensation, suggesting that generous compensation may impair a director's objectivity; but the evidence on board's "***special circumstance decisions***" (such as fund restructurings) was *mixed*: no consistent relation between director compensation and board decisions in the shareholders' interests was found.).

The courts in the *Strougo* case (SDNY 1997) and the *Krantz* case (D. MA 2000) are divided, on the impact of independent directors' multiple board memberships and receipt of substantial compensation on independence.

Bibliography

1. SEC companion releases: **1a.** Role of Independent Directors of Investment Companies, IC-24082, 64 FR 59826 (1999); **1b.** Interpretive Matters Concerning Independent Directors of Investment Companies, IC-24083, 64 FR 59877 (1999)
2. INVESTMENT COMPANY AMENDMENTS ACT OF 1970, Pub. L. 91-547, 84 Stat. 1413 (Dec. 14, 1970)
3. Lancellotta *et al.*, *Fund Governance: A Successful, Evolving Model*, 10 VA. L. & BUS. REV. 455 (2016)
4. Goldberg, *Disinterested Directors, Independent Directors and the Investment Company Act of 1940*, 9 LOY. U. CHI. L.J. 565 (1978)
5. Frankel, *The Different Design of Corporate Governance under State Law and Federal Law and the Aftermath of the Strougo Case*, 7 INV. LAW. 3 (2000)
6. Johnson, *A Fresh Look at Director "Independence": Mutual Fund Fee Litigation and Gartenburg at Twenty-Five*, 61 VAND. L. REV. 497 (2008)
7. Nutt, *A Study of Mutual Fund Independent Directors*, 120 U. PA. L. REV. 179 (1971)
8. Hanks, *Straightening Out Strougo: The Maryland Legislative Response to Strougo v. Scudder, Stevens & Clark*, 1 VILL. J.L. & INV. MGMT. 21 (1999)
9. Tufano & Sevick, *Board Structure and Fee Setting in the U.S. Mutual Fund Industry*, 46 J. FIN. ECON. 321 (1997)
10. Guercio, Dann & Partch, *Governance and Boards of Directors in Closed-End Investment Companies*, 69 J. FIN. ECON. 111 (2003)

Case Study 1:

Case holdings: While multiple directorships within the same fund complex *do not necessarily imply* a lack of independence, receipt of significant amounts of compensation from funds managed by the same adviser ***calls into question*** whether the directors desired to "please [the adviser] to retain their lucrative directorships," *i.e.*, the directors' independence from the manager of that fund complex.

Strougo v. Scudder, Stevens & Clark, Inc.
964 F. Supp. 783 (SDNY 1997)

[***Procedural history***: Strougo v. Scudder, Stevens & Clark, Inc., 964 F. Supp. 783 (SDNY 1997), *discovery stayed sub nom.* Strougo v. Padegs, 986 F. Supp. 812 (SDNY 1997), *discovery ordered*, 1 F. Supp.2d 276 (SDNY 1998), *dismissed*, 27 F. Supp.2d 442 (SDNY 1998)]

Case Study 2:

Case holdings: The IC Act defines "*control*" as "the power to exercise a controlling influence over the management or policies of a company, unless such power is solely the result of an official position with such company." The Act expressly creates a *presumption* that a natural person is not a controlled person within the meaning of the statute. While well-compensated membership on multiple boards within a fund complex is one factor in the control crucible, it is not sufficient evidence by itself to rebut the statutory presumption of no control. Thus, an independent director's multiple board memberships in the same fund family and his receipt of substantial compensation alone are ***insufficient to rebut*** the statutory presumption that he is not controlled by the investment adviser.

Krantz v. Fidelity Mgmt. & Research Co.

98 F. Supp.2d 150 (D. Mass. 2000)

Research Topics:

Roles of mutual fund board and independent directors in China; regulatory mechanisms to ensure director independence.

Strougo v. Scudder, Stevens & Clark, Inc.

964 F. Supp. 783 (SDNY 1997)

OPINION

ROBERT W. SWEET, USDJ:

In this action alleging violations of the Investment Company Act of 1940, as amended ("ICA"), and breach of fiduciary duty under the common law, defendants Scudder, Stevens & Clark, Inc. ("Scudder"), Padegs, Bratt, Villani, Fiedler, Nolen, Da Costa, Nogueira, and nominal defendant the Brazil Fund ("the Fund"), have moved to dismiss the complaint of Robert Strougo for failure to state a claim, pursuant to Fed. R. Civ. P. 12(b)(6), for failure to make pre-suit demand, pursuant to Fed. R. Civ. P. 23.1, and for failure to plead with particularity, pursuant to Fed. R. Civ. P. 9(b). For the reasons set forth below, the motions will be granted in part and denied in part.

Parties

Strougo purchased 1,000 shares of the Fund on January 11, 1993, and has held shares continuously thereafter.

The Fund, a nominal defendant in this action, is a Maryland corporation whose principal executive office is located in New York, New York. The Fund is a non-diversified, closed-end investment company that invests in the securities of Brazilian companies. Shares in the Fund trade on the New York Stock Exchange. Scudder is a Delaware corporation whose principal offices are located in New York, New York. Scudder serves as investment advisor to and manager of the Fund. It is a registered investment advisor under the Investment Advisers Act of 1940, as amended.

Padegs is chairman of the board and a director of the Fund. He is also a managing director of Scudder and serves on both Scudder's board and the boards of other funds managed by Scudder. Bratt is president and a director of the Fund. Bratt is also a managing director of Scudder and serves on the boards of other funds managed by Scudder. Villani is a director of the Fund. He is also president and managing director of Scudder and serves on both Scudder's board and the boards of other funds managed by Scudder. Scudder, Padegs, Bratt and Villani will be referred to as the "*Scudder Defendants.*"

Fiedler is a director of the Fund and serves on the boards of seven other funds managed by Scudder. He received $30,003 in compensation for serving on boards of funds managed by Scudder and accrued $366,075 in deferred compensation for service on two Scudder funds. Nolen is a director of the Fund. He also serves on the boards of fourteen other funds managed by Scudder. Nolen's aggregate compensation for service on these boards was $132,023 in 1994. Nogueira is a director and resident Brazilian director of the Fund. He serves on the boards of three other funds managed by Scudder. Nogueira's aggregate compensation for serving on these boards was $54,997 in 1994. Da Costa is a director and resident Brazilian director of the Fund. Da Costa was compensated $13,868 for serving on the Fund's board in 1994. * * * *

The Facts

On a motion to dismiss under rule 12(b)(6), the facts alleged in the complaint are presumed to be true, and all factual inferences are drawn in the plaintiff's favor. *Mills v. Polar Molecular Corporation*, 12 F.3d 1170 (2d Cir. 1993). Accordingly, the facts presented here are drawn from the allegations of the Complaint and do not constitute findings of fact by the Court.

This action arises from the 1995 decision by the board of directors of the Brazil Fund, a closed-end investment company incorporated under Maryland law and traded on the New York Stock Exchange, to increase the Fund's capital by offering the Fund's existing shareholders rights to purchase additional shares of newly issued stock (the "Rights Offering"). Strougo asserts that Scudder and each of the directors of the Fund breached their respective fiduciary duties of loyalty and due care as a result of the development and implementation of the Rights Offering.

Scudder created the Brazil Fund in 1988. * * * * Because closed-end funds operate with a fixed number of shares, they have limited options for obtaining capital to make new investments. Once a fund's initial capital has been fully invested, new investments generally can be made only if the fund sells existing portfolio holdings. Other options for raising capital include secondary public offerings at net asset value, or rights offerings to current investors at or below NAV. Scudder is paid a fee equal to a percentage of the Fund's net assets. From December 1994 through November 1995, the Fund's net assets declined significantly, dropping to $271 million on November 16, 1995, from $377 million on December 31, 1994. As the Fund's net assets materially declined, so did Scudder's fee.

As a result of the decline in net assets, as well as in Scudder's fees, Strougo alleges that defendants decided to raise additional capital to increase the Fund's net assets, and thereby restore Scudder's annual compensation. On October 13, 1995, defendants announced that the Fund would conduct the Rights Offering, whereby the Fund would issue transferable rights to its shareholders. Each Fund shareholder received one right for each share held; three rights entitled the holder to purchase an additional share at the "Subscription Price" of $15.75. The rights were transferrable; that is, if the shareholders did not wish to exercise their rights to purchase additional shares, they were entitled to sell the rights to any purchaser. The rights expired on December 15, 1995.

The Subscription Price was 30.19% below the Fund's NAV and resulted in per share NAV being reduced by $1.88. This $1.88 per share dilution was accompanied by a contemporaneous decline in the market price of the Fund's shares. The price of the Fund's stock declined, dropping $2.125 per share from $25.125 the day before the Rights Offering was announced to $23.25 one week later. Strougo alleges that as a result of the "coercive" Rights Offering, plaintiff and the other shareholders of the Fund, as well as the Fund itself, suffered harm in the form of market and dilution damages. The Complaint alleges that Rights Offerings "cause a loss to existing shareholders" because they "dilute the pro rata holdings of ... stock held by the fund allocable to existing shares, and because investment banking fees and other transactional costs are incurred by the closed-end fund." Moreover, Strougo alleges that the market value of the Fund's shares was depressed below what it would have been had the Rights Offering not been made.

The Complaint alleges six separate claims.... Claims V and VI, also brought derivatively on behalf of the Fund, and against all defendants except the fund, allege breaches of fiduciary duty owed to the Fund. Claim V is brought pursuant to ICA § 36(a) and Claim VI is brought pursuant to the common law.... With respect to Claims V and VI, which are derivative in nature,[1] the Complaint alleges that demand would be futile for the following reasons: (1) the board participated or acquiesced in the alleged wrongful acts or intentionally or recklessly failed to inform themselves of the harms and benefits associated with the Rights Offering; (2) a majority of board members are "controlled by or financially dependent" on Scudder, by virtue of their compensation for sitting on the

[1] Although Claim I, for violation of § 36(b), is "derivative," in the sense that it is brought on behalf of the corporation, demand is not required, because the shareholders are asserting a right the statute vests in the shareholders on behalf of the company, not in the company itself. *Daily Income Fund, Inc. v. Fox*, 464 U.S. 523 (1984).

boards of other Scudder funds; (3) because the entire board was responsible for the wrongful acts, the directors cannot independently determine whether a suit should be brought against themselves; (4) the wrongful acts constituted a waste of the Fund's assets, which is unprotected by the business judgment rule; (5) the wrongful acts constituted violations of federal securities law and fiduciary duties, which are not protected by the business judgment rule; and (6) the Fund's directors' and officers' insurance coverage would be voided if the Fund commenced proceedings against the directors.

Discussion

* * * *

III. *The Derivative Claims Under ICA § 36(a) & Maryland Law*

III-A. Exhaustion of Intracorporate Remedies

The defendants contend that the derivative claims under § 36(a) and the common law of Maryland should be dismissed for failure to allege with particularity, as required by Fed. R. Civ. P. 23.1, the reasons he has not made a demand on the Fund's directors and shareholders prior to instituting this action.

As the Fund is a Maryland corporation, Maryland law governs whether demand is required and the conditions that will excuse demand. See *Kamen v. Kemper Fin. Servs.*, 500 U.S. 90 (1991); see also .... As a matter of federal law, Fed. R. Civ. P. 23.1 itself requires that the grounds for excusing demand under state law be pleaded with particularity. See *Grill v. Hobiltzell*, 771 F. Supp. 709, 710 n.2 (D. Md. 1991), citing *Kamen*. Under Maryland law, courts ordinarily "will not entertain a derivative suit by a stockholder on behalf of a corporation until it appears that the intra-corporate remedies have been unsuccessfully pursued by the complaining stockholder." *Parish v. Maryland & Virginia Milk Producers Ass'n, Inc.*, 242 A.2d 512 (Md. 1968). This means that, in general, the stockholder must make a demand for remedial action on the corporation itself, first by application to the directors, and then by application to the body of the stockholders. *Id.*, citing *Eisler v. Eastern States Corp.*, 35 A.2d 118 (Md. 1943). However, prior demand on the directors and shareholders is excused when it would be futile. The futility exception is to be applied in a practical, common-sense manner. *Parish.*

III-A-1. Demand on Directors

Strougo's principal argument for excusing demand against the directors is that six of the Brazil Fund's seven directors have disqualifying financial and professional interests as a result of their paid service on the boards of other Scudder-managed funds, such that they could not impartially consider a demand or impartially prosecute this action against Scudder or themselves.

Under Maryland law, demand is excused where the directors are "dominated and controlled" by persons alleged to be guilty of the misconduct charged in the complaint. See *Grill, supra*; see also *Rales v. Blasband*, 634 A.2d 927 (Del. 1993) (under Delaware law, to establish lack of independence excusing demand, plaintiff must show that directors are "beholden" to interested party or so under interested party's influence that discretion is "sterilized"). Padegs, Bratt and Villani, who are all employed directly by Scudder, are concededly "interested" in the Rights Offering. However, the defendants contend that the remaining board members, Fiedler, Nolen, Nogueira and Da Costa, are "independent" of Scudder, and therefore are able evaluate a demand and prosecute any action on behalf of the Fund. They contend that the receipt of director's fees and service on the boards of multiple funds managed by Scudder are insufficient to render these defendants "interested" in the transaction.

Ordinarily, allegations that directors receive fees for their services are not sufficient to demonstrate demand futility. See *Kamen v. Kemper Fin. Servs.*, 939 F.2d 458 (7th Cir. 1991); (applying Maryland law). If the opposite were true, the futility exception would swallow the demand rule, since most corporate directors receive remuneration for their service. *Id.* Similarly, allegations of business relationships among directors are generally insufficient to overcome the presumption of independence enjoyed by corporate directors. See *Id.* (fact that independent directors come to board on recommendation of corporate insiders does not excused demand); *Grill, supra* (vague assertions that "personal relationships" among directors make it unlikely that board would authorize suit against current or former members insufficient to excuse demand); see also *Langner v. Brown*, 913 F. Supp. 260 (SDNY 1996) (under Delaware law, cross-directorships insufficient to create "interest" excusing demand).

Here, however, Strougo has alleged not only that the purportedly independent directors receive remuneration for their service on the Brazil Fund, but that three of the four—Fiedler, Nolen and Nogueira—receive substantial remuneration from their service on the boards of other mutual funds managed by Scudder. He characterizes Fiedler, Nolen and Nogueira as Scudder's "house directors," essentially as interested in benefitting Scudder (at the potential expense of fund shareholders) as Scudder's own employees.

In *Olesh v. Dreyfus Corp.*, 1995 WL 500491 (EDNY 1995), the district court for the Eastern District of New York held that demand upon the directors was futile because the complaint sought a determination that the directors were "interested" by virtue of their receipt of directors fees for sitting on multiple boards managed by a single advisor. *Olesh* involved a merger that, under the ICA, required the approval of 75% of the non-interested directors of the fund. The court reasoned that demand was futile under these circumstances because, in order for the merger to be approved, the purportedly disinterested directors would have to be replaced if the suit were successful. Thus, the directors' interests in retaining their remuneration and positions were directly at odds with instituting a suit that might ultimately deprive them of these benefits; *id.*[2]

Although *Olesh* is distinguishable on the grounds that the suit there would pose a more direct threat to the directors' board positions and remuneration than the present suit would present to the directors of the Brazil Fund, *Olesh* provides some support for the proposition that holding multiple paid directorships of funds managed by the same advisor can compromise a director's independence from the advisor sufficiently to excuse demand under some circumstances. See also, *Rales, supra* (court excused demand because of "reasonable doubt" as to independence of board members who were employed by corporations of which the alleged wrongdoers were directors or majority stock-holders).

The leading commentator on Maryland Corporation Law has stated that demand should not be excused "so long as there are two directors whose involvement in the facts underlying the claim is not so great as to call into question their compliance with the standard of conduct of § 2-405.1" of the Maryland Corporations and Associations Code. HANKS, MARYLAND CORPORATION LAW, § 7.21[c] at 269 (1994-1 Suppl.). Section 2-405.1(a) provides that a director shall perform his or her duties "in good faith," "in a manner he reasonably believes to be in the best interests of the corporation" and "with the care that

---

[2] In dictum, the court also stated that demand would not be excused by allegations that the directors' "close business ties" to the fund advisor spoiled their independence; id. However, the court engaged in no explicit discussion of whether the allegations that paid service on the boards of multiple funds managed by the advisor would be sufficient to call into question the directors' independence from the advisor.

an ordinarily prudent person in a like position would use under similar circumstances." These statutory provisions are Maryland's codification of the fiduciary duties of a director. "Good faith" is "the absence of any desire to obtain a personal benefit or a benefit for some person other than the corporation." HANKS, MARYLAND CORP. LAW, § 6.6[b] at 163 (1992 Suppl.).

Here, the fact that all but one of the directors who approved the Rights Offering received substantial compensation from funds managed by Scudder, and the allegation that, in approving the rights offering, these directors put the interests of Scudder in increasing their advisor's fees before the interests of the Fund and its shareholders "call into question" whether there was a desire on the part of the directors to benefit Scudder, rather than the Fund, in order to please Scudder to retain their lucrative directorships. In Maryland, two is the minimum number of directors necessary to form a committee to consider a demand. HANKS, MARYLAND CORPORATION LAW, § 7.21[c] at 269, n.173 (1994-1 Suppl.). Because only one of the directors does not serve on multiple Scudder boards, the Board could not appoint a committee of sufficiently disinterested directors to consider a demand by a shareholder to institute litigation, and thus demand would be futile.

The defendants contend that imposing a rule that would effectively eliminate multiple directorships in complexes of funds managed by a single advisor is inappropriate for several reasons. First, they contend that such practices are common and provide substantial benefits to investors, such as reduced costs and the ability of directors to use their knowledge gained from one fund in the service of others. Moreover, they contend, the ICA's definitions of an "interested person" do not include a limitation on directorships of multiple funds in a fund complex. Similarly, the SEC has not prohibited such multiple directorships, but merely required their disclosure in proxy materials. See *Amendments to Proxy Rules for Registered Investment Companies*, 57 SEC Dock. 2019, 2025 & n.26 (Oct. 13, 1994) ("receipt of substantial amount of compensation from a fund complex is not necessarily determinative of the director's independence").

Although multiple directorships are not necessarily determinative of a director's independence, either under the statute or the SEC's interpretations, where, as here, a director's actions are alleged to establish that he or she may be acting in the interests of the advisor, the receipt of substantial remuneration from a fund complex does call into question the director's independence from the manager of that complex. Moreover, the rule would not eliminate multiple directorships. It would require only that a sufficient number of directors without such multiple directorships serve on a board so that a litigation committee could be convened to consider proposed litigation.

Accordingly, demand on the board of directors is excused as futile.

* * * *

III-B. Failure to State a Claim

* * * *

III-B-2. "Personal Misconduct" Under § 36(a)

Defendants urge that the § 36(a) claim should be dismissed because Strougo has failed to allege "personal misconduct" within the meaning of the statute.

Congress enacted the ICA in response to concerns that the existing securities laws did not protect mutual fund shareholders from potential abuse by fund advisors, whose relationships with the funds they manage are "fraught with potential conflicts of interest." *Burks v. Lasker*, 441 U.S. 471 (1979). Most of the provisions of the ICA prohibit narrowly defined conduct; § 36, in contrast, was designed as a "reservoir of fiduciary obligations" to prevent more "subtle abuses ... not otherwise specifically dealt with in the Act." *Brown v. Bullock*, 194 F. Supp. 207 (SDNY 1961), *aff'd* 294 F.2d 415 (2d Cir. 1961). Such abuses include a director's "lack of independence resulting in the subordination of the stockholders' interest to that of management"; *id.* Strougo has alleged that precisely such a lack of independence led the directors to approve the Rights Offering to benefit Scudder, without regard to the consequences for the Fund.

Defendants read the phrase "involving personal misconduct" to require that a plaintiff allege more than a "mere" breach of fiduciary duty. They note that most cases imposing liability under § 36(a) have involved allegations of fraud, self-dealing, or some likelihood of direct personal financial advantage to be derived from the transactions in question. See, *e.g., SEC v. Commonwealth Chem. Sec. Inc.*, 410 F. Supp. 1002 (SDNY 1976) (Section 36(a) violation for self-dealing), *aff'd in relevant part, modified in part*, 574 F.2d 90 (2d Cir. 1978); *Fogel v. Chestnutt*, 533 F.2d 731 (2d Cir. 1975) ("*Fogel I*") (violation for failure to adequately disclose possibility of recapture).

In further support of this argument, the defendants refer to the legislative history of the 1970 amendments to § 36. Section 36(a) formerly permitted suits only if they were based upon "gross misconduct or abuse of trust." In 1967, the SEC proposed that the standard be lowered to a simple "breach of fiduciary duty." The Senate rejected this proposal, noting that the lower standard would permit SEC sanctions "based on 'nothing more than a difference of opinion about the most debatable management problems.' " S. 1659, 90th Cong., 1st Sess. § 20 (1967).

The SEC's proposed bill did not pass, and when reintroduced in the next Congress it contained the additional words "involving personal misconduct." In reporting the revised bill, the Senate committee stated:

> The amended § 36(a) will enable the Commission to move against officers, directors, and advisory board members of an investment company and its investment advisers or principal underwriters if they engage in conduct which violates prevailing standards of fiduciary duty involving personal misconduct.
>
> This section is intended to deal only with such violations committed by individuals. It is not intended to provide a basis for the Commission to undertake a general revision of the practices or structures of the investment company industry. On the other hand, your committee does not intend to limit the Commission under this section to situations where actual intent to violate the law can be shown or to acts of affirmative misconduct. In appropriate cases, nonfeasance of duty or abdication of responsibility would constitute a breach of fiduciary duty involving personal misconduct.

Senate Report at 34, S. 3724, 90th Cong., 2d Sess., § 20. (July 1, 1968).

However, the Second Circuit has concluded that § 36(a), as amended, imposes fiduciary duties "at least as stringent as those at common law." *Tannenbaum v. Zeller*, 552 F.2d 402 (2d Cir. 1977). Common law breach of fiduciary duty is properly pleaded where, as here, corporate directors are alleged to have put their interests or the interests of another before the interests of the corporation. The legislative history cited by the defendants is not to the contrary. First, consistent with *Tannenbaum*'s equation of § 36(a)'s standards with common law standards, the Senate report quoted above indicates that a defendant will be liable if he "engage[s] in conduct which violates *prevailing standards of fiduciary duty* ...." Moreover, the "personal misconduct" language appears to be intended to prevent generalized SEC attacks on industry practices that would not violate traditional standards of fiduciary duty, as opposed to individual suits involving accepted breaches of fiduciary duty. The legislative history does not indicate an intention to require allegations of fraud or self-dealing. Indeed, the Senate Committee noted that the section did not require a showing of "affirmative misconduct," such as fraud. Instead, the Committee stated that "in appropriate cases, nonfeasance of duty or abdication of responsibility would constitute a breach of fiduciary duty involving personai misconduct." Senate Report at 34; see also *In re Nuveen Fund Litig.*, 1996 WL 328006 (ND Ill. 1996) ("*Nuveen IV*").

Although, as defendants note, most of the cases finding § 36(a) liability involved fraud or self-dealing, defendants do not cite any case law squarely rejecting a claim under § 36(a) for failure to allege fraud or self-dealing.[3] Moreover, the court in Nuveen held that a claim of violation of § 36(a) was stated by allegations that arguably involve less "personal misconduct" than that charged here. See *In re Nuveen Fund Litig.*, 1996 WL 328003 (ND Ill. 1996) ("*Nuveen III*"). * * * *

Here, Strougo has alleged not only that the directors were negligent in failing to scrutinize Scudder's proposed Rights Offering, but that they affirmatively acted to benefit Scudder by approving the Rights Offering without regard to the Fund's interests because of the financial benefits they received from sitting on the boards of multiple Scudder funds. By placing the interests of self or management before the interests of the corporation, such conduct violates the "prevailing standards of fiduciary duty" Congress intended to incorporate into § 36(a).

Accordingly, as to the Scudder Defendants and defendants Fiedler, Nolen and Nogueira, there are sufficient allegations of "personal misconduct" to satisfy § 36(a). As to defendant Da Costa, however, there is no basis for inferring that he is so beholden to Scudder that he would not act in the Fund's best interests. Therefore, the § 36(a) claim against Da Costa will be dismissed.

* * * *

III-B-4. Breach of Fiduciary Duty Under Maryland Law

Under Maryland law, corporate directors owe a fiduciary duty to the corporation and its shareholders. [citations omitted]. To plead a claim for breach of fiduciary duty, a plaintiff must allege: "(1) the presence of [a] fiduciary relationship between the parties; (2) a duty created in the fiduciary by this relationship, to act on behalf of the other party; (3) a

---

[3] *Olesh* is not to the contrary. In *Olesh*, the court rejected plaintiffs' attempt to invoke § 36(a), because the plaintiffs did not allege any misconduct against the officers of the fund manager, who were not even named as defendants. Here, in contrast, the Fund's directors are named as defendants and alleged to have personally breached their duty of loyalty to the funds.

breach of this duty by the fiduciary; and (4) damage to the other party caused by the breach." [citations omitted]. Defendants contend that Strougo has not alleged a breach of any fiduciary duty.

MARYLAND CORPS. AND ASSN'S CODE ANN. § 2-405.1(a)(1) requires corporate directors to perform their duties in "good faith." "Good faith" is generally synonymous with the duty of loyalty or the duty of fair dealing. HANKS, MARYLAND CORPORATION LAW, § 6.6(b) (1995-1 Supp.). Whether a director breached his duties of loyalty and good faith are fact-intensive questions. It is ordinarily inappropriate to resolve such questions on a motion to dismiss. [citations omitted]. * * * *

Directors seeking the protection of the business judgment rule "can neither appear on both sides of a transaction nor expect to derive any personal financial benefit from it in the sense of self-dealing, as opposed to a benefit which devolves upon the corporation or all stockholders generally." *Aronson v. Lewis*, 473 A.2d 805 (Del. 1984). Thus, to enjoy the benefits of the business judgment rule and avoid judicial inquiry into a director's decision, the director must be independent of the interested director(s); *id.* (requirement of director independence from interested persons inheres in business judgment rule). To be independent, the director's decision must be based on the merits of the transaction under consideration rather than extraneous considerations or influences that would "convert an otherwise valid business decision into a faithless act"; *id.* A director who is dominated or otherwise controlled by or beholden to an individual or entity interested in the transaction at issue is interested; *id.* A proper allegation that a director has an interest in an action creates a *prima facie* case that the director did not act in good faith. HANKS, MARYLAND CORPORATION LAW, § 6.6(b).

Here, as discussed above, all of the Scudder Defendants are interested in the Rights Offering and three of the four purportedly "independent" directors are alleged to be Scudder's "house" directors, receiving substantial compensation for service given to other Scudder managed funds. This close and financially rewarding relationship with Scudder is sufficient to call into question the independence and disinterestedness of these directors with respect to a Rights Offering that would admittedly benefit Scudder and dilute non-participating shareholders' interests. Accordingly, the motion to dismiss the Maryland breach of fiduciary duty claims will be denied. However, because defendant Da Costa is not alleged to have received compensation for service on multiple boards of Scudder-managed funds, the state law claims against him will be dismissed. * * * *

V. *The Control Person Claim*

Strougo also alleges that the Scudder Defendants caused violations of the ICA by the other directors, in violation of § 48(a) of the ICA, which provides:

> It shall be unlawful for any person, directly or indirectly, to cause to be done any act or thing through or by means of any other person which it would be unlawful for such person to do under the provisions of this subchapter or any rule, regulation, or order thereunder.

Strougo contends that the purportedly "independent" directors of the Fund were in fact controlled by the Scudder Defendants, who "caused" the independent directors to approve the Rights Offering. In support of this contention, he alleges that three of the four independent directors earned very substantial compensation from various Scudder-managed funds, and thus could exert control over their votes.

In *Harriman v. E.I. DuPont de Nemours & Co.*, 372 F. Supp. 101 (D. Del. 1974), a case alleging control person liability under both § 48(a) of the ICA and § 20(a) of the Securities Exchange Act of 1934, the court observed that the "control person" provision of the Securities Exchange Act "is remedial and is to be construed liberally. It has been interpreted as requiring only some indirect means of discipline or influence short of actual direction"; *id.* Such indirect means of discipline or influence may include "business relationships [other than stock ownership], interlocking directors, family relationships and a myriad of other factors"; *id.*

The allegation that, through their control of the substantial payments made for service on the boards of multiple Scudder funds, the Scudder Defendants had the means to indirectly discipline or influence Fieldler, Nolen and Nogueira is sufficient to survive a motion to dismiss.

Conclusion

For the reasons set forth above, defendants' motions are hereby granted in part and denied in part. Specifically:

1. The Complaint as to Da Costa is dismissed in its entirety; * * * *

3. The motions to dismiss the derivative claims under § 36(a) and Maryland law (Claims V and VI) are denied, except with respect to defendant Da Costa;

4. The Scudder Defendants' motion to dismiss the § 48(a) control person claim (Claim III) is denied; and * * * * It is so ordered.

Krantz v. Fidelity Mgmt. & Research Co.

98 F. Supp.2d 150 (D. Mass. 2000)

OPINION BY: SARIS, U.S. District Court Judge.

MEMORANDUM AND ORDER

I. Introduction

Plaintiff Richard T. Krantz, a shareholder in two Fidelity mutual funds, claims that the directors are under the control of the investment adviser in violation of § § 10(a), 15(c) and 36(a) of the Investment Company Act of 1940 ("ICA"), as amended, and that the investment adviser's fees are excessive under § 36(b) of the ICA.[1] The linchpin of these claims is that the same nine "independent" directors serve on the twelve-person boards of all 237 Fidelity investment companies and receive substantial annual salaries ranging from $220,500 to $273,500. Plaintiff seeks to recover the "excessive compensation" received by defendants pursuant to agreements with the two funds.

The defendants move to dismiss the amended complaint pursuant to Fed. R. Civ. P. 12(b)(6), arguing that allegations of multiple board membership and substantial compensation—absent other indicia of control—are insufficient to support inferences that the directors are controlled by the funds' investment adviser or that the fees are excessive. After hearing, the defendants' motion to dismiss is ***ALLOWED*** except with respect to the last count alleging excessive investment adviser's fees.

II. Facts

When all reasonable inferences are drawn in favor of the nonmoving party, the amended complaint alleges the following facts (many of which are disputed by defendants).

The plaintiff is a shareholder in two Fidelity mutual funds ("Two Funds"), the Fidelity Equity-Income II Fund and the Fidelity Value Fund. The defendants are the investment adviser to the Fidelity group of mutual funds, Fidelity Management and Research Company; the underwriter of the funds, Fidelity Distributors Corporation; and Fidelity's

---

[1] The plaintiff's verified amended complaint asserts: a claim under § § 10(a) and 15(c)(Count I); a claim under § 36(a) (Count II); and an excessive fees claim under § 36(b) (Count III).

parent company, FMR Corporation (collectively "Fidelity").[2]

Nine members of the twelve-person boards within the Fidelity fund complex serve on the boards of all of Fidelity's 237 investment companies and each receives a substantial annual salary ranging from $220,500 to $273,500. Their compensation exceeds the amounts paid to other, similarly situated trustees. Most of these "independent" trustees have other full-time employment as well as directorial positions. They were all appointed by the defendants, and as a "practical matter," according to the amended complaint, they serve "at the pleasure" of the defendants. Fidelity has designated these directors as independent, that is, not affiliated with, or controlled by defendants. The prospectus for each of the Two Funds states: "The trustees serve as trustees for other Fidelity Funds. The majority of trustees are not otherwise affiliated with Fidelity."

As evidence of the trustees' lack of disinterestedness, the amended complaint asserts that the trustees failed to oppose defendants in the following respects. *First*, although three funds within the 237 fund complex have performed abysmally, the trustees have never replaced FMR. *Second*, the trustees have never considered internalizing the Two Funds' management. *Third*, the trustees have permitted FMR to receive and retain compensation from the broker-dealers who execute portfolio transactions for the Two Funds (*i.e.*, soft dollars), and as a result have caused the Two Funds to pay higher commissions than they otherwise would have. "Soft dollar" arrangements are the packaging of research services fees with brokerage commissions by investment advisers. The adviser often receives a "rebate" as a part of the packaged deal. These practices increased the average commission rate per share for the Two Funds from 1996 to 1997, and resulted in an excessive volume of portfolio transactions.

The amended complaint also asserts that the adviser's fees are excessive....

III. Discussion

* * * *

III-B. *Multiple Board Membership*

The ICA establishes a scheme designed to address potential conflicts of interests

---

[2] The original complaint in this action was filed on September 30, 1998, and the defendants moved to dismiss the complaint on January 11, 1999. The Court heard oral argument on April 28, 1999, and on the following day, plaintiff moved to amend the complaint. Plaintiff filed an amended complaint on June 14, 1999, and on August 6, 1999, the defendants again moved to dismiss.

inherent in the management of investment companies which provide mutual fund services and "typically are organized and underwritten by the same firm that serves as the company's 'investment adviser.' " *Kamen v. Kemper Fin. Serv., Inc.*, 500 U.S. 90 (1991). Among other things, the Act requires that at least forty percent of an investment company's directors be financially independent of the investment adviser. See 15 USC § § 80a-10(a) & 80a-2(a)(19)(A). Specifically, § 10(a) provides:

> No registered investment company shall have a board of directors more than 60 per centum of the members of which are persons who are interested persons of such registered company.

This provision is the "cornerstone of the ICA's effort to control conflicts of interest within the mutual funds." *Burks v. Lasker*, 441 U.S. 471 (1979). Its purpose is "to place unaffiliated directors in the role of 'independent watchdogs,' " who would "furnish an independent check upon the management of investment companies"; *id.*

The term "interested person" is defined to include "any affiliated person" of an investment company, investment adviser, or principal underwriter. See 15 USC § § 80a-2(a)(19)(A)(i) & (B)(i). The term "affiliated person," in turn, is defined to include "any person directly or indirectly ... controlled by ... such other person"; § 80a-2(a)(3)(C). The Act defines "control" as "the power to exercise a controlling influence over the management or policies of a company, unless such power is solely the result of an official position with such company"; § 80a-2(a)(9). The statute expressly creates a presumption against control: "[a] natural person shall be presumed not to be a controlled person within the meaning of this subchapter"; *id.* The statute states that any such presumption may be rebutted by "evidence," *id.*, but it does not state what kind. Any agreement entered into by an investment company must be approved by a majority of these independent directors; § 80a-15(c).[3] Section 36(a)[4] has been construed to provide a cause of action against any

---

[3] 15 USC § 80a-15(c) states in relevant part:

It shall be unlawful for any registered investment company having a board of directors to enter into, renew, or perform any contract or agreement, written or oral, whereby a person undertakes regularly to serve or act as investment adviser of or principal underwriter for such company, unless the terms of such contract or agreement and any renewal thereof have been approved by the vote of a majority of directors, who are not parties to such contract or agreement or interested persons of any such party, cast in person at a meeting called for the purpose of voting on such approval.

[4] Section 36(a) provides:

The Commission is authorized to bring an action in the proper district court of the United States, or in the

director who engages in an act "constituting a breach of fiduciary duty involving personal misconduct."

Neither the ICA nor the SEC proscribes the use of interlocking boards within mutual fund complexes. Although the SFC does not regulate multi-board membership, it requires disclosure of the aggregate compensation received by directors who serve on multiple fund boards. See *Amendments to Proxy Rules for Registered Investment Companies*, IC-20614 (1994). The pivotal issue is whether well-compensated service by non-employee directors on multiple boards of mutual funds within a fund complex managed by a single fund adviser can, in some circumstances, rebut the statutory presumption of non-control and render the directors "interested" persons within the meaning of the ICA. Essentially, plaintiffs press the view that mutual fund directors can never truly be disinterested when they serve on multiple boards and are paid well.

Courts have looked at various factors to determine whether directors are controlled persons. First, the mere fact that a director is compensated, even handsomely, for service does not constitute a disqualifying interest. See *Kamen v. Kemper Fin. Servs.*, 939 F.2d 458 (7th Cir. 1991). However, director compensation might be relevant if the investment adviser has the power to set, or even influence, the level of compensation received by the directors or remove them from office. See *Verkouteren v. Blackrock Fin. Mgmt., Inc.*, 37 F. Supp. 2d 256 (SDNY 1999), *aff'd* 208 F.3d 204 (2d Cir. 2000). Second, allegations that non-employee directors failed to resist a course of action suggested by the investment adviser which prejudiced the funds' shareholders might serve as evidence to rebut the statutory presumption; *id.* However, an allegation is insufficient if it "more plausibly suggests a dereliction of duty on the part of the outside directors than the fact that said

---

United States court of any territory or other place subject to the jurisdiction of the United States, alleging that a person serving or acting in one or more of the following capacities has engaged within five years of the commencement of the action or is about to engage in any act or practice constituting a breach of fiduciary duty involving personal misconduct in respect of any registered investment company for which such person so serves or acts—

(1) as officer, director, member of any advisory board, investment adviser, or depositor; or

(2) as principal underwriter, if such registered company is an open-end company, unit investment trust, or face-amount certificate company.

If such allegations are established, the court may enjoin such persons from acting in any or all such capacities either permanently or temporarily and award such injunctive or other relief against such person as may be reasonable and appropriate in the circumstances, having due regard to the protection of investors and to the effectuation of the policies declared in § 80a-1(b) of this title.

directors are being 'controlled' by defendant"; *id.* Third, while well-compensated membership on multiple boards within a fund complex is one factor in the control crucible, most courts have concluded that it is not sufficient evidence by itself to rebut the statutory presumption. See *id.* (rejecting a control claim where the complaint alleged service by "independent directors" on twenty-one boards with compensation ranging from $140,000 to $160,000); *Krantz v. Prudential Invs. Fund Mgmt. LLC*, 77 F. Supp.2d 559 (D. NJ 1999) (rejecting a claim that overlapping service on between 15 and 38 boards with an average compensation of $90,000 constituted control); *Langner v. Brown*, 913 F. Supp. 260 (SDNY 1996) (holding that "just as the mere receipt of director fees does not constitute a disqualifying interest as a matter of law, so too are cross-directorships insufficient to create interests"); *Olesh v. Dreyfus Corp.*, 1995 WL 500491 (EDNY 1995) (holding that directors who sat on over fifteen boards and received over $50,000 in compensation were not interested.).

One court took a more jaundiced view of lucrative multiple directorships:

> Although multiple directorships are not necessarily determinative of a director's independence, either under the statute or the SEC's interpretations, where, as here, a director's actions are alleged to establish that he or she may be acting in the interests of the adviser, the receipt of substantial remuneration from a fund complex does call into question the director's independence from the manager of the complex.

Strougo v. Scudder, Stevens & Clark, Inc., 964 F. Supp. 783 (SDNY 1997) (excusing a demand on the board of directors as futile under Maryland law where three directors sat on between four and fifteen boards and made between $54,000 and $81,753), *reh'g denied*, 1997 WL 473566 (SDNY 1997) (reiterating that "well-compensated service on multiple boards of funds managed by a single fund adviser can, in some circumstances, be indistinguishable in all relevant respects from employment by the fund manager which, admittedly renders a director interested"); *accord Strougo v. Bassini*, 1 F. Supp.2d 268 (SDNY 1998) (refusing to dismiss for refusal to make a demand where all the directors sat on between 5 and 9 boards and made $42,000).

The SEC has set forth factors relevant to a determination of control over directors: 1) selection or nomination of the director by the controlling party; 2) existence of family ties; 3) social relations; 4) former business associations between the director and the controlling person; 5) the amount of time spent by directors at meetings; 6) respective ages; 7) participation in recommending, evaluating and terminating policies; 8) independent knowledge of corporate affairs; 9) interlocking directors and officers, together with share ownership; and 10) actual domination and operation. See *First Australia Fund, Inc.*, SEC No-Action Letter (Oct. 8, 1987). Recently, the SEC reaffirmed that "a director of a fund who also is a director of another fund managed by the same adviser generally would not be viewed as an interested person of the fund under § 2(a)(19) solely as a result of this relationship." *Interpretive Matters Concerning Independent Directors of Investment Companies*, IC-24083 (1999) (citing H.R. Rep. No. 1382, 91st Cong., 2nd Sess. 15 (1970); S. Rep. No. 184, 91st Cong., 1st Sess. 34 (1969)).

The SEC has proposed a rule that: (1) fund boards should have a majority of independent directors; (2) that independent directors should select and nominate any new independent directors; (3) the directors should have outside legal counsel to insure they get objective advice; and (4) fund shareholders should have more specific information on which to judge the independence of their funds' directors. See *Role of Independent Directors of Investment Companies*, IC-24082 (1999) (proposing rule changes emphasizing disclosures to shareholders). With respect to the last proposal, the SEC stated:

> The Commission now is proposing to require disclosure of the total number of portfolios, rather than registered investment companies, that a director oversees. In today's environment, where a complex may choose between organizing a single series company with multiple portfolios or multiple investment companies each with a single portfolio, we believe that requiring disclosure of the number of portfolios that a director oversees would provide a more accurate picture of the director's responsibilities.

Id. The proposed rule does not include a prohibition against service on multiple boards.

Plaintiff makes three arguments to support his claim that the Fidelity directors are not disinterested. The first argument is semantic. He argues that the statement in the prospectus that the trustees serve as trustees for other Fidelity funds but are not "otherwise affiliated with Fidelity" amounts to an "admission" that the directors and the adviser are affiliated. This statement cannot reasonably be read as an admission of an affiliation as that term is defined in the ICA. Rather, it only admits the obvious—the majority of Fidelity directors serve on multiple boards within the Fidelity fund complex.

Second, Krantz relies on allegations that the directors' lack of disinterestedness is established by their refusal to resist actions of the investment adviser that allegedly prejudiced the shareholders. He criticizes the "soft dollar" arrangements that are being allowed to flourish at Fidelity unchecked by the directors. As defendants point out, "soft dollar" arrangements are permitted by securities law. See 15 USC § 78bb(e) (creating "safe harbor" for brokerage commissions that include research fees paid in good faith). Plaintiff has not alleged any improprieties in Fidelity's soft dollar arrangements, and he admitted at oral argument that he has no information regarding the extent of these arrangements. Also, his criticism of the refusal to ditch the investment adviser, or internalize management to save costs, because of the poor performance of three funds is unsound because apparently 234 Fidelity funds have fared well. Finally, his complaint about excessive compensation (discussed more fully in the next section) is insufficient to support an inference of control, rather than mere dereliction of duty.

The plaintiff's strongest argument is the extent of the Fidelity directors' multiplicity and compensation. The plaintiff's point is well-taken that the number of boards and the amount of the compensation involved in this case is more than four times larger than has been considered previously in reported cases. Nonetheless, I am persuaded by the majority view that the directors' well-compensated multiple board membership is insufficient to rebut the statutory presumption against control without other indicia of control. My conclusion is consistent with *Burks v. Lasker*, 441 U.S. 471 (1979), which eschews reliance on assumptions of partiality based on the structure of the governing board rather than the facts of an individual case. In *Burks*, the Supreme Court noted the view that mutual fund directors could "never be truly disinterested in suits involving their co-directors," but continued:

> While lack of impartiality may or may not be true as a matter of fact in individual cases, it is not a conclusion of law required by the ICA. Congress surely would not have entrusted such control functions as approval of advisory contracts and selection of accountants to the statutorily disinterested directors had it shared the Court of Appeals' view that such directors could never be "disinterested" where their co-directors or investment advisers were concerned.

Id. The Supreme Court predicated this analysis, in part, on the statutory presumption against control of a natural person in the ICA. See 15 USC § 80a-2(a)(9). Even the *Strougo* line of cases declines to rely solely on multiple board membership, but emphasizes the allegations of business decisions which so substantially prejudiced the shareholders to the benefit of the investment adviser that the court could reasonably draw an inference of control, rather than of poor business judgment or mere oversight.

While there is an allegation that the investment adviser appointed the directors (thus implicating SEC factor five), there is no allegation that the investment adviser sets the level of compensation or determines director retention or re-election, or actually controls the directors. Because the allegations in the Amended Complaint do not surmount the hurdle erected by the statutory presumption, plaintiff's claims under § § 10(b), 15(c), 36(a) of the ICA are ***DISMISSED***. * * * *

Section 2.3 Regulatory Strictures Protecting Funds from Affiliate Overreaching

Laws & Rules Highlight:

IC Act (15 USC 80a-1 *et seq.*)

- § 2(a)(3) "***affiliated person***" of another person means:
  - **(A)** any person directly or indirectly owning, controlling, or holding with power to vote, ***5% or more*** of the outstanding voting securities of such other person;
  - **(B)** any person ***5% or more*** of whose outstanding voting securities are directly or indirectly owned, controlled, or held with power to vote, by such other person;
  - **(C)** any person directly or indirectly ***controlling, controlled by, or under common control*** with, such other person;
  - **(D)** any ***officer, director, partner, copartner, or employee*** of such other person;
  - **(E)** if such other person is an IC, any ***IA*** of such IC, and any ***member of an advisory board*** of such IC; and
  - **(F)** if such other person is an unincorporated IC not having a board of directors, the ***depositor*** of such IC.
- § 2(a)(9) (*def.* "***control***")
  - ◆ Means the *power to exercise a* ***controlling influence*** *over the management or policies* of a company, unless such power is solely the result of an official position with such company. A ***natural person*** shall be ***presumed not to be*** a controlled person.
  - ◆ Beneficial owner of ***more than 25%*** of the voting securities of a company ***shall be presumed to control*** such company; beneficial owner of ***not more than 25%*** of the voting securities of any company ***shall be presumed not to control*** such company.
  - ◆ Any such presumption may be ***rebutted*** by evidence.

Both ***first-tier affiliates*** (*i.e.*, affiliates of a registered investment company) and ***second-tier affiliates*** (*i.e.*, affiliates of the first-tier affiliates), but ***not more-distantly affiliated*** entities, are subject to the Investment Company Act's restrictions on affiliated transactions. The two-tier restrictions are designed to protect funds from ***overreaching*** by affiliates, without costing the funds arms-length business opportunities.*

*Ref. [DIV. OF INV. MGMT, SEC. & EXCH. COMM'N, PROTECTING INVESTORS: A HALF CENTURY OF INVESTMENT COMPANY REGULATION, Ch.12 Affiliated Transactions (1992)]

Diagram:* First-Tier, Second-Tier, and More-Distant Affiliates

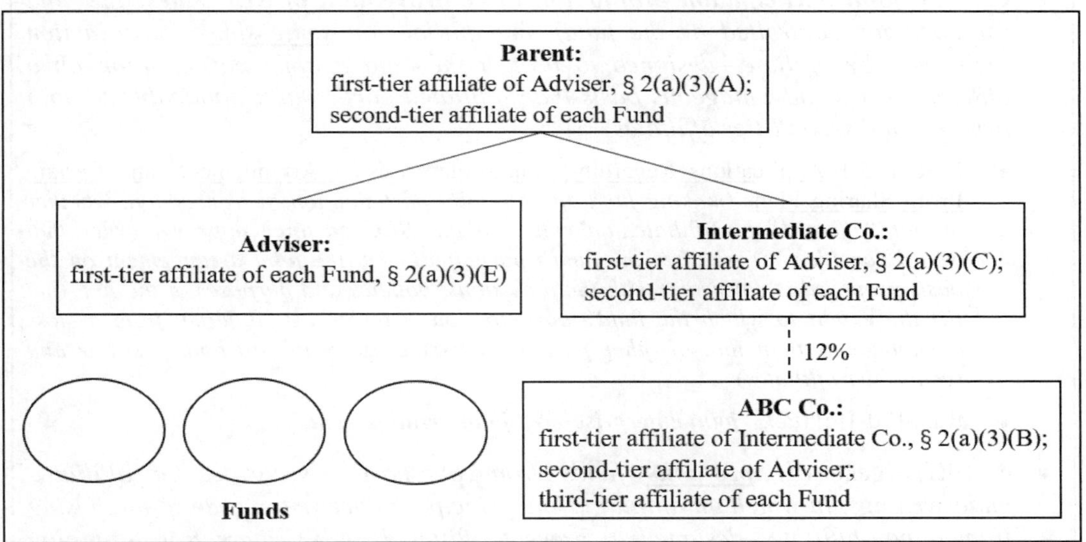

****Graph:*** Adapted from Geffen, *Classifying Affiliates Under the Investment Company Act*, 16 INV. LAW. 1 (2009)

Topic 1 Prior Exemption Required of Affiliate "Acting as Principal" Involving Fund

Laws & Rules Highlight:

IC Act (15 USC 80a-1 *et seq.*) & Rules (17 CFR §§ 270.0-1 *et seq.*)

- § 17(a) (***principal transaction bar:*** *the fund (or company controlled by the fund) and affiliate on* ***opposite sides*** *of transaction—designed to prevent affiliate from overreaching the fund; applicable to both first-tier and second-tier affiliates*)
    - § 17(b) (*SEC shall issue an* ***order of exemption*** *from § 17(a) bar* ***if*** *the proposed transaction: (i) does not involve overreaching; (ii) is consistent with the policy of the fund; and (iii) is consistent with the general purposes of the IC Act*)
- § 17(d) (***joint participation prohibition in contravention of SEC rules:*** *the fund (or company controlled by the fund) and affiliate on* ***same side*** *of transaction "effected" by affiliate—designed to protect the fund against participation on a different or less advantageous basis than affiliated participant; applicable to both first-tier and second-tier affiliates*)
    - Rule 17d-1 Applications Regarding Joint Enterprises or Arrangements and Certain Profit-Sharing Plans (*making fund-affiliate joint participation in transaction, whether or not "effected" by affiliate, unlawful without* ***SEC advance approval order*** *that would consider: (i)* ***whether*** *the fund's participation in the joint arrangement on the basis proposed is consistent with the provisions, policies and purposes of the Act, and (ii)* ***the extent*** *to which the fund's participation is on a basis different from or less advantageous than that of other participants; rule applicable to both first-tier and second-tier affiliates*)
    - Rule 17d-1(c) (*def.* ***"joint enterprise"*** *&* ***"joint arrangement"***)
- § 10(f) (*generally* ***prohibits*** *funds from purchasing securities in affiliated underwritings, in which an affiliate is the principal underwriter, even if purchasing from a non-affiliate—designed to prevent affiliated underwriters from* ***dumping*** *unmarketable securities on funds*)
    - Rule 10f-3 Exemption for the Acquisition of Securities During the Existence of an Underwriting or Selling Syndicate (*exempts a fund's purchase of securities from affiliated underwriting subject to* ***conditions*** *relating to nature of offering and terms of fund participation—designed to both protect funds from dumping and enhance investment opportunities available to funds*)
- § 6(c) (*grants SEC authority to exempt by rule, regulation, or order*)

Pre-Case Background Note:[Biblio]

Affiliated Transaction Restrictions: the "Heart"[1] of the IC Act

Viewed as the "***heart***" of the Investment Company Act,[1; 2 (§II.A); 3] § 17 is designed to protect investment companies from self-dealing and overreaching by insiders. It ***prohibits*** various conflict of interest transactions between a registered investment company and its first-tier or second-tier affiliates ("affiliates") unless ***advance*** exemption or approval order has been obtained from the SEC. Specifically:[2 (§II.A)]

Section **17(a)** ***generally prohibits*** any affiliate from knowingly selling to, or purchasing or borrowing securities or other property from the investment company (*i.e.*, fund and affiliate on ***opposite sides*** of the transaction). Section **17(b)** permits the SEC to grant ***exemptive orders*** from § 17(a) prohibition where:

- The terms of the proposed transaction are *reasonable and fair*, and do not involve *overreaching* on the part of any person concerned;
- The proposed transaction is consistent with the formal *investment policy* of each registered investment company participant; and
- The proposed transaction is consistent with the general purposes of the *Investment Company Act*.

To obviate the need for case-by-case exemptive order applications under § 17(b), the SEC has adopted a series of ***exemptive rules*** pursuant to its general exemptive authority under § 6(c), exempting specified types of transactions from the prohibitions of § 17(a) in circumstances where the need for SEC review is remote.

Section **17(d)** ***authorizes the SEC*** to adopt rules ***prohibiting*** any affiliate *acting as principal* from effecting any transaction in which the investment company (or a company controlled by the investment company) is a *joint or joint and several participant* with the affiliate on a basis *different from or less advantageous* than the other participants (*i.e.*, fund and affiliate on ***same side*** of the transaction). SEC **Rule 17d-1** adopted under § 17(d) defines the term "joint enterprise or other joint arrangement or profit-sharing plan." Rule 17d-1 sets forth the standard for review of each application for exemption from § 17(d); it also automatically exempts specified types of transactions from the prohibition of § 17(d) in circumstances where the possibility of the investment company being in disadvantageous arrangements is remote.

Comparing the scope of the SEC inquiry under a § 17(b) application for an exemption from § 17(a), to permit fund-affiliate on opposite sides of the transaction, **with** the scope of the SEC inquiry under a Rule 17d-1 application for an exemption from § 17(d), to permit fund-affiliate on the same side of the transaction: the former inquiry examines a direct conflict of interest between an affiliate and the fund and potential ***unfairness and overreaching***, and is thus wider in scope than the latter, which examines an affiliate having conflicts of interest and the power to influence decisions of the fund, and the fund and its affiliate's participation on ***equal terms***.

Commenting on the "regulation by exemption" and "case-by-case mode of operation" of § 17(a) and § 17(d) which have been criticized as an "unduly cumbersome" and "overbroad" approach,[1; 2 (§II.B.3); 4; 5 (§III.J.4)] commentators, as well as the SEC itself, have the following views:

- SEC (1992)[1 (§§III-IV)] ("From the standpoint of ***cost and efficiency***," it is desirable to limit the circumstances requiring the Commission's approval; "from the standpoint of ***investor protection***," affiliated transaction restrictions lie at the "***heart***" of the Act and remain "***fundamental***" to fund investor protection. Thus the Division of Investment Management does not recommend any "wholesale changes" to the current regulatory system; specifically: (1) the Division does not recommend any changes to § 17(a) prohibiting fund-affiliate opposite side transactions without ***prior SEC exemption order***, because such transactions "almost invariably carry the risk of overreaching"; (2) the Division recommends additional exclusions under § 17(d) governing fund-affiliate same side or joint transactions, to permit review and approval by the ***fund board including independent directors*** of joint transactions that do not involve overreaching.).
- Rosenblat & Lybecker (1976)[2 (§II.B.3)] (recommending a ***three-tiered regulation*** of § 17(b) opposite side transactions and § 17(d) same side transactions: de minimus exemption; approval by fund independent directors subject to § 36(a)(1) fiduciary duty provisions; and traditional SEC exemptive order application.).
- Lemke *et al.* (2017)[3] ("While ***exemptive rules*** under § 17 permit greater flexibility in the financial dealings of investment companies and their affiliates, they also impose responsibilities on the ***board of directors*** for monitoring exempted transactions.").
- Kroll (1972)[6] (in lieu of the current cumbersome case-by-case application procedure under Rule 17d-1, recommending the adoption of: (1) ***a self-operating 10b-5 type Rule***, making overreaching in joint transactions unlawful; (2) ***a***

self-operating blanket exemptive rule, covering transactions where there is an absence of overreaching.).

Bibliography:

1. DIV. OF INV. MGMT, SEC. & EXCH. COMM'N, PROTECTING INVESTORS: A HALF CENTURY OF INVESTMENT COMPANY REGULATION, Ch. 12. Affiliated Transactions (1992)
2. Rosenblat & Lybecker, *Some Thoughts on the Federal Securities Laws Regulating External Investment Management Arrangements and the ALJ Federal Securities Code Project*, 124 U. PA. L. REV. 587 (1976)
3. LEMKE, LINS & SMITH, REGULATION OF INVESTMENT COMPANIES, § 8.01 Transactions Involving Affiliates: Section 17 (2017)
4. Bartlett & Dowd, *Section 17 of the Investment Company Act—An Exemple of Regulation by Exemption*, 8 DEL. J. CORP. L. 449 (1983)
5. Request for Comments on Reform of the Regulation of Investment Companies, IC-17534, IA-1234, 55 FR 25322 (1990)
6. Kroll, *The "Portfolio Affiliate" Problem*, THIRD ANN. INST. ON SEC. REG. 261, 290-291 (PLI Mundheim & Fleischer eds. 1972)

Case Study 1: Fund and Affiliate on Opposite Sides of Transaction

Registered closed-end fund **Christiana** Securities Company owned ***28.3%*** of the common stock of operating company E.I. **du Pont** de Nemours & Co.—its ***downstream portfolio affiliate***; and ***98%*** of Christiana's assets consisted of du Pont common stock. Christiana and du Pont made a joint application to the SEC under § 17(b) for an exemption order from the § 17(a) statutory prohibition, to permit their proposed tax-free merger of Christiana into du Pont, in which Christiana shares would be exchanged for newly issued shares of du Pont common stock. Christiana's shares were trading in the OTC market at a substantial discount from the fund's NAV, ranging from 20% to 25%; but Christiana was able to secure merger terms providing for a discount of 2.5% of the market value of Christiana's net assets.

Collins *et al.* (du Pont's dissenting shareholders) objected to the proposed merger, arguing that it would confer great benefits to Christiana's stockholders and injure du Pont's stockholders. The **SEC,** while recognizing the clear "imbalance of benefit" inherent in the merger terms, noted that the proposed discount was within the ***"range" of fairness***: It would work no harm on the du Pont shareholders; would maintain substantially all of the value of Christiana shareholders' investment; whereas a significant increase in the discount would unfairly deprive Christiana stockholders of a substantial portion of the value of their fund's assets—a result contrary to the purpose of the Investment Company Act. Thus, overriding Collins' objection, the SEC granted an order of exemption, finding the proposed merger "*reasonable and fair; free from* *overreaching on the part of any person concerned; and consistent with the general purposes of the Act.*"

The **Eighth Circuit** set aside the SEC's exemptive order. It made its own determination of "***fairness***" as to be within the range of "arm's length bargaining"; and held: "The plain language of the [IC] Act does not permit the Commission to establish a rule of law that closed-end, non-diversified companies should be presumptively worth the value of their net assets." Such a presumption, the court found, was "central" to the SEC's exemptive order. The **U.S. Supreme Court** reversed. It found that the SEC "did not employ a mechanical application of a rule or 'presumption,' " but that the SEC's reliance on NAV in this case and the SEC's determination that the proposed merger met the statutory standards was a "product of administrative experience, appreciation of the complexities of the problem, realization of the statutory policies, and responsible treatment of the uncontested facts," "entitled to the greatest amount of weight by appellate courts."

E.I. du Pont de Nemours & Co. v. Collins

432 U.S. 46 (1977)

[***Procedural history***: In *re* Christiana Sec. Co., IC-8615, 45 SEC 649 (1974), *rev'd*, Collins v. SEC, 532 F.2d 584 (8th Cir. 1976), *rev'd on other grounds sub nom.*, E.I. du Pont de Nemours & Co. v. Collins, 432 U.S. 46 (1977)]

Case Study 2: Fund and Affiliate on Same Side of Transaction

Registered open-end fund **American Investors Fund, Inc.** owned ***9%*** of operating company **Talley Industries, Inc.**—its ***downstream portfolio affiliate***. During the specified period, Fund, Talley, and certain affiliates of Talley (*i.e.*, second-tier affiliates of Fund) each purchased shares of common stock of **General Time Corporation** under the following circumstances: The second-tier affiliates and Talley each purchased General Time common stock. One second-tier affiliate then informed Fund's investment adviser of the affiliates' earlier purchases, planned additional purchases by Talley, and possible future merger of Talley and General Time. Thereafter, Fund also purchased General Time common stock.

Subsequent to the transactions, Fund and its affiliate Talley filed a ***joint application*** with the SEC for an order: either declaring that their purchases were not a "joint enterprise or arrangement" subject to § 17(d) and Rule 17d-1, or granting approval of the transactions pursuant to § 17(d) and Rule 17d-1. In its order denying the application, the **SEC:**

- Found the concurrent stock purchases by Fund and by Talley through a common broker not "*a mere happenstance*," but "*a joint arrangement*" within the meaning of § 17(d) and Rule 17d-1: Fund and Talley made the purchases at Talley's instigation; Fund was aware of, and was influenced by, its affiliate's ultimate goal of a merger with General Time;
- Found § 17(d) and Rule 17d-1 thus applicable to the transactions, and the joint acquisition of the General Time stock without the requisite prior approval from the SEC a violation of the Act;
- Stating: one who fails to comply with the pre-approval requirement bears the burden of presenting "a compelling showing" that the failure was justified, and that retroactive approval is not inconsistent with the statutory policies and purposes.

Following its order, the SEC brought an action in court to invoke the court's injunctive powers, alleging that Talley had "*effected*" a transaction in which Fund was "*a joint or a joint and several participant*" in violation of § 17(d) and Rule 17d-1, and enjoining future violations. Applying the standard that "some element of combination" be required to find the "jointness" within the meaning of the statute, the **Second Circuit** found that there was substantial evidence to support the SEC's factual determination of joint participation by Fund and Talley. Enunciating the rationale of § 17(d) and addressing appropriate relief, the Second Circuit reasoned:

> Congress has declared "that the national public interest and the interest of investors are adversely affected ... when investment companies are organized, operated, managed, or their portfolio securities are selected, in the interest of directors, officers, investment advisers, depositors, or other affiliated persons thereof ... rather than in the interest of all classes of such companies' security holders," * * *
>
> [While the need to effectuate the statutory purpose is clearer in the case of upstream affiliates], the same language cannot be read one way in the case of upstream and another way in the case of downstream affiliation. Moreover, Congress could have thought that downstream affiliation also involved some danger that the investment company's stockholders might be put upon for the benefit of other stockholders of the affiliate. * * *
>
> The objective of § 17(d) is to prevent affiliated persons from injuring the interests of stockholders of registered investment companies by causing the company to participate "on a basis different from or less advantageous than that of such other participant." While the Court does not undertake to particularize the form of a

decree in this suit in equity, a prohibition against Talley's sale of its shares without according Fund a fair opportunity to participate would be one obvious device to the end that § 17(d) is not violated in the future.

SEC v. Talley Indus., Inc.

399 F.2d 396 (2d Cir. 1968)

[*Procedural history*:

Private actions:

General Time Corp. v. American Investors Fund, Inc., 283 F. Supp. 400 (SDNY 1968) & General Time Corp. v. Talley Indus., Inc., 283 F. Supp. 832 (SDNY 1968), *aff'd on other ground sub nom.*, General Time Corp. v. Talley Indus., Inc., 403 F.2d 159 (2d Cir. 1968), *cert. denied*, 393 U.S. 1026 (Jan 13, 1969)

SEC actions:

Talley Indus., Inc. and American Investors Fund, Inc.: Adm. Proc. 812-2302, IC-5333, 33 FR 5439 (1968) (Notice); Adm. Proc. 812-2302, IC-5358, 43 SEC 773 (1968) (Order); SEC v. Talley Indus., Inc., 286 F. Supp. 50 (SDNY 1968), *rev'd*, 399 F.2d 396 (2d Cir. 1968), *cert. denied sub nom.*, General Time Corp. v. SEC, 393 U.S. 1015 (1969); *decree on remand aff'd*, SEC v. General Time Corp., 407 F.2d 65 (2d Cir. 1968), *cert denied sub nom.*, General Time Corp. v. SEC, 393 U.S. 1026 (1969)

Post-court action SEC proceedings:

In re Talley Indus., Inc.: Findings and Opinion of the Commission, Adm. Proc. 812-2500, IC-5953, 44 SEC 165 (Jan 9, 1970); In re Talley Indus., Inc.: Order Granting Application as Amended, Adm. Proc. 812-2500, IC-5977 (Feb 10, 1970)]

Research Topic:

Regulatory mechanisms to prevent affiliates from overreaching funds under the Chinese investment management laws.

E.I. du Pont de Nemours & Co. v. Collins

432 U.S. 46 (1977)

JUDGES: Burger, Brennan, Stewart, White, Marshall, Blackmun, Powell, Rehnquist, Stevens. Mr. Justice Brennan dissented with an opinion.

OPINION

Mr. Chief Justice BURGER delivered the opinion of the Court:

We granted certiorari[1] in these cases to determine whether the Securities and Exchange Commission, in approving the merger of a closed-end investment company into an affiliate company, reasonably exercised its discretion under the Investment Company Act of 1940. The Commission valued the investment company essentially on the basis of the market value of the securities which constituted substantially all of its assets rather than on the lower basis of its own outstanding stock.

The statutory scheme here is relatively straightforward. Section 17 of the Investment Company Act of 1940 forbids an "affiliated person," as defined in the Act,[2] to purchase any securities or other property from a registered investment company unless the Commission finds, *inter alia*, that the "evidence establishes that ... the terms of the proposed transaction, including the consideration to be paid or received, are reasonable and fair and do not involve over-reaching on the part of any person concerned...."[3]

A.

The merger in this litigation involves Christiana Securities Co., a closed-end,

---

[1] 429 U.S. 815 (1976).

[2] Title 15 USC § 80a-2(a)(3) defines an "affiliated person" as follows:

"(3) 'Affiliated person' of another person means (A) any person directly or indirectly owning, controlling, or holding with power to vote, 5 per centum or more of the outstanding voting securities of such other person; (B) any person 5 per centum or more of whose outstanding voting securities are directly or indirectly owned, controlled, or held with power to vote, by such other person; (C) any person directly or in directly controlling, controlled by, or under common control with, such other person; (D) any officer, director, partner, copartner, or employee of such other person; (E) if such other person is an investment company, any investment adviser thereof or any member of an advisory board thereof; and (F) if such other person is an unincorporated investment company not having a board of directors, the depositor thereof."

[3] Section 17(b) also requires that the proposed transaction be (1) consistent with the policy of each registered investment company concerned, and (2) consistent with "the general purposes of this title." 15 USC § § 80a-17(b)(2), (3). These criteria are not contested here.

nondiversified management investment company, and E.I. du Pont de Nemours & Co., a large industrial operating company engaged principally in the manufacture of chemical products. Christiana was formed in 1915 in order to preserve family control of Du Pont & Co. At the time the present merger negotiations were announced in April 1972, 98% of Christiana's assets consisted of Du Pont common stock.[4] This block of Du Pont stock in turn comprised approximately 28.3% of the outstanding common stock of Du Pont.[5] For purposes of this litigation, Christiana has been presumed to have at least the potential to control Du Pont, although it submits that "this potential lies dormant and unexercised and that there is no actual control relationship." IC-8615 (1974).

Christiana itself has 11,710,103 shares of common stock outstanding[6] and has about 8,000 shareholders. Unlike Du Pont stock, which is traded actively on the New York and other national stock exchanges, Christiana shares are traded in the over-the-counter market. Since virtually all of its assets are Du Pont common stock, the market price of Christiana shares reflects the market price of Du Pont stock. However, as is often the case with closed-end investment companies, Christiana's own stock has historically sold at a discount from the market value of its Du Pont holdings.[7] Apparently, this discount is primarily tax related since Christiana pays a federal intercorporate tax on dividends. Its stockholders are also subject to potential capital-gains tax on the unrealized appreciation of Christiana's Du Pont stock which has a very low tax base. Additionally, the relatively limited market for Christiana stock likely influences the discount.

In 1972, Christiana's management concluded that, because of the tax disadvantages and the discount at which its shares sold, Christiana should be liquidated and its stockholders become direct owners of Du Pont stock. Christiana's board of directors proposed liquidation of Christiana by means of a tax-free merger into Du Pont. Du Pont

---

[4] Christiana owns 13,417,120 shares of Du Pont. It also holds a relatively small amount of Du Pont preferred stock. Its other assets consist of two daily newspapers in Wilmington, Del., and 3.5% of the stock of the Wilmington Trust Co., which, in turn, holds more than one-half of Christiana's common stock as trustee. IC-8615 (1974).

[5] According to the applicants' Notice of Filing of Application, IC-7402 (1972), Du Pont has 47,566,694 shares of common stock outstanding held by approximately 224,964 shareholders.

[6] Ninety-five and one-half percent of these shares are held by 338 people. IC-8615, *supra*.

[7] In the two years preceding the date of the announcement of the merger negotiations, this discount was generally in the range of 20%-25%; *ibid*.

would purchase Christiana's assets by issuing to Christiana shareholders new certificates of Du Pont stock. In more concrete terms, Du Pont would acquire Christiana's $2.2 billion assets and assume its liabilities of approximately $300,000. In so doing, Du Pont would acquire from Christiana 13,417,120 shares of its own common stock. Du Pont would then issue 13,228,620 of its shares directly to Christiana holders. This would be 188,500 shares less than DuPont would receive from Christiana. As a result of the merger, each share of Christiana common stock would be converted into 1.123 shares of Du Pont common stock. That ratio was ascertained by taking the market price of Christiana's Du Pont stock and its other assets, subtracting Christiana's relatively nominal liabilities, and making certain other minor adjustments. Direct ownership of Du Pont shares would increase the market value of the Christiana shareholders' holdings and Du Pont would have acquired Christiana's assets at a 2.5% discount from their net value. The Internal Revenue Service ruled the merger would be tax free.

Du Pont and Christiana filed a joint application with the Commission for exemption under § 17 of the Investment Company Act. Administrative proceedings followed. The Commission's Division of Investment Management Regulation supported the application. A relatively small number of Du Pont shareholders, including the respondents in this case, opposed the transaction. Their basic argument was that, since Christiana was valued on the basis of its assets, Du Pont stock, rather than the much lower market price of its own outstanding stock, the proposed merger would be unfair to the shareholders of Du Pont since it provides relatively greater benefits to Christiana shareholders than to shareholders of Du Pont. The objecting stockholders argued that Du Pont & Co. should receive a substantial share of the benefit realized by Christiana shareholders from the elimination of the 23% discount from net asset value at which Christiana stock was selling. They also argued that the merger would depress the market price of Du Pont stock because it would place more than 13 million marketable Du Pont shares directly in the hands of Christiana shareholders.

After the hearing, the parties waived the initial administrative recommendations and the record was submitted directly to the Commission. The Commission unanimously granted the application. Basically, it viewed the proposed transaction as an exchange of equivalents—Christiana's Du Pont stock to be acquired by Du Pont in exchange for Du Pont stock issued directly to Christiana shareholders. It held that, for purposes of § 17(b), the proper guide for evaluating Christiana was the market price of Christiana's holdings of Du Pont stock:

> "Here justice requires no ventures into the unknown and unknowable. An investment company, whose assets consist entirely or almost entirely of securities the prices of which are determined in active and continuous markets, can normally be presumed to be worth its net asset value.... The simple, readily usable tool of net asset value does the job much better than an accurate gauge of market impact (were there one) could." IC-8615.

The fact that Du Pont might have obtained more favorable terms because of its strategic bargaining position or by use of alternative methods of liquidating Christiana was considered not relevant by the Commission. In its view, the purpose of § 17 was to prevent persons in a strategic position from getting more than fair value. The Commission found no detriment in the transaction to Du Pont or to the value of its outstanding shares. Any depressing effects on the price of Du Pont would be brief in duration and the intrinsic value of an investment in Du Pont would not be altered by the merger. Moreover, in the Commission's view, any valuation involving a significant departure from net asset value would "run afoul of § 17(b)(1) of the Act"; it would strip long-term investors in companies like Christiana of the intrinsic worth of the securities which underlie their holdings.

A panel of the United States Court of Appeals for the Eighth Circuit divided in setting aside the Commission's determination. *Collins v. SEC*, 532 F.2d 584 (1976).[8] The majority held that the Securities and Exchange Commission had erred, as a matter of law, in determining that Christiana should be presumptively valued on the basis of the market value of its principal asset, common stock of Du Pont. "[I]n judging transactions between dominant and subservient parties, the test is 'whether or not under all the circumstances the transaction carries the earmarks of an arm's length bargain,' *Pepper v. Litton*, 308 U.S. 295 (1939)"; *id.* Employing this standard, the Court of Appeals majority concluded that the record did not support the Commission's finding that the terms of the merger were "reasonable and fair" since the "economic benefits to Christiana shareholders from the merger are immediate and substantial," *id.*, while "benefits to present Du Pont shareholders are minimal"; *id.* The court concluded that, from Du Pont's viewpoint, "the degree of [control] dispersion attained ... does not justify the substantial premium paid for

---

[8] A petition for rehearing en banc was denied by an equally divided court.

the Christiana stock"; *id.* The panel also held that the Commission had erred in failing to give weight to the "occasional detriment to Du Pont shareholders," *id.*, caused by the increase of available Du Pont stock in the market.

B.

In determining whether the Court of Appeals correctly set aside the order of the Commission, we begin by examining the nature of the regulatory process leading to the decision that court was required to review. In *United States v. National Assn. of Securities Dealers*, 422 U.S. 694 (1975), we noted that the Investment Company Act of 1940 "vests in the SEC broad regulatory authority over the business practices of the investment companies." The Act was the product of congressional concern that existing legislation in the securities field did not afford adequate protection to the purchasers of investment company securities. Prior to the enactment of the legislation, Congress mandated an intensive study of the investment company industry.[9] One of the problems specifically identified was the numerous transactions between investment companies and persons affiliated with them which resulted in a distinct advantage to the "insiders" over the public investors.[10] Section 17 was the specific congressional response to this problem.[11] Congress therefore charged the Commission, in scrutinizing a merger such as this, to take into account the peculiar characteristics of such a transaction in the investment company industry. Recognizing that an "arm's length bargain," cf. *Pepper v. Litton*, 308 U.S. 295 (1939), is rarely a realistic possibility in transactions between an affiliate and an investment company, Congress substituted, in effect, the informed judgment of the Commission to determine, inter alia, whether the transaction was "reasonable and fair and [did] not involve overreaching on the part of any person concerned."[12]

Given the wide variety of possible transactions between an investment company and

---

[9] Section 30 of the Public Utility Holding Company Act mandated that the SEC undertake such a study. See *United States v. National Assn. of Securities Dealers*, 422 U.S. 694 (1975).

[10] See generally REPORT ON INVESTMENT TRUST AND INVESTMENT COMPANIES, H.R.Doc. No. 279, 76th Cong., 1st Sess., 1017-1561 (1940).

[11] While the House and Senate Reports indicate that the Congress' chief concern was protection of the public investors of the investment company, S. Rep. No. 1775, 76th Cong., 3d Sess., 11-12 (1940); H.R. Rep. No. 2639, 76th Cong., 3d Sess., 9 (1940), the statute has been construed to afford protection to the stockholders of the affiliate as well. See *Fifth Avenue Coach Lines, Inc.*, 43 SEC 635 (1967).

[12] 15 USC § 80a-17(b)(1).

its affiliates, Congress, quite understandably, made no attempt to define this standard with any greater precision. Instead, it followed the practice frequently employed in other administrative schemes. The language of the statute was cast in broad terms and designed to encompass all situations falling within the scope of the statute; an agency with great experience in the industry was given the task of applying those criteria to particular business situations in a manner consistent with the legislative intent.[13]

C.

In this case, a judgment as to whether the terms of the merger were "reasonable and fair" turned upon the value assigned to Christiana. In making such an evaluation, the Commission concluded that "[t]he single, readily usable tool of net asset value does the job much better than an accurate gauge of market impact...." IC-8615. Investment companies, it reasoned, are essentially a portfolio of securities whose individual prices are determined by the forces of the securities marketplace. In determining value in merger situations, "asset value" is thus much more applicable to investment companies than to other corporate entities. The value of the securities surrendered is, basically, the real value received by the transferee.

In reviewing a decision of the Commission, a court must consider both the facts found and the application of the relevant statute by the agency. Congress has mandated that, in review of § 17 proceedings, "[t]he findings of the Commission as to the facts, if supported by substantial evidence, shall be conclusive." 15 USC § 80a-42. A reviewing court is also to be guided by the "venerable principle that the construction of a statute by those charged with its execution should be followed unless there are compelling indications that it is wrong...." *Red Lion Broadcasting Co. v. FCC*, 395 U.S. 367, 381 (1969). "[C]ontemporaneous construction is entitled to great weight ... even though it was applied in cases settled by consent rather than in litigation." *FTC v. Mandel Bros.*, 359 U. S. 385 (1959). Here, however, the Court of Appeals held, as a matter of law, that the Commission erred in the method applied in passing on the merger, thus all but ignoring

---

[13] This situation is quite different from that which confronted the Court earlier this Term in *Piper v. Chris-Craft Industries, Inc.*, 430 U.S. 1 (1977). There, the Court held that "the narrow legal issue" of implying a private right of action under the securities laws was "one peculiarly reserved for judicial resolution" and that the experience of the Commission on such a question was of "limited value." By contrast, this case involves an assessment as to whether a given business arrangement is compatible with the regulatory scheme which the agency is charged by Congress to administer.

the congressional limitations on judicial review of agency action.

The Commission has long recognized that the key factor in the valuation of the assets of a closed-end investment company should be the market price of the underlying securities. This method of setting the value of investment companies is, as Congress contemplated, the product of the agency's long and intimate familiarity with the investment company industry. For instance, in issuing an advisory report to the United States District Court pursuant to § 173 of Chapter X of the Bankruptcy Act, the Commission advised that "it is natural that net asset value based upon market prices should be the fundamental valuation criterion used by and large in the investment company field." [citation omitted]. Similarly, in mergers like the one presented in this litigation, the Commission has used "net asset value" as a touchstone in its analysis. [citations omitted].[14]

Moreover, despite the characterization of the Court of Appeals to the contrary, the Commission did not employ a mechanical application of a rule or "presumption." It considered carefully the contentions of the respondents that a departure from the use of net asset value was warranted in this case. Upon analysis, it concluded that the central and controlling aspect of the merger remained the fact that it consisted of an exchange of Du Pont common stock for Du Pont common stock; it was not Christiana stock but Du Pont stock which Du Pont was receiving in the merger. As to the claim that Du Pont stock would be adversely affected over an extended period of time by volume selling, the Commission concluded there was no indication of a long-term adverse market impact. It noted that Christiana stock was held principally by long-term investors. There was no evidence that Christiana stockholders, who for years had been indirect investors in Du Pont, would now change the essential nature of their investment.

The Commission's reliance on "net asset value" in this particular case and its consequent determination that the proposed merger met the statutory standards thus rested "squarely in that area where administrative judgments are entitled to the greatest

---

[14] This method of valuation of closed-end investment companies was similarly employed in [citations omitted]. The Commission has, of course, required that such valuations be adjusted to reflect such factors as expenses of the merger and tax considerations. *Talley Industries, Inc.*, IC-5953 (1970); and *Electric Bond & Share Co.*, IC-5215 (1967), cited by the Court of Appeals, did not rely on net asset value since the companies held substantial assets other than securities. While Christiana also had some assets other than Du Pont stock, they amounted to only 2% of its assets.

amount of weight by appellate courts. It is the product of administrative experience, appreciation of the complexities of the problem, realization of the statutory policies, and responsible treatment of the uncontested facts." *SEC v. Chenery Corp.*, 332 U.S. 194 (1947). In rejecting the conclusion of the Commission, the Court of Appeals substituted its own judgment for that of the agency charged by Congress with that responsibility.

We note that after receiving briefs and hearing oral argument, the Court of Appeals—over the objection of the Commission, Christiana, and Du Pont—undertook the unique appellate procedure of employing a university professor to assist the court in understanding the record and to prepare reports and memoranda for the court. Thus, the reports relied upon by that court included a variety of data and economic observations which had not been examined and tested by the traditional methods of the adversary process. We are not cited to any statute, rule, or decision authorizing the procedure employed by the Court of Appeals. Cf. Fed. Rule App. Proc. 16.

In our view, the Court of Appeals clearly departed from its statutory appellate function and applied an erroneous standard in its review of the decision of the Commission. The record made by the parties before the Commission was in accord with traditional procedures and that record clearly reveals substantial evidence to support the findings of the Commission. Moreover, the agency conclusions of law were based on a construction of the statute consistent with the legislative intent. Accordingly, the judgment of the Court of Appeals is

Reversed.

SEC, Plaintiff-Appellant v. Talley Indus., Inc., *et al.*, Defendants-Appellees

399 F.2d 396 (2d Cir. 1968)

JUDGES: Friendly, Hays and Feinberg, Circuit Judges.

OPINION

FRIENDLY, Circuit Judge:

For the second time this term, see *SEC v. Sterling Precision Corp.*, 393 F.2d 214 (2 Cir. 1968), we are confronted with a close question of interpretation of § 17 of the Investment Company Act of 1940, setting limits on "Transactions of Certain Affiliated Persons and Underwriters." On this occasion we believe the district judge construed the relevant clause, § 17(d), too narrowly, reverse his judgment dismissing the complaint, and direct further appropriate proceedings.

I.

Section 17(d), so far as here relevant, provides as follows:

> (d) It shall be unlawful for any affiliated person of or principle underwriter for a registered investment company (other than a company of the character described in § 80a-12(d)(3)(A) and (B) of this title), or any affiliated person of such a person or principal underwriter, acting as principal to effect any transaction in which such registered company, or a company controlled by such registered company, is a joint or a joint and several participant with such person, principal underwriter, or affiliated person, in contravention of such rules and regulations as the Commission may prescribe for the purpose of limiting or preventing participation by such registered or controlled company on a basis different from or less advantageous than that of such other participant.

Defendant Talley Industries, Inc. (hereafter **Industries**) is an "affiliated person" of defendant American Investors Fund, Inc. (hereafter **Fund**), a registered investment company, by virtue of Fund's owning 9% of Industries' voting shares, see § 2(a)(3)(B). As a result of discussions between Talley, president of Industries, a company having a net worth of some $10 million, and Kimelman, a partner in the brokerage firm of M. Kimelman & Co., in which Kimelman advanced General Time Corporation, a much larger corporation, as a candidate for acquisition by a merger with Industries, Talley gave Kimelman an order under which he bought 24,800 shares of General Time for Industries on December 26 and

27, 1967; the price was around $23 or $24 per share. This was only some 1% of the outstanding stock of General Time, a long way from what Talley thought would be needed to afford a prospect of success if he should decide to go forward with an acquisition or merger proposal.

On December 29, 1967, Talley telephoned Fund's office, and ultimately spoke to Chestnutt, president of Fund and of Chestnutt Corporation, its investment adviser. Talley told him that Industries had bought stock in a certain company which he viewed as a possible merger candidate and that he had in mind that Fund also might wish to buy some stock. Chestnutt broke off the conversation to consult his counsel. The latter advised that Fund could follow Talley's suggestion so long as it "maintained complete independence in our acquisition of stock and didn't make any promises or arrangements" as to voting, disposition or otherwise. Chestnutt relayed this to Talley, who accepted Fund's proceeding in this manner. Talley then named the company, saying he thought it a good investment that might become better under a more aggressive management. He indicated that Industries intended to buy more General Time stock in the market, with an eye toward a merger; Chestnutt got the impression that Talley was thinking of terms that would yield around $45 in Industries securities for each share of General Time. Talley proposed that Kimelman get in touch with Chestnutt; the latter, after telling Talley that 10% of the General Time stock would be his legal limit, said he would study his own data on the company, would like to see Kimelman, and would think the whole thing over. Shortly thereafter Industries bought 42,000 shares of General Time.

Kimelman visited Chestnutt on January 3. Next day Chestnutt determined that Fund should take a position in General Time. He was motivated both by study of the company's earnings and by a belief that if Industries sought a merger, the stock would rise as a result of that offer or of others it might stimulate. On January 5 Fund placed an order with Kimelman for 205,000 shares, subsequently increased to 210,000, just under Fund's 10% limit, on a "not-held" basis, *i.e.*, with the time of execution at the broker's discretion. Chestnutt reported this to Talley.

Chestnutt maintained close supervision of Kimelman's purchases, insisting that on days when Kimmelman had "not held" orders from other customers, shares should be allocated so as not to favor another customer over Fund. Industries was also making some purchases of General Time through Kimelman but at least on one occasion agreed to forego allocation and accept the most expensive shares. By February 15 Fund had acquired 210,000 shares at an average cost of $28.49 per share.

During the first week of January 1968, Talley discussed the situation, including his initial conversation with Chestnutt, with his counsel, who did not mention § 17(d). After some backing and filling unnecessary to recount, Industries resumed purchases of General Time toward the end of January. Talley talked to Chestnutt four or five times during January and reported how many shares he thought "were being acquired by the Kimelmans and himself and his friends and so on." He would give Chestnutt percentage figures of what "we have" and these rather obviously included the holdings of Fund. On February 5 Industries sold 40,000 shares to Donald Harrington, a friend of Talley's, who later increased his holdings to 104,500 shares. Finding that the record date for General Time's annual meeting was March 1, somewhat earlier than he had believed, and that Industries' own holding were only some 52,000 shares, about 2 1/2% of the stock as against the 10% he considered necessary for a meaningful merger proposal, Talley made a special bid on the advice of his investment bankers, Smith, Barney & Co., and against that of Chestnutt who thought this would drive the price up and would not get Industries the amount of stock it wanted. The bid, on February 19, 1968, was for 200,000 shares at 36 1/2. General Time denounced this as "grossly inadequate" and said it had a higher offer, on a tax-free basis, from another company. Only 66,437 shares were acquired.

On the afternoon of February 19, a meeting was held at Smith, Barney & Co. at the instance of the management of General Time. Talley proposed a merger and said "We and our associates own about a third of the stock"—a figure which included Fund's holdings. Later that evening the management sent word to Talley it had decided to fight. Industries, which then owned 118,537 shares, about 5 1/2% of the total, went back into the market and quickly bought another 139,400 shares at prices ranging from 41 1/2 to 43 1/2. This brought its holdings to 257,937 shares, about 12 1/2%, at an average cost of $36.76 per share.

General Time's response was an action in the District Court for the Southern District of New York alleging *inter alia* a violation of § 17(d) of the Investment Company Act and seeking an injunction against the voting of the stock, the obtaining of more, or any merger. Judge Bryan dismissed the action for lack of standing; General Time appealed. Meanwhile Industries selected ten nominees of an "Independent Stockholders Committee" for election as directors at the annual meeting of General Time on April 22, obtained a stockholders list only after litigation in Delaware, and sought to clear its proxy material with the SEC. On March 25 the SEC staff advised that the material would not be cleared unless Industries filed an application for approval of the acquisition of General Time stock by Fund and Industries under Rule 17d-1, which we reproduce in relevant part in the margin.[1] Industries filed such an application, with appropriate disclaimers of the need for doing so; a hearing was set for April 16; and the proxy material was cleared.

General Time then started a new action in the District Court for the Southern District of New York, claiming the proxy material was false and misleading in violation of § 14 of the Securities Exchange Act of 1934. Judge Tyler denied a preliminary injunction on April 11. On the next day Chestnutt was asked whether he would consider an offer for Fund's holdings in General Time from Coleman, president of Seeburg Corporation having its headquarters in Illinois. He countered by saying that he would be "down in front of the SEC testifying on the General Time situation next week, probably Tuesday" and might have to reveal anything that was said. Coleman first drew back but then asked whether Chestnutt would entertain a cash offer of $40 a share. Chestnutt replied that he would

---

[1] Rule 17d-1. Applications Regarding Joint Enterprises or Arrangements and Certain Profit-Sharing Plans

(a) No affiliated person of or principal underwriter for any registered investment company (other than a company of the character described in § 12(d)(3)(A) and (B) of the Act) and no affiliated person of such a person or principal underwriter, acting as principal, shall participate in, or effect any transaction in connection with, any joint enterprise or other joint arrangement or profit-sharing plan in which any such registered company, or a company controlled by such registered company, is a participant, and which is entered into, adopted or modified subsequent to the effective date of this rule, unless an application regarding such joint enterprise, arrangement or profit-sharing plan has been filed with the Commission and has been granted by an order entered prior to the submission of such plan or modification to security holders for approval, or prior to such adoption or modification if not so submitted, except that the provisions of this rule shall not preclude any affiliated person from acting as manager of any underwriting syndicate or other group in which such registered or controlled company is a participant and receiving compensation therefor.

(b) In passing upon such application, the Commission will consider whether the participation of such registered or controlled company in such joint enterprise, joint arrangement or profit-sharing plan on the basis proposed is consistent with the provisions, policies and purposes of the Act and the extent to which such participation is on a basis different from or less advantageous than that of other participants.

(c) "Joint enterprise or other joint arrangement or profit-sharing plan" as used in this rule shall mean any written or oral plan, contract, authorization or arrangement, or any practice or understanding whereby a registered investment company or a controlled company thereof and any affiliated person of or a principal underwriter for such registered investment company, or any affiliated person of such a person or principal underwriter, have a joint or a joint and several participation or share in the profits of such enterprise or undertaking, but shall not include an investment advisory contract subject to § 15 of the Act.

have to compare this with what anyone else might offer.[2]

April 13 saw the announcement of a plan to merge General Time and Seeburg Corporation, "contingent upon the continuation of General Time's present management." The details appeared on April 15. Chestnutt found the terms "shockingly unattractive"; he thought they would work out at not more than $28 per share of General Time as against a current market of $35. This, according to Chestnutt, was what made him decide to vote Fund's shares for the Committee's nominees and against the management.

The SEC hearings were held April 16, 17, and 18, oral argument was had before the Commission on April 19, and the Commission issued a Memorandum Opinion and Order that afternoon.[3] Concluding that Industries and Fund had entered into and carried out a joint arrangement under § 17(d), that application for approval should have been made under Rule 17d-1, and that there was "no warrant for granting retroactive approval of the transactions effected in such violation," the Commission denied the application. It made no direction beyond an assertion in a footnote of its "continuing jurisdiction ... over any future transfers by Industries of the GTC stock it has acquired...."[4]

On April 22, after a further unsuccessful attempt by General Time to secure an injunction from Judge Tyler, the stockholders met, the ballots were cast, and the meeting was adjourned to May 3 so that the inspectors could count the votes and certify the result. Preliminary reports indicate a victory for Industries' slate, although by a margin considerably less than the shares voted by Fund.

On May 1, the SEC began this action in the District Court for the Southern District of

---

[2] Chestnutt also testified that a representative of Seeburg said, "You just name a price between 35 and 50 and we will talk business." Chestnutt named no price because he didn't feel "in a position to make such an offer without talking to counsel." Counsel advised that a sale at a premium might present a problem under *Perlman v. Feldmann*, 219 F.2d 173 (2 Cir. 1955), *cert. denied*, 349 U.S. 952 (1955).

[3] The opinion of the district judge states the facts as to an April 3 letter written to the Commission by the junior Senator from Illinois on stationery of the Senate Committee on Banking and Currency of which he is a member, avowedly at the instance of General Time, "an important factor in the economy of Illinois and other States, as well as a producer of essential military and other items." While we do not suppose this letter had the slightest effect, it was unnecessary, to say the least. Senators and Representatives who are importuned by constituents to engage in such epistolary efforts might do well to keep at hand Senator George Norris' classic letter of declination, quoted in LANDIS, THE ADMINISTRATIVE PROCESS, 101-04 (1938).

[4] Industries has filed a petition in the 9th Circuit to review this order.

New York. Asserting violation of § 17(d) and Rule 17d-1 by Industries and Fund, the complaint sought temporary and permanent relief enjoining further acquisition of General Time stock, requiring Industries and Fund to withdraw any votes cast at the stockholders' meeting, enjoining the voting of such shares for nominees proposed by Industries or for any merger with Industries, and enjoining future violations by Industries and Fund. The parties agreed that the court should order the trial to be advanced and consolidated with the hearing on the application for a preliminary injunction, see F.R.Civ.P. 65(a)(2). After trial Judge Wyatt delivered an opinion directing dismissal of the complaint, this appeal followed, and we have given it expedited treatment. Meanwhile the stockholders' meeting of General Time has been adjourned at first by stipulation and later by a stay issued by this court.

II.

The first issue is whether the SEC may lawfully conclude that when an affiliated person and a registered investment company engage in a plan to achieve together a substantial stock position in another company, they can have effected "any transaction in which such registered company ... is a joint or a joint and several participant" with the affiliate even though there is no legally binding agreement between them; we postpone the related issue whether if that proposition be affirmed, the facts here sufficiently disclose such a plan.

Little purpose would be achieved by tired-eye scrutiny of the word "transaction." This is not a technical term; "transact" means "To prosecute negotiations; to carry on business; to have dealings ...." WEBSTER'S NEW INTERNATIONAL DICTIONARY (2d ed.). If any investment company and an affiliate agreed that each would buy 20% of the stock of a third company and would not sell without the other's consent, the case would evidently come within § 17(d), and it would be altogether immaterial whether "transaction" was read to refer to each purchase or the entire course of dealing or both. The real issue concerns the phrase "is a joint or a joint and several participant."[5]

---

[5] We thus find it unnecessary to discuss the issue, much debated by the parties, whether the SEC went beyond the statute when it added the words in Rule 17d-1(a), "in connection with, any joint enterprise or other joint arrangement or profit-sharing plan...." In defining these terms subdivision (c) requires that the affiliate and the investment company "have a joint or a joint and several participation" or—not here contended—"share in the profits of such enterprise or undertaking." Hence, as to this case the critical question under the Rule is the same as under the statute.

We begin by conceding that, on a quick reading, such black-letter words call up an image of situations where there is a considerable degree of common understanding. Industries argues, in a conspicuously able brief, that this conclusion is reinforced by § 12(a)(2) which forbids any registered investment company, in contravention of Commission rules, regulations or orders, "to participate on a joint or a joint and several basis in any trading account in securities ....," this rather obviously contemplating a situation where definite legal obligations are fixed. Against this, however, § 17(d) must have been intended to reach situations not already covered by § 12(a). Furthermore any idea that § 17(d) is limited to the typical joint venture in which each of the parties has a fractional share is negated by the point that its very bite is to limit or prevent participation by the investment company "on a basis different from or less advantageous than that" of the affiliated person.

We find it hard to believe that a Congress which had declared "that the national public interest and the interest of investors are adversely affected ... when investment companies are organized, operated, managed, or their portfolio securities are selected, in the interest of directors, officers, investment advisers, depositors, or other affiliated persons thereof ... rather than in the interest of all classes of such companies' security holders," § 1(b)(2), meant "a joint or a joint and several participant" to be read in light of common law concepts of jointness. The need for a liberal construction in order to effectuate the statutory purpose would be clearer if, for example, Industries had been an affiliate because of its holding of 5% or more of the voting securities of Fund, § 2(a)(3)(A), rather than the reverse. Yet if "joint" embraces a loose kind of combination in cases of the former type where the case for a liberal construction is strong, as held by Judge Nordbye with respect to directors in *SEC v. Midwest Technical Development Corp.* (D. Minn. 1963), it must also do that here where the case is less so[6]—and this even though the strict letter of the statutory command is limited to the affiliate. Moreover, Congress could have thought that downstream affiliation also involved some danger that the investment company's

---

[6] *SEC v. Sterling Precision Corp., supra,* does not support the view that the same language can be read one way in the case of upstream and another way in the case of downstream affiliation. We there declined to expand the word "purchase" in § 17(a)(2) to include a redemption by a downstream affiliate of its securities held by the investment company when a "sale" to the investment company of securities of the investment company held by an affiliate, whether downstream or upstream, admitted by the SEC to include a redemption, had been expressly excluded by Congress in § 17(a)(1).

stockholders might be put upon for the benefit of other stockholders of the affiliate.[7] "Joint" can mean not only "joined" or "united" but "combined." WEBSTER'S NEW INTERNATIONAL DICTIONARY (2d ed.). The case is thus appropriate for application of the settled principle that when administration of a statute has been confided to a regulatory agency and a statutory term is reasonably capable of the interpretation the agency has given, a court will sustain this even though it might have reached a different conclusion if the issue had arisen otherwise. [citations omitted].

Even on that view, however, some element of "combination" is required. Industries forcefully contends this to be negated, particularly by Chestnutt's statement to Talley before Fund had even decided to make purchases of General Time. But here Industries encounters the Commission's decision to the contrary. Passing for the moment the question of the validity of the portion of Rule 17d-1 authorizing the hearing conducted by the SEC, we cannot subscribe to Industries' argument that in any event the administrative proceeding was "without legal significance," so that, as in *SEC v. Frank*, 388 F.2d 486 (2 Cir. 1968), the Commission was cast in the district court in the same role as a private litigant as regards factual issues. To be sure the case is not here on a petition to review the SEC's order denying Industries' application for retrospective approval, and the provision of § 43(a) making its findings conclusive if supported by substantial evidence thus is not applicable by its terms. But the principle underlying that rule—that a factual determination by an agency responsible for the execution of Congressional policy and vested with expertise shall not be disturbed by a court where there is substantial evidence to support it—applies none the less, and it would be little short of absurd for us to decline to follow the same standard by which a court reviewing the Commission's order would be bound. Cf. *SEC v. Central-Illinois Securities Corp.*, 338 U.S. 96 (1949).

Our summary of the facts shows there was substantial evidence here. While no one has cast doubt on the veracity of Chestnutt's testimony as to his initial conversation with Talley, this did not preclude the Commission's drawing a contrary inference of intention from what the parties actually did. Indeed developments may well have brought Industries and Fund into a "combination" not clearly envisioned by either at the outset; war and the threat of war have always been powerful forgers of alliances. The

---

[7] We have noted the Commission's Proposal, IC-5128 (1967), to modify Rule 17d-1 "to provide more precise standards for the determination whether and when an application must be filed" and in that connection to narrow the cases where application must be made. See particularly proposed paragraph (e).

Commission was justified in using its knowledge of the unspoken customs of the business world to conclude that, after Chestnutt had seen Industries spend over $8,300,000 in acquiring the 205,837 shares purchased in the special offer and on February 21 and 23, he was no longer a completely free agent as to the 210,000 shares Fund had purchased, on Talley's recommendation, for about 70% of that price. Experienced business men must have known at the outset that such a situation might arise. "An administrative agency with power after hearings to determine on the evidence in adversary proceedings whether violations of statutory commands have occurred may infer within the limits of the inquiry from the proven facts such conclusions as reasonably may be based upon the facts proven. One of the purposes which lead to the creation of such boards is to have decisions based upon evidential facts under the particular statute made by experienced officials with an adequate appreciation of the complexities of the subject which is entrusted to their administration." *Republic Aviation v. NLRB*, 324 U.S. 793 (1945).

III.

The other serious issue of construction is whether, in seeking to implement § 17(d) by a general requirement of advance application and approval, Rule 17d-1 exceeds the authority granted by Congress. Industries contends that the power conferred by § 17(d) was to prescribe *substantive* rules and regulations "for the purpose of limiting or preventing participation by such registered or controlled company on a basis different from or less advantageous than that of such other participant"; that the Commission has prescribed none but rather has unlawfully insisted on advance application and approval in every case; . . . .

Here again, while initial reaction may favor Industries' contention, reflection sustains the Commission's view. The varieties in which participation by an investment company may be "different from or less advantageous than that" of an affiliate are infinite. The Commission could well have concluded that an attempt to specify these might fail to accomplish the Congressional purpose in some instances and in others accomplish more than Congress desired, and that the only effective method of regulation was to require advance disclosure and individual decision, at least until a pattern emerged, cf. note 7. Furthermore, as the Commission points out in brief, the public notice and opportunity for interested persons to come forward provided by the application procedure may lead to the development of significant facts that would not otherwise have been disclosed. * * * *

IV.

Our reversal of the judgment dismissing the complaint does not imply any belief on our part that the SEC is entitled to the drastic relief sought. Cf. *SEC v. Midwest Technical Development Corp., supra*. This action is not one for enforcement of an order making such directions, where weight must be given to the agency's selection of remedy. It is a suit in equity, whose essence lies in "the power of the Chancellor to do equity and mould each decree to the necessities of the particular case." *Hecht Co. v. Bowles*, 321 U.S. 321 (1944).

The objective of § 17(d) of the Investment Company Act is to prevent affiliated persons from injuring the interests of stockholders of registered investment companies by causing the company to participate "on a basis different from or less advantageous than that of such other participant." On the face of things that has not happened here up to this time, and the objective for a court of equity must be to insure that it does not happen in the future. While we do not undertake to particularize the form of a decree, a prohibition against sale of its shares by Industries without according Fund a fair opportunity to participate would be one obvious device to that end. On the other hand, as at present advised, we fail to perceive how the interest of Fund's stockholders would be advanced by such provisions as requiring Industries and Fund to withdraw votes cast at the April 22 stockholders' meeting of General Time and enjoining further voting by them. Requirements of that sort would have a strong tendency to induce forced liquidation at least on the part of Industries, which surely did not make its large investment in order to be a voteless minority stockholder in General Time, and this might well be detrimental rather than advantageous to the stockholders of Fund. Whether or not General Time had sufficient standing to direct judicial attention to the violation of § 17(d), an issue on which we have no occasion to pass, protection of the interests of its management in retention in office is not an objective of that section. While an order going beyond what would otherwise be the necessities of the case may sometimes be justified as against a deliberate flouter of regulatory statutes, Industries and Fund cannot be so regarded. Section 17(d) had been rarely construed, the only reported cases cited to us in addition to *SEC v. Midwest Technical Development Corp., supra*, being one portion of a decision of the Commission under the Securities Exchange Act, *Imperial Financial Services, Inc.*, 33-7684 (1965), and a portion of a very recent case dealing primarily with § 17(a), *Fifth Ave. Coach Lines, Inc.*, IC-5214 (1967). No decided case had ever applied § 17(d) to a situation like that here, and conscientious counsel could well have believed the reservations Chestnutt stated were sufficient to make it inapplicable.

The judgment dismissing the complaint is reversed, with directions to the District Court to proceed promptly to formulate an injunction consistent with this opinion. The stay of the reconvening of the annual meeting of General Time will remain in effect until such injunction is issued.

Topic 2 Remuneration Limitation on Affiliate "Acting as Broker" for Fund

Laws & Rules Highlight:

IC Act (15 USC 80a-1 *et seq.*) & Rules (17 CFR §§ 270.0-1 *et seq.*)

IC Act § 17 Transactions of Certain Affiliated Persons and Underwriters

- § 17(e)(2) (*limits compensation of a fund affiliate (first-tier or second-tier) when "**acting as broker**" to "usual and customary broker's commission"*)
- Rule 17e-1 Brokerage Transactions on a Securities Exchange (***safe harbor*** *rule defining when an affiliated broker's remuneration shall be deemed as "not exceeding usual and customary broker's commission"; design of the safe harbor is to permit an affiliated broker to receive no more than the amount an unaffiliated broker would receive in an arm's length transaction; availability of safe harbor conditions on the fund board satisfying* ***Fund Governance Standards***)

Research Note:[Biblio]

Managing Conflicts of Interest: Remuneration Limitation on Affiliated Brokers

IC Act § 17(e)(2) provides:

(e) It shall be ***unlawful*** for any affiliated person of a registered investment company, or any affiliated person of such person— * * *

(2) ***acting as broker***, in connection with the sale of securities to or by such registered company or any controlled company thereof, to receive from any source a commission, fee, or other remuneration for effecting such transaction which ***exceeds*** **(A)** the ***usual and customary broker's commission*** if the sale is effected on a securities exchange, **or (B)** *2 per centum* of the sales price if the sale is effected in connection with a secondary distribution of such securities, **or (C)** *1 per centum* of the purchase or sale price of such securities if the sale is otherwise effected unless the Commission shall, by rules and regulations or order in the public interest and consistent with the protection of investors, permit a larger commission.

Section 17(e)(2) addresses the conflicts of interest that may arise when funds effect portfolio trades through affiliated brokers (whether first-tier or second-tier affiliates), by limiting the amounts of compensation affiliated brokers may receive from the funds.[1a]

With respect to **§ 17(e)(2)(A)** securities transactions effected on a stock exchange, the SEC has adopted a safe harbor Rule 17e-1 to determine whether brokerage commissions paid by a fund to an affiliated broker-dealer satisfy the ***statutory standard*** of "*usual and customary broker's commission*."[1] The ***regulatory standard*** prescribed in the safe harbor is whether:[2]

> "[t]he commission, fee, or other remuneration received or to be received is ***reasonable and fair*** compared to the commission, fee or other remuneration received by *other brokers* in connection with *comparable transactions* involving *similar securities* being purchased or sold on a securities exchange during *a comparable period of time*."

In the event that the Rule 17e-1 regulatory standard is not met, the fund and its affiliated broker are required to establish compliance ***directly*** with § 17(e)(2)(A) statutory standard, in order for the affiliated broker to retain lawfully the brokerage commission it received.[1a (n.9)]

To rely on Rule 17e-1's regulatory standard, the fund must satisfy the following ***conditions***:[2]

- ***fund governance condition:*** the fund board satisfies *Fund Governance Standards* specified in IC Rule 0-1(a)(7).
- ***compensation procedure and review condition:*** the fund board, including a majority of its independent directors, *establishes procedures reasonably designed* to provide that affiliated brokerage compensation is consistent with the regulatory standard, and *reviews and determines at least quarterly* that all transactions effected pursuant to Rule 17e-1 in the preceding quarter were *in compliance* with such procedures.
- ***recordkeeping condition:*** the fund shall maintain copies of the procedures, and records of each transaction setting forth (1) *amount and source* of compensation received or to be received, (2) *identity* of the broker, (3) *terms* of the transaction, and (4) *information and materials supporting the board's quarterly findings* of compliance with the procedures.

In addition, information concerning aggregate brokerage commissions paid by a fund to any first-tier and second-tier affiliates must be ***disclosed*** in the fund's prospectuses.[1a; 3]

Bibliography:

1. Rule 17e-2 Rels.: **1a.** Agency Transactions by Affiliated Persons on a Securities Exchange, IC-10605, 44 FR 12202 (1979); **1b.** IC-10741, 44 FR 37202 (1979); **1c.** Transactions of Investment Companies with Portfolio and Subadviser Affiliates, IC-25557, 67 FR 31081 (2002); **1d.** IC-25888, 68 FR 3142 (2003)
2. IC Rule 17e-1 Brokerage Transactions on a Securities Exchange (2018)
3. Form N-1A—Part B, Item 21 Brokerage Allocation and Other Practices (2018)

Topic 3 Prohibition of Affiliate "Acting as Agent" Compensated by Third Party

Laws & Rules Highlight:

IC Act (15 USC 80a-1 *et seq.*) & Rules (17 CFR §§ 270.0-1 *et seq.*)
IA Act ((15 USC 80b-1 *et seq.*) & Rules (17 CFR §§ 275.0-2 *et seq.*)

IC Act: § 17 Transactions of Certain Affiliated Persons and Underwriters

- § 17(e)(1) (*prohibits any fund affiliate when "**acting as agent**" for the fund from accepting compensation from a third party—designed to protect agent's judgment and fidelity from impairment; prohibition applicable to both **first-tier and second-tier** affiliates*)

IC & IA Acts: Codes of Ethics

- IC Act § 17(j) (*prohibits fraudulent trading activities by: any affiliated person of registered IC; principal underwriter for the fund; any affiliated person of fund's IA or of fund's principal underwriter*)
    - Rule 17j-1 Personal Investment Activities of Investment Company Personnel (*requires a **Code of Ethics** to be adopted respectively by: **fund; fund's IA; fund's principal underwriter**; regulates **personal investing** activities of "access persons"—designed to prevent insiders' trading which conflicts with the fund's investment program*)
    - Rule 17j-1(a)(1) (*def. "**access person**" to include portfolio management personnel and others having access to the fund's investment decision making process*)
- IA Act § 204A Prevention of Misuse of Nonpublic Information
    - Rule 204A-1 Investment Adviser Codes of Ethics (*requires registered IA to adopt a **Code of Ethics** governing its "supervised persons"; IA Rule 204A-1 being modeled on IC Rule 17j-1*)
    - § 202(a)(5) (*def. "**supervised person**"*)

IC & IA Acts: Compliance Programs

- IC Act § 38 Rules, Regulations, and Orders; General Powers of Commission
    - Rule 38a-1 Compliance Procedures and Practices of Certain Investment Companies
- IA Act § 206(4) (*grants SEC rulemaking authority to define fraud and to prescribe means reasonably designed to prevent fraud*)
    - Rule 206(4)-7 Compliance Procedures and Practices (*requires registered IA to adopt and implement compliance policies and procedures*)

Pre-Case Background Note:[Biblio]

Prohibited Conflicts of Interest: Fund Affiliate "*Acting as Agent*" Accepting "*Compensation*" from Third Party

IC Act § 17(e)(1) provides:

(e) It shall be ***unlawful*** for any affiliated person of a registered investment company, or any affiliated person of such person—

(1) ***acting as agent***, to *accept from* any source any *compensation* (*other than* a regular salary or wages *from* such registered company) for the purchase or sale of any property to or for such registered company or any controlled company thereof, *except* in the course of such person's business as an underwriter or broker;

Section 17(e)(1) thus ***prohibits*** any first-tier or any second-tier affiliate from accepting any "*compensation*" from a third party, in connection with that affiliate's purchase or sale of any property for the fund when "*acting as agent*" for the fund, other than "*acting as broker*" the latter being governed by § 17(e)(2). Section 17(e)(1) prohibition addresses the ***abuse*** where the *benefit* of a reciprocal relationship between the affiliated person and a third party is diverted to the affiliated person, while the *burden* of that relationship is borne by the investment company.[1] The ***objective*** of § 17(e)(1) prohibition is to prevent affiliated persons from operating under, and having their judgment and fidelity impaired by, conflicts of interest.[2]

There are ***four elements*** to a violation of § 17(e)(1): an "*affiliated person*" of a registered IC, who is "*acting as agent*" for the IC, accepts "*compensation*" from any source other than his regular salary or wages, "*for*" the purchase or sale of any property to or for the IC.[3] For the purposes of § 17(e)(1):[2; 4]

- "***affiliated person***" includes both first-tier affiliate and second-tier affiliate;
- "***acting as agent***" element is satisfied when the affiliate is not "***acting as broker***" within the meaning of § 17(e)(2);
- "***compensation***" is broadly construed to include any item received and regarded by the recipient at the time of receipt as a benefit, regardless of its market value; "*compensation*" shall be distinguished from "*disgorgement*" calculation, which shall be based on cost to the benefit provider rather than the recipient's personal belief of the benefit of the compensation;

- "*for*" element is met and the offense is complete when the compensation is delivered and received with the "*forbidden intent*," *i.e.*, intent that the compensation be given and accepted in appreciation of past or in anticipation of future conduct; § 17(e)(1) offense does not require "*an intent to influence*" the affiliate's conduct, or that the affiliated person acted as a result of receiving the prohibited compensation.

Bibliography:

1. Investors Research Corp. v. SEC, 628 F.2d 168 (DC Cir. 1980), *cert. denied*, 449 U.S. 919 (1980)
2. United States v. Deutsch, 451 F.2d 98 (2d Cir. 1971)
3. In *re* Scott E. Desano *et al.*: Initial Decision as to Robert L. Burns, Adm. Proc. 3-12978 (2011)
4. United States v. Ostrander, 999 F.2d 27 (2d Cir. 1993)

Case Study 1: "Acting as Agent"

Issuer officer (Jerome Deutsch) was criminally convicted for ***aiding and abetting*** an **agent for mutual funds** (Frank Mills) in knowingly accepting unlawful "*compensation*": agent purchased a note from the issuer at *discount price* for himself while purchasing the same note from the issuer at *full price* for the funds. *Deutsch* is the first criminal prosecution brought under § 17(e)(1).

Jerome Deutsch was a senior officer of issuer Realty Equities Corporation. During the period in question, Deutsch was in charge of Realty's sale of an issue of securities consisting of units of promissory notes attached with warrants, but was having difficulty selling any unit. Then, **Frank Mills**, a senior officer of the Fidelity mutual fund complex, committed **Fidelity Puritan Fund** to purchase two notes—resulting in Realty's first sale, and further permitted Deutsch to use Puritan's prestigious name in his selling efforts. Use of Puritan's name as a "sales pitch" was effective: not only was the original offering amount immediately and fully subscribed but an additional amount of the notes was also all sold. Subsequently, Mills purchased one unit of the note from Deutsch for his **personal account** at about half of the note's market price, while merely three days later Mills caused the purchase of two units for **Fidelity Trend Fund** at the full market price. **Deutsch** was convicted of violating the ***Aider & Abettor Act***, for aiding and abetting Mills in knowingly accepting compensation from the issuer while acting as agent for registered investment companies in violation of § 17(e)(1). To sustain Deutsch's *aider and abettor conviction*, the Second Circuit construed ***§ 17(e)(1)*** to find **Mills** committing the *principal offense*.

Defining the scope of the statutory phrase "***acting as agent***," the Second Circuit enunciated:

> [The term "Agent"] defines a subclass of affiliated persons. Within the statutory scheme of § 17(e), affiliated persons who are ***acting as brokers*** may receive limited compensation in connection with portfolio transactions of the registered investment company. If affiliated persons are ***not acting as brokers***, however, but ***otherwise are acting as agents*** of the investment company, they cannot accept compensation in connection with the purchase or sale of securities. [A]n affiliated person is acting as agent within the meaning of § 17(e)(1) in all cases when he is not acting as broker for the investment company.

Likening § 17(e)(1) to the federal bribery, kickback, and gratuity statutes where the crime is complete upon the acceptance of the payment and no proof of "intent to influence" is required, the Second Circuit concluded: under § 17(e)(1) "***the paying of compensation is an evil in itself***." "An offense under § 17(e)(1) is ***complete*** when the compensation is delivered and received with ***the forbidden intent***"—the "intent to give and accept a gratuity in appreciation of past or future conduct."

United States v. Deutsch
451 F.2d 98 (2d Cir. 1971)

[***Procedural history***: United States v. Deutsch, 321 F. Supp. 1356 (SDNY 1971), *aff'd*, 451 F.2d 98 (2d Cir. 1971), *cert. denied*, 404 U.S. 1019 (1972)]

Case Study 2: Unlawful "Compensation" and Portfolio Manager Personal Investing Activity

Mutual fund portfolio manager (Patricia Ostrander) was criminally convicted for violations of §§ 17(e) and 17(j) of the IC Act. Section **17(e)(1)** makes it unlawful for any fund affiliate to accept any "***compensation***" in exchange for investing assets of the fund. Section **17(j)** and SEC **Rule 17j-1** regulate ***personal investing activities*** of fund "*access persons*" (*i.e.*, fund personnel such as portfolio managers, analysts, and traders, who, in performing their day-to-day responsibilities, may have access to information about impending fund transactions); and prohibit ***fraudulent, deceptive or manipulative*** acts by access persons in connection with their investment activities on behalf of the investment companies.*

**Ref.* [REPORT OF THE DIV. INV. MGMT., PERSONAL INVESTMENT ACTIVITIES OF INVESTMENT COMPANY PERSONNEL (1994)]

Underwriting firm **Drexel Burnham Lambert** publicly offered for sale ***LBO securities*** consisting of zero coupon bonds, debenture bonds, and preferred stock; it simultaneously conducted a private offering of ***LBO warrants*** as equity sweeteners, but only to those institutions which had purchased the LBO securities. **Patricia Ostrander**, a portfolio manager at the Fidelity mutual fund complex, purchased from Drexel hundreds of millions of dollars worth of the LBO securities on behalf of Fidelity mutual funds. Shortly thereafter, Drexel offered Ostrander the opportunity, which she accepted, to make a personal investment in **MacPherson Investment Partners L.P.**, a partnership that owned the LBO warrants.

While the LBO warrants were highly speculative at the time of her purchase and no witnesses were able to provide a valuation, the court found that a jury *need not determine* if Ostrander's warrant investment was made at *less than market value* in order to constitute "***compensation***." **Under § 17(e)**, it is enough if the item received was ***regarded as a benefit by the recipient***, whether or not others might have taken a different view of its value. Thus, it was enough that Ostrander was offered an opportunity to purchase the LBO warrants which was offered to only a few; and Ostrander clearly regarded the opportunity to purchase as a benefit by investing in the warrants. Under **§ 17(j)** and **Rule 17j-1**, Ostrander's failure to report her personal investment in the MacPherson partnership was found a crime.

United States v. Ostrander

999 F.2d 27 (2d Cir. 1993)

[***Procedural history & related proceedings***: United States v. Ostrander, 792 F. Supp. 241 (SDNY 1992), *aff'd*, 999 F.2d 27 (2d Cir. 1993); In *re* Patricia A. Ostrander, Respondent, Adm. Proc. 3-8035, 34-32254, IA-1371 (1993)]

Research Topics:

Regulation, supervision, and reporting of personal trading activities of registered funds' personnel under Chinese investment management laws; compliance and ethics programs of registered investment companies, investment advisers, and fund underwriters in China.

United States, Appellee v. Deutsch, Appellant

451 F.2d 98 (2d Cir. 1971)

Before FEINBERG, MULLIGAN and TIMBERS, Circuit Judges.

OPINION

TIMBERS, Circuit Judge:

This appeal presents questions of first impression under the Investment Company Act of 1940 (the Act). It involves the first criminal prosecution charging violations of § 17(e)(1) of the Act, during the thirty years the Act has been on the books—willful violations of the Act being punishable by a fine of not more than $10,000 and/or imprisonment of not more than two years. 15 USC § 80a-48 (1964).

Jerome Deutsch appeals from a judgment of conviction entered upon a jury verdict after a six day trial in the Southern District of New York, Charles M. Metzner, *District Judge*, finding him guilty, in violation of 18 USC § 2 (1964), of aiding and abetting one Frank D. Mills in knowingly accepting compensation from the issuer of certain securities while Mills was acting as agent for certain registered investment companies, in violation of 15 USC § 80a-17(e)(1)(1964). Deutsch also appeals from Judge Metzner's order denying his postconviction motion for *coram nobis* relief, 321 F. Supp. 1356. Finding no reversible error, we affirm.

OFFENSES CHARGED

Deutsch was tried on one count of a seven-count indictment charging violations of § 17 of the Act,[1] and of 18 USC § 2 (1964).

---

[1] Sections 17(d) and (e) of the Investment Company Act of 1940, provide:

"(d) It shall be unlawful for any affiliated person of or principal underwriter for a registered investment company (other than a company of the character described in § 80a-12(d)(3)(A) and (B) of this title), or any affiliated person of such a person or principal underwriter, acting as principal to effect any transaction in which such registered company, or a company controlled by such registered company, is a joint or a joint and several participant with such person, principal underwriter, or affiliated person, in contravention of such rules and regulations as the Commission may prescribe for the purpose of limiting or preventing participation by such registered or controlled company on a basis different from or less advantageous than that of such other participant. * * * *

(e) *It shall be unlawful for any affiliated person of a registered investment company*, or any affiliated person of such person—

(1) *acting as agent, to accept from any source any compensation* (other than a regular salary or wages from such

Counts One and Two charged Deutsch's co-defendant, Frank D. Mills, with knowingly effecting purchases of securities for his personal account and for the accounts of two registered investment companies of which he was an affiliated person, Puritan Fund, Inc. and Fidelity Trend Fund, Inc., in violation of § 17(d) of the Act. Counts Three and Four charged Deutsch with aiding and abetting these crimes, in violation of 18 USC § 2 (1964).

Count Five charged Mills with knowingly accepting compensation from Realty Equities Corporation in New York, the issuer of the securities, while Mills was acting as agent for the registered investment companies, in violation of 15 USC § 80a-17(e)(1)(1964). Count Six charged Deutsch with aiding and abetting this crime.

Count Seven charged both defendants with use of the mails in making false statements and omitting material statements regarding the transactions between Realty Equities and the investment companies with which Mills was affiliated, in violation of the Securities Exchange Act of 1934, 15 USC § 78j(b) (1964), and of 18 USC § 2 (1964). The government consented to a dismissal of Count Seven prior to trial.

Mills pleaded guilty to Count One on April 7, 1970. After Deutsch's trial, Mills was fined $7,500 on May 19, 1970, and Counts Two and Five were dismissed. Trial of Deutsch alone commenced April 20 and ended April 27, 1970. Counts Three and Four were dismissed at the close of the government's case. The jury found Deutsch guilty on the remaining count, Count Six. Deutsch was fined $10,000 on August 4, 1970.

TRANSACTIONS UNDERLYING OFFENSES CHARGED

Before discussing the claims raised on appeal, a narration of the events beginning in the summer of 1967 and culminating in the indictment returned April 11, 1969 is necessary to an understanding of the rather sophisticated crimes with which Mills and Deutsch were charged. Upon the record before us, the jury could have found as follows.

During the summer of 1967, Deutsch was executive vice president and a member of the three-man board of directors of Realty Equities Corporation in New York, a real estate investment company listed on the American Stock Exchange. Realty had been founded by Deutsch and others in 1959. By 1968 it had consolidated assets of $137 million.

---

registered company) *for the purchase* or sale *of any property* to or *for such registered company* or any controlled company thereof, except in the course of such person's business as an underwriter or broker; or

(2) acting as broker, * * * *

(Italicized provisions are those directly involved herein.)

In the summer of 1967, Realty anticipated a forthcoming merger in connection with which it needed to raise a substantial amount of capital. Realty decided to finance the merger by a private placement, limited to institutional investors only, of $12 million in promissory notes with warrants attached. This security was to be issued in units of $500,000. Each unit was to consist of a $500,000 7 1/2% 15-year promissory note, a warrant for the purchase of 37,500 shares of Realty stock at a gradually ascending price, and the right to use the note in lieu of cash when exercising the warrant. The purchase price of the unit was to be the face amount of the note. The initial exercise price of the warrant was to be the market price of Realty stock on the day before the first closing.

Deutsch was in charge of selling the issue. His initial efforts met with failure. As of December 4, 1967, he had not succeeded in selling a single note. While peddling this issue, however, Deutsch had his first contact with the co-defendant, Frank D. Mills, a contact which resulted in the first sale of Realty notes.

During the summer of 1967 and throughout 1968, Mills was a senior officer of Fidelity Management and Research Company in Boston, and of twelve mutual funds for which it acted as investment adviser. Mills was a member of the six-man investment committee of all the funds, whose aggregate assets exceeded $3.5 billion and whose combined stockholders numbered over 500,000. As such, he participated in the preparation of periodic guidelines listing securities and maximum dollar values which the fund account managers could buy or sell without approval; he also was one of the two men whose approval was needed for any transaction outside the guidelines. Mills was the account manager of one of the funds, the Puritan Fund, and, as such, he had authority to buy or sell up to $2 million in any bond and up to the guideline limits for approved stocks. Mills also was vice president of eight of the funds, including Puritan Fund and Fidelity Trend Fund. It is undisputed that Puritan and Fidelity Trend were registered investment companies and that Mills was an affiliated person of each of them within the meaning of the Act. 15 USC § § 80a-2(3), 80a-3, 80a-8 (1964).

Deutsch's first contact with Mills occurred as a result of Deutsch's attempt, in the summer of 1967, to sell some of the issue to Massachusetts Mutual Life Insurance Company in Boston. Homer Chapin, executive vice president in charge of investments, was also a director of Fidelity Management and the chairman of its investment committee. He told Deutsch that state insurance law barred Massachusetts Life from purchasing that type of security; but a few days later, Chapin recommended the issue to Mills, saying that from what he knew Realty was satisfactory in every way and that if he were interested he should contact Deutsch directly. The first sale of Realty notes ensued.

On December 8, 1967, Mills committed the Puritan Fund to purchase two notes. This first sale appeared to be the shot in the arm that Realty needed. With Mills' permission, Deutsch used Puritan's prestigious name in talking to prospective buyers. As Deutsch testified at trial, this was "a good sales pitch" and "very helpful." The entire offering was soon fully subscribed, and an additional $5 million in notes was authorized. This offering, too, was fully subscribed, with Puritan itself taking an additional $700,000 on June 14, 1968, bringing its investment up to the statutory limit of 10% of the offering. By August 9, 1968, Realty had thus succeeded in borrowing $17 million.

On August 29, 1968, Deutsch again called Chapin who had recently joined Realty's board of directors at Deutsch's invitation. Realty had contracted to repurchase five units from Republic National Life Insurance Company in Texas, one of the original subscribers, and had an option to repurchase seven more, the balance of Republic's interest, at prices which were advantageous in view of an appreciable rise in the market price of Realty stock. Meanwhile, Massachusetts law had changed, and the notes were now permissible purchases for insurance companies. Deutsch was thus able to offer to sell Massachusetts Life some of the Republic National Life units. Deutsch did not disclose the repurchase contract between Realty and Republic National Life. He led Chapin to believe that the seller was Republic National Life and that the price had not yet been negotiated. Deutsch pointed out to Chapin that the exercise price was 15 1/4 whereas the stock was trading at 32. Chapin said he was interested and asked for more information.

On September 11, Richard Dooley, a Massachusetts Life securities analyst to whom Chapin had referred the matter, told Deutsch that Massachusetts Life was rejecting the offer because of house counsel's opinion that the price was so advantageous it gave the transaction the appearance of being a corporate gift in view of Chapin's interlocking directorships.[2] Deutsch renewed the offer at a higher price, 7 3/4 premium per warrant

---

[2] On September 4, 1968, Deutsch told Chapin that the resale price of the notes had not yet been fixed, but that he thought Republic National Life would charge a relatively small premium for the warrants. A few days later, in a telephone conversation with Dooley, Deutsch said the premium to be charged was $3 per share, so that the effective conversion price would be 18 1/4. Dooley, aware that the stock was trading at 30 1/4, calculated that on a $1 million note the company would make an immediate paper profit of $900,000, and recommended purchase of what he thought was an exceptional bargain. It was the size of this "profit" which made house

instead of 3, saying that it brought the price into line with what he was told was the customary discount.[3] Counsel for Massachusetts Life still thought the price was too advantageous. On September 25, Dooley relayed his company's final rejection.

Some time between September 23 and September 26, Chapin told Mills about Realty's exceptional offer and suggested that Mills call Deutsch. However, unknown to Chapin, Mills already knew about Deutsch's offer and had taken steps to seize the opportunity for himself. On September 16, five days after the initial rejection by Massachusetts Life, Mills had approached the president of the National Shawmut Bank in Boston for the purpose of borrowing enough cash to buy a unit of the Realty securities for himself. Mills told the bank that he wanted the transaction kept strictly confidential. To insure confidentiality, Mills asked the bank to make an exception to its general practice and to place the transaction in a nominee account. Shortly after September 24, the bank agreed to lend Mills $572,000 as the entire purchase price of a unit. On September 30, a few days after the Shawmut Bank agreed to lend Mills the $572,000, the Banque de Paris bought two identical units from Republic National Life at a price per unit of $928,125.

Some time in early October, Mills took two steps with respect to Realty securities. First, he gave a 50% participation in his private deal with Realty to a real estate investor named Philip Levin.[4] Second, he tried unsuccessfully to interest Richard Smith, the account manager of one-half of Fidelity Trend, to buy two notes for the fund. On October 15, after his unsuccessful approach to Richard Smith, Mills approached the account manager of the other half of Fidelity Trend, Ross Sherbrooke. Mills said two units would

---

counsel reject the tempting offer.

[3] Deutsch may have had ulterior motives in making this strenuous effort to sell the Realty securities to Massachusetts Life at such an advantageous price. During the negotiations, Deutsch explained to Richard Dooley why he was offering this exceptional bargain to Massachusetts Life. Dooley testified at trial that Deutsch told him:

> "Mass. Mutual and Realty Equities had a good business relationship, that he hoped this would continue, that the Realty Equities people loved Homer Chapin, that he hoped by extending this possible investment to us it would cement our relations over a period of time."

[4] Levin estimated that the date upon which Mills first offered him half a note was "approximately" August 1968. Deutsch argues that Levin's testimony supports his contention that he, Deutsch, had made a commitment to sell a note to Mills in February or March 1968. There was evidence, however, from which the jury could have found that Levin was mistaken about the date. If Mills had approached Levin in August, why would Mills ask the Shawmut Bank for a loan to finance the purchase of an entire unit on September 16? Moreover, Mills did not inform the bank until October 17 that he would require only half the money since he was buying only half the unit.

be available for a little over $900,000 per unit, but that there was some urgency and that Sherbrooke had to make up his mind by October 17, after which the notes would no longer be available. Mills did not disclose that he and Levin were about to buy a unit themselves at a substantially lower price. On the same day, Mills told the Shawmut Bank that he was ready to proceed with the loan and would require only half the money since he was buying only half the unit.

Mills undoubtedly was influential in Sherbrooke's decision to buy the Realty notes. Sherbrooke had never heard of Realty before. He looked up the company in standard reference books, asked a Fidelity specialist about it, and a day or so later told Mills he would take the two units. Mills was considerably senior to Sherbrooke. Since Sherbrooke had been on the job for only four months, he may well have been reluctant to reject his senior's suggestion. Sherbrooke at trial conceded that Mills' high opinion of Realty played a "significant role in influencing my judgment." Mills' and Levin's purchase and Fidelity Trend's purchase closed three days apart. Mills and Levin paid $537,000 for one unit on October 21; Fidelity Trend paid $928,125 per unit for two units—a total of $1,856,250—on October 24.

After his purchase was made, Mills continued to try to conceal the transaction. In violation of the Fidelity group's internal code of ethics, Mills did not report his purchase of the Realty note. Moreover, Mills had not requested advance approval of the transaction from the SEC, in violation of the regulations governing joint and several transactions of an affiliated person such as Mills and a fund such as Fidelity Trend. 15 USC § 80a-17(d) (1964); 17 CFR § 270.17d-1 (1971).

Deutsch also tried to conceal the transaction. He insisted that Levin use a nominee. When called before the SEC on November 22, 1968, he falsely testified that the two nominees were "two banks in the United States," when in fact Levin's nominee was Saul and Co. and Mills' nominee was Harris and Co. Deutsch also supplied the SEC with what he said was an office memorandum listing all subscribers and purchasers at resale. With respect to other nominees, this memorandum indicated the real parties in interest in parentheses; but with respect to Mills' and Levin's nominees, the real parties were not indicated.

At trial, the main thrust of Deutsch's defense was that he had agreed to sell a Realty note to Mills in February or March 1968 and that the actual sale the following October was the fulfillment of a promise made at a time when Deutsch had no idea that the notes would be worth so much more than face value. Deutsch testified that on February 29, 1968, after the closing of the sale of two Realty notes to Puritan, Mills told him he wanted personally to buy a note; that the next day, Deutsch told Realty's president, Morris Karp, about Mills' request and that Karp said it could not be done on original issue, but that Mills could purchase one of the notes on resale; and that several weeks later, near the end of March, Deutsch told Mills, "I got approval from Morris that if there is ever a resale you can have it for whatever price we get it for," to which Mills' response was, "Great. You got a deal."

Despite Deutsch's customary practice of making notes on his way home from negotiations, he made none of this commitment. His promise was not reflected in any contemporaneous writing. Moreover, this alleged oral agreement was not binding on Realty. See N.Y. UNIFORM COMMERCIAL CODE, § § 8-319 and 2-201 (McKinney 1964). Morris Karp, Realty's president, and David Stein, Realty's counsel, testified on Deutsch's behalf. While their testimony generally corroborated that of Deutsch, several inconsistencies between their testimony and Deutsch's could have led the jury to disbelieve Deutsch's story of the February-March commitment.

CLAIM THAT TRIAL COURT MISINTERPRETED § 17(e)(1) OF THE ACT

The essential issues on this appeal require interpretation of § 17(e)(1) of the Act. While this is the first criminal prosecution under § 17(e)(1), the SEC has had occasion at the administrative level to construe this section of the statute.[5] Prior to the instant case, however, no court, so far as we know, has discussed the intent of Congress in enacting § 17(e)(1).[6]

---

[5] Some of the SEC's more recent decisions involving § 17(e)(1) are: *Cornfield*, 34-9091 (March 1, 1971); *Provident Management Corp.*, 34-9028 (Dec. 1, 1970); *Dishy, Easton and Co.*, 34-8702 (Sept. 23, 1969); *Consumer-Investor Planning Corp.*, 34-8542 (Feb. 20, 1969); *Imperial Financial Services, Inc.*, 34-7684 (Aug. 26, 1965).

[6] In *Entel v. Guilden*, 223 F. Supp. 129 (SDNY 1963), *aff'd sub nom. Neuwirth v. Allen*, 338 F.2d 2 (2 Cir. 1964), the court decided that § 17(e) of the Act created a private right of action for the benefit of an investment company and that the right could be exercised secondarily by holders of perpetual warrants issued by the investment company. The court, however, did not attempt to unravel the proper meaning of § 17(e)(1).

Several district courts also have entered decrees enjoining violations of § 17(e), but they have not attempted to construe that section of the Act. See *SEC v. Bernhard & Co.*, (SDNY 1971); *SEC v. Commonwealth Security Investors, Inc.* (ED Ky. 1970).

Our Court has dealt with other subsections of § 17: *SEC v. Sterling Precision Corp.*, 393 F.2d 214 (2 Cir. 1968) (§ 17(a)(2)); *SEC v. Talley Indus., Inc.*, 399 F.2d 396 (2 Cir. 1968) (§ 17(d)). But these opinions do not help us in

Unfortunately, the legislative history affords little help in our present task of construing § 17(e)(1). While enactment of the Act was preceded by lengthy hearings, the section in question was explained only once during these proceedings, and this brief comment sheds little light on Congressional intent. The Senate and House Reports on the Act[7] also fail to deal specifically with § 17(e)(1). Congress did set forth in the Act a declaration of Congressional policy and specific findings, based on the SEC Report mentioned below. Section 1 of the Act.

The Act resulted from a four-year study of the investment company industry by the SEC.[8] The SEC Report depicted fantastic abuse of trust by investment company management and wholesale victimizing of security holders. The Act evolved from a bill which was based on the conclusions and recommendations of the SEC Report. After hearings had been held on a bill drafted by the SEC, the industry and the Commission worked out a compromise bill which passed without a dissenting vote.[9]

The Senate and House Reports indicate that the Act was designed primarily to correct the abuses of self-dealing which had produced injury to stockholders of investment companies.[10] Four sections of the Act, including § 17, were aimed specifically at insuring

---

interpreting § 17(e)(1).

[7] S. Rep. No. 1775, 76th Cong., 3d Sess. (1940) (Senate Report); H.R. Rep. No. 2639, 76th Cong., 3d Sess. (1940) (House Report).

[8] SEC REPORT ON THE STUDY OF INVESTMENT TRUSTS AND COMPANIES (SEC Report). The SEC Report was issued in five parts: The Nature, Classification and Origin of Investment Companies, H.R. Doc. No. 707, 75th Cong., 2d Sess. (1939); Statistical Survey of Investment Trusts and Investment Companies, H.R. Doc. No. 70, 76th Cong., 1st Sess. (1939); Abuses and Deficiencies in the Organization and Operation of Investment Trusts and Investment Companies, H.R. Doc. No. 279, 76th Cong., 2d Sess. (1940); Control and Influence Over Industry and Economic Significance of Investment Companies and Conclusions and Recommendations, H.R. Doc. No. 246, 77th Cong., 2d Sess. (1942).

[9] For a discussion of the events leading to the enactment of the Act and about the Act generally, see Motley *et al.*, *Federal Regulation of Investment Companies Since 1940*, 63 HARV. L. REV. 1134 (1950); Jaretzki, *The Investment Company Act of 1940*, 26 WASH. U.L.Q. 303 (1941); Comment, *The Investment Company Act of 1940*, 50 YALE L.J. 440 (1941).

[10] The Senate Committee on Banking and Currency reported:

"Basically the problems flow from the very nature of the assets of investment companies. The assets of such companies invariably consist of cash and securities, assets which are completely liquid, mobile and readily negotiable. Because of these characteristics, control of such funds offers manifold opportunities for exploitation by the unscrupulous managements of some companies." Senate Report, *supra* note 7.

the independence of management and its fidelity to stockholders.[11] Congress recognized that its existing laws were inadequate to prevent the abuses of self-dealing. Several times during the hearings, Senators questioned SEC attorneys on their inability to obtain convictions, thus evincing a concern about the difficulties of obtaining convictions for abuse of trust in the investment company industry. The Act was thus designed in part quite clearly to establish broad standards which would more easily enable the government to convict affiliated persons for self-dealing in the management of investment companies—an industry the very nature of which made it particularly difficult to gather proof.

Interpretation of the Phrase "Acting as Agent"

Section 17(e)(1), so far as here relevant, provides as follows: "It shall be unlawful for any affiliated person of a registered investment company, ... acting as agent, to accept from any source any compensation ... for the purchase ... of any property ... for such registered company...."

Deutsch does not dispute the fact that Mills was an affiliated person within the meaning of the Act and that Puritan and Fidelity Trend were registered companies. He contends, however, that the trial court misconstrued the phrase "acting as agent." He argues that this phrase makes the violation proscribed by § 17(e)(1) incomplete unless the compensation actually caused a fund to purchase or sell securities. The trial court rejected Deutsch's proposed construction and charged the jury that:

> "The Government does not have to show that Mills was influenced by the compensation he received or that as a result of receiving it Mills caused either of the funds to purchase the notes or influenced others in either of the funds to make such purchase."

Moreover, the trial court, interpreting the phrase as being merely descriptive of a subclass of affiliated persons, instructed the jury on the element of acting as agent in the following manner:

> "You may find that he acted as an agent if you determine that he had the power to make investment decisions for Puritan Fund at the time of its purchases or that as a result of his position in the company he could influence the decisions regarding the purchases by Fidelity Trend of Realty Equities notes."

---

[11] The others were § § 9, 10 and 15(c) and (d).

We believe that the trial court's interpretation of the phrase "acting as agent" was incorrect but that, if anything, it imposed a greater burden on the government in proving its case than was necessary and therefore Deutsch was not prejudiced.

Section 17(e)(1) does not explicitly make it an element of the offense that the recipient of the compensation take any action as a result thereof. Deutsch argues that the draftsman's use of a verb in the phrase "acting as agent" expresses a Congressional intent to prohibit only gratuities which succeed in influencing the recipient's conduct. We find it hard to believe, however, that a Congress which had recognized that the investment company industry "offer[ed] manifold opportunities for exploitation by unscrupulous managements ...," Senate Report, *supra* note 7, meant that an offense was complete only when the affiliated person acted as a result of receiving something of value. Rather, we believe that the more reasonable interpretation is that an offense under § 17(e)(1) is complete when the compensation is delivered and received with the forbidden intent. The objective of § 17(e)(1) is to prevent affiliated persons from having their judgment and fidelity impaired by conflicts of interest. It is clear that, as soon as Mills purchased the Realty note at a reduced price, he was inhibited by a conflict of interest which could easily becloud his judgment to the detriment of the beneficiaries of the funds. The abuse which § 17(e)(1) was designed to prevent—affiliated persons operating under conflicts of interest—was complete when Mills received the compensation, even if he never exerted any influence on Realty's behalf. Moreover, to accept Deutsch's construction would emasculate § 17(e)(1). Given the nature of the investment company industry, it would be extremely difficult to prove that the payment of compensation actually caused a particular purchase. It is most unlikely that Congress intended a construction which would rob § 17(e)(1) of its effectiveness.

Our interpretation of the phrase "acting as agent," namely, that it is a descriptive phrase and does not require a showing that the recipient of the compensation took any action as a result thereof, appears to be buttressed by the SEC's administrative views. In *Provident Management Corp.*, *supra* note 5, the SEC found a violation of § 17(e)(1) when an investment adviser to a registered investment company retained fees which rightfully belonged to the company. On three occasions, when the investment company tendered its holdings of securities in certain companies pursuant to public tender offers, Porteous, the president of the investment adviser, caused his company to be designated as soliciting agent and received and retained approximately $42,000 in tender fees from those inviting the tenders. The SEC held that the retention of the tender fees by Porteous constituted an impermissible form of compensation derived from the investment company's portfolio transactions. In so holding, however, the Commission did not find that the retention of the tender fees had caused Porteous to take any improper action. Instead, the mere retention of the fees constituted a violation of § 17(e)(1), because the SEC recognized that to permit the investment adviser to retain the fees would create a conflict of interest which might influence the adviser's future advice to the investment company: "To countenance such conduct would permit the determination whether an investment company's portfolio securities should be tendered to be influenced by considerations relating to the affiliate's compensation, and thereby create a conflict of interest between those acting in a fiduciary capacity for the investment company and the fund." *Id.*

Similarly, in *Imperial Financial Services, Inc., supra* note 5, the SEC found that actual conduct as a result of being compensated was not an essential element of the offense proscribed by § 17(e)(1). There the SEC held that it was a violation of § 17(e)(1) for an officer of an investment adviser to an investment company to buy securities at a discount from a broker-dealer, because the officer "was in a position to influence" the choice of broker-dealers who would be granted business through transactions in the investment company's portfolio securities; *id.* See also *Consumer-Investor Planning Corporation, supra* note 5. It is true that in the latter two cases the affiliated person probably acted as a result of receiving compensation, but the opinions do not turn on this.

Our interpretation of the phrase "acting as agent," that it is not necessary to show actual conduct as a result of the compensation, further appears to be consistent with decisions of this Court and of other Courts of Appeals interpreting statutes analogous to § 17(e)(1) which likewise are designed to prevent officials and other "insiders" from operating under conflicts of interest. In *United States v. Irwin*, 354 F.2d 192 (2 Cir. 1965), *cert. denied*, 383 U.S. 967 (1966), we held that it was not necessary to show actual conduct to prove the unlawful payment of a gratuity to a public official under 18 USC § 201(f) (1964): "It is not necessary for the Government to show that the gift caused or prompted or in any way affected the happening of the official act." In *Howard v. United States*, 345 F.2d 126 (1 Cir.), *cert. denied*, 382 U.S. 838 (1965), the First Circuit said that under the anti-kickback statute, 41 USC § 51 (1964), the crime is "complete upon the acceptance of a bribe regardless of whether or not improper action is thereafter taken." See also *Krogmann v. United States*, 225 F.2d 220 (6 Cir. 1955) (the offense defined by the predecessor to 18 USC § 201(b) "was complete upon the payment of money to Krueger ..."); *Smith v. United States*, 305 F.2d 197 (9 Cir. 1962), *cert. denied*, 371 U.S. 890 (1962) (the statute, 18 USC § 434, superseded by 18 USC § 208, "is directed not only at dishonor, but also at conduct that tempts dishonor ..." and "whether he actually gives or withholds instructions ... is immaterial").

Rejection of Deutsch's construction does not make the phrase "acting as agent" superfluous. It defines a subclass of affiliated persons. Within the statutory scheme of § 17(e), affiliated persons who are acting as brokers may receive limited compensation in connection with portfolio transactions of the registered investment company. 15 USC § 80a-17(e)(2) (1964). If affiliated persons are not acting as brokers, however, but otherwise are acting as agents of the investment company, they cannot accept compensation in connection with the purchase or sale of securities. While § 17(e) is far from a model of clarity, we believe that an affiliated person is acting as agent within the meaning of § 17(e)(1) in all cases when he is not acting as broker for the investment company.

The government and the trial court believed that the phrase "acting as agent" defined a more limited subclass of affiliated persons: those who have the capacity to influence investment decisions. This construction, we believe, is inconsistent with other sections of the Act and with other subsections of § 17 itself. One of the primary objectives of the Act was to prevent affiliated persons, and affiliated persons of such persons, from self-dealing and from operating under conflicts of interest. To achieve this objective, Congress thought it necessary to prohibit affiliated persons from engaging in certain types of conduct; accordingly, all other sections of the Act, including the other subsections of § 17, prohibit all affiliated persons from engaging in the unlawful conduct. There is no reason to believe that Congress intended to allow certain affiliated persons to accept compensation with the forbidden intent and be immune from violating § 17(e)(1).[12] We believe that the more reasonable interpretation of "acting as agent" is that it is a

---

[12] The government contends that subsection (e)(1) is more stringent than the other subsections of § 17 in that § 17(b) allows for exemptions for some subsections, but not for subsection (e)(1). From this, the government concludes that § 17(e)(1) applies to a more limited class of affiliated persons than the other subsections of § 17. However, § 6(c) of the Act permits the SEC to exempt any person from any provision of the Act. This section has been used by the SEC to exempt certain transactions which might otherwise have violated § 17(e)(1). See *Drexel & Co.*, 37 SEC 574 (1957); *Axe-Houghton Fund, Inc.*, 25 SEC 133 (1947); *Bankers Securities Corp.*, 24 SEC 398 (1946); *Pathe Film Corp.*, 10 SEC 483 (1941).

descriptive phrase distinguishing affiliated persons acting as brokers from those who are not acting as brokers in connection with a sale or purchase of securities for an investment company.

In view of our interpretation of the phrase "acting as agent," we believe that the trial court erred in submitting to the jury the issue of whether Mills was acting as agent. As we have indicated, "acting as agent" does not require a showing that Mills took any action as a result of being compensated. Since Deutsch did not dispute the facts that Mills was an affiliated person and that Mills was not acting as broker, we believe that the government established, as a matter of law, that Mills was acting as agent for the investment companies within the meaning of § 17(e)(1). While the trial court erred in submitting this issue to the jury, it was harmless error, for Deutsch suffered no prejudice. [citations omitted] .... Accordingly, we hold that Deutsch was not prejudiced by the trial court's interpretation of the phrase "acting as agent."

Requisite Intent Under § 17(e)(1)

Deutsch maintains that the evidence was insufficient to prove that compensation was given with the intent to influence. We find it unnecessary to reach this issue, because we believe that the trial court erred in charging the jury that, in order to convict, they must find that the compensation was given and received with the intent to influence Mills.[13]

The language of § 17(e)(1) makes no mention of intent to influence; the subsection is cast in the familiar "for" terminology of the gratuity statutes (*e.g.*, 18 USC § § 201(f-i) (1964)) where the only intent required is that the payment be given and accepted in appreciation of past, or in anticipation of future, conduct. We have held that intent to influence is not an element of 26 USC § 7214(a)(2) (1964), which makes it a crime for a federal officer "acting in connection with" the revenue laws to receive "compensation ... for the performance of any duty." *United States v. Cohen*, 387 F.2d 803, 806 (2 Cir. 1967),

---

[13] The trial court's charge on this point was as follows:

" ... you must determine whether or not the compensation was accepted for the purchase of securities by either Puritan Fund in February or June or by Fidelity Trend Fund in October.

"If the evidence persuades you beyond a reasonable doubt that Mills held a position where he could influence the purchase of these securities by Puritan Fund or Fidelity Trend Fund and that he was given this compensation because of this position with the intent of influencing him, and that Mills knew that this was the purpose of the compensation, then you may find that this aspect ... is established."

cert. denied, 390 U.S. 996 (1968). Similarly, we have held that the government does not have to show intent to influence to prove an offense under 18 USC § 201(f) (1964), which makes it a crime to give a public official something of value "for and because of any act performed or to be performed." *United States v. Irwin*, 354 F.2d 192 (2 Cir. 1965), *cert. denied*, 383 U.S. 967 (1966). See also, *United States v. Umans*, 368 F.2d 725 (2 Cir. 1966), *cert. dismissed as improvidently granted*, 389 U.S. 80 (1967).

The statute in the instant case is similar in this respect to the gratuity statutes. We do not believe that Congress intended that intent to influence should be read into § 17(e)(1) of the Act. The paying of compensation is an evil in itself, even though the payor does not corruptly intend to influence the affiliated person's acts, for it tends to bring about preferential treatment in favor of the payor which can easily injure the beneficiaries of investment companies. Congress recognized that affiliated persons had manifold opportunities for self-dealing and designed a statute to remove the potential for conflicts of interest by prohibiting the receipt of compensation "for the purchase or sale of any property...." 15 USC § 80a-17(e)(1) (1964). We hold that to read into § 17(e)(1) a requirement of intent to influence would frustrate this statutory purpose.

Since the requisite intent under § 17(e)(1) is intent to give and accept a gratuity in appreciation of past or future conduct, we believe that the evidence was sufficient to prove the necessary intent with respect to the transactions by both Puritan Fund and Fidelity Trend Fund. The jury was justified in finding that the sale of the note at a discounted price was compensation in appreciation of past conduct "which met with [Deutsch's] satisfaction." *United States v. Cohen, supra*. Deutsch's efforts to sell the issue were unsuccessful until Mills, by committing Puritan to purchase two notes, gave Realty the boost which eventually turned the issue into an overwhelming success. It is equally clear that the jury was entitled to infer that the compensation was "for" the purchase by Fidelity. Mills' conduct in urging the Realty notes on the two managers of the Fidelity Trend Fund is not readily understandable except in the context of Deutsch's relationship to Mills. It would seem unlikely that Mills would want Fidelity Trend to purchase Realty notes at the same time he did, because he would thereby create an invidious comparison between the bargain opportunity he received and the far more expensive purchase he recommended for the fund with which he was affiliated.

The trial court's error in charging the jury that intent to influence was a necessary element of the offense did not prejudice Deutsch, for the erroneous charge merely "exacted a higher standard of proof than the law required." .... At most, the erroneous charge here imposed on the government the burden of proving an additional element of the offense. The instructions on intent therefore could only have been favorable to Deutsch and do not necessitate reversal. [citations omitted].

CLAIM THAT STATUTE IS VOID FOR VAGUENESS

Deutsch claims that § 17(e)(1) of the Act is unconstitutional because the language is so vague as to be void under the due process clause of the Fifth Amendment. This claim is without merit.

The applicable test is whether the language conveys "sufficiently definite warning as to the proscribed conduct when measured by common understanding and practices." A statute violates due process if "men of common intelligence must necessarily guess at its meaning and differ as to its application." Even in criminal cases, however, where the vagueness standard is most stringently applied, the statute must only present "ascertainable standard[s] of guilt." [citations omitted].

We do not believe that Deutsch was "required at peril of life, liberty or property to speculate as to the meaning of penal statutes." *Lanzetta v. State of New Jersey*, 306 U.S. 451 (1939). Section 17(e)(1) clearly places men of reasonable intelligence on notice that affiliated persons cannot accept compensation in connection with the purchase or sale of property to or for their affiliated investment companies. The phrase "acting as agent" is not so vague as to make men of common intelligence guess at its meaning.[14] We believe that § 17(e)(1) establishes standards of guilt which are at least as definite as those in a gratuity statute, *e.g.*, 18 USC § 201(f) (1964), which withstood this same constitutional challenge in *United States v. Irwin, supra.*

CLAIM THAT THERE WAS INSUFFICIENT EVIDENCE TO PROVE COMPENSATION

Deutsch argues that the evidence was insufficient to prove the statutory element of compensation. He admits that he sold Mills a note at a substantial discount in October and he does not dispute the trial court's definition of compensation as a "benefit or thing of value [including] being granted an opportunity to purchase securities at a discount price." He claims, however, that he made a commitment to sell one of the notes to Mills in

---

[14] Deutsch's claim that § 17(e)(1) fails to establish an ascertainable standard of guilt is undermined by his and Mills' evasive conduct in trying to conceal the transaction.

February or March 1968 and that when he made this commitment he had no idea that the Realty note and attached warrant would be so valuable eight or nine months later. He contends that, since compensation must be paid and accepted knowingly and willfully to render him guilty, he did not violate § 17(e)(1) by fulfilling an oral agreement which was made with no intention of selling at a discount price.

The trial court, accepting Deutsch's contention that the jury must acquit if they found Deutsch had agreed to sell Mills a Realty note in February or March 1968, instructed the jury as follows:

> "If you find that Mills was granted the opportunity for the first time in September or thereafter to purchase these securities at a price which was significantly lower than the price charged other buyers at the same time, then you may find that Mills received compensation in the form of this reduced price.
>
> If, on the other hand, you find that the commitment to Mills was made in February, then you should acquit the defendant."[15]

In view of the jury's verdict, they evidently chose to disbelieve Deutsch's story of a February-March commitment. Deutsch now contends that the issue of compensation should never have gone to the jury, because the government failed to challenge his affirmative defense with directly contradictory proof, and because there was insufficient evidence to prove that the first time Deutsch offered the deal to Mills was in September 1968. These contentions are without merit.

Deutsch's claim that the government was required to offer proof which directly contradicted his testimony about the February-March commitment is frivolous.... That no February-March agreement existed could be proved by evidence of objective facts and circumstances having a rational tendency to show, and from which the jury rationally and logically could find, that no agreement was made. In light of the inherent implausibility that Realty would orally contract, without consideration, to sell a valuable security, at some indefinite time in the future, at an indefinite price, the jury was warranted in

---

[15] Deutsch argues on appeal that the trial court's instructions on the February-March commitment improperly placed the burden of proof on him. However, the instructions given were substantially those requested; and in colloquy prior to summations, defense counsel specifically requested the charge on the February-March commitment, despite the trial judge's warning that the jury might misunderstand and think the defense had the burden. There being no plain error, Deutsch's failure to make timely objection below precludes him from raising this issue on appeal. [citations omitted].

disbelieving Deutsch's story. The jury's disbelief is further supported by inconsistencies within Deutsch's own testimony and between his testimony and that of his colleagues, Karp and Stein.

There also was sufficient evidence to entitle the jury to find that the first time Deutsch offered the deal to Mills was in September 1968. The alleged commitment was that Mills could purchase a Realty note on resale when one became available. Notes did become available for resale in August 1968. But Deutsch contacted Massachusetts Life, not Mills, about the possibility of purchasing the securities. Mills did not approach the Shawmut Bank for a loan until September 16, five days after the initial rejection of Deutsch's offer by Massachusetts Life. The jury could logically find that Deutsch did not make an offer to Mills until Massachusetts Life had first turned it down and that Mills had then gone to the bank to see if he could borrow money to purchase the note. Thus, there was sufficient evidence for the jury to find that the offer to Mills was first made between September 11 and 16.

In any event, the trial court's instructions on this issue were more favorable than those to which Deutsch was entitled. He was entitled to an instruction merely that the jury could not convict without being persuaded beyond a reasonable doubt that the agreement to buy a Realty note was made with the knowledge that it constituted something of value. The jury would have been justified in finding that the alleged February-March commitment was something of value. It was an option, obliging Mills to do nothing, but entitling him to buy a Realty note if circumstances made it profitable for him to do so. Options to purchase securities constitute a significant form of executive compensation. Since Deutsch viewed the commitment as binding, the jury would have been entitled to find that the alleged February-March commitment satisfied the statutory element of compensation.

CLAIM THAT EVIDENCE OF MILLS' CRIME WAS IMPROPERLY ADMITTED

Deutsch argues that he was denied his Sixth Amendment right of confrontation when the trial court admitted evidence which tended to prove that Mills failed to report his personal investment in Realty. We hold that the trial court properly admitted this evidence.

The challenged evidence consists of three documentary exhibits: a copy of an internal code of ethics circulated among all Fidelity officers and employees which required them to make monthly reports of securities they purchased; Mills' monthly reports for the period December 1967 through December 1968, which failed to reflect his purchase of the Realty note; and an SEC statement that there was no record of Mills ever having sought SEC permission to purchase the security. The trial court admitted the three documents and carefully instructed the jury that they were received solely as proof of the guilt of Mills.[16]

We believe that the trial court's ruling was correct. Proof of the guilt of the principal is admissible at the trial of an accomplice. The documents could be considered by the jury as independent evidence of Mills' guilt, for they showed evasive conduct aimed at concealing the transaction and constituted circumstantial evidence of guilty consciousness; as such, they were independently probative of his guilt. [citations omitted].

Deutsch's reliance on *Bruton v. United States*, 391 U.S. 123 (1968), is misplaced. The documents did not constitute hearsay, for they were not offered for the truth of the matter asserted. Rather, the government offered the documents as circumstantial evidence of Mills' failure to report the transaction, from which the jury could infer consciousness of guilt. Assuming that the documents constituted hearsay, however, there are good reasons why *Bruton* should not apply here. The trial court's prompt and clear explanation of the limited purpose for which the records were received was sufficient to negate any possibility of prejudice. Moreover, since these documents did not contain any inculpatory statements as to Deutsch, *Bruton* is not applicable. See *United States ex rel. Nelson v. Follette*, 430 F.2d 1055 (2 Cir. 1970). [additional citations omitted].

* * * *

---

[16] The trial court's instructions when the three documentary exhibits were admitted were as follows:

"Ladies and gentlemen of the jury, as I think I indicated to you in the beginning, Mr. Mills is charged with violation of the law. Mr. Deutsch is charged with aiding and abetting Mr. Mills in the violation of the law. In order for Mr. Deutsch to be convicted, the government will have to prove that Mr. Mills violated the law. That is one of the burdens the government will have, in addition to certain others.

"So these exhibits are being offered solely proving that Mr. Mills violated the law. You have to get over that hurdle first before you can ever take up the question of whether Mr. Deutsch aided and abetted Mr. Mills in violating the law."

CLAIM THAT
DISMISSAL OF COUNT FIVE PRECLUDED CONVICTION ON COUNT SIX

Finally, Deutsch argues that he could not be convicted as an aider and abettor on Count Six, because Count Five charging Mills as principal subsequently was dismissed. This claim is without merit.

At Deutsch's trial in April 1970, the trial court instructed the jury that, in order to find Deutsch guilty as an aider and abettor, they first had to find that Mills had committed the principal offense, *i.e.*, had violated § 17(e)(1) of the Act. In view of the verdict, the jury must have found that Mills had violated § 17(e)(1). The fact that Count Five subsequently was dismissed when Mills was sentenced the following month does not undermine the conviction of Deutsch on Count Six.

To sustain the conviction of one who has been charged as an aider and abettor, it is necessary that there be evidence showing an offense to have been committed by the principal, and that the principal was aided and abetted by the accused. It is not incumbent upon the prosecution, however, to prove that the principal has been either convicted or acquitted of the offense. *Hendrix v. United States*, 327 F.2d 971 (5 Cir. 1964); *Perkins v. United States*, 315 F.2d 120 (9 Cir. 1963); *Meredith v. United States*, 238 F.2d 535 (4 Cir. 1956); *Colosacco v. United States*, 196 F.2d 165 (10 Cir. 1952). In the instant case, the government presented sufficient evidence to establish that Mills had committed the offense. That was all the government was required to show.

We have considered Deutsch's other claims of error and find them to be without merit.[17]

Affirmed.

---

[17] Except to the extent mentioned in the foregoing opinion, we do not find it necessary to discuss separately Deutsch's claims raised on the appeal from denial of his post-conviction motion seeking *coram nobis* relief. His claims on that appeal are not materially different from those raised on the appeal from his judgment of conviction. We have considered them carefully and find them without merit.

United States, Appellee v. Ostrander, Defendant-Appellant

999 F.2d 27 (2d Cir. 1993)

Before VAN GRAAFEILAND and WINTER, Circuit Judges, and POLLACK, District Judge.*

*(The Honorable Milton Pollack, United States District Judge for the Southern District of New York, sitting by designation).

OPINION

WINTER, Circuit Judge:

Patricia Ostrander was charged with two counts of accepting unlawful "compensation" or a "thing of value" from a source other than her employer in connection with the performance of her duties as a portfolio manager, see 15 USC § 80a-17(e), 18 USC § 1954, and one count of failing to report a personal investment to her employer, see 15 USC § 80a-17(j), 17 CFR § 270.17j-1. After an eight-day trial, the jury convicted Ostrander on all three counts. Judge Owen sentenced her to concurrent terms of two months' imprisonment. We affirm.

BACKGROUND

Most of the pertinent events occurred during 1985 and 1986. When all permissible inferences are drawn in favor of the government, the evidence showed the following. Ostrander was a portfolio manager for Fidelity Management Research and Fidelity Management Trust Company (collectively "**Fidelity**"), investment advisers registered with the Securities and Exchange Commission, from 1970 to 1987. As a manager of Fidelity's funds, Ostrander purchased hundreds of millions of dollars worth of securities from Drexel Burnham Lambert, Inc. ("**Drexel**").

During early 1985, Kohlberg Kravis Roberts & Co. ("**KKR**"), a firm specializing in leveraged-buyouts ("LBOs"), decided upon an LBO of Storer Communications, Inc. ("**Storer**"). KKR hired Drexel to underwrite the securities for the financial transactions. The publicly offered securities included zero coupon bonds, debenture bonds paying fifteen percent per annum, and preferred stock. The preferred stock "paid-in-kind," meaning that it paid dividends of preferred stock rather than cash. It was the most junior of the securities and the most difficult of the securities to sell.

In addition to these publicly offered securities, 67,840,000 warrants were created. Their holders were entitled to exchange each warrant for one share of common stock in the Storer holding company at an exercise price of $2.05. The warrants represented thirty-two percent of the Storer holding company's common stock. They were described as "equity sweeteners" or "equity kickers" because they were designed to assist in the sale of the debentures and preferred stock. Drexel thus told KKR that they would be offered for private sale only to those institutions who had purchased zero coupon bonds, debentures, or preferred stock. This intent also was stated in the prospectus. Thereafter, the head of Drexel's High Yield Bond Department, Michael Milken, falsely indicated to KKR that the warrant price was too high and that potential bond or stock purchasers were "balking" at a price of fourteen cents per warrant. The warrants then were sold for seven cents each and offered only to a few select investors, including Drexel employees. Many of these Drexel employees kept the warrants in partnerships, one of which was MacPherson Investment Partners L.P.

On behalf of Fidelity, Ostrander attended a Drexel roadshow on October 28, 1985. She agreed to purchase for Fidelity Storer securities issued pursuant to the LBO. On December 5, 1985, KKR executed the Storer LBO. On behalf of Fidelity, Ostrander purchased $10 million of the zero coupon bonds, $26 million of the preferred stock (ten percent of the preferred stock offering), and $59 million of the fifteen percent senior subordinated debentures. During late December 1985, Drexel's Michael Milken offered Ostrander the opportunity to invest her personal funds in MacPherson Investment Partners L.P., a partnership holding some of the Storer warrants. She was not alone. Sixty-five percent of MacPherson was owned by fiduciaries for institutions that purchased other securities issued in the Storer LBO. Ostrander invested $13,200 in MacPherson (paying approximately nine cents per warrant) during January 1986. When purchased, the warrants were highly speculative, and no witnesses were able to value them even as of late December 1985. KKR sold Storer's stations and cable systems at the top of the market in 1987 and 1988 and realized a profit that surpassed prior expectations. The value of Ostrander's $13,200 investment grew to roughly $750,000.

On October 11, 1991, Ostrander was indicted on three counts. Count One charged her with accepting unlawful compensation in connection with her purchases or sales of securities for registered investment companies that she managed as an affiliated person in violation of 15 USC § 80a-17(e). Because the funds she managed for Fidelity Management Trust Company ("FMTC") were primarily pension plans, Count Two charged that she, acting as "an officer, agent, or employee" of FMTC received "things of value" in connection with purchases of securities for pension plans in violation of 18 USC § 1954.

The third count charged that Ostrander, an access person, failed to report the securities at issue to her employer, a registered investment advisory company, as required by 15 USC § 80a-17(j) and 17 CFR § 270.17j-1(c). The jury convicted her on all counts. Judge Owen sentenced Ostrander to concurrent terms of two months' imprisonment and to a $100,000 fine.

DISCUSSION

On appeal, Ostrander challenges the convictions on four grounds: (1) an erroneous jury charge stating that the opportunity to purchase the warrants was "a thing of value" even though the actual value of the warrants was not proven, (2) insufficient evidence, (3) erroneous evidentiary rulings, and (4) a claim that Count Three does not allege a crime.

Section 17(e) of the Investment Companies Act makes it unlawful for an "affiliated person" of a registered investment company, acting as its agent, to accept "from any source any compensation (other than a regular salary or wages from such registered company) for the purchase or sale" of property, including securities, by such investment company. 15 USC § 80a-17(e). Section 1954 of Title 18 prohibits administrators, officers, and employees of employee welfare benefit plans or employee pension benefit plans from receiving "any fee, kickback, commission, gift, loan, money, or thing of value because of or with intent to be influenced with respect to, any of [her] actions, decisions, or other duties relating to" the plan. 18 USC § 1954.

Ostrander challenges the trial court's instruction that the "opportunity" to purchase the warrants might constitute a violation of § 17(e) and § 1954 even though there was no proof that the warrants were purchased at a price below their market value. The challenged instruction is set out in full in the margin.[1] Specifically, Ostrander argues that

---

[1] The challenged instruction stated:

Compensation is anything of benefit or anything of value, whether directly or indirectly received. It may take several forms and is not limited to money or tangible things with an identifiable commercial price tag.

To prove that compensation was received the government must prove that what Mrs. Ostrander received constituted something of value at the time she received it. You need not concern yourselves with finding a precise value in the marketplace. But you may look to the value the recipient here, Mrs. Ostrander, placed on the thing at the time she received it. In other words, the value of something can well be judged and set by the desire of that recipient to have the thing and depends upon that individual and all the circumstances surrounding its receipt.

On this issue you may consider whether or not the defendant herself attached a value to the opportunity to purchase MacPherson and, if she did, whether the value she placed on it was materially above the price being

Counts One and Two require proof of receipt of "compensation" or a "thing of value" for a price less than its market value. She argues that the judge charged on a faulty legal theory in stating that "you [jurors] need not concern yourself with finding [the warrants'] precise value in the marketplace." We disagree.

In *United States v. Deutsch*, 451 F.2d 98 (2d Cir. 1971), *cert. denied*, 404 U.S. 1019 (1972), the case upon which Ostrander primarily relies, we upheld a trial court's definition of the term compensation as a "benefit or thing of value [including] being granted an opportunity to purchase securities at a discounted price." Our holding that this kind of benefit was included among "things of value" did not limit that definition to securities sold at a discount. In fact, the panel stated that the instructions "were more favorable" to Deutsch than necessary. "He was entitled to an instruction merely that the jury could not convict without being persuaded beyond a reasonable doubt that the agreement to buy [the note] was made with the knowledge that it constituted something of value." *Id.*

Nor do other cases require that the "thing of value" received be shown to have been transferred at a discount somehow calculated. In *United States v. Williams*, 705 F.2d 603 (2d Cir.), *cert. denied*, 464 U.S. 1007 (1983), we upheld an instruction that the jury should disregard the stock's "worth in the commercial world"; see also *United States v. Crozier*, 987 F.2d 893 (2d Cir. 1993); *United States v. Blitz*, 533 F.2d 1329 (2d Cir. 1976), *cert. denied*, 429 U.S. 819 (1976) (construing "thing of value" under § 17(e) of the Investment Companies Act to include loans repaid with interest); *United States v. Roth*, 333 F.2d 450 (2d Cir. 1964) (upholding instruction that jury must "find more than a loan [and] substantial monetary benefit or thing of value" because, "if anything, [it was] *too favorable* to defendants"), *cert. denied*, 380 U.S. 942 (1965).

These decisions take a common sense view of § 17(e) and § 1954. Under these statutes, it is enough if the item received was regarded as a benefit by the recipient, whether or not others might have taken a different view of its value. Based on the evidence before it, the jury could reasonably conclude that Ostrander regarded the

---

asked to pay for it. Here the defendant contends that MacPherson ... had all of the attendant risks and therefore was not a thing of value as defined. The government, on the other hand, contends that the mere opportunity to invest in MacPherson was itself compensation or a thing of value because the MacPherson interests were by their nature scarce or available to only a few individuals....

It is sufficient that the government prove that the compensation at issue here, namely, the opportunity to invest in MacPherson, was connected to the sale of securities to the funds she managed or, in other words, that it was given and received by her in appreciation of past or in anticipation of future conduct by her.

opportunity to purchase the warrants as a benefit. This opportunity was carefully limited by Milken to selected persons, including himself, other Drexel employees, firms, and fiduciaries for institutions that had purchased securities in the Storer LBO. There was no market price set by public trading in which all were free to engage, and the opportunity to purchase the warrants was at Milken's whim and at a price set by him. Ostrander's claim that the legal theory underlying her conviction would criminalize transactions in heavily traded securities at open market prices is simply wrong. Such transactions are not benefits within the meaning of the statutes because the purchaser obtains nothing unavailable elsewhere at the same price. Such a transaction cannot influence a fiduciary's decisionmaking. Although Ostrander got no guarantee of profit, she did get an opportunity offered only to a few that she clearly believed to be a good buy. That is a thing of value, or so a jury might find.

Without irony, she also contends that the warrants had no value and that the judge erred by instructing the jury to "look to the value [she] placed on the thing at the time she received it." We disagree. First, the warrants had value, if for no other reason because numerous investment professionals, including Drexel employees and fiduciaries for investors, were willing to, and did, purchase them. See *Williams, supra.* Indeed, the "they-had-no-value" argument rings particularly hollow from one who actually paid value and then made a profit of nearly $750,000 on an investment of $13,200. Second, the instruction was proper according to our decision in *Williams*, which upheld an instruction "to focus on the value that the defendants subjectively attached to the items received"; *id.*

The jury might easily have found that the warrants were compensation for her past and future purchases of securities from Drexel for Fidelity. She had purchased on behalf of Fidelity large blocs of the securities offered in the LBO, including ten percent of the preferred, the most difficult securities of the package to sell. We are unpersuaded by her argument that, because she purchased no Storer bonds after agreeing to buy the warrants, the jury could not as a matter of law find a connection to her purchase of the Storer securities or to potential future purchases from Drexel of securities in other companies.[2]

---

[2] Because we reject Ostrander's theory that the payment of a fair market value for the warrants was a defense, we need not consider her two related arguments: (i) she was deprived of presenting her defense that she did not know that the warrants may have been sold below their market value; if the law does not recognize a legal argument as a valid defense, the court has no duty to instruct the jury on that argument; (ii) the government lacked sufficient evidence that the warrants were sold below their actual value; that is not an element of the crime and thus need

Ostrander also challenges the admission of evidence concerning two conversations that purportedly are inadmissible hearsay. The first conversation occurred between Michael Milken and Ted Ammon, a general partner from KKR. During the telephone conversation, Milken told Ammon that potential bond or preferred stock buyers were "balking" because the warrants were too expensive. This conversation induced Ammon to agree to reduce the initial offering price for the warrants from fourteen to seven cents. Because this evidence was not offered by the government to prove the truth of its contents, it was not hearsay. See Fed. R. Evid. 801(c). The evidence was intended to show that Milken had made such statements and persuaded KKR to authorize a drop in price, not that the contents of the statements were true. Indeed, Milken's statements were false and were offered to show only that he successfully induced Storer to reduce the price and, by implication, that he believed the warrants, which he intended to appropriate for himself, co-workers and other selected purchasers, were of value. Craig Cogut, a witness, testified about the second conversation. He stated that he had overheard Michael Milken's brother Lowell tell Milken "words to the effect that you better get moving selling the preferred or we are going to be long a whole lot of it," a statement with which Michael did not disagree. This statement reflected the state of mind of each brother that the preferred was a hard sell, see Fed. R. Evid. 803(3), a fact that was relevant to their motive to pay compensation to Ostrander.

Finally, Ostrander argues that Count III does not allege a crime. Count III charged that she had violated 15 USC § 80a-17(j) and 17 CFR § 270.17j-1 by failing to report her MacPherson investment to Fidelity. Section 17(j) of the Investment Companies Act states in pertinent part:

> It shall be unlawful [for a person in Ostrander's position] to engage in any act, practice, or course of business in connection with the purchase or sale, directly or indirectly, by such person of any security held or to be acquired by such registered investment company in contravention of such rules and regulations as the Commission may adopt to define, and prescribe means reasonably necessary to prevent, such acts, practices, or courses of business as are fraudulent, deceptive or manipulative.

Title 17 CFR § 270.17j-1(c)(1), promulgated pursuant to § 17(j), states in pertinent part:

> Every [portfolio manager for] a registered investment company ... shall report to such

---

not be proven.

> investment company, ... [the date of a purchase or sale of a security, the price, and the broker] with respect to transactions in any security in which such access person has, or by reason of such transaction acquires, any direct or indirect beneficial ownership ....

Both the statutory provision and the regulation may be enforced through criminal proceedings. 15 USC § 80a-49.

Ostrander does not dispute that she failed to inform Fidelity of her MacPherson investment, thus violating a company rule as well as § 270.17j-1(c)(1). Rather, she argues that § 17(j) applies only to securities "held or to be acquired" by Fidelity. Because Fidelity never held an interest in MacPherson, she concludes, she was under no duty to report. The argument is entirely frivolous. Any payment to a portfolio manager intended to induce the purchase of a firm's securities on behalf of an investment company easily qualifies as a "fraudulent, deceptive or manipulative" act "in connection with" the investment company's acquisition of securities, whether or not the payment consists of an opportunity to purchase securities in a different firm. Moreover, § 17(e) expressly invites the Commission to flesh out its general prohibitions by regulation. The regulation in question, which requires portfolio managers to report to their companies their interests in various securities, is a prophylactic measure reasonably related to the enforcement of § 17(j). See *United States v. Chestman*, 947 F.2d 551 (2d Cir. 1991). Ostrander's failure to report her interest in MacPherson was thus a crime.

Affirmed.

Chapter 3 Mutual Fund Distribution; Trading; Investments

> " . . . the national public interest and the interest of investors are adversely affected . . . (3) when investment companies issue securities containing inequitable or discriminatory provisions, or fail to protect the preferences and privileges of the holders of their outstanding securities; (4) when the control of investment companies is unduly concentrated through pyramiding or inequitable methods of control, or is inequitably distributed, or when investment companies are managed by irresponsible persons; . . ."
>
> ----Investment Company Act of 1940, §§ 1(b)(3)-(4)

Section 3.1 Mutual Fund Distribution

Topic 1 Structure of Mutual Fund Distribution Finance

Laws & Rules Highlight:

IC Act (15 USC 80a-1 *et seq.*) & Rules (17 CFR §§ 270.0-1 *et seq.*)
Financial Industry Regulatory Authority (FINRA) Rules

SEC and FINRA Respective Authority

- § 22 Distribution, Redemption, and Repurchase of Redeemable Securities
  - §§ 22(a)-(b) (*authorizes* ***national securities association*** *to issue rules* ***governing*** *member activities with respect to the pricing and distribution of redeemable securities, and* ***prohibiting*** *"excessive sales loads"*)
  - § 22(c) (*authorizes the* ***SEC*** *to issue rules relating to redeemable securities issued by open-end companies; provides that* ***SEC rules preempt*** *any conflicting rules adopted by national securities association*)

Mutual Fund Distribution Finance Regulation

- § 22(d) (*establishes a* ***retail price maintenance system*** *for mutual fund distribution: requires a mutual fund to sell its shares to or through a principal underwriter if it levies a* ***sales load****; permits a mutual fund to sell its shares directly to the public if it sells at* ***a current public offering price*** *described in the prospectus*); § 2(a)(35) (*def.* ***"sales load"***)

- Front-End Sales Loads
  - Rule 22d-1 Exemption from Section 22(d) to Permit Sales of Redeemable Securities at Prices Which Reflect Sales Loads Set Pursuant to a Schedule (***permits*** *funds to use scheduled variations in, or elimination of, front-end sales loads;* ***permits*** *mutual funds to charge different amounts of sales loads for different classes*)
- Back-End Sales Loads
  - Rule 6c-10 Exemption for Certain Open-End Management Investment Companies to Impose Deferred Sales Loads (***permits*** *contingent deferred sales loads CDSLs and other forms of deferred sales loads*)
- 12b-1 Asset-Based Fees
  - § 12(b) (***requires*** *any mutual fund acting as an* ***issuer-distributor*** *to adhere to SEC rules and regulations—intended to protect mutual funds from bearing excessive sales and promotion expenses, by granting authority to the SEC to regulate the use of fund assets to finance distribution*)
  - Rule 12b-1 Distribution of Shares by Registered Open-End Management Investment Company (***permits*** *mutual fund acting as an issuer-distributor to bear distribution expenses pursuant to a* ***12b-1 plan***)
- Prohibition of Excessive Sales Charges (FINRA Rules)
  - Rule 2341 Investment Company Securities (***prohibits*** *"****excessive****" sales charges; prescribing "****maximum****" aggregates sales charges"*)
  - Rule 2341(b)(8) (*def. "****sales charges****" to include front-end, deferred and asset-based sales charges*); (8)(A) (*def. "****asset-based sales charge****"*); (8)(B) (*def. "****deferred sales charge****"*); (8)(C) (*def. "****front-end sales charge****"*)
  - Rule 2341(d)(4) (*prohibited use of "****no load****" or "****no sales charge****"*)
  - Rule 2342 "Breakpoint" Sales (***prohibits*** *below breakpoint sales abuse*)

Fund Distribution: Broker-Channel Distribution Structure

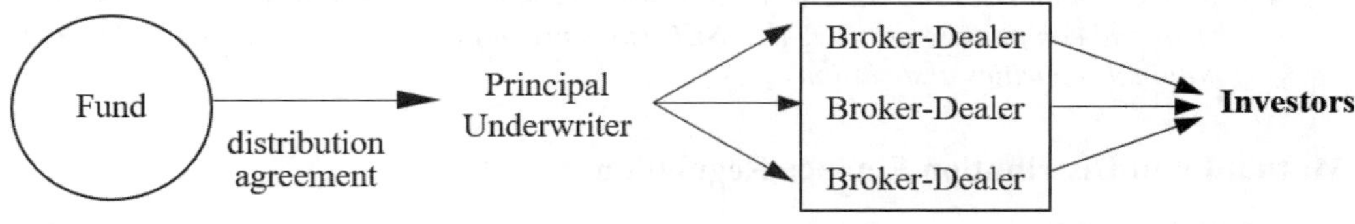

Source of graph: MUTUAL FUNDS AND EXCHANGE TRADED FUNDS REGULATION Fig. 1-3 (Kirsch ed. 2017)

Fund Distribution: Direct Distribution Structure

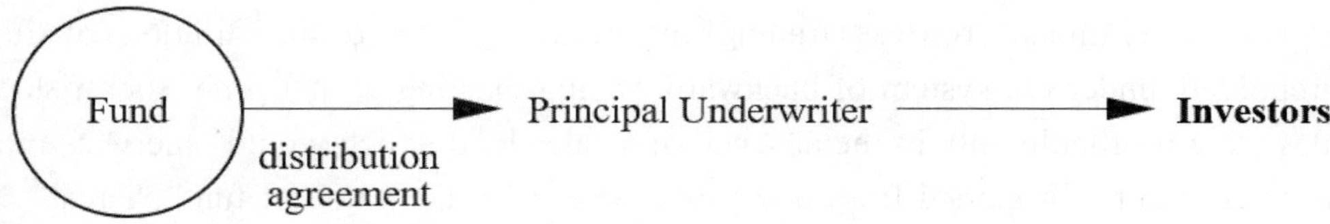

Source of graph: MUTUAL FUNDS AND EXCHANGE TRADED FUNDS REGULATION Fig. 1-4 (Kirsch ed. 2017)

Multi-Class Fund Load Structure: Class A; Class B; Class C

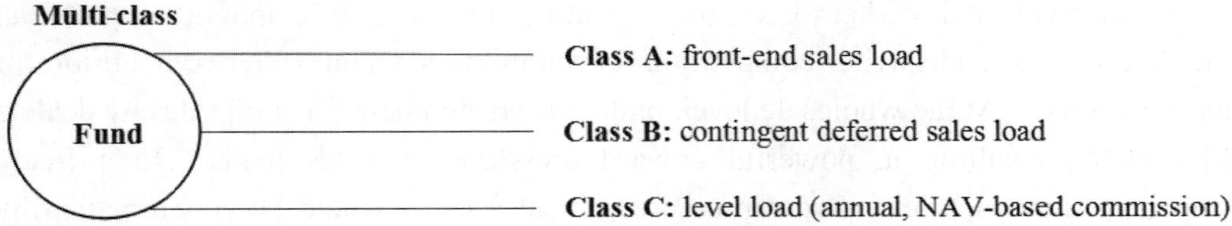

Source of graph: MUTUAL FUNDS AND EXCHANGE TRADED FUNDS REGULATION Fig. 1-9 (adapted) (Kirsch ed. 2017)

Research Note:[Biblio]

Structure of Mutual Fund Distribution Finance: Dynamics of Competition and Regulation

The Statutory Retail Price Maintenance System[1; 2a]

Referred to as an "***anticompetitive***," "***retail price maintenance***" provision,[1] § 22(d) of the IC Act requires that all sales of mutual fund shares be made at a fixed offering price specified in the prospectus. Since the current offering price of redeemable securities is determined by adding a sales load to the net asset value of the securities, § 22(d) effectively fixes the sales load component of the public offering price and prohibits sales loads competition in mutual fund sales. To protect investors against excessive sales charges under such a retail price maintenance system, Congress decided to rely on the national securities association, which is given statutory authority to prescribe maximum sales charges subject to SEC oversight under the Securities Exchange Act.

According to the SEC's interpretation, when enacted § 22(d) was primarily designed to eliminate riskless trading by fund insiders to the dilution of fund shareholders under the system of backward pricing existing at that time: such riskless trades were profitable only in the absence of a sales load which would otherwise more than offset the profit gained from one day's increase in the value of fund shares. By requiring all investors to pay the same sales load, the enactment of § 22(d) reduced the economic incentive of insiders to engage in riskless trading by exploiting backward pricing. The SEC acknowledged, however, that it would have cured such backward-pricing based riskless trading abuse by requiring forward pricing but the industry vigorously resisted, and that § 22(d) as enacted was a "***compromise***."[1 (p.301 n.43)]

Subject to normal market forces, there would be two types of competition in mutual fund distribution: underwriter competition for mutual funds, and dealer competition for investor assets. At the wholesale level, underwriters compete for fund sales by dealers and brokers, resulting in powerful upward pressures on sales loads. In a freely competitive market, such upward pressures on sales loads would be countervailed by downward pressures stemming from price competition among dealers for investors at the retail level. However, since § 22(d) prohibits competition among retail dealers, the countervailing downward pressures on sales loads otherwise exerted by retail price competition cannot operate. As a result, the intense competition among principal underwriters in the mutual fund industry becomes a "***perverse competition***" for investors—raising rather than lowering prices to fund investors.[3 (p.836 n.652)]

In 1992, with a view to eliminating impediments to vigorous price competition, the SEC's Division of Investment Management recommended (1) legislative amendment to § 22(d) to end the mandatory retail price maintenance system, and (2) SEC rulemaking to introduce price competition among dealers at the retail level. In making its recommendations, the IM Division noted ***three factors*** critical to the interplay of regulation and competition on distribution pricing:[1]

- the continuous pressures on mutual funds to sell shares to avoid net redemption;
- the external management structure and the fund asset percentage-based advisory fee structure with their structural built-in conflicts of interest in the decision to use fund assets to promote distribution;
- the variety of fund distribution financing methods and the impact of regulation on

each.

Front-End Loads[2]

Among the variety of methods of mutual fund distribution financing, "***front end loads***" remain the traditional and the most prevalent method of distribution financing. A front-end load is expressed as a percentage of the public offering price of the fund shares. It is a commission charged to an investor upon purchasing fund shares; the load is generally divided among the individual broker who actually sold the fund shares, the broker's firm, and the fund's distributor/underwriter.[4]

SEC exemptive Rule 22d-1 permits scheduled variations in sales loads. Mutual funds charging front-end loads typically offer discounts based on pre-determined levels of investment called "***breakpoints***." An investor can become entitled to breakpoint discounts in a number of ways: by his *current purchase* at or exceeding a breakpoint investment threshold; by way of *a letter of intent* counting his future purchases over a specified period of the same fund or fund(s) in the same fund family toward a breakpoint investment threshold; or by way of *rights of accumulation* linking and aggregating his own purchases with those of related accounts toward a breakpoint investment threshold.[5] FINRA Rule 2342 prohibits broker-dealer firms from selling fund shares to investors just below the breakpoint investment thresholds so as to charge and share in higher sales loads ("***breakpoint sales***").

Back-End Loads[6]

In contrast to front-end loads paid by investors at the time of purchase, ***back-end loads*** are sales loads to be paid after purchase but before or upon redemption. SEC exemptive Rule 6c-10 permits the use of back-end loads. The variety of back-end loads includes "***contingent deferred sales load***" or CDSL; "***spread load***" or a combination of CDSL with Rule 12b-1 asset-based distribution fee; "***installment load***" or a load payable in installments during the term of a shareholder's investment in a fund; as well as other forms of "***deferred sales loads***." A CDSL is paid, if at all, at redemption; the amount of a CDSL declines to zero if redemption does not occur before a period of time specified by the fund, reflecting the rate at which the shareholder is paying for distribution through the fund's 12b-1 plan.

To reduce investor uncertainty about the amount of deferred load to be paid, to facilitate investor comparison of various load structures, and to assure any NAV growth post-purchase inuring to the benefit of investors, Rule 6c-10 requires that the total amount of any deferred load paid by an investor may not exceed the amount represented by the specified percentage of the fund NAV at the time of purchase. From the ***investor perspective***, a back-end sales load arrangement would leave investors with greater amounts of money for investment at the time of purchase, compared with a front-end load arrangement; however, a back-end load may potentially leave investors with higher ongoing sales charges. Thus FINRA rules governing broker-dealer suitability obligations apply not only to suitability of funds but also to suitability of fee structures to the brokerage customers.[7] From the ***fund principal underwriter perspective***, since selling brokers are paid their commissions at the time of sale in both front-end and back-end load arrangements, fund principal underwriters generally finance their deferred sales load distributions.[8]

"12b-1 Fees" *aka* "Asset-Based Sales Loads"[9e]

Under traditional mutual fund underwriting arrangements, underwriters receive their compensation from sales loads paid by purchasers of fund shares. Use of fund assets to finance distribution generally raises ***three concerns***:[9c; 9d]

- the ***conflicts*** that may exist between the interests of a fund, and the interests of fund adviser whose compensation is based on the size of the fund, who may be a primary beneficiary of increased sales of fund shares, and who might be inclined to cause the fund to spend excessive amounts to finance distribution in an effort to increase fund assets and consequently the adviser's own compensation;
- the ***uncertain or even speculative*** nature of any benefit inuring to the fund for financing the distribution costs, and
- the ***fairness*** to all fund shareholders.

Congressional concern with mutual fund distribution financing is reflected in § 12(b) of the IC Act, which authorizes the SEC to regulate the use of fund assets to pay for the distribution of fund shares.

In 1980, the SEC adopted Rule 12b-1 "Distribution of Shares by Registered Open-End Management Investment Company," which ***permits*** mutual funds to finance distribution subject to substantive standards and procedural safeguard designed to address those concerns. A fund which decides to bear distribution expenses must formulate a written plan ("***12b-1 plan***"). Initially, the 12b-1 plan must be approved, separately, by (1) holders of a majority of the fund's outstanding voting securities, (2) a majority of the fund's full board, and (3) a majority of fund's disinterested directors who have no direct or indirect financial interest in the operation of the plan or in any agreements related to the plan ("***12b-1 disinterested directors***"). To continue in effect, the 12b-1 plan must be reapproved annually by the last two categories. At any time, the plan may be terminated by either holders of a majority of the fund's outstanding voting securities, or a majority of the 12b-1 disinterested directors. Rule 12b-1 ***prohibits*** a fund from making any distribution payment not made pursuant to a 12b-1 plan.[9d]

Where a **mutual fund adviser finances distribution** of fund shares, questions of ***indirect distribution financing*** may arise, *i.e.*, whether the fund is incurring distribution expenses indirectly. On the one hand, under the external management structure and advisory compensation system, fund advisers have an entrepreneurial interest in the sale of fund shares and the development of the advisory business. It would be "*anomalous*" to suggest that any profits of the adviser from performing the advisory contract would be the adviser's money if used to pay dividends to the management firm's shareholders, but would be the fund's money if used to finance sales of fund shares. If an adviser makes distribution related payments out of its ***own resources***, there is no indirect use of fund assets. On the other hand, if the advisory fee was inflated in order to provide the adviser with money to finance fund sales, it would clearly constitute an ***indirect use of fund assets*** for distribution. Such indirect use of fund assets for distribution may exist, for example, where the advisory fee makes allowance for the adviser's distribution expenses by designating any specific or readily determinable portion of the adviser's fee as a source of compensation for sellers of fund shares, or contemplating unspecified payments by the adviser for distribution. Thus the fund board must determine in conjunction not only whether fund assets are being used for distribution but also whether the advisory fee is excessive in violation of § 36(b) fiduciary standard and a "conduit" for distribution financing.[9c; 9d; 9e]

Certain types of **distribution plans between a fund and its principal underwriter** may be "***a cause for regulatory concern***."[9e] One such example is a "***compensation plan***," under which the fund's principal underwriter fixes in advance the annual level of payments to be made by a fund to the principal underwriter. Such compensation plans entail an impermissible delegation of the fundamental decision on fund distribution spending to the very recipient of the payments—from the fund disinterested directors, who are required to conclude, in the exercise of their reasonable business judgment and in light of their fiduciary duties, that there is a reasonable likelihood that the plan will benefit both the fund and its shareholders. Another example is a "***reimbursement plan***," under which the fund agrees to reimburse the fund's principal underwriter for specific expenses subject to a stated annual ceiling, with any "excess distribution spending" to be "carried forward" in anticipation of repayment under the plan in future years. The "carry-forward" feature of such reimbursement plans puts constraint on the ability, and undermines the crucial "prior approval" role, of fund disinterested directors to make decisions in the best interest of the fund relating to distribution financing. The "carry-forward" feature may also result in future shareholders of the fund bearing the burden of reimbursing the principal underwriter for distribution spending that primarily benefits current, vis-à-vis future, fund shareholders.

Mutual funds financing distributions via 12b-1 fees remains controversial. Critics of 12b-1 fees include:

- Freeman (2007)[10] (arguing that SEC's handling of Rule 12b-1 shows a case of "*regulatory capture*"; and that "Rule 12b-1 fees allow fund sponsors to off-load entrepreneurial risk" but no decrease in management fee profitability levels has been observed).
- Rubinstein (1995)[11] (advocating that the problem of excessive fees to fund advisers through fund distributions can be solved by *abolishing 12b-1 plans entirely*).
- Burgunder & Hartmann (1988)[12] (comparing the original intent of Rule 12b-1 plans as "*supplemental plans*" with its current use as "*reimbursement plans*" and "*compensation plans*"; recommending *retaining but modifying* Rule 12b-1, to tie up with directors and advisers' fiduciary standards under § 36).
- Ferris & Chance (1987)[13] (refuting 12b-1 proponents' claim of value of "*economies of scale*," and offering expense ratio evidence suggesting that 12b-1 plan "*is only a dead-weight cost*" to fund shareholders).

An SEC staff report (2000)[14] acknowledged that, as adopted, Rule 12b-1 contemplated a fund's 12b-1 plan as "a temporary measure ... to solve a particular distribution problem ... such as net redemptions." Today, however, many funds use a 12b-1 plan as "an ongoing method of paying for marketing and distribution." The SEC staff report recommended a review of the requirements of Rule 12b-1.

Bibliography:

1. DIV. OF INV. MGMT, SEC. & EXCH. COMM'N, PROTECTING INVESTORS: A HALF CENTURY OF INVESTMENT COMPANY REGULATION, Ch.8 The Sale of Open-End Investment Company Shares (1992)
2. Rule 22d-1 Rels.: Exemption from Section 22(d) to Permit the Sale of Redeemable Securities at Prices

That Reflect Different Sales Loads: **2a.** IC-13183, 48 FR 19887, Appendix (1983); **2b.** IC-14390, 50 FR 7909 (1985)

3. Farina, Freeman & Webster, *The Mutual Fund Industry: A Legal Survey*, 44 NOTRE DAME LAW. 732 (1969)
4. Lemke *et al.*, REGULATION OF INVESTMENT COMPANIES, § 9.03 Sales Loads and Broker Activities: Section 22(d), FINRA Regulations (2017)
5. REPORT OF THE JOINT NASD/INDUSTRY TASK FORCE ON BREAKPOINTS (2003)
6. Rule 6c-10 Rels.: Exemptions for Certain Registered Open-End Management Investment Companies to Impose Deferred Sales Loads: **6a.** IC-16619, 53 FR 45275 (1988); **6b.** IC-20916, 60 FR 11887 (1995); **6c.** IC-20917, 60 FR 11890 (1995); **6d.** IC-22202, 61 FR 49011 (1996)
7. MUTUAL FUNDS AND EXCHANGE TRADED FUNDS REGULATION, Ch.23 Regulation of Mutual Fund Sales Practices (Kirsch ed. 2017)
8. Plesset & Ambler, *The Financing of Mutual Fund "B Share" Arrangements*, 52 BUS. LAW. 1385 (1997)
9. Rule 12b-1 Rels.: Bearing of Distribution Expenses by Mutual Funds: **8a.** IC-9915, 42 FR 44810 (1977); **8b.** IC-10252, 43 FR 23589 (1978); **8c.** IC-10862, 44 FR 54014 (1979); **7d.** IC-11414, 45 FR 73898 (1980); **8e.** Payment of Asset-Based Sales Loads by Registered Open-End Management Investment Companies, IC-16431, 53 FR 23258 (1988); **8f.** Technical Amendments to Rule Relating to Payments for the Distribution of Shares by a Registered Open-End Management Investment Company, IC-22201, 61 FR 49010 (1996); **8g.** Prohibition on the Use of Brokerage Commissions to Finance Distribution, IC-26591, 69 FR 54728 (2004); **8h.** Mutual Fund Distribution Fees; Confirmations, 33-9128, 34-62544, IC-29367, 75 FR 47064 (2010)
10. Freeman, *The Mutual Fund Distribution Expense Mess*, 32 J. CORP. L. 739 (2007)
11. Rubinstein, *Excessive Mutual Fund Advisory Fees: Give-Ups in Rule 12b-1 Clothing?*, 14 ANN. REV. BANKING L. 385 (1995)
12. Burgunder & Hartmann, *The Mutual Fund Industry and Rule 12b-1 Plans: An Assessment*, 15 SEC. REG. L.J. 364 (1988)
13. Ferris & Chance, *The Effect of 12b-1 Plans on Mutual Fund Expense Ratios: A Note*, 42 J. FIN. 1077 (1987)
14. SEC DIV. OF INV. MANAGEMENT, REPORT ON MUTUAL FUND FEES AND EXPENSES (2000)

Topic 2 Prohibited Distribution Arrangement: IA Revenue Sharing for BD Shelf Space

Laws & Rules Highlight:

IC Act (15 USC 80a-1 *et seq.*) & Rules (17 CFR §§ 270.0-1 *et seq.*)
FINRA Rules

- Rule 12b-1 Distribution of Shares by Registered Open-End Management Investment Company
  - Rule 12b-1(h)(1) (***prohibits*** *a fund from directing portfolio brokerage to a BD for selling or promoting fund shares*)
  - Rule 12b-1(h)(2) (***permits*** *a fund to use a selling BD to execute portfolio transactions* ***only if*** *its selection of a selling BD for portfolio transactions is not influenced by fund sale considerations*)
- FINRA Rule 2341 Investment Company Securities
  - Rule 2341(k) Execution of Investment Company Portfolio Transactions (*"**anti-reciprocal rule**": prohibits BDs from conditioning fund distribution or promotion on receipt of fund portfolio brokerage commissions*)

Pre-Case Background Note:[Biblio]

Banning an "Unmanageable"[1] Conflict of Interest: Bartering Fund Brokerage for Fund Promotion

Fund brokerage is an asset of the fund. Thus, any use of fund brokerage to finance fund distribution would be subject to SEC Rule 12b-1, regulating the use of fund assets to finance distribution. Addressing the adviser practice of bartering fund brokerage for sales efforts, the SEC concluded in 2004 that the benefits of such practice to funds and their shareholders are unclear but the benefits to fund advisers are clear, and consequently adopted paragraph (h) of Rule 12b-1 to end the practice. Rule 12b-1(h) ***prohibits*** mutual funds from *paying for fund shares distribution with* ***fund brokerage commissions***, whether through:[1]

- ***directed brokerage***—*i.e.*, fund adviser ***directly rewards*** fund selling broker, by directing fund portfolio securities brokerage transactions and commissions to it as executing broker; or
- ***step out***—*i.e.*, fund adviser ***indirectly rewards*** fund selling broker who may lack execution capability, by selecting another broker to execute the portfolio trades but

requiring such executing broker to step out (*i.e.*, to set aside, surrender, or "*give up*"[2 (pp.169-70)]) a portion of the commissions and pay over the step-out commissions to the fund selling broker as reward for its fund promotion.

Such practices pose significant, unmanageable conflicts of interest that cannot be cured by ***disclosure***.[1; cf. 3 & 4] **Fund advisers**, whose compensation is based on a percentage of assets under management, have an incentive to promote the sale of fund shares and increase their advisory fees through directing brokerage commissions to reward fund promotion, even if fund portfolio transactions do not receive best execution (fund adviser "***revenue sharing***" practice). **Fund selling brokers** have an incentive to recommend and provide prominence to funds that best compensate the brokers, instead of funds that better meet brokerage customers' investment needs (fund selling broker "***shelf space***" practice). Such brokerage for promotion practice may also disadvantage funds that do not actively trade their portfolios due to their investment considerations. Thus, using fund portfolio brokerage in exchange for fund share promotion may enrich fund advisers and fund selling brokers, but harm funds and fund shareholders.[1]

The following two enforcement cases, one against a fund adviser (*investment adviser* or **IA**) and one against a fund selling broker (*broker-dealer firm* or **BD**), address IA's provision of "***revenue sharing***" for "***shelf space***" at BD. As the cases related to practices before the Rule 12b-1(h) prohibition took effect in 2004, the enforcement actions proceeded on the grounds of fraud for ***failure to disclose*** the conflicted distribution arrangements.

For academic literature comparing disclosure as "***a remedy***" for conflicts of interest, with the "***perverse effects***" of such disclosure, see for example, Cain *et al.* (2011),[5] concluding: Disclosure is likely to be helpful when information is made available to intermediaries, and is much less likely to help individuals such as personal investors who are unlikely to possess the knowledge or experience to know how much they should discount conflicted advice. Transparency may be good, but objectivity is even better. Regulators should focus less on disclosing sources of bias but more on ensuring that objective information reaches the audience, if not in lieu of biased information, at least directly alongside it.

Bibliography:

1. Prohibition on the Use of Brokerage Commissions to Finance Distribution: **1a.** IC-26356, 69 FR 9726 (2004); **1b.** IC-26591, 69 FR 54728 (2004)

2. Report of the Securities and Exchange Commission on the Public Policy Implications of Investment Company Growth, H.R. Rep. No. 89-2337 (1966)
3. Payment for Investment Company Services with Brokerage Commissions: **3a.** IC-20472, 59 FR 42187 (1994); **3b.** IC-21221, FR-46, 60 FR 38918 (1995)
4. Request for Comments on Measures to Improve Disclosure of Mutual Fund Transaction Costs; Concept Release, 34-48952, IC-26313, 68 FR 74820 (2003)
5. Cain *et al.*, *When Sunlight Fails to Disinfect: Understanding the Perverse Effects of Disclosing Conflicts of Interests*, 37 J. Consumer Res. 836, 850-51 (2011)

Case Study 1: IA Revenue Sharing

Enforcement against adviser and principal underwriter for Franklin Templeton Investments, a global mutual fund complex, for failure to adequately disclose directing fund brokerages to thirty-nine broker-dealers to gain shelf space.

In *re* Franklin Advisers, Inc. and Franklin/Templeton Distributors, Inc., Respondents

Adm. Proc. 3-11769, 34-50841A, IA-2337A, IC-26692A (Dec. 13, 2004)

Case Study 2: BD Shelf Space

Enforcement against Edward D. Jones & Co., L.P., one of the largest sellers of brokerage-sold mutual funds in the United States, for failure to disclose seeking directed brokerages in return for providing "Preferred Fund Families" space.

In *re* Edward D. Jones & Co., L.P., Respondent

Adm. Proc. 3-11780, 33-8520, 34-50910 (Dec. 22, 2004)

Selected Literature Debating Propriety of IA-BD Shelf Space Practices

Legal Literature:

Pro—Retail Grocery Industry Shelf Space Analogy:

- Johnsen (2008)[1] (comparing IA using fund brokerage to pay BD for shelf space arrangement to retail grocery industry's "***slotting contracts***" arrangement, arguing that there is no indication that the slotting contracts practice harms consumers).

Con—Conflicts of Interest Theory:

- Langevoort (2010)[2] (citing evidence that investors pay significantly more for mutual fund investments sold via broker channel without receiving any better fund performance; pointing to "***conflicts of interest***" as tempting brokers to push funds that pay for "shelf space" to increase brokerage firm's profitability; doubting efficacy of any "simple disclosure" as solution to such conflicts of interest).

- Birdthistle (2006)[3] (arguing: IA-BD "prominent shelf space" arrangement puts advisers' interest ***in conflict*** with fund shareholders' interest; the managerial ***power*** of advisers gives them the ***ability*** to extract value surreptitiously at fund shareholders' expense).

Economics Literature:

- Christoffersen *et al.* (2013)[4] (found "***significant evidence***" that revenue sharing and similar payments skew brokers' incentives; identified "***a cost***" of the industrial organization of investment advice, where the latitude fund sponsors enjoy to pay more or less to their brokers has real consequences for the brokers' clients).
- Marx & Shaffer (2010)[5] (investigating the pro- and anti-competitive effects of "***slotting allowances***"—payments made by manufacturers to supermarkets to obtain shelf space for their products, and constructing model to demonstrate: contrary to the ***conventional view*** that takes as given scarcity of shelf space and that assumes slotting allowances as a response to such scarcity, ***the opposite causality*** may also be true, *i.e.*, (1) scarcity of shelf space itself may be induced by the feasibility of slotting allowances; and (2) the retailer is more likely to limit its shelf space in an environment with slotting allowances than without, leading to a total welfare loss even if slotting allowances have no effect on retail prices).

Bibliography:

1. Johnsen, *The SEC's Mistaken ban on Directed Brokerage: A Transaction Cost Analysis*, 40 ARIZ. ST. L.J. 1241, 1284 n.170 (2008)
2. Langevoort, *Brokers as Fiduciaries*, 71 U. PITT. L. REV. 439, 448 n.32 (2010), *citing* Bergstresser *et al.*, *Assessing the Costs and Benefits of Brokers in the Mutual Fund Industry*, 22 REV. FIN. STUD. 4129 (2009)
3. Birdthistle, *Compensating Power: An Analysis of Rents and Rewards in the Mutual Fund Industry*, 80 TUL. L. REV. 1401, §V-E (2006)
4. Christoffersen *et al.*, *What Do Consumers' Fund Flows Maximize? Evidence from Their Brokers' Incentives*, 68 J. FIN. 201 (2013)
5. Marx & Shaffer, *Slotting Allowances and Scarce Shelf Space*, 19 J. ECON. & MGMT. STRATEGY 575 (2010)

Research Topic:

Mutual fund distribution structure, financing arrangements, and their regulation in China.

In *re* Franklin Advisers, Inc. and Franklin/Templeton Distributors, Inc., Respondents

Adm. Proc. 3-11769, 34-50841A, IA-2337A, IC-26692A (Dec. 13, 2004)

I.

The United States Securities and Exchange Commission deems it appropriate and in the public interest that administrative and cease-and-desist proceedings be, and hereby are, instituted pursuant to § § 203(e) and 203(k) of the Investment Advisers Act of 1940, § § 9(b) and 9(f) of the Investment Company Act of 1940 and § 15(b) of the Securities Exchange Act of 1934 against Franklin Advisers, Inc. ("**FA**") and Franklin/Templeton Distributors, Inc. ("**FTDI**") (collectively, the "**Respondents**").

II.

In anticipation of the institution of these proceedings, Respondents have submitted an Offer of Settlement (the "**Offer**") that the Commission has determined to accept. Solely for the purpose of these proceedings and any other proceedings brought by or on behalf of the Commission or in which the Commission is a party, and without admitting or denying the findings, except those findings pertaining to the jurisdiction of the Commission over them and the subject matter of these proceedings, Respondents consent to the entry of this Order Instituting Administrative and Cease-and-Desist Proceedings, Making Findings, and Imposing Remedial Sanctions and a Cease-and-Desist Order Pursuant to § § 203(e) and 203(k) of the Investment Advisers Act of 1940, § § 9(b) and 9(f) of the Investment Company Act of 1940, and § 15(b) of the Securities Exchange Act of 1934 ("**Order**") as set forth below.

III.

On the basis of this Order and Respondents' Offer, the Commission finds[1] that:

Respondents

1. FA is an investment adviser registered with the Commission and headquartered in San Mateo, California. FA provides investment advisory, portfolio management, and administrative services to a majority (though not all) of the mutual funds in the Franklin

---

[1] The findings herein are made pursuant to Respondents' Offer and are not binding on any other person or entity in this or any other proceeding.

Templeton Investments complex.[2] As of January 31, 2004, FA had $138.4 billion in assets under management.

2. FTDI is a broker-dealer registered with the Commission and headquartered in St. Petersburg, Florida. FTDI provides sales and marketing services and acts as the principal underwriter and distributor of shares of most of the U.S.-registered mutual funds in the Franklin Templeton Investments complex. FTDI earns fees and commissions in connection with the sale of the FT Fund shares.

Summary

3. Between 2001 and 2003, Franklin Templeton Investments ("**Franklin**" or "**FT**"), a global mutual fund complex, entered into inadequately disclosed agreements with 39 broker-dealer firms. Pursuant to those agreements, FT used $52 million in brokerage commissions—which were fund assets—to compensate those broker-dealers for providing preferential marketing of the funds. The use of fund brokerage commissions in lieu of cash payments by FTDI for these marketing arrangements created potential conflicts of interest that should have been, but were not, adequately disclosed to the FT Fund Boards of Directors and FT fund shareholders. These agreements with the broker-dealers, known as "shelf space" agreements, bought placement on certain broker-dealers' lists of recommended mutual funds and on the brokers-dealers' websites, among other things. The objective in entering into the shelf space agreements was to increase sales of the FT funds.

4. FTDI, the principal underwriter and distributor of shares of most of the FT mutual funds, negotiated the terms of the shelf space arrangements and attempted to have each broker-dealer receive the amount contemplated in its agreement with FTDI. FA, which provides investment advisory, portfolio management, and administrative services to a majority of the FT mutual funds, had the duty to inform the fund directors and shareholders of potential conflicts of interest.

5. FA, aided and abetted by FTDI, failed to adequately disclose that the shelf space

---

[2] FA and FTDI are wholly owned subsidiaries of Franklin Resources, Inc., a Delaware corporation headquartered in San Mateo, California, which has securities registered under § 12(g) of the Securities Exchange Act of 1934 and files periodic reports with the Commission. Franklin Resources, Inc. and its subsidiaries operate under the name "**Franklin Templeton Investments**," here shortened to "**FT**." Through its subsidiaries, FT provides a broad range of investment advisory, investment management, and related services to open-end investment companies, including a family of over 100 retail mutual funds, referred to herein as the "**FT funds**."

arrangements shifted marketing expenses from FTDI to fund shareholders. They also failed to disclose that if the shelf space agreements successfully increased fund sales, FA would benefit from an increase in its compensation, which was calculated as a percentage of total assets under management. In addition, because FTDI asked FT's traders to meet specific directed brokerage targets for certain broker-dealers, FT risked executing trades in a manner inconsistent with shareholder interests. Finally, without knowledge of these agreements, the Boards were unable adequately to evaluate the funds' overall marketing expenses and other issues.

6. By engaging in the inadequately disclosed practice of using fund assets for shelf space, FA and FTDI violated the securities laws. FA and FTDI also violated the law by not ensuring that the commission payments for shelf space were assets of the specific fund promoted by the broker-dealer. As a result, some funds may have been improperly disadvantaged in that the assets of those funds were used for the benefit of other funds.

FTDI Used Brokerage Commissions to Pay for Shelf Space

7. Between January 2001 and the end of 2003, FTDI negotiated shelf space agreements with banks and broker-dealers. Under these agreements, FTDI agreed to pay the broker-dealers for heightened access to the broker-dealers' distribution or sales systems. The heightened access included placement of certain Franklin funds on the brokers' websites and lists of preferred mutual funds, access to brokers, participation in broker conferences, and other advantages. Senior FTDI officers negotiated these deals for FTDI.

8. For the period 2001 through 2003, FTDI sent 39 broker-dealers a total of $52 million in brokerage commissions "directed" as a credit for shelf space arrangements. When the FT traders directed brokerage to the broker-dealers with whom they had shelf space agreements, commissions on mutual fund portfolio trades were used to offset shelf space payments. These brokerage commissions were fund assets. FTDI made some payments in cash, but cash payments were an expense to FTDI. So, FTDI preferred to avoid the cost through the use of directed brokerage. This use of commissions created potential conflicts of interest that needed to be adequately disclosed.

9. When FTDI paid for shelf space with brokerage commissions, it did so according to a ratio calculation. If, for example, the shelf space agreement contemplated that FTDI would pay $100,000 in cash to a broker-dealer for fund sales and assets, some

broker-dealers would allow FTDI to satisfy the agreement with $130,000 in brokerage commissions pursuant to an agreed ratio of 1:1.3. If the brokerage commission payments did not cover the specified amount for shelf space, FTDI would pay the balance in cash. It was more beneficial for FTDI to pay for shelf space with brokerage commissions than cash because FTDI was able to avoid using its own assets for the marketing expense.

10. FA also benefited from the payment of directed brokerage commissions for shelf space agreements insofar as increased fund sales generated increased assets under management, which in turn generated increased management fees for FA.

11. FTDI tracked compliance with the shelf space agreements, most of which were oral, though still definite and specific. FTDI recorded the terms and brokerage targets on a spreadsheet identifying all the broker-dealers who had agreed to accept brokerage in lieu of hard cash payments. FT's trading department established targets for brokerage commissions that would be directed to the various broker-dealers pursuant to the negotiated agreements. As the year progressed, the targets were circulated to the FT trading department as a monthly update showing progress toward the shelf space targets. Toward the end of the year, these reports were distributed weekly rather than monthly to ensure that the traders received up-to-date information on target completion. Toward the end of the fiscal year, the FTDI account managers responsible for maintaining specific broker-dealer relationships would sometimes tell the FT trading department that they were short of reaching that year's brokerage target for one of the broker-dealers. They would ask the FT traders to direct more brokerage to that broker-dealer in order to meet the target and subject to best execution, the FT traders were generally able to comply. The traders were aware of the targets, and FTDI's progress in meeting them, when allocating their trades.

The Inadequately Disclosed Shelf Space Payments Created Potential Conflicts of Interest

12. Between 2001 and late 2003, FA did not adequately disclose to the FT Boards and FT Shareholders that brokerage commissions were being used as a credit for shelf space. As a fiduciary responsible for informing the FT Boards of important matters and approving the funds' written disclosures to FT Shareholders, FA had a duty to ensure adequate disclosures were made.

13. The Boards were not specifically advised of the practice of paying for shelf space with directed brokerage and were never made aware of several potential conflicts of interest, including that FTDI had a choice about whether to pay for the shelf space from its own assets or the funds' assets and that FA stood to profit from higher fees resulting from increased assets under management. As a result, the Boards were unable to adequately evaluate the funds' overall marketing expenses in approving the funds' marketing plans as required by the Commission pursuant to Rule 12b-1. Because they were not given the opportunity to approve the practice of using fund assets to pay for shelf space, the Boards could not adequately evaluate whether this use of fund assets was in accordance with the best interests of the FT shareholders. Nor could they evaluate the funds' overall marketing expenses.

14. The shelf space arrangements also were not adequately disclosed to the FT Shareholders. FA was responsible for ensuring that the disclosures made in the funds' prospectuses and Statements of Additional Information ("SAIs") accurately described how FTDI chose the broker-dealers with which it worked. Item 16(c) of the SEC's Form N-1A requires a description in the SAI of "how the Fund will select brokers to effect securities transactions in the Fund" and requires that "if the Fund will consider the receipt of products or services other than brokerage or research services in selecting brokers, [the Fund should] specify those products or services."

15. In the "*Dealer Compensation*" section of its SAIs, FT disclosed, in pertinent part:

> Distributors and/or its affiliates may provide financial support to securities dealers that sell share of Franklin Templeton Investments. This support is based primarily on the amount of sales of fund shares and/or total assets with Franklin Templeton Investments. The amount of support may be affected by: total sales; net sales; levels of redemptions; the proportion of a securities dealer's sales and marketing efforts in Franklin Templeton Investments; a securities dealer's sales and marketing efforts in Franklin Templeton Investments; a securities dealer's support of, and participation in, Distributors' marketing programs; a securities dealer's compensation programs for its registered representatives; and the extent of a securities dealer's marketing programs relating to Franklin Templeton Investments. Financial support to securities dealers may be made by payments from Distributor's own resources, from Distributors' retention of underwriting concessions and, in the case of funds that have Rule 12b-1 plans, from payments to Distributors under such plans. In addition, certain securities dealers may receive brokerage commissions generated by fund portfolio transactions

in accordance with the rules of the National Association of Securities Dealers, Inc.

The "*Portfolio Transactions*" section of FT's SAIs states, in pertinent part:

> If the Funds' officers are satisfied that the best execution is obtained, the sale of Fund shares, as well as shares of other funds in Franklin Templeton Investments, also may be considered a factor in the selection of broker-dealers to execute the Funds' portfolio transactions.

Although the SAIs stated that FT could consider a broker-dealer's sales of fund shares when selecting a broker-dealer to execute portfolio transactions, they did not describe FTDI's practice of annually negotiating shelf space arrangements with certain broker-dealers. They did not make clear to fund shareholders that brokerage commissions were used to offset shelf space payment obligations under at least some of these shelf space arrangements. They also did not make clear that use of brokerage payments in this manner was not specifically authorized by the funds' distribution plans approved by the FT Fund Boards pursuant to Rule 12b-1.

Respondents Engaged in Improper Joint Arrangements

16. Each time FT directed a fund's brokerage commissions to obtain credit for the shelf space arrangements, they made no effort to ensure that these commissions came from the specific fund promoted by the broker-dealer in connection with a shelf space arrangement. Accordingly, Respondents made no efforts to ensure that the directed brokerage commissions from any given fund were used to promote the sale of that fund, as opposed to the sale of other funds. As a result, some funds may have been improperly disadvantaged in that the assets of those funds were used for the benefit of other funds. FTDI and FA thus participated in a joint distribution arrangement whereby they improperly pooled and directed brokerage from the FT Funds.

Respondents' Remedial Actions

17. In November 2003, Respondents voluntarily stopped the practice of paying for shelf space with directed brokerage, citing uncertainty in the industry regarding the appropriateness of the practice. Respondents continued to pay for shelf space with cash payments from FTDI.

Violations

18. As a result of the conduct described above:

a. FA:

i. Willfully[3] violated § 206(2) of the Advisers Act, which provides that it is "unlawful for any investment adviser, by the use of the mails or any means or instrumentality of interstate commerce, directly or indirectly ... to engage in any transaction, practice, or course of business which operates as a fraud or deceit upon any client or prospective client."

ii. Willfully violated § 34(b) of the Investment Company Act, which provides in pertinent part that it is "unlawful for any person to make any untrue statement of a material fact in any registration statement ... filed or transmitted pursuant to" the Investment Company Act and to "omit to state therein any fact necessary in order to prevent the statements made therein, in light of the circumstances under which they were made, from being materially misleading."

iii. Willfully violated § 17(d) of the Investment Company Act and Rule 17d-1 thereunder, which provide in pertinent part that it is unlawful for any "affiliated person of or principal underwriter for any registered investment company ..., acting as principal, [to] participate in, or effect any transaction in connection with, any joint enterprise or other joint arrangement or profit-sharing plan in which any such registered company ... is a participant ... unless an application regarding such joint enterprise or profit-sharing plan has been filed with the Commission and has been granted by an order entered prior to the submission of such plan[.]"

b. FTDI:

i. Willfully[4] aided and abetted and caused FA's violation of § 206(2) of the Advisers Act.

ii. Willfully violated § 17(d) of the Investment Company Act and Rule 17d-1 thereunder. * * * *

---

[3] "Willfully" as used with respect to the direct violations in this Order means intentionally committing the act that constitutes the violation. See *Wonsover v. SEC*, 205 F.3d 408, 414 (DC Cir. 2000); *Tager v. SEC*, 344 F.2d 5, 8 (2d Cir. 1965). There is no requirement that the actor also be aware that it is violating one of the Rules or Act.

[4] "Willfully" as used with respect to the aiding and abetting violations in this Order means knowingly committing the act which constitutes the violation, see *Wonsover v. SEC*, 205 F.3d 408, 418 (D.C. Cir. 2000); *Tager v. SEC*, 344 F.2d 5, 8 (2d Cir. 1965).

IV.

In view of the foregoing, the Commission deems it appropriate and in the public interest to impose the sanctions specified in the Offer submitted by Respondents. Accordingly, it is hereby ORDERED that: * * * *

D. FTDI and FA shall pay, jointly and severally, within 30 days of the entry of the Order, disgorgement in the amount of $1 ("Disgorgement"). FTDI and FA shall each pay, within 30 days of the entry of the Order, civil money penalties in the amount of $10 million ("Penalties"), for a total payment of $20,000,001. * * * *

In *re* Edward D. Jones & Co., L.P., Respondent

Adm. Proc. 3-11780, 33-8520, 34-50910 (Dec. 22, 2004)

I.

The Securities and Exchange Commission deems it appropriate and in the public interest that public administrative and cease-and-desist proceedings be, and hereby are, instituted pursuant to §8A of the Securities Act of 1933 and §§15(b) and 21C of the Securities Exchange Act of 1934 against Edward D. Jones & Co., L.P. ("**Edward Jones**" or "**Respondent**").

II.

In anticipation of the institution of these proceedings, Respondent has submitted an Offer of Settlement (the "Offer") which the Commission has determined to accept. Solely for the purpose of these proceedings and any other proceedings brought by or on behalf of the Commission, or to which the Commission is a party, and without admitting or denying the findings herein, except as to the Commission's jurisdiction over it and the subject matter of these proceedings, Respondent consents to the entry of this Order Instituting Administrative and Cease-and-Desist Proceedings, Making Findings, and Imposing Remedial Sanctions and a Cease-and-Desist Order Pursuant to §8A of the Securities Act of 1933 and §§15(b) and 21C of the Securities Exchange Act of 1934 ("Order"), as set forth below.

III.

On the basis of this Order and Respondent's Offer, the Commission finds[1] that:

Respondent

1. Edward Jones is a Missouri limited partnership that has been registered with the Commission as a broker-dealer pursuant to §15 of the Exchange Act since 1941. It is also a member of the National Association of Securities Dealers and the New York Stock Exchange. Edward Jones' principal offices are located in St. Louis, Missouri. It has more than 8,000 branch offices staffed primarily by one or two registered Investment Representatives ("*IRs*") that provide retail brokerage services throughout the United States, Canada and the United Kingdom. Edward Jones is the principal operating subsidiary of

---

[1] The findings herein are made pursuant to Respondent's Offer of Settlement and are not binding on any other person or entity in this or any other proceeding.

the Jones Financial Companies, L.L.L.P. ("**Jones Financial**"), a Missouri limited partnership whose limited partnership interests are registered under § 12(g) of the Exchange Act. Jones Financial holds all of Edward Jones' partnership equity. Jones Financial is comprised of approximately 275 general partners, 5,021 limited partners and 146 subordinated limited partners.

Overview

2. Edward Jones is one of the largest sellers of brokerage-sold mutual funds in the United States. Half of all of Edward Jones' customers' assets are invested in mutual funds held in brokerage accounts and college savings plans established under § 529 of the Internal Revenue Code ("*529 plans*"). Edward Jones' customers hold onto their investments for a lengthier period of time than customers at other broker-dealers. Edward Jones has selling agreements with approximately 240 mutual fund families which permit its IRs to sell at least 1,930 different mutual funds.

3. Prior to the late 1980s, Edward Jones had internally designated certain of the mutual fund families with which it had selling agreements as "recommended." In the late 1980s, Edward Jones approached certain of those mutual fund families ("*Preferred Families*") with which it had long-standing relationships and sought to obtain revenue sharing from them. Edward Jones set an internal revenue sharing target of 25% of the advisory fees earned by those mutual fund families on the mutual fund assets purchased or held by Edward Jones' customers, plus in most instances sought an equity interest in their advisers or distributors.

The Preferred Mutual Fund Family Program

4. By the early 1990s, six mutual fund families had agreed to make revenue sharing payments to Edward Jones. Between 1993 and 1996, Edward Jones removed one of these fund families and added two new fund families to the list of Preferred Families, raising the total number of Preferred Families to seven.

5. Each of these fund families agreed to make revenue sharing payments to Edward Jones in varying amounts up to and in several cases meeting Edward Jones' target of 25% of the advisory fees for assets purchased or held by Edward Jones' customers. These fees were calculated in various ways and by various measures, including: a flat fee determined by the fund family based on the total fund assets held by Edward Jones' customers; 7.5 to 10 basis points of average fund assets held by Edward Jones' customers in a given year;

12.5 basis points on the gross sales of a Preferred Families' mutual funds made by Edward Jones to its customers in a given year; or 25% of the advisory fee attributable to the average assets of certain Preferred Families' mutual funds held by Edward Jones' customers in a given year. One of the Preferred Families also agreed to provide Edward Jones an equity interest of at least 5% in the distributor of its mutual funds if Edward Jones reached a certain threshold of sales of its mutual funds, this was later changed to profit participation.

6. Revenue sharing was a material factor, among others, in the selection of at least two of the Preferred Families. Revenue sharing was also a material factor, among others, with respect to the retention of fund families as Preferred Families. Edward Jones periodically sought to negotiate additional revenue sharing payments from its Preferred Families.

7. Edward Jones' revenue sharing agreements with the Preferred Families are and have been highly profitable to Edward Jones. Between 1999 and the present, the firm has collected tens of millions of dollars in revenue sharing payments from the Preferred Families each year. Most of these payments have been paid directly to Edward Jones from the assets of the advisers or distributors associated with the Preferred Families. However, for a portion of this time period, Edward Jones also accepted millions of dollars in directed brokerage commissions or "step-outs" from three of the Preferred Families for distribution of mutual fund shares. In these instances, the advisers of these Preferred Families instructed the brokerage firm executing portfolio transactions for their mutual funds to "step out" of the transactions and direct a portion of the commissions for the transactions to Edward Jones. These directed brokerage payments ceased in 2003.

8. Edward Jones' distributed 11% to 12% of its net income, which includes net revenue sharing, to its limited partners and 10% to 12% of its net income to its subordinated limited partners each year and the residual is distributed to the general partners. Thus, the majority of any revenue sharing received by Edward Jones, after operating expenses, was distributed to the firm's general partners, some of whom make decisions regarding which mutual fund families become "Preferred Families" and others of whom are Edward Jones IRs who recommend the Preferred Families to their customers. During 2003 alone, the revenue sharing received by Edward Jones was equivalent to 33% of the net income of Edward Jones' parent holding company, Jones Financial.

9. Out of the approximately 240 mutual fund families with which Edward Jones has selling agreements, only the seven Preferred Families make revenue sharing payments to

Edward Jones. These payments are in addition to standard sales loads, commissions, Rule 12b-1 fees, expense reimbursements and sub-transfer-agent fees for maintaining customer account information. Edward Jones does not receive any revenue sharing payments from any non-preferred mutual fund families. Historically, 95% to 98% of Edward Jones' sales of mutual fund shares have been sales of the Preferred Families.

10. Edward Jones and its partners have a financial incentive to internally promote the sales of mutual funds from the Preferred Families over other mutual funds that its IRs can sell. Edward Jones promoted to IRs the existence of revenue sharing by the Preferred Families and encouraged IRs on a case-by-case basis to consider revenue sharing in making recommendations to their customers to purchase certain mutual funds.

11. For example, during the relevant time period, Edward Jones' Director of Mutual Fund Marketing described his "greatest contribution to the Firm's bottom line" as "the Department's ability to continue the focus on selling preferred fund families and the subsequent leverage this gives us to negotiate revenue sharing programs with vendors." He also represented to the IRs that Edward Jones directly passes the revenue sharing income along to the "IRs who did the work to get the money in the first place."

12. During the "rollouts" of the two newest Preferred Families, a general partner of the firm also made broadcast presentations to IRs throughout the country further extolling the benefits the IRs receive from the revenue sharing agreements negotiated with these Preferred Families.

13. At least one newsletter distributed by an Edward Jones regional leader conveyed this message by describing how "revenue sharing can contribute large benefits to the firm in terms of profit and bonus." In a January 2000 regional newsletter, a regional leader further promoted the sales of mutual funds from Preferred Families that provide revenue sharing payments over those that do not provide revenue sharing by describing how, over a ten year period, an IR would receive an additional $256,369 in profit from the sales of such mutual funds. During regional and other meetings, another of Edward Jones' regional leaders, who was also a general partner, encouraged IRs in his region to sell the mutual funds of one Preferred Family over the funds of another Preferred Family that paid less revenue sharing.

14. Edward Jones' IRs receive credits for the amount of revenue sharing that Edward Jones receives from the IRs' proportionate sales and customer holdings of funds from the

Preferred Families. These credits were not directly paid to IRs, but were applied as a separate line item to the profit and loss statements ("*P&Ls*") prepared for each IR's office. These P&Ls are distributed monthly to the IRs and track their profitability to the firm. An IR's profitability to the firm determines whether the IR is successful at Edward Jones and is used as a factor in determining whether the IR will be considered for status as a limited partner. In addition, three times per year, Edward Jones' IRs are eligible to receive bonuses based, in part, on their overall profitability which is impacted by their revenue sharing credits. For an IR to receive a bonus in any of Edward Jones' three annual bonus periods, both the firm and the particular IR's office must be profitable during the period. In addition, if an IR has worked for Edward Jones for more than 30 months, the IR also needs to make at least $4,000 in profits to become eligible for a bonus. Edward Jones' top-producing IRs have received as much as an additional $5,000 per bonus period as the part of their bonuses based directly on revenue sharing payments attributable to the IRs' sales and customer holdings of funds from the Preferred Families to their retail customers.

15. Edward Jones further offers "diversification contest" trips to its IRs twice each year. During these contests, the IRs can qualify for a trip by earning points based on, among other things, their sales of mutual funds. Once an IR earns a specific number of points, the IR "wins" a trip. Although the IRs generally can earn contest points for selling any mutual funds or other investment product, for a 90-day period in the fall of 2002, Edward Jones only gave mutual fund contest points for the sale of a subset of mutual funds from the Preferred Families. One or more of the Preferred Families always participate in the sponsorship of the diversification trips and make one short training presentation for the IRs during each trip. Sponsorship of these trips and other meetings provide the Preferred Families with exclusive access to and visibility with the IRs.

16. The Preferred Families receive certain benefits not otherwise available to non-preferred families. First, Edward Jones exclusively promotes the seven Preferred Families on its public website and exclusively provides links to the Preferred Families' websites on Edward Jones' internal computer system accessible only to its IRs. Second, Edward Jones exclusively lists the Preferred Families in sales literature and newsletters provided to its customers. Third, Edward Jones provides its IRs with research on only the seven Preferred Families and maintains a "Preferred Funds List" containing the names of approximately 110 mutual funds within the Preferred Families that Edward Jones' Product Review department recommends for sale to Edward Jones' retail customers. Only funds

from the seven Preferred Families are considered for inclusion on this list. The Product Review department does not review any mutual funds from fund families that are not Preferred Families for this "Preferred Funds List." Fourth, Edward Jones uses only the Preferred Families as examples in its internal training sessions for new IRs and only invites representatives from the Preferred Families to make presentations at these training sessions. Finally, Edward Jones facilitates exclusive direct access for the Preferred Families to its IRs for the dissemination of marketing materials and to answer IRs' questions regarding the funds offered by the Preferred Families.

Edward Jones Did Not Disclose Its Financial Incentives to Sell Mutual Funds from the Preferred Families

17. The mutual fund section of Edward Jones' public website lists only the seven Preferred Families and provides links to only the Preferred Families' websites. In addition, since approximately 1997, Edward Jones has claimed on its public website that it focuses on the seven Preferred Families because: "With nearly 11,000 mutual funds available, it can be difficult to know which fund(s) to pick. That's why at Edward Jones, we focus on seven preferred mutual fund families that share our same commitment to service, long-term investment objectives, and long-term performance."

18. During the same time period, Edward Jones did not disclose on its website or in any other written document that it prepared, the revenue sharing, directed brokerage payments and other payments received from the Preferred Families for distribution of mutual fund shares as described above. Edward Jones also did not disclose the dimensions of the potential financial conflict created by these payments.

19. Edward Jones and its IRs do not orally disclose to customers the revenue sharing, directed brokerage or other payments received by Edward Jones in connection with the distribution of mutual fund shares or the potential conflict of interest such payments create.

20. Instead, Edward Jones claimed to rely on language contained in the Preferred Families' prospectuses and Statements of Additional Information ("*SAIs*") to disclose revenue sharing arrangements. At all relevant times, Edward Jones required its IRs to provide customers with a prospectus at the point-of-sale or with the confirmation of sale of any mutual fund; however, the firm did not require its IRs to provide and IRs did not provide customers with copies of SAIs unless a customer specifically requested a copy.

21. Many of the Preferred Families' prospectuses and SAIs fail to disclose adequate information about the source and the amount of the revenue sharing payments to Edward Jones and the dimensions of the resulting potential conflicts of interest. Although the Preferred Families' prospectuses and SAIs contained various disclosures concerning payments to broker-dealers distributing their funds, few of these disclosures adequately described Edward Jones' potential conflict of interest.

22. During the relevant time period, Edward Jones also has not had sufficient procedures in place to ensure that someone with appropriate knowledge, experience and authority reviews the prospectuses and SAIs of the mutual funds offered by the Preferred Families to determine if they adequately disclose revenue sharing and directed brokerage payments made to Edward Jones or the other incentives offered to Edward Jones by the Preferred Families.

Edward Jones' 529 College Savings Plan Sales and Disclosures

23. Since 2000, Edward Jones has offered and sold 529 college savings plans to its customers. Offers and sales of 529 plans are municipal securities transactions. Prior to September 2004, Edward Jones stated on its public website that "the 529 plans available through Edward Jones" were three plans offered by three of its Preferred Families. Also, prior to September 2004, Edward Jones provided additional detailed information on its public website about only these three 529 plans. Edward Jones did not list or provide information on its website regarding any of the other numerous 529 plans that it could sell.

24. Edward Jones currently has selling agreements with 14 mutual fund companies to sell their 529 plans. However, Edward Jones promotes only the 529 plans of the Preferred Families that offer 529 plans, two of which pay additional revenue sharing to Edward Jones for sales of 529 plans. Edward Jones expressly encourages its IRs to sell only the 529 plans of the Preferred Families. In internal notices to its IRs announcing the availability of 529 plans from non-preferred families, Edward Jones explicitly states: "Edward Jones will continue to promote only our preferred vendors' 529 plans ... Although we have a selling agreement with [another 529 plan], they are not one of our preferred vendors. However, if one of your clients feel [sic] the advantages of [another 529 plan] are important factors in their decision, you can sell it." In addition, Edward Jones has made it easier for its IRs to sell and service the Preferred Families' 529 plans versus non-preferred 529 plans.

25. At the same time, Edward Jones has failed to disclose on its website or in any other written documents prepared by Edward Jones, including confirmations of 529 plan sales, the material financial incentives to Edward Jones, its partners and its IRs to sell 529 plans from certain of the Preferred Families over other 529 plans that Edward Jones could sell.

[***Violations***]

26. Based on the conduct described above, Edward Jones willfully violated:

a. Section 17(a)(2) of the Securities Act, which provides that it is "unlawful for any person in the offer or sale of any securities ... by the use of any means or instruments of transportation or communication in interstate commerce or by use of the mails, directly or indirectly ... to obtain money or property by means of any untrue statement of a material fact or any omission to state a material fact necessary in order to make the statements made, in light of the circumstances under which they were made, not misleading";

b. Rule 10b-10 under the Exchange Act, which provides in pertinent part that it is "unlawful for any broker or dealer to effect for or with an account of a customer any transaction in, or to induce the purchase or sale by such customer of, any security ... unless such broker or dealer, at or before completion of such transaction, gives or sends to such customer written notification disclosing ... the source and amount of any other remuneration received or to be received by the broker in connection with the transaction"; and

c. Section 15B(c)(1) of the Exchange Act, which provides that "no broker, dealer, or municipal securities dealer shall make use of the mails or any means or instrumentality of interstate commerce to effect any transaction in, or to induce or attempt to induce the purchase or sale of, any municipal security in contravention of any rule of the [Municipal Securities Rulemaking] Board."

27. By virtue of its sales of 529 college savings plans, as described above, Edward Jones also contravened the dictates of Municipal Securities Rulemaking Board ("MSRB") Rule G-15, which requires a broker or dealer to send or give a written confirmation to its customer, at or before the completion of a municipal securities transaction, that discloses, among other things, either: "(A) the source and amount of any remuneration received or to be received ... by the broker [or] dealer ... in connection with the transaction from any person other than the customer, or (B) a statement indicating whether any such remuneration has been or will be received and that the source and amount of such other

remuneration will be furnished upon written request of the customer." * * * *

IV.

In view of the foregoing, the Commission deems it appropriate and in the public interest to impose the sanctions agreed to in Edward Jones' Offer. Accordingly, pursuant to §8A of the Securities Act and §§15(b) and 21C of the Exchange Act, it is hereby ORDERED that: * * * *

C. IT IS FURTHER ORDERED that:

1. Edward Jones shall pay disgorgement plus prejudgment interest in the total amount of $37.5 million ("Disgorgement") and a civil monetary penalty in the amount of $37.5 million ("Penalties"), for a total payment of $75 million. * * * *

Section 3.2 Trading in Mutual Fund Shares

Laws & Rules Highlight:

IC Act (15 USC 80a-1 *et seq.*) & Rules (17 CFR §§ 270.0-1 *et seq.*)

- § 22 Distribution, Redemption, and Repurchase of Redeemable Securities
  - § 22(c) (*authorizes SEC pricing rulemaking, for the purpose of eliminating or reducing* ***dilution of value*** *of fund outstanding securities or other* ***unfair results*** *to holders of fund outstanding securities*)
  - § 22(e) (*limits suspension or delay in redemption to no more than* ***seven days****—designed to prevent* ***abusive redemption barriers*** *such as: to stop net redemptions and attendant management fee decrease; to prevent shareholders from switching to other funds*)
- Rule 22c-1 Pricing of Redeemable Securities for Distribution, Redemption and Repurchase (*requires NAV* ***"forward pricing"*** *and prohibits* ***"backward pricing"****—designed to* ***eliminate*** *riskless trading by insiders and dilution of fund assets*)
  - § 2(a)(41) (*def. "value": (i) "market value"; (ii) "fair value" determined "in good faith" by fund board*)
- Rule 22c-2 Redemption Fees for Redeemable Securities (*authorizes fund board to impose up to* ***2% short-term redemption fee****—designed to* ***discourage*** *market timing*)
- Rule 22c-1(a)(3) (***NAV swing pricing rule:*** *permits mutual funds, other than MMF and ETF, to adjust its current NAV by a swing factor not exceeding 2% if a swing threshold is triggered, effectively passing on fund's liquidity and transaction costs to shareholders effecting significant net purchases or redemptions—designed to* ***mitigate fund value dilution***)

Topic 1 Late Trading: Insider's Illegal Profits

Research Note:[Biblio]

Late Trading—Betting Today on Yesterday's Horse Races[1]

Since prior to the passage of the IC Act, open-end funds practised "***backward pricing***" resulting in a "***two-price system***." Fund NAVs were typically calculated at 4:00 p.m. EST, but were not published and did not become effective until 10:00 a.m. the following day. During the period from 10:00 a.m. to 4:00 p.m. on a trading day, two prices could be ascertained: the price of the present trading day (day 2), which was based on the NAV of the preceding day (day 1) and which was still in effect; the price of the next trading day (day 3), which was based on the NAV of the present trading day (day 2) but which had not yet gone into effect. Fund insiders, who were allowed to buy and sell without paying a load, thus created a riskless arbitrage by simultaneously buying at the low price and selling at the high price: In a rising market, the fund insiders could purchase shares based on the lower, previous day's NAV, and turn around redeeming their shares at the higher, that day's NAV. In a falling market, the fund insiders could redeem their shares based on the higher, previous day's NAV, and turn around repurchasing shares at the lower, that day's NAV. The backward pricing system enabled fund insiders to time their purchases and redemptions and make riskless profits, to the dilution of fund's other shareholders.[2; 3e; 4]

In 1968, the SEC instituted a mandatory "***forward pricing***" requirement and outlawed the "backward pricing" practice, by adopting Rule 22c-1—the forward pricing rule. Rule 22c-1 prohibits any mutual fund, its principal underwriter, or any dealer from selling, redeeming, or repurchasing fund shares "*except at a price based on the current net asset value of such security which is next computed after receipt of a tender of such security for redemption or of an order to purchase or sell such security*." Rule 22c-1 imposes a minimum of *once daily* computation requirement, with the specific time or times to be decided by each fund board as most appropriate to the fund's particular investment portfolio. Rule 22c-1 is designed to eliminate or reduce the dilution of value of the fund outstanding securities or other unfair results to the holders of the fund outstanding securities, under the "backward pricing" system.[3; 2]

Mutual funds are sold through ***five principal distribution channels***, with the intermediated channels being the most significant measured by their respective share of asset distribution (rounded numbers):[5]

<table>
<tr><td rowspan="2">Retail Investors</td><td rowspan="2">Fund Direct Channel: 12%</td><td>Intermediated Channels: 76%</td></tr>
<tr><td>• Advice Channel (provided by investment adviser firms, banks, insurance companies, and financial planning firms): 55%
• Retirement Plan Channel (provided by employers): 16%
• Fund Supermarket Channel (provided by discount brokers): 5%</td></tr>
<tr><td>Institutional Investors</td><td colspan="2">Institutional Channel: (transacting through Fund Direct Channel or Intermediated Channels): 13%</td></tr>
</table>

Rule 22c-1's specification of the "***price ... next computed after receipt of a tender***" and trade processing reality have presented an operational loophole to late trading and a challenge to regulators. Funds typically calculate NAV, reflecting the closing prices or fair values of fund portfolio securities, at 4:00 p.m. EST when the major U.S. stock exchanges close. Investor orders of purchase and redemption, submitted by 4:00 p.m., may pass through a chain of fund intermediaries before finally reaching the funds, typically by midnight. Since Rule 22c-1's adoption in 1968, the SEC has interpreted the "*next computed*" price to mean "*the next price which goes into effect after receipt of the order.*" "*The rule contemplates that the time of receipt of the order by the retail dealer is controlling.*"[3b; 3g]

Permitting "***late trading***" is unlawful, and a violation of the forward pricing rule. Late trading occurs when a trader places a purchase or redemption order after 4:00 p.m. fund NAV pricing and yet receives that day's price or stale NAV, to exploit events that occurred after the 4:00 p.m. pricing and obtain risk-free arbitrage profits. The late trader buys on good news at the stale NAV and below the "next computed" NAV, and sells on bad news at the stale NAV and above the "next computed" NAV, diluting the value of fund's other investors to the very extent of the late trader's profits.[3g; 6]

While late trading can involve fund personnel, ***late trading violations have typically occurred at fund intermediaries***. Broker-dealers collect fund orders from their customers throughout the day; net purchase and redemption orders for the same funds among their customers; aggregate all the customer orders in their omnibus accounts under their own names with funds; and transmit such net, aggregated order information to the funds after 4:00 p.m. In performing such trade processing, broker-dealers are required to segregate all as of 4:00 p.m. orders—which will receive the same day's NAV, from all post-4:00 p.m. orders—which will receive the next day's NAV. Receiving such net, aggregated order information from fund intermediaries, funds generally do not have information of either the identities, or the individual transactions, of the investors represented in the intermediaries' omnibus accounts.[7] The SEC investigations in 2003 had uncovered "*not isolated*" instances where intermediaries abused order processing, to facilitate and conceal customer late trading by blending late trades (*i.e.*, orders received after 4:00 p.m.) with legitimate trades (*i.e.*, orders received by 4:00 p.m.).[3g] An academic study (Zitzewitz 2006)[8] investigating late trading between 1998 and 2003 presented evidence that "mutual fund trades purportedly placed before 4:00 p.m. were *correlated* with market movements from 4:00 p.m. to 9:00 p.m." and identified illegal late trading as the likely source of the correlation; and found "statistically significant evidence of late trading in *39 out of 66 fund families*."

Designed as a means "*to eliminate late trading through fund intermediaries*," the SEC in 2003 proposed a "***4:00 p.m. hard close rule***": all purchase and redemption orders be received by the fund or its designee by fund pricing time (*e.g.*, 4:00 p.m.) in order to receive the current day's price.[3g] The SEC's proposal met with concerns from fund intermediaries about costs of compliance. Instead of the SEC's "***hard 4***" approach, a "***smart 4***" approach had been put forward, including proposals to:[7]

- retain the current order "receipt" time approach but *beef up late trading compliance at the intermediaries*—an approach met with the SEC's concern: due to its "lack of regulatory jurisdiction" over some fund intermediaries, such as banks and pension plans; or
- establish a *central clearinghouse for mutual fund trades whose electronic time stamp* on an order before market close would entitle the order to receive that day's fund price—a proposal met with opposition by many fund intermediaries: due to the "prohibitively expensive" costs in developing links to such a clearing house.

As of the time of this book, the SEC has not acted on its 2003 "hard close" proposal as a means to combat late trading at the fund intermediary level.

For an ***insider trading theory*** of a fund adviser's selective disclosure of fund portfolio holdings to facilitate a third party's late trading or arbitrage trading, see the debate:

- SEC (2000)[9] (In the case of ***public operating companies***: "*issuer selective disclosure*" bears a close resemblance to "*ordinary tipping and insider trading.*"

The economic effects of the two practices are essentially the same: In both cases, a privileged few gain an informational edge from their superior access to corporate insiders, rather than from their skill, acumen, or diligence. In both cases, investors lose confidence in the fairness of the markets when they know that other participants may exploit "unerodable informational advantages" derived not from hard work or insights, but from their access to corporate insiders.).

- SEC (2003; 2004)[10a; 10b] (In the case of ***mutual funds***: when a mutual fund's portfolio holdings are selectively disclosed and professional traders are given the opportunity to use this information to their advantage and to the detriment of fund shareholders, misuse of material, nonpublic information may occur. Consistent with their obligations to prevent the misuse of material, nonpublic information and their fiduciary duties, funds and advisers may divulge nonpublic portfolio holdings to selected third parties *only when* the fund has legitimate business purposes for doing so *and* the recipients are subject to a duty of confidentiality, including *a duty not to trade on the nonpublic portfolio information*.).
- Bullard (2005)[11] (arguing: selective disclosure of ***fund's portfolio transactions*** to facilitate front running the fund transactions *in portfolio securities* is insider trading; however, selective disclosure of ***fund's portfolio holdings*** to facilitate arbitrageur trading *in fund shares* is not insider trading, because "portfolio information often is not necessary and is never by itself sufficient for fund arbitrage to succeed.").
- Langevoort (2012)[12] (Where advisory personnel use their knowledge of the make-up of the fund's portfolio to, or tip favored hedge funds or others to, make timing trades, it would be a fairly straightforward violation under the ***misappropriation theory***; IA Rule 204A-1 defines "***reportable security***" to include both mutual fund portfolio securities and shares of mutual funds advised by the adviser).
- Ortman (2014)[13] (noting no federal court having ruled on the issue of whether ***traditional insider trading theories*** apply to ***mutual fund redemptions***).

Bibliography

1. State of New York v. Canary Capital Partners, *et al.* (NYAG Compl., NY Sup. Ct. Sept. 3, 2003)
2. DIV. OF INV. MGMT, SEC. & EXCH. COMM'N, PROTECTING INVESTORS: A HALF CENTURY OF INVESTMENT COMPANY REGULATION, Ch. 11 § II.A.2. Pricing and Redemption of Open-End Shares (1992)
3. Rule 22c-1 Rels: **3a.** Pricing of Redeemable Securities for Distribution, Redemption and Repurchase and Time-Stamping of Orders by Dealers, IC-5519, 34-8429, 33 FR 16331 (1968); **3b.** Staff Interpretive Positions Relating to Rule 22c-1, IC-5569, 34 FR 383 (1969); **3c.** Pricing of Investment Company Shares Generally, IC-10691, 44 FR 29678 (1979); **3d.** IC-10827, 44 FR 48659 (1979); **3e.**

Pricing of Redeemable Securities for Distribution, Redemption, and Repurchase, IC-14244, 49 FR 46558 (1984); **3f.** Amendment to Pricing Rule and Adoption of Rule on Pricing of Redemptions, IC-14559, 50 FR 24762 (1985); **3g.** Amendments to Rules Governing Pricing of Mutual Fund Shares, IC-26288, 68 FR 70388 (2003); **3h.** Investment Company Swing Pricing, IC-32316, 81 FR 82084 (2016)

4. Heffernan & Jorden, *Section 22(d) of the Investment Company Act of 1940—Its Original Purpose and Present Function*, 1973 DUKE L.J. 975 (1973)
5. ICI, *Mutual Fund Distribution Channels and Distribution Costs*, PERSPECTIVE 09-03 (2003)
6. Mahoney, *Manager-Investor Conflicts in Mutual Funds*, 18 J. ECON. PERSP. 161 (2004)
7. GAO (05-313), MUTUAL FUND TRADING ABUSES: LESSONS CAN BE LEARNED FROM SEC NOT HAVING DETECTED VIOLATIONS AT AN EARLIER STAGE (2005)
8. Zitzewitz, *How Widespread Was Late Trading in Mutual Funds?*, 96 AM. ECON. REV. 284 (2006)
9. Selective Disclosure and Insider Trading, 33-7881, 34-43154, IC-24599, 65 FR 51716 (2000)
10. Disclosure Regarding Market Timing and Selective Disclosure of Portfolio Holdings: **10a.** 33-8343, IC-26287, 68 FR 70402 (2003); **10b.** 33-8408, IC-26418, 69 FR 22300 (2004)
11. Bullard, *Insider Trading in Mutual Funds*, 84 OR. L. REV. 821 (2005)
12. LANGEVOORT, INSIDER TRADING: REGULATION, ENFORCEMENT & PREVENTION § 12:20 n.17 (2012)
13. Ortman, *SEC v. Bauer: If the Glove Fits, It's Insider Trading*, 63 CATH. U.L. REV. 1075 (2014)

Topic 2 Abusive Market Timing: Unfair Short-Term Arbitrage Profit

Research Note:[Biblio]

Market Timing and Shareholder Dilution Protections

In contrast to illegal late trading, market timing is ***not per se illegal***.[1a; 1d (n.4); 2; 3 (§44:2.2); 4] Market timing issue arises when the last-sale prices of securities used to calculate the fund's current NAV had become "***stale***"—most acutely occurring with mutual funds investing in *non-U.S. stocks* or in *U.S. domestic less liquid assets* (*e.g.*, corporate bonds or small capitalization stocks)—when significant information is released after the foreign market close or after the U.S. domestic assets' last trade, but before the fund pricing at 4:00 p.m. Eastern time. If the calculated NAV were to deviate both predictably and systematically from the value of the fund's underlying assets, fund short-term traders could exploit the mispricing, to the dilution of interests of fund long-term investors: Predictability enables the trader to know "whether" to buy or sell; systematicness enables the trader to know "when" to buy or sell.[1a; 1b; 5]

Market timing ***can constitute illegal conduct*** if, for example, it is the result of undisclosed agreements between fund investment advisers and favored customers permitting the latter to engage in market timing, in contravention of the funds' stated trading limits, funds' policies or prospectus disclosures, or in breach of the advisers' fiduciary obligations. By November 2003, an estimated "*50 percent of the 80 largest mutual fund companies*" in the United States had such undisclosed market timing arrangements; and some such arrangements had existed "*for as long as 5 years*." In a report to Congress, the U.S. Government Accountability Office (US GAO) called the undisclosed market timing arrangements and late trading abuses detected in late 2003 "*one of the most widespread and serious scandals in the history of the mutual fund industry*."[2] Market timing enforcement actions have revealed two patterns in abusive market timing activities:[6]

- Target mutual funds were unaware of the market timers' presence, who used the services of *intermediaries to camouflage* their market-timing trades;
- *Mutual fund managers deliberately* permitted market-timing their managed funds for *quid pro quo* from the market timers, effectively exacting extra management compensation by selling the right to trade at stale prices.

To reduce arbitrage and curb market timing, the SEC (1970)[6] emphasized the fund board's obligation, in pricing fund shares, to "***fair value***" "in good faith" a portfolio security when the security's market quotations are not readily available or are not reliable. Fair value pricing thus takes after-market-close events into account in determining the fund's daily NAV. The SEC (2004)[1a; 1b] has required that ***fund prospectuses disclose*** fund policies and procedures with respect to frequent purchases and redemptions of fund shares (*e.g.*, whether the fund permits, accommodates, discourages, or deters frequent purchases and redemptions); the circumstances under which funds will use fair value pricing (*e.g.*, specifying the types of events occurring after the close of the overseas exchange, designed to minimize time-zone arbitrage in the case of foreign stock funds), and the effects of using fair value pricing. The SEC (2005)[1c; 1d] adopted **IC Rule 22c-2**, authorizing mutual fund boards to impose on short-term traders a redemption fee up to 2% of the amount of fund shares redeemed within seven days of purchase. The "***7-day minimum holding period with a 2% maximum redemption fee***" mechanism is designed to:

- *offset* the costs of short-term trading to the fund, and reduce or eliminate the profitability of market timing and other types of short-term trading strategies;
- *reconcile* conflicts between shareholders who use the fund as a short-term trading vehicle, and shareholders who use the fund for long-term investments;
- *strike a balance* between two competing goals, *i.e.*, preserving redeemability of mutual fund shares, and preventing abusive market timing transactions by short-term traders to profit at the expense of fund long-term investors.

In 2016,[8] the SEC acknowledged that the Rule 22c-2 redemption fee mechanism was "unpopular with investors and intermediaries"; was utilized by only a "limited number of funds"; entailed "operational complexities"; and had "not become prevalent" as a means of addressing dilution due to shareholder transaction activity. As a "*complement or alternative*" to the redemption fee mechanism, and "*another anti-dilution tool available*" to funds, the SEC adopted an optional ***NAV swing pricing rule***, **Rule 22c-1(a)(3)**. If a fund elects to use swing pricing:

- ***swing pricing:*** whenever a fund's level of net purchases or net redemptions has exceeded a "swing threshold," the fund must "*swing price*," *i.e.*, *adjust its current NAV* by the "swing factor" applicable to that swing threshold, to lessen the dilution effects caused by redeeming and subscribing shareholders on non-transacting shareholders' interests;

- ***swing threshold*:** set by each fund, it reflects the *estimated level* of net purchases or net redemptions which would trigger the fund to trade its portfolio assets in the near term, thus likely generating material liquidity and/or transaction costs to the fund;
- ***swing factor:*** expressed as a percentage of the fund's NAV, it must bear a reasonable relationship to the *near-term costs expected* to be incurred by the fund in meeting the net purchases or net redemptions transacted on that day, subject to an upper limit of 2% of the fund's NAV per share;
- ***tiered swing pricing:*** to more precisely target the costs of managing shareholder trading activity and better mitigate the fund dilution effects, a fund may set *multiple, escalating swing thresholds*, each associated with a specific swing factor; whichever swing threshold is triggered on a given day would determine *the single swing factor* to be used to adjust the fund's NAV on that day.

Academic literature has commented on the various approaches adopted by the SEC to reduce NAV arbitrage and dilution to fund long-term shareholders:

- Ciccotello *et al.* (2002)[5] (recommending ***a combination of ex ante and ex post techniques*** to combat dilution resulting from stale-price traders "cohabiting" with long-term shareholders: (1) ***ex ante***, the SEC should permit broader use of "fair value" pricing to determine NAV; (2) ***ex post***, the SEC should sanction trading restrictions and costs on stale price traders, and require adequate disclosure of a fund's ex post policies necessary for investors to make informed decision and efficient selection of funds.).
- Zitzewitz (2003)[9] (empirical study ***showing*** (1) "*short term trading fees*" have to be fairly large and of long duration to eliminate the arbitrage opportunity; (2) "*trading frequency restrictions and monitoring*" entail detection difficulty for transaction activities effected through distribution channels such as fund supermarkets or retirement plans, and do not eliminate dilution opportunities; (3) "*partial fair-value pricing*" removes only part of the arbitrage opportunity; ***recommending:*** "***true fair-value pricing***" properly constructed should completely eliminate dilution and should substantially reduce market timing activity and the associated costs to funds.).
- Alexander (2007)[10] (empirical study indicating: when funds *trade for valuation* reasons, they perform well; when funds are forced to *trade for liquidity* reasons, such trading results in not only transaction costs but also significant trading losses; the ***2% redemption fee*** imposed on short-term arbitrage trading not only addresses

the *dilution loss* but also makes it easier for funds to *manage liquidity* hence leading to improved performance.).

Bibliography

1. Market timing rels. (Rule 22c-2): **1a.** Disclosure Regarding Market Timing and Selective Disclosure of Portfolio Holdings, IC-26287, 68 FR 70402 (2003); **1b.** IC-26418, 69 FR 22300 (2004); **1c.** Mandatory Redemption Fees for Redeemable Fund Securities, IC-26375A, 69 FR 11762 (2004); **1d.** Mutual Fund Redemption Fees, IC-26782, 70 FR 13328 (2005); **1e.** IC-27255, 71 FR 11351 (2006); **1f.** IC-27504, 71 FR 58257 (2006)
2. GAO (05-313), MUTUAL FUND TRADING ABUSES: LESSONS CAN BE LEARNED FROM SEC NOT HAVING DETECTED VIOLATIONS AT AN EARLIER STAGE (2005)
3. MUTUAL FUNDS AND EXCHANGE TRADED FUNDS REGULATION, Ch.44 The Mutual Fund Market Timing and Late Trading Scandal of 2003 (Kirsch ed. 2017)
4. LEMKE ET AL., REGULATION OF INVESTMENT COMPANIES, § 9.02 [2][a][vi] Market Timing and Late Trading (2017)
5. Ciccotello *et al.*, *Trading at Stale Prices with Modern Technology: Policy Reasons for Mutual Funds in the Internet Age*, 7 VA. J.L. & TECH. 6 (2002)
6. Mahoney, *Manager-Investor Conflicts in Mutual Funds*, 18 J. ECON. PERSP. 161 (2004)
7. Accounting for Investment Securities by Registered Investment Companies, AS-118, 40-6295, 35 FR 19986 (1970)
8. Investment Company Swing Pricing, IC-32316, 81 FR 82084 (2016)
9. Zitzewitz, *Who Cares about Shareholders? Arbitrage-Proofing Mutual Funds*, 19 J.L. ECON. & ORG. 245 (2003)
10. Alexander *et al.*, *Does Motivation Matter When Assessing Trade Performance? An Analysis of Mutual Funds*, 20 REV. OF FIN. STUD. 125 (2007)

Illegal Late Trading—A Timeline Illustration

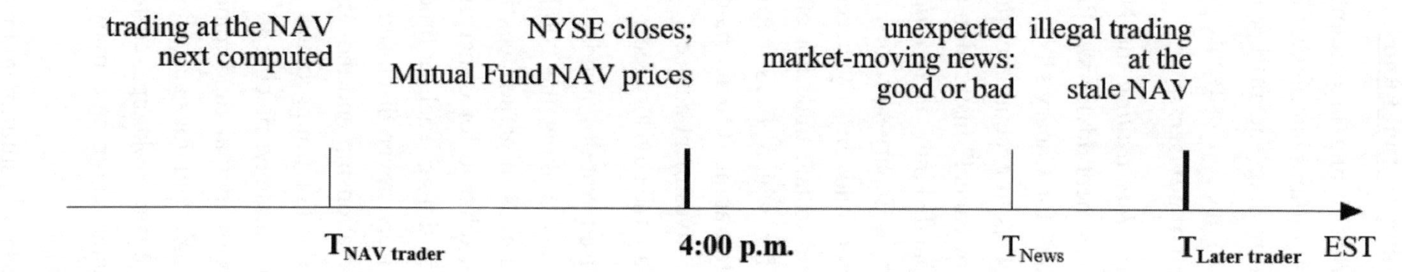

Late Traders:

- On good news: place buy order or cancel sell order, at the lower stale NAV, diluting gains otherwise enjoyed by the existing fund shareholders.
- On bad news: place sell order or cancel buy order, at the higher stale NAV, avoiding a certain loss.

Market-Timing via Time-Zone Arbitrage—A Timeline Illustration

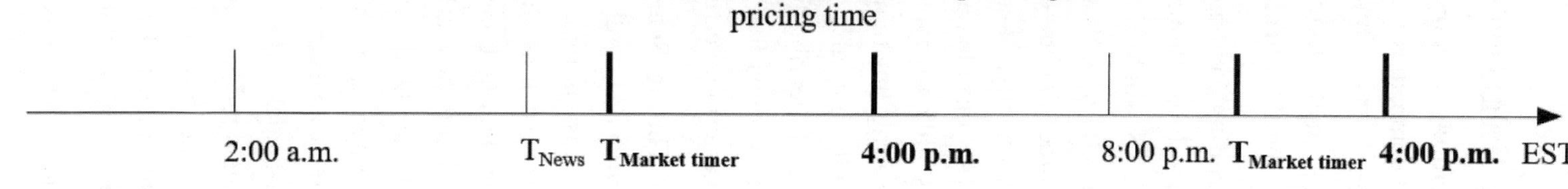

Market Timing Arbitrageurs:

- On good news: buy fund shares before Tokyo stock price adjusts and fund price rises, locking in guaranteed gains.
- On bad news: sell fund shares before Tokyo stock price adjusts and fund price falls, avoiding a certain loss.

Case Study: Hedge Funds Late Trading and Market Timing Mutual Funds

Hedge funds Canary effected late trading and market timing in a number of mutual fund companies via *quid pro quo* and in collusion with fund intermediaries and fund advisers. The following gist features Canary's late trading and market timing arrangements with **Bank of America**'s broker-dealer and investment adviser subsidiaries: the **BAS broker-dealer**, and the **BAC investment advisers**.

Late Trading Scheme. Canary began by ***"manually" late trading*** the Nations Funds—a family of mutual funds advised by the BAC investment advisers: Prior to 4:00 p.m., BAS would prepare and time stamp order tickets for Canary's "proposed" trades; after 4:00 p.m., BAS would either use the order tickets to execute the trades or discard the order tickets—to carry out Canary's "confirm or cancel" instruction at that time. Subsequently, Canary's manual late trading was expanded into ***"electronic" late trading***: BAS installed an electronic direct access system in Canary's offices, so that Canary was able to bypass the order time recording step and directly access the system's clearing function, to late trade until 6:30 p.m. and to late trade not only the Nations Funds but also other mutual funds families for which BAS performed distribution and clearing functions. In return for such late trading, Canary paid BAS broker-dealer various fees and charges, and left with BAC investment advisers "sticky assets"—long-term investments to remain in place to generate the advisory fees.

Market Timing Scheme. For timing the BAC-advised Nations Funds, Canary made a ***timing deal*** with BAC investment advisers: Canary making the "dollar for dollar" sticky assets investment in certain of the Nations Funds to garner fees for the BAC advisers (such as short-term government funds), in exchange for Canary timing certain other Nations Funds which were more vulnerable to timing (such as time-zone arbitrage and liquidity arbitrage). BAC investment advisers never disclosed to the mutual fund shareholders and investors Canary's timing relationship and the advisers' conflicts of interest, in the fund prospectuses or otherwise. For timing other mutual fund families, Canary pursued a "***timing under the radar***" strategy: placing its trades with broker-dealers who each day process large numbers of mutual fund trades and submit all such trades to the fund companies en masse through "omnibus accounts" (*i.e.*, accounts in the broker-dealers' own names which aggregate brokerage customers' individual accounts at the broker-dealers); and intending that such timing activity would be camouflaged by the "noise" of the omnibus accounts.

Epilogue:* The NYAG complaint resulted in $1.5 billion in restitution to investors,

$966 million in civil penalties, $945 million in anticipated reductions in mutual fund fees, criminal prosecutions, and multiple settlements.

**Ref.* [Frankel, THE REGULATION OF MONEY MANAGERS—MUTUAL FUNDS AND ADVISERS, Ch.1 n.326 (3d. 2017)]

State of New York v. Canary Capital Partners, *et al.*

(NYAG Compl., NY Sup. Ct. Sept. 3, 2003)

[***Related proceedings***: SEC v. Sec. Trust Co., N.A., *et al.* (SEC Compl. CV 03-2323 PHX JWS, D. Ariz. 2003); In *re* Banc of Am. Capital Mgmt., LLC, *et al.*, Adm. Proc. 3-11818 (2005); In *re* Theodore Charles Sihpol III, Adm. Proc. 3-11261 (2005)]

Research Topics:

Mutual fund pricing regulation, and regulatory mechanisms to detect and prevent abusive trading practices and to protect long-term investors under the Chinese investment management laws.

State of New York v. Canary Capital Partners, *et al.*

(NYAG Compl., NY Sup. Ct. Sept. 3, 2003)

Plaintiff, the State of New York, by Eliot Spitzer, Attorney General of the State of New York, complaining of the above-named defendants, alleges upon information and belief, that:

PARTIES

1. This action is brought in the name of the State of New York pursuant to Civil Practice Law and Rules § 1301.

2. Defendant Edward J. **Stern**, a resident of New York County, New York is, and was at all relevant times, the Managing Principal of defendants Canary Capital Partners, LLC and Canary Investment Management, LLC (collectively, "**Canary**").

3. Defendant **Canary Capital Partners, LLC** is a limited liability company organized and existing under the laws of the State of New Jersey, with offices at 400 Plaza Drive, Secaucus, New Jersey.

4. Defendant **Canary Investment Management, LLC** is a limited liability company organized and existing under the laws of the State of New Jersey, with offices at 400 Plaza Drive, Secaucus, New Jersey.

5. Defendant **Canary Capital Partners, Ltd.** is a Bermuda limited liability company. Stern is also the Managing Principal of Canary Capital Partners, Ltd. * * * *

PRELIMINARY STATEMENT

8. From 1999 to 2003, Canary engaged in two fraudulent schemes and benefitted to the extent of tens of millions of dollars at the expense of mutual fund investors. Both schemes involved the complicity of mutual fund management companies that violated their fiduciary duties to their customers in return for substantial fees and other income for themselves and their affiliates.

9. The first scheme was Canary's "*late trading*" of mutual fund shares. As described in greater detail below, the daily price of mutual fund shares is generally calculated as of 4:00 p.m. EST. Orders to buy, sell or exchange mutual fund shares placed at or before 4:00 p.m. EST on a given day receive that day's price. Conversely, orders placed after 4:00 p.m. EST are supposed to be priced using the following day's price. Canary agreed with certain financial institutions (including the Bank of America) that orders Canary

placed after 4 p.m. on a given day would illegally receive that day's price (as opposed to the next day's price, which the order would have received had it been processed lawfully). This allowed Canary to capitalize on post-4:00 p.m. information while those who bought their mutual fund shares lawfully could not.

10. Late trading can be analogized to betting today on yesterday's horse races.

11. The second scheme involved "*timing*" of mutual funds. "Timing" is an investment technique involving short-term, "in and out" trading of mutual fund shares. The technique is designed to exploit inefficiencies in the way mutual fund companies price their shares. This practice is by no means limited to Canary. Indeed: (1) it is widely acknowledged that timing inures to the detriment of long-term shareholders; (2) because of this detrimental effect, mutual fund prospectuses typically state that timing is monitored and the funds work to prevent it; and (3) nonetheless, in return for investments that will increase fund managers' fees, fund managers enter into undisclosed agreements to allow timing.

12. In fact, certain mutual fund companies have employees (generally referred to as the "timing police") who are supposed to ferret out "timers" and put a stop to their short-term trading activity. Nonetheless, the mutual fund managers arranged to give Canary and other market timers a "pass" with the timing police, who would look the other way rather than attempt to shut down their short-term trading.

13. The mutual fund prospectuses created the misleading impression that mutual funds were vigilantly protecting investors against the negative effects of timing. In fact, the opposite was true: managers sold the right to time their funds to Canary and other hedge fund investors. The prospectuses were silent about these arrangements.

14. As a result of "late trading" and "timing" of mutual funds, Canary, the mutual fund companies and their intermediaries profited handsomely. The losers were unsuspecting long-term mutual fund investors. Canary's excess profits came dollar-for-dollar out of their pockets.

A. Late Trading

15. Canary's practice of late trading exploited the unique way in which mutual funds set their prices. Mutual funds are valued once a day, usually at 4:00 p.m. EST, when the New York market closes. The price, known as the Net Asset Value or "NAV," generally reflects the closing prices of the securities that comprise a given fund's portfolio, plus the

value of any cash that the fund manager maintains for the fund. A mutual fund stands ready to buy or sell (the mutual fund industry refers to sales as "redemptions") its shares at the NAV with the public all day, any day—but unlike a stock, the price of a mutual fund does not change during the course of the day. Accordingly, orders placed at any time during the trading day up to the 4:00 p.m. cutoff get that day's NAV, but an order placed at 4:01 p.m. or thereafter receives the next day's NAV. This is the rule of "forward pricing", which became law in 1968.

A-1. The Purpose of "Forward Pricing"

16. This system assures a level playing field for investors. Mutual fund investors do not know the exact price at which their mutual fund orders will be executed at the time they place the orders (unlike stock investors), because NAVs are calculated after the market closes. Orders placed on or before 4 p.m. on a given day are filled at the NAV determined that day while orders placed after 4 p.m. are filled at the NAV calculated the next day. Thus, all investors have the same opportunity to assemble "pre-4:00 p.m. information" before they buy or sell. And no investor has (or at least is supposed to have) the benefit of "post-4:00 information" prior to making an investment decision. The importance of this protection becomes clear when, for example, there is an event after 4:00 p.m. (like an unexpectedly positive corporate earnings announcement) that makes it highly probable that the market for the stocks in a given fund will open sharply higher the next day. Forward pricing ensures fairness: those who bought the fund during the day, before the information came out, will enjoy a gain. Those who buy shares in the fund ***after*** the announcement are not supposed to share in this profit. Their purchase order should receive the NAV set at the end of the next day, when the market will have digested the news and reflected its impact in (1) higher prices for the stock held by the fund and therefore (2) a higher NAV for the fund.

17. An investor who has the ability to avoid forward pricing and buy at the ***prior*** NAV enjoys a significant trading edge. He or she can wait until after the market closes for significant news such as the above earnings announcement to come out, and then buy the fund at the old, low NAV that does not reflect the impact of the new information. When the market goes up the next day, the lucky investor would be able to sell and realize an arbitrage profit based solely on the privilege of trading on the "stale" NAV.

18. Where does the late trader's arbitrage profit come from? Dollar for dollar, it comes out of the mutual fund that the late trader buys. In essence, the late trader is being

allowed into the fund after it is closed for the day to participate in a profit that would otherwise have gone completely to the fund's buy-and-hold investors. When the late trader redeems his shares and claims his profit, the mutual fund manager has either to sell stock or use cash on hand—stock and cash that used to belong to the long-term investors—to give the late trader his gain. This makes late trading basically a zero-sum game. Putting to one side the investment results of the mutual fund for the brief time that the late trader actually holds it, the late trader's gain is the long-term investors' loss. The forward pricing rule was enacted to prevent this kind of abuse. See 17 CFR § 270.22c-1(a).

A-2. Summary of Canary's Late Trading

19. Canary engaged in late trading on a daily basis from in or about March 2000 until this office began its investigation in July of 2003. It targeted dozens of mutual funds and extracted tens of millions of dollars from them. During the declining market of 2001 and 2002, it used late trading to, in effect, sell mutual fund shares short. This caused the mutual funds to overpay for their shares as the market went down, serving to magnify long-term investors' losses.

20. Canary obtained some of its late trading "capacity" (the opportunity to engage in late trading) directly from one mutual fund manager, the **Bank of America**. Bank of America installed special computer equipment in Canary's office that allowed it to buy and sell Bank of America's own mutual funds—the Nations Funds—and hundreds of other mutual funds at the 4:00 p.m. price until 6:30 p.m. New York time. In return, Canary agreed to leave millions of dollars in Bank of America bond funds on a long-term basis. These parked funds are known in the trade as "sticky assets."

21. Canary obtained additional late trading capacity from intermediaries, including Security Trust Company ("**STC**"), an Arizona company providing trust administrative services (including access to mutual funds) to retirement plans. STC gave Canary the ability to trade hundreds of additional mutual funds as late as 9:00 p.m. New York time. So profitable was this opportunity that STC ultimately demanded, and received, a percentage of Canary's winnings.

B. Timing

22. Mutual funds are meant to be long-term investments. They are designed for buy-and-hold investors, and are therefore the favored homes for Americans' retirement

and college savings accounts. Nevertheless, quick-turnaround traders routinely try to trade in and out of certain mutual funds in order to exploit inefficiencies in the way they set their NAVs.

23. This strategy works only because some funds use "stale" prices to calculate the value of securities held in the fund's portfolio. These prices are "stale" because they do not necessarily reflect the "fair value" of such securities as of the time the NAV is calculated. A typical example is a U.S. mutual fund that holds Japanese shares. Because of the time zone difference, the Japanese market may close at ***2:00 a.m.*** New York time. If the U.S. mutual fund manager uses the closing prices of the Japanese shares in his or her fund to arrive at an NAV at ***4:00 p.m.*** in New York, he or she is relying on market information that is fourteen hours old. If there have been positive market moves during the New York trading day that will cause the Japanese market to rise when it later opens, the stale Japanese prices will not reflect them, and the fund's NAV will be artificially low. Put another way, the NAV does not reflect the true current market value of the stocks the fund holds. On such a day, a trader who buys the Japanese fund at the "stale" price is virtually assured of a profit that can be realized the next day by selling. This and similar strategies are known as "time zone arbitrage." Taking advantage of this kind of short-term arbitrage repeatedly in a single mutual fund is called "timing" the fund.[1]

24. A similar type of timing is possible in mutual funds that contain illiquid securities such as high-yield bonds or small capitalization stocks. Here, the fact that some of the fund's securities may not have traded for hours before the New York closing time can render the fund's NAV stale, and thus open it to being timed. This is sometimes known as

---

[1] A particularly striking historical example of time zone arbitrage is described in a June 10, 2000 article in TheStreet.Com entitled "*Your International Fund May Have the 'Arbs Welcome' Sign Out*":

On Oct. 28, 1997, on the heels of a 10% decline in the U.S. stock market, Asian markets dropped precipitously. By 4 p.m. ET, however, the U.S. markets had recovered. To anyone following the Asian markets, it was clear that those markets would follow suit when they opened for trading. Unfortunately, this was not so clear to some mutual funds that invest in securities traded in Asian markets. These funds calculated their NAVs at the lower, 13 hours' stale closing prices on the exchange. Many arbitragers, knowing the funds' next-day NAV would rise, stood ready to exploit this pricing discrepancy.... They poured money into Asia/Pacific funds and sold them the next day, pocketing a one-day profit of around 10%. This profit came directly out of the pockets of the remaining shareholders. How much did shareholders in Asia-Pacific funds lose because the funds used stale prices to value their portfolios? Not surprisingly, the funds aren't talking. But based on methodology suggested by the SEC, shareholders in many of these funds would have seen their accounts drop by up to 2.5% overnight.

See also "*International Funds Still Sitting Ducks for Arbs,*" TheStreet.com (July 1, 2000).

"liquidity arbitrage."

B-1. The Effect on Long Term Shareholders

25. Like late trading, effective timing captures an arbitrage profit. And like late trading, the arbitrage profit from timing comes dollar-for-dollar out of the pockets of the long-term investors: the timer steps in at the last moment and takes part of the buy-and-hold investors' upside when the market goes up, so the next day's NAV is reduced for those who are still in the fund. If the timer sells short on bad days—as Canary did—the arbitrage has the effect of making the next day's NAV lower than it would otherwise have been, thus magnifying the losses that investors are experiencing in a declining market.

26. Timing is not entirely risk free, however. For example, the timer has to keep his or her money in the target fund for at least a day, so he or she may enjoy additional gains or incur losses, depending on the market. But such gains and losses are distinct from the timer's arbitrage profit, which is essentially crystallized at the moment of purchase.

27. Besides the wealth transfer of arbitrage (called "dilution"), timers also harm their target funds in a number of other ways. They impose their transaction costs on the long-term investors. Indeed, trades necessitated by timer redemptions can also lead to realization of taxable capital gains at an undesirable time, or may result in managers having to sell stock into a falling market. Accordingly, fund managers often seek to minimize the disruptive impact of timers by keeping cash on hand to pay out the timers' profits without having to sell stock. This "strategy" does not eliminate the transfer of wealth out of the mutual fund caused by timing; it only reduces the administrative cost of those transfers. However, at the same time it can also reduce the overall performance of the fund by requiring the fund manager to keep a certain amount of the funds' assets in cash at all times, thus depriving the investors of the advantages of being fully invested in a rising market. Some fund managers even enter into special investments as an attempt to "hedge" against timing activity (instead of just refusing to allow it), thus deviating altogether from the ostensible investment strategy of their funds, and incurring further transaction costs.

B-2. Tools to Combat Market Timing

28. Mutual fund managers are aware of the damaging effect that timers have on their funds. And while the effects on individual shareholders may be small once they are

spread out over all the investors in a fund, their aggregate impact is not: for example, one recent study estimates that U.S. mutual funds lose $4 billion each year to timers. Zitzewitz, *Who Cares About Shareholders? Arbitrage-Proofing Mutual Funds* (2002). While it is virtually impossible for fund managers to identify every timing trade, large movements in and out of funds—like those made by Canary—are easy for managers to spot. And mutual fund managers have tools to fight back against timers.

29. Fund managers typically have the power simply to reject timers' purchases. Many funds have also instituted short-term trading fees ("early redemption fees") that effectively wipe out the arbitrage that timers exploit. Generally, these fees go directly into the affected fund to reimburse it for the costs of short term trading. In addition, fund managers are required to update NAVs at the end of the day in New York when there have been market moves that might render the NAV stale. This is called giving the fund a "fair value." It eliminates the timer's arbitrage. As fiduciaries for their investors, mutual fund managers are obliged to do their best to use these weapons to protect their customers from the dilution that timing causes.

B-3. Incentives for Allowing Market Timing

30. Given the harm that timing causes, and the tools available to put a stop to it, why would a mutual fund manager allow his fund to be timed? The answer lies in the way that mutual funds are organized. Typically a single management company sets up a number of mutual funds to form a family. For example, **Banc of America Capital Management, LLC** is the manager for the **Nations Funds family**, including Nations International Equity fund, Nations Small Cap fund and so on. While each mutual fund is in fact its own company, as a practical matter the management company runs it. The portfolio managers who make the investment decisions for the funds and the executives to whom they report are all typically employees of the management company, not the mutual funds themselves. Still, the management company owes fiduciary duties to each fund and each investor.

31. The management company makes its profit from fees it charges the funds for financial advice and other services. These fees are typically a percentage of the assets in the fund, so the more assets in the family of funds, the more money the manager makes. The timer understands this perfectly, and frequently offers the manager more assets in exchange for the right to time. Fund managers have succumbed to temptation and allowed investors in the target funds to be hurt in exchange for additional money in their

own pockets in the form of higher management fees.

32. Canary found many mutual fund managers willing to take that deal.[2] In the period from 2000 to 2003, Canary entered into agreements with dozens of mutual fund families allowing it to time many different mutual funds. Typically, Canary would agree with the fund manager on target funds to be timed—often international and equity funds offering time zone or liquidity arbitrage—and then move the timing money quickly between those funds and a resting place in a money market or similar fund in the same fund family. By keeping the money—often many million dollars—in the family, Canary assured the manager that he or she would collect management and other fees on the amount whether it was in the target fund, the resting fund, or moving in between. In addition, sometimes the manager would waive any applicable early redemption fees. By doing so, the manager would directly deprive the fund of money that would have partially reimbursed the fund for the impact of timing.

33. As an additional inducement for allowing the timing, fund managers often received "sticky assets." These were typically long-term investments made not in the mutual fund in which the timing activity was permitted, but in one of the fund manager's financial vehicles (*e.g.*, a bond fund or a hedge fund run by the manager) that assured a steady flow of fees to the manager.

B-4. Failure to Disclose Timing Arrangements

34. These arrangements were never disclosed to mutual fund investors. On the contrary, many of the relevant mutual fund prospectuses contained materially misleading statements assuring investors that the fund managers discouraged and worked to prevent mutual fund timing. For example, the "*Excessive Trading Policy*" in the February 25, 2002 prospectus for the Janus Income Funds states:

> Frequent trades in your account or accounts controlled by you can disrupt portfolio investment strategies and increase Fund expenses for all Fund shareholders. The Funds are not intended for market timing or excessive trading. To deter these activities, the Funds or their agents may temporarily or permanently suspend or terminate exchange privileges of any investor who makes more than four exchanges out of a Fund in a calendar year and bar future purchases into the Fund by such

---

[2] Indeed, many fund managers contacted by Canary had active, preexisting timing businesses entirely separate from their relationship with Canary.

> investor. In addition, the Funds or their agents also may reject any purchase orders (including exchange purchases) by any investor or group of investors indefinitely for any reason, including, in particular, purchase orders that they believe are attributable to market timers or are otherwise excessive or potentially disruptive to the Fund.
>
> Orders placed by investors in violation of the exchange limits or the excessive trading policies or by investors that the Fund believes are market timers may be revoked or cancelled by a Fund....

Nevertheless, as described further below, Canary was allowed to time a Janus fund subject to such a prospectus.

35. Canary realized tens of millions of dollars in profits as a result of these timing arrangements. In many cases these profits also reflect late trading, as Canary would frequently negotiate a timing agreement with a mutual fund management company, and then proceed to late trade the target funds through Bank of America, STC or another intermediary.

FACTUAL ALLEGATIONS

* * * *

C. Canary's Trading Strategies

44. Stern evolved and improved his trading strategies over time to achieve these above-market results. Prior to 2000, Stern followed a simple timing strategy that consisted largely of buying a small cap technology fund (subject to "liquidity arbitrage") in a certain fund family on days when the market was up, and selling it when the market began to decline. Stern was able to do this over and over again—systematically transferring wealth out of the fund—because of an understanding he had with a senior executive of the fund family, who allowed Stern unlimited timing privileges and received a "sticky asset" private equity fund investment in return.

45. Canary's interest in similar negotiated timing capacity deals never flagged, and it continued to devote considerable energy to finding such opportunities in 2000, 2001, 2002 and 2003. Indeed, starting in late 2000 Canary engaged a consultant who was devoted exclusively to looking for timing capacity. By July of 2003, Canary had negotiated (sometimes directly, and sometimes through intermediaries) timing capacity agreements with approximately thirty mutual fund families, many of which involved "sticky assets" of one kind or another.

46. In 2000, Canary also began to expand its timing capacity through an approach called "*timing under the radar.*" This refers to placing trades in mutual fund shares in such a way that the timing activity is difficult for the mutual fund family whose funds are targets to detect. Timers pursuing this strategy trade through brokers or other intermediaries (for instance, **STC** and **Bank of America** provided this service in addition to late trading) who process large numbers of mutual fund trades every day through omnibus accounts where trades are submitted to mutual fund companies *en masse*. The timer hopes that his activity will not be noticed among the "noise" of the omnibus account.
* * * *

49. In 2001, faced with dropping markets, Canary developed a complex strategy that allowed it to in effect sell mutual funds short and profit on declining NAVs. To achieve this, Canary first needed to determine the exact portfolio makeup of a target mutual fund. Mutual fund managers were happy to provide this information to Canary. Canary would then (1) sell these securities short to create a negative mirror image of the fund and (2) buy the fund in an offsetting amount. As a result, Canary would own the shares of the fund, but be overall "market neutral." It would then wait, fully hedged, until there was a market event that would drive down the fund's price and create an opportunity for arbitrage. Canary would sell the shares back to the fund that day at an artificially high price (because the NAV would not yet fully reflect the market movement downward) and then close out the short position with cheaper, market price shares. The cash left over was Canary's profit. To reduce the transaction costs of the strategy, Canary worked with derivatives dealers (including Bank of America) to create "equity baskets" of short positions in fund holdings that mimicked the effect of shorting every stock in the fund, with one customized "basket" per fund. This strategy served Canary well through the market drops in 2001 and 2002.

D. The Bank of America

50. Canary's most extensive late trading and timing relationship was with the Bank of America. Starting in 2001, the Bank of America (1) set Canary up with a state-of-the-art electronic late trading platform, allowing it to trade late in the hundreds of mutual funds that the bank offers to its customers, (2) gave Canary permission to time its own mutual fund family, the "Nations Funds," (3) provided Canary with approximately $300 million of credit to finance this late trading and timing, and (4) sold Canary the derivative short positions it needed to time the funds as the market dropped. None of these facts were

disclosed in the Nations Funds prospectuses. In the process, Canary became one of Bank of America's largest customers. The relationship was mutually beneficial: Canary made tens of millions through late trading and timing, while the various parts of the Bank of America that serviced Canary made millions themselves. All of this activity was coordinated through the Bank of America broker who brought Canary in as a client, Theodore C. Sihpol, III.

D-1. Setting Up the Stern Relationship

* * * * [¶ ¶ 59-61: Robert H. Gordon, co-President of **Banc of America Capital Management, LLC** ("BACAP"), investment manager of the Nations Funds, confirmed to various BACAP personnel that Canary was "*an approved timer*." In addition, Gordon's e-mail granting a special market timing dispensation to Canary was forwarded to the BACAP "*timing police*" responsible for protecting the Nations Funds from market timers.].

D-2. Late Trading at the Bank of America

62. At first, Canary conducted its late trading with the Bank of America "manually." Prior to 4:00 p.m. New York time, Canary sent Sihpol or a member of his team a series of "proposed" mutual fund trades by e-mail or fax. Upon receipt, Sihpol or a member of his team filled out an order ticket, time stamped it, and set it to one side until that evening. Sometime after 4 p.m. New York time, Canary telephoned Sihpol or a member of his team to either confirm or cancel the "proposed" order. If confirmed, the order (with its pre-close time stamp) was sent by fax to Bank of America's mutual funds clearing department for processing, and received that day's NAV. If the order was cancelled, Sihpol or a member of his team would destroy the ticket. * * * *

64. The manual trading system was cumbersome, and Canary soon began using ADP, the "direct link." After Bank of America technicians installed it in Canary's offices in June of 2001, the link became the preferred route for Canary's late trading (although the manual procedure was still followed occasionally for certain orders and when Canary experienced technical problems). The link enabled Canary to trade late not just in the Nations Funds where it had negotiated capacity, but in the many other mutual fund families with which the bank had clearing agreements. When there was a significant market event after 4:00 p.m. EST but before the ADP trading window closed at 6:30 p.m., the NAVs of many of these funds would be stale and potentially ripe for arbitrage trading by Canary.

65. Sihpol and his team collected a so called "wrap fee" of one percent of the Canary assets in Nations Funds and one half of one percent of the assets in other funds traded through the platform.[3] Throughout 2001, 2002 and up until July 2003, Canary placed late orders for hundreds of mutual fund trades through ADP. Each evening, summaries of Canary's late trades were faxed to Sihpol's team, which used them to reconcile trading reports and then discarded them. * * * *

D-6. Disclosures in the Nations Funds Prospectuses

73. At no time did the Nations Funds disclose to shareholders (1) the agreements with Canary, (2) Canary's extensive market timing activities pursuant to these agreements, (3) the "sticky asset" deals, (4) the fact that Canary had access to a Banc of America Securities trading platform that enabled Canary to trade late, or (5) the other financial services the Bank of America had provided Canary (and the revenues the Bank of America derived therefrom) in connection with Canary receiving timing capacity in the Nations Funds. * * * *

SEVENTH CAUSE OF ACTION

102. The acts and practices of the Defendants relating to *late trading* and *timing* violated § 63(12) of the Executive Law, in that Defendants engaged in repeated fraudulent or illegal acts or otherwise demonstrated persistent fraud or illegality in the carrying on, conducting or transaction of a business.

WHEREFORE, plaintiff demands judgment against the defendants as follows: * * * *

C. That defendants, pursuant to General Business Law § 353(3) and Executive Law § 63(12), disgorge profits obtained and pay damages caused by the fraudulent acts complained of herein; . . . .

---

[3] [T]he "wrap fee" was compensation [to Bank of America] for timing capacity and late trading.

Section 3.3 Mutual Fund Trading in Portfolio Securities

Topic 1 Soft Dollar Practices

Laws & Rules Highlight:

Securities Exchange Act of 1934 (SEA) (15 USC 78a *et seq.*)
Investment Advisers Act of 1940 (15 USC 80b-1 *et seq.*)

- SEA § 28(e) (***statutory safe harbor*** *to money managers of discretionary accounts from charges of breach of fiduciary duty for failing to obtain the lowest available commission rate,* ***if*** *the amount of commissions charged is reasonable in relation to the value of brokerage and research services provided*)
  - § 3(a)(34)(F) (*def. "appropriate regulatory agency"*); § 3(a)(35) (*def. "investment discretion"*)
  - §§ 28(e)(3)(A)-(B) (*def. "**research services**"*); *cf.* IA Act § 202(a)(11) (*def. "**investment adviser**"*)
- IA Act § 202(a)(11)(C) (***B/D exclusion from statutory IA:*** *any broker or dealer whose performance of investment advisory services is "solely incidental" to the conduct of its broker or dealer business and who receives "no special compensation therefor"*)

"CLASSIC" SOFT DOLLAR ARRANGEMENT

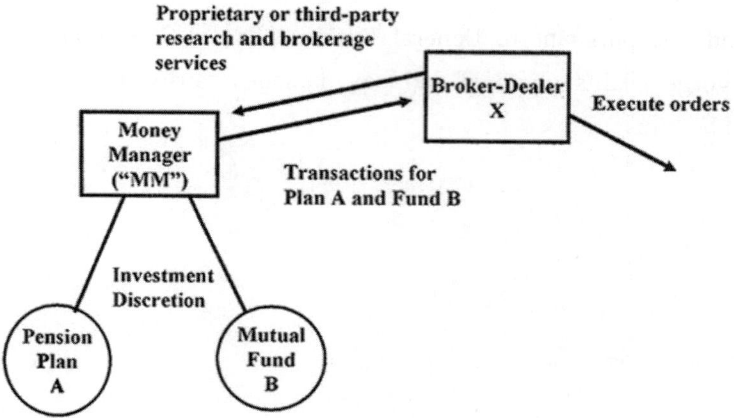

Source of diagram: LEMKE & LINS, SOFT DOLLARS AND OTHER TRADING ACTIVITIES § 1:3 (2013-2014)

Pre-Case Background Note[Biblio]

"Soft Dollars": Historical Origin and Current Controversy

Government regulation of the securities trading markets in the United States began with the Securities Exchange Act of 1934. The Securities Acts Amendments of 1975 revised the 34 Act and opened a new era: ***government regulation*** of the trading markets aimed to assure effective performance of the ***market's functions***.[1; 2]

I. Fixed Minimum Commission Era (Ending in May 1975)

Prior to and continuing after the 34 Act's enactment, an anticompetitive fixed minimum commission rate system or "***cartel pricing***" existed.[2] Members of an exchange jointly sought to maximize their income: by fixing the minimum commission rate per share charged to the public and non-members at higher than the preferential rate charged intra-membership, and by restricting exchange membership. Price fixing induced service competition; and the use of ***soft dollars*** developed as a means of ***indirect price negotiation***. Since the fixed rate structure ignored economies of scale existing in large order executions, brokers competed for institutional business by furnishing additional service or benefit to institutional managers, employing the "*fat*" in the minimum commission charged to, or the "*soft dollars*" component of the nominal commission paid by, institutional brokerage customers and the ultimate investor beneficiaries of the fiduciary managers.[1; 2]

A series of events and forces **in the 1960's** heralded the ultimate abolition of the fixed commission rates. Institutional investors had emerged as the most important customers of the equity markets, who shopped and negotiated soft dollars, commission rebates, reciprocity of business and similar arrangements to circumvent the fixed minimum commission rates. A 1963 U.S. Supreme Court case *Silver v. New York Stock Exchange* challenged NYSE's group boycott of non-members, although the case left open antitrust validity of the fixed commission rate structure.[3] By the end of 1968, pressure was mounting against the fixed minimum commission practices: The Department of Justice attacked the fixed commission rates for propriety under antitrust laws; private antitrust actions were brought challenging the validity of fixed commission rates; mutual fund shareholders were suing fund directors for permitting fund managers to reap the benefit of commission rebates generated by the fixed minimum commissions paid by the funds.[2]

During **1972-1973**, in its broader study of "a central market system" for the U.S. securities markets, ***Congress*** noted:[4 (nn.22-23 & text)]

> The side-by-side existences of fixed commission rates and competition-driven efforts to circumvent the effect of fixed rates "cause inefficient allocations of economic resources, exacerbate conflicts of interest, foster anticompetitive business practices and impede the development of a central market system for securities trading." "The abolition of fixed minimum rates will facilitate the speedy development of a central market system."

In September 1974, the ***SEC*** sent "a letter to all registered national securities exchanges," "formally requesting": all exchanges eliminate fixed minimum commission rates by their own rulemaking, or the SEC would commence appropriate proceedings "promptly."[5a] A month later, only one of the thirteen exchanges indicated that it "would comply" with the SEC's request; three indicated that they "do not intend to comply fully"; nine did not respond. "Accordingly," in October 1974 the SEC proposed its own Rule 19b-3 "*Prohibiting Fixing of Rates of Commission by Exchanges*," which the SEC adopted in January 1975 to become effective **May 1, 1975**. Rule 19b-3 of 1975 abolished the fixed minimum commission rate structure, various forms of which had existed for over a century and a half since stock brokers' Buttonwood Tree Agreement of 1792.[5b; 5c]

II. <u>Competitive Commission Era</u> (Beginning June 1975 Accompanied by Safe Harbor for Soft Dollars)

On the heels of the historic "*May Day 1975*"[6a (§3:2)]—the May 1, 1975 advent of freely negotiable rates—Congress in June 1975 enacted **Securities Acts Amendments of 1975** amending the Securities Exchange Act of 1934. Declared to be an act to "remove barriers to competition" and "foster the development of a national securities market system," the 1975 Amendments prohibit commission fixing by national securities exchanges.[7] In the fixed minimum commission era, money managers paid "***soft dollars***" for research. Brokerage commission ***bundled*** in one "undifferentiated" fee charge for trade execution for the client and charge for research provision to the money manager. The client account paying the bundled fee may not even have utilized the research. The introduction of competitive commission era "created the potential for a highly visible and economically sensible system" of payment for research in "***hard dollars***": by ***unbundling*** the brokerage commission into "distinguishable" execution charge and research charge, and having money managers pay for research with their own cash. However, "in response to pleas from the financial community," the 1975 Amendments added ***§ 28(e)*** to the Exchange Act, which allows money managers continued use of soft dollar payment for research.[8]

Before abolition of fixed minimum rates, soft dollars were "*fat*" contained in the fixed minimum commission charged by brokers to public investors.[2] After abolition of fixed minimum rates, soft dollars are generated by investment advisers "***paying up for research***," *i.e.*, paying more than the competitively available lowest commission rate in order to purchase research, using their clients' commission dollars.[9; 10a (p.16005 n.3)] **Section 28(e) provides a conditional safe harbor** for "*persons who exercise investment discretion with respect to an account*" (*e.g.*, investment advisers, portfolio managers of mutual funds, fiduciaries of bank trust funds, money managers of pension plans, and money managers of hedge funds—collectively "discretionary money managers").[11] Section 28(e) protects such a paying-up-for-research money manager from claims of

> "hav[ing] acted unlawfully or hav[ing] breached a fiduciary duty ... solely by reason of his having caused the account to pay a [broker-dealer] an amount of commission for effecting a securities transaction in excess of the amount of commission another [broker-dealer] would have charged for effecting that transaction, if such person determined in good faith that such amount of commission was reasonable in relation to the value of the brokerage and research services provided by such [broker-dealer] ...." [**§ 28(e)(1)**]. Such money manager "shall make such disclosure ... as the appropriate regulatory agency ... may prescribe ..." [**§ 28(e)(2)**]. "Provid[ing] brokerage and research services" means "(A) furnish[ing] advice ... as to the value of securities, the advisability of investing in, purchasing, or selling securities, and the availability of securities or purchasers or sellers of securities; (B) furnish[ing] analyses and reports concerning issuers, industries, securities, economic factors and trends, portfolio strategy, and the performance of accounts; or (C) effect[ing] securities transactions and performs functions incidental thereto ... or required in connection therewith ..." [**§ 28(e)(3)**].

The SEC interprets the term "***fiduciary duty***" in the context of "paying up" as follows: "***The determinative factor***" of a fiduciary's obligation to obtain "best execution" of clients' transactions *is not* "the lowest possible commission cost," *but is* whether the transaction represents "the best qualitative execution" for the managed account, considering the full range and quality of the broker's services including execution capability and value of research.[10a]

The SEC interprets § 28(e)-eligible "***research***" and "***brokerage***" as follows:

- "*The controlling principle*" is whether the research and/or brokerage services provide "lawful and appropriate assistance to the money manager in the performance of his investment decision-making responsibilities."[10a; 10c]
- "*Research*" must meet "*substantive content standard*," *i.e.*, research must reflect "the expression of reasoning or knowledge" relating to "the advisability of investing in securities."[10c]
- "*Brokerage*" must meet "*temporal standard*," *i.e.*, brokerage services begin when an order is transmitted to a broker-dealer and end at the conclusion of clearance and settlement of the transaction—a standard designed to distinguish between § 28(e) eligible brokerage services related or incidental to the securities execution, and ineligible overhead expenses not integral to order execution and falling outside the temporal standard.[10c]

The SEC interprets § 28(e)-compliant use of soft dollars as contemplating "***cross subsidization***," *i.e.*, commissions paid by one set of clients may be used to purchase research benefiting another set of clients, such as using equity client commissions to pay for fixed-income research.[12 (§V.E.2)] However, "*to eliminate, or at least expose, all potential or actual conflicts of interest which might incline an investment adviser consciously or unconsciously to render advice which was not disinterested*," any cross subsidization practice—whether inside or outside § 28(e) safe harbor—***must be disclosed***.[10a] Cross subsidization disclosure by investment advisers:

> "Disclose whether you use soft dollar benefits to service all of your clients' accounts or only those that paid for the benefits. Disclose whether you seek to allocate soft dollar benefits to client accounts proportionately to the soft dollar credits the accounts generate."[13]

Cross subsidization disclosure by mutual funds:

> "If applicable, explain that research services provided by brokers through which the Fund effects securities transactions may be used by the Fund's investment adviser in servicing all of its accounts and that not all of these services may be used by the adviser in connection with the Fund. If other policies or practices are applicable to the Fund with respect to the allocation of research services provided by brokers, explain those policies and practices."[14]

While **unregistered hedge funds and their managers** are not subject to the same requirements under the federal securities laws as registered entities, they remain subject to the antifraud provisions of the federal securities laws and state fiduciary laws, which may mandate extensive ***disclosure*** of soft dollar practices to participants.[12 (§VII)] For **registered investment companies**, regardless of any disclosure, soft dollar arrangements ***must stay within § 28(e) safe harbor***; or an IA's receipt of research or other benefits may violate the following provisions of the IC Act:[10a; 10d]

- § 17(e)(1), prohibiting any affiliate of a registered IC when "acting as agent" for the IC from receiving *any* "*compensation*" (*e.g.*, any economic benefit) from a third party;
- § 36(b), imposing liability on IA for breach of fiduciary duty in receiving *excessive management* "*compensation*" (*e.g.*, advisory fee and research or other services from soft dollar arrangements combined).

III. The Unbundling Debate

Basic fiduciary principles prohibit a fiduciary from taking an interest that is potentially adverse to the beneficiary without the beneficiary's informed consent.[15a; 15b] As fiduciary, a money manager is prohibited from enriching itself at the expense of beneficiaries/clients, such as using client assets for its own benefit.[6a (§3:3); 10a] Soft dollars represent "*client commission dollars*."[10c (p.41978 n.4)] The research in the "*bundle*"[10c] of "brokerage and research services" purchased with client commission dollars, while benefitting the beneficiaries/clients, also benefits the money manager, in that the money manager is relieved of the obligation to produce the research itself or to purchase the research with its own money at an "*unbundled*," component price.[10] Thus, whether money managers should be allowed to "pay up" for research with client commission dollars, and whether § 28(e) safe harbor should be repealed—this issue was debated vigorously before the passage of § 28(e) safe harbor in 1975, and has continued unabated since.[1; 6b (§§1:18-1:40)]

Supporters of soft dollar practice emphasize the benefits of soft dollar arrangement, as:[6b (§§1:18-1:28)]

- *encouraging* ***broker-dealers*** to provide more and better research, while third-party soft dollar arrangements provide sources of independent research free from investment banking-research conflicts of interest;
- *enabling* ***money managers*** to provide more effective management of client accounts;

- *benefiting* ***clients*** when their asset managers have the broadest possible access to research and can arrive at the most informed investment decisions.

Critics of soft dollar practice counter that soft dollars:[6b (§§1:29-1:40)]

- incentivize money managers and soft dollar broker-dealers to ***churning***;
- bring possible ***unjust enrichment*** to the money manager, who uses client assets to reduce its own expense;
- cause clients to pay ***"a hidden, second" advisory fee***, which obfuscates the true market value of each of the services clients received (advisory; research; execution); and ***unfairly allow for cross subsidization*** among clients.

Unbundling "***brokerage***" and "***research***" services and charges would present a novel regulatory issue. Under § 202(a)(11) of the Investment Advisers Act, an "***investment adviser***":

> **means** any person ***who***, for compensation, engages in the business of advising others, either directly or through publications or writings, as to the value of securities or as to the advisability of investing in, purchasing, or selling securities, ***or who***, for compensation and as part of a regular business, issues or promulgates analyses or reports concerning securities; **but does not include** ... **(C)** any ***broker or dealer*** whose performance of such services is *solely incidental* to the conduct of his business as a broker or dealer and who receives *no special compensation therefor*; (D) ...

"*Special compensation*" is found "where there is a clearly definable charge for investment advice."[16; 17 (p.490 n.7)] By ***unbundling***, or breaking down, the overall research and execution services into component parts, with an approximate value assigned to each component, the broker-dealer may be found to be "providing research for compensation other than commissions," thus becoming a statutory IA. To date, very few have chosen the unbundling arrangements.[6b (§1:10)]

Bibliography

1. DIV. MARKET REGULATION, UNITED STATES SEC. & EXCH. COMM'N., MARKET 2000—AN EXAMINATION OF CURRENT EQUITY MARKET DEVELOPMENTS, § V-B-3 Soft Dollar Practices (1994)
2. Werner, *Adventure in Social Control of Finance: The National Market System for Securities*, 75 COLUM. L. REV. 1233 (1975)
3. Silver v. New York Stock Exchange, 373 U.S. 341 (1963) (*Stewart, J., dissenting*); *cf.* Gordon v. New York Stock Exchange, 422 U.S. 659 (1975) (*Stewart, J., concurring*)
4. Fixed Commission Rates on Exchange Transactions, 34-11093 (Nov 1974), *quoting* (1) REGULATION OF SECURITIES TRADING BY MEMBERS OF NATIONAL SECURITIES EXCHANGES AND THE SALE OF

INVESTMENT ADVISERS OF REGISTERED INVESTMENT COMPANIES, A REPORT OF THE SENATE COMMITTEE ON BANKING, HOUSING AND URBAN AFFAIRS TO ACCOMPANY S. 470, Sen. Doc. No. 93-187, 93d Cong., 1st Sess. (1973); (2) SECURITIES INDUSTRY STUDY, REPORT OF THE SUBCOMMITTEE ON COMMERCE AND FINANCE OF THE HOUSE COMMITTEE ON INTERSTATE AND FOREIGN COMMERCE, H.R. Doc. No. 92-1519, 92nd Cong., 2d Sess. (1972)

5. **5a.** Announcement of Written Requests Concerning Commission Rates Sent to Registered National Securities Exchanges, 34-11019, 39 FR 35214 (1974); **5b.** Proposal to Adopt Securities Exchange Act Rules 19b-3 and 10b-22, 34-11073 (1974); **5c.** Adoption of Securities Exchange Act Rule 19b-3, 34-11203 (1975)
6. LEMKE & LINS, SOFT DOLLARS AND OTHER TRADING ACTIVITIES, **6a.** (2013-2014); **6b.** (2016-2017)
7. Securities Acts Amendments of 1975, Pub. L. No. 94-29, 89 Stat. 97 (1975)
8. Pozen, *Money Managers and Securities Research*, 51 N.Y.U. L. REV. 923 (1976)
9. Herzel, *"Paying Up" on Stock Brokerage Commissions under Section 28(e) of the Securities Exchange Act of 1934*, 31 BUS. LAW. 1479 (1976)
10. 28(e) Rels.: **10a.** Securities; Brokerage and Research Services, 34-23170, 51 FR 16004 (1986); **10b.** Commission Guidance Regarding Client Commission Practices Under Section 28(e) of the Securities Exchange Act of 1934, 34-52635, 70 FR 61700 (2005); **10c.** 34-54165, 71 FR 41978 (2006); **10d.** Commission Guidance Regarding the Duties and Responsibilities of Investment Company Boards of Directors with Respect to Investment Adviser Portfolio Trading Practices, 34-58264, IC-28345, IA-2763 (2008)
11. Office of the Comptroller of the Currency, *Description: Use of Commission Payments by Fiduciaries*, OCC BULLETIN NO. 2007-7 (2007)
12. SEC OCIE, INSPECTION REPORT ON THE SOFT DOLLAR PRACTICES OF BROKER-DEALERS, INVESTMENT ADVISERS AND MUTUAL FUNDS (1998)
13. IA Rule 204-3 Delivery of Brochures and Brochure Supplements; Form ADV—Part 2, Item 12
14. Form N-1A—Part B, Item 21
15. **15a.** RESTATEMENT (THIRD) OF TRUSTS § 78 Duty of Loyalty (2007); **15b.** RESTATEMENT (THIRD) OF AGENCY § 8.01 General Fiduciary Principle (2006)
16. Applicability of the Investment Advisers Act to Certain Brokers and Dealers, 34-15215, IA-640 (1978)
17. Fin. Planning Ass'n v. SEC, 482 F.3d 481 (DC Cir. 2007)

Case Study 1: Fixed Commission Era

Mutual fund investment adviser *interposed* broker between adviser and market maker to obtain research, and incurred additional cost to the fiduciary accounts; found to violate best execution and antifraud statutes.

In *re* Delaware Mgmt. Co., Inc. *et al.*

33-4875, 34-8128, 43 SEC 392 (1967)

Case Study 2: Competitive Commission Era

In a soft dollar clearing house arranged by Investment Information, Inc. ("III"), a non-registered entity: *participating brokers* effecting trades did not "provide" research within the meaning of § 28(e) safe harbor; *participating money managers* purchasing research directly from vendors with soft dollars failed to make adequate disclosure to clients and violated antifraud statutes.

Report of Investigation in the Matter of Investment Information, Inc.
Relating to the Activities of
Certain Investment Advisers, Banks, and Broker-Dealers

34-16679, 19 SEC Docket 926 (1980) (*aka* "III Report")

In *re* Delaware Mgmt. Co., Inc. *et al.*

33-4875, 34-8128, 43 SEC 392 (1967)

FINDINGS AND OPINION OF THE COMMISSION

On May 1, 1967, in consolidated proceedings, we issued orders pursuant to § 15(b) of the Securities Exchange Act of 1934 which suspended the registrations as brokers and dealers of **Delaware Management Company, Inc.** ("*Management*") and **Mutual Funds Associates, Inc.** ("*Associates*") for periods of 45 days and 15 business days, respectively. We also suspended from association with any broker or dealer, Nelson, president of Management, Schellenger, a vice-president, Bowman, investment vice-president, and Ganz who succeeded Bowman as investment vice-president, for 60 days, 30 days, 30 days, and 10 days, respectively, and Mallin, president of Associates, and Fischer, its secretary-treasurer, for 15 business days.[1] In addition, we issued orders pursuant to § 8(d) of the Securities Act of 1933 suspending the effectiveness of registration statements, as amended, filed by **Delaware Fund, Inc.** ("*Delaware*") and **Decatur Income Fund, Inc.** ("*Decatur*"), registered open-end investment companies, and denying effectiveness to a certain post-effective amendment, as amended, filed by Decatur.[2]

Management is the investment adviser to and principal underwriter for Delaware and Decatur, and its officers hold or held corresponding positions in those companies. Such officers were vested by the Funds with the executive and supervisory responsibility for conducting the affairs of the Funds, which responsibility embraced but was not limited to the direction of their day-to-day operations, including the selection of portfolio securities for purchase and sale pursuant to the Funds' stated investment policies, and the placement of orders for the purchase and sale of such portfolio securities. Associates is a dealer in the shares of the two Funds and executed portfolio transactions for them on a continuous and regular basis.

Our orders were entered pursuant to offers of settlement and upon consideration of the record as stipulated by the parties. Under those offers, the Management respondents, solely for the purpose of these proceedings, admitted and consented to certain findings of fact and violations of anti-fraud provisions of the Securities Act, the Exchange Act and the Investment Advisers Act of 1940 and to such inferences and conclusions as we might

---

[1] See 34-8071 (May 1, 1967).

[2] *Id.*

deem appropriate. The Associates respondents, solely for the purpose of these proceedings and without admitting or denying violations of anti-fraud provisions of the securities acts, admitted and consented to certain findings of fact and to such inferences and conclusions as we might deem appropriate. Delaware and Decatur, for purposes of these proceedings only, admitted and consented to findings that their registration statements which became effective under the Securities Act on April 23, 1954 and March 14, 1957, respectively, as amended by certain post-effective amendments filed between 1962 and 1966, contained materially false and misleading statements. Decatur further admitted and consented to a finding that a certain post-effective amendment as amended, filed in 1967, which had not been declared effective, was also materially incomplete and inaccurate. In addition, the Funds admitted and consented to the findings set forth in Management's offer of settlement and to such inferences and conclusions as might be drawn therefrom. In accordance with those orders, we now issue our detailed findings and opinion.

Management and its officers admit that between October 1961 and September 1966, in the placement of about 400 orders for the purchase and sale of listed and unlisted portfolio securities in the over-the-counter market on behalf of Delaware and Decatur, they caused the Funds to incur unnecessary brokerage costs and charges by interposing Associates between the Funds and other broker-dealers who make markets in securities or specialize in accumulating and liquidating blocks of securities.[3] The Management respondents further admit that they knew or should have known that Associates, which was a substantial dealer in Delaware and Decatur shares,[4] did not maintain markets in listed or unlisted securities.

The Funds admittedly were in a position, in substantially all instances, to deal directly with the same broker-dealers used by Associates in executing over-the-counter portfolio

---

[3] During the period, Delaware and Decatur paid to Associates unnecessary brokerage costs and charges not exceeding $214,210 and $11,030, respectively.

[4] From 1961 to 1966, Associates ranked among the eight dealers who sold the largest amount of shares of Delaware and Decatur. In three of those years it ranked second in the sale of Delaware shares, and first or second in the sale of Decatur shares. During the five-year period, it sold a total of about 369,901 Delaware shares for $5,290,879 and 149,430 Decatur shares for $1,842,317. In dollar volume, those sales amounted to about 9% of Associates' sales of mutual fund shares during the period. The dealer concessions received by Associates from Management, which ranged from 6% to 1.125% of the offering price on sales of Delaware shares and from 6.5% to 1.15% on sales of Decatur shares, totalled about $414,105.

transactions for the Funds, on as favorable a basis as Associates without incurring the brokerage costs and charges charged to them by Associates. The Funds maintained a joint trading department consisting of two traders and other administrative personnel,[5] and had direct telephone wires to various broker-dealers who were market makers or specialists in large blocks of securities.[6] In some instances, the Funds in fact did trade in both listed and unlisted portfolio securities in the over-the-counter market directly with such broker-dealers. These instances included transactions in portfolio securities in which they also effected transactions through Associates.

It is clear that the officers of the Funds had a fiduciary responsibility to the Funds and their shareholders to seek the most favorable execution of portfolio transactions. In handling the Funds' portfolio transactions those officers, who as stated were also Management's officers, disregarded that responsibility by engaging in the practice of interposing Associates between the Funds and the best market. Moreover, Management, which undertook the placement of portfolio transactions for the Funds, violated its own responsibility to the Funds to secure the best execution. Associates was interposed, despite the fact that the Funds maintained their own trading department, in order to compensate it for selling the Funds' shares and to stimulate further sales.[7] Under the circumstances, we are of the opinion that such practice was largely motivated by the Management respondents' desire to increase Management's underwriting concessions on sales of the Funds' shares[8] and its advisory fees which would increase as Associates' sales increased the size of the Funds.[9] We find that the course of conduct engaged in here,

---

5 The estimated annual cost of such trading department to Delaware ranged from $21,759 in 1961 to $35,598 in 1966, and to Decatur from $2,277 to $3,920 in those years.

6 The telephone wires are paid for by the various broker-dealers.

7 The obligation to secure the best execution exists irrespective of whether or not a trading unit is maintained by the investment fund.

8 From 1961 to 1966, Management's underwriting concessions on Associates' sales of the Funds' shares totalled about $165,243.

9 Management's investment advisory contracts with the Funds, it is paid approximately 1/2 of 1% per year of the Funds' average net assets as compensation for "management research and statistical services." In 1966, Management as investment adviser to Delaware received $1,466,961, and as underwriter $894,260 before expenses after reallowing $2,231,659 to dealers. In the fiscal year ending November 30, 1966, Management for the same services to Decatur received, respectively, $162,473 and $115,529 before expenses after reallowing $ 369,320 to dealers. Management also received as dividend disbursing and transfer agent during those periods

which involved the use of a broker-dealer to execute transactions on behalf of the Funds in securities in which such broker-dealer did not make a market, constituted a fraud upon the Funds and their shareholders.[10]

The execution of portfolio transactions of investment companies through some broker-dealers who sell their shares has become a well-established practice in the investment company industry. Implicit in any consideration of the propriety of a reciprocal practice of this nature, however, is the overriding requirement that the investment company and its shareholders benefit and certainly that they not be injured. Where transactions are effected in a manner calculated to promote the sale of investment company shares, as in the case before us, at the cost of sacrificing the best executions on portfolio transactions, the ultimate effect of such trades is to increase the cost of securities purchased by investment companies and reduce the amount the investment companies receive for portfolio securities sold as compared with the costs of purchase and proceeds of sale they might reasonably have expected to realize had a bona fide effort been made to execute transactions at the lowest cost. The growth in size of the investment company so induced operates primarily to increase the profits of the principal underwriter and investment adviser, and at the same time dilutes the interest of the fund shareholder in terms of asset value per share. While we recognize there may be certain economies of size, it should be emphasized that such growth cannot be promoted at the expense of shareholders.[11]

$85,933 from Delaware and $13,248 from Decatur.

[10] Cf. *H.C. Keister & Co.*, 34-7988 (1966). Even if a fund and its adviser-underwriter do not have interlocking officers or directors, and the adviser-underwriter has not undertaken to manage the fund's portfolio transactions, the underwriter may be found to have committed a fraud in the offer and sale of the fund's shares if it knew or should have known that a broker-dealer was interposed between the fund and the best market to the detriment of the fund's shareholders.

[11] The use of allocation of portfolio brokerage as extra compensation for the sale of fund shares may be potentially harmful in other respects. As we pointed out in our recent report on the PUBLIC POLICY IMPLICATIONS OF INVESTMENT COMPANY GROWTH (H. Rep. No. 2337, 89th Cong., 2d Sess., pp.16-17 (1966)), the practice of allocating brokerage for sales of fund shares may not only "lead fund managers to eschew those markets where the best prices in portfolio transactions might have been obtained and may cause them to pay unnecessary charges for the execution of such transactions." It may also, among other things, cause Fund managers to generate brokerage commissions by excessive sales and purchases of portfolio securities, and impair the integrity of dealer recommendations upon which customers rely "by tempting dealers to base their recommendations on the amount of brokerage ... received rather than on the investment needs of their customers."

Management, Nelson, Schellenger, and Bowman also caused Delaware to sell 202,000 shares of stock of Libby, NcNeill & Libby ("Libby") at $13.50 per share on March 5, 1965, through a broker-dealer firm, although Delaware had theretofore been offered $14 per share by another broker-dealer firm and could have obtained that price for such shares on the same day. The executing broker was selected because it had provided Management with research and statistical services and recommendations with respect to the purchase and sale of portfolio securities for the two Funds, while the other firm neither supplied such services nor dealt in the Funds' shares.[12] The sale of the Libby stock at the lower price, through that particular firm, was designed to and did benefit Management at the expense of Delaware and its shareholders, by compensating that firm for research services even though Management was contractually obligated to provide such services and received advisory fees for them. Such conduct was incompatible with the duty of the Funds' managers to obtain the best prices for Delaware and constituted a fraud upon that Fund and its shareholders.

The execution of portfolio transactions through broker-dealers who provide research or statistical services to investment advisers of investment companies is also common practice. Where the investment company, however, receives something less than the best prices and executions solely because the executing broker provides research services to the investment adviser, the assets of the investment company are in effect used to enrich the investment adviser at the expense of the fund shareholders.

The interpositioning of Associates and the sale of the Libby stock at an unfavorable price also rendered materially false and misleading the statements in the Funds' prospectuses, used by the Management respondents in the offer and sale of the Funds' shares, that the Funds would seek the most favorable prices and executions of orders in portfolio securities. It is apparent that the Management respondents in handling portfolio transactions for the Funds complied with neither the spirit nor the letter of the Funds' stated policy as to brokerage.[13] In fact, those respondents not only failed to seek

---

[12] The firm which handled the transaction received one-half of the $41,410 in commissions charged to Delaware, with the balance being allocated to 18 other broker-dealers who either sold shares of the Funds or provided research services to Management. In 1964, that firm ranked ninth, and in 1965 eighth, among the largest participating brokers in commissions paid by Delaware for executions of portfolio transactions.

[13] The prospectuses of Delaware and Decatur represented that "While there is no undertaking or agreement to do so, it is the practice of the Fund, so far as possible while seeking the most favorable prices and executions of orders,

the most favorable price for the Libby stock, but actually rejected a better price.

On the basis of the foregoing, we conclude that Management, Nelson, Schellenger, Bowman, and Ganz willfully violated the anti-fraud provisions of § 17(a) of the Securities Act and § 10(b) of the Exchange Act and Rule 17 CFR 240.10b-5 thereunder, and that those individuals caused Management willfully to violate § § 206(1) and (2) of the Advisers Act.[14]

The Associates respondents, in executing portfolio transactions for Delaware and Decatur on a regular basis over a period of about five years, admittedly should have known in substantially all such transactions that the Funds were in a position to obtain as favorable a price as Associates without incurring unnecessary brokerage costs and charges. Thus, the interpositioning of Associates was inconsistent not only with Management's obligation to obtain the best execution for the Funds, but with Associates' duty not to participate in an arrangement designed to defeat such an obligation.[15] It was also inconsistent with Associates' own obligations both to the Funds as its customers and to the customers whom Associates solicited to purchase the Funds' shares. In addition, the Associates respondents sold the Funds' shares through the use of prospectuses which, since Associates was the interposed dealer, they knew or at least should have known were materially false and misleading. We conclude, based on their admissions and consents, that the Associates respondents willfully violated the anti-fraud provisions of § 17(a) of the Securities Act and § 10(b) of the Exchange Act and Rule 17 CFR 240.10b-5 thereunder.

As we have seen, various prospectuses filed by Delaware and Decatur contained materially false and misleading statements with respect to their seeking the most

---

to place orders for transactions in portfolio securities resulting from investment decisions with eligible dealers who have sold Fund shares using their relative sales of such shares as a factor in the allocation and with firms who have supplied research information, quotes or other services to Delaware Fund, Decatur Income Fund, and Delaware Management Company." In our opinion, even absent such representation, the prospectuses would be materially misleading in failing to disclose that the Funds did not seek the most favorable prices and executions and sustained unnecessary costs in portfolio transactions.

[14] While the Management respondents did not specifically admit violations of § 17(a)(1) of the Securities Act, Rule 10b-5(1) under the Exchange Act, and § 206(1) of the Advisers Act, making unlawful a scheme to defraud, we have found willful violations of those subsections pursuant to respondents' consent to such conclusions as we might draw from their admissions.

[15] See *H.C. Keister & Co., supra.*

favorable prices and executions of orders for transactions in portfolio securities. The Funds' respective prospectuses were also materially misleading in failing to disclose that Associates was interposed between the Funds and the best available market, and the Delaware prospectuses filed after the Libby transaction were further materially misleading in failing to disclose that the Libby shares were sold at a price lower than could have been obtained. We also find that the Funds' prospectuses were misleading in failing to disclose that Associates was interposed and the Libby transaction effected for the purpose of securing benefits for Management to the detriment of the Funds and their shareholders.[16]

The Management and Associates respondents urged in mitigation that they believed, "whether or not justified," that the placement of portfolio transactions through Associates, which had employed a trader with an asserted reputation for competency, was in accord with the Funds' stated practice of placing such transactions with dealers in the Funds' shares while seeking so far as possible the most favorable prices and executions of orders; and that the best execution was being obtained through Associates because it could obtain better prices than were available to the Funds. The Management respondents further stated that they believed that Associates was securing broker's discounts from primary market houses that were not available to the Funds, while the Associates respondents claimed they believed that Associates did in fact obtain the best prices and executions for the Funds and that its acceptance of orders from the Funds and receipt of brokerage commissions for executing such orders were in accordance with industry practice and applicable law.

Respondents, however, had no reasonable basis for believing that Associates, which was not a market maker in any listed or unlisted securities, could effect portfolio transactions for the Funds at better prices than the Funds could have obtained by dealing directly with primary market makers.[17] This is not a case of the execution of isolated transactions by a non-market maker who as agent may be able to find an institutional or other substantial customer with whom to effect the transaction. Here, Associates' portfolio transactions for the Funds extended over a period of about five years and involved various securities, and it became the practice to execute over-the-counter trades

---

[16] Following our orders of May 1, 1967, the two Funds filed amendments to their respective registration statements as amended which corrected the deficiencies upon which our orders were based, and the stop orders have been lifted. 33-4866 (May 3, 1967).

[17] Cf. *H.C. Keister & Co., supra.*

through Associates. Respondents should have known that the prices Associates obtained were at best not better than those obtainable by the Funds and that Associates caused the Funds to incur unnecessary costs and charges, to the detriment of the Funds' shareholders including its own customers to whom it sold the Funds' shares.

Moreover, the Associates respondents did not have a legitimate basis for believing that their transactions in portfolio securities on behalf of the Funds were in accordance with industry practice and applicable law. Persons engaged in the securities business cannot be unaware of their obligation to serve the best interests of customers,[18] and that interpositioning is bound to result in increased prices or costs. The Special Study of Securities Markets[19] was critical of the justification claimed for interpositioning to obtain reciprocal business. It cited a decision of the National Association of Securities Dealers, Inc., in 1952 which held that interpositioning, done without justification, was a violation of its Rules of Fair Practice, and stressed the fiduciary standards with respect to diligence of execution in order to obtain the best price for the customer.[20] Indeed, as early as 1942, we held that an interposed dealer had willfully violated the anti-fraud provisions of the securities acts.[21]

In determining to accept the offers of settlement submitted by the Management and Associates respondents, we gave consideration to Management's agreement to pay a total of $319,127 to the Funds in reimbursement of their excess costs as a result of executing portfolio transactions through Associates and of the loss sustained by Delaware in the Libby stock transaction. We also considered the fact that Management, during our staff investigation, ceased executing portfolio transactions through Associates in September 1966, six months before the proceedings were instituted, and caused the Funds at that time to adopt the policy of executing such transactions directly with or through brokers who make primary markets in the securities. In addition, we took into account Management's suspension of sales of the Funds' shares, pending disposition of the proceedings, two days after the proceedings were instituted,[22] and the Funds' consent to

---

[18] See *Thomas Brown III*, 34-8032 (1967).

[19] H. Doc. No. 95, 88th Cong., 1st Sess. (1963).

[20] Pt. 2, pp.620-24.

[21] *W.K. Archer & Co.*, 11 SEC 635 (1942), *aff'd*, 133 F.2d 795 (CA 8, 1943).

[22] Management, which is also sponsor of Delaware Variable Investment Plans for the Accumulation of Shares of

stop orders suspending the effectiveness of their registration statements as amended. We further considered the fact that these proceedings were being decided upon the basis of offers of settlement containing admissions and consents, and that our staff had recommended acceptance of the offers. Under all the circumstances, we deemed it appropriate in the public interest and for the protection of investors to dispose of the proceedings in accordance with such offers.

Delaware Fund, a registered unit investment trust, likewise suspended the further sale of units of such trust.

Report of Investigation in the Matter of Investment Information, Inc. Relating to the Activities of Certain Investment Advisers, Banks, and Broker-Dealers

34-16679, 19 SEC Docket 926 (1980) (*aka* **"III Report"**)

I. Introduction

As the result of a private investigation In the Matter of **Investment Information, Inc.** ("III"), the Commission deems it appropriate that this public report of investigation ("Report") be made pursuant to § 21(a) of the Securities Exchange Act of 1934 with respect to the activities of certain investment advisers, banks, and broker-dealers that did business with III. The investigation on which this Report is based was in no sense an adjudicatory or disciplinary proceeding and no hearing has been conducted by the Commission, nor does this Report make any finding or determination with respect to the liabilities of any person. The individuals and entities named herein have consented to the issuance of this Report without admitting or denying the statements or conclusions contained herein.[1] In addition, they have undertaken to effect certain remedial actions which are described below.

In issuing this Report, the Commission addresses certain practices by which fiduciary money managers have obtained goods and services with brokerage commissions ("**soft dollars**") paid from client accounts. In particular, the Report focuses upon an arrangement established by III which enabled money managers to acquire goods and services by executing trades for their clients through brokers participating in the III arrangement. The participating brokers remitted 50%[2] of the commissions on such trades to III, which in turn paid for goods and services independently purchased by the money managers. The Report expresses the Commission's belief that the III and similar arrangements established by others in claimed reliance upon § 28(e) of the Exchange Act[3]

---

[1] Simultaneously with the issuance of this Report, the Commission filed a civil injunctive action in the United States District Court for the District of Columbia against III and Frederick P. Oman, its chief executive officer and majority stockholder. III and Oman, without admitting or denying the allegations in the Commission's Complaint, consented to the entry of Judgments of Permanent Injunction.

[2] In some instances the amount remitted was less than 50% of the commission.

[3] Section 28(e)(1) states, in part, that:

"No person using the mails or any means or instrumentality of interstate commerce, in the exercise of investment discretion with respect to an account shall be deemed to have acted unlawfully or to have breached a

do not fall within the exemptive provisions of that section.

II. Background: III Activities Prior to May 1975

III, which was founded by Oman in 1969, originally engaged in the sale of goods and services to money managers and broker-dealers. III sold these products as a representative of the manufacturer or publisher, and did not assist in their preparation or selection. While most sales were for cash, III also offered to a limited number of money managers the option of paying for the goods and services with brokerage commissions on trades executed for their clients. A money manager who elected this option directed such brokerage transactions to a single registered broker-dealer, designated by III, who then paid for the services selected and rebated a portion of the commissions to III.

In August 1970, the arrangement between III and the broker-dealer referred to above was terminated. III then entered into an arrangement with approximately ten brokers that enabled it to continue offering a method by which money managers could obtain goods and services with commission dollars. Under this arrangement, a money manager could receive credit towards the purchase of goods and services by directing transactions on behalf of his clients to any of the brokers designated by III. The broker receiving such orders was then obligated to purchase from III an amount of goods and services which provided III with revenues, in excess of III's cost, equal to 50% of the commissions received by the broker.[4] III used from 66 to 80% of the excess amount to pay for the goods and services ordered by the money manager who directed the transaction.

III. The III Arrangement After May 1975

With the abolition of fixed commission rates and exchange anti-rebate rules in May

---

fiduciary duty under State or Federal law unless expressly provided to the contrary by a law enacted by the Congress or any State subsequent to the date of enactment of the Securities Acts Amendments in [sic] 1975 solely by reason of his having caused the account to pay a member of an exchange, broker, or dealer an amount of commission for effecting a securities transaction in excess of the amount of commission another member of an exchange, broker, or dealer would have charged for effecting that transaction, if such person determined in good faith that such amount of commission was reasonable in relation to the value of the brokerage and research services provided by such member, broker, or dealer, viewed in terms of either that particular transaction or his overall responsibilities with respect to the accounts as to which he exercises investment discretion."

[4] Most of the brokers satisfied this obligation by purchasing subscriptions to and advertisements in RESEARCH Magazine, a trade directory which listed institutional sources of information concerning approximately 1,500 issuers of securities. RESEARCH Magazine, which was published quarterly by III at a nominal cost, was discontinued in May 1975.

1975, III modified the "soft dollar" arrangement, which by that time accounted for 90% of its revenues. Under the revised arrangement, money managers who did business with participating brokers could either acquire goods and services with brokerage commissions or recapture in cash a portion of the brokerage commissions for the benefit of their clients.[5]

The revised arrangement was similar to its predecessor in that a money manager directly contacted a participating broker to place an order and to negotiate the commission without any participation by III and generally without any solicitation by the broker. The broker retained 50% of each commission and remitted the remaining 50% to III.[6] Of the portion remitted by the broker, III retained 20 to 34% as its fee and credited the remaining 66-80% to the money manager's account. The money manager could either recapture in cash the funds credited to his account, resulting in a return of 33 to 40% of each commission dollar to the person for whose benefit the trade had been made, or use the credit to purchase goods and services.

A money manager who chose the latter option selected the goods and services that he wished to acquire and placed an order directly with the supplier. Upon receipt of an invoice from the supplier, the money manager directed it to III for payment. The money manager thereafter had the option of reimbursing III directly with his own funds or indirectly with brokerage commissions.[7]

As indicated above, the role of a broker who participated in the III arrangement was limited to executing the transaction placed by a participating money manager and remitting 50% of the commission to III. The participating brokers did not select the

---

[5] The money managers and brokers whose activities are described in this Report testified that they were not aware that III offered the alternative of cash payments. Oman, however, testified that he generally informed money managers of the cash option, and that he would have paid cash whenever requested to do so provided the cash was given to the beneficial owner of the securities. Although it should have been apparent that there was no legal impediment to the recapture of cash for the beneficial owners of the securities, the money managers whose activities are discussed herein did not request that cash be returned.

[6] III mailed to each broker a monthly invoice which stated that it was for "services provided" by III to money managers on behalf of the broker. In fact, the amount billed to the broker was simply equal to 50% of the commissions received by the broker from money managers as part of the III arrangement.

[7] The acquisition of goods and services by a money manager could either precede or follow the placement of brokerage transactions with participating brokers. Thus, a money manager's account with III could have either a positive or a negative balance.

goods and services acquired by the money managers. In fact, the participating brokers generally were not aware of the specific goods and services actually purchased through III by their money manager customers.

The staff's investigation has revealed that brokerage commissions aggregating more than $11,500,000 were paid to brokers, including those brokers whose activities are discussed herein, between January 1973 and June 1978. Approximately 33% to 40% of that amount was ultimately returned to money managers in the form of goods and services. The total amount includes commissions generated with respect to non-fiduciary accounts (which are not a subject of this Report) as well as those generated from fiduciary accounts. The amount of commissions received by participating brokers varied considerably.

IV. Participating Money Managers

During the course of its investigation, the staff examined the participation of, among others, the following money managers in the III arrangement:

Andrecom Advisers Corporation ("Andrecom"), a registered investment adviser located in Deerfield, Illinois, commenced its participation in the III arrangement in June 1976. Andrecom acquired goods and services worth approximately $14,000 as a result of its participation in the III arrangement. Andrecom has undertaken to make restitution of $84,000 to its clients, in connection with the III and other "soft dollar" arrangements,[8] and to refrain from soliciting or accepting any new advisory clients for a period of 45 days.

Investment & Capital Management, Inc. ("ICM"), a registered investment adviser located in Chicago, Illinois, commenced its participation in the III arrangement in September 1975 and thereby acquired goods and services worth approximately $11,000. ICM has undertaken to make restitution of $13,300 to its clients, in connection with the III and other "soft dollar" arrangements,[9] and to refrain from soliciting or accepting any new advisory clients for a period of 45 days.

John H. Lee & Co. ("Lee"), a registered investment adviser located in Houston, Texas, commenced its participation in the III arrangement in January 1975 and thereby acquired

---

[8] Andrecom also participated in three other arrangements in which brokers receiving brokerage commissions paid invoices for approximately $200,000 in goods and services acquired by Andrecom.

[9] ICM also participated in two other arrangements in which brokers that received brokerage commissions paid invoices for approximately $22,500 in goods and services acquired by ICM.

goods and services worth approximately $6,266. Lee has undertaken to make restitution of $6,266 to its clients and to refrain from soliciting or accepting any new advisory clients for a period of 45 days.

Norris Perne & French ("NPF"), a registered investment adviser located in Grand Rapids, Michigan, commenced its participation in the III arrangement in November 1975 and thereby acquired goods and services worth approximately $24,000. NPF has undertaken to make restitution of $15,000 to its clients and to refrain from soliciting or accepting any new advisory clients for a period of 45 days.

John Edison Sloane, Inc. ("Sloane"), a registered investment adviser located in Westfield, New Jersey, commenced its participation in the III arrangement in August 1974 and thereby acquired goods and services worth approximately $7,800. Sloane has undertaken to offer restitution of $7,800 to its clients and to refrain from soliciting or accepting any new advisory clients for a period of 45 days.

Daniel H. Renberg & Associates, Inc. ("Renberg"), a registered investment adviser located in Los Angeles, California, commenced its participation in the III arrangement in December 1971 and thereby acquired goods and services worth approximately $6,600. Renberg has undertaken to make restitution of $6,600 to its clients and to refrain from soliciting or accepting any new advisory clients for a period of 45 days.

Towneley Capital Management, Inc. ("Towneley"), a registered investment adviser located in New York, New York, commenced its participation in the III arrangement in 1974 and thereby acquired goods and services worth approximately $120,000. Towneley has undertaken to make restitution of $75,000 to its clients, in connection with the III and other "soft dollar" arrangements,[10] and to refrain from soliciting or accepting any new advisory clients for a period of 45 days.

Beverly Bank ("Beverly"), a state chartered bank located in Chicago, Illinois, commenced its participation in the III arrangement in August 1976 and thereby acquired goods and services worth approximately $16,600. Beverly has undertaken to make

---

[10] Towneley also participated in another soft dollar arrangement under which it acquired goods and services worth approximately $65,000. Pursuant to this arrangement, Towneley executed transactions for managed accounts through broker, not one of the brokers named herein, who credited 40% of the commissions to a segregated bank account in the name of the broker for the benefit of Towneley. Towneley then submitted invoices to the broker for services which it had purchased, and the broker authorized payment of those invoices from the bank account.

restitution of $16,600 to its clients, to review existing procedures concerning its use of brokerage commissions paid by clients, and, if necessary, to implement and maintain new procedures designed to ensure compliance with the federal securities laws.

Eagle Management & Trust Co. ("Eagle"), a state chartered trust company located in Houston, Texas, commenced its participation in the III arrangement in December 1974 and thereby acquired goods and services worth approximately $35,300. Eagle has undertaken to make restitution of $28,730 to its clients, to review existing procedures concerning its use of brokerage commissions paid by clients, and, if necessary, to implement and maintain new procedures designed to ensure compliance with the federal securities laws.

First National Bank in Grand Junction ("FNBGJ") commenced its participation in the III arrangement in June 1974 and thereby acquired services worth approximately $45,000. FNBGJ has undertaken to make restitution of $45,000 to its clients, to review existing procedures concerning its use of brokerage commissions paid by clients, and, if necessary, to implement and maintain new procedures designed to ensure compliance with the federal securities laws.

First National Bank & Trust Company of Oklahoma City ("FNBOkla") commenced its participation in the III arrangement in January 1979 and thereby acquired goods and services worth approximately $32,581. FNBOkla has undertaken to make restitution of $32,581 to its clients, to review existing procedures concerning its use of brokerage commissions paid by clients, and, if necessary, to implement and maintain new procedures designed to ensure compliance with the federal securities laws.

Maryland National Bank ("MNB"), located in Baltimore, Maryland, commenced its participation in the III arrangement in January 1976 and thereby acquired goods and services worth approximately $24,000. MNB has undertaken to make restitution of $50,000 to its clients in connection with the III and other "soft dollar" arrangements,[11] to review existing procedures concerning its use of brokerage commissions paid by clients, and, if necessary, to implement and maintain new procedures designed to ensure

---

[11] MNB participated in two other soft dollar arrangements which were similar to the III arrangement except that MNB submitted the invoices for goods and services acquired to the executing broker-dealers, who made payment in return for trust department brokerage transactions. MNB acquired goods and services worth approximately $26,000 as a result of its participation in such arrangements.

compliance with the federal securities laws.

V. Participating Brokers

During the course of its investigation, the staff examined the participation of the following brokers in the III arrangement: Bateman Eichler, Hill Richards Inc. ("**Bateman**"); Cowen & Company ("**Cowen**"); Ernst & Company, Inc. ("**Ernst**"); Jefferies & Company, Inc. ("**Jefferies**");[12] Kelly Associated, Ltd. ("**Kelly**"); Mesirow & Company ("**Mesirow**"); Morgan, Olmstead, Kennedy & Gardner Incorporated ("**Morgan**"); Rauscher Pierce Refsnes, Inc. ("**Rauscher**"); Rotan Mosle Inc. ("**Rotan**"); Roulston & Company, Inc. ("**Roulston**"); Shumagco, formerly doing business as Shuman Agnew & Co., Inc. ("**Shumagco**");[13] and Sloate, Weisman, Murray & Company, Inc. ("**Sloate**").

Those firms which participated in the III arrangement as of May 1975 were Shumagco, Sloate, Jefferies, Rauscher, Cowen, Roulston, and Rotan. The following firms did not commence participation until the later dates indicated: Morgan (December 1976), Ernst (December 1976), Mesirow (December 1976), Kelly (July 1977) and Bateman (November 1977).

In connection with the issuance of this Report, the brokers listed above have undertaken to limit certain profits on brokerage transactions executed for certain fiduciary accounts over a period of ten days. The amount of reduction in profits effected by such limitation is $5,000 for each broker for all such profits during such period, and is to be disposed of in accordance with a plan satisfactory to the Commission.

VI. Discussion

VI-A. Section 28(e)

The common law imposes a stringent fiduciary obligation upon a money manager, and

---

[12] In addition to participating in the arrangement with III, Jefferies commenced a soft dollar business of its own during 1974. All arrangements for acquiring the services were made by the money managers and the vendors of the services. The money managers independently selected and ordered goods and services and forwarded the suppliers' invoices to Jefferies for payment. Jefferies personnel testified that commissions negotiated with clients who participated in this arrangement were comparable to commissions negotiated with other clients, and that Jefferies relied on the advice of its outside securities counsel with respect top its arrangement and the III arrangement. It is the Commission's position that the Jefferies arrangement did not fall within the safe harbor of § 28(e).

[13] Shumagco's participation in these activities ceased in mid-1977, at which time Shumagco sold substantially all of its assets. Thereafter, Shumagco withdrew its broker-dealer registration with the Commission.

requires that he exercise the utmost care to avoid improperly enriching himself at the expense of his client. The Investment Advisers Act of 1940 imposes a similar obligation upon investment advisers.[14] It is the responsibility of an investment adviser to assure that he does not breach this fiduciary obligation.

Before the elimination of exchange-prescribed minimum rates of commissions on stock exchange transactions, money managers had developed the practice of purchasing, with commission dollars, services beyond those involving simply execution, clearance and settlement of a securities transaction. After the elimination of fixed commission rates in May 1975, the concern of money managers and research-oriented brokerage firms was that, in an environment of fully negotiated commission rates, a money manager would be subject to suit alleging breach of fiduciary duty if he effected securities transactions involving payment of commissions at rates in excess of the lowest rates available.[15]

In response to these concerns Congress added, as part of the Securities Acts Amendments of 1975,[16] § 28(e) of the Exchange Act. Section 28(e)(1) does not establish a legal standard the violation of which is a breach of fiduciary duty. Rather, § 28(e) provides a "safe harbor" that applies in certain circumstances where money managers use brokerage commissions generated by client accounts to pay for brokerage and research services.

This Report deals with an arrangement whereby money managers received benefits through the use of brokerage commissions generated from clients' accounts, and the claim that the receipt of such benefits was permitted under § 28(e). Since § 28(e) involves a statutory exemption for conduct which might otherwise constitute a breach of fiduciary duty owed by a money manager to his client, the Commission believes that the section should be construed in light of its limited purposes. Particularly in view of otherwise applicable fiduciary law, a money manager who seeks to extend the safe harbor provided by § 28(e) to its outer boundaries assumes the risk that his perception of those boundaries may be imperfect and that his conduct may not be within permissible limits.

After the enactment of § 28(e), III represented that its arrangement came within the

[14] Section 206 of the Investment Advisers Act of 1940; see *SEC v. Capital Gains Research Bureau, Inc.*, 375 U.S. 180 (1963).

[15] See 34-12251 (March 24, 1976).

[16] Pub. L. No. 94-29 (June 5, 1975).

safe harbor provided by that section. The Commission believes that the facts of the III arrangement were such that those involved should have realized that the arrangement was not permitted by § 28(e), regardless of whether the goods and services involved were or were not "brokerage and research services" within the meaning of § 28(e)(3).[17]

As noted above, § 28(e) was enacted to address certain fiduciary problems that were thought to arise from a continuation, after the elimination of fixed commissions, of the practice whereby brokers provided money managers with brokerage and research services. The section expressly states, however, that the services must be provided by a broker effecting the transaction. The general legislative history of § 28(e) emphasizes the requirement that such broker was to provide the research services:

> The conferees analyzed the possibility that the fiduciary provision would be asserted as a shield behind which the give-ups and reciprocal practices which were so notorious during the late 1960's could be reinstituted. The conferees believe the new language would not permit such a result. The provision agreed to provide [sic] that a money manager may pay a broker or dealer an amount of commission, for ***that*** broker or dealer's executing a transaction, if the money manager determines that the services it received from ***that*** broker or dealer justify the payment. The provisions have no application whatsoever to a situation in which payments is made by a money manager to one broker or dealer for service rendered by another broker or dealer. The give-up was a regrettable chapter in the history of the securities industry and the limited definition of fiduciary responsibility added to the law by this bill will in no way permit its return.[18] [Emphasis in original]

The brokers involved in the III arrangement in no significant sense provided the money managers with research services. They only executed the transactions and paid 50% of the commissions to III. All arrangements for acquiring the services were made by the money managers and the vendors of the services. III simply held the money for the money managers and paid the bills as requested. The services were selected and ordered

---

[17] Certain of the services received by some participating money managers were not research services, or were readily and customarily available and offered to the general public on a commercial basis. These included such items as periodicals, newspapers, quotation equipment and general computer services. In the Commission's view, the provision of such goods and services was not protected by § 28(e). See 34-12251, *supra*.

[18] Securities Act Amendments of 1975, Conference Report to Accompany S. 249, Joint Explanatory Statement of the Comm. of Conference, H.R. Rep. No. 229, 94th Cong., 1st Sess. 108 (1975).

by the money managers. The money managers were obligated to pay the vendors for the services, and the brokers generally were not aware of the specific services which the managers acquired. Accordingly, the Commission believes that the brokers did not "provide" services within the meaning and intent of § 28(e).

It is not necessary that a broker produce the research services "in house" in order to obtain the protection afforded by § 28(e). As the Commission has previously stated:

> Section 28(e) might under appropriate circumstances, be applicable to situations where a broker provides money manager with research produced by third parties....[19]

It is necessary, however, in order to satisfy the statutory requirement, that the research services be "provided by" the broker. While a broker may under appropriate circumstances arrange to have research materials or services produced by a third party, it is not "providing" such research services when it pays obligations incurred by the money manager to the third party.

VI-B. Disclosure

With few exceptions, the money managers who participated in the III arrangement failed to disclose adequately to their clients the facts and circumstances surrounding that arrangement. The Commission believes that such inadequate disclosure constituted a violation of § 10(b) of the Exchange Act and Rule 10b-5 promulgated thereunder. In the case of investment advisers the inadequate disclosure also violated § 206 of the Investment Advisers Act of 1940.[20]

---

[19] See 34-12251, *supra*.

[20] Even assuming the III arrangement was within the safe harbor of § 28(e), that Section does not eliminate whatever disclosure obligations may arise under other provisions of the federal securities laws. See, *e.g.*, § 17 of the Securities Act of 1933, § 10(b) and § 206. Section 28(e)(2) also provides that the appropriate regulatory authority may adopt disclosure regulations relating to the exercise of investment discretion under § 28(e)(1). Except for banks, which are regulated by the various banking authorities, the Commission is the appropriate regulatory authority with respect to other investment advisers exercising investment discretion under § 28(e)(1).

Although they were not in effect during the period when the III arrangement was operating, the Commission has recently adopted certain brokerage placement disclosure regulations as part of its "brochure rule" for advisers registered under the Investment Advisers Act. See generally, IA-664 (1979) adopting Rule 204-3 and amending Form ADV. Registered advisers are now required to deliver a written disclosure statement to prospective clients when entering into an advisory contract. Part of the required disclosure relates to brokerage placement practices. In particular, if the registered adviser determines or suggests the broker or brokers through whom, or the commission rates at which, securities transactions for client accounts are executed, the adviser is required to

A number of the money managers used a consent form suggested and distributed by III, which gave their clients the option of approving or disapproving the money managers' use of commissions to acquire goods and services. That consent form contained the following language:

> As you may or may not know, when we place buy and sell orders for your account, as a fiduciary and a registered investment advisor, we are obligated to obtain the best price and execution as well as to pass on to you, directly or indirectly, any additional benefits we might be able to receive from the broker who handles the orders for your account.
>
> If the best price also happens to be the same price at more than one brokerage firm, then we will do business with the brokerage firm that offers additional benefits to us in the form of research or investment-related services, thereby obtaining these benefits at no cost to us or yourself....

This consent form was deficient in at least three different ways. First, it stated that the money manager obtained benefits "at no cost" to the client and implied that the client had received the maximum benefits available from the broker. Those statements were erroneous, inasmuch as III was willing to return cash to the money manager's client instead of paying invoices for services acquired by the money manager, a fact which the consent form failed to disclose. The cost to the money manager's client was thus increased by every dollar the manager elected to use for the purchase of goods and services rather than recapture for his client's benefit. The money managers have stated that they were unaware of the recapture possibility, but it is the Commission's position that even if they were unaware, they had a duty to inquire and to ascertain that cash could be obtained for their clients' benefit. In the context of obtaining benefits which, through reduction of expenses, result in benefits to them, advisers are held to the high standards of inquiry and disclosure applicable to fiduciaries generally. The consent form also failed to describe how the specific arrangement was structured or to identify actual services that were received by the money manager. Further, it failed to disclose the value of the services and the amount of commissions subject to recapture through III.

---

describe how the broker or brokers will be selected to effect securities transactions and how evaluations will be made of the overall reasonableness of brokerage commissions paid, including factors considered in these determinations. If the receipt of research services is such a factor, the adviser must describe the nature of the research services. The adviser must also describe any arrangement in effect during the preceding fiscal year whereby the adviser directed brokerage transactions to a broker or brokers because of research services provided.

Many of the participating money managers acted as advisers to pension or profit-sharing funds covered by the Employee Retirement Income Security Act of 1974 ("ERISA"). Part 4 of Title 1 of ERISA imposes various duties and prohibitions on the persons managing and advising such funds. Specifically, § 406(b)(3) of that statute prohibits a fiduciary from receiving any consideration for his own account from any party dealing with the fund in connection with a transaction involving the assets of the fund. It is the Commission's position that the III arrangement was not within the safe harbor provided by § 28(e). Therefore any exemption from the obligations imposed by ERISA § 406(b)(3) which § 28(e) might otherwise offer would not have been available to the money managers participating in the III arrangement. In this regard, money managers should be sensitive to the fact that certain transactions between money managers and their clients may be prohibited by ERISA regardless of consent.

VI-C. Participation of the Brokers

As the Commission stated in Release 34-12251, *supra*, § 28(e) was intended to apply to those situations where research was provided by the executing broker, including certain third party arrangements, and not to those arrangements in which brokers were paying other operating expenses of a money manager in return for commissions. The Commission went on to state that in its view such arrangements might constitute fraudulent acts and practices by fiduciaries and that:

> [B]rokers should recognize that compliance with any direction or suggestion by a fiduciary which would appear to involve a violation of the fiduciary's duty to its beneficiaries could implicate them in a course of conduct violating the antifraud provisions of the federal securities laws.

A similar admonition to brokers was included in Release 34-11629 (1975), which stated:

> A broker which causes or assists an institution to violate a duty to the investor may be aiding or abetting a fraudulent or deceptive act or practice. Furthermore, a broker would have a duty to inquire with respect to his participation in a course of conduct which, to a reasonable person, would raise a question of fraudulent or deceptive acts or practices.

The participating brokers in this instance were aware that money managers were receiving benefits from III in return for directing brokerage transactions. The brokers were also aware of the limited extent of their own participation in the provision of those benefits. Accordingly, it is the Commission's view that the brokers should have been alerted to the possibility of conduct which contravened applicable fiduciary principles and the federal securities laws and that, under these circumstances, they should have ascertained whether there were provisions to insure that adequate disclosure was being made to clients of the money managers. In addition, all brokers were required by then applicable Rule 15c1-4[21] to disclose their compensation on confirmations of transactions. Under the III arrangement, the actual compensation retained by a participating broker for executing a transaction was 50% of the amount reflected on the confirmation, with the balance remitted for ultimate use by III and the money managers. Given the nature of the transaction it is the Commission's view that the confirmations should have reflected the fact that 50% of the commission had been remitted to III.

VII. Conclusion

The Commission notes that the money managers and brokers mentioned in this Report have cooperated with the Commission's investigation of this matter. In the course of the Commission's investigation the money managers and brokers testified that the commission rates charged to their III customers were actively negotiated and were comparable to those rates charged to other customers. The money managers further testified that the goods and services acquired through the III and other arrangements were used by them to service their clients' accounts. Finally the money managers and brokers testified that they relied upon advice from III and its outside securities counsel that the III arrangement did not violate the federal securities laws. The Commission believes that, in the circumstances, reliance on such advice was not justified.

Money managers, brokers and others who deal with them must at all times be attentive to the fiduciary obligations of money managers to their clients. Section 28(e) does not provide a general exemption from these fiduciary obligations; it provides only a limited exemption as to particular decisions concerning the purchase of brokerage services, and it should be relied on only after careful attention to its limited nature.

[21] This Rule has been replaced by Rule 10b-10. The analysis is the same under either provision.

Section 3.4 Mutual Fund Investment and Leverage Restrictions

Topic 1 Fund of Funds: Pyramid *vs* Hub-and-Spokes

Laws & Rules Highlight:

IC Act (15 USC 80a-1 *et seq.*) & Rules (17 CFR §§ 270.0-1 *et seq.*)

§ 12(d)(1) (*anti-pyramiding provisions*)

- **§ 12(d)(1)(A)** [**purchase limits of registered fund**: *mutual fund (or other registered fund) as "acquiring company"* (defined to include companies controlled by the acquiring company); *registered and unregistered ICs as "acquired companies"*]—**prohibits "*acquiring company*"** from:
  - **i** acquiring more than **3%** of the voting stock of an acquired company;
  - **ii** investing more than **5%** of its total assets in any one acquired company; or
  - **iii** investing more than **10%** of its total assets in acquired companies.
- **§ 12(d)(1)(B)** [**sales limits of registered mutual fund**: *mutual fund as "acquired company"; IC registered or unregistered as "acquiring company"* (defined to include companies controlled by the acquiring company)]—**prohibits "*acquired company*"** from selling its securities to the "*acquiring company*" if immediately following the sale:
  - **i** the acquiring company would own more than **3%** of the voting stock of the acquired company; or
  - **ii** the acquiring company, and other ICs (defined to include companies controlled by such other ICs) together would own more than **10%** of the voting stock of the acquired company.
- **§ 12(d)(1)(E)** (**exemption**: ***"master-feeders"*** *fund structure*)—**three conditions:**
  - **i** feeder fund's principal underwriter is, or is controlled by, a U.S.-registered broker-dealer;
  - **ii** feeder fund holds shares of the master fund as its only investment securities; and
  - **iii** feeder fund's shareholders are given pass-through voting rights, as if they were direct shareholders in the master fund.
- **§ 12(d)(1)(J)** (*grants SEC authority to provide exemption from § 12(d)(1), in order to continually adapt regulatory control to the evolving use of fund of funds structure*)

Master-Feeders Structure*

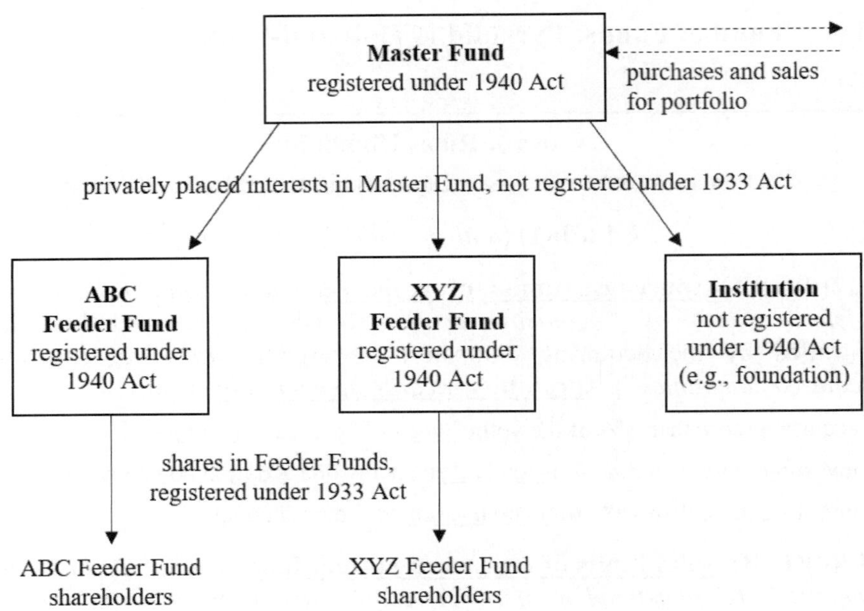

****Graph:*** Adapted from LEMKE, LINS & SMITH, REGULATION OF INVESTMENT COMPANIES § 7.07 (2017)

Manager-of-Managers Fund Structure*

(*aka* Multi-Manager Structure)

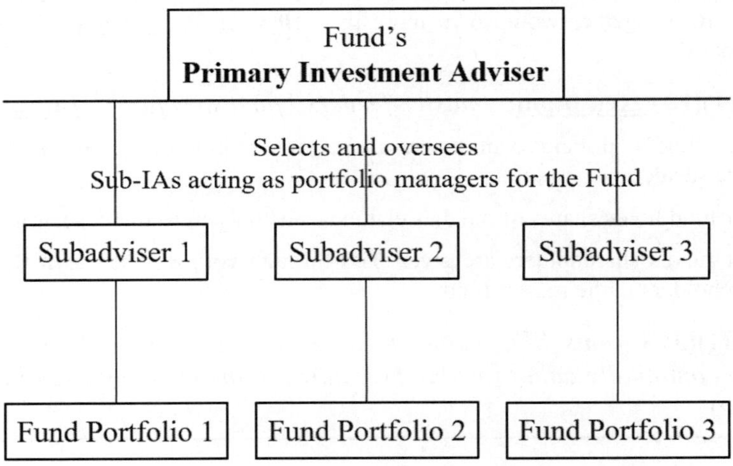

****Reference:*** *Multi-Manager Funds—Aggregate Advisory Fee Rate*, IM GUIDANCE UPDATE 2014-03 (2014)

Research Note:[Biblio]

Unlawful Pyramid *vs* Legitimate Master-Feeders Structure

Fund pyramiding schemes occurred before the 1940 enactment of the Investment Company Act, when a fund was free to purchase an unlimited number of shares of another fund. Unscrupulous individuals would gain control of a fund, which could use its assets to acquire control of another fund, which, in turn, could use its assets to acquire control of a third fund. Thus a few individuals using a relatively small amount of money could effectively control millions of dollars in shareholder assets in the chain of acquired funds. The pyramiding schemes yielded numerous ***abuses and harms*** to fund public investors: undue concentration of control by the acquiring fund without commensurate commitment of capital; undue influence by the acquiring fund on the investments of the acquired funds through threat of mass redemptions; layering and duplication of advisory fees, sales charges, and fund expenses at both acquiring and acquired fund levels, enriching the controlling individuals at the expense of fund public shareholders; opaqueness of the true value of shareholder investments resulting from the structural complexities.[1; 2]

In **IC Act § 1(b)(4)**, Congress declares: "the national public interest and the interest of investors are adversely affected ... when the control of investment companies is unduly concentrated through pyramiding or inequitable methods of control, or is inequitably distributed." In § 12(d)(1), as amended over the years,[3] Congress prohibits "fund of funds" investments beyond the statutory limits, provides specific statutory exemptions, and grants the SEC with exemptive authority to be exercised *"in a progressive way as the fund of funds concept continues to evolve"*—designed both to prevent unlawful and harmful pyramiding, and to allow legitimate and beneficial fund of funds structures.[1a]

Master-feeder structure is permitted by § 12(d)(1)(E) statutory exception from § 12(d)(1)'s general prohibition of "fund holding companies." The structure is often used to facilitate the master fund's access to various distribution channels and target investor markets to sell its shares. Under this structure, the master fund issues its shares to feeder funds only, and feeder funds hold shares of the master fund as their only investment securities. The master fund is an open-end management investment company registered under the IC Act. Feeder funds may be U.S. entities: such as registered ICs, or non-registered bank common trusts, or bank collective investment funds for pension fund assets. Feeder funds may also be offshore funds for non-U.S.

investors. Investment management takes place at the master fund level only: the master fund invests all the proceeds from feeder funds in a single master portfolio in accordance with the shared investment policies and objectives of master and feeder funds, realizing economies of scale. Public distribution of interests in the master portfolio takes place at the feeder funds level only: each feeder fund targets its own investor market, where a stand-alone fund may not otherwise be feasible due to limited asset base. Master-feeder funds are also called "hub-and-spoke" funds: the Signature Financial Group is the originator and patent licensor of the **Hub and Spoke**® form of the master-feeder structure.[4; 4b (n.2); 5]

Distinct from a fund-of-funds structure is a **manager-of-managers fund structure** (or a **multi-manager structure**), under which a fund's primary investment adviser selects and oversees one or more subadvisers who serve as day-to-day portfolio managers for the fund. In terms of advisory fee structure, there are two models of manager-of-managers fund structure. Under the "traditional multi-manager model," the fund enters into one advisory contract with and pays advisory fees only to the primary adviser; the primary adviser in turn enters into separate contracts with subadvisers and pays the subadvisers out of its advisory fees received from the fund. Under the "direct-pay multi-manager model," the fund enters into separate advisory contracts with and pays advisory fees to each of the subadvisers, as well as entering into an advisory contract with and paying advisory fees to the primary adviser. Under either model, the aggregate advisory fee rates are subject to § 15(a) of the IC Act governing investment advisory contracts.[6; 7] While **master-feeders structure** benefits fund investors in different market segments who gain from economies of scale in asset management, **manager-of-managers structure** benefits fund investors who gain access to a broad array of subadvisers with particular expertise.[5; 8]

Bibliography

1. Fund of Funds Investments: **1a.** 33-8297, IC-26198, 68 FR 58226 (2003), *citing* SEC, PUBLIC POLICY IMPLICATIONS OF INVESTMENT COMPANY GROWTH, H.R. Rep. No. 2337, 89th Cong., 2d Sess. 316-320 (1966); **1b.** 33-8713, IC-27399, 71 FR 36640 (2006)
2. FRANKEL & LABY, THE REGULATION OF MONEY MANAGERS—MUTUAL FUNDS AND ADVISERS, § 22.01[F] Investing in Other Investment Companies' Securities (Investment Company Holding Companies) (3rd. 2017)
3. INVESTMENT COMPANY AMENDMENTS ACT OF 1970, PL 91-547, 84 Stat. 1413, 1417 § 7 (1970); NATIONAL SECURITIES MARKETS IMPROVEMENT ACT OF 1996, PL 104-290, 110 Stat. 3416, 3426 § 202 (1996)
4. Exemption for Open End Management Investment Companies Issuing Multiple Classes of Shares; Disclosure by Multiple Class and Master-Feeder Funds: **4a.** IC-19955, 58 FR 68074 (1993); **4b.** 33-7143, IC-20915, 60 FR 11876 (1995)

5. MUTUAL FUNDS AND EXCHANGE TRADED FUNDS REGULATION, § 2:2.3 Structural Issues: Master-Feeder Funds; § 8:3.2[C][1] Excepted Fund Types: Section 12(d)(1)(E), n.79 (Kirsch ed. 2017)
6. Exemption from Shareholder Approval for Certain Subadvisory Contracts, 33-8312, 34-48683, IC-26230, 68 FR 61720 (2003)
7. *Multi-Manager Funds—Aggregate Advisory Fee Rate*, IM GUIDANCE UPDATE 2014-03 (2014)
8. Flynn, *So You Want to Be a Manager of Managers*, 9 INV. LAW. 3 (2002)

Case Study 1:

"Hub-and-Spoke" Funds:
A Report Prepared by the Division of Investment Management (1992)
[Lexis cite: 1993 SEC No-Act. LEXIS 766 (June 2, 1993)]

Case Study 2:

Foreign Feeder Funds; U.S. Master Fund
2017 SEC No-Act. LEXIS 240 (Mar. 8, 2017)

"Hub-and-Spoke" Funds:
A Report Prepared by the Division of Investment Management

Submitted to Committee on Energy and Commerce, U.S. House of Representatives

(1992)

I. INTRODUCTION

The phrase "hub-and-spoke" refers to a two-tiered arrangement in which one or more collective investment vehicles with substantially identical investment objectives pool their assets by investing in a single investment company having the same investment objective. The bottom tier, or the "hub," is a single open-end management investment company. The companies making up the second tier, the "spokes," are typically open-end investment companies, commonly known as mutual funds. The spoke funds sell their shares to the public and invest all of their assets in shares of the corresponding hub fund. This structure is permitted under a provision of the Investment Company Act of 1940 that excludes a registered investment company from the restrictions upon fund holding companies, or "funds of funds," if it invests exclusively in the securities of another investment company.[1]

The first registration statement by a spoke fund became effective in January 1990. Since then, the number of hub-and-spoke arrangements has increased rapidly. As of March 15, 1992, 34 hub funds and 54 spoke funds were registered under the 1940 Act. Signature Financial Group, Inc., which filed the first registration and is now the largest promoter of hub-and-spoke arrangements, has 39 spoke funds investing in 24 hub funds with total assets of $5.902 billion.[2]

Spoke funds can be sold through various distribution channels to different targeted markets such as retail investors, brokerage sweep accounts, foreign investors, or bank trust funds. Distribution costs are paid through front-end sales loads, deferred sales charges, rule 12b-1 fees,[3] or a combination of these charges, depending upon the method chosen by the spoke fund's promoters. Similarly, administrative and service fees can vary

---

[1] See § 12(d)(1)(E) of the 1940 Act and the discussion *infra*.

[2] Signature Financial Group claims to have developed the hub-and-spoke concept, and has registered the phrase "Hub and Spoke" as a service mark.

[3] Rule 12b-1 under the 1940 Act permits an investment company to distribute its own shares and to pay the costs of distribution with fees assessed against the investment company's assets ("rule 12b-1 fees") pursuant to a plan complying with the rule.

from spoke to spoke depending upon the level of services sought by the fund's investors.[4]

Although traditional "stand alone" funds can also be marketed to a targeted group of investors with different sales charge and fee structures, they may not attract enough investment dollars for efficient operation. By enabling a spoke fund to pool its assets with other spoke funds, however, the hub-and-spoke structure may offer certain advantages over more traditional investment companies:

- Participating spoke funds may achieve economies of scale by sharing among a greater number of investment dollars fixed expenses of portfolio management and fund administration.
- Participating funds may participate in securities transactions involving larger denominations than would be available to individual investment companies.
- Spoke funds can achieve greater diversification, by means of a larger portfolio of securities, than could be achieved directly by individual funds. This is particularly important for certain types of funds such as money market funds or index funds that are simply not viable without a significant asset base.
- Even small spoke funds may obtain the benefit of highly sophisticated investment management and compliance personnel usually available only to large fund complexes.

To date, hub-and-spoke arrangements have been adopted primarily by banks offering spoke funds in conjunction with their other financial and investment services. In the future, some spokes may not be registered investment companies but pension funds, or large institutional investors. The hub-and-spoke structure may also enable the United States' mutual fund industry to clear many of the regulatory hurdles involved in selling mutual funds overseas, by organizing an off-shore spoke to comply with the tax and regulatory requirements of the host country while managing the assets in a hub in the United States. The Division's review of hub-and-spoke arrangements has focused

---

[4] In this regard, hub-and-spoke arrangements are similar to "multi-class" distribution systems offering two or more classes of shares in the same investment company portfolio. In a multi-class system, each class has its own distribution channel, and sales load and fee structure. The hub-and-spoke arrangement offers certain advantages over "multi-class" funds, however. For example, unlike hub-and-spoke arrangements, multi-class distribution systems require fairly elaborate accounting systems to assure the proper allocation of expenses among the classes. The hub-and-spoke arrangement also avoids the time and expense of seeking from the Commission the exemptive order required for the operation of a multi-class fund.

primarily upon three areas of concern:

- whether the hub-and-spoke structure creates additional risks of investment beyond those associated with investment in a single tier mutual fund;
- whether the information regarding these arrangements in a fund's prospectus is adequate; and,
- whether the hub-and-spoke structure deprives investors of any rights they would otherwise have as investors in a single tier mutual fund under the 1940 Act or the Securities Act of 1933.

In general, the Division has treated hub and spoke funds, to a great extent, as functionally one combined entity. As discussed below, for example, the fee table in the front of a spoke fund's prospectus summarizes combined hub-and-spoke expenses. Similarly, when the hub seeks a shareholder vote, investors in the spokes are treated as shareholders of the hub. The Division believes that, by treating hub-and-spoke arrangements in this fashion, investors enjoy all the protections of the 1933 and 1940 Act that they would have as investors in a traditional mutual fund. This treatment also enables investors to weigh investment in a spoke fund against investment in a traditional, single tier fund.

II. THE HUB-AND-SPOKE STRUCTURE

II-A. Organization

In the typical hub-and-spoke arrangement, the hub fund registers under the 1940 Act as an open-end management investment company.... The hub fund invests in portfolio securities (*e.g.*, money market instruments, tax free municipal bonds, equities) in accordance with the investment objectives in its registration statement. The hub's portfolio is managed by an investment adviser like other open-end investment companies. The hub sells its shares to the spoke funds only, and therefore has no distribution costs.

At present, all spoke funds are open-end investment companies.[5] The spoke fund registers under the 1940 Act as a separate entity with its own board of directors and management, but with an investment policy identical to that of the corresponding hub fund. The spoke fund invests exclusively in shares of the hub fund. The spoke needs no

[5] In theory, a spoke could be a pension fund, bank collective trust fund or other commingled fund, as well as any other public or private investment vehicle.

investment adviser, and pays no advisory fees. The spoke typically offers its shares to the public, thereby incurring distribution costs just like ordinary funds.

II-B. Hub-and-Spoke Arrangements under the "Fund of Funds" Provisions of the 1940 Act

Section 12(d)(1) of the 1940 Act restricts the ability of one investment company to invest in another investment company or companies.[6] As adopted in 1940, the section was intended to prevent one investment company from buying control of other investment companies and creating complicated pyramidal structures.[7] In 1966, because of the emergence of the "fund of funds," the Commission recommended amendments to strengthen the restrictions of § 12(d)(1) to prevent such abuses as the unnecessary layering of costs, undue influence by the fund holding company over its underlying funds, and the threat of large scale redemptions of the securities of the underlying investment companies.[8]

When § 12(d)(1) was amended in 1970, however, Congress added § 12(d)(1)(E) to preserve the existing exception for unit investment trusts, and to extend that exception to

---

[6] Section 12(d)(1) prohibits one investment company (the "*acquiring company*") from acquiring more than three percent of the outstanding stock of another investment company (the "*acquired company*"); prohibits the acquiring company from investing more than ten percent of its total assets in other investment companies; and prohibits the acquiring company from investing in excess of five percent of its total assets in the securities issued by the acquired company.

[7] The section reflects the policy of § 1(b)(4) of the 1940 Act which declares that the national public interest and the interest of investors are adversely affected when the control of investment companies is unduly concentrated through pyramiding or inequitable methods of control, or is inequitably distributed.

[8] See REPORT OF THE SEC ON THE PUBLIC POLICY IMPLICATIONS OF INVESTMENT COMPANY GROWTH: Hearings on H.R. 2337 before the House Comm. on Interest and Foreign Commerce, 89th Cong., 2d Sess. 311-24 (1966) (the "**PPI Report**"). The PPI Report gave particular attention to the emergence of the Fund of Funds, Ltd. and its sponsor I.O.S., Ltd (S.A.), a Panamanian corporation headquartered in Geneva, Switzerland and controlled by Bernie Cornfeld.

Despite this concern over fund holding companies, Congress has twice refused to prohibit ownership of the securities of one investment company by another. The original draft of § 12(d)(1) flatly prohibited an investment company from acquiring any securities of another investment company. Because fund holding companies were not a significant problem in 1940, however, Congress permitted limited investment in other companies in order to permit investment companies to take advantage of good business opportunities. During reconsideration of the 1940 Act following publication of the PPI study in 1966, a flat prohibition on funds of funds was again proposed. Again, however, the final version of the amended § 12(d)(1) did not include such a flat prohibition.

similar vehicles not organized in trust form. Section 12(d)(1)(E) in effect permits an acquiring investment company (*e.g.*, the spoke) to own the shares of another investment company (*e.g.*, the hub) so long as those shares are the only investment securities owned by the acquiring investment company.

Thus, although Congress probably did not envision the hub-and-spoke structure, it is expressly permitted by § 12(d)(1)(E) of the 1940 Act. Because the Division believes that the major abuses at which § 12(d)(1) was aimed are either not present in these arrangements or have been addressed during our review of hub-and-spoke registrations, it has not challenged hub-and-spoke registrants' reliance on § 12(d)(1)(E).

II-B-1. Duplication of Fees and Expenses

Layering of expenses in a hub-and-spoke arrangement is minimal. Portfolio management and related functions are consolidated at the hub level. The investment adviser's fees, and the expenses of portfolio securities transactions agent fees are also paid at this level, but they are low because the few shareholders (*i.e.*, the spokes) bunch their purchase and redemption orders. Because the hub fund sells its shares only to the spokes, its distribution costs are minimal or non-existent.

Marketing and distribution take place at the spoke level. The distribution expenses that spoke funds incur are usually paid for by front-end or deferred sales loads and/or rule 12b-1 fees. Most transfer agency fees are incurred at the spoke level as well. Because the spoke invests only in securities issued by the hub fund, it pays no investment advisory fees. In addition, because the spoke's only assets are shares of the hub fund, maintained on a book-entry system, its custodial and accounting expenses are minimal.

Thus, investors pay for advisory services and portfolio transactions at the hub level and for distribution and most transfer agency fees at the spoke level. Because two funds are involved, some layering of fees appears unavoidable: each fund bears its own custodial fees; expenses of preparing and mailing reports to shareholders; expenses of shareholder meetings; and any other costs of administering the fund. Nevertheless, the aggregate of these expenses appears to be less than the cost of establishing and operating an individual fund, rather than a spoke, because of the inefficiencies of operation and the cost of advisory services for each fund.

Accordingly, even if § 12(d)(1)(E) did not permit hub-and-spoke arrangements, these arrangements would comport with the policy of § 12(d)(1) with respect to layering of fees.

Section 12(d)(1) limits, but does not prohibit, duplication of expenses. Furthermore, unlike the complicated pyramidal structures addressed in § 12(d)(1), a hub-and-spoke is a fairly simple two tier arrangement, capable of being understood by investors. The Division has therefore addressed the risk of undue layering of expenses by requiring clear disclosure of all expenses in the spoke fund's prospectus.

II-B-2. Risk of Large Scale Redemptions

The Commission's 1966 PPI Report also identified the threat of large-scale redemptions as another potential abuse associated with a fund of funds. After evaluating the likelihood and the magnitude of this risk, however, the Division has concluded that it is not appreciably greater in hub-and-spoke arrangements than in traditional mutual funds.

Many mutual funds have large investors whose redemptions may affect the expense ratio of the fund. In some cases these large shareholders are individuals; more frequently they are institutions—for example, bank trustees who maintain omnibus accounts with a mutual fund on behalf of a number of beneficial owners. The value of these accounts may amount to a large percentage of the fund's assets. It is true that the departure of a very large spoke could cause some per share increase in expenses for the remaining shareholders. A large redemption could also cause a hub to lose the advantage of reduced advisory fees because its assets would fall below certain "break points." Again, however, the risk that break points will be lost by redemption of a few large shareholders (or by a large number of small shareholders) is present in a single tier mutual fund.

Indeed, the hub-and-spoke structure may reduce the risks associated with large scale redemptions. A large shareholder in a traditional, single tier mutual fund can redeem its shares unilaterally at any time without notice to the fund. In contrast, investment in a hub fund is an investment policy of a spoke fund. Before the spoke may deviate from this policy and redeem its shares in the hub it needs, at a minimum, approval of its board of directors, and possibly its shareholders. Obtaining this approval might prevent, and would certainly slow, large scale redemptions. Thus, even if a large redemption was approved, the additional time required for the approval, and the advance notice that the hub likely would receive, should permit the hub to manage its portfolio in anticipation of the redemption in such a way as to reduce any disruption affecting the other shareholders of the hub.

The Division believes that the possibility of large scale redemptions requires prospectus disclosure that the economies of scale expected from the hub-and-spoke structure may not be achieved. Because the probability of such redemptions is slight and because the impact would likely be minimal,[9] however, greater disclosure is not necessary.

II-C. Voting Rights

II-C-1. "Pass-Through" Voting

All hub-and-spoke arrangements registered with the Commission provide that when the hub fund requests a vote of its security holders (*i.e.*, the spoke funds), the spoke fund will vote its hub fund shares proportionately in accordance with the votes cast by the spoke fund shareholders. Thus, voting rights at the hub level are effectively "passed through" the spoke fund to its shareholders. The vote of each share in every spoke is dual and the spokes, as spokes, have no control over those matters required to be submitted to a shareholder vote. In effect, the spoke fund security holders have the same voting rights they would have as direct security holders of the hub fund.

Some spoke funds also represent in their registration statements that they will vote shares for which they receive no voting instructions in the same proportion as the shares for which they do receive voting instructions. This "echo" voting procedure is the same as that required of unregistered investment companies relying on § 12(d)(1)(E).[10] For reasons that are not clear echo voting is not required for registered companies such as a spoke fund. The Division is currently considering appropriate disclosure for spokes that do not provide for echo voting and for hub-and-spoke structures where the individual spokes are not consistent with regard to their echo voting provisions. We are also considering recommending an amendment to § 12(d)(1)(E) to require echo voting for all "spoke" companies.

II-C-2. Changes in the Hub Fund's Investment Policies

A hub's board of directors may approve a change in investment objectives without submitting the issue to the spoke shareholders. Even if the investment policies of a hub were submitted for a shareholder vote, because of the pass-through voting procedure, the

---

[9] Fixed expenses are but a small percentage of a fund's assets, so even a large redemption would not increase these expenses significantly per share, or notably diminish the return to investors.

[10] This echo voting procedure is also consistent with the treatment of voting by the trustees of periodic payment plans and life insurance separate accounts of their shares in an underlying fund.

hub's policies could be approved by the voters of all spokes collectively even though the shareholders of one spoke voted against the change. In either case, the spoke fund could take one of two alternative courses. The spoke fund could subsequently vote to change its fundamental investment objective to correspond to the new objectives of the hub. Or the directors of the fund could determine that it was in the spoke's best interest to redeem its hub shares and either seek a new hub with matching objectives or retain its own adviser to manage its portfolio consistently with those objectives.

The inability of the spoke to find a substitute hub or equivalent management might significantly affect shareholders' investments in the spoke. This is a very different risk than one which investors in a mutual fund would ordinarily expect. The Division has therefore insisted that disclosure of this risk be included in the prospectuses of hub-and-spoke funds.

III. REGISTRATION OF HUB-AND-SPOKE FUNDS UNDER THE SECURITIES ACT OF 1933 AND THE INVESTMENT COMPANY ACT OF 1940

III-A. Compliance with Disclosure Requirements

Under current practice, a spoke fund offering its shares to the public registers as an open-end management investment company under § 8 of the 1940 Act. It also registers its securities under § 5 of the 1933 Act.

The hub fund registers under the 1940 Act only. * * * * For these [tax treatment] reasons, the Division has not insisted that the hub fund register its shares under the 1933 Act.[11] Instead, the Division has viewed the hub fund as the co-issuer of the spoke fund's securities in accordance with rule 140 under the 1933 Act. As co-issuer of the spoke fund's Securities, the hub fund signs the spoke fund's registration statement registering the spoke fund's securities, as do the hub's officers and directors. That registration statement must also include disclosure about the hub equivalent to that which investors would receive if the hub registered its securities separately. Thus, the registration statement describes the investment objectives and policies of the hub; the management of

[11] In nearly all of the hub-and-spoke arrangements reviewed by the Division, the hub funds sell their securities to one or more spoke funds only. Counsel for most hub funds have therefore taken the position that the offer and sale of the hub's securities to a spoke or spokes constitutes a private placement under § 4(2) of the 1933 Act and does not require registration of the hub fund's shares. The Division has expressed no view regarding this position, however.

the hub, including its investment adviser, administrator and custodian; and how transactions in the portfolio securities of the hub are effected, including brokerage commissions and allocations. The registration statement also includes the hub's financial statement, including its balance sheet, statement of operations, statement of changes in net assets, and a list of its portfolio investments.[12]

III-B. Liability of Responsible Parties

III-B-1. Liability for Misstatements or Omissions in Disclosure Documents

In determining not to require the hub to register its securities separately under the 1933 Act, the Division carefully considered whether the hub-and-spoke structure insulates responsible parties at the hub level from liability in a Commission enforcement action or from suit by a shareholder in the spoke. Because the directors and principal officers of the hub fund sign each spoke fund's registration statement, they are exposed to liability under § 11 of the 1933 Act just as if the hub fund filed its own registration statement under the Act. The hub fund itself also signs the spoke fund's registration statement and has potential liability under § 11 for any material misstatement or omission in the spoke fund's registration statement regarding the hub fund. Accordingly, we do not believe the hub-and-spoke structure insulates any parties at the hub level for misstatements or omissions in the spoke's disclosure documents.

III-B-2. Liability for Proxy Violations

As described previously, a spoke fund's shareholders effectively have the same voting rights they would have if they held shares of the hub fund. A proxy statement issued by the spoke fund soliciting approval of a proposed action at the hub level contains the same

---

[12] In general, the division looks for the following disclosure peculiar to hub-and-spoke arrangements:

- A general description of the hub-and-spoke arrangement in the prospectus summary. For example, a prospectus should include a statement to the effect that the spoke fund intends to achieve its investment objective by investing exclusively in another investment company, rather than in a portfolio of securities.
- A discussion of the investment policies of the hub and an explanation that the investment experience of the spoke will correspond directly with the investment experience of the hub.
- A statement as to whether the directors have considered whether the aggregate of the hub and spoke fees will be more or less than if the spoke were invested directly in the securities held by the hub.
- A unified fee table disclosing all fees at both the hub and the spoke level and explaining that the table summarizes both hub and spoke expenses with a cross-reference to the text of the prospectus that describes these expenses in detail and identifies the recipient of particular fees.
- A per share table summarizing combined hub fund and spoke fund financial information.

information that would be required if the hub fund were directly issuing a proxy statement to the spoke fund's shareholders, including all the information about the hub fund's officers directors, and investment adviser that would be required by rules 20a-2 and 20a-3 under the 1940 Act. Moreover, in accordance with rule 14a-9 under the 1933 Act, the spoke fund's proxy statement must disclose any other information about the hub fund and its affairs that is necessary to prevent the statement made from being materially false or misleading.

When hub-and-spoke proposals first came to the Division's attention, we considered whether investors in the spoke fund could bring a private action under § 20(a) of the 1940 Act against the hub fund and its affiliates directly, or whether they must bring a derivative action on behalf of the spoke fund.[13] Section 20(a) of the 1940 Act provides in relevant part that it is unlawful for "any person ... to solicit or to permit the use of his name to solicit any proxy or consent or authorization in respect to any security of which a registered investment company is the issuer in contravention of such rules and regulations as the Commission may prescribe...."

The Division has concluded that the hub-and-spoke structure does not in any way impair the rights of spoke fund security holders under § 20(a). If the hub fund participates in a proxy violation against the spoke fund's security holders, the hub (and other responsible parties) may be sued directly by the spoke fund's shareholders. The courts have made it clear that, in actions under § 14(a) of the 1934 Act, security holders may sue not only parties who are technically soliciting proxies but also third parties who participate in a proxy violation.[14] Nor does the hub-and-spoke structure alter the

---

[13] It is well settled that there is an implied right of action under § 14(a) of the Securities Exchange Act of 1934 and that such an action may be brought directly or derivatively, since the victims of a proxy violation are the security holders who are asked to vote. See *J.I. Case Co. v. Borak*, 377 U.S. 426 (1964). The Commission has expressed the view that there is a private right of action under § 20(a) and that it is direct, rather than derivative, since the action seeks to vindicate the shareholder right to fair corporate suffrage. See *Kamen v. Kemper Financial Services, Inc.*, 111 S.Ct. 1711 (1991) (reserving judgment on this issue).

[14] See, *e.g.*, *SEC v. Falstaff Brewing Corp.*, 629 F.2d 62 (DC Cir. 1980), *cert. denied*, 449 U.S. 1012 (1980) (held, a person who permitted his name to be used in a merger proxy statement was directly liable for his failure to correct materially false and misleading statements that appeared in the statement since, "in reality," it was he "who was seeking the shareholders' votes to approve" the merger.); *Herskowitz v. Nutri/System, Inc.*, 857 F.2d 179 (3rd Cir. 1988), *cert. denied*, 489 U.S. 1054 (1989) (held, investment bank could be sued directly where its name appeared in the proxy statement and it was responsible for supplying materially false and misleading information therein.); *In re Caesar's Palace Sec. Lit.*, 360 F. Supp. 366 (SDNY 1973) ("Even [where] persons have not actually solicited

remedies available to spoke fund shareholders for violations of § 20(a). The federal courts have the requisite power to grant complete relief where a proxy violation has occurred.[15]

III-B-3. Liability under § 36(b) of the 1940 Act

Section 36(b) authorizes any "security holder" of a registered investment company to bring an action on behalf of the company to recover excessive compensation paid to any investment adviser, or any affiliate of the adviser. Although any recovery goes to the investment company, a shareholder may bring suit directly without demand on the company's directors.[16] The Division has considered whether the hub-and-spoke structure introduces a demand requirement in an action under § 36(b) against the hub fund's investment adviser because investors are shareholders of the spoke fund, rather than the hub.

The courts should construe the term "security holder" in § 36(b) as not restricted to the spoke funds, but as including the spoke fund shareholders. Section 36(b) is intended to provide an "independent" shareholder check on excessive fees. Granting spoke shareholders standing to bring suit directly on the hub fund's behalf would promote this independent check, and would be consistent with broad concepts of standing applied in other contexts.[17]

Even if the courts did consider § 36(b) claims against the hub fund's adviser by a spoke fund's shareholders to be derivative in nature, we do not believe they would require that the spoke shareholders make demand upon the spoke's board of directors prior to

---

proxies but merely participated in their preparation or in other related ways brought about such solicitation, they must share the responsibility with those persons who are primarily vulnerable ....").

[15] *Borak, supra*; MAGNUSON, SHAREHOLDER LITIGATION, § 6.11 p.22 (1984) ("In a word, courts have carte blanche, once a violation is found, to fashion a remedy they feel is just.").

[16] *Daily Income Fund, Inc. v. Fox*, 464 U.S. 523 (1984).

[17] For example, in cases brought under § 10(b) of the Securities Exchange Act of 1934 and Rule 10b-5 thereunder, beneficiaries of securities held by pension trust funds or broker-dealers in "street name" have standing to sue for damages caused by the purchase or sale of such securities. See *Kirshner v. United States*, 603 F.2d 234 (2d Cir. 1978), *cert. denied*, 442 U.S. 909 (1979); *Drachman v. Harvey*, 453 F.2d 722 (2d Cir. 1971) (en banc); *Klamberg v. Roth*, 425 F. Supp. 440 (SDNY 1976) (While the trust beneficiary is not the actual seller or purchaser, the beneficiary is the one "who immediately stood to gain or lose by the sale."); 3B MOORE'S FEDERAL PRACTICE § 23.1.17 p. 23.1-67 (1991).

suit. The demand requirement in a derivative action under the 1940 Act is determined by reference to state law unless the application of that law would be inconsistent with the federal policy underlying the cause of action.[18] A demand requirement would be inconsistent with the policy of providing an independent shareholder check on excessive fees.

IV. CONCLUSION

The organization of mutual funds in hub-and-spoke arrangements is an import evolution in the mutual fund industry. The Division believes that, with adequate disclosure and certain structural safeguards for investors, these arrangements can offer benefits to both investors and the mutual fund industry without any significant risk to investors. The staff will continue to monitor developments in this area, however, to assure that these arrangements do not deprive investors of the protections of the 1933 and 1940 Acts.

---

[18] *Kamen, supra*; see also *Burks v. Lasker*, 441 U.S. 471 (1979).

Foreign Feeder Fund

IC Act § § 12(d)(1)(A) & (B), SEC No-Action Letter (Mar. 8, 2017)

Response of Chief Counsel's Office
Division of Investment Management

Your letter dated March 8, 2017 requests assurance that we would not recommend enforcement action to the Securities and Exchange Commission under § 12(d)(1)(A) or (B) of the Investment Company Act of 1940 against: (i) a foreign investment company (a "**Foreign Feeder Fund**") that acquires securities of an open-end investment company registered under the 1940 Act (a "**U.S. Master Fund**") in excess of the limits in § 12(d)(1)(A) of the 1940 Act; or (ii) the U.S. Master Fund, its principal underwriter ("Master Fund Principal Underwriter") and any broker or dealer, that sells [*sic*] the U.S. Master Fund's securities to the Foreign Feeder Fund in excess of the limits in § 12(d)(1)(B) of the 1940 Act, if it does so in compliance with the conditions of § 12(d)(1)(E) of the 1940 Act, modified as described in your letter.

Section 12(d)(1)(E) is a conditional exemption from the restrictions in § § 12(d)(1)(A) and (B) that is relied upon by, among others, private funds and foreign investment companies to invest in U.S.-registered funds. In sum, your proposed structure (the "**Proposed Structure**") would deviate from the conditions of § 12(d)(1)(E) in that a **Foreign Feeder Fund**:

- may not have a principal underwriter or depositor that is a broker or dealer registered under the Securities Exchange Act of 1934 or a person controlled by such broker or dealer, as required by § 12(d)(1)(E)(i), but: (a) may have a principal underwriter that either controls or is under common control with a broker or dealer registered under the 1934 Act ("*Foreign Principal Underwriter*"); and (b) will have as its investment adviser an investment adviser that (i) controls, is controlled by, or is under common control with ("Control Affiliate"), the investment adviser to the U.S. Master Fund ("*Master Fund Adviser*") and the Master Fund Principal Underwriter and (ii) may be registered under the Investment Advisers Act of 1940 ("*Feeder Fund Adviser*");
- may hold certain investment securities that are not limited to the securities of the U.S. Master Fund, as required by § 12(d)(1)(E)(ii), but will do so solely for purposes of hedging either: (a) the performance of the U.S. Master Fund, measured in the U.S. dollar, against the currency of the foreign jurisdiction in which the

Foreign Feeder Fund's securities are primarily offered and sold ("Designated Currency"); or (b) if the U.S. Master Fund seeks to approximate the return of an index, the U.S. dollar and/or foreign currency exposure of the U.S. Master Fund to the Foreign Feeder Fund's Designated Currency; and

- may either abstain from voting or withhold voting the U.S. Master Fund's shares, rather than pass through such vote to the Foreign Feeder Fund's shareholders or vote proportionately to the vote of the U.S. Master Fund's other shareholders, which is a condition of § 12(d)(1)(E)(iii)(aa).

Based on the representations in your letter, and for the reasons set forth below, we are providing such assurance.

BACKGROUND

You state the following:

- A number of global investment managers are seeking to offer Foreign Feeder Funds in various foreign jurisdictions as vehicles for investing in a U.S. Master Fund using a master-feeder fund arrangement. The Proposed Structure potentially could help attract significant assets to the benefit of all investors in the U.S. Master Fund. The Master Fund Adviser will be registered under the Advisers Act and the U.S. Master Fund will have a Master Fund Principal Underwriter that is a broker-dealer registered under the 1934 Act.
- A Foreign Feeder Fund will be a foreign publicly offered investment company whose securities are generally redeemable upon demand to the fund (*i.e.*, a foreign mutual fund) or whose securities are listed on one or more foreign securities exchanges (*i.e.*, a foreign exchange traded fund or foreign closed-end fund).[1] The Foreign Feeder Fund will have as its investment adviser a Feeder Fund Adviser that is a Control Affiliate of the Master Fund Adviser and the Master Fund Principal Underwriter.
- A Foreign Feeder Fund may: (i) have a principal underwriter that is a broker or dealer registered under the 1934 Act or a person controlled by such broker or dealer; (ii) have a Foreign Principal Underwriter that controls or is under common

[1] The Foreign Feeder Fund would not be registered under the 1940 Act consistent with § 7(d) of the 1940 Act and prior SEC and Staff guidance. See, *e.g.*, *Exemptions for Advisers to Venture Capital Funds, Private Fund Advisers With Less Than $150 Million in Assets Under Management, and Foreign Private Advisers*, IA-3222, 76 FR 39645, n.294 (2011).

control with a broker or dealer registered under the 1934 Act; or (iii) not have a principal underwriter or depositor at all. Any Foreign Principal Underwriter to the Foreign Feeder Fund will be a Control Affiliate of the Feeder Fund Adviser, Master Fund Adviser, and Master Fund Principal Underwriter.

- Each Foreign Feeder Fund will invest in the securities of a single U.S. Master Fund and may hold cash and other assets that are not investment securities. The Foreign Feeder Fund also may invest in foreign currency and certain foreign currency-related instruments ("Foreign Currency Instruments")[2] to mitigate the effects of currency fluctuations in two situations.[3] First, a Foreign Feeder Fund may hedge the performance of the U.S. Master Fund, as measured in the U.S. dollar, against the Foreign Feeder Fund's Designated Currency ("*Feeder-level Hedging*").[4] Second, a Foreign Feeder Fund that invests in a U.S. Master Fund that seeks to approximate the return of an index, may hedge the U.S. dollar and/or foreign currency exposure associated with the U.S. Master Fund's portfolio to the Foreign Feeder Fund's Designated Currency[5] ("*Master-level Hedging*").[6]

---

[2] Such Foreign Currency Instruments may include foreign currency futures contracts, options on foreign currency futures contracts, forward foreign currency contracts, options on foreign currency and foreign currency swap agreements.

[3] The Foreign Feeder Fund may invest in Foreign Currency Instruments only for the specific hedging purposes described in your letter and not for speculative purposes (*i.e.*, generating excess investment returns). A Foreign Feeder Fund that does not engage in any currency hedging would not invest in Foreign Currency Instruments.

[4] The Feeder-level Hedging would enable the security holders of the Foreign Feeder Fund to achieve a return on their investment, as measured in the Designated Currency, similar to that of the security holders of the U.S. Master Fund, as measured in the U.S. dollar.

[5] The Master-level Hedging would enable the security holders of the Foreign Feeder Fund to achieve a return on their investment, as measured in the Designated Currency, similar to that of the index whose returns the U.S. Master Fund seeks to approximate, by reducing the impact of currency fluctuations between or among the Designated Currency and the U.S. Dollar or other foreign currency exposure of the index.

[6] Such Foreign Feeder Fund may engage in Master-level Hedging only so long as: (i) the provider of the index is not an affiliated person or an affiliated person of an affiliated person, of the U.S. Master Fund, the Master Fund Adviser, any subadviser or promoter of the U.S. Master Fund, or the Master Fund Principal Underwriter; (ii) the currency exposure of the U.S. Master Fund does not materially deviate from the currency exposure of the index, whether through sampling or otherwise; and (iii) the investment objectives of the Foreign Feeder Fund and the U.S. Master Fund are substantially the same, except to the extent necessary to permit the currency hedging as described in your letter.

LEGAL ANALYSIS

Sections 12(d)(1)(A) and (B) of the 1940 Act

Section 12(d)(1)(A), in relevant part, prohibits a Foreign Feeder Fund from: (i) acquiring more than three percent of the total outstanding voting stock of a U.S. Master Fund; (ii) investing more than five percent of the value of its total assets in the U.S. Master Fund; or (iii) investing more than ten percent of the value of its total assets in investment companies registered under the 1940 Act.

Section 12(d)(1)(B), in relevant part, prohibits a U.S. Master Fund, Master Fund Principal Underwriter and any broker or dealer registered under the 1934 Act from knowingly selling the U.S. Master Fund's securities to a Foreign Feeder Fund if immediately after such sale the Foreign Feeder Fund would own more than three percent of the U.S. Master Fund's total outstanding voting stock, or more than ten percent of the U.S. Master Fund's total outstanding voting stock would be owned by the Foreign Feeder Fund and other investment companies.

These prohibitions were enacted out of concerns about undue influence by the acquiring fund and its affiliates over the acquired fund and its affiliates, the pyramiding of control, the layering of fees, and overly complex fund structures.[7] Specifically with respect to foreign funds investing in U.S. funds, it was also noted that "redemptions could be unduly escalated by the instability of certain foreign economies, political upheaval, currency reform, or other factors which are not really relevant to investment in domestic mutual funds."[8]

Section 12(d)(1)(E) of the 1940 Act

Section 12(d)(1)(E) provides an exemption from the prohibitions in § § 12(d)(1)(A) and (B) of the 1940 Act, subject to the following conditions designed to address the concerns underlying those prohibitions:

---

[7] See REPORT OF THE SECURITIES AND EXCHANGE COMMISSION ON THE PUBLIC POLICY IMPLICATIONS OF INVESTMENT COMPANY GROWTH, H.R. Report No. 2337, 89th Cong., 2d Sess., at 311-324 (1966) ("PPI Report"). Moreover, with respect to protecting *foreign* acquiring funds and their security holders, you point out that the SEC generally has no significant U.S. regulatory interest in protecting such *foreign* acquiring funds and their security holders from certain potential abuses that § § 12(d)(1)(A) and (B) were designed to address (*i.e.*, duplicative fees and unnecessary complexity). See *Dechert LLP*, SEC No-Action Letter (Aug. 4, 2009).

[8] PPI Report, *supra* note 7, at 318.

- The principal underwriter for the Foreign Feeder Fund must be a broker or dealer registered under the 1934 Act, or a person controlled by such broker or dealer;
- The U.S. Master Fund's securities are the only investment security held by the Foreign Feeder Fund; and
- The Foreign Feeder Fund purchases or otherwise acquires securities issued by the U.S. Master Fund pursuant to an arrangement with the U.S. Master Fund or its principal underwriter whereby the Foreign Feeder Fund is obligated: (i) to either seek instructions from its security holders with regard to the voting of all proxies with respect to the U.S. Master Fund's securities and vote such proxies only in accordance with such instructions, or vote the shares held by it in the same proportion as the vote of all other holders of the U.S. Master Fund's securities; and (ii) to refrain from substituting the U.S. Master Fund's securities unless the Commission shall have approved such substitution in the manner provided in § 26 of the 1940 Act.

You state that in the Proposed Structure a Foreign Feeder Fund would deviate from the conditions set forth in § 12(d)(1)(E) in the following manner.[9]

Foreign Feeder Fund Might Not Have a Principal Underwriter or Depositor

You state that a Foreign Feeder Fund might not have a principal underwriter or depositor at all, or have a Foreign Principal Underwriter, and therefore would not meet the condition in § 12(d)(1)(E) that the principal underwriter or depositor be a broker or dealer registered under the 1934 Act or a person controlled by such broker or dealer. You state that this condition appears to have been designed to ensure that the Commission has jurisdiction over and the ability to pursue claims against the principal underwriter or depositor of the acquiring fund in connection with their activities relating to the master-feeder fund structure.

You argue that the following factors in the Proposed Structure serve to address these jurisdictional concerns:

- The Foreign Feeder Fund will have an investment adviser[10] that is a Control

---

[9] You represent that, in complying with § 12(d)(1)(E)(iii)(bb), a Foreign Feeder Fund will not substitute its investment in the U.S. Master Fund unless the Commission shall have approved such substitution by order issued to the Foreign Feeder Fund.

[10] In the case of a Foreign Feeder Fund that also has a Foreign Principal Underwriter, you note that the Commission previously has viewed such relationship as addressing the jurisdictional concern. See *World of*

Affiliate of the Master Fund Adviser and Master Fund Principal Underwriter;[11]

- To the extent the Feeder Fund Adviser is not registered under the Advisers Act, such Feeder Fund Adviser will make its books and records with respect to the activities of the Foreign Feeder Fund available to the Commission and its staff, designate the Master Fund Adviser as its agent for service of process in the United States with respect to the Foreign Feeder Fund, and consent to the jurisdiction of the U.S. courts and the Commission with respect to its activities in connection with the Foreign Feeder Fund;[12]
- The Foreign Feeder Funds will be organized in, and regulated under the laws of, jurisdictions whose securities regulators have entered into a cooperation arrangement with the Commission;[13] and
- No Foreign Feeder Fund will offer or sell its securities in the United States, either publicly or privately, or sell its securities to any "U.S. person," as defined in Rule 902(k) of Regulation S under the 1933 Act; each Foreign Feeder Fund's transactions with its shareholders will be consistent with the definition of "offshore transactions" in Rule 902(h) of Regulation S; and no Foreign Feeder Fund, Feeder Fund Adviser, Foreign Principal Underwriter, any of their respective affiliates, or any person acting on behalf of any of the foregoing, will engage in any "directed selling efforts," as defined in Rule 902(c) of Regulation S, with respect to securities of the Foreign Feeder Fund in the United States.[14]

Currency Hedging by a Foreign Feeder Fund

You state that, because a Foreign Feeder Fund might hold Foreign Currency Instruments, it might not meet the requirement in § 12(d)(1)(E) that the U.S. Master

---

Technology, Inc. and Financial Programs, Inc., IC-13459 (Aug. 23, 1983) (notice) ("Applicants assert that § 12(d)(1)(E)(i) insures that the Commission has administrative recourse under the [1934 Act] against principal underwriters of fund holding companies. Applicants contend that such recourse remains where the principal underwriter is a foreign dealer under common control with a registered broker-dealer....").

[11] Your letter details the manner in which these relationships would address the jurisdictional concerns.

[12] You state that a Foreign Principal Underwriter to a Foreign Feeder Fund will do the same. The details of these arrangements are set forth in your letter.

[13] These jurisdictions will be limited to the following: France, Germany, Ireland, Luxembourg, Switzerland, United Kingdom, Canada, Mexico, Brazil, Australia, Hong Kong, Japan, Singapore, and South Africa.

[14] You state that, over time, a Foreign Feeder Fund may include investors that are U.S. Persons, consistent with § 7(d) of the 1940 Act and SEC and Staff guidance thereunder.

Fund's securities be the only investment security held by the Foreign Feeder Fund.[15] You note that, under the Proposed Structure, Foreign Currency Instruments may be held by a Foreign Feeder Fund solely in order to engage in either Feeder-level Hedging or Master-level Hedging.

With respect to Feeder-level Hedging, you argue that the Foreign Feeder Fund's proposed use of Foreign Currency Instruments would not create any incentive to exercise any improper influence over the U.S. Master Fund and is the only efficient way for the Foreign Feeder Fund to accomplish the foreign currency management objective that you describe in your letter (*i.e.*, the Foreign Feeder Fund, by entering into the Foreign Currency Instruments, would be able to isolate the effects of the fluctuations in the exchange rate between the Designated Currency and the U.S. dollar for its shareholders, without affecting the return for other shareholders of the U.S. Master Fund).[16]

With respect to Master-level Hedging, you acknowledge that the potential for improper influence might exist. For example, as a Foreign Feeder Fund seeks to hedge the currency exposure of the U.S. Master Fund's portfolio to the Foreign Feeder Fund's Designated Currency, the investment interests of the Foreign Feeder Fund and the U.S. Master Fund could diverge because the Foreign Feeder Fund might be more or less affected by the currency exposure of the U.S. Master Fund's portfolio. A Foreign Feeder Fund might seek to influence the U.S. Master Fund's choice of currency exposure for its own interest, to the potential detriment of the U.S. Master Fund and its other shareholders.

You argue, however, that the Proposed Structure mitigates this concern by limiting Master-level Hedging solely to a Foreign Feeder Fund that invests in a U.S. Master Fund that seeks to approximate the return of an index. In such case, the U.S. Master Fund would have very limited ability to vary its currency exposure to benefit a Foreign Feeder Fund and would not be susceptible to potential undue influence by a Foreign Feeder Fund.[17]

Voting of U.S. Master Fund's Shares Held by the Foreign Feeder Fund

Under § 12(d)(1)(E)(iii)(aa), a Foreign Feeder Fund is required to either: (i) seek

---

[15] In this letter, we are not interpreting what constitutes "investment securities" under § 12(d)(1)(E)(ii).

[16] You note that the Feeder-level Hedging is similar to that addressed in *PIMCO Funds*, SEC No-Action Letter (July 9, 2002).

[17] See also *supra* note 6.

instructions from its security holders with regard to the voting of all proxies with respect to the securities of the U.S. Master Fund and vote such proxies only in accordance with such instructions; or (ii) vote the securities held by it in the same proportion as the vote of all other holders of the U.S. Master Fund's securities. You state that these voting requirements were intended to address the concern about undue influence that may be exercised by the acquiring fund and its affiliates over the acquired fund.[18]

You state that the laws and/or market practices of a foreign jurisdiction in which a Foreign Feeder Fund operates might not permit, or may be interpreted as prohibiting, voting in the manner required by § 12(d)(1)(E)(iii)(aa). In such case, under the Proposed Structure, the Foreign Feeder Fund will either abstain from voting or withhold voting the shares of the U.S. Master Fund. You state that this alternative neutralizes the vote of the Foreign Feeder Fund in the same manner as voting in the same proportion as the vote of all holders of the U.S. Master Fund's securities and therefore accomplishes the objective of the requirement in § 12(d)(1)(E)(iii)(aa).

CONCLUSION

Based on the facts and representations set forth in your letter, we would not recommend. enforcement action to the Commission under § 12(d)(1)(A) or (B) of the 1940 Act against a Foreign Feeder Fund that acquires securities of a U.S. Master Fund in excess of the limits in § 12(d)(1)(A) of the 1940 Act, or against the U.S. Master Fund, Master Fund Principal Underwriter and any broker or dealer, that sells [*sic*] the U.S. Master Fund's securities to the Foreign Feeder Fund in excess of the limits in § 12(d)(1)(B) of the 1940 Act, if it does so in compliance with the conditions of § 12(d)(1)(E) of the 1940 Act, modified as described in your letter. Because this position is based on all of the facts and representations made in your letter, any different facts or circumstances might require a different conclusion. This letter expresses our position only with respect to enforcement action, and does not express any legal conclusions on the issues presented.

---

[18] See PPI Report, *supra* note 7, at 314-315. See also, *e.g.*, H.R. Rep. 622, 104th Cong., 2d Sess., at 41 (1996) (noting that originally this voting requirement [under § 12(d)(1)(E)(iii)] [...] was enacted to address abusive practices of the 1970s involving off-shore [...] funds that invested in U.S. funds.").

Chapter 4 Investment Adviser Regulation and Enforcement Under Advisers Act

> " . . . investment advisers are of national concern, in that, among other things—(1) their advice, . . . analyses, and reports are furnished and distributed, and their contracts, . . . with clients are negotiated and performed, by the use of the mails and means and instrumentalities of interstate commerce; (2) their advice, . . . analyses, and reports customarily relate to the purchase and sale of securities . . . ; and (3) the foregoing transactions occur in such volume as substantially to affect interstate commerce, national securities exchanges, and other securities markets, the national banking system and the national economy."
>
> ----Investment Advisers Act of 1940, § 201

Section 4.1 Investment Adviser Conduct Regulation

Topic 1 Statutory Investment Adviser and Exclusions

Laws & Rules Highlight:

IA Act ((15 USC 80b-1 *et seq.*) & Rules (17 CFR §§ 275.0-2 *et seq.*)

- § 202(a)(11) (***def.*** *"investment adviser"*)
- § 202(a)(11)(A)-(H) (***exclusions*** *from statutory "investment adviser"*)
  - **§ 202(a)(11)(A)** (***bank and bank holding company*** *exclusions, unless acting as IA to registered IC*)
    - ✓ § 202(a)(2) (*def. "bank"*)
  - § 202(a)(11)(B) (*professionals (lawyer, accountant, engineer, and teacher) exclusion*)
  - § 202(a)(11)(C) (*broker-dealer exclusion*)
  - **§ 202(a)(11)(D)** (***bona fide publisher exclusion***)
  - § 202(a)(11)(E) (*exclusion for investment advice solely relating to government or agency securities*)
  - § 202(a)(11)(F) (*nationally recognized statistical rating organization NRSRO exclusion, unless the NRSRO issues recommendation about or manages assets of securities on behalf of others*)
  - § 202(a)(11)(G) (*family office exclusion*)

◆ § 202(a)(11)(H) (*exclusion by SEC rule, regulation, or order of persons not within the intent of IA definition*)

<u>**Pre-Case Background Note 1**</u>:[Biblio]

"Bona Fide Publisher Exclusion"—Investment Adviser Status of Certain Investment Advisory Publications and Computer Software Services

Under **§ 202(a)(11)** of the Investment Advisers Act, an "***investment adviser***":

"**means** any person ***who***, for compensation, engages in the business of advising others, either directly or through publications or writings, as to the value of securities or as to the advisability of investing in, purchasing, or selling securities, ***or who***, for compensation and as part of a regular business, issues or promulgates analyses or reports concerning securities; **but does not include** (A) ...; ***(D)*** the publisher of any bona fide newspaper, news magazine or business or financial publication of general and regular circulation; (E) ...; or (H) ...."

The statutory definition of "***investment adviser***" contains three analytical elements:[1]

- whether the person provides advice, or issues reports or analyses, regarding securities (*i.e.*, ***advising as to securities***);
- whether the person is ***in the business*** of providing such services; *e.g.*, by holding out as IA, or receiving clearly definable or transaction-based compensation for the investment advice, or providing specific investment advice on a basis other than rare, isolated, and non-periodic instances; and
- whether the person provides such services ***for compensation*** (*i.e.*, the person's receipt of any economic benefit for his services from some source).

To qualify for **§ 202(a)(11)(D)** ***bona fide publisher exclusion*** from statutory IA, an investment advisory publication must be:[2; 3]

- "*impersonal*";
- "*bona fide*"; and
- "*of general and regular circulation*."

In *Lowe v. SEC*,[3] a case interpreting ***bona fide newspaper exclusion*** from statutory adviser, the U.S. Supreme Court distinguished between regulating impersonal investment periodicals, and regulating personal and fiduciary relationship. Regulation of the former through licensing would implicate the First Amendment concerns of prior restraints on speech. Regulation of the latter—being the essence of an investment advisory relationship—is the subject of the Investment Advisers Act.

In *Datastream International, Inc.*,[4] an SEC no-action letter interpreting "***advising as to securities***" element of statutory adviser definition in the case of provision to subscribers of databases and software analytic tools with which to manipulate the data, the SEC states: the presentation of securities data or information to subscribers does not constitute "*furnishing investment advice or an analysis or report*" within the meaning of § 202(a)(11) if (1) the information is readily available to the public in its raw state, (2) the categories of information presented are not highly selective, and (3) the information is not organized or presented in a manner which suggests the purchase, holding, or sale of any security or securities.

Bibliography

1. Applicability of the Investment Advisers Act to Financial Planners, Pension Consultants, and Other Persons Who Provide Investment Advisory Services as a Component of Other Financial Services; statement of staff interpretive position, IA-1092, 52 FR 38400 (1987)
2. Lee, *The Effects of Lowe on the Application of the Investment Advisers Act of 1940 to Impersonal Investment Advising Publications*, 42 BUS. LAW. 507 (1987)
3. Lowe v. SEC, 472 U.S. 181 (1985)
4. Datastream Int'l, Inc., IA Act § 202(a)(11), 1993 SEC No-Act. LEXIS 735 (March 15, 1993)

Case Study 1a: Financial Publisher

Financial publisher providing *impersonal* rather than *personalized* investment advice excluded from coverage of the Advisers Act, under the bona fide newspaper exclusion.

Lowe, *et al.*, Petitioners v. SEC
472 U.S. 181 (1985)

[***Procedural history and related case materials:*** *In re* Lowe Mgmt. Corp., Adm. Proc. 3-5823, IA-759 (May 11, 1981); SEC v. Lowe, 556 F. Supp. 1359 (EDNY 1983), *rev'd*, 725 F.2d 892 (2d Cir. 1984); Brief of the American Civil Liberties Union, 1983 U.S. Briefs 1911 (Nov 15, 1984); *rev'd*, 472 U.S. 181 (1985)]

Case Study 1b: Financial Database Vendor

Economic and financial information services vendor licensing databases and software analytic tools to subscribing investment managers and institutional investors, enabling subscribers to select and retrieve data, manipulate the data, and produce analyses for themselves. SEC no-action granted allowing the information services vendor to withdraw its registration as an investment adviser.

Datastream Int'l, Inc.

IA Act § 202(a)(11), 1993 SEC No-Act. LEXIS 735 (March 15, 1993)

Pre-Case Background Note 2:[Biblio]

"Bank Exclusion" and SEC Enforcement Power Over Banks under Securities Laws

IA Act § 202(a)(11)(A) excludes **banks** and **bank holding companies**, but not **non-bank subsidiaries** of the bank holding companies, from the statutory definition of "*investment adviser*," unless the bank or the bank holding company acts as IA to registered ICs, in which case the bank or the bank holding company as the case may be must be registered under the IA Act. A bank may, however, house its investment company advisory activities such as acting as IA to registered mutual funds in a "*separately identifiable department or division*" (**SID**) as the term is defined in IA Act § 202(a)(26); and have its SID, instead of the bank itself, register as an IA.[1; 2] Nevertheless, the SEC may exercise enforcement power over a **non-IA bank's wealth management business** under other provisions of the federal securities laws.[3]

Bibliography

1. Evans, *Regulation of Bank Securities Activities*, 91 BANKING L.J. 611 (1974)
2. FEIN, SECURITIES ACTIVITIES OF BANKS, § 5.03 Regulation of Investment Advisers (4th ed. 2014)
3. In *re* JPMorgan Chase Bank, N.A. and J.P. Morgan Securities LLC, Respondents Adm. Proc. 3-17008, 33-9992, 34-76694, IA-4295 (Dec. 18, 2015)

Case Study 2: Commercial Bank's Wealth Management Business

In *re* JPMorgan Chase Bank, N.A. and J.P. Morgan Securities LLC, Respondents

Adm. Proc. 3-17008, 33-9992, 34-76694, IA-4295 (Dec. 18, 2015)

[***Related proceedings and case materials:*** SEC Press Rel. 2015-283, *J.P. Morgan to Pay $267 Million for Disclosure Failures* (Dec. 18, 2015); CFTC Press Rel. 7297-15, *CFTC Orders JPMorgan Chase Bank, N.A. to Pay $100 Million for Failure to Disclose Conflicts of Interest* (Dec. 18, 2015); In *re* JPMorgan Chase Bank, N.A., Respondent, CFTC Docket No. 16-05 (Dec 18, 2015)]

Research Topics:

Investment adviser status of banks, broker-dealers, family offices, and financial information data and analytics software providers under the Chinese investment management laws and regulations.

Lowe, *et al.*, Petitioners v. SEC

472 U.S. 181 (1985)

JUDGES: STEVENS, J., delivered the opinion of the Court, in which BRENNAN, MARSHALL, BLACKMUN, and O'CONNOR, JJ., joined. WHITE, J., filed an opinion concurring in the result, in which BURGER, C. J., and REHNQUIST, J., joined. POWELL, J., took no part in the decision of the case.

OPINION

Justice STEVENS delivered the opinion of the Court:

The question is whether petitioners may be permanently enjoined from publishing nonpersonalized investment advice and commentary in securities newsletters because they are not registered as investment advisers under § 203(c) of the Investment Advisers Act of 1940.

Christopher Lowe is the president and principal shareholder of Lowe Management Corporation. From 1974 until 1981, the corporation was registered as an investment adviser under the Act.[1] During that period Lowe was convicted of misappropriating funds of an investment client, of engaging in business as an investment adviser without filing a registration application with New York's Department of Law, of tampering with evidence to cover up fraud of an investment client, and of stealing from a bank. Consequently, on May 11, 1981, the Securities and Exchange Commission, after a full hearing before an Administrative Law Judge, entered an order revoking the registration of the Lowe Management Corporation, and ordering Lowe not to associate thereafter with any investment adviser.

In fashioning its remedy, the Commission took into account the fact that petitioners "are now solely engaged in the business of publishing advisory publications." The Commission noted that unless the registration was revoked, petitioners would be "free to engage in all aspects of the advisory business" and that even their publishing activities afforded them "opportunities for dishonesty and self-dealing."[2]

---

[1] In *re Lowe Management Corp.* (1981).

[2] The Commission wrote:

"We do not seek to punish respondents but, in light of their egregious misconduct, we must protect the public from the future harm at their hands. In evaluating the public interest requirements in this case, we have taken into account respondents' statement that they are now solely engaged in the business of publishing advisory

A little over a year later, the Commission commenced this action by filing a complaint in the United States District Court for the Eastern District of New York, alleging that Lowe, the Lowe Management Corporation, and two other corporations,[3] were violating the Act, and that Lowe was violating the Commission's order. The principal charge in the complaint was that Lowe and the three corporations (petitioners) were publishing two investment newsletters and soliciting subscriptions for a stock-chart service. The complaint alleged that, through those publications, the petitioners were engaged in the business of advising others "as to the advisability of investing in, purchasing, or selling securities ... and as a part of a regular business ... issuing reports concerning securities." Because none of the petitioners was registered or exempt from registration under the Act, the use of the mails in connection with the advisory business allegedly violated § 203(a) of the Act. The Commission prayed for a permanent injunction restraining the further distribution of petitioners' investment advisory publications; for a permanent injunction enforcing compliance with the order of May 11, 1981; and for other relief.

Although three publications are involved in this litigation, only one need be described. A typical issue of the Lowe Investment and Financial Letter contained general commentary about the securities and bullion markets, reviews of market indicators and investment strategies, and specific recommendations for buying, selling, or holding stocks and bullion. The newsletter advertised a "telephone hotline" over which subscribers could call to get current information. The number of subscribers to the newsletter ranged from 3,000 to 19,000. It was advertised as a semimonthly publication, but only eight issues were published in the 15 months after the entry of the 1981 order.[4]

---

publications. However, respondents are still free to engage in all aspects of the advisory business. And, as the Administrative Law Judge noted, even their present activities afford numerous 'opportunities for dishonesty and self-dealing.'

"Under all the circumstances, we are convinced that the public interest requires the revocation of registrant's investment adviser registration, and a bar of Lowe from association with any investment adviser." *Supra* note 1.

[3] The other two corporations are the Lowe Publishing Corporation and the Lowe Stock Chart Service, Inc.

[4] The Lowe Stock Advisory had only 278 paid subscribers and had published only four issues between May 1981 and its last issue in March 1982. It also analyzed and commented on the securities and bullion markets, but specialized in lower-priced stocks. Subscribers were advised that they could receive periodic letters with updated recommendations about specific securities and also could make use of the telephone hotline. 556 F. Supp. 1359 (EDNY 1983). Petitioners advertised the Lowe Chart Service as a weekly publication that would contain charts for all securities listed on the New York and American Stock Exchanges, and for the 1,200 most actively traded over-the-counter stocks, as well as charts on gold and silver prices and market indicators. Unlike the other two

Subscribers who testified at the trial criticized the lack of regularity of publication, but no adverse evidence concerning the quality of the publications was offered. There was no evidence that Lowe's criminal convictions were related to the publications;[5] no evidence that Lowe had engaged in any trading activity in any securities that were the subject of advice or comment in the publications; and no contention that any of the information published in the advisory services had been false or materially misleading.

For the most part, the District Court denied the Commission the relief it requested; 556 F. Supp. 1359 (EDNY 1983). The court did enjoin petitioners from giving information to their subscribers by telephone, individual letter, or in person, but it refused to enjoin them from continuing their publication activities or to require them to disgorge any of the earnings from the publications.[6] The District Court acknowledged that the face of the statute did not differentiate between persons whose only advisory activity is the "publication of impersonal investment suggestions, reports and analyses," and those who rendered person-to-person advice, but concluded that constitutional considerations suggested the need for such a distinction. After determining that petitioners' publications were protected by the First Amendment, the District Court held that the Act must be construed to allow a publisher who is willing to comply with the existing reporting and disclosure requirements to register for the limited purpose of publishing such material and to engage in such publishing.[7]

A splintered panel of the Court of Appeals for the Second Circuit reversed; 725 F.2d 892 (1984). The majority first held that petitioners were engaged in business as "investment advisers" within the meaning of the Act. It concluded that the Act does not distinguish between person-to-person advice and impersonal advice given in printed publications. Rather, in its view, the key statutory question was whether the exclusion in

---

publications, it did not propose to offer any specific investment advice. Although there were approximately 40 subscribers, no issues were published. The regular subscription rate was $325 for 3 months or $900 for 1 year.

[5] In addition to the 1977 and 1978 convictions that gave rise to the Commission's 1981 order, in 1982, Lowe was convicted on two counts of theft by deception through the issuance of worthless checks.

[6] The District Court also rejected the Commission's claim that the publications were fraudulent because they did not disclose Lowe's criminal convictions or the revocation of the registration of Lowe Management Corporation, noting that the Commission had not promulgated any rules requiring such disclosure.

[7] The District Court wrote: "When a publisher who has been denied registration or against whom sanctions have been invoked fully complies with the record, reporting and disclosure requirements under the Act, he must be allowed to register for the purpose of publishing and to publish."

§ 202(a)(11)(D), for "the publisher of any bona fide newspaper, news magazine, or business or financial publication of general and regular circulation" applied to the petitioners. Relying on its decision in *SEC v. Wall Street Transcript Corp.*, 422 F.2d 1371, *cert. denied*, 398 U.S. 958 (1970), the Court of Appeals concluded that the exclusion was inapplicable.

Next, the Court of Appeals rejected petitioners' constitutional claim, reasoning that this case involves "precisely the kind of regulation of commercial activity permissible under the First Amendment."[8] Moreover, it held that Lowe's history of criminal conduct while acting as an investment adviser justified the characterization of his publications "as potentially deceptive commercial speech." The Court of Appeals reasoned that a ruling that petitioners "may not sell their views as to the purchase, sale, or holding of certain securities is no different from saying that a disbarred lawyer may not sell legal advice." Finally, the court noted that its holding was limited to a prohibition against selling advice to clients about specific securities.[9] Thus, the Court of Appeals apparently assumed that petitioners could continue publishing their newsletters if their content was modified to exclude any advice about specific securities.[10]

---

[8] The court additionally rejected petitioners' claim that "the Act violates equal protection by subjecting investment newsletters, but not bona fide newsletters, to regulation."

[9] At the end of its opinion, the Court of Appeals wrote:

> "Finally, we note what this holding does not entail. Lowe is not prohibited from publishing or stating his views as to any matter of current interest, economic or otherwise, such as the likelihood of war, the trend in interest rates, whether the next election will affect market conditions, or whether future enforcement of the Anti-Dumping Act to protect basic American smokestack industry from foreign competition is likely. He is not prohibited from publishing a newspaper of general interest and circulation. Nor is he prohibited from publishing recommendations in somebody else's bona fide newspaper as an employee, editor, or writer. What he is prohibited from doing is selling to clients advice and counsel, analysis and reports as to the value of specific securities or as to the advisability of investing in, purchasing or selling or holding specific securities."

It appended the following footnote:

> "We leave to another day the question whether a publication dealing only with market indicators generally or making recommendations only as to groups of securities (*e.g.*, air transport, beverages-brewers, mobile homes) could be barred on facts such as those of this case." n.7.

[10] The Court of Appeals did not explain whether its apparent unwillingness to grant the Commission all of the relief requested was based on its opinion that a modification in the content of the publication would avoid the statutory definition of "investment adviser" or on the assumption that petitioners have a constitutional right to publish newsletters omitting specific recommendations.

One judge concurred separately, although acknowledging his agreement with the court's opinion. The dissenting judge agreed that Lowe may not hold himself out as a registered investment adviser and may not engage in any fraudulent activity in connection with his publications, but concluded that the majority had authorized an invalid prior restraint on the publication of constitutionally protected speech. To avoid the constitutional question, he would have adopted the District Court's construction of the Act.

I.

We granted certiorari to consider the important constitutional question whether an injunction against the publication and distribution of petitioners' newsletters is prohibited by the First Amendment; 469 U.S. 815 (1984).[11] Petitioners contend that such an injunction strikes at the very foundation of the freedom of the press by subjecting it to license and censorship, see, *e.g.*, *Lovell v. City of Griffin*, 303 U.S. 444 (1938); *Brief for Petitioners.* In response the Commission argues that the history of abuses in the securities industry amply justified Congress' decision to require the registration of investment advisers, to regulate their professional activities, and, as an incident to such regulation, to prohibit unregistered and unqualified persons from engaging in that business; *Brief for Respondent*; cf. *Konigsberg v. State Bar of California*, 366 U.S. 36 (1961). In reply, petitioners acknowledge that person-to-person communication in a commercial setting may be subjected to regulation that would be impermissible in a public forum, cf. *Ohralik v. Ohio State Bar Assn.*, 436 U.S. 447 (1978), but contend that the regulated class—investment advisers—may not be so broadly defined as to encompass the distribution of impersonal investment advice and commentary in a public market; *Reply Brief for Petitioners.*

In order to evaluate the parties' constitutional arguments, it is obviously necessary first to understand, as precisely as possible, the extent to which the Act was intended to

---

[11] Petitioners' submission in this Court does not challenge the validity of the Commission's order revoking the registration of Lowe Management Corporation and barring Lowe from future association with an investment adviser. Section 203(e) of the Act authorizes the Commission to revoke the registration of any investment adviser if it finds, after notice and an opportunity for hearing, that such revocation is in the public interest and that the investment adviser has committed certain types of crimes. Section 203(f) authorizes the Commission to bar the association of any person with an investment adviser if he has committed acts that would justify the revocation of an investment adviser's registration. Moreover, petitioners do not challenge the District Court's holding that they may not operate a direct "hot line" for subscribers desiring personalized advice.

regulate the publication of investment advice and the reasons that motivated Congress to authorize such regulation. Moreover, in view of the fact that we should "not decide a constitutional question if there is some other ground upon which to dispose of the case,"[12] and the further fact that the District Court and the dissenting judge in the Court of Appeals both believed that the case should be decided on statutory grounds, a careful study of the statute may either eliminate, or narrowly limit, the constitutional question that we must confront. We therefore begin with a review of the background of the Act with a particular focus on the legislative history describing the character of the profession that Congress intended to regulate.

II.

As we observed in *SEC v. Capital Gains Research Bureau, Inc.*, the "Investment Advisers Act of 1940 was the last in a series of acts designed to eliminate certain abuses in the securities industry, abuses which were found to have contributed to the stock market crash of 1929 and the depression of the 1930's."[13] The Act had its genesis in the Public Utility Holding Company Act of 1935, which "authorized and directed" the Commission "to make a study of the functions and activities of investment trusts and investment companies ... and to report the results of its study and its recommendations to the Congress on or before January 4, 1937." Pursuant to this instruction, the Commission transmitted to Congress its study on investment counsel, investment management, investment supervisory, and investment advisory services.[14] The Report focused on "some of the more important problems of these investment counsel organizations"; significantly, the Report stated that it "was intended to exclude any person or organization which was engaged in the business of furnishing investment analysis, opinion, or advice solely through publications distributed to a list of subscribers and did not furnish specific advice to any client with respect to securities."

The Report traced the history and growth of investment counsel, noting that the

---

[12] *Escambia County, Florida v. McMillan*, 466 U.S. 48 (1984) (per curiam); see also *Atkins v. Parker*, 472 U.S. 115 (1985); *Ashwander v. TVA*, 297 U.S. 288 (1936) (Brandeis, J., concurring).

[13] 375 U.S. 180 (1963).

[14] See INVESTMENT TRUSTS AND INVESTMENT COMPANIES, Report of the Securities and Exchange Commission, Pursuant to § 30 of the Public Utility Holding Company Act of 1935, Investment Counsel, Investment Management, Investment Supervisory, and Investment Advisory Services, H.R. Doc. No. 477, 76th Cong., 2d Sess. (1939) (hereinafter cited as Report).

profession did not emerge until after World War I. In the 1920's "a distinct class of persons ... held themselves out as giving only personalized investment advisory service"; rapid growth began in 1929, and markedly increased in the mid-1930's in response "to the demands of the investing public, which required supervision of its security investments after its experience during the depression years."[15]

Regarding the functions of investment counselors, the Report stated that "[some] of the representatives of investment counsel firms urged that the primary function of investment counselors was 'to render to clients, on a personal basis, competent, unbiased, and continuous advice regarding the sound management of their investments.' " Nevertheless, it noted that one investment counselor conceded:

> "[You] have a gradation from individuals who are professed tipsters and do not make any pretense of being anything else, all the way up the scale to the type of individual, who, as you say, desires to give the impartial scientific professional advice to persons who are trying to plan their economic situation in the light of accomplishing various results, making provision for old age, education, and so forth. However, you can readily see ... that a very significant part of that problem, as far as we are concerned, and possibly the most vital one, is, shall we say, the individuals on the fringes...."

Representatives of the industry viewed the functions of investment counselors slightly differently, concluding that they should serve "individuals and institutions with substantial

---

[15] After detailing the geographic distribution, the forms, and the sizes of investment-counsel firms, the Report analyzed the affiliations of the firms. It noted that "[all] investment counsel firms have not restricted their business interests or activities to the supervision of the accounts of their investment clients." Of the investment-counsel firms surveyed, approximately 5% published investment manuals and periodicals; of these latter firms, 80% were without investment-company clients. The Commission posited that affiliations with publishers of investment manuals and periodicals "may be attributable to the fact that research and statistical organizations are not uncommon with these businesses." The Report also analyzed the nature of services of investment-counsel firms to their clients:

> "The powers of investment counsel firms with respect to the management of the funds of their investment company clients were either discretionary or advisory. Discretionary powers imply the vesting with an investment counsel firm control over the client's funds, with the power to make the ultimate determination with respect to the sale and purchase of securities for the client's portfolio. In contrast, vesting advisory powers with an investment counsel firm merely means that the firm may make recommendations to its client, with whom rests the ultimate power to accept or reject such recommendations."

Approximately one-third of the firms surveyed had discretionary powers; however, all firms surveyed rarely assumed "custody of the portfolio securities of their investment company clients."

funds who require continuous supervision of their investments and a program of investment to cover their entire economic needs."[16] Turning to the problems of investment counselors, the Report concluded that they fell within two categories: "(a) the problem of distinguishing between bona fide investment counselors and 'tipster' organizations; and (b) those problems involving the organization and operation of investment counsel institutions."[17]

Commission's work "culminated in the preparation and introduction by Senator Wagner of the bill which, with some changes, became the Investment Advisers Act of

---

[16] Moreover, the representatives pointed out that there was a difference between the functions of investment counselors and investment companies: ".... [The] ordinary investment trust of the management type gives its holder a diversification, probably beyond the ability of the small investor to obtain on his own capital. It also gives him management. It does not take any cognizance—the distinction is that it takes no cognizance of his total financial position in investing his money for him, and is distinguished from investment counsel, in that it gives him no judgment in the matter whatever...."

"Q. *Now, you say the true function as you conceive it, of an investment counselor, is to give advice in connection with the specific condition of a particular individual*

"A. *Yes.*

"Q. *While the investment trust does not have that personal element in it, that it manages the funds more on an impersonal basis*

"A. *That is right.*

"Q. 'Impersonal' being used in the sense that they may try to get a common denominator, or what they envision their stockholders' condition may be, or what would be best for a cross-section of the American public, but does not give the advice with the peculiar, particular, specific financial condition of the individual and what he hopes to accomplish, or what purpose.

"A. Might I also add that in a number of cases at least, as Mr. Dunn said yesterday, the investment trust managers do not consider their funds as a proper repository for all of an individual's capital. It is not that it doesn't consider only his personal peculiarities and needs, but it does not give him a complete financial program." (testimony of James N. White of Scudder, Stevens & Clark) (emphasis added)

[17] Moreover, industry representatives "felt that investment counsel organizations could not completely perform their basic function—furnishing to clients on a personal basis competent, unbiased, and continuous advice regarding the sound management of their investments—unless all conflicts of interest between the investment counsel and the client were removed." The Report, near its conclusion, summarized:

> "It was the unanimous opinion of the representatives at the public examination ... that, although a voluntary organization would serve some salutary purpose, such an organization could not cope with the most elemental and fundamental problem of the investment counsel industry—the investment counsel 'fringe' which includes those incompetent and unethical individuals or organizations who represent themselves as bona fide investment counselors. These individuals and organizations not only could not meet the requirements of membership, but because of the nature of their activities would not even consider voluntarily submitting to supervision or policing."

1940."[18] Senator Wagner's bill, S.3580, contained two Titles; the first, concerning investment companies, contained a definition of "investment adviser,"[19] but the second, concerning investment advisers, did not. After the introduction of S.3580, a Senate Subcommittee held lengthy hearings at which numerous statements concerning investment advisers were received.[20] One witness distinguishing the investment-counsel profession from investment firms and businesses, explained:

> *"It is a personal-service profession and depends for its success upon a close personal and confidential relationship between the investment-counsel firm and its*

---

[18] *SEC v. Capital Gains Research Bureau, Inc., supra.*

[19] S.3580 contained the following definition of "investment adviser":

" 'Investment adviser' means any person who, for compensation, engages in the business of advising others, either directly or through publications or writings, as to the value of securities or as to the advisability of investing in, purchasing or selling securities, or who, for compensation and as part of a regular business, issues or promulgates analyses or reports concerning securities; but does not include (A) a bank; (B) any lawyer, accountant, engineer, or teacher whose performance of such services is solely incidental to the practice of his profession; (C) the publisher of any bona fide newspaper or newsmagazine of general circulation; or (D) such other persons, not within the intent of this paragraph, as the Commission may designate by rules and regulations or order." Hearings on S.3580 before the Subcommittee on Securities and Exchange of the Senate Committee on Banking and Currency, 76th Cong., 3d Sess. (1940) (Senate Hearings).

It is noteworthy that the exclusion for publishers in clause (C) in S.3580 is not as broad as the exclusion in the final draft of the Act. See n.24, *infra*.

[20] Douglas T. Johnston, Vice President of the Investment Counsel Association of America, stated in part:

"The definition of 'investment adviser' as given in the bill, in spite of certain exclusions, is quite broad and covers a number of services which are entirely different in their scope and in their methods of operation. For example, as we read the definition, among others, it would include those companies which publish manuals of securities such as Moody's, Poor's, and so forth; it would include those companies issuing weekly investment letters such as Babson's, United Business Service, Standard Statistics, and so forth; it would include those tipsters who through newspaper advertisements offer to send, for a nominal price, a list of stocks that are sure to go up; it would include certain investment banking and brokerage houses which maintain investment advisory departments and make charges for services rendered; and finally it would include those firms which operate on a professional basis and which have come to be recognized as investment counsel.

"Just why it is thought to be in the public interest at this time to require all the above services to register with, and be regulated by, the Federal Government we do not know.

"I have mentioned certain important exceptions or exclusions in the definition of 'investment advisers'; one of the principal of these is lawyers. Probably in the aggregate more investment advice is given by lawyers than by all other advisers combined. I only want to point out that in so acting they are not functioning strictly as lawyers. So far as I know, no courses on investments are part of a law school curriculum, nor in passing bar examinations does a lawyer have to pass a test on investment." Senate Hearings.

client. It requires frequent and personal contact of a professional nature between us and our clients. * * * *

"*We must establish with each client a relationship of trust and confidence designed to last over a period of time because economic forces work themselves out slowly.* Business and investment cycles last for years and our investment plans have to be similarly long-range. No investment counsel firm could long remain in business or be of real benefit to clients except through such long-term associations. * * * *

".... Judgment of the client's circumstances and of the soundness of his financial objectives and of the risks he may assume. Judgment is the root and branch of the decisions to recommend changes in a client's security holdings. If the investment counsel profession, as we have described it, could not offer this kind of judgment with its supporting experience and information, it would not have anything to sell that could not be bought in almost any bookstore....

"Furthermore, our clients are not unsophisticated in financial matters. They are resourceful men and women of means who are very critical in their examination of our performance. If they disapprove of our activities, they cancel their contracts with us, which eliminates our only source of income. * * * *

"We are quite clearly not 'hit and run' tipsters, nor do we deal with our clients at arms' length through the advertising columns of the newspapers or the mails; in fact, we regard it as a major defeat if we are unable to have frequent personal contact with a client and with his associates and dependents. We do not publish for general distribution a statistical service or compendium of general economic observations or financial recommendations. To use a hackneyed phrase, our business is 'tailor-made.' "[21]

David Schenker, Chief Counsel of the Commission's Investment Trust Study, summarized the extent of the proposed legislation: "If you have been convicted of a crime, you cannot be an investment counselor and you cannot use the mails to perpetrate a fraud," Senate Hearings 996. Schenker provided the Subcommittee with a significant report[22] prepared by the Research Department of the Illinois Legislative Council.

---

[21] *Id.* (testimony of Charles M. O'Hearn); [additional testimony quotations omitted].

[22] It should be noted that the Illinois report was submitted by Schenker on April 26, 1940, more than three weeks after the statement quoted by JUSTICE WHITE, post, at 219. Contrary to JUSTICE WHITE's suggestion, there is nothing in the legislative history to indicate that Congress rejected the report's proposed distinction between

Referring to possible regulation of investment counselors in the State of Illinois, the report stated in part:

"Regulatory statutes concerning investment counselors appear to exempt from their provisions those who furnish advice without remuneration or valuable consideration, apparently because it is thought impracticable to regulate such gratuitous services. Newspapers and journals generally also seem to be excluded although this is not explicitly stated in the statutes, the exemption apparently being based on general constitutional and legal principles. * * * *

"*A particular problem in defining the application of a law regulating investment counselors arises from the existence of individuals and firms who furnish investment advice solely by means of publications. Insofar as such individuals and firms also render specialized advice to individual clients, they might be subject to any regulatory measure that may be adopted.* The question arises, however, as to whether or not services which give the same general advice to all their clients, by means of some circular or other publication, are actually engaged in a type of investment counseling as to which regulation is feasible. * * * *

"These investment services which function through publications sent to their subscribers, rather than through individualized advice, would present several difficulties not found in regulating investment counselors generally. In the first place, the large number of agencies publishing investment facts and interpretations is well known, and a very large administrative staff would be required to enforce detailed registration. Secondly, such information is supplied both by newspapers and by specialized financial journals and services. *The accepted rights of freedom of the press and due process of law might prevent any general regulation and perhaps also supervision over particular types of publications, even if the advertisements of these publications occasionally quite exaggerate the value of the factual information which is supplied. That the constitutional guarantee of liberty of the press is applicable to publications of all types, and not only to newspapers, has been clearly indicated by the United States Supreme Court* [citing *Lovell v. City of Griffin*, 303 U.S. 444 (1938)]. * * * *

"To the problem of formulating reasonable and practicable regulations for the

---

advice distributed solely "to a list of subscribers" and advice to "clients." It is undisputed that Congress broadened the scope of the "bona fide publications" exclusion after the Commission submitted the Illinois report. See n.19, *supra*, and n.24, *infra*.

factual services must, accordingly, be added the legal and constitutional difficulties inherent in the attempted regulation of any individual or organization functioning primarily by means of published circulars and volumes. However, liberty of the press is not an absolute right, and some types of regulation may be both constitutional and feasible, assuming that regulation of some sort is thought desirable. Such regulation could probably not legally take the form of licensing publications or prohibiting certain types of publications. Regulation of the publishing of investment advice in order to conform with constitutional requirements, would probably have to be confined to punishing, by civil or criminal penalties, those who perpetrate or attempt to perpetrate frauds or other specific acts declared to be contrary to law. * * * *

"*It may be thought desirable specifically to exclude from regulation the publishers of generalized investment information, along with those who furnish economic advice generally. This may be done by carefully defining the term 'investment counselor' so as to exclude 'any person or organization which engages in the business of furnishing investment analysis, opinion, or advice solely through publications distributed to a list of subscribers and not furnishing specific advice to any client with respect to securities, and also persons or organizations furnishing only economic advice and not advice relating to the purchase or sale of securities.'*"

After the Senate Subcommittee hearings on S.3580, and after meetings attended by representatives of investment-adviser firms, a voluntary association of investment advisers, and the Commission, a revised bill, S.4108, was reported by the Senate Committee on Banking and Currency. In the Report accompanying the revised bill, the Committee on Banking and Currency wrote:

"Not only must the public be protected from the frauds and misrepresentations of unscrupulous tipsters and touts, but the bona fide investment adviser must be safeguarded against the stigma of the activities of these individuals. Virtually no limitations or restrictions exist with respect to the honesty and integrity of individuals who may solicit funds to be controlled, managed, and supervised. Persons who may have been convicted or enjoined by courts because of perpetration of securities fraud are able to assume the role of investment advisers. * * * *

"*Title II recognizes that with respect to a certain class of investment advisers, a type of personalized relationship may exist with their clients. As a consequence, this relationship is a factor which should be considered in connection with the enforcement by the Commission of the provisions of this bill.*"[23]

S.4108 was introduced before the House of Representatives as H.R. 10065.[24] After additional hearings,[25] the Committee on Interstate and Foreign Commerce wrote in its Report accompanying the bill:

> "The essential purpose of Title II of this bill is to protect the public from the frauds and misrepresentations of unscrupulous tipsters and touts and to safeguard the honest investment adviser against the stigma of the activities of these individuals by making fraudulent practices by investment advisers unlawful. *The title also recognizes the personalized character of the services of investment advisers and especial care has been taken in the drafting of the bill to respect this relationship between investment*

---

[23] S. Rep. No. 1775, 76th Cong., 3d Sess., 21-22 (1940).

[24] Hearings on H.R. 10065 before a Subcommittee of the House Committee on Interstate and Foreign Commerce, 76th Cong., 3d Sess. (1940). The bill contained two definitions of "investment adviser," one in Title I (investment companies) and the other in Title II (investment advisers). The latter definition read, in part:

> " 'Investment adviser' means any person who, for compensation, engages in the business of advising others, either directly or through publications or writings, as to the value of securities or as to the advisability of investing in, purchasing, or selling securities, or who, for compensation and as part of a regular business, issues or promulgates analyses or reports concerning securities; but does not include ... (D) the publisher of any bona fide newspaper, news magazine or business or financial publication of general and regular circulation...."

Whereas the exclusion for publishers in clause (C) of the exclusion in S.3580 only mentioned newspapers of general circulation, the exclusion in clause (D) of H.R. 10065 includes newspapers "of general and regular circulation" and also encompasses "business or financial" publications. See n.19, *supra*.

[25] Hearings on H.R. 10065 before a Subcommittee of the House Committee on Interstate and Foreign Commerce, 76th Cong., 3d Sess. (1940). During the hearings, testimony about the personal nature of the investment-counseling profession was again emphasized:

"When the hearings were held on this bill before the Senate committee the association opposed it. We opposed it for three general reasons: First, in the original bill there was a confusion between investment counsel and investment trusts. We felt that the personal confidential relationship existing between investment counsel and his client was so very different from the commodity of investment trust shares which investment trusts were engaged in selling, that any legislation to regulate these two different activities should be incorporated in separate acts. In the bill we felt that our clients were not properly protected in their confidential relationship. * * * * Following the hearings before the Senate subcommittee, we had conferences with the Securities and Exchange Commission, and all of our objections have been satisfactorily adjusted. * * * * The Investment Counsel Association of America unqualifiedly endorses the present bill." (statement of Dwight Rose, representing Investment Counsel Association of America, New York, NY).

advisers and their clients."[26]

The definition of "investment adviser" included in Title II when the Act was passed, 54 Stat. 848-849, is in all relevant respects identical to the definition before the Court today.

III.

The basic definition of an "investment adviser" in the Act reads as follows:

> " 'Investment adviser' means any person who, for compensation, engages in the business of advising others, either directly or through publications or writings, as to the value of securities or as to the advisability of investing in, purchasing, or selling securities, or who, for compensation and as part of a regular business, issues or promulgates analyses or reports concerning securities...."[27]

Petitioners' newsletters are distributed "for compensation and as part of a regular business" and they contain "analyses or reports concerning securities." Thus, on its face, the basic definition applies to petitioners. The definition, however, is far from absolute. The Act excludes several categories of persons from its definition of an investment adviser, lists certain investment advisers who need not be registered, and also authorizes the Commission to exclude "such other person" as it may designate by rule or order.[28]

One of the statutory exclusions is for "the publisher of any bona fide newspaper, news magazine or business or financial publication of general and regular circulation."[29]

---

[26] H.R. Rep. No. 2639, 76th Cong., 3d Sess. (1940). The terms "investment counsel," "investment counselor," and "investment adviser" were used interchangeably throughout the legislative history. That the terms were understood to share a common definition is best demonstrated by the testimony of the Commission's David Schenker. While describing the Commission's initial report to Congress, he stated that "we learned of the existence of 394 investment counselors." Senate Hearings 48. On the very next page of the hearings, he stated that "we learned of the existence of 394 investment advisers." *Id.*, at 49. JUSTICE WHITE, however, *post*, at 221-223, n.7, correctly observes that the statutory definition of an "adviser" encompasses persons who would not qualify as investment counsel because they are not primarily engaged in the business of rendering "***continuous*** advice as to the investment of funds...." 15 USC § 80b-2(a)(13) (emphasis added). But it does not follow, as JUSTICE WHITE seems to assume, that the term "investment adviser" includes persons who have no personal relationship at all with their customers. The repeated use of the term "client" in the statute, see n.34, *infra*, contradicts the suggestion that a person who is merely a publisher of nonfraudulent information in a regularly scheduled periodical of general circulation has the kind of fiduciary relationship the Act was designed to regulate.

[27] 15 USC § 80b-2(a)(11).

[28] § § 80b-2(a)(11)(F), 80b-3(b), 80b-6a.

[29] § 80b-2(a)(11)(D).

Although neither the text of the Act nor its legislative history defines the precise scope of this exclusion, two points seem tolerably clear. Congress did not intend to exclude publications that are distributed by investment advisers as a normal part of the business of servicing their clients. The legislative history plainly demonstrates that Congress was primarily interested in regulating the business of rendering personalized investment advice, including publishing activities that are a normal incident thereto. On the other hand, Congress, plainly sensitive to First Amendment concerns, wanted to make clear that it did not seek to regulate the press through the licensing of nonpersonalized publishing activities.

Congress was undoubtedly aware of two major First Amendment cases that this Court decided before the enactment of the Act. The first, *Near v. Minnesota ex rel. Olson*, 283 U.S. 697 (1931), established that "liberty of the press, and of speech, is within the liberty safeguarded by the due process clause of the Fourteenth Amendment from invasion by state action." In *Near*, the Court emphatically stated that the "chief purpose" of the press guarantee was "to prevent previous restraints upon publication," and held that the Minnesota nuisance statute at issue in that case was unconstitutional because it authorized a prior restraint on publication.

Almost seven years later, the Court decided *Lovell v. City of Griffin*, 303 U.S. 444 (1938), a case that was expressly noted by the Commission during the Senate Subcommittee hearings. In striking down an ordinance prohibiting the distribution of literature within the city without a permit, the Court wrote:

> "We think that the ordinance is invalid on its face. Whatever the motive which induced its adoption, its character is such that it strikes at the very foundation of the freedom of the press by subjecting it to license and censorship. The struggle for the freedom of the press was primarily directed against the power of the licensor. It was against that power that John Milton directed his assault by his 'Appeal for the Liberty of Unlicensed Printing.' And the liberty of the press became initially a right to publish '*without* a license what formerly could be published only *with* one.' While this freedom from previous restraint upon publication cannot be regarded as exhausting the guaranty of liberty, the prevention of that restraint was a leading purpose in the adoption of the constitutional provision. . . .
>
> "The liberty of the press is not confined to newspapers and periodicals. It necessarily embraces pamphlets and leaflets. These indeed have been historic

weapons in the defense of liberty, as the pamphlets of Thomas Paine and others in our own history abundantly attest. The press in its historic connotation comprehends every sort of publication which affords a vehicle of information and opinion. What we have had recent occasion to say with respect to the vital importance of protecting this essential liberty from every sort of infringement need not be repeated. *Near v. Minnesota....*"

The reasoning of *Lovell*, particularly since the case was cited in the legislative history, supports a broad reading of the exclusion for publishers.[30]

The exclusion itself uses extremely broad language that encompasses any newspaper, business publication, or financial publication provided that two conditions are met. The publication must be "bona fide," and it must be "of regular and general circulation." Neither of these conditions is defined, but the two qualifications precisely differentiate "hit and run tipsters" and "touts" from genuine publishers. Presumably a "bona fide" publication would be genuine in the sense that it would contain disinterested commentary and analysis as opposed to promotional material disseminated by a "tout." Moreover, publications with a "general and regular" circulation would not include "people who send out bulletins from time to time on the advisability of buying and selling stocks," see Hearings on H.R.10065, or "hit and run tipsters."[31] Because the content of petitioners' newsletters was completely disinterested, and because they were offered to the general public on a regular schedule, they are described by the plain language of the exclusion.

The Court of Appeals relied on its opinion in *SEC v. Wall Street Transcript Corp.*, 422 F.2d 1371 (CA2), *cert. denied*, 398 U.S. 958 (1970), to hold that petitioners were not bona

---

30 "It is always appropriate to assume that our elected representatives, like other citizens, know the law." *Cannon v. University of Chicago*, 441 U.S. 677 (1979). Moreover, "[in] areas where legislation might intrude on constitutional guarantees, we believe that Congress, which has always sworn to protect the Constitution, would err on the side of fundamental constitutional liberties when its legislation implicates those liberties." *Regan v. Time, Inc.*, 468 U.S. 641 (1984) (STEVENS, J., concurring in part and dissenting in part).

31 The term "tipsters" is explained in the testimony of Douglas T. Johnston, n.20, *supra*—persons "who through newspaper advertisements offer to send, for a nominal price, a list of stocks that are sure to go up." JUSTICE WHITE is unable "to imagine" any workable definition of the exclusion "that does not sweep in all publications that are not personally tailored to individual clients," post, at 216. The definition Congress actually wrote, however, does not sweep in bulletins that are issued from time to time in response to episodic market activity, advertisements that "tout" particular issues, advertised lists of stocks "that are sure to go up" that are sold to individual purchasers, or publications distributed as an incident to personalized investment service.

fide newspapers and thus not exempt from the Act's registration requirement. In *Wall Street Transcript*, the majority held that the "phrase 'bona fide' newspapers ... means those publications which do not deviate from customary newspaper activities to such an extent that there is a likelihood that the wrongdoing which the Act was designed to prevent has occurred." It reasoned that whether "a given publication fits within this exclusion must depend upon the nature of its practices rather than upon the purely formal 'indicia of a newspaper' which it exhibits on its face and in the size and nature of its subscription list." The court expressed its concern that an investment adviser "might choose to present [information to clients] in the guise of traditional newspaper format." The Commission, citing *Wall Street Transcript*, has interpreted the exclusion to apply "only where, based on the content, advertising material, readership and other relevant factors, a publication is not primarily a vehicle for distributing investment advice."[32]

These various formulations recast the statutory language without capturing the central thrust of the legislative history, and without even mentioning the apparent intent of Congress to keep the Act free of constitutional infirmities.[33] The Act was designed to apply to those persons engaged in the investment-advisory profession—those who provide personalized advice attuned to a client's concerns, whether by written or verbal communication.[34] The mere fact that a publication contains advice and comment about

---

[32] IA-563, 42 FR 2953, n.1 (1977) (codified at 17 CFR § 276 (1984)). The Commission's reformulation of the definition of the exclusion was not drafted until 1977—37 years after the passage of the Act—and therefore is not entitled to the deference due a contemporaneous construction of the Act. *SEC v. Sloan*, 436 U.S. 103 (1978). JUSTICE WHITE attaches significance to the fact that in the first year of the Act's operation, 165 publishers of investment advisory services registered under the Act. *Post*, at 215. The fact that those firms deemed it advantageous to register does not demonstrate that the statute required them to do so.

[33] The Commission's focus on the content of the publication to determine whether a publisher is within the exclusion represents a dramatic departure from the objective criteria in the statute itself. As far as content is concerned, the statutory exclusion broadly encompasses every "business or financial publication" but then limits the category by a requirement that it be "bona fide," and a further requirement that it be "of general and regular circulation." JUSTICE WHITE makes no attempt to explain the meaning of either of these requirements, *post*, at 215-216, but, instead, merely emphasizes the breadth of the basic definition of an investment adviser, *post*, at 216-219, which admittedly is broad enough to encompass publishers. However, the basic definition must be read together with the exclusion in order to locate the place where Congress drew the line; in other words, we must give effect to every word that Congress used in the statute.

[34] It is significant that the Act repeatedly refers to "clients," not "subscribers." See, *e.g.*, 15 USC § § 80b-1(1), 80b-3(b)(1), 80b-3(b)(2), 80b-3(b)(3), 80b-3(c)(1)(E), 80b-6(1), 80b-6(2), 80b-6(3).

specific securities does not give it the personalized character that identifies a professional investment adviser. Thus, petitioners' publications do not fit within the central purpose of the Act because they do not offer individualized advice attuned to any specific portfolio or to any client's particular needs. On the contrary, they circulate for sale to the public at large in a free, open market—a public forum in which typically anyone may express his views.

The language of the exclusion, read literally, seems to describe petitioners' newsletters. Petitioners are "publishers of any bona fide newspaper, news magazine or business or financial publication." The only modifier that might arguably disqualify the newsletters are the words "bona fide." Notably, however, those words describe the publication rather than the character of the publisher; hence Lowe's unsavory history does not prevent his newsletters from being "bona fide." In light of the legislative history, this phrase translates best to "genuine"; petitioners' publications meet this definition: they are published by those engaged solely in the publishing business and are not personal communications masquerading in the clothing of newspapers, news magazines, or financial publications. Moreover, there is no suggestion that they contained any false or misleading information, or that they were designed to tout any security in which petitioners had an interest. Further, petitioners' publications are "of general and regular circulation."[35] Although the publications have not been "regular" in the sense of consistent circulation, the publications have been "regular" in the sense important to the securities market: there is no indication that they have been timed to specific market activity, or to events affecting or having the ability to affect the securities industry.[36]

---

35 JUSTICE WHITE relies on the testimony of witness James White to support his interpretation of the legislative history. *Post*, at 219-220. However, significantly, White stated that the term "investment adviser" includes "people who send out bulletins from time to time on the advisability of buying or selling stocks." Such people would not fit within the exclusion for bona fide publications of regular and general circulation. Tipsters who send out bulletins from time to time on the advisability of buying or selling stocks presumably would not satisfy the requirement of "general and regular circulation" and would fall within the basic definition of investment adviser. Thus, we do not agree with JUSTICE WHITE's assumption that petitioners should be equated with distributors of "tout sheets," *post*, at 217, n.3. Additionally, it is extremely doubtful that any "tipsheet" or "tout sheet" could be a "bona fide," *i.e.*, genuine, publication so as to claim the benefits of the exclusion.

36 Without actually determining how the exception is "supposed to mesh" with the basic definition, *post*, at 215, and without any consideration of the "general and regular" publication requirement, JUSTICE WHITE would adopt an extremely narrow, content-based, interpretation of the exclusion in order to preserve the Commission's ability to deal with the practice of "scalping," *post*, at 224. That practice is, of course, most dangerous when engaged in

The dangers of fraud, deception, or overreaching that motivated the enactment of the statute are present in personalized communications but are not replicated in publications that are advertised and sold in an open market.[37] To the extent that the chart service contains factual information about past transactions and market trends, and the newsletters contain commentary on general market conditions, there can be no doubt about the protected character of the communications,[38] a matter that concerned Congress when the exclusion was drafted. The content of the publications and the audience to which they are directed in this case reveal the specific limits of the exclusion. As long as the communications between petitioners and their subscribers remain entirely impersonal and do not develop into the kind of fiduciary, person-to-person relationships that were discussed at length in the legislative history of the Act and that are characteristic of investment adviser-client relationships, we believe the publications are, at least presumptively, within the exclusion and thus not subject to registration under the Act.[39]

We therefore conclude that petitioners' publications fall within the statutory exclusion for bona fide publications and that none of the petitioners is an "investment adviser" as defined in the Act. It follows that neither their unregistered status, nor the Commission order barring Lowe from associating with an investment adviser, provides a justification for restraining the future publication of their newsletters. It also follows that we need not specifically address the constitutional question we granted certiorari to decide.

---

by a publication with a large circulation—perhaps by a columnist in an admittedly exempt publication. Cf. *Zweig v. Hearst Corp.*, 594 F.2d 1261 (CA9 1979). Moreover, it is incorrect to assume that the only remedies against scalping are found in the Act. The mail-fraud statute would certainly be available for many violations, and the SEC has recently had success using Rule § 10b-5 against a newsletter publisher. See *SEC v. Blavin*, 557 F. Supp. 1304 (ED Mich. 1983), *aff'd*, 760 F.2d 706 (CA6 1985).

[37] Cf. *Ohralik v. Ohio State Bar Assn.*, 436 U.S. 447 (1978). It is significant that the Commission has not established that petitioners have had authority over the funds of subscribers; that petitioners have been delegated decisionmaking authority to handle subscribers' portfolios or accounts; or that there have been individualized, investment-related interactions between petitioners and subscribers.

[38] Moreover, because we have squarely held that the expression of opinion about a commercial product such as a loudspeaker is protected by the First Amendment, *Bose Corp. v. Consumers Union of U.S., Inc.*, 466 U.S. 485 (1984), it is difficult to see why the expression of an opinion about a marketable security should not also be protected.

[39] The Commission suggests that an investment adviser may regularly provide, in newsletter form, advice to several clients based on recent developments, without tailoring the advice to each client's individual needs, and that this is the practice of investment advising. Brief for Respondent. However, the Commission does not suggest that this "practice" is involved here; thus, we have no occasion to address this concern.

The judgment of the Court of Appeals is reversed.

It is so ordered.

Datastream Int'l, Inc.

IA Act § 202(a)(11), SEC No-Action Letter (March 15, 1993)

Response of the Office of Chief Counsel
Division of Investment Management
Ref. No. 93-33-CC: Datastream International, Inc. & Datastream International Limited

Your letters of January 18, 1993 and March 12, 1993, request our assurance that we would not recommend enforcement action to the Commission if each of the above-captioned registrants (collectively, "**Datastream**") withdraws its registration as an investment adviser under the Investment Advisers Act of 1940.

You state that Datastream provides economic and financial information services to the securities and financial industries worldwide through a series of linked databases. Datastream's customers, principally investment managers and institutional investors, pay fixed subscription fees quarterly in advance, based on the specific on-line services they receive. Datastream also provides to subscribers software packages that contain analytic tools that enable customers to retrieve data series from the databases and manipulate the data to produce graphics, statistics, time series analysis, and other analyses. Customers can use the analytic tools to perform various calculations ranging from simple arithmetic to complex algebraic equations.

Section 202(a)(11) of the Advisers Act defines an "investment adviser" as any person who, for compensation, engages in the business of advising others, either directly or through publications or writings, as to the value of securities, or who, for compensation and as part of a regular business, issues or promulgates analyses or reports concerning securities. The staff takes the position that the presentation of securities data or information to subscribers does not constitute furnishing investment advice or an analysis or report within the meaning of § 202(a)(11) if: (1) the information is readily available to the public in its raw state, (2) the categories of information presented are not highly selective, and (3) the information is not organized or presented in a manner which suggests the purchase, holding, or sale of any security or securities. [citations to SEC no-action letters omitted].

You state that the information in Datastream's databases is readily available in its raw state. Datastream collects the information from wire services, international agencies, government departments, stock, options and futures exchanges, brokers, dealers, banks, issuers, and other information vendors. An institutional investor or a money manager, theoretically, could contract with each of Datastream's sources to obtain the information in Datastream's databases. You state, however, that the proliferation of economic and financial data now relevant to investment decisions has made it impracticable, if not impossible, for investment decision-makers to access sufficient raw data directly.

You also state that the categories of information made available to Datastream's subscribers are not highly selective. Datastream collects over 720 million data items, including approximately 2,000 market indices from 20 different countries, 850 international interest rates, and 1,600 international end-of-day currency exchange rates. In addition, Datastream includes data relating to 30,000 stocks and 44,000 bond issues in its databases. Datastream's objective is to furnish subscribers with a database that is as comprehensive as possible, and there is no restriction on the data that is collected and made available to the subscribers.

In addition, you state that the information in the databases and the software packages is not organized or presented in a manner which suggests the purchase, holding, or sale of any security or securities. Datastream's customers select the criteria for retrieving data series from the databases and the analytic tools that will be used to manipulate that data, and data delivery is not timed to any specific market activity. Datastream and its affiliates have no direct or indirect financial interest in whether a subscriber uses Datastream data and analytic tools to purchase, sell, or hold a particular security.

In addition to providing no-action assurance as previously discussed, the staff has given no-action assurance to providers of various computer software services offering calculations and pricing models. In not requiring these providers to register as investment advisers, the staff considered a number of factors, including the sophistication of the users, the degree to which the users themselves perform the calculations, the degree to which the product is pre-packaged and not personalized for each customer, and whether the calculations or models are based on traditional or standard calculations. [citations to SEC no-action letters omitted]. These factors are relevant in determining whether computer software services function merely as mathematical tools to facilitate a user's own analytical efforts or whether they involve the recommendation of securities. You state that the analytic tools, in some cases, are standardized mathematical formulae that are already in the public domain; in other cases, the tools are considered proprietary products or intellectual property protected by patent or copyright. You represent that

Datastream does not attach any value judgment to its data. You further represent that Datastream's software is licensed as a package and is not tailored to the personal interests of any user. Datastream's subscribers are sophisticated users who may arrange the various elements in a package to suit their particular needs.

In addition, you state that **Nomura Securities Co. Ltd.** ("Nomura"), a Japanese brokerage firm, has contracted with Datastream to make Nomura-generated data available exclusively to Nomura brokerage customers who are also Datastream subscribers at no extra cost.[1] Datastream has a similar arrangement with **Hoare Govette**, a British brokerage firm, which has contracted with Datastream to make Hoare Govette-generated data available exclusively to other Hoare Govette brokerage customers in the form of a hard-copy quarterly book published by Datastream. Datastream has no control over the Nomura-and Hoare Govette-generated data.[2] You represent that Datastream will act merely as a passive communications conduit between these brokerage firms and their customers.[3]

On the basis of the facts and representations in your letters, and without necessarily agreeing with your legal analysis, we would not recommend enforcement action to the Commission if Datastream withdraws its registration as an investment adviser. Because our position is based on the facts and representations in your letters, you should note that different facts or representations may require a different conclusion. Further, this response expresses the Division's position on enforcement action only and does not purport to express any legal conclusions on the issues presented.

---

1 You represent that Datastream's U.S. subscribers cannot access the Nomura-generated data through Datastream's technical facilities and, therefore, Nomura's use of Datastream's services to provide investment advice to some of Datastream's non-U.S. subscribers does not subject Nomura to regulation under the Advisers Act.

2 You represent that ABN-AMRO Securities (USA), Inc., a registered investment adviser, issues this book in the United States through its Hoare Govette division.

3 See *EJV Partners, L.P.; UniVu System* (Dec. 7, 1992) (customers transmit their own proprietary products, such as financial models, research reports, information on bond indexes, and securities information directed at dealers, to other customers through the UniVu's Private Pages service). Cf. *Reuters Information Services, Inc.* (Jan. 17, 1991) (video information network marketed to institutional investors featuring presentations by financial services firms).

In *re* JPMorgan Chase Bank, N.A. and J.P. Morgan Securities LLC, Respondents

Adm. Proc. 3-17008, 33-9992, 34-76694, IA-4295 (Dec. 18, 2015)

I.

The Securities and Exchange Commission deems it appropriate and in the public interest that public administrative and cease-and-desist proceedings be, and hereby are, instituted pursuant to § 8A of the Securities Act of 1933, § 15(b) of the Securities Exchange Act of 1934, and § § 203(e) and 203(k) of the Investment Advisers Act of 1940 against **JPMorgan Chase Bank, N.A.** and **J.P. Morgan Securities LLC** (together, **Respondents**).

II.

In anticipation of the institution of these proceedings, Respondents have submitted *Offers of Settlement* ("*Offers*") which the Commission has determined to accept. Respondents admit the facts set forth in § III.B below, acknowledge that the conduct set forth in § III.B violated the federal securities laws, admit the Commission's jurisdiction over them and the subject matter of these proceedings, and consent to the entry of this *Order Instituting Administrative and Cease-and-Desist Proceedings, Pursuant to § 8A of the Securities Act of 1933, § 15(b) of the Securities Exchange Act of 1934, and § § 203(e) and 203(k) of the Investment Advisers Act of 1940, Making Findings, and Imposing Remedial Sanctions and a Cease-and-Desist Order* ("*Order*"), as set forth below.

III.

On the basis of this Order and Respondents' Offers, the Commission finds that:

A. Summary

1. This matter concerns the negligent failure of **JPMorgan Chase & Co.'s** wealth management businesses, **JPMorgan Chase Bank, N.A.** and **J.P. Morgan Securities LLC**, to disclose conflicts of interest arising from, as applicable, preferences for (i) JPMorgan-managed mutual funds ("*Proprietary Mutual Funds*"), (ii) JPMorgan-managed private hedge funds ("*Proprietary Hedge Funds*," and, together with Proprietary Mutual Funds, "*Proprietary Funds*"), and (iii) third-party-managed private hedge funds that shared client fees with a JPMCB affiliate. * * * *

Respondents

4. **JPMorgan Chase Bank, N.A. (JPMCB)**, a wholly-owned subsidiary of JPMorgan, is a nationally-chartered bank, incorporated in 1824, and headquartered in New York, New York. JPMCB acts as the investment manager for certain discretionary portfolios offered primarily to clients of the **JPM U.S. Private Bank**, the marketing name for JPMorgan's U.S. business unit that provides banking and investment services to high net worth and ultra-high net worth clients. JPMCB is not registered under the Advisers Act, as it is excluded from the definition of investment adviser pursuant to § 202(a)(11)(A) of the Advisers Act.

5. **J.P. Morgan Securities LLC (JPMS)**, a wholly-owned subsidiary of JPMorgan, is a Delaware company headquartered in New York, New York. JPMS has been registered with the Commission as an investment adviser since 1965 and as a broker-dealer since 1985. JPMS or its affiliates[1] have offered CSP through more than 2,800 financial advisors located in Chase bank branches nationwide from CSP's launch in 2008 to the present.

Other Relevant Entities and Lines of Business

6. **JPMorgan Chase & Co. (JPMorgan)** is a Delaware corporation headquartered in New York, New York. JPMorgan is a global financial services firm and bank with $2.6 trillion in assets as of December 31, 2014.

7. **JPMorgan Asset Management (JPMAM)** is one of JPMorgan's primary business units and oversees, among other businesses, JPM U.S. Private Bank and JPMorgan's Proprietary Funds business. As of December 31, 2014, JPMAM had $1.7 trillion in assets under management.

8. **J.P. Morgan's U.S. Private Bank (JPM U.S. Private Bank)** is the marketing name of a business unit within JPMAM that operates in the U.S. and provides banking and investment management services to high net worth and ultra-high net worth individuals through JPMCB. As of December 31, 2014, JPM U.S. Private Bank had approximately $207 billion in assets under management. (This excludes JPMorgan-managed funds purchased in self-directed brokerage accounts.) Hereinafter, reference to JPMCB will

---

[1] From CSP's inception in 2008 through September 2012, **Chase Investment Services Corp.** (*CISC*), an affiliate of JPMS that was registered as an investment adviser and broker-dealer from 1990 to 2012, offered and managed CSP. On October 1, 2012, CISC was merged into JPMS, and JPMS became the investment adviser for CSP.

encompass both JPMCB and JPM U.S. Private Bank.

B. Facts

9. As set out more fully below, during the relevant period, JPMS and JPMCB failed to adequately disclose certain conflicts of interest to their clients.

Chase Strategic Portfolio ("CSP")

10. In early 2007, **JPMS** and **JPMAM** (which, among other things, oversees JPMorgan's Proprietary Funds business), began developing CSP, a unified managed account program, for distribution to retail investors through JPMS-affiliated advisors located in Chase bank branches across the country. CSP's minimum account value has always been $50,000 and its current median account value is approximately $110,000.

11. As a unified managed account program, CSP comprised a set of standardized, risk-weighted portfolios of predominantly registered funds. JPMS (or, beginning in September 2013, an affiliate of JPMS engaged to serve as sub-adviser) selected the constituent holdings for each CSP portfolio and set the percentage of assets invested in each holding in the various CSP portfolios. For example, the entry-level "Conservative" portfolio in late 2009 held 12 mutual funds, seven of which were Proprietary Mutual Funds. JPMS allocated 57% of this portfolio's assets to Proprietary Mutual Funds.

JPMS Failed to Disclose That It Preferred to Invest CSP Assets in Proprietary Mutual Funds

12. JPMS and JPMAM designed CSP with an expectation that a majority of CSP's assets would be in Proprietary Mutual Funds, as well as JPMAM-managed money market funds and separately managed accounts (together with Proprietary Mutual Funds, "*Proprietary CSP Assets*"). JPMAM correspondingly would benefit from the management fees earned from these allocations.

13. From approximately June 2007 to March 2008, the fund research team servicing CSP conducted quantitative and qualitative due diligence. The team first applied a quantitative scoring methodology that awarded points to potential funds based on a series of analytical metrics. It next conducted a qualitative review which, among other things, included fund manager interviews and incorporated judgments about those managers' investment philosophies. As part of its review, the fund research team exercised a preference for Proprietary Mutual Funds.

14. JPMS launched CSP in May 2008 and, consistent with an expectation that a majority of CSP's assets would be in Proprietary CSP Assets, JPMS invested approximately 60% of CSP client assets in Proprietary CSP Assets. Since that time, JPMS has continuously operated CSP with a preference for Proprietary Mutual Funds.

15. From 2008 to 2013, CSP grew rapidly and by December 2013, JPMS had invested approximately $10 billion in Proprietary Mutual Funds out of a total of $32.6 billion of CSP client mutual fund assets. From early 2009 until early 2012, JPMS invested approximately 47% to 51% of CSP client mutual fund assets in Proprietary Mutual Funds. Thereafter, the percentage began to decrease, falling to 45% by mid-2012, to approximately 31% by year-end 2013 and 27% by year-end 2014.

16. From 2008 through August 5, 2013, neither CSP's Schedule H or its successor Form ADV Part 2A (collectively, "*CSP ADV*") nor CSP marketing materials disclosed that JPMS preferred Proprietary Mutual Funds. JPMS also failed to disclose that JPMS and JPMAM had designed CSP to feature Proprietary Mutual Funds, that JPMS had an expectation that it would invest a majority of CSP client assets in Proprietary CSP Assets at the beginning of the program, and that JPMAM had this expectation from the beginning of the program until early 2013.

***JPMS Failed to Disclose** That JPMAM Provided Discounted Services to CSP Based on the Amount of CSP Assets JPMS Invested in Proprietary CSP Assets*

17. JPMS contracted with an affiliate in JPMAM to provide various services to CSP, including "overlay services" (*i.e.*, trading and reporting services related to the management of CSP portfolios) and, later, asset allocation, portfolio construction, and tactical trading advice.

18. JPMAM tied both its willingness to provide services to JPMS and the pricing for those services to the amount of CSP's assets that JPMS invested in Proprietary CSP Assets. Between 2008 and 2013, JPMS failed to disclose that the discounted pricing of services provided to JPMS by a JPMAM affiliate was tied to the amount of CSP assets that JPMS invested in Proprietary CSP Assets. JPMS also did not disclose for a period of time that JPMAM's provision of services to CSP was tied to JPMS's investment of the majority of CSP assets in Proprietary CSP Assets.

***JPMS Failed to Disclose** the Availability of Lower Cost Share Classes*

19. When selecting mutual funds for CSP, JPMS typically negotiated with the funds'

advisers regarding, among other things, the share class into which it would invest CSP clients. Different share classes have different minimum investment amounts and fee structures, but otherwise reflect an identical interest in the funds. For example, institutional share classes usually require a minimum $1 million investment and have lower distribution and shareholder servicing fees than share classes available to retail investors. The difference in fees between institutional and retail share classes is typically 65 basis points or more.

20. JPMS's CSP ADV described the share classes available in the program as follows: "Fund shares sold in [CSP] are generally investor or institutional class shares, or no load or load-waived Class A shares that are sold at net asset value." CSP clients were informed in writing prior to account opening of the share class they would be receiving and the fees associated with that share class.

21. Certain of the Proprietary Mutual Funds used in CSP offered, in addition to retail share classes, two different institutional share classes: (a) a "Select" share class (with an investment minimum of $1 million) and (b) an "Institutional" share class (with an investment minimum of $3 million). For a majority of the Proprietary Mutual Funds used in CSP, the "Select" share class was the only institutional share class offered by the fund.

22. From 2008 to 2013, a minority of the Proprietary Mutual Funds used in CSP offered both Select and Institutional classes. In certain of these funds, JPMS invested CSP client assets in the Select share class even though the lower cost Institutional class was available. The Select share class typically had a shareholder servicing fee that was 15 basis points higher than the Institutional share class offered by those Proprietary Mutual Funds. As a result, JPMAM earned higher fees when JPMS invested CSP client assets in the Select share class. In November 2013, JPMS converted all CSP client investments in Select shares to Institutional shares where the Proprietary Mutual Funds offered Institutional shares.

23. Between 2008 and 2013, JPMS failed to disclose that certain of the Proprietary Mutual Funds purchased for CSP clients offered Institutional shares that were less expensive, and would generate less revenue for a JPMS affiliate, than the Select shares JPMS chose for CSP clients.

***JPMS's Forms ADV Failed to Adequately Disclose** Conflicts of Interest*

24. From May 2008 to February 2013, JPMS filed nine CSP ADVs with the

Commission.

25. JPMS's CSP ADVs described the quantitative and qualitative criteria used during the fund selection process. For example, the CSP ADV dated March 2011 stated: "Both affiliated and non-affiliated [Mutual] Funds ... are evaluated and monitored using the same criteria."

26. In its CSP ADV filings, JPMS disclosed certain conflicts of interest. For example, JPMS disclosed that an affiliate performed overlay services for CSP. Additionally, JPMS disclosed the conflict of interest arising from the use of Proprietary Mutual Funds. For example, the versions of the CSP Schedule H in effect in 2009 and 2010 provided that JPMS "may have a conflict of interest in including affiliated [Mutual] Funds ... because [JPMS] and/or its affiliates will receive additional compensation."

27. In addition, in advance of account opening, CSP clients were informed which funds were proposed for their CSP portfolio, and how much of the portfolio's assets were to be allocated to each Proprietary Mutual Fund and each third-party mutual fund. Once the account was open, CSP clients were informed of which funds were in their account and the amount of assets allocated to those funds through, for example, periodic account statements and client reviews. Marketing materials used with potential CSP clients also disclosed which funds were to comprise a portfolio and the amount of portfolio assets allocated to each fund.

28. However, in its CSP ADV filings, JPMS did not disclose that it had exercised a preference for Proprietary Mutual Funds in CSP. JPMS also failed to disclose that the discounted pricing of services provided to JPMS for CSP by a JPMAM affiliate was tied to the amount of CSP assets that JPMS invested in Proprietary CSP Assets. Finally, JPMS's CSP ADV filings did not disclose that, for certain of the Proprietary Mutual Funds in which it invested CSP clients, less expensive share classes were available.

29. On August 5, 2013, JPMS filed an amended CSP ADV that disclosed there "may" be a preference for Proprietary Mutual Funds in CSP. On December 31, 2013, JPMS further amended the CSP ADV to disclose that "[a]s a general matter, we prefer" Proprietary Mutual Funds.

***JPMS Failed to Implement** Written Policies and Procedures Reasonably Designed to Prevent Violations of the Advisers Act and the Rules Thereunder*

30. JPMS did not implement its written policies and procedures to ensure adequate

disclosure of the conflicts of interest discussed above. From 2008 to 2012, JPMS's written policies and procedures required that JPMS avoid any actual or potential conflict of interest and that any such conflict be disclosed to clients with discretionary managed accounts. On certain occasions, the disclosure concerning the use of Proprietary Mutual Funds in CSP was raised, and discussed among JPMS personnel, but was not adequately addressed. Policies and procedures were insufficiently implemented to ensure that (a) the disclosures relating to the above conflicts of interest were sufficiently reviewed and (b) the above conflicts of interest were adequately disclosed to CSP clients. As a result, JPMS did not implement written policies and procedures reasonably designed to prevent violations of the Advisers Act and the rules thereunder.

JPMorgan Chase Bank, N.A. (JPMCB)

31. JPMCB provides wealth management services to clients with three progressively higher levels of wealth: affluent, high net worth, and ultra-high net worth. Through **JPM U.S. Private Bank**, JPMCB serves high net worth and ultra-high net worth clients. JPMCB serves as the fiduciary investment manager for discretionary, diversified, risk-adjusted investment management accounts ("*IM accounts*") that can hold, among other investments, mutual funds and hedge funds.

32. JPMCB also serves as investment manager to certain private funds, known as the Global Access Portfolios ("*GAP*"), that offer to JPM U.S. Private Bank clients diversified portfolios comprised of, among other underlying investments, mutual funds and/or hedge funds. The GAP private funds may be held in an IM account ("*GAP IM Holdings*").

33. In 2007, JPMCB and JPMS jointly developed **J.P. Morgan Investment Portfolio** ("*JPMIP*"), a new managed account product to be marketed as part of a new banking and wealth management business called Chase Private Client. JPMIP was offered to affluent Chase banking clients. JPMIP accounts were identical to certain IM accounts, with investments in mutual funds, for example.

***JPMCB Failed to Disclose** Its Preference for Proprietary Funds*

34. JPMCB prefers Proprietary Funds in IM accounts, GAP private funds, and JPMIP and expects that a significant percentage of relevant portfolio assets will be invested in Proprietary Funds. For example, in early 2011, JPMCB had invested 47% of mutual fund assets and 35% of hedge fund assets in JPMCB IM client accounts in Proprietary Funds.

35. From December 2006 to February 2011, JPMCB disclosed its preference for

Proprietary Mutual Funds in what was entitled "JPMorgan general investment principles regarding the use of JPMorgan Funds and external managers" (the "*Investment Principles*"). The Investment Principles were distributed to relevant clients through various means including the incorporation of the Investment Principles into the JPMorgan Fund Disclosure Statement ("*FDS*"), a document provided to new IM account clients (including those with GAP IM Holdings), JPMIP clients, and to clients with existing accounts in an annual mailing. In January 2011, JPMCB mistakenly removed the Investment Principles (including language stating "we prefer to use JPMorgan-affiliated managers") from the FDS while amending the FDS for reasons unrelated to the language on a preference. By January 2011, the FDS was the sole means by which the Investment Principles were being affirmatively distributed to clients on a systematic basis. Therefore, from February 2011 until January 2014, JPMCB did not disclose a preference for Proprietary Mutual Funds in account documentation.

36. JPMCB disclosed that it had a conflict of interest when it invested its clients' discretionary portfolio assets in Proprietary Funds, as such investments increased revenue to affiliates. In addition, clients were informed of which funds were in their discretionary portfolios, as well as the amount of assets held in each Proprietary Fund and third-party fund through, for example, periodic account statements and client reviews. However, during the time period of February 2011 to January 2014, no account opening documents or marketing materials disclosed to IM account clients (including those with GAP IM Holdings) or JPMIP clients that JPMCB preferred to invest client assets in Proprietary Mutual Funds.

37. With respect to those portfolios that might be invested in private hedge funds, account opening documents disclosed JPMCB's conflict of interest when investing client assets in Proprietary Hedge Funds. However, from 2008 through January 2014, JPMCB did not disclose its preference for investing IM account or GAP IM Holding assets in Proprietary Hedge Funds.

38. Beginning in January 2014, language providing that "[a]s a general matter, we prefer" Proprietary Funds was incorporated into account opening documentation, the FDS, account statements, marketing materials and other documentation used with IM account clients (including those with GAP IM Holdings) and JPMIP clients.

JPMCB Failed to Disclose *Its Preference for Retrocession-Paying Third-Party Hedge Fund Managers*

39. For the IM accounts, GAP private funds, and JPMIP accounts, JPMCB uses the investment funds on what is known as the "Private Bank Platform." With respect to most of the private hedge funds on the Private Bank Platform, a broker-dealer affiliate of JPMCB acts as the placement agent and earns fees for placement, shareholder servicing and other ongoing services. These placement agent fees are typically referred to as "retrocessions" and are usually a portion of the private hedge fund managers' management and/or performance fees earned on relevant client assets. The standard retrocession that the broker-dealer affiliate of JPMCB receives from a third-party hedge fund is approximately 1.0% of the market value of relevant client assets invested, paid on an annual basis. Retrocessions are not additional fees paid by JPM U.S. Private Bank clients; rather, the retrocessions are paid by the hedge funds and/or their sponsors.

40. Beginning in at least 2005, JPMCB sought retrocessions from third-party private hedge fund managers under consideration for inclusion on the Private Bank Platform. During introductory meetings, the third-party hedge fund managers were typically asked about their willingness to pay retrocessions. If a manager declined to pay retrocessions, an alternative manager with a similar investment strategy that would pay retrocessions was typically sought. Currently all but one of the third-party-managed hedge funds on the Private Bank Platform and available for direct investment in IM accounts pay retrocessions to JPMCB affiliates.

41. JPMCB disclosed to its IM account clients (including those with GAP IM Holdings) that its affiliates may receive retrocessions in connection with investments in third-party hedge funds and informed some clients that retrocessions lowered client fees by reducing the clients' total costs to access the hedge funds on the Private Bank Platform. However, JPMCB did not disclose its preference for retrocession-paying third-party hedge fund managers in IM accounts and GAP IM Holdings until August 2015, when it added additional language to certain client documentation regarding the extent to which such funds are used in certain discretionary portfolios.

C. Remedial Actions

42. In determining to accept Respondents' Offers, the Commission considered remedial acts promptly undertaken by Respondents and cooperation afforded the Commission staff. Respondents retained an independent compliance consultant ("*ICC*") to review policies and procedures concerning disclosures of conflicts of interest; the ICC has completed its review and issued recommendations; and Respondents have accepted and

implemented the ICC's recommendations.

43. Respondents have agreed to provide notice of these proceedings to their JPMS and JPM U.S. Private Bank clients and prospective clients with CSP, JPMIP, and IM accounts (including IM accounts with GAP IM Holdings) ("*relevant client(s)*") as follows: * * * *

D. Violations

44. As a result of the conduct described above, **JPMS** willfully[2] violated § 206(2) of the Advisers Act, which prohibits an investment adviser from, directly or indirectly, engaging in any transaction, practice, or course of business which operates as a fraud or deceit upon any client or prospective client.

45. As a result of the conduct described above, **JPMS** willfully violated § 206(4) of the Advisers Act and Rule 206(4)-7 thereunder, which require investment advisers to adopt and implement written policies and procedures reasonably designed to prevent violation of the Advisers Act and its rules.

46. As a result of the conduct described above, **JPMS** willfully violated § 207 of the Advisers Act, which makes it "unlawful for any person willfully to make any untrue statement of a material fact in any registration application or report filed with the Commission ... or willfully to omit to state in any such application or report any material fact which is required to be stated therein."

47. As a result of the conduct described above, **JPMCB** willfully violated § § 17(a)(2) and 17(a)(3) of the Securities Act, which, respectively, prohibit making untrue statements of material fact or material omissions in the offer or sale of securities and engaging in a course of business which operates as a fraud or deceit in the offer or sale of securities.

IV.

In view of the foregoing, the Commission deems it appropriate and in the public interest to impose the sanctions agreed to in Respondents' Offers. Accordingly, pursuant

---

[2] A willful violation of the securities laws means merely " 'that the person charged with the duty knows what he is doing.' " *Wonsover v. SEC*, 205 F.3d 408, 414 (D.C. Cir. 2000) (quoting *Hughes v. SEC*, 174 F.2d 969, 977 (DC Cir. 1949)). There is no requirement that the actor " 'also be aware that he is violating one of the Rules or Acts.' " *Id.* (quoting *Gearhart & Otis, Inc. v. SEC*, 348 F.2d 798, 803 (DC Cir. 1965)). The actor may be found to have acted willfully even if, as here, the violations resulted from negligent conduct.

to § 8A of the Securities Act, § 15(b) of the Exchange Act, and § § 203(e) and 203(k) of the Advisers Act, it is hereby ORDERED that:

A. Respondent **JPMorgan Chase Bank, N.A.** cease and desist from committing or causing any violations and any future violations of § § 17(a)(2) and 17(a)(3) of the Securities Act.

B. Respondent **J.P. Morgan Securities LLC** cease and desist from committing or causing any violations and any future violations of § § 206(2), 206(4) and 207 of the Advisers Act and Rule 206(4)-7 promulgated thereunder.

C. Respondent **J.P. Morgan Securities LLC** is censured.

D. **Respondents, jointly and severally**, shall, within 14 days of the entry of this Order, pay *disgorgement*, which represents profits gained as a result of the conduct described herein of $127,500,000 and prejudgment interest of $11,815,000 to the Securities and Exchange Commission for transfer to the general fund of the United States Treasury in accordance with Exchange Act § 21F(g)(3). **Respondents, jointly and severally**, shall, within 14 days of the entry of this Order, pay a *civil money penalty* in the amount of $127,500,000 to the Securities and Exchange Commission for transfer to the general fund of the United States Treasury in accordance with Exchange Act § 21F(g)(3). *
* * *

Topic 2 Registration, Exemption, and Reporting Regime for Statutory Advisers

Laws & Rules Highlight:

IA Act ((15 USC 80b-1 *et seq.*) & Rules (17 CFR §§ 275.0-2 *et seq.*)
IC Act (15 USC 80a-1 *et seq.*) & Rules (17 CFR §§ 270.0-1 *et seq.*)

IA Act

- **Statutory Investment Advisers**
  - § 203(a) (*generally **prohibits** any investment adviser from using U.S. jurisdictional means in connection with its business as an IA, **unless** it is registered, or is exempted or excluded from the requirement to register, under the IA Act*)
    - ✓ § 202(a)(11) (*def. "investment adviser"*); § 203(c)(1) (*filing of registration application*)
  - § 204 Annual and Other Reports (*recordkeeping and reporting requirements of statutory IAs*)
    - ✓ Rule 204-1 Amendments to Form ADV; Rule 204-2 Books and Records to Be Maintained by Investment Advisers (*applicable to § 203 registered IAs*)
- **Exempt Advisers (AUM < $25 mm)**
  - § 203(b)(3) (*"**foreign private adviser**": registration exemption*)
    - ✓ § 202(a)(30) (*def. "foreign private adviser"—AUM from **U.S.** clients and investors **less than $25 mm***)
    - ✓ Rule 202(a)(30)-1 Foreign Private Advisers (*defines terms used in § 202(a)(30) statutory definition*)
  - § 204(a) (*IA "**specifically exempted**" from registration under **§ 203(b)** not subject to recordkeeping and reporting requirements of § 204*)
- **Exempt Reporting Advisers (AUM < $150 mm)**
  - § 203(l) Exemption of Venture Capital Fund Advisers (*IA **solely to venture capital funds**: registration exemption but subject to reporting; applicable equally to **U.S. and foreign advisers** to qualified VC funds*)
    - ✓ Rule 203(l)-1 Venture Capital Fund Defined
  - § 203(m) Exemption of and Reporting by Certain Private Fund Advisers (*IA **solely to small private funds**—AUM **in the U.S. less than $150 mm**: registration exemption but subject to reporting*)
    - ✓ § 202(a)(29) (*def. "**private fund**," referring to IC Act § 3(c)(1) fund & § 3(c)(7) fund*); ***cf.*** Rule 203(m)-1(d)(5) (*def. "**qualifying private fund**"*)
    - ✓ Rule 203(m)-1 Private Fund Adviser Exemption (*interprets and implements § 203(m); territorial application to foreign advisers*)

- ◆ Rule 204-4 Reporting by Exempt Reporting Advisers (***Form ADV*** *reporting requirement for § 203(l) venture capital fund advisers and § 203(m) small private fund advisers*)

- **Registered Advisers to Large-and Mid-Sized Private Funds (AUM ≥ $150 mm)**
  - ◆ § 204(b) Records and Reports of Private Funds; Rule 204(b)-1 Reporting by Investment Advisers to Private Funds (***Form PF*** *reporting requirements for registered advisers to large and mid-sized private funds*)
    - ✓ § 202(a)(29) (*def. "**private fund**," referring to IC Act § 3(c)(1) 100-person fund & § 3(c)(7) qualified purchaser fund*)
  - ◆ Form PF (*scaled reportings*):
    - ✓ Large Private Equity Adviser: AUM ≥ $2 bn
    - ✓ Large Hedge Fund Adviser: AUM ≥ $1.5 bn
    - ✓ Large Liquidity Fund Adviser: AUM ≥ $1 bn
    - ✓ Other Private Fund Adviser: AUM ≥ $150 mm

IC Act

- § 3(c)(1) (*exclusion from § 3(a) IC status: **privately offered** fund having **100 or fewer** beneficial owners*)
- § 3(c)(7) (*exclusion from § 3(a) IC status: **privately offered** fund owned **exclusively** by unlimited number of "**qualified purchasers**"*)
  - ◆ § 2(a)(51) (*def. "qualified purchaser"*)
- § 7 Transactions by Unregistered Investment Companies
  - ◆ § 7(a) (*prohibits **U.S. domestic IC** from making **any offering** of its securities in the U.S. unless it is registered under the IC Act*)
  - ◆ § 7(d) (*prohibits **foreign IC** from **public offering** of its securities in the U.S. unless it is permitted to register under the IC Act by SEC exemptive order*)

Research Note:[Biblio]

A Scaled Reporting Regime for Foreign Private Advisers; Venture Capital Fund Advisers; Large, Midsize, and Small Private Fund Advisers

Private Funds

Based on **legal classification**, the term "private fund" as defined by the Investment Advisers Act § 202(a)(29) refers to two types of pooled investment vehicles excluded from the definition of "investment company" under the Investment Company Act: a §

3(c)(1) "100-beneficial owner" private investment fund (the fund is held by *no more than* 100 beneficial owners and is not offered publicly); and a § 3(c)(7) "qualified purchaser" private investment fund (the fund is *exclusively* held by "qualified purchasers" and is not offered publicly). Based on **investment strategies**, private funds can be classified into private equity funds, and hedge funds.[1] Most of U.S. private equity funds and U.S. hedge funds and almost all foreign funds rely on IC Act §§ 3(c)(1) and 3(c)(7) private fund exclusions to avoid registration under the IC Act.[2 (§9:17)]

Venture Capital Fund: A Type of Private Equity Funds

"***Private equity***" generally refers to the following four forms of investment:[3 (§16, pp.535-537)]

- *Venture capital* (VC): It is an equity investment in *less mature nonpublic* companies, to fund the launch, early development, or expansion of a business. A VC fund pursues a portfolio of high-risk, high-reward investments, although a majority of VC's individual investments may fail.
- *Leveraged buyout* (LBO): It has the opposite profile from a VC fund: seeking to acquire *mature* businesses or taking a *public* company private, and leveraging its thin equity slice infusion with large amounts of debt by tapping into the high-yield bond market, as vehicles to produce an attractive medium-term return on its investment.
- *Mezzanine capital*: It typically provides small amounts of *subordinated debt* financing to *growth* companies: "mezzanine" meaning *between* equity and senior debt, and *between* the portfolio company's start-up phase and its becoming public phase.[2 (§13.4)]
- *Growth capital*: It is a *minority equity* investment in *mature* companies, without a change of control of the company.

"***Venture capital fund***" is defined by IA Act Rule 203(l)-1 to mean a private fund that, among other qualifications, pursues a venture capital strategy. Venture capital (**VC**) has five characteristics:[4 (§1.1)]

- A VC is a *financial intermediary*, taking the investors' capital and invests it directly in portfolio companies—differing from angel investors who use their own capital.
- A VC invests only in *private companies*, defining VC as a type of private equity.

- A VC takes an active role in *monitoring* its portfolio companies (*e.g.*, via a board representation)—a role central to the success of a VC.
- A VC's primary goal is to maximize its financial return by *exiting* investments through an IPO or private sales—differing from a strategic investor who has strategic objectives other than financial returns and may maintain its stake indefinitely without the need to exit.
- A VC invests to fund the *internal growth* of the portfolio companies, by building new businesses rather than acquiring existing businesses.

The first true VC firm, the American Research and Development (ARD), was established in 1946 by Harvard Business School professor General Georges F. Doriot and MIT president Karl Compton together with local business leaders, to make high-risk investments in emerging companies developing technology for World War II. Formed as a ***corporation*** and structured as a ***publicly traded closed-end fund***, ARD invested in illiquid assets while providing liquidity to investors, most of whom were retail investors. After the Soviet launch of the *Sputnik* satellite in 1957 and spurred by fears of lagging American technological competitiveness, the U.S. government began its own VC efforts. The Small Business Investment Act of 1958 launched the federal small business investment company (SBIC) program, authorizing SBICs to be licensed and regulated by the Small Business Administration (SBA), to provide capital to SBA-qualified small businesses. In the 1960's the most common form of modern VC funds took shape—***limited partnerships***, in which the general partner (GP) is the venture capitalist, and the limited partners (LPs) are mostly institutional investors.[4 (§1.3, Ch.2); 5; 6]

Hedge Fund

In contrast to private equity funds which invest only in private companies and are long-term investors, ***hedge funds*** tend to invest in public securities and are short-term traders.[4 (§1.1)] Hedge fund saw its origin in the late 1940s in a magazine article written by the fund's founder, Albert Winslow Jones; and the first widely cited article about hedge funds appeared in *Fortune* in April 1966, titled: "*The Jones Nobody Keeps Up With*." Jones proposed the uses of short selling to hedge stock positions, leverage as part of hedge fund strategies, and incentive fees.[7 (pp.6, 12, Ch.6)] Early hedge funds were predominantly "*market neutral*" or creating a leveraged exposure—taking long positions on undervalued (in their view) stocks and short positions on overvalued stocks, and other hedging strategies; hence the name "hedge fund." Although today's hedge funds are characterized by their high-risk trading strategies, typically involving short selling, short-term trading, arbitrage, and the use of futures and options, the "hedge fund" name sticks.[3 (pp.539-540)] As Franklin R. Edwards, a Columbia University professor of economics and finance, famously quipped: "*It is hard to imagine a greater misnomer than 'hedge fund,' since hedge funds typically do just the opposite of what their name implies: they speculate*."[7]

Hedge funds' ***arbitrage*** activities include three areas:[3 (pp.539-540)]

- *convertible arbitrage*: This strategy involves investing in corporate debt convertible into common stock and simultaneously selling the common stock short—trying to find an arbitrage value between two securities issued by the same corporation, or to realize the "optionality" value embedded in the convertible security.
- *risk arbitrage*: This strategy involves betting on consummation as planned of an announced merger or acquisition, by taking long on the target company and short on the would-be acquiror; and exploiting the difference between the target-acquiror stock spread reflecting market view of the probability of deal success, and the target-acquiror stock spread reflecting the hedge fund's own estimate of the probability of deal success.
- *distressed debt trading*: In the past hedge funds bought defaulted or near-default bonds and resold the distressed bonds at a profit as the issuer moved to the restructuring stage. Today some hedge funds specializing in bankruptcy hang on to their distressed investments through the entire restructuring process, and end up holding substantial or controlling equity stakes in the portfolio company as it emerges from bankruptcy. Here the line between hedge fund trading and LBO private equity fund investing begins to blur.

Like private equity funds, hedge funds are typically ***organized*** as private limited partnerships. The *general partner* (GP) is the person (individual or entity) who starts the hedge fund and usually acts as the fund's manager. The *limited partners* (LPs) are investors, generally high net-worth individuals and institutions, whose investments are usually locked up for a period of time between six months to three years.[7 (pp.6, 12, Ch.6)]

Offshore Fund (Foreign Investment Company)

In this Note, "offshore fund" broadly refers to an investment company organized under the laws of a jurisdiction ***foreign*** to the United States.[9] While some literature uses "offshore" to refer to a jurisdiction perhaps perceived to be a "tax haven," other literature uses "offshore" to refer to any location outside of a fund manager's home jurisdiction, to not only seek tax advantage but also to utilize strategic advantage in the target markets.[10 (§7.1)] Many U.S.-based fund managers manage offshore funds parallel to, and with identical investment strategy with, their U.S. domestic hedge funds; the offshore fund allows the U.S.-based manager to access non-U.S. investors.[2 (§§9:1-9:2, 9:16-9:17)]

Section 7(d) of the Investment Company Act ***prohibits*** a foreign investment company from making a ***public offering*** of its securities in the United States unless the SEC issues an exemptive order permitting such foreign fund to register under the IC Act. The purposes of § 7(d) are to ensure the integrity of the U.S. investment company industry, and to enable the SEC to enforce investor protections of the IC Act against foreign funds operating in the United States. The SEC, through interpretation of the statute, has "***married***" § 7(d) to §§ 3(c)(l) and 3(c)(7): A foreign fund ***may*** privately sell its securities ***in the U.S.*** relying on the § 3(c)(l) private fund exemption (where the fund has no more than 100 beneficial owners resident in the U.S.), or the § 3(c)(7) private fund exemption (where the fund's U.S. resident shareholders are exclusively "qualified purchasers" as defined by § 2(a)(51)); and simultaneously conduct a public offering of its securities ***outside of the United States***—without violating § 7(d) prohibition.[11; 12]

"Specifically Exempted" Adviser: Foreign Private Adviser

"***Foreign private adviser***" is specifically exempted by § 203(b)(3) from IA Act registration requirement. Section 202(a)(30) defines "foreign private adviser" to mean any adviser who:[13 (§II.C)]

- has ***no*** place of business in the U.S.; *and*
- has, in total, ***fewer than 15*** clients in the U.S. and investors in the U.S. in § 3(c)(1) and/or § 3(c)(7) private funds advised by the adviser; *and*
- has ***less than $25 million*** in AUM (assets under management) attributable to its U.S. clients and U.S. investors in the private funds advised by it; *and*
- ***neither*** holds itself out generally to the public in the U.S. as an investment adviser; ***nor*** acts as an investment adviser to a registered investment company or to a business development company under the IC Act.

Thus, for example, a foreign adviser having AUM $25 million or more from U.S.

clients will be required to register under the IA Act, irrespective of the number of its U.S. clients.[14 (§§1:32, 1:41)]

Under § 204 "Annual and Other Reports," any investment adviser "specifically exempted from registration pursuant to § 203(b)" is not subject to recordkeeping and reporting requirements of § 204. Thus, § 203(b)(3) exempt foreign private advisers are not subject to reporting requirements under the IA Act; neither are they subject to SEC staff examination.[13 (pp.39646-47 nn.5, 21)]

Section 203(l) Exempt Reporting Adviser: Venture Capital Fund Adviser

A "***venture capital fund adviser***" who provides investment advice ***solely*** to one or more venture capital funds is exempted by § 203(l) from registration under the IA Act. Under the "solely" requirement, for example, an adviser cannot simultaneously rely on or combine multiple exemptions, such as by combining § 203(l) VC fund adviser exemption with § 203(m) small private fund adviser exemption.[13 (p.39667); 14 (§1:35)] Furthermore, § 203(l) does not distinguish between U.S. and foreign advisers: A foreign adviser may meet the "*solely*" requirement if *all* of its clients—both U.S. and non-U.S.—are venture capital funds within the meaning of SEC Rule 203(l)-1.[13 (§II.A.9)] Under definitional Rule 203(l)-1, to qualify as a "***venture capital fund***":[13 (§II.A)]

- The fund must be a *§ 3(c)(1) or § 3(c)(7) private fund* (whether a U.S. fund or an offshore fund) that pursues a *venture capital strategy*.
- The fund is neither a *registered investment company* nor a *business development company* under the IC Act.
- The fund does *not* provide its investors with *redemption or similar liquidity rights* other than in extraordinary circumstances.
- The fund's borrowing and other leverage are capped at *15%* of its aggregate capital contributions and commitments and are limited to a *short-term* basis.
- Of the fund's aggregate capital contributions and commitments after deduction of its short-term holdings of cash and cash equivalents, the fund's ***non-qualifying investments*** are capped at 20%. The fund's "***qualifying investments***" generally consist of equity securities issued by a "***qualifying portfolio company***," which is an operating company, which does not use leverage in exchange for the VC fund's investment in the company, and which is neither a reporting company under the Exchange Act nor listed or traded in a foreign securities market, and does not have, directly or indirectly, a control relationship with an Exchange Act reporting

company or a foreign traded company—investment limitations designed to distinguish VC funds from other types of private equity funds and from hedge funds, and to preclude "VC fund of funds" from the scope of qualifying "VC fund."

Being exempt from registration under § 203(l), VC fund advisers remain subject to certain reporting requirements under the IA Act (hence "***exempt reporting advisers***"). IA Rule 204-4 "*Reporting by Exempt Reporting Advisers*" requires § 203(l) VC fund advisers and § 203(m) small private fund advisers to electronically file certain reports on Form ADV with the SEC using the same process as used by registered IAs. Compared with full reporting by a registered IA on Form ADV:[15]

- **Form ADV** is now dually-titled for dual uses by registered IAs and by exempt reporting IAs: "Uniform Application for Investment Adviser Registration" & "Report by Exempt Reporting Advisers."
- Exempt reporting advisers are ***required*** to complete selected items in **Part 1A** of Form ADV concerning:
  - ✓ *exemption(s)* on which the exempt reporting adviser is relying to report, and not to register (**Item 2.B** SEC Reporting by Exempt Reporting Advisers);
  - ✓ *basic identification details* (**Item 1** Identifying Information; **Item 3** Form of Organization; **Item 10** Control Persons);
  - ✓ *other business activities* of the adviser and its affiliates to reveal significant conflicts with advisory clients (**Item 6** Other Business Activities; **Item 7** Financial Industry Affiliations and Private Fund Reporting, **7.A**);
  - ✓ *disciplinary history* of the adviser and its employees, and details of each disciplinary event (**Item 11** Disclosure Information);
  - ✓ information about *each private fund* the adviser advises (**Item 7** Financial Industry Affiliations and Private Fund Reporting, 7.B; **Schedule D**, Section 7.B).
- Exempt reporting advisers are ***not required***, as registered advisers are, to comply with **Part 2** of Form ADV requiring disclosure of certain current information about the adviser to advisory and prospective clients.
- All information reported on Form ADV, by registered IAs and exempt reporting IAs alike, is publicly accessible through the ***IAPD system*** (Investment Adviser Public Disclosure System) on the SEC's website, http://www.adviserinfo.sec.gov.

Section 203(m) Exempt Reporting Adviser: Small Private Fund Adviser

An adviser who provides investment advice ***solely to*** one or more § 3(c)(1) and/or § 3(c)(7) "private funds," and has assets under management (AUM) in the United States of less than $150 mm ("***small private fund adviser***") is exempted by § 203(m) and SEC Rule 203(m)-1 from registration under the IA Act. Under the "solely" condition, for example, a single non-private fund client would disqualify the adviser from reliance on the exemption.[14 (§1:36)] Furthermore, the "solely" requirement precludes simultaneous reliance on multiple exemptions, such as by combining § 203(m) small private fund adviser exemption with § 203(b)(3) foreign private adviser exemption.[13 (p.39667 n.322)]

While § 203(m) does not separately address U.S. advisers and foreign advisers, under SEC interpretive and implementing Rule 203(m)-1:[13 (§II.B)]

- In the case of a **U.S. adviser**: the adviser must provide advisory services *solely to* one or more "***qualifying private funds***" (including a private fund of funds),[14 (§1:36)] and manage "***private fund assets***" (*i.e.*, AUM attributable to the qualifying private funds) of less than $150 mm.
- In the case of a **foreign adviser**: all *U.S.-person clients* of the adviser must be qualifying private funds, and all *AUM of the adviser in the U.S.* must be solely attributable to the private fund assets the total value of which is less than $150 mm. That is, a foreign adviser may enter the U.S. market and rely on § 203(m) exemption, without regard to the type or number of its *non-U.S. clients* or the amount of its *AUM outside of the United States*—reflecting appropriate limits on the extraterritorial application of the IA Act.

As "exempt reporting adviser," § 203(m) small private fund advisers are subject to the same reporting requirements as § 203(l) VC fund advisers described above.[15]

Registered Adviser to Large-or-Mid Sized Private Funds

Prior to the Dodd-Frank Wall Street Reform and Consumer Protection Act of 2010,[16] most hedge fund advisers were not required to and did not register under the IA Act, relying on the "fewer than fifteen clients" statutory exemption from registration (provided in the since then repealed IA Act § 203(b)), where each hedge fund was counted as one client (pursuant to the since then rescinded SEC Rule 203(b)(3)-1). Such non-registered hedge fund advisers were not subject to any reporting requirements or examination by the SEC, which in turn caused the SEC to be unable to evaluate the effect of hedge fund strategies on the U.S. financial markets.[17] The ***Private Fund***

Investment Advisers Registration Act of 2010 (*i.e.*, Title IV of the Dodd-Frank Act) repealed the old § 203(b)(3) broad "private adviser exemption" (and SEC rescinded Rule 203(b)(3)-1 thereafter).[15 (§II.D.2.a)] In its stead, the Dodd-Frank Act created three limited exemptions from registration: a new § 203(b)(3) "foreign private adviser" exemption; § 203(l) adviser "solely" to qualifying VC funds exemption; and § 203(m) adviser "solely" to small private funds exemption (with its aggregate AUM in the United States being less than $150 million). Consequently, most private fund advisers previously relying on the "private adviser exemption" must since 2011 register under the IA Act.[13]

To "promote the financial stability of the United States," the Dodd-Frank Act established the Financial Stability Oversight Council (**FSOC**), directing it to monitor risks to the U.S. financial system. The Dodd-Frank Act amended § 204(b) of the IA Act, directing the SEC to establish—based on the type or size of the private funds the advisers advise—different reporting and recordkeeping requirements for different classes of advisers to private funds, and to share such information with the FSOC for the assessment of systemic risk.[18b] Under SEC's implementing Rule 204(b)-1, an investment adviser must, in addition to **Form ADV** which is required of all registered advisers and exempt reporting advisers,[19] file a **Form PF** if such adviser (referred to in this Note as "***registered adviser to large-or-mid sized private funds***"):[18b (§II.A.7)]

- is registered or required to be registered under § 203 of the IA Act;
- acts as an investment adviser to one or more private funds; and
- has aggregate private fund AUM in the U.S. of at least $150 million.

Form PF reporting adopts a scaled approach, based on the size of the adviser and the types of private funds managed:[18b (§II); 14 (§§3:19-3:20, 4:2-4:3)]

- registered IAs to ***large*** private funds must provide more details on Form PF, sub-categorized into:
    - ✓ large *hedge* fund adviser: with at least $1.5 billion AUM attributable to hedge funds;
    - ✓ large *liquidity* fund adviser: with at least $1 billion combined AUM attributable to liquidity private funds and registered money market funds;
    - ✓ large *private equity* fund adviser: with at least $2 billion AUM attributable to private equity funds.
- registered IAs to ***mid-sized*** private funds (*i.e.*, not meeting the above thresholds for

large private funds but having private fund assets of at least $150 million) are subject to less extensive reporting on Form PF.

Form PF data collection is designed to provide the FSOC with necessary information to monitor systemic risk across the private fund industry. It elicits non-public information about the operations and trading strategies of the private funds. Thus, unlike Form ADV, an adviser's Form PF filings are not individually accessible to the public.[18a (p.8071 n.39); 18b (§§II.A, C-D)] However, aggregate data on the private fund industry statistics and trends based on Form PF and Form ADV filings are publicly available on the SEC's website: ***Private Funds Statistics***, (https://www.sec.gov/divisions/investment/private-funds-statistics.shtml).

Bibliography

1. SEC Division of Investment Management, Private Fund Adviser Resources (Modified: Oct. 21, 2016), https://www.sec.gov/divisions/investment/guidance/private-fund-adviser-resources.htm
2. LEMKE ET AL., HEDGE FUNDS AND OTHER PRIVATE FUNDS: REGULATION AND COMPLIANCE (Thomson Reuters 2015)
3. STOWELL, INVESTMENT BANKS, HEDGE FUNDS, AND PRIVATE EQUITY (2nd ed. Academic Press 2013)
4. METRICK & YASUDA, VENTURE CAPITAL & THE FINANCE OF INNOVATION (2nd ed. Wiley 2011)
5. Gompers & Lerner, *The Venture Capital Revolution*, 15 J. ECON. PERSP. 145 (2001)
6. Murphy & Netter, *The Small Business Investment Act of 1958*, 19 FED. B. J. 162 (1959)
7. CLOSED-END FUNDS, EXCHANGE-TRADED FUNDS, AND HEDGE FUNDS—ORIGINS, FUNCTIONS, AND LITERATURE (Anderson et al. eds. Springer 2010)
8. Edwards, *Hedge Funds and the Collapse of Long-Term Capital Management*, 13.2 J. ECON. PERSP. 189 (1999)
9. Hugh F. Owens, Commissioner of the SEC, *A Regulator Looks at Some Unregulated Investment Companies—The Exotic Funds* (Address Before the North American Securities Administrators Association, Oct. 21, 1969), https://www.sec.gov/news/speech/1969/102169owens.pdf
10. HUDSON, FUNDS: PRIVATE EQUITY, HEDGE AND ALL CORE STRUCTURES (Wiley 2014)
11. DIV. INV. MGMT, SEC. & EXCH. COMM'N, PROTECTING INVESTORS: A HALF CENTURY OF INVESTMENT COMPANY REGULATION (1992), Ch.4 Internationalization and Investment Companies
12. Goodwin, Procter & Hoar: IC Act §§ 3(c)(1), 3(c)(7) & 7(d), SEC No-Action Letter (Feb. 28, 1997)
13. Exemptions for Advisers to Venture Capital Funds, Private Fund Advisers With Less Than $150 Million in Assets Under Management, and Foreign Private Advisers, IA-3222, 76 FR 39646 (2011)
14. LEMKE & LINS, REGULATION OF INVESTMENT ADVISERS (Thomson Reuters 2015)
15. Rules Implementing Amendments to the Investment Advisers Act of 1940, IA-3221, 76 FR 42950 (2011)
16. DODD-FRANK WALL STREET REFORM AND CONSUMER PROTECTION ACT, PUB. L. NO. 111-203, 124 STAT. 1376 (2010), TITLE IV—PRIVATE FUND INVESTMENT ADVISERS REGISTRATION ACT OF 2010
17. STAFF REPORT TO THE UNITED STATES SEC. & EXCH. COMM'N, IMPLICATIONS OF THE GROWTH OF HEDGE FUNDS (2003)
18. Reporting by Investment Advisers to Private Funds and Certain Commodity Pool Operators and Commodity Trading Advisors on Form PF: **18a.** IA-3145, 76 FR 8068 (Feb. 2011) (Prop. Rel.); **18b.** IA-3308, 76 FR 71128 (Nov. 2011) (Adopt. Rel.)
19. Investment Advisers Act of 1940: **19a.** § 204 Annual and Other Reports (2012); **19b.** IA Rule 204-4 Reporting by Exempt Reporting Advisers

Case Study:

Two non-registered statutory advisers: TL Ventures, claiming ***§ 203(l) VC fund adviser exemption***; Penn Mezzanine, claiming ***§ 203(m) small private fund adviser exemption***—were found to be under common control and not operationally independent of each other. Integration theory applied to treat the two advisers as a single adviser for purposes of applicable exemptions and registration requirement under the IA Act.

TL Ventures Inc.; Penn Mezzanine Partners Mgmt., L.P.

[In *re* TL Ventures Inc., Respondent, IA-3859, Adm. Proc. 3-15940 (June 20, 2014); In *re* Penn Mezzanine Partners Mgmt., Respondent, L.P., IA-3858, Adm. Proc. 3-15939 (June 20, 2014)]

Research Topics:

Regulatory framework governing advisers to private funds and foreign funds under the Chinese investment management laws.

In *re* TL Ventures Inc., Respondent

IA-3859, Adm. Proc. 3-15940 (June 20, 2014)

I.

The Securities and Exchange Commission deems it appropriate and in the public interest that public administrative and cease-and-desist proceedings be, and hereby are, instituted pursuant to § § 203(e) and 203(k) of the Investment Advisers Act of 1940 against **TL Ventures Inc.** ("*Respondent*"). * * * *

III.

On the basis of this Order [*Instituting Administrative and Cease-and-Desist Proceedings Pursuant § § 203(e) and 203(k) of the Investment Advisers Act of 1940, Making Findings, and Imposing Remedial Sanctions and a Cease-and-Desist Order*] and Respondent's Offer [of Settlement], the Commission finds[1] that:

A. SUMMARY

* * * *

6. Section 203(a) of the Advisers Act prohibits an investment adviser from using the mails or any means or instrumentality of interstate commerce in connection with its business as an investment adviser unless it is registered with the Commission or exempt from registration. Section 208(d) of the Advisers Act makes it unlawful for any person indirectly, or through or by any other person, to do any act or thing which would be unlawful for such person to do directly under the provisions of the Act or rule or regulation thereunder.

7. Effective March 30, 2012, TL Ventures and **Penn Mezzanine Partners Management, L.P.**, a related investment adviser, each claimed to be exempt from the Advisers Act's registration requirements. However, the facts and circumstances surrounding their relationship indicate that the two advisers were under common control, were not operationally independent of each other and thus should have been integrated as a single investment adviser for purposes of the applicable registration requirement and the applicability of any exemption. Once integrated, TL Ventures and Penn Mezzanine would not have qualified for any exemption from registration and therefore should have

---

[1] The findings herein are made pursuant to Respondent's Offer of Settlement and are not binding on any other person or entity in this or any other proceeding.

been registered effective March 30, 2012.

8. By using the mails or any means or instrumentality of interstate commerce in connection with its business as an investment adviser and not being registered with the Commission, TL Ventures, acting through or by Penn Mezzanine, violated § § 203(a) and 208(d) of the Advisers Act.

B. RESPONDENT

9. TL Ventures is a Delaware corporation located in Wayne, Pennsylvania. TL Ventures is not registered with the Commission as an investment adviser. Prior to March 30, 2012, TL Ventures was exempt from Commission registration in reliance on § 203(b)(3) of the Advisers Act and Rule 203-1(e) under the Advisers Act.[2] From March 29, 2012, TL Ventures claimed to be an investment adviser solely to one or more venture capital funds and thus to be exempt under **§ 203(l)** of the Advisers Act from registration as an investment adviser. It has reported to the Commission as an "exempt reporting adviser" under **§ 204(a)** of the Advisers Act and **Rule 204-4** thereunder.[3] In its exempt reporting adviser report on Form ADV dated March 31, 2014, TL Ventures reported regulatory assets under management of approximately $178 million in **venture capital funds**.

C. BACKGROUND

TL Ventures Is an Adviser to "Covered Investment Pools"

10. TL Ventures is an adviser to venture capital funds which invest in early-stage technology companies. TL Ventures raised its last venture capital fund in 2008. TL Ventures acted as the investment adviser to several venture capital funds, including TL Ventures IV and TL Ventures V, both of which constitute "covered investment pools" as defined in Advisers Act Rule 206(4)-5(f)(3) because they would be investment companies

---

[2] The exemption from registration formerly contained in § 203(b)(3) was repealed effective July 21, 2011 by the Dodd-Frank Wall Street Reform and Consumer Protection Act, and Rule 203-1(e) in effect extended that exemption until March 30, 2012. See *Rules Implementing Amendments to the Investment Advisers Act of 1940*, IA-3221, 76 FR 42950 (2011).

[3] The Dodd-Frank Act created a category of advisers known as exempt reporting advisers (which generally were formerly advisers relying on the private adviser exemption contained in § 203(b)(3), which has been repealed). Although exempt from Commission registration, exempt reporting advisers are required by Rule 204-4 under the Advisers Act to file reports with the Commission electronically on Form ADV through the IARD using the same process used by registered investment advisers.

under § 3(a) of the Investment Company Act of 1940 but for the exclusion from the definition of investment company provided by § 3(c)(1) of the Investment Company Act of 1940. The funds have terms of 10 years, with the possibility of two one-year extensions following the initial term if approved by a majority-in-interest of the limited partners in the fund. * * * *

TL Ventures and Penn Mezzanine Should Have Been Registered

The Advisers Claimed to Be Exempt From Registration

20. The Dodd-Frank Act repealed a prior exemption from registration under § 203(b)(3) of the Advisers Act but mandated other exemptions. In connection with implementing the new exemptions, investment advisers that were previously exempt from registration under § 203(b)(3) of the Advisers Act were required to be registered or file as exempt reporting advisers by March 30, 2012. On March 29, 2012, TL Ventures and Penn Mezzanine filed separate exempt reporting adviser reports on Form ADV with the Commission each claiming to be an exempt reporting adviser, and neither TL Ventures nor Penn Mezzanine registered with the Commission as an investment adviser under § 203 of the Advisers Act. TL Ventures claimed that it qualified for an exemption from registration with the Commission based on **§ 203(l)** of the Advisers Act because it was an adviser solely to one or more venture capital funds. Penn Mezzanine claimed that it qualified for an exemption from registration with the Commission based on **Rule 203(m)-1** under the Advisers Act because it acted solely as an adviser to private funds and had regulatory assets under management in the U.S. of less than $150 million.

The Advisers were Operationally Integrated

21. On their exempt reporting adviser reports filed with the Commission, both TL Ventures and Penn Mezzanine report that they are under common control with each other. In addition, various employees and associated persons of TL Ventures held ownership stakes in TL Ventures and in the general partner and management company entities of Penn Mezzanine; among those, the Covered Associate[4] and a managing director of TL

[4] "Covered associates" are officers and employees of the adviser who have a direct economic stake in the business relationship with the government client. Covered associates are defined to include: (i) any general partner, managing member or executive officer, or other individual with a similar status or function; (ii) any employee who solicits a government entity for the investment adviser and any person who supervises, directly or indirectly, such employee; and (iii) any political action committee controlled by the investment adviser or by any of its covered associates. Under the ["pay-to-play"] Rule, executive officers include: (i) the president; (ii) any vice president in

Ventures held in the aggregate a majority ownership interest in TL Ventures and indirectly held in the aggregate more than a 25%, but less than a majority, ownership interest in Penn Mezzanine.

22. TL Ventures and Penn Mezzanine had several overlapping employees and associated persons, including individuals who provided investment advice on behalf of both TL Ventures and Penn Mezzanine. For example, two of the three members of Penn Mezzanine's investment committee, which had sole and exclusive authority to approve any investment by Penn Mezzanine's fund, also served as managing directors at TL Ventures and were significantly involved in providing investment advice on behalf of TL Ventures.

23. TL Ventures and Penn Mezzanine had significantly overlapping operations without any policies and procedures designed to keep the entities separate. Marketing materials for Penn Mezzanine made reference to TL Ventures and Penn Mezzanine as being a "partnership" and referenced Penn Mezzanine's ability to leverage and benefit from this relationship, including outsourcing its back office functions to TL Ventures. In addition, Managing Directors of TL Ventures, who served on Penn Mezzanine's investment committee, solicited potential investors for Penn Mezzanine's funds, including soliciting past investors in TL Ventures' funds. Moreover, neither adviser had adequate information security policies and procedures in place to protect investment advisory information from disclosure to the other. Also, employees and associated persons of Penn Mezzanine routinely used their TL Ventures email addresses to conduct business and communicate with outside parties about and on behalf of Penn Mezzanine.

The Advisers Did Not Qualify for Exemption From Registration

24. The Commission has stated that it will treat as a single adviser two or more affiliated advisers that are separate legal entities but are operationally integrated, which could result in a requirement for one or both advisers to register.[5] Based upon the facts and circumstances, TL Ventures and Penn Mezzanine were operationally integrated and, therefore, were not eligible to rely on the claimed exemptions from registration.

---

charge of a principal business unit, division or function (such as sales, administration or finance); (iii) any other officer of the investment adviser who performs a policy-making function; or (iv) any other person who performs similar policy-making functions for the investment adviser. Rule 206(4)-5(f)(2), (4).

[5] See *Exemptions for Advisers to Venture Capital Funds, Private Fund Advisers With Less Than $150 Million in Assets Under Management, and Foreign Private Advisers*, IA-3222, 76 FR 39645, 39680 (2011).

25. When integrated with Penn Mezzanine, TL Ventures did not qualify for an exemption from registration with the Commission under **§ 203(l)** of the Advisers Act because it was not an adviser solely to venture capital funds. Accordingly, as of March 30, 2012, TL Ventures should have registered with the Commission as an investment adviser under the Advisers Act.

D. VIOLATIONS

* * * *

27. Section 203(a) of the Advisers Act makes it unlawful for any investment adviser, unless registered or exempt from registration, to make use of the mails or any means or instrumentality of interstate commerce in connection with its business as an investment adviser. Section 208(d) of the Advisers Act makes it unlawful for any person indirectly, or through or by any other person, to do any act or thing which would be unlawful for such person to do directly under the provisions of the Advisers Act.[6] As described above, TL Ventures acted through or by Penn Mezzanine to engage in the business of providing investment advice without registering as an investment adviser and, as a result, TL Ventures willfully[7] violated § § 203(a) and 208(d) of the Advisers Act.

REMEDIAL EFFORTS: In determining to accept the Offer, the Commission considered remedial acts that the Respondent is undertaking, including steps to reorganize operations and separate its advisory functions **from Penn Mezzanine**, as well as the adoption of policies and procedures reasonably designed to ensure compliance with the applicable rules. * * * *

---

[6] Advisers Act § § 203(a) and 208(d) do not require a showing of scienter.

[7] A willful violation of the securities laws means merely " 'that the person charged with the duty knows what he is doing.' " *Wonsover v. SEC*, 205 F.3d 408 (DC Cir. 2000). There is no requirement that the actor " 'also be aware that he is violating one of the Rules or Acts.' " *Id.*

In *re* Penn Mezzanine Partners Mgmt., L.P., Respondent

IA-3858, Adm. Proc. 3-15939 (June 20, 2014)

I.

The Securities and Exchange Commission deems it appropriate and in the public interest that public administrative and cease-and-desist proceedings be, and hereby are, instituted pursuant to § § 203(e) and 203(k) of the Investment Advisers Act of 1940 against **Penn Mezzanine Partners Management, L.P.** ("*Respondent*"). * * * *

III.

On the basis of this Order [*Instituting Administrative and Cease-and-Desist Proceedings Pursuant to Sections 203(e) and 203(k) of the Investment Advisers Act of 1940, Making Findings, and Imposing Remedial Sanctions and a Cease-and-Desist Order*] and Respondent's Offer [of Settlement], the Commission finds[1] that:

A. SUMMARY

1. These proceedings involve violations of the Advisers Act's registration requirement by Penn Mezzanine. Section 203(a) of the Advisers Act prohibits an investment adviser from using the mails or any means or instrumentality of interstate commerce in connection with its business as an investment adviser unless it is registered with the Commission or exempt from registration. Section 208(d) of the Advisers Act makes it unlawful for any person indirectly, or through or by any other person, to do any act or thing which would be unlawful for such person to do directly under the provisions of the Act or rule or regulation thereunder.

2. Effective March 30, 2012, Penn Mezzanine and **TL Ventures Inc.**, a related investment adviser, each claimed to be exempt from the Advisers Act's registration requirements. However, the facts and circumstances surrounding their relationship indicate that the two advisers were under common control, were not operationally independent of each other and thus should have been integrated as a single investment adviser for purposes of the applicable registration requirement and the applicability of any exemption. Once integrated, Penn Mezzanine and TL Ventures would not have qualified for any exemption from registration and therefore should have been registered

[1] The findings herein are made pursuant to Respondent's Offer of Settlement and are not binding on any other person or entity in this or any other proceeding.

effective March 30, 2012.

3. By using the mails or any means or instrumentality of interstate commerce in connection with its business as an investment adviser and not being registered with the Commission, Penn Mezzanine, acting through or by TL Ventures, violated § § 203(a) and 208(d) of the Advisers Act.

B. RESPONDENT

4. Penn Mezzanine is a Delaware limited partnership located in Wayne, Pennsylvania. Penn Mezzanine is not registered with the Commission as an investment adviser. Prior to March 30, 2012, Penn Mezzanine was exempt from Commission registration in reliance on § 203(b)(3) of the Advisers Act and Rule 203-1(e) under the Advisers Act.[2] From March 29, 2012, Penn Mezzanine claimed to be an investment adviser solely to private funds with less than $150 million in regulatory assets under management and thus to be exempt under **Rule 203(m)-1** under the Advisers Act from registration as an investment adviser. It has reported to the Commission as an "exempt reporting adviser" under § **204(a)** of the Advisers Act and **Rule 204-4** thereunder.[3] In its exempt reporting adviser report on Form ADV dated March 31, 2014, Penn Mezzanine reported regulatory assets under management of approximately $51 million in **private capital funds.**

C. BACKGROUND

Penn Mezzanine and TL Ventures Should Have Been Registered

The Advisers Claimed to Be Exempt From Registration

5. The Dodd-Frank Act repealed a prior exemption from registration under § 203(b)(3) of the Advisers Act but mandated other exemptions. In connection with implementing the new exemptions, investment advisers that were previously exempt from registration

---

[2] The exemption from registration formerly contained in § 203(b)(3) was repealed effective July 21, 2011 by the Dodd-Frank Wall Street Reform and Consumer Protection Act, and Rule 203-1(e) in effect extended that exemption until March 30, 2012. See *Rules Implementing Amendments to the Investment Advisers Act of 1940*, IA-3221, 76 FR 42950 (2011).

[3] The Dodd-Frank Act created a category of advisers known as exempt reporting advisers (which generally were formerly advisers relying on the private adviser exemption contained in § 203(b)(3), which has been repealed). Although exempt from Commission registration, exempt reporting advisers are required by Rule 204-4 under the Advisers Act to file reports with the Commission electronically on Form ADV through the IARD using the same process used by registered investment advisers.

under § 203(b)(3) of the Advisers Act were required to be registered or file as exempt reporting advisers by March 30, 2012. On March 29, 2012, Penn Mezzanine and TL Ventures filed separate exempt reporting adviser reports on Form ADV with the Commission each claiming to be an exempt reporting adviser, and neither Penn Mezzanine nor TL Ventures registered with the Commission as an investment adviser under § 203 of the Advisers Act. Penn Mezzanine claimed that it qualified for an exemption from registration with the Commission based on **Rule 203(m)-1** under the Advisers Act because it acted solely as an adviser to private funds and had regulatory assets under management in the U.S. of less than $150 million. TL Ventures claimed that it qualified for an exemption from registration with the Commission based on **§ 203(l)** of the Advisers Act because it was an adviser solely to one or more venture capital funds.

The Advisers were Operationally Integrated

6. On their exempt reporting adviser reports filed with the Commission, both Penn Mezzanine and TL Ventures report that they are under common control with each other. In addition, various employees and associated persons of TL Ventures held ownership stakes in TL Ventures and in the general partner and management company entities of Penn Mezzanine; among those, two managing directors of TL Ventures held in the aggregate a majority ownership interest in TL Ventures and indirectly held in the aggregate more than a 25%, but less than a majority, ownership interest in Penn Mezzanine.

7. Penn Mezzanine and TL Ventures had several overlapping employees and associated persons, including individuals who provided investment advice on behalf of both Penn Mezzanine and TL Ventures. For example, two of the three members of Penn Mezzanine's investment committee, which had sole and exclusive authority to approve any investment by Penn Mezzanine's fund, also served as managing directors at TL Ventures and were significantly involved in providing investment advice on behalf of TL Ventures.

8. Penn Mezzanine and TL Ventures had significantly overlapping operations without any policies and procedures designed to keep the entities separate. Marketing materials for Penn Mezzanine made reference to TL Ventures and Penn Mezzanine as being a "partnership" and referenced Penn Mezzanine's ability to leverage and benefit from this relationship, including outsourcing its back office functions to TL Ventures. In addition, Managing Directors of TL Ventures, who served on Penn Mezzanine's investment committee, solicited potential investors for Penn Mezzanine's funds, including soliciting

past investors in TL Ventures' funds. Moreover, neither adviser had adequate information security policies and procedures in place to protect investment advisory information from disclosure to the other. Also, employees and associated persons of Penn Mezzanine routinely used their TL Ventures email addresses to conduct business and communicate with outside parties about and on behalf of Penn Mezzanine.

The Advisers Did Not Qualify for Exemption From Registration

9. The Commission has stated that it will treat as a single adviser two or more affiliated advisers that are separate legal entities but are operationally integrated, which could result in a requirement for one or both advisers to register.[4] Based upon the facts and circumstances, Penn Mezzanine and TL Ventures were operationally integrated and, therefore, were not eligible to rely on the claimed exemptions from registration.

10. When integrated with TL Ventures, Penn Mezzanine did not qualify for an exemption from registration with the Commission under **Rule 203(m)-1** under the Advisers Act because the combined operations of Penn Mezzanine and TL Ventures exceeded $150 million in regulatory assets under management in the U.S. Accordingly, as of March 30, 2012, Penn Mezzanine should have registered with the Commission as an investment adviser under the Advisers Act.

D. VIOLATIONS

11. Section 203(a) of the Advisers Act makes it unlawful for any investment adviser, unless registered or exempt from registration, to make use of the mails or any means or instrumentality of interstate commerce in connection with its business as an investment adviser. Section 208(d) of the Advisers Act makes it unlawful for any person indirectly, or through or by any other person, to do any act or thing which would be unlawful for such person to do directly under the provisions of the Advisers Act.[5] As described above, Penn Mezzanine acted through or by TL Ventures to engage in the business of providing investment advice without registering as an investment adviser and, as a result, Penn Mezzanine willfully[6] violated §§203(a) and 208(d) of the Advisers Act.

---

[4] See *Exemptions for Advisers to Venture Capital Funds, Private Fund Advisers With Less Than $150 Million in Assets Under Management, and Foreign Private Advisers*, IA-3222, 76 FR 39645, 39680 (2011).

[5] Advisers Act §§203(a) and 208(d) do not require a showing of scienter.

[6] A willful violation of the securities laws means merely " 'that the person charged with the duty knows what he is doing.' " *Wonsover v. SEC*, 205 F.3d 408 (DC Cir. 2000). There is no requirement that the actor " 'also be aware

REMEDIAL EFFORTS: In determining to accept the Offer, the Commission considered remedial acts that the Respondent is undertaking, including steps to reorganize operations and separate its advisory functions **from TL Ventures**, as well as the adoption of policies and procedures reasonably designed to ensure compliance with the applicable rules. * * * *

---

that he is violating one of the Rules or Acts.' " *Id.*

Topic 3 Standards of Conduct: Investment Adviser *vs* Broker-Dealer

Laws & Rules Highlight:

IA Act ((15 USC 80b-1 *et seq.*) & Rules (17 CFR §§ 275.0-2 *et seq.*)
Exchange Act (15 USC 78a *et seq.*) & Rules (17 CFR §§ 240.0-1 *et seq.*)

IA Act:

- § 202(a)(11) (*def. "**investment adviser**"*)
  - § 202(a)(11)(C) (***B/D exclusion from statutory IA**: any broker or dealer whose performance of investment advisory services is "**solely incidental**" to the conduct of its broker or dealer business and who receives "**no special compensation therefor**"*)
- § 206 Prohibited Transactions by Registered Investment Advisers (*IA Act's antifraud provisions; applicable to "**any**" statutory IA—whether or not required to register under § 203(a)*)
  - § 206(1) (*prohibits "any device, scheme, or artifice **to defraud** any client or prospective client"*)
  - § 206(2) (*prohibits "any transaction, practice, or course of business which **operates as a fraud or deceit** upon any client or prospective client"*)
  - § 206(3) (*prohibits **principal or agency cross** transaction by an IA with client without advance written disclosure and client consent; prohibition not applicable to **a BD not acting as an IA** in relation to the transaction*)
    - ✓ Rule 206(3)-1 Exemption of Investment Advisers Registered as Broker-Dealers in Connection with the Provision of Certain Investment Advisory Services (*exempts such IAs from §206(3) when providing solely **impersonal** investment advisory services*)
    - ✓ Rule 206(3)-2 Agency Cross Transactions for Advisory Clients (***safe harbor** for IA effecting agency cross transaction for advisory client*)
  - § 206(4) (*prohibits "any act, practice, or course of business which **is** fraudulent, deceptive, or manipulative; grants **SEC rulemaking authority** to define, and to prescribe means reasonably designed to prevent, fraud by advisers*)
- § 211(g) Standard of Conduct
  - § 211(g)(1) (*authoring the SEC rulemaking to provide for standard of conduct for **all brokers, dealers, and investment advisers**, when providing **personalized** investment advice about securities to **retail customers**: "to act in the best interest of the customer without regard to the financial or other interest of the broker, dealer, or investment adviser providing the advice."*)
  - § 211(g)(2) (*def. "retail customer"*)

Exchange Act:

- § 3(a)(4) (*def. "**broker**"*); § 3(a)(5) (*def. "**dealer**"*)
- certain antifraud provisions under Securities Act and Exchange Act governing broker-dealer transactions
  - ◆ § 17 (SA) Fraudulent Interstate Transactions
    - ✓ §§ 17(a)(1)-(3)
  - ◆ § 10 (SEA) Regulation of the Use of Manipulative and Deceptive Devices
    - ✓ § 10(b) (*general antifraud provisions of the Exchange Act*)
    - ✓ Rule 10b-5 Employment of Manipulative and Deceptive Devices
  - ◆ § 15 (SEA) Registration and Regulation of Brokers and Dealers
    - ✓ Rule 15c1-2 Fraud and Misrepresentation (*specific antifraud rule governing over-the-counter market transactions*)
- § 15(k) Standard of Conduct
  - ◆ § 15(k)(1)-(2) (*same as IA Act § 211(g)(1); **three provisos** with respect to compensation, continuing duty of care or loyalty, and sale of proprietary or other limited range of products*)

Investor Protection and Securities Reform Act of 2010:

[Dodd-Frank Wall Street Reform and Consumer Protection Act, Pub. L. No. 111-203, 124 Stat. 1376, Title IX (July 21, 2010)]

- § 913 Study and Rulemaking Regarding Obligations of Brokers, Dealers, and Investment Advisers
  - ◆ § 913(f) Rulemaking
  - ◆ § 913(g) Authority to Establish A Fiduciary Duty for Brokers and Dealers (*adding § 15(k) to the Exchange Act and § 211(g) to the Advisers Act*)
  - ◆ § 913(h) Harmonization of Enforcement

Investment Advisers Act of 1940 § 211(g) Standard of Conduct	Securities Exchange Act of 1934 § 15(k) Standard of Conduct
(1) IN GENERAL.—The Commission may promulgate rules to provide that the standard of conduct for all brokers, dealers, and investment advisers, when providing personalized investment advice about securities to retail customers (and such other customers as the Commission may by rule provide), shall be to act in the best interest of the customer without regard to the financial or other interest of the broker, dealer, or investment adviser providing the advice. * * * Such rules shall provide that such standard of conduct shall be no less stringent than the standard applicable to investment advisers under section 206(1) and (2) of this Act when providing personalized investment advice about securities, * * * The receipt of compensation based on commission or fees shall not, in and of itself, be considered a violation of such standard applied to a broker, dealer, or investment adviser. (2) RETAIL CUSTOMER DEFINED.	(1) IN GENERAL.—Notwithstanding any other provision of this Act or the Investment Advisers Act of 1940, the Commission may promulgate rules to provide that, with respect to a broker or dealer, when providing personalized investment advice about securities to a retail customer (and such other customers as the Commission may by rule provide), the standard of conduct for such broker or dealer with respect to such customer shall be the same as the standard of conduct applicable to an investment adviser under section 211 of the Investment Advisers Act of 1940. The receipt of compensation based on commission or other standard compensation for the sale of securities shall not, in and of itself, be considered a violation of such standard applied to a broker or dealer. Nothing in this section shall require a broker or dealer or registered representative to have a continuing duty of care or loyalty to the customer after providing personalized investment advice about securities. (2) DISCLOSURE OF RANGE OF PRODUCTS OFFERED.

Investment Advisers Act of 1940 § 211(g) Standard of Conduct	Securities Exchange Act of 1934 § 15(k) Standard of Conduct
(2) RETAIL CUSTOMER DEFINED.—For purposes of this subsection, the term "retail customer" means a natural person, or the legal representative of such natural person, who— (A) receives personalized investment advice about securities from a broker, dealer, or investment adviser; and (B) uses such advice primarily for personal, family, or household purposes.	(2) DISCLOSURE OF RANGE OF PRODUCTS OFFERED.—* * * The sale of only proprietary or other limited range of products by a broker or dealer shall not, in and of itself, be considered a violation of the standard set forth in paragraph (1).

Pre-Case Background Note[Biblio]

Scalping *vs* Front-Running

"***Scalping***" refers to the practice of an investment manager's trading for its own account or for its favored managed account ("own trading"), *in advance of* its recommendation to its managed accounts to trade in the same direction ("client trading"): such as its buying in advance of a buy recommendation or selling in advance of a sell recommendation to its advisory or discretionary client accounts. By triggering subsequent client trading in the ***same direction*** as its earlier own trading, the scalper seeks to move the market price of a security. *Immediately thereafter*, the scalper trades for its own account in the ***opposite direction***, seeking to make a quick profit from the price change produced by the client trading. There may *not* be any investment merit in its recommended client investment action.[1 (§11.03[A])]

"***Front-running***" also involves an *investment manager*'s own trading in advance of, and at a price not yet impacted by, recommended client trading in the same direction (or, it may involve a *broker* "***trading ahead***" of customer orders). Different from a short-run, in-and-out scalper, a front-runner ostensibly believes in the investment merit of the recommended client investment action, and the front-runner itself invests on that investment judgment. This ***technical difference*** between scalping and front-running should not, however, obscure the same offense by scalpers and front-runners, *i.e.*, a deliberate subordination of their clients' interest to their own interest, and violations of common law agency principles and fiduciary principles.[1 (§11.03[A]); 2 (§III)]

Bibliography

1. BINES & THEL, INVESTMENT MANAGEMENT LAW AND REGULATION (3ed. 2014)
2. Lowenfels & Bromberg, *Securities Market Manipulations: An Examination and Analysis of Domination and Control, Frontrunning, and Parking*, 55 ALB. L. REV. 293 (1991)

Case Study 1: Investment Adviser as Statutory Fiduciary

The Investment Advisers Act of 1940 reflects a congressional recognition of "the delicate fiduciary nature" of the investment advisory relationship. Courts have imposed on a ***fiduciary***, which Congress recognized an **investment adviser** to be to its client, an *affirmative duty* of utmost good faith and full and fair disclosure of all material facts, and an *affirmative obligation* to employ reasonable care to avoid misleading his clients. The investment adviser's non-disclosure of scalping practice "operates as a fraud or deceit" in violation of § 206 of the Advisers Act.

SEC v. Capital Gains Research Bureau, Inc.
375 U.S. 180 (1963)

[***Procedural history***: SEC v. Capital Gains Research Bureau, Inc., 191 F. Supp. 897 (SDNY 1961), *aff'd*, 300 F.2d 745 (2d Cir. 1961), *en banc adh'd*, 306 F.2d 606 (2d Cir. 1962), *rev'd & remanded*, 375 U.S. 180 (1963)]

Case Study 2: Broker-Dealer Subject to Shingle Theory

Broker-dealers' duty to customers, whether acting in an agency or a principal capacity, historically has been in significant part* based on the ***shingle theory***. The shingle theory states, in terms of *general standards of conduct* for a broker or dealer: The customer will be dealt with fairly and in accordance with the standards of the profession.** The shingle theory also states, phrased as *misrepresentation*: One who sells securities to the public—*who hangs out his shingle*—implicitly warrants the soundness of statements of stock value, estimates of a firm's earnings potential and the like. And, when such a person conceals known information inconsistent with this implicit warranty of soundness, he has omitted a material fact without which the statements made would be misleading.

*[LIPTON, BROKER DEALER REGULATION vol.15A Ch.5 §5.1 (2016); **Duker & Duker, 34-2350, 6 SEC 386 (1939)].

Kahn v. SEC
297 F.2d 112 (2d. Cir. 1961) (Clark, J., Concurring)

Post-Case Commentary:[Biblio]

A Uniform Federal Fiduciary Duty Standard for Broker-Dealers and Investment Advisers?

An investment manager's core business is making investment decisions. A broker-dealer's core business is effecting securities transactions.[1 (§9.03)] Brokers and dealers are expressly excluded from the statutory definition of investment adviser by IA Act § 202(a)(11)(C) excepting "any broker or dealer whose performance of such [investment advisory] services is solely incidental to the conduct of his business as a broker or dealer and who receives no special compensation therefor."

Federal Fiduciary Duty Under Investment Advisers Act

Investment advisers regulated by the Investment Advisers Act have historically been recognized to be fiduciaries to their clients, and are subject to the ***federal fiduciary standard of conduct*** under the Advisers Act. Such federal fiduciary standard includes an affirmative duty of utmost good faith and full and fair disclosure of all material facts, and an affirmative obligation to employ reasonable care to avoid misleading their clients. Investment advisers perform their basic function of furnishing to clients on a personal basis competent, unbiased, and continuous advice regarding the sound management of clients' investments; and charge an asset-based fee for such a continuing relationship. The fiduciary standard applies to an investment adviser's entire relationship with its clients and prospective clients.[2; 3a (§II.A.2); 4 (§II.B.1)]

Shingle Theory and Fiduciary Concept Governing Broker-Dealers

Brokers and dealers registered under the Securities Exchange Act have traditionally been subject to the ***shingle theory*** (also known as the ***implied representation theory***), which subjects them to the obligations of fair dealing with customers and in accordance with the standards of the profession, for hanging up their shingle or doing business with the public.[5; 6 (vol.15A §5:1)] Principles underlying the shingle theory were first enunciated in 1939 by the U.S. Securities and Exchange Commission in the *Duker & Duker* administrative proceeding finding the dealer charging substantial mark-up without customers' knowledge in violation of the antifraud provisions of the Securities Act and Exchange Act. The shingle theory principles were first judicially affirmed in 1943 by the U.S. Court of Appeals for the Second Circuit in the *Charles Hughes & Co.* opinion, also supporting a finding of the dealer's charging of undisclosed substantial mark-up unrelated to the prevailing market in violations of the antifraud violations of the Securities Act and Exchange Act.[7; 8; 6 (vol.15A §5:1)] A central obligation of broker-dealers under the shingle theory is suitability of recommendations that are consistent with the best interests of their customers.[9; 10] Distinguishing between a suitability violation and an antifraud violation, one commentator characterizes the suitability doctrine as "an ethical standard" instead of "a rule of law," while there may be a "point of merger" in a given case where both suitability doctrine and antifraud rules are implicated.[11] Distinguishing a broker's suitability obligation from an adviser's fiduciary relationship, another commentator points to the discrete nature of brokerage commissions; and states that a broker's suitability obligation arises on the event of a particular securities recommendation, and that absent a recommendation no suitability obligation exists.[3a (§II.A.2)]

Fiduciary concept had also been invoked by the SEC in administrative proceedings against broker-dealers since prior to 1949; but it was in 1949 came the first judicial recognition of the fiduciary status of a broker-dealer who was dually registered as an investment adviser in the *Arleen Hughes* case, where the broker-dealer failed to disclose to her customers/clients that she was not selling securities to them at the best price obtainable.[12b; 6 (vol.15A §5:10)] In affirming the SEC's decision to revoke Arleen Hughes' broker-dealer registration while leaving her investment adviser registration intact, the Court of Appeals for the D.C. Circuit held the broker to be in a fiduciary relationship with her brokerage customers:

> When a person is registered under both the Securities Exchange Act and the Investment Advisers Act, she is amenable to regulation under both statutes. The broker was in a fiduciary relationship with clients in that she purported to render to such clients impartial investment advice for compensation under an investment advisory contract. In failing to fully disclose to such clients the nature and extent of her adverse interest in her transactions with them, the broker breached her fiduciary duty and violated the antifraud provisions of the Securities Act and the Exchange Act, § 15 of the latter Act requires the revocation of broker-dealer registration for such violations. It is immaterial that the broker's violations of the Exchange Act resulted from her conduct as an investment adviser. "The situation would be otherwise if the Commission had sought to have revoked petitioner's investment adviser registration because of violations of the Securities and Securities Exchange Acts."[12]

Subsequent case law delimits the application of fiduciary theory in the broker-dealer context. For example, the Second Circuit has held:[13]

> There is no general fiduciary duty inherent in an ordinary broker-customer relationship; but a relationship of trust and confidence does exist between a broker and a customer with respect to those matters that have been entrusted to the broker. The presence of a discretionary account automatically implies a general fiduciary duty between a broker and a customer.[13a] In a nondiscretionary account, ordinarily the customer keeps control over the account and the broker's narrowly defined duties begin and end with each transaction. Absent the transformative "special circumstances" recognized in the case law that render de facto control over the account to rest in the broker, a broker owes no fiduciary duty to give ongoing advice to the holder of a nondiscretionary account.[13b]

The ***shingle theory*** and the ***fiduciary theory*** as applied in the broker-dealer context are closely related: each is applicable whether the broker-dealer is acting in an agency or a principal capacity—in contrast to traditional agency principles which bind broker-dealers only when they act as agent for their customers. Yet each rests on a technically separate and distinguishable legal underpinning: the shingle theory arises out of the professional stature of the broker; the fiduciary theory arises out of the broker's trust and confidence relationship with his customer.[6 (vol.15A §§5:1, 5:10)]

Conduct Regulation: Providing Personalized Securities Investment Advice to Retail Customers

With respect to the provision of personalized investment advice about securities to retail customers by brokers, dealers, and investment advisers, the Investor Protection and Securities Reform Act of 2010[14] authorizes the SEC by rule to establish a federal fiduciary duty for brokers and dealers currently applicable to investment advisers; it also authorizes the SEC by rule to provide that the uniform standard of conduct shall be "*to act in the best interest of the customer without regard to the financial or other interest of the broker, dealer, or investment adviser providing the advice*."

There is debate within and among the government regulators, the industries, and academics[3b (nn.16-19)] on whether the SEC should impose a fiduciary duty on brokers and dealers and adopt a uniform standard of conduct regulating brokers, dealers, and investment advisers, when those three categories of investment professionals provide personalized investment advice about securities to retail customers.

Among the academic literature—

- propositions ***opposing*** a fiduciary duty on brokers and dealers include:
  - ✓ Langevoort (2009-2010):[15] Securities brokerage is a sales-based business, which is not a fiduciary occupation. Instead of applying blanket fiduciary norms to broker ***sales activity***, textured rules should be applied to both brokers and advisers on the crucial aspects of the ***advisory relationship***.
  - ✓ Black (2010-2011):[16] Fiduciary duty is ***too amorphous*** a concept to establish a standard of conduct. Professionalism-based, well-defined, and enforceable ***federal professional standards of care and competence*** for broker-dealers and investment advisers should be adopted, rather than a federal fiduciary duty.
- propositions ***supporting*** a fiduciary duty on brokers and dealers include:
  - ✓ Laby (2012)[3b] theorizing a ***reasonable expectations-based justification*** for imposing a federal fiduciary duty on the brokerage industry: The brokerage industry broadly holds itself out as purveyors of impartial advice. Such

holding-out creates reasonable expectations that *the brokerage industry will* act in a fiduciary capacity, and *not simply that* any individual brokers through advertising or use of titles *have created individualized fiduciary contracts* with particular investors.

✓ Wrona* (*a current lawyer with regulator FINRA, 2012)[17] advocating a "***strong universal fiduciary duty***" concept: for broker-dealers to be subject to the same "*broad disclosure obligation*" as advisers currently are, and for advisers to be subject to "*an explicit suitability rule*" as broker-dealers currently are.

- propositions for ***maintaining*** the current regulatory structure for broker-dealers include:

✓ Hazen (2011):[18] The broker-dealer regulatory rules structure is not broken and there is no need to significantly overhaul the nature of broker-dealer regulation. An *explicit legislative or regulatory declaration* that broker-dealers *are* fiduciaries will add emphasis to the obligations under existing law, but will not provide significant additional regulation.

Two SEC Commissioners (Kathleen and Paredes, 2011),[19b] in opposing the release to Congress of the SEC Staff Study on Investment Advisers and Broker-Dealers (2011) which recommended a uniform fiduciary standard of conduct for both investment advisers and broker-dealers when they provide personalized investment advice to retail customers,[19a] identified ***two failures*** as the "pervasive shortcoming" of the Staff Study:

> ***A failure*** to "adequately justify its recommendation" for a new uniform fiduciary duty standard and for harmonization of the two disparate regulatory regimes; and ***a failure*** to "adequately recognize the risk" that its recommendations could adversely impact investors. A stronger analytical and empirical foundation, and more rigorous analysis rooted in economics and data, are needed before the SEC embarks on rulemaking.

The same two failures are also pervasive in the cited academic literature advocating a "broad" and "universal" fiduciary duty standard and harmonization. Legal academic literature may as well benefit from the rigor of sound economic analysis.

Bibliography

1. BINES & THEL, INVESTMENT MANAGEMENT LAW AND REGULATION (3ed. 2014)
2. SEC v. Capital Gains Research Bureau, Inc., 375 U.S. 180 (1963)

3. Laby: **3a.** *Reforming the Regulation of Broker-Dealers and Investment Advisers*, 65 BUS. LAW. 395 (2010); **3b.** *Selling Advice and Creating Expectations: Why Brokers Should be Fiduciaries*, 87 WASH. L. REV. 707 (2012)
4. STAFF OF THE U.S. SECURITIES AND EXCHANGE COMMISSION, STUDY ON INVESTMENT ADVISERS AND BROKER-DEALERS (2011)
5. Kahn v. SEC, 297 F.2d 112 (2d Cir. 1961)
6. DAVID LIPTON, BROKER-DEALER REGULATION (2016)
7. In the Matter of Duker & Duker, 34-2350, 6 S.E.C. 386 (1939)
8. Charles Hughes & Co. v. SEC, 139 F.2d 434 (2d Cir. 1943)
9. Hanly v. SEC, 415 F.2d 589 (2d Cir. 1969)
10. SEC (OCIE), *Broker-Dealer Controls Regarding Retail Sales of Structured Securities Products*, RISK ALERT, vol. IV Issue 7 (Aug 2015)
11. Mundheim, *Professional Responsibilities of Broker-Dealers: The Suitability Doctrine*, 1965 DUKE L.J. 445 (1965)
12. **12a.** In the Matter of Arleen W. Hughes, 34-4048, 27 SEC 629 (1948); **12b.** Hughes v. SEC, 174 F.2d 969 (DC Cir. 1949)
13. Second Circuit: **13a.** U.S. v. Wolfson, 642 F.3d 293 (2d Cir. 2011); **13b.** Bear Stearns & Co., Inc. v. Kwiatkowski, 306 F.3d 1293 (2d Cir. 2002)
14. Dodd-Frank Wall Street Reform and Consumer Protection Act, Title IX §§ 913(f)(-(g), Pub. L. No. 111-203, 124 Stat. 1376 (July 21, 2010)
15. Langevoort, *Brokers as Fiduciaries*, 71 U. PITT. L. REV. 439 (2009-2010)
16. Black, *How to Improve Retail Investor Protection After the Dodd-Frank Wall Street Reform and Consumer Protection Act*, 13 U. PA. J. BUS. L. 59 (2010-2011)
17. Wrona, *The Best of Both Worlds: A Fact-Based Analysis of the Legal Obligations of Investment Advisers and Broker-Dealers and a Framework for Enhanced Investor Protection*, 68 BUS. LAW. 1 (2012)
18. Hazen, *Stock Broker Fiduciary Duties and the Impact of the Dodd-Frank Act*, 15 N.C. BANKING INST. 47 (2011)
19. SEC: **19a.** SEC Staff Study on Investment Advisers and Broker-Dealers (As Required by Section 913 of the Dodd-Frank Wall Street Reform and Consumer Protection Act) (Jan. 2011); **19b.** Commissioners Kathleen L. Casey and Troy A. Paredes, *Statement by SEC Commissioners: Statement Regarding Study On Investment Advisers And Broker-Dealers* (Jan. 21, 2011)

SEC, Petitioner v. Capital Gains Research Bureau, Inc.
375 U.S. 180 (1963)

JUDGES: Warren, Black, Clark, Harlan, Brennan, Stewart, White, Goldberg. HARLAN, J. dissented. DOUGLAS, J. took no part in the consideration or decision of this case.

OPINION

Mr. Justice GOLDBERG delivered the opinion of the Court:

We are called upon in this case to decide whether under the Investment Advisers Act of 1940 the Securities and Exchange Commission may obtain an injunction compelling a registered investment adviser to disclose to his clients a practice of purchasing shares of a security for his own account shortly before recommending that security for long-term investment and then immediately selling the shares at a profit upon the rise in the market price following the recommendation. The answer to this question turns on whether the practice—known in the trade as "scalping"—"operates as a fraud or deceit upon any client or prospective client" within the meaning of the Act.[1] We hold that it does and that the Commission may "enforce compliance" with the Act by obtaining an injunction requiring the adviser to make full disclosure of the practice to his clients.[2]

---

[1] 15 USC § 80b-6, provides in relevant part that:

"It shall be unlawful for any investment adviser, by use of the mails or any means or instrumentality of interstate commerce, directly or indirectly—

"(1) to employ any device, scheme, or artifice to defraud any client or prospective client;

"(2) to engage in any transaction, practice, or course of business which operates as a fraud or deceit upon any client or prospective client;

"(3) acting as principal for his own account, knowingly to sell any security to or purchase any security from a client, or acting as broker for a person other than such client, knowingly to effect any sale or purchase of any security for the account of such client, without disclosing to such client in writing before the completion of such transaction the capacity in which he is acting and obtaining the consent of the client to such transaction. The prohibitions of this paragraph shall not apply to any transaction with a customer of a broker or dealer if such broker or dealer is not acting as an investment adviser in relation to such transaction...."

[2] 15 USC § 80b-9, provides in relevant part that:

"(e) Whenever it shall appear to the Commission that any person has engaged, is engaged, or is about to engage in any act or practice constituting a violation of any provision of this subchapter, or of any rule, regulation, or order hereunder, or that any person has aided, abetted, counseled, commanded, induced, or procured, is aiding, abetting, counseling, commanding, inducing, or procuring, or is about to aid, abet, counsel, command, induce, or procure such a violation, it may in its discretion bring an action in the proper district court of the United States, or the proper United States court of any Territory or other place subject to the jurisdiction of the United States, to

The Commission brought this action against respondents in the United States District Court for the Southern District of New York. At the hearing on the application for a preliminary injunction, the following facts were established. Respondents publish two investment advisory services, one of which—"**A Capital Gains Report**"—is the subject of this proceeding. The Report is mailed monthly to approximately 5,000 subscribers who each pay an annual subscription price of $18. It carries the following description:

> "An Investment Service devoted exclusively to (1) The protection of investment capital. (2) The realization of a steady and attractive income therefrom. (3) The accumulation of CAPITAL GAINS thru the timely purchase of corporate equities that are proved to be undervalued."

Between March 15, 1960, and November 7, 1960, respondents, on six different occasions, purchased shares of a particular security shortly before recommending it in the Report for long-term investment. On each occasion, there was an increase in the market price and the volume of trading of the recommended security within a few days after the distribution of the Report. Immediately thereafter, respondents sold their shares of these securities at a profit. They did not disclose any aspect of these transactions to their clients or prospective clients.

On the basis of the above facts, the Commission requested a preliminary injunction as necessary to effectuate the purposes of the Investment Advisers Act of 1940. The injunction would have required respondents, in any future Report, to disclose the material facts concerning, *inter alia*, any purchase of recommended securities "within a very short period prior to the distribution of a recommendation ....," and "the intent to sell and the sale of said securities ... within a very short period after distribution of said recommendation ...."[3]

---

enjoin such acts or practices and to enforce compliance with this subchapter of any rule, regulation, or order hereunder. Upon a showing that such person has engaged, is engaged, or is about to engage in any such act or practice, or in aiding, abetting, counseling, commanding, inducing, or procuring any such act or practice, a permanent or temporary injunction or decree or restraining order shall be granted without bond."

[3] The requested injunction reads in full as follows:

"WHEREFORE the plaintiff demands a temporary restraining order, preliminary injunction and final injunction: 1. Enjoining the defendants Capital Gains Research Bureau, Inc. and Harry P. Schwarzmann, their agents, servants, employees, attorneys and assigns, and each of them, while the said Capital Gains Research Bureau, Inc. is an investment adviser, directly and indirectly, by the use of the mails or any means or instrumentalities of interstate commerce from:

The District Court denied the request for a preliminary injunction, holding that the words "fraud" and "deceit" are used in the Investment Advisers Act of 1940 "in their technical sense" and that the Commission had failed to show an intent to injure clients or an actual loss of money to clients; 191 F. Supp. 897 (SDNY 1961). The Court of Appeals for the Second Circuit, sitting *en banc*, by a 5-to-4 vote accepted the District Court's limited construction of "fraud" and "deceit" and affirmed the denial of injunctive relief.[4] The majority concluded that no violation of the Act could be found absent proof that "any misstatements or false figures were contained in any of the bulletins"; or that "the investment advice was unsound"; or that "defendants were being bribed or paid to tout a stock contrary to their own beliefs"; or that "these bulletins were a scheme to get rid of worthless stock"; or that the recommendations were made "for the purpose of endeavoring artificially to raise the market so that [respondents] might unload [their] holdings at a profit"; *id.* The four dissenting judges pointed out that "the common-law doctrines of fraud and deceit grew up in a business climate very different from that involved in the sale

---

"(a) Employing any device, scheme or artifice to defraud any client or prospective client by failing to disclose the material facts concerning

"(1) The purchase by defendant, Capital Gains Research Bureau, Inc., of securities within a very short period prior to the distribution of a recommendation by said defendant to its clients and prospective clients for purchase of said securities;

"(2) The intent to sell and the sale of said securities by said defendant so recommended to be purchased within a very short period after distribution of said recommendation to its clients and prospective clients;

"(3) Effecting of short sales by said defendant within a very short period prior to the distribution of a recommendation by said defendant to its clients and prospective clients to dispose of said securities;

"(4) The intent of said defendant to purchase and the purchase of said securities to cover its short sales;

"(5) The purchase by said defendant for its own account of puts and calls for securities within a very short period prior to the distribution of a recommendation to its clients and prospective clients for purchase or disposition of said securities.

"(b) Engaging in any transaction, practice and course of business which operates as a fraud or deceit upon any client or prospective client by failing to disclose the material facts concerning the matters set forth in demand 1(a) hereof."

[4] The case was originally heard before a panel of the Court of Appeals, which, with one judge dissenting, affirmed the District Court. 300 F.2d 745 (2d Cir. 1961). Rehearing *en banc* was then ordered. The Court of Appeals purported to recognize that "federal securities laws are to be construed broadly to effectuate their remedial purpose." 306 F.2d 606 (2d Cir. 1962). But by affirming the District Court's "technical" construction of the Investment Advisers Act of 1940 and by requiring proof of "misstatements," unsound advice, bribery, or intent to unload "worthless stock," the court read the statute, in effect, as confined by traditional common-law concepts of fraud and deceit.

of securities," and urged a broad remedial construction of the statute which would encompass respondents' conduct; *id.* We granted certiorari to consider the question of statutory construction because of its importance to the investing public and the financial community; 371 U.S. 967 (1963).

The decision in this case turns on whether Congress, in empowering the courts to enjoin any practice which operates "as a fraud or deceit upon any client or prospective client," intended to require the Commission to establish fraud and deceit "in their technical sense," including intent to injure and actual injury to clients, or whether Congress intended a broad remedial construction of the Act which would encompass nondisclosure of material facts. For resolution of this issue we consider the history and purpose of the Investment Advisers Act of 1940.

I.

The Investment Advisers Act of 1940 was the last in a series of Acts designed to eliminate certain abuses in the securities industry, abuses which were found to have contributed to the stock market crash of 1929 and the depression of the 1930's.[5] It was preceded by the Securities Act of 1933, the Securities Exchange Act of 1934, the Public Utility Holding Company Act of 1935, the Trust Indenture Act of 1939, and the Investment Company Act of 1940. A fundamental purpose, common to these statutes, was to substitute a philosophy of full disclosure for the philosophy of *caveat emptor* and thus to achieve a high standard of business ethics in the securities industry.[6] As we recently said in a related context, "It requires but little appreciation ... of what happened in this country during the 1920's and 1930's to realize how essential it is that the highest ethical standards prevail" in every facet of the securities industry. *Silver v. New York Stock Exchange*, 373 U.S. 341 (1963).

The Public Utility Holding Company Act of 1935 "authorized and directed" the Securities and Exchange Commission "to make a study of the functions and activities of investment trusts and investment companies ...."[7] Pursuant to this mandate, the

---

[5] See generally Douglas & Bates, *The Federal Securities Act of 1933*, 43 YALE L.J. 171 (1933); Loomis, *The Securities Exchange Act of 1934 and the Investment Advisers Act of 1940*, 28 GEO. WASH. L. REV. 214 (1959); Shulman, *Civil Liability and the Securities Act*, 43 YALE L.J. 227 (1933). Cf. GALBRAITH, THE GREAT CRASH (1955).

[6] See H.R. Rep. No. 85, 73d Cong., 1st Sess. 2, quoted in *Wilko v. Swan*, 346 U.S. 427 (1953).

[7] 49 Stat. 837, 15 USC § 79z-4.

Commission made an exhaustive study and report which included consideration of investment counsel and investment advisory services.[8] This aspect of the study and report culminated in the Investment Advisers Act of 1940.

The report reflects the attitude—shared by investment advisers and the Commission—that investment advisers could not "completely perform their basic function—furnishing to clients on a personal basis competent, unbiased, and continuous advice regarding the sound management of their investments—unless all conflicts of interest between the investment counsel and the client were removed." The report stressed that affiliations by investment advisers with investment bankers, or corporations might be "an impediment to a disinterested, objective, or critical attitude toward an investment by clients ...."

This concern was not limited to deliberate or conscious impediments to objectivity. Both the advisers and the Commission were well aware that whenever advice to a client might result in financial benefit to the adviser—other than the fee for his advice—"that advice to a client might in some way be tinged with that pecuniary interest [whether consciously or] subconsciously motivated ...." The report quoted one leading investment adviser who said that he "would put the emphasis ... on subconscious" motivation in such situations. It quoted a member of the Commission staff who suggested that a significant part of the problem was not the existence of a "deliberate intent" to obtain a financial advantage, but rather the existence "subconsciously [of] a prejudice" in favor of one's own financial interests. The report incorporated the Code of Ethics and Standards of Practice of one of the leading investment counsel associations, which contained the following canon:

> "[An investment adviser] should continuously occupy an impartial and disinterested position, as free as humanly possible from the subtle influence of prejudice, conscious

---

[8] While the study concentrated on investment advisory services which provide personalized counseling to investors, see INVESTMENT TRUSTS AND INVESTMENT COMPANIES, REPORT OF THE SECURITIES AND EXCHANGE COMMISSION, Pursuant to Section 30 of the Public Utility Holding Company Act of 1935, on Investment Counsel, Investment Management, Investment Supervisory, and Investment Advisory Services, H.R. Doc. No. 477, 76th Cong., 2d Sess., 1 (hereinafter cited as **SEC Report**) the Senate Committee on Banking and Currency did receive communications from publishers of investment advisory services, see, *e.g.*, Hearings on S.3580 before Subcommittee of the Senate Committee on Banking and Currency, 76th Cong., 3d Sess., and the Act specifically covers "any person who, for compensation, engages in the business of advising others, either directly or through publication or writings ...." 54 Stat. 847, 15 USC § 80b-2.

or unconscious; he should scrupulously avoid any affiliation, or any act, which subjects his position to challenge in this respect."

Other canons appended to the report announced the following guiding principles: that compensation for investment advice "should consist exclusively of direct charges to clients for services rendered"; that the adviser should devote his time "exclusively to the performance" of his advisory function; that he should not "share in profits" of his clients; and that he should not "directly or indirectly engage in any activity which may jeopardize [his] ability to render unbiased investment advice." These canons were adopted "to the end that the quality of services to be rendered by investment counselors may measure up to the high standards which the public has a right to expect and to demand." One activity specifically mentioned and condemned by investment advisers who testified before the Commission was "*trading by investment counselors for their own account in securities in which their clients were interested* ...."

This study and report—authorized and directed by statute[9]—culminated in the preparation and introduction by Senator Wagner of the bill which, with some changes, became the Investment Advisers Act of 1940.[10] In its "declaration of policy" the original bill stated that

"Upon the basis of facts disclosed by the record and report of the Securities and Exchange Commission ... it is hereby declared that the national public interest and the interest of investors are adversely affected— ... (4) when the business of investment advisers is so conducted as to defraud or mislead investors, or to enable such advisers to relieve themselves of their fiduciary obligations to their clients.

"It is hereby declared that the policy and purposes of this title, in accordance with which the provisions of this title shall be interpreted, are to mitigate and, so far as is presently practicable to eliminate the abuses enumerated in this section." S.3580, 76th Cong., 3d Sess., § 202.

Hearings were then held before Committees of both Houses of Congress.[11] In

---

[9] See text accompanying note 7, *supra*.

[10] S.3580, 76th Cong., 3d Sess.

[11] Hearings on S. 3580 before Subcommittee of the Senate Committee on Banking and Currency, 76th Cong., 3d Sess. (hereinafter cited as **Senate Hearings**). Hearings on H. R. 10065 before Subcommittee of the House Committee on Interstate and Foreign Commerce, 76th Cong., 3d Sess. (hereinafter cited as **House Hearings**).

describing their profession, leading investment advisers emphasized their relationship of "trust and confidence" with their clients[12] and the importance of "strict limitation of [their right] to buy and sell securities in the normal way if there is any chance at all that to do so might seem to operate against the interests of clients and the public." The president of the Investment Counsel Association of America, the leading investment counsel association, testified that the

> "two fundamental principles upon which the pioneers in this new profession undertook to meet the growing need for unbiased investment information and guidance were, first, that they would limit their efforts and activities to the study of investment problems from the investor's standpoint, not engaging in any other activity, such as security selling or brokerage, which might directly or indirectly bias their investment judgment; and, second, that their remuneration for this work would consist solely of definite, professional fees fully disclosed in advance." *Id.*

Although certain changes were made in the bill following the hearings,[13] there is nothing to indicate an intent to alter the fundamental purposes of the legislation. The broad proscription against "any ... practice ... which operates ... as a fraud or deceit upon any client or prospective client" remained in the bill from beginning to end. And the Committee Reports indicate a desire to preserve "the personalized character of the services of investment advisers,"[14] and to eliminate conflicts of interest between the investment adviser and the clients 36 as safe guards both to "unsophisticated investors" and to "bona fide investment counsel." The Investment Advisers Act of 1940 thus reflects a congressional recognition "of the delicate fiduciary nature of an investment advisory

---

[12] Senate Hearings.

[13] The bill as enacted did not contain a section attributing specific abuses to the investment adviser profession. This section was eliminated apparently at the urging of the investment advisers who, while not denying that abuses had occurred, attributed them to certain fringe elements in the profession. They feared that a public and general indictment of all investment advisers by Congress would do irreparable harm to their fledgling profession. See, *e.g.*, Senate Hearings. It cannot be inferred, therefore, that the section was eliminated because Congress had concluded that the abuses had not occurred, or because Congress did not desire to prevent their repetition in the future. The more logical inference, considering the legislative background of the Act, is that the section was omitted to avoid condemning an entire profession (which depends for its success on continued public confidence) for the acts of a few.

[14] H.R. Rep. No. 2639, 76th Cong., 3d Sess. 28 (hereinafter cited as **House Report**). See also S. Rep. No. 1775, 76th Cong., 3d Sess. 22 (hereinafter cited as **Senate Report**).

relationship,"[15] as well as a congressional intent to eliminate, or at least to expose, all conflicts of interest which might incline an investment adviser—consciously or unconsciously—to render advice which was not disinterested. It would defeat the manifest purpose of the Investment Advisers Act of 1940 for us to hold, therefore, that Congress, in empowering the courts to enjoin any practice which operates "as a fraud or deceit," intended to require proof of intent to injure and actual injury to clients.

This conclusion moreover, is not in derogation of the common law of fraud, as the District Court and the majority of the Court of Appeals suggested. To the contrary, it finds support in the process by which the courts have adapted the common law of fraud to the commercial transactions of our society. It is true that at common law intent and injury have been deemed essential elements in a damage suit between parties to an arm's-length transaction.[16] But this is not such an action.[17] This is a suit for a preliminary injunction in which the relief sought is, as the dissenting judges below characterized it, the "mild prophylactic," 306 F.2d, at 613, of requiring a fiduciary to disclose to his clients, not all his security holdings, but only his dealings in recommended securities just before and after the issuance of his recommendations.

The content of common-law fraud has not remained static as the courts below seem to have assumed. It has varied, for example, with the nature of the relief sought, the relationship between the parties, and the merchandise in issue. It is not necessary in a

---

[15] 2 LOSS, SECURITIES REGULATION 1412 (2d ed. 1961).

[16] See cases cited in 37 C.J.S., Fraud, 210 (1943).

Even in a damage suit between parties to an arm's-length transaction, the intent which must be established need not be an intent to cause injury to the client, as the courts below seem to have assumed. "It is to be noted that it is not necessary that the person making the misrepresentations intend to cause loss to the other or gain a profit for himself; it is only necessary that he intend action in reliance on the truth of his misrepresentations." 1 HARPER & JAMES, THE LAW OF TORTS 531 (1956). "The fact that the defendant was disinterested, that he had the best of motives, and that he thought he was doing the plaintiff a kindness, will not absolve him from liability so long as he did in fact intend to mislead." PROSSER, LAW OF TORTS 538 (1955). See 3 RESTATEMENT, TORTS, § 531, Comment *b*, illustration 3 (1938). It is clear that respondents' failure to disclose the practice here in issue was purposeful, and that they intended that action be taken in reliance on the claimed disinterestedness of the service and its exclusive concern for the clients' interests.

[17] Neither is this a criminal proceeding for "willfully" violating the Act, 15 USC § 80b-17, nor a proceeding to revoke or suspend a registration "in the public interest," 15 USC § 80b-3. Other considerations may be relevant in such proceedings. Compare *Federal Communications Comm'n v. American Broadcasting Co.*, 347 U.S. 284 (1954).

suit for equitable or prophylactic relief to establish all the elements required in a suit for monetary damages.

> "Law had come to regard fraud ... as primarily a tort, and hedged about with stringent requirements, the chief of which was a strong moral, or rather immoral element, while equity regarded it, as it had all along regarded it, as a conveniently comprehensive word for the expression of a lapse from the high standard of conscientiousness that it exacted from any party occupying a certain contractual or fiduciary relation towards another party."[18]
>
> "Fraud has a broader meaning in equity [than at law] and intention to defraud or to misrepresent is not a necessary element."[19]
>
> "Fraud, indeed, in the sense of a court of equity properly includes all acts, omissions and concealments which involve a breach of legal or equitable duty, trust, or confidence, justly reposed, and are injurious to another, or by which an undue and unconscientious advantage is taken of another."[20]

Nor is it necessary in a suit against a fiduciary, which Congress recognized the investment adviser to be, to establish all the elements required in a suit against a party to an arm's-length transaction. Courts have imposed on a fiduciary an affirmative duty of "utmost good faith, and full and fair disclosure of all material facts,"[21] as well as an affirmative obligation "to employ reasonable care to avoid misleading"[22] his clients. There has also been a growing recognition by common-law courts that the doctrines of fraud and deceit which developed around transactions involving land and other tangible items of wealth are ill-suited to the sale of such intangibles as advice and securities, and

---

[18] HANBURY, MODERN EQUITY 643 (8th ed. 1962). See *Letter of Lord Hardwicke to Lord Kames*, dated June 30, 1759, printed in PARKES, HISTORY OF THE COURT OF CHANCERY 508 (1828), quoted in SNELL, PRINCIPLES OF EQUITY 496 (25th ed. 1960):

> "Fraud is infinite, and were a Court of Equity once to lay down rules, how far they would go, and no farther, in extending their relief against it, or to define strictly the species or evidence of it, the jurisdiction would be cramped, and perpetually eluded by new schemes which the fertility of man's invention would contrive."

[19] DE FUNIAK, HANDBOOK OF MODERN EQUITY 235 (2d ed. 1956).

[20] *Moore v. Crawford*, 130 U.S. 122 (1889), quoting 1 STORY, EQUITY JUR. § 187.

[21] PROSSER, LAW OF TORTS 534-535 (1955) (citing cases). See generally Keeton, *Fraud—Concealment and Non-Disclosure*, 15 TEXAS L. REV. 1 (1936).

[22] 1 HARPER & JAMES, THE LAW OF TORTS 541 (1956).

that, accordingly, the doctrines must be adapted to the merchandise in issue.[23] The 1909 New York case of *Ridgely v. Keene*, 119 NY Supp. 451, illustrates this continuing development. An investment adviser who, like respondents, published an investment advisory service, agreed, for compensation, to influence his clients to buy shares in a certain security. He did not disclose the agreement to his client but sought "to excuse his conduct by asserting that ... he honestly believed, that his subscribers would profit by his advice ...." The court, holding that "his belief in the soundness of his advice is wholly immaterial," declared the act in question "a palpable fraud."

We cannot assume that Congress, in enacting legislation to prevent fraudulent practices by investment advisers, was unaware of these developments in the common law of fraud. Thus, even if we were to agree with the courts below that Congress had intended, in effect, to codify the common law of fraud in the Investment Advisers Act of 1940, it would be logical to conclude that Congress codified the common law "remedially" as the courts had adapted it to the prevention of fraudulent securities transactions by fiduciaries, not "technically" as it has traditionally been applied in damage suits between parties to arm's-length transactions involving land and ordinary chattels.

The foregoing analysis of the judicial treatment of common-law fraud reinforces our conclusion that Congress, in empowering the courts to enjoin any practice which operates "as a fraud or deceit" upon a client, did not intend to require proof of intent to injure and actual injury to the client. Congress intended the Investment Advisers Act of 1940 to be construed like other securities legislation "enacted for the purpose of avoiding frauds,"[24] not technically and restrictively, but flexibly to effectuate its remedial purposes.

II.

We turn now to a consideration of whether the specific conduct here in issue was the type which Congress intended to reach in the Investment Advisers Act of 1940. It is arguable—indeed it was argued by "some investment counsel representatives" who testified before the Commission—that any "trading by investment counselors for their own

---

[23] See generally Shulman, *Civil Liability and the Securities Act*, 43 YALE L.J. 227 (1933).

[24] 3 SUTHERLAND, STATUTORY CONSTRUCTION 382 *et seq.* (3d ed. 1943) (citing cases). See Note, *Intrastate Telephone Call Held to Be Use of an Interstate Instrumentality under Section 10(b)*, 38 N.Y.U.L. Rev. 985 (1963); Comment, *Insider Liability under Securities Exchange Act Rule 10b-5: The "Cady, Roberts" Doctrine*, 30 U. CHI. L. REV. 121 (1962).

account in securities in which their clients were interested ..." creates a potential conflict of interest which must be eliminated. We need not go that far in this case, since here the Commission seeks only disclosure of a conflict of interests with significantly greater potential for abuse than in the situation described above. An adviser who, like respondents, secretly trades on the market effect of his own recommendation may be motivated—consciously or unconsciously—to recommend a given security not because of its potential for long-run price increase (which would profit the client), but because of its potential for short-run price increase in response to anticipated activity from the recommendation (which would profit the adviser).[25] An investor seeking the advice of a registered investment adviser must, if the legislative purpose is to be served, be permitted to evaluate such overlapping motivations, through appropriate disclosure, in deciding whether an adviser is serving "two masters" or only one, "especially ... if one of the masters happens to be economic self-interest." *United States v. Mississippi Valley Co.*[26] Accordingly, we hold that the Investment Advisers Act of 1940 empowers the courts, upon a showing such as that made here, to require an adviser to make full and frank disclosure of his practice of trading on the effect of his recommendations.

III.

Respondents offer three basic arguments against this conclusion. They argue first that Congress could have made, but did not make, failure to disclose material facts unlawful in the Investment Advisers Act of 1940, as it did in the Securities Act of 1933,[27]

---

[25] For a discussion of the effects of investment advisory service recommendations on the market price of securities, see Note, *Securities Regulation: Stock Scalping by the Investment Adviser: Fraud or Legitimate Business Practice?—SEC v. Capital Gains Research Bureau*, 51 Calif. L. Rev. 232 (1963).

[26] This Court, in discussing conflicts of interest, has said:

"The reason of the rule inhibiting a party who occupies confidential and fiduciary relations toward another from assuming antagonistic positions to his principal in matters involving the subject matter of the trust is sometimes said to rest in a sound public policy, but it also is justified in a recognition of the authoritative declaration that no man can serve two masters; and considering that human nature must be dealt with, the rule does not stop with actual violations of such trust relations, but includes within its purpose the removal of any temptation to violate them....

"... In *Hazelton v. Sheckells*, 202 U.S. 71(1906), we said: 'The objection ... rests in their tendency, not in what was done in the particular case.... The court will not inquire what was done. If that should be improper it probably would be hidden and would not appear.' " *United States v. Mississippi Valley Co.*, 364 U.S. 520 (1961).

[27] 15 USC § 77q(a), provides:

"It shall be unlawful for any person in the offer or sale of any securities by the use of any means or

and that absent specific language, it should not be assumed that Congress intended to include failure to disclose in its general proscription of any practice which operates as a fraud or deceit. But considering the history and chronology of the statutes, this omission does not seem significant. The Securities Act of 1933 was the first experiment in federal regulation of the securities industry. It was understandable, therefore, for Congress, in declaring certain practices unlawful, to include both a general proscription against fraudulent and deceptive practices and, out of an abundance of caution, a specific proscription against nondisclosure. It soon became clear, however, that the courts, aware of the previously outlined developments in the common law of fraud, were merging the proscription against nondisclosure into the general proscription against fraud, treating the former, in effect, as one variety of the latter. For example, in *Securities & Exchange Comm'n v. Torr*, 15 F. Supp. 315 (DCSD NY 1936), *rev'd on other grounds*, 87 F.2d 446 (2d Cir. 1937), Judge Patterson held that suppression of information material to an evaluation of the disinterestedness of investment advice "operated as a deceit on purchasers," *id.* Later cases also treated nondisclosure as one variety of fraud or deceit.[28] In light of this, and in light of the evident purpose of the Investment Advisers Act of 1940 to substitute a philosophy of disclosure for the philosophy of caveat emptor, we cannot assume that the omission in the 1940 Act of a specific proscription against nondisclosure was intended to limit the application of the antifraud and anti-deceit provisions of the Act so as to render the Commission impotent to enjoin suppression of material facts. The more reasonable assumption, considering what had transpired between 1933 and 1940, is that Congress, in enacting the Investment Advisers Act of 1940 and proscribing any practice which operates "as a fraud or deceit," deemed a specific proscription against nondisclosure

---

instruments of transportation or communication in interstate commerce or by the use of the mails, directly or indirectly—

"(1) to employ any device, scheme, or artifice to defraud, or

"(2) to obtain money or property by means of any untrue statement of a material fact or any omission to state a material fact necessary in order to make the statements made, in the light of the circumstances under which they were made, not misleading, or

"(3) to engage in any transaction, practice, or course of business which operates or would operate as a fraud or deceit upon the purchaser."

[28] See *Archer v. Securities & Exchange Comm'n*, 133 F.2d 795 (CA 8th Cir. 1943), *cert. denied*, 319 U.S. 767 (1943); *Charles Hughes & Co. v. Securities & Exchange Comm'n*, 139 F.2d 434 (CA 2d Cir. 1943), *cert. denied*, 321 U.S. 786 (1944); *Hughes v. Securities & Exchange Comm'n*, 174 F.2d 969 (1949); *Norris & Hirshberg v. Securities & Exchange Comm'n*, 177 F.2d 228 (DC Cir. 1949); *Speed v. Transamerica Corp.*, 235 F.2d 369 (CA 3d Cir. 1956).

surplusage.

Respondents also argue that the 1960 amendment[29] to the Investment Advisers Act of 1940 justifies a narrow interpretation of the original enactment. The amendment made two significant changes which are relevant here. "Manipulative" practices were added to the list of those specifically proscribed. There is nothing to suggest, however, that with respect to a requirement of disclosure, "manipulative" is any broader than fraudulent or deceptive.[30] Nor is there any indication that by adding the new proscription Congress intended to narrow the scope of the original proscription. The new amendment also authorizes the Commission "by rules and regulations [to] define, and prescribe means reasonably designed to prevent, such acts, practices, and courses of business as are fraudulent, deceptive, or manipulative." The legislative history offers no indication, however, that Congress intended such rules to substitute for the "general and flexible" antifraud provisions which have long been considered necessary to control "the versatile inventions of fraud-doers."[31] Moreover, the intent of Congress must be culled from the events surrounding the passage of the 1940 legislation. "Opinions attributed to a Congress twenty years after the event cannot be considered evidence of the intent of the Congress of 1940." *Securities & Exchange Comm'n v. Capital Gains Research Bureau, Inc.*, 306 F.2d 606 (2d Cir. 1962) (dissenting opinion). See *United States v. Philadelphia Nat'l Bank*, 374 U.S. 321 (1963).

Respondents argue, finally, that their advice was "honest" in the sense that they believed it was sound and did not offer it for the purpose of furthering personal pecuniary objectives. This, of course, is but another way of putting the rejected argument that the elements of technical common-law fraud—particularly intent—must be established before an injunction requiring disclosure may be ordered. It is the practice itself, however, with

---

[29] 74 Stat. 887, 15 USC § 80b-6(4). The amendment, as it is relevant here, made it unlawful for an investment adviser:

> "(4) to engage in any act, practice, or course of business which is fraudulent, deceptive, or manipulative. The Commission shall, for the purposes of this paragraph (4) by rules and regulations define, and prescribe means reasonably designed to prevent, such acts, practices, and courses of business as are fraudulent, deceptive, or manipulative."

[30] See, *e.g.*, 15 USC § 78o(c)(1), which refers to such devices "as are manipulative, deceptive, or *otherwise* fraudulent." (Emphasis added.)

[31] *Stonemets v. Head*, 154 SW 108 (1913). See also note 18, *supra*.

its potential for abuse, which "operates as a fraud or deceit" within the meaning of the Act when relevant information is suppressed. The Investment Advisers Act of 1940 was "directed not only at dishonor, but also at conduct that tempts dishonor." *United States v. Mississippi Valley Co., supra.* Failure to disclose material facts must be deemed fraud or deceit within its intended meaning, for, as the experience of the 1920's and 1930's amply reveals, the darkness and ignorance of commercial secrecy are the conditions upon which predatory practices best thrive. To impose upon the Securities and Exchange Commission the burden of showing deliberate dishonesty as a condition precedent to protecting investors through the prophylaxis of disclosure would effectively nullify the protective purposes of the statute. Reading the Act in light of its background we find no such requirement commanded. Neither the Commission nor the courts should be required "to separate the mental urges," *Peterson v. Greenville*, 373 U.S. 244 (1963), of an investment adviser, for "the motives of man are too complex ... to separate ...." *Mosser v. Darrow*, 341 U.S. 267 (1951). The statute, in recognition of the adviser's fiduciary relationship to his clients, requires that his advice be disinterested. To insure this it empowers the courts to require disclosure of material facts. It misconceives the purpose of the statute to confine its application to "dishonest" as opposed to "honest" motives. As Dean Shulman said in discussing the nature of securities transactions, what is required is "a picture not simply of the show window, but of the entire store ... not simply truth in the statements volunteered, but disclosure."[32] The high standards of business morality exacted by our laws regulating the securities industry do not permit an investment adviser to trade on the market effect of his own recommendations without fully and fairly revealing his personal interests in these recommendations to his clients.

Experience has shown that disclosure in such situations, while not onerous to the adviser, is needed to preserve the climate of fair dealing which is so essential to maintain public confidence in the securities industry and to preserve the economic health of the country.

The judgment of the Court of Appeals is reversed and the case is remanded to the District Court for proceedings consistent with this opinion. *Reversed and remanded.*

---

[32] Shulman, *Civil Liability and the Securities Act*, 43 Yale L.J. 227 (1933).

Kahn, Petitioner v. SEC, Respondent

297 F.2d 112 (2d. Cir. 1961) (Clark, J., Concurring)

Before CLARK, FRIENDLY and MARSHALL, Circuit Judges. CLARK, J. concurring in the result.

OPINION

MARSHALL, Circuit Judge:

This petition for review of an SEC order arises out of the same proceedings described in our opinion in *Berko v. SEC*, 297 F.2d 116 (2d Cir. 1961). The general background may be found there. As in *Berko*, we conclude the SEC's findings and reasoning lack the clarity necessary to enable us to make a considered judgment without substituting our own findings and legal theories.

The gist of the SEC's opinion is as follows:

"We found in our previous opinion that 'Kahn told one customer, who purchased 25 shares at 3 1/2 in June 1958, that Sports expected to have ten (bowling) arenas in operation by the end of the year, and that, if such expectation were realized, its projected earnings would be about $1.18 per share based on the past performance of other bowling companies.' We noted that these optimistic representations were made before any financial information concerning Sports' operations was available, and concluded that Kahn 'had no adequate foundation' for his optimism and that he should at least have disclosed to his customer 'that no financial information was available and cautioned (him) ... as to the risk involved in purchasing the stock in the absence of such information.' We further concluded that Kahn 'should have disclosed to what companies he was comparing Sports or how long they had been in business, any material differences or similarities between Sports and such companies and any other facts necessary to make the comparison fair.'

"Kahn asserts that his projection of the number of arenas to be operated, which he now admits was 'mistaken' to the extent that it referred to 10 rather than 16 arenas, 'was based upon literature supplied to him which he referred to in good faith.' If the literature he refers to is that contained in the record, as he previously asserted, we can only repeat what we said in our earlier opinion that such literature 'had not yet been published by registrant at the time Kahn made the statement to his customer.' On the other hand, if Kahn is referring to other literature, it is not in the record before us, and cannot constitute a basis for excusing his erroneous projection.

"We accordingly reaffirm our conclusions that Kahn 'either knew there was no adequate basis for the optimistic Statements' he made or he was 'grossly careless or indifferent as to the existence of an adequate basis' for his statements, that he willfully violated or aided and abetted in registrant's willful violations of the designated anti-fraud provisions, and that he was a cause of the revocation of registrant's broker-dealer registration."

As in *Berko*, counsel for the Commission stated this case was important because of the need to end so-called "boiler room" operations. Again, as in *Berko*, we note the legal theories advanced in the agency's opinion would apply to all sales of securities whether or not effectuated in a "boiler room" context.

In the Commission's view petitioner committed two sins. The first is that on one occasion he made an optimistic statement as to stock of a new company without disclosing there was no information available as to whether it had operating profits or losses at the time.[1] When Kahn made the statements complained of only one brochure had been published and no accounting figures were yet available. Clearly, a straightforward affirmance on these grounds would establish an extraordinarily broad *per se* rule. Upon remand, the Commission, in accordance with the statute, should state which, if any, of the surrounding circumstances made this statement "misleading." Furthermore, the Commission's finding of a lack of an adequate basis for faith in Sports stock at the time of Kahn's statement should be spelled out. The only specific fact in this lengthy record yet brought to the Court's attention is that Sports had operating losses at the end of the first year. But no accounting figures were available when Kahn made the challenged statement. As in *Berko*, an analysis of Sports' overall financial condition at the time must be made. Finally, the Commission should indicate the extent to which it believes Kahn's specialization in Sports stock or his knowledge that the customer had read some material from MacRobbins created or increased the duty to disclose. If this latter factor is considered important, a finding should be made, with reasons stated, as to whether the first brochure was misleading. This is particularly necessary since this was apparently the only one published at the pertinent time and the opinion merely quotes certain portions and then leaves it without an explicit finding. It is not the form so much as the substance that is troubling, however, for no part of this lengthy record has been brought to our attention which challenges in the slightest the truthfulness of the quoted passages.

The second aspect of the Commission's findings relates to Kahn's projection of

---

[1] We cannot agree with the Commission that a lack of information as to present operating profits or losses is equivalent to a complete lack of "financial information."

earnings. The vice found here is Kahn's failure to state which other companies he was talking about, in what ways they were different, and "other facts necessary to make the comparison fair." It then rejected Kahn's defense that he had relied on certain literature in good faith solely on the grounds that the literature had not been published at the time. The implication is left, however, that such literature could "constitute a basis for excusing his erroneous projection." This is doubly confusing. First, counsel for the Commission have relied in this Court upon certain SEC decisions which apparently hold comparisons between new and old companies, even when named, *per se* misleading and reject the defense of reliance upon unverified literature. *In re American Republic Investors, Inc.*, 37 S.E.C. 287 (1956); *Whitehall Corp.*, 38 S.E.C. 259 (1958). But the Commission itself did not rely upon these cases or their holdings in framing its theory against Kahn. Second, the right to rely upon information secured from the employer would seem to be a critical issue in applying the statute to salesmen in "boiler room" operations. Indeed, in *Berko* this right is implicitly rejected. In *Kahn*, it is implicitly upheld, albeit held inapplicable on the facts. Upon remand, the Commission should clarify its views as to why Kahn's statement is misleading. It should deal with the issues outlined above and any others the Commission considers relevant.

We will remand the case to the Commission to the end that it may take such further action, including those which we have indicated, as may be required.

Remanded.

CONCUR

CLARK, Circuit Judge (concurring in the result):

With considerable doubt and not a little reluctance I have at length felt constrained to concur in the remand to the Commission, although for somewhat different reasons from those expressed by my brothers. In fact their directions for re-examination of the case seem to me vague and unoriented.... In substance [Kahn and Berko's] defense is lack of knowledge of what they were actually doing, or "I didn't know the gun was loaded." I do not care to support that defense or to throw obstacles in the way of the very necessary policing which the SEC should do and here is attempting of improper stock sales promotion. I believe they deserve the quite moderate punishment or reprimand they received. Finally I am concerned by the statement that our authority to affirm is here more limited than upon district court review; as shown by the author cited, 2 Davis, Administrative Law Treatise § § 16.05, 16.12 (1958), this is an oversimplification of a complex problem with extensive ramifications.

My trouble is somewhat different; it is more to perceive what theory of law, or which of several possible ones, the Commission is applying. And I think it will be helpful not only to reviewing courts, but to the Commission itself, if it clarifies the position it here takes and doubtless will need to take in other similar cases. Basically the question is the extent to which it would press the conclusion of fraud which we supported in *Charles Hughes & Co. v. SEC*, 139 F.2d 434 (2d Cir. 1943), *cert. denied* 321 U.S. 786 (1944). The Commission is relying on the so-called **"shingle" theory** to establish statutory fraud. The essence of this theory is that in certain circumstances one who sells securities to the public—who hangs out his shingle—implicitly warrants the soundness of statements of stock value, estimates of a firm's earnings potential, and the like. When such a person conceals known information inconsistent with this "implicit warranty of soundness" he has omitted a material fact without which the statements made would be misleading. See 3 LOSS, SECURITIES REGULATION 1490 (2d ed. 1961). One element of this warranty, the Commission held below, is that all such statements, or at least highly optimistic ones, have an "adequate basis." If the salesman makes statements, knowing they had no adequate basis, or if he is "grossly careless or indifferent to the existence of an adequate basis" for his statements, then he has violated the antifraud provisions of the securities laws, principally § 17(a)(2) of the Securities Act of 1933.

My difficulty here is not with this theory of the law, or necessarily with its application to these circumstances, but with the fact that, while the record presents a diversity of possible rules of law governing this situation, the Commission has not clearly indicated which we are to rely on for purposes of review. In oral argument counsel for the Commission pointed out that the fact that these were "boiler room" operations should be considered in review of this case, suggesting that the obligations imposed by the "shingle" theory apply here because of the special circumstances of this type of operation. Yet the opinion below does not connect Kahn explicitly with any of the "boiler room" activities; the Commission's findings do not even state that Kahn's customer had received one of MacRobbins' brochures, even though the record suggests that he did. Thus I agree with the remand, not because otherwise we would establish a *per se* rule, but because we cannot tell what rule—*per se* or otherwise—we are called upon to review. Congress has given the Commission a broad, though not limitless, grant of authority to interpret and apply the statutes under which it operates. Before we can assess the validity of the Commission's interpretation of the statute, we should know precisely what that interpretation is. Compare *SEC v. Chenery Corp.*, 318 U.S. 80 (1943).

Section 4.2 Investment Adviser Antifraud Enforcement

Topic 1 Antifraud Statute of Advisers Act

Laws & Rules Highlight:

IA Act (15 USC 80b-1 *et seq.*) & Rules (17 CFR §§ 275.0-2 *et seq.*)

- § 203 Registration of Investment Advisers
  - § 203(a) (*general **registration** requirement for statutory investment advisers*)
  - §§ 203(b)(1)-(7) (*categories of statutory IAs **specifically exempted** from registration*)
  - §§ 203(l)-(m) (*categories of **exempt reporting** IAs*)
- § 206 Prohibited Transactions by Registered Investment Advisers (*IA Act's antifraud statute; applicable to "**any**" statutory IA—whether or not required to register under § 203(a)*)
  - § 206(1) (*prohibits "any device, scheme, or artifice **to defraud** any client or prospective client"*)
  - § 206(2) (*prohibits "any transaction, practice, or course of business which **operates as a fraud or deceit** upon any client or prospective client"*)
  - § 206(3) (*prohibits **principal or agency cross** transaction by an IA with client without advance written disclosure and client consent; prohibition not applicable to **a BD not acting as an IA** in relation to the transaction*)
  - § 206(4) (*prohibits "any act, practice, or course of business which **is** fraudulent, deceptive, or manipulative; grants **SEC rulemaking authority** to define, and to prescribe means reasonably designed to prevent, fraud by advisers*)
    - ✓ Rule 206(4)-8 Pooled Investment Vehicles (*prohibits investment advisers—whether to **registered § 3(a) ICs** or to **non-registered §§ 3(c)(1) & 3(c)(7) private funds**—from defrauding "any investor or prospective investor" in such pooled investment vehicles advised by the IA*)
    - ✓ § 202(a)(29) (*def. "**private fund**," referring to IC Act §§ 3(c)(1) & 3(c)(7) funds*)
- § 211 Rules, Regulations, and Orders
  - § 211(a) (*For purposes of **§§ 206(1)-(2)**, SEC may not define "**client**" to include an **investor** in a private fund managed and advised by an investment adviser*)

Case Study 1 & 2: Varying Degrees of Liability under Antifraud Statutes

Liability for violation of § 206(1)'s prohibition of scheme "*to defraud*" any client or prospective client requires a finding of ***scienter***, or deliberate or reckless deception. Liability for violation of § 206(2)'s prohibition of practice which "*operates as a fraud* *or deceit*" upon any client or prospective client requires a finding of a lower standard of ***negligence***, or negligent deception. In contrast to §§ 206(1)-(2) which specifically define their violations, § 206(4)'s general prohibition of "any fraudulent practice" by an investment adviser without any reference to clients defers to SEC rulemaking to define its violation. A ***broad*** reading of § 206(4) is consistent with the statutory purpose of the Adviser Act "to protect the public's confidence in investment advisers."

Steadman v. SEC

603 F.2d 1126 (5th Cir. 1979)

[***Procedural history***: In re Steadman Security Corp., Adm. Proc. 3-3101, 34-13695, IC-9830, IA-593, 46 SEC 896 (1977), *aff'd in part and vacated and remanded on other grounds sub nom.* Steadman v. SEC, 603 F.2d 1126 (5th Cir. 1979), *aff'd on other grounds*, 450 U.S. 91 (1981)]

United States v. Elliott

62 F.3d 1304 (11th Cir. 1995, as amended per curiam 1996)

[***Procedural history***: United States v. Elliott, 62 F.3d 1304 (11th Cir. 1995, as amended 1996); *amended per curiam*, 82 F.3d 989 (11th Cir. 1996); *cert. denied*, 519 U.S. 859 (1996)]

Case Study 3: Fraud by Adviser to Unregistered Investment Pool*

While §§ 206(1)-(2) prohibits fraud by "*any*" investment adviser—whether or not subject to registration—against "***any client or prospective client***," their enforcement scope is limited by § 211(a) which does not allow the SEC to define the term "*client*" to include an "*investor*" in a private fund managed and advised by the adviser. On the other hand, § 206(4) broadly grants the SEC rulemaking authority to define, and to prescribe means reasonably designed to prevent, fraud by advisers. Pursuant to § 206(4) authority the SEC adopted Rule 206(4)-8, which prohibits fraud by "*any*" investment adviser—whether or not subject to registration—against "***any investor or prospective investor***" in a pooled investment vehicle advised by the adviser. Thus Rule 206(4)-8 extends an adviser's ***duty to refrain from fraud*** from the "client" relationship to the ultimate "investor" relationship; however, the Rule does not create a ***fiduciary duty*** to investors or prospective investors in a pooled investment vehicle not otherwise imposed by law.*

*[Prohibition of Fraud by Advisers to Certain Pooled Investment Vehicles, IA-2628, 72 FR 44756 (2007)]

SEC v. Overseas Chinese Fund L.P., WinWin Capital Mgmt., *et al.*

3:09-cv-00614B (SEC Compl., ND Texas Apr 3, 2009)

[***Related materials:*** SEC v. Overseas Chinese Fund L.P., WinWin Capital Mgmt., et al., 3:09-cv-00614B (SEC Compl., ND Texas Apr. 3, 2009); Lit. Rel. 20988, *SEC Halts On-Going Multi-Million Dollar Ponzi*

Scheme and Affinity Fraud Involving Investments in a Canadian-Based Hedge Fund (Apr. 6, 2009); Press Rel 2009-74, *SEC Obtains Asset Freeze In Ponzi Scheme Targeting Chinese-American Community in Dallas Area* (Apr. 6, 2009); In *re* Weizhen Tang, Adm. Proc. 3-15060, IA-3505 (Nov. 21, 2012)]

Steadman, Petitioner v. SEC, Respondent

603 F.2d 1126 (5th Cir. 1979)

Before WISDOM, GODBOLD and TJOFLAT, Circuit Judges.

OPINION

TJOFLAT, Circuit Judge:

The petitioner in this case, Charles W. Steadman, is the president, chairman of the board, and sole beneficial owner of all the voting stock in **Steadman Security Corporation** (SSC), an investment adviser registered with the Securities and Exchange Commission. SSC, either directly or through wholly-owned subsidiaries, is the adviser to and manager of several mutual funds known collectively as the **Steadman Funds**. Steadman petitions for review of the SEC's decision of June 29, 1977, *In re Steadman Security Corp.*, 46 SEC 896 (1977), which found Steadman, SSC, and the subsidiaries in violation of several provisions of the securities laws.[1] Because of these violations, the Commission entered an order that would (1) bar Steadman permanently from associating with any investment adviser, (2) prohibit his affiliation with any registered investment company, and (3) suspend him for one year from associating with any broker or dealer. No sanctions were ordered against

---

[1] The Commission found the following violations:

1. Steadman, SSC, and SSC's wholly-owned broker-dealer subsidiary, Republic Securities Corp. (RSC), violated or aided and abetted violations of section 17(a) of the Securities Act of 1933 (Securities Act), section 10(b) of the Securities Exchange Act of 1934 and rule 10b-5 thereunder, and § § 206(1) and (2) of the Investment Advisers Act of 1940 (IAA) by failing to disclose that Steadman and SSC had borrowed money from the banks that maintained the custodian accounts for the Steadman Funds;

2. Steadman and SSC violated or aided and abetted violations of § § 20(a), 30, and 34 of the Investment Company Act of 1940 (ICA) by failing to disclose the bank loans in proxy solicitation materials and annual and quarterly reports;

3. Steadman and SSC violated or aided and abetted violations of § 17(a) of the Securities Act, § 10(b) of the Exchange Act, and rule 10b-5 thereunder, § § 206(1) and (2) of the IAA, and § 15(a)(1) of the ICA by failing to disclose that SSC had received compensation from the mutual funds not precisely described in its management contracts;

4. Steadman and RSC violated or aided and abetted violations of § 17(e) of the ICA by receiving tender solicitation fees in connection with the tender of shares held by the funds and not remitting the fees to the funds;

5. Steadman, SSC, and its subsidiaries violated and aided and abetted violations of § 30(a) of the ICA and rules 30a-1 and 30a-2 thereunder, and § 17(a) of the Exchange Act and rule 17a-5 thereunder by failing to file annual reports of three mutual funds and four brokerage firms on time; and

6. Steadman and SSC aided and abetted technical violations of § 17(a) of the ICA by causing one fund under their control to buy and sell securities directly from other funds to which SSC was the adviser.

the corporate respondents, and they do not join in this appeal. Steadman raises several points of error in his petition, most of which we find to be without merit. We grant the petition in part, however, and remand the case to the Commission for reconsideration of the sanctions. * * * *

I. The Banking Relationships

Between 1965 and 1968, Steadman and SSC borrowed substantial amounts of money from the Riggs Bank of Washington, D.C.,[2] the same bank where the Steadman Funds kept their checking accounts.[3] In 1968, SSC began an expansion program to acquire the management rights to additional mutual funds. To finance these acquisitions, SSC applied to the Riggs Bank for a $2 million unsecured loan. The bank turned down the request, finding that the additional debt load on SSC, whose operations had not been profitable, would be too large. Steadman then retained two prominent investment bankers to aid his quest for capital; one of them successfully arranged a $3 million loan to SSC from the Chase Manhattan Bank in New York.

At about the time the Chase loan was negotiated, Steadman and SSC recommended to the directors of several of the mutual funds that the funds transfer their bank accounts to Chase. The directors were told that the New York bank's custodial fees were lower, that it would be advantageous to be closer to the New York securities market, and that there had been problems with the Riggs Bank. They were not told about the loan to SSC. The transfer of accounts was approved.

Riggs called its personal loans to Steadman when the accounts were transferred (SSC had no loans outstanding from this bank at the time). Steadman obtained a collateralized loan from the First National Bank of Washington to repay the Riggs loans. The First National loan was called in 1970 when the value of the collateral declined, but Steadman received a 90-day extension. Two days later, one of the funds purchased a 90-day certificate of deposit from First National in an amount in excess of the loan. To repay his First National loan, Steadman obtained a loan from yet another bank, the National Bank of

[2] The Commission's opinion does not specify any of the banks involved in these dealings, but the Administrative Law Judge's Initial Decision identifies them and their names are not in dispute.

[3] The Riggs Bank was the custodian for the securities and other investments owned by the funds and it also kept the funds' cash assets on deposit. Cash assets of a fund include proceeds from the sale of portfolio securities and any judgments realized by the fund. Checking accounts are used by the funds principally to pay dividend distributions and redemptions to fund shareholders.

Washington. Soon afterwards, the custodial accounts for one of the Steadman funds were transferred from St. Louis to the National Bank. The fund's directors were not told about the loan to Steadman when they approved the transfer.

Neither Steadman's nor SSC's loans were disclosed in the mutual funds' prospectuses. The Commission found that this was material information that Steadman had a duty to reveal. His failure to do so was in willful violation of § 17(a) of the Securities Act of 1933, § 10(b) of the Securities Exchange Act of 1934, rule 10b-5, and § § 206(1) and (2) of the Investment Advisers Act of 1940 (**IAA**). Steadman contends that the Commission erred in finding the omitted information material, and that even if it were material, he cannot be held in violation of these statutes absent a finding that he acted with scienter, *i.e.*, an intent to deceive or defraud.

I-A. Materiality

Steadman agrees that *TSC Industries, Inc. v. Northway, Inc.*, 426 U.S. 438 (1976), defines the applicable standard of materiality but argues that the Commission misapplied that standard in this case. The *TSC* case states: "An omitted fact is material if there is a substantial likelihood that a reasonable shareholder would consider it important in deciding (the matter before him)." The Commission concluded that Steadman's practice of borrowing heavily, for himself and SSC, from the same banks where the funds had accounts created a potential for subordinating the funds' interests to his own. Deposits are the source of money that banks lend out for interest. Steadman needed large loans. His self-interest in currying the good favor of the banks might have led him, the Commission speculated, to keep unduly large amounts idle in the funds' non-interest-bearing accounts to the benefit of the banks but the detriment of the funds' shareholders. The SEC made no finding that this had in fact occurred and specifically declined to find that the funds' custodial accounts were a *quid pro quo* for the loans. Regardless of whether there was a connection between the loans and the accounts, the Commission decided that "Steadman had disabled himself from looking at the funds' checking account balances in a wholly disinterested way, with an eye single to the funds' best interest. Investors had a right to know this." Therefore, the loans were material under the *TSC* standard.

Steadman argues that the SEC found only a potential conflict of interest, and *TSC* requires an actual conflict before liability may be imposed. This misreads *TSC.* The relevant part of the *TSC* opinion involved the nondisclosure of facts that may have indicated possible market manipulation in the context of a proxy solicitation, a completely different context than what is involved here. More importantly, the Court was addressing the sufficiency of the plaintiff's case for summary judgment, *i.e.*, whether the omission was material as a matter of law. The Court was not called upon to decide the quantum of evidence necessary to establish a material omission at trial. The Court reaffirmed in *TSC* that the issue of materiality is a mixed question of law and fact and that divining the significance of the inferences a reasonable investor would draw from a given set of facts is peculiarly within the competence of the trier of fact. Turning again to the facts of the case before it, the Court said that facts suggesting that one corporation controls another may be material even though in actuality there is no control; the influence of the one company over the affairs of the other would be of importance to shareholders. Here, the Commission is the trier of fact. It decided that, under the circumstances of this case, the potential for Steadman's abuse of his influence over where the funds did their banking was sufficiently great that shareholders would want to know about the loans. That finding is not wrong as a matter of law, and we affirm it.[4]

I-B. Scienter

Steadman strenuously urges that scienter, an intent to deceive, manipulate, or defraud, is a necessary element of any enforcement action by the SEC under the antifraud provisions of the securities laws. Since the Commission failed to find that Steadman acted with the requisite intent, he would have us set aside its decision and order. There is some support for this position. In *Ernst & Ernst v. Hochfelder*, 425 U.S. 185 (1976), the Supreme Court decided that scienter must be proved in a private damage action under rule 10b-5. Whether that holding should be extended to Commission enforcement actions under the statutes that Steadman was found to have violated is the question before us. We turn to an examination of each relevant section.

I-B-1. Section 10(b) of the Exchange Act

The Commission found that Steadman violated § 10(b) of the Exchange Act and rule 10b-5, § 17(a) of the Securities Act, and § § 206(1) and (2) of the IAA. In *SEC v. Blatt*,

[4] *McDonough v. Champburger Corp.*, 488 F.2d 948 (5th Cir. 1974), does not require a contrary result. We there decided that the omitted facts were not material because other disclosed facts adequately revealed the possible conflict of interest, if indeed there was one at all. Steadman and SSC disclosed no facts concerning their borrowings from the banks.

583 F.2d 1325 (5th Cir. 1978), we held that the Commission must prove scienter in an injunctive action under § 10(b). Steadman contends that this holding compels the conclusion that scienter also is required in a disciplinary enforcement action such as this one.[5] Because the Commission failed to indicate whether it considered the other violations independent and sufficient bases for the sanctions imposed, the argument continues, we should reverse the decision.

We need not decide what state of mind must be shown in a disciplinary action for a violation of § 10(b), for the Commission has indicated to our satisfaction that the § 10(b) violation is mere surplusage in this case. In its opinion, in the context of distinguishing the *Hochfelder* case, the Commission stated:

> The instant case does not resemble *Hochfelder*. This is not a private action for money damages. It is a proceeding initiated by a public authority for the prophylactic purpose of preventing future harm to the public interest. Nor does this case rest solely on Rule 10b-5. Indeed, it does not turn on 10b-5 at all. The references to that rule in the order for proceedings and in this opinion are merely cumulative. Section 17(a) of the Securities Act and the provisions of the Investment Company Act ... are independent bases for liability.

The clear import of these words is that § 10(b) and rule 10b-5 are not essential to the opinion and order.

1-B-2. Section 17(a) of the Securities Act

Section 17(a) of the Securities Act provides:

> It shall be unlawful for any person in the offer or sale of any securities by the use of any means or instruments of transportation or communication in interstate commerce or by the use of the mails, directly or indirectly
>
> (1) to employ any device, scheme, or artifice to defraud, or
>
> (2) to obtain money or property by means of any untrue statement of a material fact or any omission to state a material fact necessary in order to make the statements made, in the light of the circumstances under which they were made, not misleading, or

---

[5] The *Blatt* case was brought pursuant to § 21(d) of the Exchange Act, which authorizes the Commission to seek injunctive relief in district court for violations of that Act. The case before us is an administrative proceeding under § 15(b) of the Exchange Act, § 9(b) of the ICA, and § 203(f) of the IAA.

> (3) to engage in any transaction, practice, or course of business which operates or would operate as a fraud or deceit upon the purchaser.

In *Hochfelder* the Court noted that the language of rule 10b-5 appears to have been derived in significant part from this section.[6] *Hochfelder* held that scienter is required under rule 10b-5. Petitioner argues that this indicates strongly that scienter also is required under § 17(a).

Hochfelder exposes the sophistry in this argument. The Court imposed a scienter element on rule 10b-5 because the rule can be no broader than its parent statute, § 10(b) of the Exchange Act, whose language the Court interpreted to require an intent to defraud.[7] Section 17(a) is, of course, a congressional enactment, not an administrative rule, and its language is quite different from that of § 10(b). Indeed, in a passage that cuts against Steadman's position, the Court stated:

> Viewed in isolation the language of subsection (b), and arguably that of subsection (c) (of rule 10b-5), could be read as proscribing, respectively, any type of material misstatement or omission, and any course of conduct, that has the effect of defrauding investors, whether the wrongdoing was intentional or not.

Hochfelder, supra. Subsections (b) and (c) of rule 10b-5 are nearly word-for-word identical with subsections (2) and (3) of § 17(a), respectively. We think that the Court would regard these subsections of § 17(a) as requiring no intent to defraud.

---

[6] Rule 10b-5 provides:

It shall be unlawful for any person, directly or indirectly, by the use of any means or instrumentality of interstate commerce, or of the mails or of any facility of any national securities exchange,

(a) To employ any device, scheme, or artifice to defraud,

(b) To make any untrue statement of a material fact or to omit to state a material fact necessary in order to make the statements made, in the light of the circumstances under which they were made, not misleading, or

(c) To engage in any act, practice, or course of business which operates or would operate as a fraud or deceit upon any person, in connection with the purchase or sale of any security.

[7] Section 10(b) provides:

It shall be unlawful for any person, directly or indirectly, by the use of any means or instrumentality of interstate commerce or of the mails, or of any facility of any national securities exchange

(b) To use or employ, in connection with the purchase or sale of any security registered on a national securities exchange or any security not so registered, any manipulative or deceptive device or contrivance in contravention of such rules and regulations as the Commission may prescribe as necessary or appropriate in the public interest or for the protection of investors.

Steadman responds that the Securities Act and the Exchange Act have traditionally been construed *in pari materia*, and that to impose a scienter requirement under one but not the other would disrupt the "single comprehensive scheme of regulation" that these statutes form. *Globus v. Law Research Service, Inc.*, 418 F.2d 1276 (2d Cir. 1969), *cert. denied*, 397 U.S. 913 (1970). But *Hochfelder* observes that Congress fashioned standards of fault under these acts on a particularized basis. "Ascertainment of congressional intent with respect to the standard of liability created by a particular section of the Acts must therefore rest primarily on the language of that section." We turn then to an examination of the language of § 17(a).

We are not the first to travel this road. In *SEC v. Coven*, 581 F.2d 1020 (2d Cir. 1978), *cert. denied*, 440 U.S. 950 (1979), the Second Circuit, in a well-reasoned opinion that included a canvass of the legislative history, concluded that scienter is not required in an SEC injunctive action under § 17(a)(2). We adopt that conclusion for the reasons given in the *Coven* opinion. Accord, *SEC v. American Realty Trust*, 586 F.2d 1001 (4th Cir. 1978); *SEC v. Southwest Coal & Energy Co.*, 439 F. Supp. 820 (WD La. 1977), Appeal docketed, No. 78-1130 (5th Cir. 1978). Moreover, we adopt the further suggestion in *Coven* that "the clear import of the critical phrase in subsection (3), 'operates as a fraud,' is to focus attention on the effect of potentially misleading conduct on the public, not on the culpability of the person responsible." *Coven, supra.* When construing identical language in § 206(2) of the IAA, language which was undoubtedly copied from § 17(a)(3), the Supreme Court said: "Congress, in empowering the courts to enjoin any practice which operates 'as a fraud or deceit' upon a client, did not intend to require proof of intent to injure ...." *SEC v. Capital Gains Research Bureau, Inc.*, 375 U.S. 180 (1963).[8] Steadman objects that *Coven* is distinguishable as an injunctive action in which the Commission need only prove that the defendant is about to engage in unlawful conduct, *i.e.*, not every element of a § 17(a) violation need be proved. We think that *Coven*'s analysis of the statutory language does not depend on the character of relief sought; the words used by Congress carry the same meaning regardless of whether the SEC seeks an injunction or a

---

[8] Read literally, § 17(a)(3) requires a finding that the course of business in which Steadman engaged operated as a fraud on the funds' shareholders. The Commission made no such finding in this case. A remand for rectification of this lapse would be a wasted gesture, however, because Capital Gains holds that nondisclosure of a material fact is conduct that "operates as a fraud or deceit" within the meaning of § 206(2) of the IAA. We think the same conclusion is inescapable under § 17(a)(3).

stronger sanction. As we shall discuss, the severity of the sanctions affects the factual showing necessary to support them, but it does not affect the basic elements of the offense. Accordingly, we hold that scienter need not be proved to establish violations of § § 17(a)(2) and (3).[9]

We come now to § 17(a)(1). This clause contains the word "device" that the Supreme Court in *Hochfelder* found to be suggestive of intentional conduct when read together with "manipulative" and "deceptive." The latter two words do not appear in § 17(a)(1), but the three words of that section device, scheme, and artifice must each be read in conjunction with the words "to defraud." The resulting phrases device to defraud, scheme to defraud, artifice to defraud carry strong implications of intentional conduct. We do not think Congress would have used such language if it meant to reach merely negligent actions. The use of the term "employ" further supports our reading of the section. See *Hochfelder, supra.*

In adjudicating a violation of § 17(a), the Commission failed to find that Steadman acted with an intent to defraud, and thus an essential element of a § 17(a)(1) violation is missing. There is an indication in a footnote to the Commission's opinion (n.31) that the § 17(a) infraction rests only on subsections (2) and (3). Perhaps this oblique footnote sufficiently conveys the SEC's intent to disclaim reliance upon § 17(a)(1). To the extent that the SEC relied upon subsections (2) and (3) of § 17(a), under which scienter is not a requirement, the violations are supported by substantial evidence and we would affirm; nevertheless, since we find other reasons to send this case back for reconsideration, the Commission on remand can clarify its opinion with regard to the subsections of § 17(a) that it considers were violated.

1-B-3. Sections 206(1) and (2) of the IAA

---

[9] Steadman argues that *Sanders v. John Nuveen & Co.*, 554 F.2d 790 (7th Cir. 1977), suggests a contrary result. On the assumption that a private right of action for damages exists under § 17(a)(2), a question it did not resolve, the Seventh Circuit there commented that scienter must be proved in such an action, for to interpret the subsection otherwise would nullify other sections of the Securities Act that specifically provide for private actions. We cannot agree with Steadman's contention that the logic in Sanders should control in the type of proceeding now before us. Even if scienter may be required to harmonize a hypothetical implied private cause of action with the rest of the act, there is no reason to hold scienter an element of the action specifically contemplated by the statute.

What we have said in discussing § 17(a) of the Securities Act applies equally to the language of subsections (1) and (2) of § 206 of the IAA.[10] The wording of these provisions, which make it unlawful for an investment adviser "(1) to employ any device, scheme, or artifice to defraud any client or prospective client; (2) to engage in any transaction, practice, or course of business which operates as a fraud or deceit upon any client or prospective client," is drawn from § § 17(a)(1) and (3), respectively. As we already have noted, the Supreme Court has ruled that scienter is not required under **§ 206(2)**. *Capital Gains Research Bureau, supra.* The Court in that case said nothing about part (1) of § 206. We think that the language of this subsection must be construed to have the same meaning as § 17(a)(1), for to do otherwise would produce a serious anomaly; language copied directly from the Securities Act would have a different meaning under the IAA. We are aware that in *Capital Gains*, the Court emphasized that the intent of the IAA was to impose fiduciary standards on investment advisers. This general purpose for the statute argues in favor of liability for negligence alone, but "ascertainment of congressional intent with respect to the standard of liability created by a particular section ... must ... rest primarily on the language of that section." *Hochfelder, supra.* The language of **§ 206(1)** clearly connotes intentional conduct and nothing in either the House or Senate Committee reports indicates that this phrase in the IAA is to be interpreted differently than the same phrase in the Securities Act. See H.R. Rep. No. 2639, 76th Cong., 3d Sess. (1940); S. Rep. No. 1775, 76th Cong., 3d Sess. (1940). Although the violation of § 206(2) can be supported without a showing of scienter, here the Commission found a violation of § 206(1) without finding the requisite scienter. Because the Commission's findings do not support some of the violations, we remand so that the Commission can reconsider whether it would impose the same sanctions under the violations we uphold.

[omitted: II. Advisory Fees; III. Tender Solicitation Fees; IV. Reporting Violations; V. Sanctions and Burden of Proof]

---

[10] Section 206 provides in part:

It shall be unlawful for any investment adviser, by use of the mails or any means or instrumentality of interstate commerce, directly or indirectly

(1) to employ any device, scheme, or artifice to defraud any client or prospective client;

(2) to engage in any transaction, practice, or course of business which operates as a fraud or deceit upon any client or prospective client.

VI. Conclusion

We summarize here our holdings adverse to the Commission, which will affect the proceedings on remand:

1. Scienter is an element of a violation of § 17(a)(1) of the Securities Act, and § 206(1) of the IAA.

* * * *

The petition for review is therefore granted in part and denied in part; the order is set aside and the cause is remanded for reconsideration consistent with this opinion.

Remanded.

United States v. Elliott

62 F.3d 1304 (11th Cir. 1995, as amended per curiam 1996)

Before ANDERSON and BIRCH, Circuit Judges, and JOHNSON, Senior Circuit Judge.

Opinion

BIRCH, Circuit Judge:

In this appeal, we decide the first-impression issue for our circuit of the requirements for qualification as an investment adviser under the Investment Advisers Act of 1940, 15 USC § §80b-2(a)(11) and 80b-6. Because we conclude that managers of a number of investment companies were investment advisers who violated the anti-fraud provisions of the Investment Advisers Act, we AFFIRM their convictions. The district court, however, erred in formulating the restitution ordered. We VACATE the previous restitution orders and REMAND for the district court to order restitution consistent with this opinion.

I. BACKGROUND

From 1980 to 1987, defendants-appellants Charles Phillip Elliott and William H. Melhorn managed a collection of investment companies that included Elliott Real Estate, Inc., Elliott Securities, Elliott Mortgage Company, Inc., and Elliott Group, Inc. (collectively, "**Elliott Enterprises**"). During the relevant period, Elliott was president and owner of Elliott Enterprises; Melhorn began as a special assistant to Elliott and was promoted to chief executive officer of Elliott Enterprises. While **Elliott Securities** operated as a securities broker, the rest of Elliott Enterprises marketed a range of investment vehicles created and managed by Elliott Enterprises.

Elliott Enterprises lost millions of dollars each year between 1980 and 1987. Nevertheless, Elliott and Melhorn retained their current investors and attracted new ones by making false claims regarding the safety and performance of Elliott Enterprises investments. For example, Elliott and Melhorn represented to current and prospective investors that Elliott Enterprises had a good track record and was financially sound. The two men also falsely represented Elliott Enterprises as being a regulated bank. They assured investors that particular investments were insured or secured when, in fact, the investments often were backed with insufficient, worthless or nonexistent collateral. In several instances, Elliott and Melhorn falsely told investors that income from investments was tax-free. The two also stated that Elliott Enterprises had "always received a clean bill of health by periodic audits by the Florida Department of Professional Regulation," when no such audits were performed.

Significantly, Elliott Enterprises "lulled" its investors by sending regular, competitive interest payments at rates just above the market rate. Elliott Enterprises was able to maintain these payments, despite huge, mounting losses, by the use of a Ponzi, or pyramid, scheme: interest payments were funded not only by returns from underlying investments, but also by the principal from newer investor funds. On some occasions, Elliott and Melhorn and their employees solicited new investments in Elliott Enterprises in order to cover interest payments that were coming due.

Both Elliott and Melhorn profited enormously from this arrangement. Elliott's extravagant lifestyle included multimillion dollar residences, resort homes, and luxury automobiles. Although Elliott's sole employment during this period was as president of Elliott Enterprises, he did not receive a salary. Instead, he compensated himself by commingling investor funds with personal funds.[1] Melhorn's compensation came from commissions on sales of Elliott Enterprises investment products; in some years, income from those commissions exceeded one million dollars.

In 1987, following an investigation by the Securities Exchange Commission, a receiver took control of Elliott Enterprises. An audit taken at that time revealed liabilities exceeding assets by more than twenty million dollars. As a result, Elliott and Melhorn were no longer able to attract new investments; the Ponzi scheme collapsed, and interest payments ceased. Following the failure of Elliott Enterprises, investors and creditors have recovered from the receiver ten-and-a-half cents on the dollar.

Elliott and Melhorn were indicted on twenty-two counts of fraud under the Investment Advisers Act, 15 USC § § 80(b)-3(d) and 80b-6 and 18 USC § 2, six counts of securities fraud under the Securities Act, 15 USC § 77q(a) and 18 USC § 2, ten counts of mail fraud, 18 USC § § 2 and 1341, and one count of conspiracy, 18 USC § 371. The thirty-nine charges in the indictment stemmed from misrepresentations allegedly made by Elliott and Melhorn to nineteen[2] individuals. In March, 1990, a jury returned a verdict of guilty on

---

[1] Elliott maintained a separate personal account, which was carried on the books of Elliott Enterprises; as of 1987, that account had a balance exceeding one million dollars. Additionally, because Elliott Enterprises was an unincorporated business, Elliott could draw upon the other Elliott Enterprises bank accounts as though they were his personal funds. In this way, Elliott used investor funds to pay for his personal living expenses, including medical expenses, and mortgage and interest payments on his various houses.

[2] At resentencing, Melhorn's counsel stated that there were approximately twenty-three victims named in the

all but two charges of mail fraud. In July, 1990, the district court sentenced Elliott and Melhorn to prison terms[3] and ordered each defendant "to make full restitution as determined by U.S. Probation."

On first appeal, this court determined that the original restitution orders were impermissibly vague. Consequently, we remanded the case for further proceedings on the restitution issue and retained jurisdiction over the remainder of the appeal. The district court referred the case to a magistrate judge solely to calculate the amount of loss to the victims. After two status conferences, the magistrate judge recommended that the district court accept the government's estimate of victim loss, which was based on claims made to the receiver by approximately 940 Elliott Enterprises investors. The district court adopted the magistrate judge's report and recommendation without vacating the original restitution orders, setting an actual restitution amount, or making any other findings of fact. Elliott and Melhorn now appeal from this order. At the government's request, we consolidated this new appeal with the remainder of their original appeals pending before this court.

II. DISCUSSION

II-A. Exclusion of Relevant Evidence

Elliott and Melhorn contend that the district court erred by excluding proffered testimony from satisfied Elliott Enterprises customers.[4] These customers, none of whom

---

indictment. Our review of the Amended Indictment reveals only nineteen individuals.

[3] Elliott was sentenced to three, consecutive five-year prison terms for one count of investment adviser fraud, one count of securities fraud, and the count of conspiracy; he received concurrent five-year prison terms for each of the remaining counts. Melhorn received three, consecutive four-year prison terms for one count of investment adviser fraud, one count of securities fraud, and the count of conspiracy; he received concurrent five-year prison terms for each of the remaining counts.

[4] .... Elliott and Melhorn also argue that the court improperly excluded evidence regarding the receiver's conduct in handling the assets of Elliott Enterprises; they attempted to show that the investors' losses were because of the receiver's mismanagement rather than any wrongdoing by Elliott and Melhorn. It is the financial status of Elliott Enterprises before the receiver took over and while defendants were still representing that the businesses were financially sound that is significant; the financial status of Elliott Enterprises after the receiver had taken over is irrelevant. Fed. R. Evid. 401. Subsequent mismanagement by the receiver would in no way diminish the fraud perpetrated by Elliott and Melhorn against their investors before Elliott Enterprises entered into receivership, and the record contains ample evidence that Elliott Enterprises was suffering huge financial losses at the same time that Elliott and Melhorn were representing that their investments were profitable and secure....

were named in the indictment, were to have testified to their belief that Elliott and Melhorn had committed no wrongdoing; they also would have testified that the two defendants had kept their promise to secure these particular investments with collateral. We review evidentiary rulings by the district court for abuse of discretion. *United States v. Adair*, 951 F.2d 316 (11th Cir. 1992).

Although the admission and exclusion of evidence falls within the broad realm of judicial discretion, such discretion "does not extend to the exclusion of crucial relevant evidence necessary to establish a valid defense." *United States v. Williams*, 954 F.2d 668 (11th Cir. 1992). Relevant evidence is evidence that has "any tendency to make the existence of any fact that is of consequence to the determination of the action more probable or less probable than it would be without the evidence." Fed. R. Evid. 401. To the extent that Elliott and Melhorn proffered the witnesses to show that these investors did not believe that they had been defrauded, that they had received a portion of their money back upon request, that Elliott had told these investors to testify truthfully before the SEC, or that Elliott had backed these investors with the appropriate collateral as he had promised, the district court properly excluded this testimony as irrelevant. See Fed. R. Evid. 402. The fact that Elliott and Melhorn avoided wrongdoing in their dealings with five customers not named in the indictment is inconsequential in determining whether both made fraudulent representations to the nineteen victims listed in the indictment.

Elliott and Melhorn's main contention, however, is that the testimony of satisfied customers is relevant to the issue of their intent to defraud. In support of this proposition, they rely on the Ninth Circuit's decision in *United States v. Thomas*, 32 F.3d 418 (9th Cir. 1994). In *Thomas*, the defendant was charged with mail fraud for implementing an "averaging scheme." Under the scheme, the defendant quoted false prices to fruit growers to even out fluctuations in the market. The growers affected by this scheme collectively came out ahead by approximately $175,980, but the trial court in *Thomas* excluded testimony from growers, who had benefitted under the scheme but were not named in the indictment. The Ninth Circuit reversed the district court and held that the testimony of all growers impacted by the scheme was relevant to the defendant's intent in devising the scheme. The court further noted that there was "no basis for concluding that the scheme defendant had devised was intended to impact unnamed individuals any differently than those the government chose to name." *Id.*

While Elliott and Melhorn proffered the same type of testimony as that excluded in

Thomas, we note that the scheme and intent at issue in *Thomas* differ significantly from the scheme and intent at issue in this case. In *Thomas*, the defendant made two, distinct misrepresentations: when fruit prices rose above an "average" price, the defendant falsely quoted a lower price to growers; when fruit prices dropped below average, the defendant falsely quoted a higher price. Overall, the growers impacted by the averaging scheme actually came out ahead by approximately $175,980; thus, testimony from "satisfied" growers could have helped the defendant establish that he did not intend to profit from his admittedly fraudulent representations.

Proving intent in this case, however, is not a simple matter of accounting for economic surplus. The material misrepresentations here center on the purported financial health of the Elliott Enterprises businesses and the performance and safety of its investments. No amount of testimony from satisfied customers could "average out" Elliott and Melhorn's intent to defraud when they continued to solicit new investments and reassure old investors while concealing millions of dollars in losses per year with fictitious audits and phantom collateral. To a much greater degree than was the case in *Thomas*, the proof of Elliott and Melhorn's intent to defraud lies in the substance of their misrepresentations, not in the cumulative impact of those misrepresentations on all of their customers. Thus, the district court did not err by excluding the proffered testimony as irrelevant.[5]

II-B. Applicability of the Investment Advisers Act of 1940

Elliott and Melhorn contend that the evidence was insufficient to support their convictions for investment adviser fraud. They argue that a defendant and his alleged victim must be in an adviser-client relationship before the antifraud provisions of the Investment Adviser Act can apply. * * * *

II-B-2. Necessity of Adviser-Client Relationship

Elliott and Melhorn maintain that, even if they were investment advisers, they were not in an adviser-client relationship with any of the customers named in the indictment.

---

[5] Despite Elliott and Melhorn's arguments to the contrary, such a calculus of victims would be especially inappropriate in the case of a Ponzi or pyramid scheme. A Ponzi scheme impacts individual investors differently, depending on how much of their initial investment particular investors had recovered before the pyramid's inevitable collapse. As the district court observed "if ... this, in fact, was a Ponzi scheme, obviously the first people ... are going to make money. That's the nature of the Ponzi scheme."

They cite not only the lack of a clearly identified investment advisory fee, but also lack of an investment adviser contract as proof that no such relationship existed. In the absence of an adviser-client relationship, they argue that they cannot be convicted under the antifraud provisions of the Investment Advisers Act. The Act in relevant part provides:

> It shall be unlawful for any investment adviser, by use of the mails or any means or instrumentality of interstate commerce, directly or indirectly—
>
> (1) to employ any device, scheme, or artifice to defraud any *client or prospective client*;
>
> (2) to engage in any transaction, practice, or course of business which operates as a fraud or deceit upon any *client or prospective client* …
>
> (4) *to engage in any act, practice, or course of business which is fraudulent, deceptive, or manipulative.*

15 USC § 80b-6 (emphasis added). Subsections (1) and (2) describe offenses specifically affecting a "client or prospective client." In contrast, subsection (4) requires the government to prove only that the defendant was an investment adviser and that the defendant "engaged in any act, practice, or course of business which is fraudulent, deceptive, or manipulative." *Id.* § 80b-6(4). Lacking any reference to clients, subsection (4) appears to be a general prohibition against certain conduct by an investment adviser. See *United States v. Jordan*, 915 F.2d 622 (11th Cir. 1990), *cert. denied*, 499 U.S. 979 (1991) ("Where Congress includes particular language in one section of a statute but omits it in another section of the same Act, it is generally presumed that Congress acts intentionally and purposefully in the disparate inclusion or exclusion.") (quoting *Rodriguez v. United States*, 480 U.S. 522 (1987) (per curiam)).

The legislative history of the Investment Advisers Act does not contradict this reading of § 80b-6. In 1960, Congress amended the Investment Advisers Act by adding subsection (4). PL 86-750, § 9, 74 Stat. 885, 887 (Sept. 13, 1960). The Senate Report accompanying the 1960 amendment stated that the purpose of the new subsection was to "empower the [SEC] by rule to define and prescribe means reasonably designed to prevent *fraudulent practices*." S. Rep. No. 1760, 86th Cong., 2d Sess. (1960) (emphasis added).

> Because of the general language of the statutory antifraud provision and the absence of any express rulemaking power in connection with them, it is not clear what fraudulent and deceptive activities are prohibited by this act and as to how far the Commission is limited in this area by common-law concepts of fraud and deceit.

> These include proof of a (1) false representation of; (2) a material; (3) fact; (4) the defendant must make it to induce reliance; (5) the plaintiff must rely on the false representation; (6) and suffer damage as a consequence.
>
> In order to overcome this difficulty, § 9 of the bill would amend [15 USC § 80b-6] to add a prohibition against *engaging in conduct which is fraudulent, deceptive, or manipulative* and to authorize the Commission by rules and regulations to define, and prescribe means reasonably designed to prevent, such acts and practices as are fraudulent, deceptive, or manipulative.

Id. (emphasis added). Thus, the legislative history of the 1960 amendment also indicates an intent to prohibit fraudulent practices or conduct, without regard to whether the victim is in an adviser-client relationship with the investment adviser. Indeed, Congress's primary concern appeared to be the possible limitations imposed by common-law concepts of fraud and deceit, which require reliance but no other relationship between the plaintiff and the defendant.[6]

As demonstrated above, both Elliott and Melhorn were investment advisers within the meaning of 80b-2(a)(11). There is ample evidence in the record to show that they both engaged in acts, practices, or courses of business in violation of § 80b-6(4). Therefore, we conclude that the evidence was sufficient to support Elliott and Melhorn's convictions under the Investment Advisers Act.[7]

---

[6] Such a broad reading of § 80b-6 is also consistent with the goal of the original Investment Advisers Act of 1940. One of the main purposes of the Investment Advisers Act was to protect the public's confidence in investment advisers. As the Senate Report accompanying the Act warned:

> "Not only must the public be protected from the frauds and misrepresentations of unscrupulous tipsters and touts, but the bona fide investment adviser must be safeguarded against the stigma of the activities of these individuals."

S. Rep. No. 1775, 76th Cong., 3d Sess. 21 (1940); see also *SEC v. Capital Gains Research Bureau*, 375 U.S. 180 (1963) ("A fundamental purpose, common to these statutes, was to substitute a philosophy of full disclosure for the philosophy of *caveat emptor* and thus to achieve a high standard of business ethics in the securities industry. As we recently said in a related context, 'It requires but little appreciation ... of what happened in this country during the 1920's and 1930's to realize how essential it is that the highest ethical standards prevail' in every facet of the securities industry." See generally *Lowe v. SEC*, 472 U.S. 181 (1985) (describing legislative background to the Investment Advisers Act). One method of safeguarding the integrity of investment advisers is by criminalizing any fraudulent or deceptive behavior by an investment adviser, regardless of whether the victim of the fraud can establish an adviser-client relationship.

[7] Our decision implicitly confirms the jury instructions given by the district court regarding the Investment Advisers Act, since these instructions are in accordance with our analysis.

* * * *

III. CONCLUSION

Elliott and Melhorn contest their convictions and sentences for investment adviser fraud, securities fraud, mail fraud, and conspiracy. Because the district court did not err in its evidentiary rulings and because the evidence in the record was sufficient to support the jury's verdict, we AFFIRM Elliott and Melhorn's convictions. * * * *

SEC v. Overseas Chinese Fund L.P., WinWin Capital Mgmt., *et al.*

3:09-cv-00614B (SEC Compl., ND Texas Apr 3, 2009)

COMPLAINT

The Securities and Exchange Commission, Plaintiff, files this Complaint against **Defendants** Overseas Chinese Fund Limited Partnership, Weizhen Tang & Associates, Inc., Weizhen Tang Corp., WinWin Capital Management, LLC, WinWin Capital Limited Partnership, J.O.R. & Associates, LLC, and Weizhen Tang, and **Relief Defendants** WinWin Capital Partners, LP, and Bluejay Investment, LLC, d/b/a Vintage International Investment, LLC, and would respectfully show the Court as follows:

SUMMARY

1. This emergency matter involves an on-going Ponzi scheme and affinity fraud targeting members of the Chinese-American community. Weizhen Tang, the self-described "*Chinese Warren Buffet*" recently admitted to investors that since at least 2006 his Toronto-based hedge fund, **Oversea Chinese Fund Limited Partnership** (the "Hedge Fund"), operated as a *Ponzi* scheme. In February 2009, Tang told investors that he and the Hedge Fund posted false profits on investors' account statements for the purpose of concealing substantial trading losses, and, more insidiously, to attract new investors to his fund. Tang further admitted that he used funds from new investors to return principal and payout purported profits to other investors. Tang admitted to investors that the Hedge Fund paid out at least $8 million in purported profits in 2006, 2007, and 2008—despite significant trading losses incurred during that time. Since at least as early as 2004, more than 200 investors have collectively invested between $50 and $75 million in the Hedge Fund.

2. Tang specifically targeted members of the Chinese-American community and solicited U.S. investors to directly and indirectly invest in the Hedge Fund. Several U.S. investors directly invested in the Hedge Fund. Since at least November 2007, Tang raised capital for the Hedge Fund from U.S. investors by offering and selling limited partnership interests in **WinWin Capital Limited Partnership** ("WinWin Partners"), a Texas-based limited partnership he controls. WinWin Partners' sole business is investing partnership capital in the Hedge Fund. As of March 10, 2009, WinWin Partners had raised almost $17.3 million in principal investments from approximately 75 investors, most of which are located in the Dallas area, but also include investors in California. These investors have

withdrawn approximately $8.4 million from the Hedge Fund, of which at least $700,000 was paid out as purported profits. Nearly $9.6 million in investor principal remains unaccounted for. Consistent with his recent confession to investors, funds invested with WinWin Partners were used to pay other investors in a *Ponzi* fashion.

3. In an effort to prey on the panic generated by his admissions of wrongdoing, Tang has sent e-mails to investors to persuade them to trust him with even more of their money and allow him to continue trading on their behalf. Within the last two weeks, Tang has informed investors that he is actively raising an additional $1 million to "recoup" investor losses and creating new business entities, bank accounts, and brokerage accounts to circumvent action by the Commission and/or the Ontario Securities Commission.

4. The Commission, in the interest of protecting investors from any further illegal activity, brings this action against the Defendants and Relief Defendants, seeking as applicable permanent injunctive relief, disgorgement of all illicit profits and benefits Defendants or Relief Defendants have received plus accrued prejudgment interest, civil monetary penalties, the appointment of a receiver over assets traceable to investor funds and other emergency and equitable relief. * * * *

PARTIES

6. **Weizhen Tang**, age 50, of Toronto, Ontario, Canada, is the manager of Oversea Chinese Fund Limited Partnership, a Toronto-based hedge fund, whose general partner is Weizhen Tang & Associates, Inc. Tang is also the owner and co-CEO of Weizhen Tang Corp., the owner of J.O.R & Associates, LLC, and the owner of WinWin Capital Management, LLC.

7. **Oversea Chinese Fund Limited Partnership** (the "***Hedge Fund***") is a limited partnership organized in December 2001 under the laws of the province of Ontario.

8. Weizhen Tang & Associates, Inc. ("WTA"), is an Ontario corporation that serves as the general partner of the Hedge Fund. WTA's officers and directors are Tang and Hong Xiao, his wife.

9. Weizhen Tang Corp. ("WTC") is an Ontario corporation that, according to its website (www.wtang.com), is primarily engaged in the management of private equity funds and hedge funds. WTC's officers and directors are Tang (chairman and secretary), his daughter Wenyi Tang (director and secretary), and Jiehua "Jay" Yu (officer).

10. **WinWin Capital Management, LLC** (the "***Adviser***"), a Texas limited liability company with its principal office in Plano, Texas, has been registered as an investment adviser with the Texas State Securities Board since July 2008. While Tang owns the Adviser, it is managed by Jiehua "Jay" Yu.

11. **WinWin Capital Limited Partnership** ("***WinWin Partners***"), a Texas limited partnership with its principal office in Plano, Texas, was created to invest partnership funds in the Hedge Fund. The limited partners of WinWin Partners, located primarily in the Dallas, Texas, area are the individual investors who, along with investors directly solicited by Tang, are the victims of the fraud in this case. WinWin Partners' sole general partner is J.O.R & Associates, LLC.

12. J.O.R & Associates, LLC ("JOR"), a Texas limited liability company located in Plano, Texas, is the general partner of WinWin Partners. JOR was created in October 2006 and listed Jiehua "Jay" Yu, Xiaohong Peng, and Richard Gu as members of the LLC. On January 1, 2007, Yu, Gu, and Peng transferred their ownership interests in JOR to Tang. Tang retained Yu, Gu, and Peng as managers of JOR to manage the day-to-day operations of WinWin Partners. Pursuant to the partnership agreement of WinWin Partners, JOR retains sole discretion to invest the partnership capital.

13. WinWin Capital Partners, L.P., a Delaware limited partnership authorized to do business in the State of Texas, lists as its principal office the Adviser's address in Plano, Texas. The general partner of WinWin Capital Partners, LP is the Adviser. A private offering memorandum for WinWin Capital Partners, LP, dated July 1, 2008, states that the minimum investment in WinWin Capital Partners, LP is $250,000. WinWin Capital Partners, LP, was formed to provide Tang's U.S. investors with greater transparency over his investment decisions using their funds. WinWin Capital Partners, L.P. is named as a relief defendant solely for the purpose of obtaining equitable relief.

14. Bluejay Investment, LLC, d/b/a Vintage International Investment, LLC ("Bluejay Investment"), a Texas limited liability company, lists as its principal office the Adviser's address in Plano, Texas. U.S. investor funds were diverted to an account in the name of Bluejay Investment. Bluejay Investment is named as a relief defendant solely for the purpose of obtaining equitable relief.

BACKGROUND FACTS

15. Weizhen Tang, a Chinese Canadian living in the Greater Toronto Area, is a

prominent figure in the Chinese community in North America. In December 2001, Tang created the Hedge Fund under the laws of the province of Ontario. Hedge Fund offering documents provide that: (i) the Hedge Fund has been active since 2004; (ii) Tang is the trading manager and WTA is the general partner; (iii) the offering started in May 2004; (iv) "prospected partners must be qualified accredit [sic] investors only" [citing Rule 501 of Reg. D]; (v) the minimum initial investment in the Hedge Fund is $150,000; and (vi) "[b]ased on past performance ... the system the Trading Manager will utilize has produced an average return of 32% per year for index and currencies."

16. According to the Hedge Fund's website (www.wtang.com), Tang, during the four years since the Hedge Fund was established, achieved an "average annual return rate [of] over 40%" by:

- integrating stock indexes, foreign exchanges, and futures into reliable short-term speculations;
- seeking consistent returns with minimum risk: 1% weekly profit; and
- keeping 99% of the total investment pool outside the market for safekeeping, while amplifying the remaining 1% with certain leverage.

Tang's purported investment strategy is to invest 99% of the total investment pool in conservative, out-of-the market investments like bonds and certificates of deposit and 1% of the investment pool in speculative short-term investments. The Hedge Fund provides investors with periodic account statements via its website, and investors use personalized user names and passwords to monitor their accounts. The Hedge Fund is comprised of more than 200 investors who have collectively invested between $50 and $75 million. The Hedge Fund does not charge investors a fee on the first 6% of profit, but it charges a 25% "management" fee on any additional profit.

17. Since at least November 2007, Tang has directly and indirectly solicited U.S. investors to invest in the Hedge Fund. At least two U.S. investors have directly invested in Oversea Chinese Fund through Tang's website solicitation.

18. Tang has further indirectly solicited U.S. investors by causing the creation of WinWin Capital Limited Partners ("WinWin Partners") and by offering and selling limited partnership interests in the entity. WinWin Partners' sole business is investing partnership capital in the Hedge Fund. The minimum investment in WinWin Partners is $100,000 and partnership interests are sold in units; each unit costing $50,000. Investors sign partnership agreements with WinWin Partners, which set forth that the

"purpose of the partnership is to invest the capital of the Partnership in such investments as [JOR] shall determine in its sole discretion to be advisable or advantageous to the Partnership." WinWin Partners funds were held in a bank account, invested in a certificate of deposit or invested solely with the Hedge Fund.

19. The WinWin Partners' partnership agreement provides that JOR, as general partner, does not charge a fee on the first 6% of profit, but charges a 25% fee on any additional profit, mirroring the fee arrangement described on the Hedge Fund's website. JOR was created in late 2006 and listed Jiehua "Jay" Yu, Xiaohong Peng, and Richard Gu as its members. Effective January 1, 2007, Tang acquired from Yu, Gu, and Peng their ownership interests in JOR. Pursuant to a compensation agreement, Tang retained Yu, Gu, and Peng as managers of JOR to manage the day-to-day operations of WinWin Partners.

20. As of March 10, 2009, WinWin Partners raised almost $17.3 million from investors in Texas and California. Even though Tang's U.S. investors were limited partners in WinWin Partners, Tang created an account for each investor on his website in Canada. Using this Internet access, each U.S. investor was shown an account that purported to represent the investor's current investment results, including daily and cumulative trading results. If a U.S. investor desired to withdraw some, or all, of the investment with Tang, a form was submitted to WinWin Partners to redeem the investor's interest in the Hedge Fund. These redemption requests were processed in Texas but were not paid unless Tang personally approved the redemption request. Once approved, a check or a wire transfer was arranged by WinWin Partners to deliver funds pursuant to the redemption request. Of the funds raised from investors, Tang returned approximately $8.4 million to investors, of which at least $700,000 was characterized as profits and used to compute management fees due to JOR. Nearly $9.6 million in investor principal remains unaccounted for.

21. On January 26 through January 30, 2009, Tang conducted a public, real-time demonstration of his trading operations and strategy at his office in Toronto. Tang invited prospective investors, existing investors, and the media to attend. Individuals who could not attend the demo live in Toronto were able to watch it online. After watching Tang's public demonstration, many investors became very concerned about their investments, because Tang was unable to duplicate the percentage returns that the Hedge Fund had purported to achieve—as reflected on the investors' account statements on the

Hedge Fund website.

22. On February 7, 2009, Tang sent an e-mail to all Hedge Fund investors, acknowledging that the public demonstration had failed. Although Tang claimed not to have lost money during the demo, he conceded that the results were far from his stated goal of one percent per week. As an apparent result of the demonstration's failure, many investors lost confidence in his trading abilities and closed their accounts or attempted to withdraw large amounts of money from the Hedge Fund. Tang informed investors that the Hedge Fund had insufficient assets from which to pay the withdrawal requests. And, Tang vowed to return all principal to investors within six months and noted that it would not affect the Hedge Fund's normal operation.

23. On February 27, 2009, approximately 200 Hedge Fund investors met with Tang in Toronto. Among the attendees at the meeting was a contingent of the Dallas-area investors. During the meeting, many investors confronted Tang about his repeated failures to honor withdrawal requests. In response, Tang admitted that (i) the Hedge Fund had no more money, (ii) deposits into the Hedge Fund by new investors had been used to pay withdrawals and purported profits to earlier investors, and (iii) the information posted on the Hedge Fund website, showing the daily value of each investor's account, was false. Hedge Fund investors in the Toronto area elected individuals to serve on a volunteer committee (the "Toronto Committee") to act on their behalf to investigate Tang's fraud. Likewise, the Dallas-area investors elected 12 investors to serve on a similar committee (the "Dallas Committee").

24. Tang further admitted to fraudulently operating the Hedge Fund in two March 6, 2009, telephone calls between Tang and investors. During these phone calls, Tang admitted that:

- he and the Hedge Fund sustained trading losses of $15 million in 2006 and 2007;
- he and the Hedge Fund posted fake profits on the Hedge Fund's website in order to conceal losses and to attract more investors and more money;
- because of the huge trading losses in 2006 and 2007, he was not able to follow his Trading Strategy and he conducted very little trading in 2008;
- he used deposits from newer investors (which included most of the Dallas-area investors) to pay earlier investors (which included mostly Toronto-area investors) when they sought to withdraw funds (principal and fake profits) from their accounts;

- investor deposits were pooled together and commingled in a Hedge Fund account at Bank of Montreal; and
- he was unable to access his bank statements online because a group of Toronto-area investors convinced him to sign over authority in the accounts.

25. On March 8, 2009, Tang sent an e-mail to Hedge Fund investors, acknowledging that the purported profits he and the Hedge Fund listed in each investor's account statement on the Hedge Fund's website were false. Tang also claimed that, during the last three years, he and the Hedge Fund distributed over $30 million in principal and $8 million of purported profits to investors. Further, Tang implored investors to give him a year to repay each investor's debt. To persuade investors to afford him some time to repay investor losses, Tang claimed to have borrowed money from a friend, traded in her account, made $2 million in 12 days of trading, and used $1 million to repay some investors.

26. On March 19, 2009, Tang sent another e-mail to Hedge Fund investors, revealing, among other things, that "[e]ven if I have to go to jail, I still hope that I can go after I have repaid all of you. Now finally I have a chance to trade again." Tang also represented:

> "[u]nder the close monitoring of the client committee, I will be able to give you convincing results using my trading skill. By then, a lot of investors will be willing to let me trade for them under such a transparent system. As a result, this will be no problem to repay all of your money. Please gave me some time and please give me this last chance."

27. Tang-related entities currently control more than $750,000 of investor funds in U.S. accounts in the names of WinWin Capital Partners, LP and Bluejay Investment, LLC. Despite the revelations of his fraud, Tang is creating and attempting to create additional entities and accounts for the purpose of moving investor funds to evade government intervention that would prevent his trading activities. Tang and Tang-related entities have opened and attempted to open new brokerage accounts within the last several weeks for the purpose of trading, and have recently lost more than $500,000 in trading in U.S. accounts.

28. In response to his fraudulent conduct, the Ontario Securities Commission (OSC) instituted a Temporary Order that ordered all trading by Tang, WTC, WTA, and the Hedge Fund to cease. The Temporary Order is limited to Tang's Canadian entities and has no apparent effect on U.S. assets, entities or trading activities.

CLAIMS * * *

Fourth Claim: Violations of § § 206(1) and 206(2) of the Investment Advisers Act

44. Defendants Tang, Weizhen Tang & Associates, Inc., J.O.R. & Associates, LLC and WinWin Management, LLC, as investment advisers, used the mails and means or instrumentalities of interstate commerce, directly and indirectly: 1) to employ devices, schemes or artifices to defraud clients or prospective clients; or 2) to engage in transactions, practices and courses of business which operated as a fraud or deceit upon clients and prospective clients. * * * *

Fifth Claim: Violations of § 206(4) of the IA Act and Rule 206(4)-8 thereunder

47. Defendants Tang, Weizhen Tang & Associates, Inc. and J.O.R. & Associates, LLC, as investment advisers, 1) engaged in acts, practices, or courses of business which were fraudulent, deceptive or manipulative; and 2) as advisers to a pooled investment vehicle: a) made untrue statements of a material fact or omitted to state a material facts necessary to make statements made, in light of the circumstances under which they were made, not misleading to investors or prospective investors in the pooled investment vehicle; and/or b) otherwise engaged in acts, practices and courses of business that were fraudulent, deceptive, or manipulative with respect to investors or prospective investors of the pooled investment vehicle. * * * *

RELIEF REQUESTED

The Commission seeks the following relief: * * * *

53. An order of the Court appointing a receiver to take control of all assets of the Defendants WinWin Capital Management, LLC, WinWin Capital Limited Partnership, J.O.R. & Associates, LLC, and the Relief Defendants, to marshal and preserve assets for the benefits of investors.

54. An order of the Court directing Defendants to disgorge an amount equal to the funds and benefits obtained illegally as a result of the violations alleged, plus prejudgment interest on that amount.

55. An order of the Court directing Defendants, as appropriate, to pay civil monetary penalties in an amount determined as appropriate by the Court pursuant to § 20(d) of the Securities Act, § 21(d) of the Exchange Act and § 209(e)(2) of the Investment Advisers Act for their violations of the federal securities laws as alleged herein.

Topic 2 Fraudulent "Pay to Play" Practices

Laws & Rules Highlight:

IA Act (15 USC 80b-1 *et seq.*) & Rules (17 CFR §§ 275.0-2 *et seq.*)
Exchange Act (SEA) (15 USC 78a *et seq.*) & Rules (17 CFR §§ 240.0-1 *et seq.*)
MSRB Rules, http://www.msrb.org/Rules-and-Interpretations/MSRB-Rules.aspx
FINRA Manual, www.finra.org

IA Act

- Rule 206(4)-5 Political Contributions by Certain Investment Advisers (*"**Pay-to-Play**" Rule applicable to **statutory investment advisers**, including registered or required to be registered with the SEC, exempt, and exempt reporting advisers, in connection with investment advisory services provided to government entities*)
  - ◆ Rule 206(4)-5**(a)(1)** (***"two-year compensation ban"***)
    - ✓ Rule 206(4)-5(f)(2) (*def. "covered associate"*)
  - ◆ Rule 206(4)-5**(a)(2)(i)** (***"third-party solicitor ban"***)
    - ✓ Rule 206(4)-5(f)(9) (*def. "regulated person" to mean registered "investment adviser", registered "broker" or "dealer," and registered "municipal advisor"*)
  - ◆ Rule 206(4)-5**(a)(2)(ii)** (***"solicitation and coordination ban"***)
- Rule 204-2 Books and Records to Be Maintained by Investment Advisers
  - ◆ Rule 204-2(a)(18) & Rule 204-2(h)(1) (*books and records requirements pertaining to pay-to-play rule compliance*)

FINRA Rules

- Rule 2030 Engaging in Distribution and Solicitation Activities with Government Entities (*"**Pay-to-Play**" Rule applicable to **member firm broker-dealers** acting as placement agents or solicitors, assisting investment advisers with obtaining investment advisory business from government entities*)
- Rule 4580 Books and Records Requirements for Government Distribution and Solicitation Activities (*books and records requirements pertaining to pay-to-play rule compliance*)

MSRB Rules

- Rule G-37 Political Contributions and Prohibitions on Municipal Securities Business and Municipal Advisory Business & Rule G-38 Solicitation of Municipal Securities Business (*"**Pay-to-Play**" Rules applicable to **brokers, dealers, municipal securities dealers**, and **municipal advisors** in connection with municipal securities business and municipal advisory business*)

- Rule G-8 Books and Records to be Made by Brokers, Dealers, and Municipal Securities Dealers and Municipal Advisors & Rule G-9 Preservation of Records (*books and records requirements pertaining to pay-to-play rule compliance*)

Exchange Act

- § 3(a)(4) (*def. "broker"*); § 3(a)(5) (*def. "dealer"*); § 3(a)(30) (*def. "municipal securities dealer"*)
- § 15B(e)(4) (*def. "municipal advisor"*); § 15B(e)(5) (*def. "municipal financial product"*); § 15B(e)(8) (*def. "municipal entity"*); § 15B(e)(9) (*def. "solicitation of a municipal entity or obligated person"*); § 15B(e)(10) (*def. "obligated person"*)

Pre-Case Background Note[Biblio]

Functional Regulation-Based "Pay-to-Play" Regulatory Scheme

"Pay to play" in the public funds management area distorts and manipulates the public market for advisory services.[1b] On the demand side of corruption,[2] elected government officials allow political contributions to play a role in the management of public pension plan assets, and use the public assets to reward contributors. On the supply side of corruption,[2] investment advisers make or solicit political contributions to the government officials, and seek to thereby influence such officials' awards of advisory contracts. "Pay to play" thus corrupts both the government electoral process and the adviser selection process. The government officials violate the public trust, and undermine the fairness of public contract awarding process. The investment advisers are selected not based on their merit, performance, and cost but based on their campaign contributions. The pay-to-play advisers compromise their fiduciary duties to the public pension plans they advise, and defraud prospective clients.[1b] More generally in the securities law of public finance, "*pay to play*" refers to the practices where the contractors "***pay***" (the contribution to public officials) to "***play***" (obtain the government business).[3 (§53:5); 4 (§1:7, Ch15)]

In the municipal securities market, ***issuers*** include states, their political subdivisions (*e.g.*, cities, towns, counties, and school districts), and their instrumentalities (*e.g.*, housing, health care, airport, port, and economic development authorities and agencies). ***Intermediaries*** include brokers, dealers, municipal securities dealers, municipal advisors, and investment advisers. **Broker-dealers** effect transactions in securities. Broker-dealers are regulated under the Securities Exchange

Act of 1934. They are required to register with the SEC (Securities and Exchange Commission), be members of FINRA (Financial Industry Regulatory Authority, an SRO), and additionally register with and be subject to the rules of the MSRB (Municipal Securities Rulemaking Board, an SRO) if they act as municipal securities dealers, effecting transactions in or underwriting municipal securities.[5] **Municipal advisors** advise municipal entities or "obligated persons" (*i.e.*, persons obligated to pay the debt service on municipal securities issued for their benefit, *e.g.*, issuers of municipal securities), on their "*issuance of municipal securities*" or with respect to their use of "*municipal financial products*" (such as municipal derivatives); and undertake solicitations of municipal entities or obligated persons on behalf of brokers, dealers, municipal securities dealers, other municipal advisors, and investment advisers. Municipal advisors are regulated under the Exchange Act. They are required to register with both the SEC and the MSRB, and are subject to the MSRB rules. **Investment advisers** advise investors including municipal entities, and advise investment companies including municipal bond funds. Investment advisers are regulated under the Investment Advisers Act of 1940. Exchange Act § 15B(e)(4) excludes from the statutory definition of "municipal advisor" investment advisers registered with the SEC and their associated persons providing "*investment advice*" to municipal entities or obligated persons.[3 (§55:1)]

IA Act "Pay-to-Play Rule" (Rule 206(4)-5) regulates the pay-to-play practices of all statutory investment advisers (except small and mid-sized investment advisers that are state-registered and subject to state regulation).[1b; 1c] Designed to protect public pension plans and other government investors and to deter advisers from participating in "pay to play," the Rule contains three general prohibitions:[1b]

- "***two-year compensation ban***": it prohibits an adviser from ***receiving*** compensation for providing advice to a "government entity" for two years after a contribution was made by the adviser or any of its "covered associates" to an official of that government entity;
- "***third-party solicitor ban***": it prohibits an adviser from ***paying*** any third party to solicit a government entity for investment advisory services on its behalf, unless such *third-party solicitor* itself is a "regulated person" subject to "pay to play" rules; (examples of third-party solicitors are "*pension consultants*" who provide advice to pension plans and their trustees; "*finders*" who locate buyers and sellers of securities on behalf of broker-dealers; "*solicitors*" who locate investment advisory clients on behalf of investment advisers; and "*placement agents*" who find investors

for private securities offerings of issuers);[1a (n.137)]

- "***soliciting and coordinating ban***": it prohibits an adviser from soliciting or coordinating contributions or payments from others to elected officials or political parties in the locality where the adviser is providing or seeking government business.

The Rule's prohibitions operate both where an adviser directly manages the assets of a government entity as ***separately managed advisory accounts***, and where an adviser indirectly manages the public assets through ***pooled investment vehicles*** which the adviser sponsors or advises and in which public funds invest.[1b]

Under IA Act pay-to-play recordkeeping requirements (Rule 204-2(a)(18)), an IA must keep records of: **(A)** names, titles, business addresses, and residence addresses of all its "*covered associates*"; **(B)** all *government entities* to which the IA has provided investment advisory services in the past five years; **(C)** all direct or indirect *contributions or payments* made by the IA or its covered associates to an official of a government entity or to a political party, specifically listing name and title of each *contributor*, name and title of each *recipient* of a contribution or payment, and the *amount and date* of each contribution or payment; and **(D)** name and business address of each "*regulated person*" to whom the IA provides or agrees to provide payment to solicit a government entity for investment advisory services on the adviser's behalf.

MSRB "Pay-to-Play Rule" (Rule G-37) regulates pay-to-play practices of broker-dealers, municipal securities dealers, and municipal advisors in connection with their municipal securities business with government issuers, their provision of municipal securities underwriting services to government entities, their advisory services to municipal entities with respect to the issuance of municipal securities or the use of municipal financial products, and their solicitations of municipal entities or obligated persons. Rule G-38 prevents such persons from circumventing Rule G-37 through the use of consultants. MSRB "Pay-to-Play Rule" imposes "substantially equivalent or more stringent restrictions" on such broker-dealers and municipal advisors than the restrictions imposed by the IA Act "Pay-to-Play Rule" on investment advisers; and "is consistent with the objectives" of the IA Act "Pay-to-Play" Rule.[6]

FINRA "Pay-to-Play Rule" (Rule 2030) regulates pay-to-play practices of member firm broker-dealers who engage in distribution or solicitation activities for compensation with government entities, on behalf of investment advisers who provide or seek to provide investment advisory services to such government entities. FINRA "Pay-to-Play Rule" imposes "substantially equivalent or more stringent restrictions" on member firm broker-dealers than the restrictions imposed by the IA Act "Pay-to-Play Rule" on investment advisers; and "is consistent with the objectives" of the IA Act "Pay-to-Play" Rule.[7]

A functional regulation-based, or financial service-based, pay-to-play regulatory scheme thus prevents "*migration*" of pay-to-play practices to areas not covered by a single regulation.[1a] On the other hand, as firms engage in multiple businesses in municipal securities, a functional regulation-based pay-to-play regulatory scheme may intersect or overlap. A firm that underwrites municipal securities, provides financial advisory services to municipal entities, and acts as an investment adviser to government entities may be subject to MSRB's pay-to-play rule governing municipal securities dealers and municipal advisors, FINRA's pay-to-play rule governing broker-dealer placement agents and solicitors, and SEC's pay-to-play rule governing investment advisers.[3 (§55:4)]

Bibliography

1. IA Pay-to-Play Rule: **1a.** Political Contributions by Certain Investment Advisers, IA-2910, 74 FR 39840 (2009); **1b.** IA-3043, 75 FR 41018 (2010); **1c.** Rules Implementing Amendments to the Investment Advisers Act of 1940, IA-3221, 76 FR 42950, II.D.1 Amendments to "Pay to Play" Rule (2011)
2. **2a.** Butler *et al.*, *Corruption, Political Connections, and Municipal Finance*, 22 REV. FIN. STUD. 2673 (2009); **2b.** Low *et al.*, *The Demand Side of Transnational Bribery and Corruption: Why Leveling the Playing Field on the Supply Side Isn't Enough*, 84 FORDHAM L. REV. 563 (2015)
3. INVESTMENT ADVISER REGULATION—A STEP-BY-STEP GUIDE TO COMPLIANCE AND THE LAW (Kirsch ed., 3d ed. PLI 2015)
4. FIPPINGER, THE SECURITIES LAW OF PUBLIC FINANCE (3d ed. PLI 2017)
5. SEC, COMMISSION REPORT ON THE MUNICIPAL SECURITIES MARKET, II. Overview of the Municipal Securities Market (July 31, 2012)
6. MSRB Pay-to-Play Rule: **6a.** SRO; Municipal Securities Rulemaking Board, 34-33868, SR-MSRB-94-2, 59 FR 17621 (1994); **6b.** In the Matter of SROs; Order Approving Proposed Rule Change by the Municipal Securities Rulemaking Board Relating to Consultants, 34-36727, SR-MSRB-95-15, 61 FR 1955 (1996); **6c.** SROs; MSRB; Notice of Filing of a Proposed Rule Change Consisting of Proposed Amendments to Rule G-37, on Political Contributions and Prohibitions on Municipal Securities Business, Rule G-8, on Books and Records, Rule G-9, on Preservation of Records, and Forms G-37 and G-37x, 34-76763, SR-MSRB-2015-14, 80 FR 81710 (2015); **6d.** Political Contributions by Certain Investment Advisers: Ban on Third-Party Solicitation; Order With Respect to MSRB Rule G-37, IA-4531, 81 FR 66526 (2016)
7. FINRA Pay-to-Play Rule: **7a.** SROs; FINRA; Order Approving a Proposed Rule Change to Adopt FINRA Rule 2030 and FINRA Rule 4580 to Establish "Pay-to-Play" and Related Rules, 34-78683, SR-FINRA-2015-056, 81 FR 60051 (2016); **7b.** Political Contributions by Certain Investment Advisers: Ban on Third-Party Solicitation; Order With Respect to FINRA Rule 2030, IA-4532, 81 FR 66526 (2016)

Case Study 1: "Pay-to-Play" Rule Adoption by Municipal Securities Rulemaking Board

Pay to play practices feed *quid pro quo* corruption or a "collective action" problem: firms feel the need to make political contributions in order to be considered for the award of valuable government business; public officials feel the need to take political contributions in order to avoid financial disadvantage relative to their political opponents. Municipal Securities Rulemaking Board (MSRB) Rule G-37 is narrowly tailored to serve a compelling government interest: protecting investors from fraud, promoting just and equitable principles of trade in the municipal securities industry, and perfecting the mechanism of a free and open market—by outlawing pay to play practices in the municipal securities market.

Blount v. SEC

61 F.3d 938 (DC Cir. 1995)

[***Procedural history & related case materials***: SRO; Municipal Securities Rulemaking Board, 34-33868, SR-MSRB-94-2, 59 FR 17621 (1994); Blount v. SEC, 61 F.3d 938 (DC Cir. 1995), *cert. denied*, 517 U.S. 1119 (1996)]

Case Study 2: "Pay-to-Play" Arrangement Involving New York State Common Retirement Fund

Henry Morris had served as the top political advisor to ***Alan Hevesi***, who became New York State Comptroller in 2002, and who was the sole trustee of assets held by the New York State Common Retirement Fund (CRF). In a fraudulent rent-seeking scheme using the CRF assets, Morris orchestrated Hevesi's installation of ***David Loglisci*** as the CRF's Chief Investment Officer. During a period of five to six years, the duo exacted $35 million dollars under the guise of business finder fee out of investment management firms seeking to do business with the CRF—creating a "**toll gate**" for entering the New York State public fund management business. The New York Attorney General's office instituted criminal prosecutions, and the Securities and Exchange Commission instituted civil fraud charges, against several participants in the public finance pay-to-play scheme.

People v. Morris

958 N.Y.S.2d 62 (Table) (NY Sup. Ct. 2010)

[*Related proceedings & materials*: **1. NYAG enforcement:** New York v. Henry "Hank" Morris and David Loglisci, Indictment No. 25/2009 (NY Sup. Ct. 2009); People v. Morris, 958 N.Y.S.2d 62 (Table) (NY Sup. Ct. 2010); **2. SEC enforcement:** SEC v. Morris & Loglisci, *et al.*, 09-CV-2518 (SEC Compl., SDNY 2009); *Seven Defendants Settle SEC Fraud Charges in "Pay to Play" Case Involving New York State Common Retirement Fund*, SEC Lit. Rel. 22938 (Mar 10, 2014)]

Research Topic:

Regulation of public finance markets in China.

Blount, Petitioner v. SEC, Respondent & MSRB, Intervenor
61 F.3d 938 (DC Cir. 1995)

Before WILLIAMS, HENDERSON and ROGERS, Circuit Judges.

OPINION

WILLIAMS, Circuit Judge:

In late 1993, regulators of the municipal securities markets began to investigate reports that brokers and dealers were engaging in a variety of ethically questionable practices in order to secure underwriting contracts. These practices, often lumped together under the label "pay to play," include as a paradigmatic example the making of political contributions to state and local officials who may influence the choice of underwriter. Concerned that such practices were becoming more prevalent and were undermining the integrity of the $250 billion municipal securities market, the **Municipal Securities Rulemaking Board** ("*MSRB*" or "*Board*") drafted several new rules, which were then approved by the Securities and Exchange Commission. Among these was Rule G-37, the rule challenged in this case. See 34-33868 (April 7, 1994) (order approving proposed rule change) ("*SEC Approval Order*").

The two principal sections of Rule G-37, (b) and (c), together restrict the ability of municipal securities professionals to contribute and to solicit contributions to the political campaigns of state officials from whom they obtain business. Section (d) serves as a loophole-closer, prohibiting indirect violations of the restrictions in (b) or (c). We describe each in turn.

Contributions. Section (b) prohibits any "broker, dealer, or municipal securities dealer" who has contributed "to an official of [an] issuer" from "engaging in municipal securities business with [that] issuer" for a period of two years after the contribution.[1] Contributions by a "municipal finance professional associated" with the broker or dealer are treated as equivalent to contributions by the broker or dealer itself; as are contributions by a political action committee "controlled" either by the broker or dealer or by "any municipal finance professional" whatsoever. The two-year restriction on business is not triggered, however, by any of these various parties' contribution of up to $250 per

[1] "Municipal securities business" is defined for most purposes as excluding issues based on competitive bids. See Rule G-37(g)(vii); see also *SEC Approval Order* at 16 n.41.

official per election to an official for whom that party is entitled to vote.

Solicitations. Section (c) prohibits brokers, dealers, and municipal securities dealers—as well as their associated municipal finance professionals—from soliciting or coordinating contributions to officials of any issuer with whom the broker, etc., is "engaging or is seeking to engage in municipal securities business."

Loophole-closer. Section (d) prohibits brokers, dealers, municipal securities dealers, and municipal finance professionals in general from "directly or indirectly" doing anything that would "result in a violation of sections (b) or (c)...."

The petitioner, William B. Blount, is the chairman of the Alabama Democratic Party and a registered broker and dealer of municipal securities. He challenges the SEC's order approving Rule G-37, claiming that each of the three sections of the rule we have described impermissibly infringes his First Amendment rights; that section (d) is, in addition, unconstitutionally vague; and that the rule as a whole violates the Tenth Amendment. The SEC rebuts each of these claims, and the MSRB, as intervenor, raises two defenses not urged by the SEC: that Blount does not have standing under the Exchange Act to pursue his claim and that the rule is not the product of government action and thus cannot violate either the First or Tenth Amendment. We find that Blount has standing to sue and that Rule G-37 is government action. We therefore meet all of Blount's arguments on the merits, though ultimately we reject them and deny the petition for review.

I. Standing and Exhaustion

Neither the Board nor the SEC claims that Blount lacks constitutional or prudential standing, and given his roles as a state party chair and municipal securities dealer, any such claim would be meritless. Instead, the Board points to § 25(c)(1) of the Securities Exchange Act, which requires that the objections in a petition for review have been "urged before the Commission," and argues that because Blount did not ***himself*** raise the present objections before the Commission, he is not a "person aggrieved" by the Commission's order within the meaning of § 25(a)(1) of the Securities Exchange Act. We see nothing in either § 25(c)(1) or § 25(a)(1) that purports to link the two subsections together as the Board suggests. In addition, § 25(c)(1) conspicuously uses the passive voice, saying only that an objection may not be considered by a reviewing court unless it was "urged before the Commission"; it shows no interest in ***who*** urged the objection, and is presumably aimed only at assuring that the Commission have had a chance to address claims before being challenged on them in court. Cf. *NRDC v. EPA*, 824 F.2d 1146 (DC Cir. 1987) (en banc).

The Commission indisputably had the necessary chance. The Board concedes that others raised and the SEC considered the "general constitutional objections to the Rule" that Blount now makes before us. See *SEC Approval Order* at 31-37 (considering constitutional objections). This quite accurate concession reduces the Board to the alternative argument that the SEC did not consider the "specific concerns identified by the Petitioner ... which arise from his particular status and duties as Chairman of the Alabama Democratic Party." While petitioner's activities may represent an unusually good example of the conduct the rule seeks to restrict, the Board does not explain, and we cannot see, how any of the issues the petitioner raises are in any salient way different from the concerns raised and considered during the rulemaking. Blount's claim is therefore not barred by the exhaustion requirement of § 25(c)(1).

II. Government Action

The Board maintains that it is a private organization and that Rule G-37 is a private rule. As such, the Board asserts, the rule cannot be found to violate the First or Tenth Amendment, since the Constitution is "a restraint on government action, not that of private persons," *CBS v. Democratic Nat'l Comm.*, 412 U.S. 94 (1973) (plurality opinion).

We put to one side the Board's questionable assertion that it is a purely private organization even though it was created by an act of Congress and directed by Congress to "propose and adopt rules to effect the purposes of [the Exchange Act]" within specified constraints, § 78o-4(b)(2). Cf. *Lebron v. National R.R. Passenger Corp.*, 115 S.Ct. 961 (1995) (fact that Amtrak was created by federal law to accomplish federal governmental objectives points toward classification as federal actor). What is critical here is that MSRB Rule G-37 operates not as a private compact among brokers and dealers but as federal law. Under § 15B of the Exchange Act, a broker or dealer may not engage in interstate trade in municipal securities unless he registers under § 15B itself or under § 15 of the Exchange Act. See 15 USC § 78o-4(a)(1) (forbidding dealers to use "instrumentality of interstate commerce" to effect or solicit transactions in municipal securities unless registered as a broker or dealer in accordance with § 15 or § 15B, 15 USC § 78o or § 78o-4). If he violates an MSRB rule, he may be sanctioned by revocation or suspension of his license to deal in municipal securities. See *id.* § 78o-4(c)(1) (forbidding brokers and dealers from contravening the rules of the MSRB in effecting or soliciting interstate transactions in municipal securities); § 78o(b)(4)(D) (authorizing the Commission to suspend or revoke the registration of any broker or dealer who "has willfully violated" or "is unable to comply with" any of the applicable rules, including those of the MSRB); § 78o-4(c)(2) (similar authority as to municipal securities dealers). Dealers who violate Rule G-37 and who persist in securities dealing after any resulting Commission suspension or revocation of their licenses are subject to federal criminal penalties. 15 USC § 78ff(a) (providing for criminal penalties up to $1,000,000 and 10-year imprisonment for natural persons who willfully violate rules). As a government-enforced condition to any participation in a municipal securities career, Rule G-37 constitutes government action of the purest sort.

III. First Amendment Challenge

We turn now to the central issue in this case, petitioner's claim that Rule G-37 violates his First Amendment rights to free speech and free association.

III-A. Rule G-37 as a restriction of speech

All three sections of Rule G-37 at issue here infringe speech. Giving money is one method of indicating one's devotion to a cause; hence the familiar challenge, "Put your money where your mouth is." The Supreme Court has characterized the campaign contribution as a "symbolic act" that "serves as a general expression of support for the candidate and his views," though noting at the same time that the contribution does not indicate the basis for the support and that a limit on contributions does not "infringe the contributor's freedom to discuss candidates and issues." *Buckley v. Valeo*, 424 U.S. 1 (1976) (per curiam); see also *Citizens Against Rent Control v. Berkeley*, 454 U.S. 290 (1981). Solicitation of campaign funds, the target of sections (c) and (d), is close to the core of protected speech, as it is "characteristically intertwined" with both information and advocacy and essential to the continued flow of both. *Village of Schaumburg v. Citizens for a Better Environment*, 444 U.S. 620 (1980).

III-B. The requisite level of scrutiny

The intensity with which we scrutinize Rule G-37 depends on whether the rule is content-based, eliciting "strict" scrutiny, or content-neutral, eliciting only "intermediate" scrutiny. *Turner Broadcasting Sys., Inc. v. FCC*, 114 S.Ct. 2445 (1994). The proper categorization of Rule G-37 is not clear-cut. As petitioner points out, under the everyday meaning of the word "content," the rule appears to be content-based, as it restricts only messages that concern one "topic," specifically, financial contributions to political campaigns. Cf., *e.g.*, *McIntyre v. Ohio Elections Comm'n*, 115 S.Ct. 1511 (1995); *Consolidated Edison Co. v. Public Serv. Comm'n of New York*, 447 U.S. 530 (1980). But the Supreme Court does not regard a rule's use of subject-based categories as automatically establishing it as content-based. The critical issue is whether the state's justification for the distinction is the "content" of the speech itself or some other concern:

> The principal inquiry in determining content neutrality ... is whether the government has adopted a regulation of speech because of disagreement with the message it conveys.... Government regulation of expressive activity is content neutral so long as it is "***justified*** without reference to the content of the regulated speech."

Ward v. Rock Against Racism, 491 U.S. 781 (1989) (quoting *Clark v. Community for Creative Non-Violence*, 468 U.S. 288 (1984)) (emphasis added). Compare, *e.g.*, *Turner Broadcasting, supra* (content-neutral regulation), and *Renton v. Playtime Theatres, Inc.*, 475 U.S. 41 (1986) (same), with *City of Cincinnati v. Discovery Network, Inc.*, 113 S.Ct. 1505 (1993) (content-based regulation), and *Boos v. Barry*, 485 U.S. 312 (1988) (same).[2]

This regulation's goals could well be described as content-neutral. Contributions and solicitation of contributions have two aspects. They may communicate support for a candidate and his ideas, but they may also be used as the cover for what is much like a bribe: a payment that accrues to the private advantage of the official and is intended to induce him to exercise his discretion in the donor's favor, potentially at the expense of the polity he serves. The SEC clearly rested its approval of Rule G-37 on a wish to curtail this latter function. In language tracking that of § 15B of the Exchange Act, it explained how the limits would, in its judgment, "prevent fraudulent and manipulative acts and practices, as well as the appearance of fraud and manipulation," perfect the mechanism of a free and open market for municipal securities, and "promote just and equitable principles of trade." *SEC Approval Order*. Petitioner himself describes these goals as "non speech-related." Petitioner's Br. at 27 n.14.

---

[2] This methodology has come to replace the distinction between speech and conduct regulations originally articulated in *United States v. O'Brien*, 391 U.S. 367 (1968). See Ely, *Flag Desecration: A Case Study in the Roles of Categorization and Balancing in First Amendment Analysis*, 88 HARV. L. REV. 1482 (1975) (noting that the *O'Brien* Court itself adopts purpose test later in its opinion, "abandoning its earlier suggestion that the constitutional answer can be found by examining O'Brien's act").

These purposes are quite different from some of the ones that have triggered strict scrutiny in other cases involving political contributions. In *Buckley v. Valeo, supra*, the interests "served by the Act included restricting the voices of people and interest groups who have money to spend and reducing the overall scope of federal election campaigns," as well as "equalizing the relative ability of all voters to affect electoral outcomes." See also *id.* (referring to "ancillary" interest in "serving to mute the voices of affluent persons and groups in the election process and thereby to equalize the relative ability of all citizens to affect the outcome of elections."); *Austin v. Michigan Chamber of Commerce*, 494 U.S. 652 (1990) (regulation said to target "corrosive and distorting effects of immense aggregations of wealth that are accumulated with the help of the corporate form and that have little or no correlation to the public's support for the corporation's political ideas"); *FEC v. Massachusetts Citizens for Life, Inc.*, 479 U.S. 238 (1986) (similar); *FEC v. National Right to Work Committee*, 459 U.S. 197 (1982) (similar). Thus the object in *Buckley* and the other campaign finance cases was not only, as here, to prevent ***direct*** quid pro quos (and the appearance thereof) but more broadly to reduce the ***indirect*** impact of wealth on the electoral process, including the ***persuasive impact*** on both candidates and the public at large of messages communicated by the wealthy in that process. The Commission notes that in keeping with the difference in objectives, Rule G-37 is targeted narrowly to a concrete business relationship between the contributors and the candidates' governmental entities:

> Unlike general campaign financing restrictions, ... which seek to combat unspecified forms of undue influence and political corruption, [these] conflict of interest provisions, ... are tied to a contributor's business relationship with governmental entities and are intended to prevent fraud and manipulation.

SEC Approval Order.

We are uncertain how much to make of this distinction. In *Buckley* the Court also said that "the primary interest served by the limitations ... is the prevention of corruption ... spawned by the real or imagined coercive influence of large financial contributions on candidates' positions and on their actions if elected to office." At no point did the Court suggest that it saw a great divide between efforts to foreclose corruption disguised as campaign contributions and more general efforts to limit the influence of wealth. Moreover, the principle that the Commission claims narrows the rule's purpose—its focus only on "business relations"—is subject in the full-blown modern interest-group state to very broad generalization. The class of people with "business relations to government entities" is plentiful, if we include all government employees; all government contractors; all who benefit in their business from government activity creating a market for their goods or services (from lawyers specializing in SEC work to suppliers of environmental control technology); all whose businesses benefit from the imposition of regulatory, tax, or tariff restrictions on competitors or potential competitors; all whose income enjoys any kind of tax advantage; and all who are employed by or otherwise economically dependent on firms fitting the description above. The principle could also embrace anyone who (directly or through some group) is seeking to receive any such benefits and anyone seeking to stave off either the cancellation of existing benefits or the imposition of new burdens.

The only other basis for distinguishing the regulatory purposes asserted (and found to be content-based) in *Buckley* and its progeny from those asserted in this case is that the rules in the former cases were intended to safeguard the political process as a whole, whereas here the effort is to safeguard a commercial marketplace. But if the object of extirpating corruption—in the particular form of implicit exchanges between political contributions and politically allocated benefits—is content-based when the focus is on politics, we are uncertain why the object would be content-neutral when the focus is on the allocation of commercial benefits. In every case where a ***quid*** in the electoral process is being exchanged for a ***quo*** in a particular market where the government deals, the corruption in the market is simply the flipside of the electoral corruption.

Thus, although the purpose of preventing corrupt bond markets might logically be considered unrelated to the suppression of speech, our difficulty in distinguishing the purposes of this rule from those animating the rules at issue in Buckley and Austin makes us hesitate to find the rule content-neutral. If the rule can withstand strict scrutiny there is no need to decide the issue. Accordingly we turn to applying such scrutiny and ask, following *Boos, supra*, and *Sable Communications v. FCC*, 492 U.S. 115 (1989), whether the rule is narrowly tailored to serve a compelling government interest.

III-C. Application of strict scrutiny

We divide the inquiry into three parts, addressing in turn (1) whether the interests the government proffers in support of the rule are properly characterized as "compelling"; (2) whether the rule effectively advances those interests, *i.e.*, whether the Commission has shown that the ills it claims the rule addresses in fact exist and the rule will materially reduce them, Turner Broadcasting, supra; and (3) whether the rule is narrowly tailored to advance the compelling interests asserted, *i.e.*, whether less restrictive alternatives to the rule would accomplish the government's goals equally or almost equally effectively, *Sable Communications v. FCC, supra.* We conclude that the rule meets all three of these requirements.

III-C-1. Legitimate and compelling nature of interests asserted

Congress has charged the Commission and the MSRB to create rules

> to prevent fraudulent and manipulative acts and practices, to promote just and equitable principles of trade, ... to remove impediments to and perfect the mechanism of a free and open market ..., and not ... to permit unfair discrimination between ... municipal securities brokers, or municipal securities dealers....

15 USC § 78o-4(b)(2)(C). The Commission claims that Rule G-37 supports two interests encompassed within this mandate: (1) protecting investors in municipal bonds from fraud and (2) protecting underwriters of municipal bonds from unfair, corrupt market practices. Both of these interests are not only substantial, see *Turner Broadcasting, supra* ("The Government's interest in eliminating restraints on fair competition is always substantial ....") (citing cases), but, we think, compelling. The Supreme Court has said that "preventing corruption or the appearance of corruption" is "the only legitimate and compelling government interest thus far identified for restricting campaign finances." *FEC v. National Conservative PAC*, 470 U.S. 480 (1985) (citing the holdings in *Buckley* and *Citizens Against Rent Control*). As we have already noted, in Buckley and Austin the legislature was interested in clean elections, whereas here the SEC is interested in clean bond markets. Petitioner insists on the importance of this distinction, saying that the latter interest is less compelling than the former. As we see it, however, one of the primary reasons people object to bought elections is that a bought politician tends to make distorted choices, and the public's concern about a particular type of distorted choice (the choice of bond underwriter) does not logically stand on a lower plane than its concern about bought politicians generally.

III-C-2. Tendency of the rule to further those interests

Petitioner also maintains that the Commission has failed to provide evidence sufficient to show "that the recited harms are real, not merely conjectural, and that the regulation will in fact alleviate these harms in a direct and material way." *Turner Broadcasting, supra.*[3] As a threshold matter, petitioner claims there is no support for the Commission's finding that pay-to-play practices are prevalent in the negotiated municipal bond business, because the record contains no evidence of specific instances of quid pro quos. But underwriters' campaign contributions self-evidently create a conflict of interest in state and local officials who have power over municipal securities contracts and a risk that they will award the contracts on the basis of benefit to their campaign chests rather than to the governmental entity. Petitioner himself remarked on national radio that "most likely [state and local officials] are gonna call somebody who has been a political contributor" and, at least in close cases, award contracts to "friends" who have contributed. *Morning Edition* (National Public Radio, June 1, 1994). While the risk of corruption is obvious and substantial, actors in this field are presumably shrewd enough to structure their relations rather indirectly—indeed, the phrase "pay to play" suggests that a contribution brings the donor merely a chance to be seriously considered, not the assurance of a contract. As the Court said of quid pro quos for campaign contributions in *Buckley v. Valeo, supra*, "the scope of such pernicious practices can never be reliably ascertained." In any event, the Commission observes that "specific abuses have been alleged in several state and local governments," *SEC Approval Order, supra*, and then cites newspaper clippings from 13 states and the District of Columbia with such headlines as "*Kentucky Official Says He Served as Middleman to Solicit Funds*," from THE BOND BUYER, September 7, 1993. Although the record contains only allegations, no smoking gun is needed where, as here, the conflict of interest is apparent, the likelihood of stealth great, and the legislative purpose prophylactic. See *FEC v. National Right to Work Committee, supra* (Court will not "second-guess a legislative determination as to the need for prophylactic measures where corruption is the evil feared.").

Even assuming the prevalence of quid pro quos, Blount maintains, the Commission has not demonstrated that eliminating such activity advances the asserted interests in protecting investors and promoting just and equitable principles of trade. As to the harm

[3] We note petitioner's suggestion that the Commission's failure to support its findings with record evidence violates, in addition to the First Amendment, the Securities and Exchange Act, 15 USC § § 78y(a)(4), 78y(b)(4) (rules must be supported by "findings ... as to the facts" and "substantial evidence"), and the Administrative Procedure Act, see 5 USC § 706(2)(e); *Tex Tin Corp. v. EPA*, 992 F.2d 353 (DC Cir. 1993) (agency is not "entitled merely to assume" that the practices it seeks to regulate cause the harm it fears). Because the First Amendment requires us to scrutinize the factual basis for the regulation at least as stringently as these statutes, we see no need to address these contentions separately.

to investors, we tend to share the petitioner's skepticism. The Commission reasoned that pay-to-play practices make underwriters "less likely or competent to perform a reasonable investigation of statements made by the issuer in connection with the offering." *SEC Approval Order, supra.* The Commission points to no data supporting the idea, and it is anything but self-evident. Two interests seem to give the underwriter an incentive to exercise due diligence in investigating municipal issuers: its interest in averting liability for fraud, see *SEC Approval Order* at n.54 (noting that securities laws impose on underwriters a legal duty to investigate), and its interest in safeguarding its reputation among bond buyers and their representatives. Neither interest would be diminished merely by an underwriter's use of sleazy means to secure the contract. And while an implicit (or even explicit) offer to refrain from investigating thoroughly might well help an underwriter win a negotiated contract, it would help regardless of whether the underwriter also used other means of ingratiating himself with the powers that be.

On the other hand, the link between eliminating pay-to-play practices and the Commission's goals of "perfecting the mechanism of a free and open market" and promoting "just and equitable principles of trade" is self-evident. The Commission explained:

> "Pay to play" practices raise artificial barriers to competition for those firms that either cannot afford or decide not to make political contributions. Moreover, if "pay to play" is the determining factor in the selection of an underwriting syndicate, an official may not necessarily hire the most qualified underwriter for the issue.... "Pay to play" practices undermine [just and equitable] principles [of trade] since underwriters working on a particular issuance may be assigned similar roles, and take on equivalent risks, but be given different allocations of bonds to sell--resulting in differing profits--based on their political contributions or contacts.

See *SEC Approval Order, supra.* Moreover, there appears to be a collective action problem tending to make the misallocation of resources persist. As beneficiaries of the practice, politicians vying for state or local office may be reluctant to stop it legislatively; some, of course, may seek to exploit their rivals' cozy relation with bond dealers as a campaign issue, but if they refuse to enter into similar relations, their campaigns will be financially handicapped. Bond dealers are in a still worse position to initiate reform: individual firms that decline to pay will have less chance to play, and may even be the object of explicit boycott if they do. See "*Politicians Are Mobilizing to Derail Ban on Muni*

Underwriters," WALL ST. J., Dec. 27, 1993, at C16 (reporting that Florida Association of Counties called for a boycott of 17 firms that had voluntarily banned political contributions).

Even if the regulation does advance the asserted interests, Blount says, it should be stricken as underinclusive. He points out that the prohibitions on contributions and on solicitation of contributions obviously will not eliminate ***all*** possible methods by which underwriters may curry favor. Municipal finance professionals remain free, for example, to solicit votes or contribute time and talents to a campaign effort. He also notes that the limitations of Rule G-37 do not apply to chief executive officers of banks with municipal securities departments or subsidiaries.

But a regulation is not fatally underinclusive simply because an alternative regulation, which would restrict ***more*** speech or the speech of ***more*** people, could be more effective. The First Amendment does not require the government to curtail as much speech as may conceivably serve its goals. While the rule chosen must "fit" the asserted goals, *City of Cincinnati, supra*, it must also, by virtue of the narrow tailoring requirement discussed below, strike an appropriate balance between achieving those goals and protecting constitutional rights. Because the primary purpose of underinclusiveness analysis is simply to "ensure that the proffered state interest actually underlies the law," *Austin, supra* (Brennan, J., concurring), a rule is struck for ***under***-inclusiveness only if it cannot "fairly be said to advance any genuinely substantial governmental interest," *FCC v. League of Women Voters*, 468 U.S. 364 (1984), because it provides only "ineffective or remote" support for the asserted goals, *id.* (citing *Central Hudson Gas & Elec. Corp. v. Public Serv. Comm'n*, 447 U.S. 557 (1980)), or "limited incremental" support, *Bolger v. Youngs Drug Prods. Corp.*, 463 U.S. 60 (1983). See also *Florida Star v. B.J.F.*, 491 U.S. 524 (1989) (government "must demonstrate its commitment to advancing [its] interest by applying its prohibition evenhandedly.... Without more careful and inclusive precautions against alternative forms of [the harm], we cannot conclude that Florida's selective ban ... satisfactorily accomplishes its stated purpose."). Thus, with regard to First Amendment ***under***-inclusiveness analysis, neither a perfect nor even the best available fit between means and ends is required.[4]

---

[4] Petitioner tosses into his opening brief a footnote contending that the Commission's failure to make Rule G-37 applicable to bank officers and bank-controlled political action committees makes for disparate treatment that violates not only the First Amendment but also the due process clause of the *Fifth* Amendment. We find it

In citing the Commission's failure to cover the CEOs of banks with municipal securities departments as evidence of fatal underinclusiveness, petitioner invokes *Carey v. Brown*, 447 U.S. 455 (1980), which he reads as requiring a "substantial interest" to justify a class's ***exemption*** from a speech restriction (under an equal protection analysis). Even assuming that that is a correct reading of *Carey*, the decision clearly related to an exemption based on the content of the subject's expression (labor matters), see *id.*, and petitioner makes no claim that ***content*** played any role whatever in the Commission's exclusion of bank CEOs.

We have already explained why and how we think the provisions of Rule G-37 at issue can be expected materially to advance compelling interests asserted by the Commission. The Commission has explained that the "loopholes" that remain are due to its "sensitivity" to First Amendment concerns; it believes that closing the supposed loopholes would broaden the regulation's scope beyond that "necessary" to accomplish its interests. In other words, the Commission adjudged the risk of corruption in the conduct left unrestrained too remote to warrant restraint. In our view, petitioner has pointed to nothing that calls that judgment into serious question.

III-C-3. Narrow tailoring

Blount asserts that Rule G-37 is too broad, arguing that the Commission could have achieved its goal with less restrictive means. Specifically, he claims, it could have confined itself to disclosure and record-keeping requirements (which the Commission instituted in Rule G-37(e) and Rules G-8 and G-9); or, at worst, to those requirements plus the contribution limits of Rule G-37(b). In other words, the Commission probably had no need to curtail ***contributions***, Rule G-37(b), and certainly had no need to curtail ***solicitation*** of contributions, Rule G-37(c).

If the Commission's goals were only to protect the investing public, disclosure and record-keeping requirements might do the job. Informed investors—insofar as they believe contributors are less likely to investigate issuers or more likely to overprice issues—could use the disclosed information to avoid buying bond issues underwritten by

---

unnecessary to evaluate this contention. The Fifth Amendment requires only that the government have a rational basis for its distinction, see, *e.g.*, *Vance v. Bradley*, 440 U.S. 93 (1979) ("Rather than abandoning its primary end completely, or unnecessarily including all federal employees within the means, it drew a line around those groups of employees it thought most generally pertinent to its objective."); and rational-basis review requires, if anything, less "mathematical nicety," *id.* at 109, than the First Amendment requires.

campaign contributors. As we pointed out above, however, it is not at all clear that investors are harmed or even perceive themselves to be harmed when underwriters obtain business through shady practices. Thus disclosure would not likely cause market forces to erode "pay to play," and the Commission's other grounds for objecting to the practice would go unmet. Just as the Court in *Buckley v. Valeo, supra*, said that Congress could have found disclosure "only a partial measure," so here the Commission could reasonably find it inadequate. Moreover, without the prohibitions of sections (c) and (d) on soliciting contributions, directly or indirectly, underwriters could easily circumvent the prohibition against direct contributions. Not only would the Commission's purpose of protecting the integrity of the market for underwriting services most certainly "be achieved less effectively," *Ward, supra*, without the limits on campaign contributions and solicitation, but none of the alternatives presented would be even ***almost*** equally effective. Cf. *Sable Communications v. FCC, supra* (narrow tailoring requirement not met when the record suggests a less restrictive and possibly "extremely effective" alternative); *Boos, supra* (requirement not met when there is evidence that Congress itself "no longer considers this statute necessary" to meet the stated objective and when "a less restrictive alternative is readily available").

Finally, the regulation is "closely drawn" and thus "avoids unnecessary abridgement" of First Amendment rights, *Buckley v. Valeo, supra*. Rule G-37 constrains relations only between the two potential parties to a quid pro quo: the underwriters and their municipal finance employees on the one hand, and officials who might influence the award of negotiated municipal bond underwriting contracts on the other.[5] Even then, the rule restricts a narrow range of their activities for a relatively short period of time. The underwriter is barred from engaging in business with the particular issuer for only two years after it makes a contribution, and it is barred from soliciting contributions only during the time that it is engaged in or seeking business with the issuer associated with the donee. A municipal finance professional may contribute up to $250 per election to

---

[5] The rule does not apply to underwriting business awarded on a competitive basis, that is, "offerings in which the securities are awarded to the underwriting syndicate presenting the best bid according to stipulated criteria set forth in the notice of sale." *SEC Approval Order* at 16 n.41; see also Rule G-37(g)(vii)(A). Although the rule might be interpreted as applying to private placement or advisory service business awarded on a competitive basis, see Rule G-37(g)(vii)(B) and (C), none of the parties mentions this possibility, and petitioner does not contend that he engages in such business. It is therefore unnecessary for us to address the constitutionality of those parts of the rule. See *Burson v. Freeman*, 504 U.S. 191 (1992).

each official for whom he or she is entitled to vote, without triggering the business bar. Furthermore, as the Commission interprets the rule, municipal finance professionals are not in any way restricted from engaging in the vast majority of political activities, including making direct expenditures for the expression of their views, giving speeches, soliciting votes, writing books, or appearing at fundraising events. *SEC Approval Order, supra* ("proposal will not restrict personal volunteer work ... in political campaigns other than soliciting or coordinating contributions"); *id.* ("proposal does not restrict uncoordinated independent expenditures"); SEC Release 34-33870 (Apr. 7, 1994) (*SEC Order Denying Preliminary Stay*: ban on solicitation applies only to "explicit solicitations of contributions, and not to generalized solicitations of support for a candidate or his views."); SEC Release 34-34008 (May 4, 1994) (*SEC Order Denying Stay*: "Applicant's concern that the provision could be triggered by inadvertently using the word 'money' in a speech urging support for a candidate, or simply by making a speech of general support at a fund-raising affair, is misplaced. Likewise, his contention that soliciting money for his political party will necessarily trigger the provision is incorrect."); but cf. *id.* (noting that Blount's complaint is that the rule will prevent him from directing contributed funds to particular state officials, which is normally a duty of the party chairman, and appearing to assume that the rule will have the feared effect).

IV. Vagueness

Petitioner argues that section (d), prohibiting anyone from "directly or indirectly, through or by any other person or means" doing what sections (b) and (c) prohibit, is unconstitutionally vague and in violation of his due process rights under the Fifth Amendment. See, *e.g., Timpinaro v. SEC*, 2 F.3d 453 (DC Cir. 1993) ("A vague rule denies due process by imposing standards of conduct so indeterminate that it is impossible to ascertain just what will result in sanctions."); see also *Hynes v. Mayor & City Council of Oradell*, 425 U.S. 610 (1976) ("The general test of vagueness applies with particular force in review of laws dealing with speech.... [A] man may less be required to act at his peril here, because the free dissemination of ideas may be the loser.").

Although the language of section (d) itself is very broad, the SEC has interpreted it as requiring a showing of culpable intent, that is, a demonstration that the conduct was undertaken "as a means to circumvent" the requirements of (b) and (c). *SEC Approval Order, supra*; see also *SEC Order Denying Stay*, supra (prohibition only affects Blount's family to the degree that "he is directing their contributions, thus seeking to evade the rule's provisions"). The SEC states its "means to circumvent" qualification in general terms. The qualification appears, therefore, to apply not only to such items as contributions made by the broker's or dealer's family members or employees, but also to gifts by a broker to a state or national party committee, made with knowledge that some part of the gift is likely to be transmitted to an official excluded by Rule G-37. In short, according to the SEC, the rule restricts such gifts and contributions only when they are intended as end-runs around the direct contribution limitations.

Moreover, the Commission has substantially reduced any remaining uncertainty about the rule's potential application by providing for informal advance rulings from SEC staff on any proposed course of conduct, see 17 CFR § § 202.1(d) & 202. This helps protect underwriters against the sort of risk that the constitutional rule against vagueness seeks to constrain. See *Civil Service Comm'n v. National Ass'n of Letter Carriers*, 413 U.S. 548 (1973) (taking existence of such a procedure into account). And, of course, if the SEC actually brings an enforcement action, the affected party may challenge the particular application of the rule as not reasonably foreseeable under the rule's language. See, *e.g.*, *General Elec. Co. v. EPA*, 53 F.3d 1324 (DC Cir. 1995) (agency's interpretation of a rule, though permissible, may yet be "so far from a reasonable person's understanding" of what the rule might mean that the rule cannot be said to give the "fair notice" necessary for due process).

V. Tenth Amendment Challenge

Finally, petitioner claims that Rule G-37 is an effort to regulate state election campaigns and, as such, usurps the states' power to control their own elections. This contention is meritless. Rule G-37 neither compels the states to regulate private parties, as the Tenth Amendment prohibits, *New York v. United States*, 505 U.S. 144 (1992), nor regulates the states directly, a question on which the Supreme Court's Tenth Amendment jurisprudence "has traveled an unsteady path," *id.* Further, the rule does not have anything resembling the kind of preemptive effect on states' ability to control their own election processes that might be perceived as "destructive of state sovereignty." See *Garcia v. San Antonio Metropolitan Transit Authority*, 469 U.S. 528 (1985); cf. *Gregory v. Ashcroft*, 501 U.S. 452 (1991). Blount points to no theory of the Tenth Amendment or the commerce clause under which Congress is disabled from regulating private persons in their conduct of interstate trade in municipal securities, see 15 U.S.C. § 78o-4(a)(1), so we need not proceed further. See generally *United States v. Lopez*, 115 S.Ct. 1624 (1995).

Because Rule G-37 withstands all of Blount's challenges, the petition for review is ***Denied***.

People v. Morris

958 N.Y.S.2d 62 (Table) (NY Sup. Ct. 2010)

Opinion

Lewis Bart STONE, J.

At the request of the **State Attorney General** (AG), acting on behalf of the People, a Grand Jury convened in New York County indicted defendants **Henry Morris** and **David Loglisci** on one hundred twenty-three felony and misdemeanor counts. Some of these counts applied only to Morris, some only to Loglisci and some to both. * * * *

FACTS

This case and the relevant issues are better understood after a consideration of the facts before and after Morris' relationship with the **New York State Common Retirement Fund (CRF)** began, *i.e.*, to the period prior to **Alan Hevesi**'s election as **Comptroller** in November 2002. Under N.Y. Const. Art. V § 1, the Comptroller is an independently elected state-wide official, vested with audit and accounting functions. The Comptroller also serves as the Administrative head of the CRF and the sole trustee of the funds held by the CRF.

The CRF was established to secure retirement benefits payable to State employees, and has been funded by State and employee[1] contributions. CRF's growth from its initial creation to date has been enormous. For example, in 1960 the CRF had more than $4 Billion in public pension funds and now has over $100 Billion in assets. Initially, the CRF funds could only be invested in a narrow range of expressly defined low-yielding investments. Following a report of a State study committee established by Governor Rockefeller in 1960, which found CRF's investment restrictions to be outmoded and unduly restrictive, the legislature enacted **Retirement and Social Security Law** (R & SSL) Art. 4-A entitled "*Investments of Public Pension Funds*," to govern and broaden investment possibilities for public pension funds including the CRF, granting them *inter alia* investment powers similar to those powers accorded Savings Banks.

Although these 1960 changes expanded the types of investments the CRF could make,

---

[1] The original State retirement system required no employee contributions. In response to ever increasing benefits and changes in longevity, Retirement and Social Security Law (**R & SSL**) has since been modified several times to create new "Tiers" for after employed employees who must also contribute their own friends to CRF to fund, in part, their retirement benefits.

the rules under which such investments were permitted were still highly prescriptive. In 1982, Governor Carey proposed a series of additional reforms for CRF investments "into areas which private plans have found profitable, thus serving the interests of the beneficiaries and participants in all public retirement systems." The legislature adopted certain of these recommendations, among them, an amendment to R & SSL Art. 4-A to authorize a public pension plan to invest up to **five percent** of its assets in investments not expressly specified by other provisions of R & SSL.[2] [The 1982 amendment], however, also limited how the investment decisions in these "alternate investments" were to be made. In 1983, at the urging of Governor Cuomo, the legislature modified [R & SSL Art. 4-A] to replace the proscriptive standards governing the alternate investments with the standard of the "prudent investor." As a result, while the list of "eligible investments" under R & SSL remains a hodge podge of proscriptive requirements, "alternative investments" may be made under "prudent investor" standards.

Over time, the specific rules for non-alternate investments were eased and the percentage of CRF assets which could be invested in alternate investments was raised. In 1991, the portion of CRF investments which could be placed in alternate investments was further expanded to **7 1/2 %**, as a partial implementation of Governor Cuomo's Task Force on Pension Fund Investments. Subsequent legislation through 1996 made technical changes and expanded other investment powers. In 1997 the Legislature, at the urging of the New York State Teacher's Retirement Board, which serves as trustee of the New York State Teachers Retirement System, a public pension fund also subject to R & SSL, raised the portion of public retirement funds' assets which could be invested in alternate investments to **15%**, and simplified and rationalized other provision of [R & SSL].

In 2005, **Hevesi**, as Comptroller, sought further legislation to amend R & SSL to increase the portion of public pension funds which could be invested in alternate investments to **25%**. While the Legislature adopted a bill to do so, **Governor Pataki** vetoed such measure on the grounds that because the Comptroller was the sole trustee of the CRF, "it would be appropriate to establish an independent board to provide greater transparency and accountability as to how CRF funds are invested." In his veto message, he noted that "[i]n the absence of governance and accountability reforms ... I am unwilling to approve the bill." In 2006, when Governor Pataki was no longer Governor, a similar

[2] These provisions are sometimes commonly referred to ad "alternate," "leeway" or "basket" investments.

bill without the governance and accountability reforms sought by Governor Pataki was introduced, passed and signed into law at the request of Comptroller Hevesi.

The concept of alternate investments allows the CRF to invest in any conceivable investment, provided that the investment would be appropriate under the "prudent Investor" rule. The prudent investor rule is now set forth in Estates, Powers and Trust Law (**ETPL**), which substantially enacted the Uniform Prudent Investors Act (**UPIA**), a Uniform Law now in force in forty-four states, the District of Columbia and the U.S. Virgin Islands, promulgated by the National Conference of Commissioners on Uniform State Laws in 1994. The UPIA represents the modern understanding that a trustee's responsibility is "to exercise reasonable care, skill and caution to make and implement enactment decisions as a prudent investor would for the entire portfolio, taking into account the purposes and the terms and provisions of the governing instrument."[3]

That standard authorizes a trustee "to invest in any type of investment consistent with the [prudent investor rule], since no particular investment is inherently prudent or imprudent for the prudent investor standard." For the CRF, the R & SSL limitations on unlimited discretion of the Comptroller now applies with respect to 75% of fund assets, the remainder effectively being subject only to the prudent investor rule. These obligations of the Comptroller to act as a trustee apply to any deputy or agent empowered by the Comptroller, such as **Loglisci**, to carry out the Comptroller's duties.

The alternate investments at issue in this case were in what are commonly known as private equity funds, hedge funds, and "fund of funds" which in turn interested in hedge and private equity funds. A **private equity fund** in this context is an investment vehicle where a manager amasses a pool of money or commitments to fund money from investors, to be used in one or more equity investments in enterprises through direct ownership of the assets or through non-traded securities of the entity owning the assets. A **hedge fund** is an investment vehicle where a manager amasses a pool of money or commitments to fund money from investors to invest in financial assets or other assets or instruments with the power to borrow at the fund level to leverage such purchases, which the manager expects will provide superior returns by reason of the manager's understanding of market anomalies. In a "**fund of funds**," the manager invests the funds committed or to be committed by investors in a portfolio of private equity or hedge funds to diversify the

---

[3] See the Prefatory Note to the UPIA which traces the evolution of trust investment law up to the UPIA.

investments being made.

To invest in these funds, investors commit their investments before the fund identifies the investments it makes. Thus the investor in such funds relies on the expertise and ability of the manager to understand the market to identify good direct investments or financial or other opportunities for greater return, through proper management of business in which equity investments are made; or in the case of fund of funds investments, in other funds which are expected to be good investors, rather than evaluating the ultimate investments itself.[4] All of these funds typically have long time horizons which, on the one hand, reduce the liquidity of investments in them and, on the other hand, may enhance the ultimate return to investors by reason of the Fund's ability to stay with an investment over an extended period. While there are successful Private Equity and Hedge funds, some are unsuccessful and some even fraudulent, and others have achieved spectacular returns by successfully reviving failing business or predicting market movements or trends. These funds generally do not raise money from the general public. Instead, they are generally marketed to and purchased by institutional and "accredited" investors under [Rule 144A and Regulation D] of the Securities Act of 1933 which permit the market for such securities to be lightly regulated at the Federal level, relying on the sophistication of institutional or accredited investors to police the investments rather than the heavy hand of Federal securities regulators to evaluate a fund's business model and the quality and experience of its managers. The explosive growth of these funds are evidence that sophisticated investors consider these funds to be proper and appropriate vehicles for their investments.

---

[4] As part of CRF's "diligence" procedures, alternate investments in funds were purportedly vetted by outside consultants. Given that CRF investments in these funds were to be made before the fund made its own investments, such vetting could be no more than an inquiry into the legitimacy of the management of the fund and its track record and capacity to carry out their proposed investment program. While this vetting process undoubtedly protected CRF from making an investment in a phony or Ponzi fund, the process which assigned diligence tasks to at least two different consultants, could not serve as a check whether CRF complied with its mandate to make and allocate CRF investments among alternate investments and between alternate and traditional investment categories, on a prudent investor standard. The consultants were not called upon to compare any proposed investments to other funds which may have been available for investment, whether the amount invested in a fund resulted in a prudent balance of investments or whether the balance between alternate and traditional investments was prudent, or whether the balance among the alternative investments was prudent. Further, because several consultants were employed, none had an overview or was in position to make such determination.

As the CRF is one of the largest institutional investors in the United States, it was not inappropriate for the CRF to consider and perhaps, in its discretion as a prudent investor, to invest in these funds, to the extent that the [entire] CRF portfolio is prudently invested to balance risk, gain and liquidity.

This history of the expansion of the Comptroller's discretionary investment authority over almost a half century tracks the expansion of narrow investment criteria for other trust funds under State Law. However, the history of gubernatorial recommendation for the modification and approval of this authority as well as veto messages, shows a continuing concern of many Governors that, although the standard under which CRF investments should be made should be regulated under a prudent investor rule, allowing the Comptroller as [the] sole trustee to invest such funds without further oversight remained problematic.

In January 2002, **Hevesi** took office as the newly elected Comptroller. **Morris** was his long time political consultant and confidant. By such time, the CRF had been regularly investing in some but not all types of "alternative investments" as authorized by R & SSL, and the Division of Alternate Investments had already been established to review and recommend which alternate investments should be made. Soon after Hevesi took office, **Loglisci** was appointed as Director of Alternate Investments, and subsequently was promoted to Chief Investment Officer of the entire CRF.

It is **the theory of the AG's case** that Morris, Loglisci and persons associated with them took control of the alternate investment process of the Comptroller's office, to capture placement fees and management fees generated by the overwhelming majority of new alternate investments for their own benefit, by conditioning the approval of most or all alternate investments on placement fees being payable [to], or fund management fees being shared with, a designee of Morris or persons associated with him, or their relatives or other persons as a compensation or reward for political or other services performed at Morris' request. The AG asserts that as a result of this scheme, Morris committed the crimes for which he was indicted. It is the AG's further theory that Morris arranged the removal of the former Chief Investment Officer of the CRF who would not "play ball" with Morris, and induced Hevesi to promote Loglisci to Chief Investment Officer to carry out the scheme.

Central to this matter is how "**placement agents**" function and how placement fees are paid to them. Any consideration of the issues raised by Morris' motion requires an understanding of what these entail. Placement agents are essentially brokers and their fees are essentially brokerage commissions. To the extent therefore that brokers play an appropriate economic function and their fees represent an appropriate recompense for their services, a market economy such as ours should expend no effort in fretting about their propriety as a general matter.

Brokers function to match counter parties and to negotiate the terms of their match in exchange for a fee. The most obvious brokers are those who provide a matching service for buyers and sellers of real estate or stock or bonds, or between landlord and tenant. Brokers, sometimes under other names, provide similar services to match parties seeking a relationship, as for example: the investment bank which brokers merger and acquisition transactions between companies; the head hunter who matches executives with businesses, universities or hospitals; or the employment agency which matches people with jobs. Placement agents in this context match Hedge funds or Private Equity funds seeking investors with capital sources seeking investments. Except for heavily regulated industries, the compensation of brokers is left to the market with the understanding that, except for such regulated industries, any collusion among brokers to fix prices or rates would violate antitrust laws.

As the market sets brokerage compensation levels, brokerage compensation should reach a general equilibrium, as those who pay brokers attempt to minimize payments and to retain more for themselves, and those who are brokers may not accept assignment from those unwilling to pay what the broker feels is a fair compensation for his efforts, which he might receive from another customer. As there are differences in the abilities of brokers to close a deal, persons who are perceived of as more successful in consummating favorable transactions will command a higher fee. It is no secret that persons perceived of as successful brokers (as is true of those perceived of a successful doctors or lawyers) may be richly compensated. There was substantial evidence before Grand Jury of this dynamic in the setting of placement agent fees.

For a legitimate broker to be successful, the broker should understand the needs of the parties he is bringing together, and if entities, their decision making process and other concerns. In large scale financial transactions especially where a number of participants are sought, individuals with specific experience and understanding of different parties is useful. Thus it is common, for example, if placing securities with nationals or entities of a foreign country, that someone familiar with that country, its culture and its financial and tax system would be employed or affiliated with the placement agent to make such sale. It is true also when dealing with governments that one with prior governmental or political experience would probably be better suited to understand governmental needs and culture in promoting and consummating a transaction with a governmental entity—while at the same time, such expertise could aid the Fund in formulating its product and approach to meet governmental requirements.

Because of the competitive nature of the business, fund managers seek out whatever brokers they believe will be successful to the extent fund management may not hire different brokers to pitch to specific capital sources and promiscuously and unsentimentally replace those unsuccessful with those who seem to be in a better position to secure investments in their fund. Multiple witnesses before the Grand Jury painted this industry as practice of musical chairs for placement agents and competition for investments, with scant regard for who the broker was or how he would be able to close the deal, as long as he was successful. If the placement agent was successful, his contingent fee was deemed earned and paid. Thus, absent some legal restriction on Morris' activities, or some crime committed by him in the course of his activities in the placement of CRF investments, his acting as placement agent and the receipt of compensation therefor was not *per se* criminal.

Alexander Wolcott, Jr, an American commentator and critic once observed that "all the things I really like to do are illegal, immoral or fattening." It is clear that the approximately $19 Million Morris received was fattening. It may be that his receipt of such funds while he continued as principal political consultant to Comptroller Hevesi, and hiding such fact, were immoral, at least to the political sensitivities of pundits.[5] However,

---

[5] It is a reality of politics that elected officials often act to reward their supporters, whether by supporting legislation favored by them or appointing supporters to positions of power, trust or prestige. Similarly, it is not rare that supporters often win the award of government contracts especially where there are few if any objective standards for their award and great discretion in the person awarding them. Where such appointments or awards are made within legal parameters, it is fair game for political commentators or opponents to complain, and where such action seems excessive, to score political points with the public. Here, the disclosure of Morris' receipt of approximately $19 Million in placement and management fees while he was Hevesi's principal political consultant, was met with political outrage by Hevesi's opponents and by press and pundit commentary as at least "immoral." Whether such a course of action was immoral, however, is a determination left to the court of public opinion after hearing from the moral arbiters of our communities, and such judgment does not and may not bind this Court. Sanctions for immoral behavior are left to be imposed, if at all, by the court of public opinion and the ballot box. Whether such behavior was also criminal is to be determined in this case.

the sole question before this Court is whether Morris' actions were illegal and whether at this stage of this case, the AG may proceed to prosecute Morris on any or all charges in the indictment.

Illustrative of the political quandry created by this system of placement fees [are] the different responses to the highly publicized disclosure of Morris' activities by **Comptroller DeNapoli**, Hevesi's successor in New York, by California Public Employee Retirement System (**CalPERS**) (the only State public pension system larger than the CRF), and by the United States Securities and Exchange Commission. The CRF has now banned placement agents, paid intermediaries and registered lobbyists from being involved in CRF investments. CalPERS has elected instead to regulate them extensively and to force public disclosure.[6] And the SEC, after a full consideration, has decided to leave placement fees and placement agents to market discipline, as under present regulation, but instead prohibited, commencing September 13, 2010, recipients of placement fees, as well as employees of funds which have received public pension fund investments from making political contributions to public officials who oversee such public pension fund.[7] What these three well publicized regulatory changes reflect is that, at the times relevant to this indictment, the payment of placement fees by funds to placement agents for the placement of CRF investments into such funds was not *per se* illegal; nor was it *per se* illegal for a placement agent to be "involved" politically, to make political contributions, or to do political favors not otherwise proscribed by campaign finance laws.

Federal Law has long recognized that placement agents are brokers of securities and requires them to be registered as such with the SEC, and further requires individuals working for placement agents who may be compensated by a share of the placement agent fees to also be licensed and tested as to their understanding of securities laws. This licensure process is currently carried out by **Financial Industry Regulation Authority** (FINRA), which has developed a testing protocol for individual brokers. FINRA issues a series of licenses; Morris applied for and received what are known as Series 7 and 63

[6] A bill has also passed the California Assembly to ban contingent placement fees for CalPERS investments and to require placement agents doing business with California public pension funds to register as lobbyists. This bill, AB1743 of 2010, is pending in the California Senate for action on August 2, 2010.

[7] Rules 206(4)-5, and amendments to Rules 204-2 and 206(4)-3 under the Investment Advisors Act of 1940. See SEC Release 1A-3043, which discusses at great length the issues and basis of their decision to adopt such rules. Such report cites the transactions covered by this indictment as a major reason for the new rules adopted.

Licenses which entitled him to act as an employee of a registered broker-dealer and to receive a share of brokerage commissions earned by such broker-dealer on business he generated. Shortly after Hevesi's election as Comptroller, and Morris' initial attempt to share in placement fees relating to a CRF investment, Morris, becoming aware of this regulatory protocol, affiliated with **Searle & Co.** (Searle), an SEC registered broker-dealer located in Connecticut, and took and passed the Series 7 and 63 License tests and therefore became eligible under Federal securities laws to share placement fees paid to Searle, his "employer." Again, such activity was itself a lawful activity. Had Morris, by himself, merely proceeded in this new endeavor as a securities salesman to introduce funds to the CRF on behalf of Searle, which had been commissioned as a placement agent by such funds and whose proposals were duly considered by the CRF under the prudent investor rule, and after such consideration the CRF made an investment in one or more of such funds, generating placement fees payable to Searle and in part paid to Morris for his services and otherwise complied with State and Federal law, there would be no basis for an indictment for such acts. However, the Grand Jury heard additional facts upon which the counts against Morris were based. While Morris challenges each count as to whether the "facts" could support a finding of criminality on such counts, issues which this Decision and Order will address below, the Grand Jury heard sufficient evidence of Morris' additional acts and behavior during the relevant period to sustain most of the charges against him.

This additional evidence showed that Morris and Loglisci, with the aid of at least one other senior official of the Comptroller's office and others, created a **corrupt operation** by which decisions of the CRF to invest in a fund were based on whether such fund had agreed to pay placement fees to or share management fees with Morris or his designees, rather than solely on the **prudent investor rule**. For example, in some cases Loglisci had already identified a fund which had otherwise sought a CRF investment, and let it be known to the fund that an investment was possible only if the fund retained **Searle** as a placement agent. On other occasions, funds seeking investments on "cold calls" to Loglisci as Director of Alternate Investments or Chief Investment Officer were returned to the Fund by Morris, "offering" his services as placement agent. Morris also agreed with other persons acting as placement agents for funds to share fees with Searle or another designee of Morris, in exchange for securing CRF investments. During the course of this activity, Morris never publicly attended meetings between the funds and the CRF personnel, and failed to disclose his role except where disclosure was made to Loglisci, who, as part of the arrangement, hid such disclosures from the public.[8] Funds which would not hire Morris or his designees were shut out of CRF investments. Finally, Morris routed payments through other persons and chains of entities to disguise the trail of funds and payments to cover his tracks for payoffs, to hide his activities and to allow the scheme continue; Morris made payments, disguised as loans, to secure the participation of the other members of the Morris group. The Grand Jury found that, as a result, the corrupt operation created by Morris and his group within and without the Comptroller's office constituted a Criminal Enterprise, and indicted Morris and Loglisci on the other counts of the indictment.

MARTIN ACT COUNTS

> * * * The **Martin Act**, in **General Business Law GBL** § 352-c(6), expressly proscribes "*fraud deception, concealment, suppression ... while engaged in inducing or promoting the issuance, distribution, exchange, sale or purchase within or from this state of any securities.*"

Fifty-one counts charge Morris with violations of the Martin Act. The twenty-three Class E felony counts under GBL § 352–c(6) relate to twenty-three investments made by the CRF during the period in question which generated placement fees paid or payable to Morris and persons acting in concert with him. * * *

The existence and functioning of the international securities and capital markets and their principal location in New York are a major source of New York jobs, wealth and tax receipts. The location of such markets in the United States also significantly contributes to American wealth, jobs and tax receipts and to the United States balance of international payments. The health of a securities and capital market depends in substantial part on investors' confidence in the market's transparency and honesty. Where transparency or honesty is lacking, investors will not invest, will seek markets elsewhere, or will at least seek risk premiums so high as to stifle investment activities. Where such is lacking, the ability of New York market to function and efficiently allocate the always scarce capital of the world to its most effective use will be adversely impacted. There is therefore a rational basis for New York to legislate to promote the honesty and effectiveness of this

[8] This "non-public" file of disclosure letters to the Comptroller's office, maintained by Loglisci, "disappeared" when the Morris/Loglisci operation was disclosed and Loglisci left the Comptroller's office.

market so as to promote wealth and jobs and the economic well being of its citizens.

The Federal Securities Acts were adopted in the 1930s to remedy market failures which were perceived to have caused or prolonged the depression of the 1930s, and State Blue Sky[9] securities acts such as the Martin Act represent considered legislative judgments of individual States to preserve the honesty and therefore investor confidence and the efficacy of the securities and capital markets. These laws expressly expand existing common law theories and common law remedies, such as what constituted actionable common law fraud, to remedy gaps in the common law structure to police properly the securities business. Thus, Morris' attempt to limit the scope of the Martin Act to common law fraud flies in the face of the legislative history and purpose of the Martin Act, as set forth in its terms, and as it has been construed by the Courts. * * *

Morris' further attempt to limit the Martin Act to concepts of common law fraud are similarly unavailing. The beneficiaries of the Martin Act are not only "investors" and the "investing public," but the general public in terms of societal economic wealth, jobs and tax receipts by reason of the world's capital market center being located in New York, rather than elsewhere. * * *

In any event, an evaluation of Morris' behavior in light of real-world economics shows that his actions may also have had a substantial likelihood of causing a material economic loss to the CRF. Morris' scheme was to create a "**toll gate**" for entry into the CRF alternate investment program where only those who paid Morris' toll could enter. While the Grand Jury was given no evidence as to how many alternative investment funds might have been suitable for CRF investment, ample evidence was presented that funds found it economically desirable to have CRF moneys invested in them. This is not surprising as managers of Hedge and Private Equity funds commonly receive a 2% annual fee for assets under management and a 20% carried interest in profits. Similarly, while fund of funds managers may receive a small percentage management fee, the size of such funds are often quite large, resulting in a potential of a large management fee. Thus a large additional investment (and there was Grand Jury testimony that CRF investments were quite large) would generate large fees and profit possibilities for a fund. The Grand Jury

[9] State Securities Laws are generally referred to as "Blue Sky" laws. This name derives from the understanding that these laws were enacted to address the sale of stock by "fast talking [sellers] selling anything including the blue sky." 1 HAZEN, TREATISE ON THE LAW OF SECURITIES REGULATION 8.1 (5th ed. 1995).

also heard evidence that many funds sought a CRF investment because, in addition to directly enhancing the earnings of the fund manager, a CRF investment would constitute a seal of approval and endorsement of such fund to other investors thus aiding the fund to secure additional investments from other investors and thus also increase fund manager's profits.

Yet, the Grand Jury testimony showed that in spite of all economic benefits to a fund's manager arising from a CRF investment, not all fund applicants to the CRF would agree to pay Morris's demanded toll. In fact, there was evidence that some of the funds who did receive investments from the CRF only did so because their own placement agents, unknown to them, secretly colluded with Morris or persons working with him to pay his toll out of their own fees, which they received for obtaining CRF investment. The effect of Morris' acts was to restrict the universe of alternate investments in which CRF could invest to only those funds where Morris' tolls were paid. It is basic economics that restricting the CRF's choices of investment opportunities to an arbitrary limited subset of the potential investments in which the CRF could otherwise properly consider for investment is economically disadvantageous to the CRF, violates the duty of the CRF to follow the prudent investor rule, and is therefore wrongful.

Under long standing rulings of New York Courts, the Martin Act has been construed to prohibit acts which would not be found to be improper under common law fraud concepts. "*Neither scienter nor an intent to defraud need be proven in order to establish liability under the Martin Act.*" The standard of behavior of persons who engage in the promotion or facilitation of the sale and purchase of securities is, under the Martin Act, set between the poles of the "**morals of the market place**" and the responsibilities of a fiduciary which require "**the punctilio of an honor most sensitive**" as the standard of behavior.

The standard imposed on such participants in the security market by the Martin Act is that they may not perform any deceitful practice "*contrary to the plain rules of common honesty and all acts tending to deceive the public.*" This enhanced level of obligation is part of the regulatory scheme imposed on persons in the business of selling, offering or dealing in securities or in their promotion or recommendation. Under Federal securities regulations and laws, such persons must be licensed and pass qualifying examinations to assure their knowledge and the knowledge of the regulatory scheme under which they operate. Under the Martin Act and similar Blue Sky laws of many states, their behavior and responsibilities are set at a higher level. Given the complexities of securities and the concomitant opportunity for fraud or deception, the securities industry has become a regulated industry and its practitioners are held to higher standards than the ordinary unregulated or unlicensed purveyor of goods and services.

There is no dispute that Morris was involved in the securities industry and in the promotion of the sale and purchase of securities. He became licensed under FINRA knowing he needed to do so to become eligible to share placement fees received by a registered broker-dealer, and became affiliated with Searle, a registered broker-dealer which was authorized to receive placement fees. To do so Morris shared the placement fees received by Searle on a commission basis, which was set at 5% for Searle and 95% for Morris. Morris knew that placement fees were only, by Federal law, payable to a licensed broker-dealer and shareable by it with a licensed person or other licensed broker-dealers; and he voluntarily became part of the securities industry and thus had acceded to its rules and standard rules. CRF investments, which are the subject of this indictment, all were investments by the CRF in securities making Morris subject to the heightened obligations placed on persons engaged in promotion or sale of such securities in or from the State. * * *

PENAL LAW COUNTS

Accomplice Liability

Many indictment counts asserted against Morris are at least partially based on a theory of accomplice liability—that Morris, acting in concert with Loglisci or others committed the charged crime. Morris asserts that such accomplice liability cannot attach to him under certain counts because no single person committed all of the elements of the crime charged under such counts.... It is an interesting theory, but one without basis under New York law. While it is clear that a person proven to be an aider or abettor who has not personally performed any of the elements of a crime may be, under **Penal Law** PL § 20.00, held responsible for the entire crime, it is also true that where accomplices act together, with the appropriate common intent, all accomplices may be found guilty of a crime under a theory of acting in concert even where separate elements of the crime are performed by different persons and no one person performed all of the elements by himself or herself. All that New York [Penal Law] requires is that, to convict a defendant, the People must prove that such defendant, alone, or acting in concert, committed each element of the crime. * * *

Enterprise Corruption

Count one of the Indictment charges Morris with Enterprise Corruption under PL § 460.20(1)(a), a Class B felony.... Under PL § 460.20(1),

> "*[a] person is guilty of* ***enterprise corruption*** *when, having knowledge of the existence of a* ***criminal enterprise*** *and the nature of its activities, and being employed by or associated with such enterprise, he intentionally conducts or participates in the affairs of an enterprise by participating in a* ***pattern*** *of criminal activity.*"

PL § 460.10 defines "**criminal enterprise**" as

> "*a group of persons sharing a common purpose of engaging in criminal conduct, associated in an ascertainable structure distinct from a pattern of criminal activity, and with a continuity of existence, structure and criminal purpose beyond the scope of individual criminal incidents.*"

Count one charges Morris of conducting and participating in the affairs of a criminal enterprise, referred to in the indictment as the "**Morris Group**," by participating in a pattern of criminal activities including seventy "pattern acts" of criminal actions set forth in such count. The enterprise is described as including Morris, Loglisci, John Doe 1 (an asset manager and family friend of Loglisci, and a placement agent finder and principal with respect to certain alternative investment transactions with the CRF, sometimes in partnership with Morris), John Doe 2 (a high-ranking official within the office of the State Comptroller and an advisor to the Comptroller), other persons known and unknown to the Grand Jury, who shared Morris' criminal purpose.

To substantiate the existence of a criminal enterprise under PL § 460.10, the People must establish that a group of persons was associated in an ascertainable structure distinct from a pattern of criminal activity. That is, the evidence before the Grand Jury must show "*[a] cognizable* ***criminal enterprise*** *that extend[s] beyond the common plan or scheme encompassing the alleged* ***pattern acts***." It must demonstrate "*[a] system of authority beyond what is minimally necessary to effectuate individual substantive criminal offenses,*" something more than and "*[d]istinct from any ad hoc association entered into for the purpose of carrying out one or more of the criminal incidents relied upon to establish its existence.*"

This Court finds that evidence presented to the Grand Jury was sufficient to sustain a finding that Morris conducted the criminal activities alleged in the indictment within the confines of an ascertainable structure, with Morris at the top of the command structure and with Loglisci directly below him. A criminal enterprise may be operated through a separate formal structure or by an organized cabal wholly or partially within a legitimate operation. Here the Office of the Comptroller is a governmental organization established by N.Y. Const. Art. 5 § 1. The indictment does not charge ***it*** to be a criminal enterprise, but does accuse Morris and persons within and without the Comptroller's office with establishing an ongoing criminal enterprise within and outside of such office.

Because criminal enterprises rarely organize under written charters, agreements or by-laws, or keep extensive written minutes or records of their criminal activity, proof of the structure and continuity of the enterprise may be inferred through evidence of the actual activities of the group. The courts have considered many different factors which may be used to prove the existence of a particular criminal enterprise. Among them are evidence of the time frame over which the illegal acts occurred, patterns of concealment, succession arrangements to replace individuals who may leave the group, explicit profit share arrangements with the group and other factors. None of these factors have been deemed to be a *sine qua non* to establish the existence of a criminal enterprise under the statute, but merely factors from which a finder of fact may reach the factual conclusion that the statutory definition of "criminal enterprise" has been met.

Here, the Grand Jury found the Morris Group participated in seventy "pattern acts" of criminal activity during a five to six year period, involving nineteen large placements of CRF money in nineteen separate alternate investments generating approximately $35 Million in placement fees or shared management fees, of which approximately $19 Million was eventually received personally by Morris or by entities owned by him, with the remainder going to other members of the Morris Group, persons recruited by Morris to front for, or to conceal payments or compensation to, persons for the performance of future, current and past political favors for Morris and his political consulting clientele. This Court finds the evidence before the Grand Jury sufficient to support their finding of a criminal enterprise having an ascertainable structure. * * * PL § 460 is not by its own terms intended solely to cover crimes committed by **classic mafias**. PL § 460.00 itself expressly states that "*the concept of criminal enterprise should not be limited to traditional criminal syndicates or crime families, and may induce persons who join together in a criminal enterprise, as defined by subdivision three of Section 460.10 of this article for the purpose of corrupting legitimate enterprises or infiltrating and illicitly* *influencing such enterprises.*"

Bribery and Rewarding Official Misconduct

Count one hundred-thirteen charges Morris with Bribery in the Second Degree in violation of PL § 200.03. Such crime occurs when a defendant confers or offers to confer a benefit of the value of more than ten thousand dollars upon a public servant, upon an agreement or understanding that such public servant's vote, opinion, judgment, action, decision or exercise of discretion as a public servant would be therefore influenced.... While the crime requires the relationship between the payment and the action of the official to be proven, the law is not so naive as to believe that bribery may only be shown by proof of a formal written contract setting forth the *quid pro quo* of the parties to the bribe as to the **payment** on the one hand, and the **official misconduct** on the other. Bribery is, instead, "*often perpetrated subtly with winks, nods and walks in the park*"; and proof may be from circumstantial and inferential evidence. Here this Court finds that the Grand Jury was presented with sufficient evidence for it to have concluded both, from inferences which may be properly drawn from such evidence to support Morris' indictment on this count. * * *

This is the Decision and Order of the Court.

Topic 3 Misleading Investment Performance Advertising

Laws & Rules Highlight:

IA Act (15 USC 80b-1 *et seq.*) & Rules (17 CFR §§ 275.0-2 *et seq.*)
IC Act (15 USC 80a-1 *et seq.*) & Rules (17 CFR §§ 270.0-1 *et seq.*)
Securities Act (15 USC 77a *et seq.*) & Rules (17 CFR §§ 230.100 *et seq.*)

IA Act

- § 206 Prohibited Transactions by Registered Investment Advisers
  - § 206(4) (*prohibits "any act, practice, or course of business which* ***is*** *fraudulent, deceptive, or manipulative; grants* ***SEC rulemaking authority*** *to define, and to prescribe means reasonably designed to prevent, fraud by advisers*)
  - Rule 206(4)-1 Advertisements by Investment Advisers (*prohibits fraudulent, deceptive, and manipulative advertisement by* ***registered*** *IAs*)
    - ✓ Rule 206(4)-1(a) (*specifying* ***five types*** *of advertisement as "fraudulent, deceptive, or manipulative" within the meaning of § 206(4)*)
    - ✓ Rule 206(4)-1(b) (*def.* ***"advertisement"***)

IC Act

- Rule 34b-1 Sales Literature Deemed to Be Misleading (*extending* ***SA Rule 482 omitting prospectus*** *standardization and disclosure requirements to* ***all fund sales literature*** *containing performance information*)

Securities Act

- § 5 Prohibition Relating to Interstate Commerce and the Mails
  - § 5(c) (***pre-filing:*** *prohibits any offer to sell or offer to buy any security*)
  - § 5(b)(1) (***post-filing pre-effectiveness:*** *requires use of § 10(b) prospectus*)
  - § 5(b)(1) & § 2(a)(10)(a) (***post-effectiveness:*** *requires § 10(a) final prospectus be "sent or given" "prior to or at the same time with" a written offer that is not a § 10(b) prospectus*)
- § 10 Information Required in Prospectus
  - § 10(a) (*final prospectus*)
  - § 10(b) (*other prospectuses*)
    - ✓ Rule 482 Advertising by an Investment Company as Satisfying Requirements of Section 10 (***Rule 482 omitting prospectus****: permits fund standardized performance advertising with required disclosure*)
- exclusions from "prospectus"
  - § 2(a)(10) (*def. "prospectus"*); § 2(a)(3) (*def. "sale," "sell," "offer"*)
    - ✓ § 2(a)(10)(a) (*excepting* ***supplemental sales literature*** *from "prospectus" if*

preceded by or accompanied with § 10(a) prospectus)

- ✓ § 2(a)(10)(b) (*excepting* ***tombstone advertising*** *from "prospectus"*)
- ◆ Rule 134 Communications Not Deemed a Prospectus (*Rule 134 tombstone ad. exception from "prospectus":* ***not available*** *to registered ICs*)
- ◆ Rule 135a Generic Advertising (***Rule 135a generic Ad.*** *exception from "prospectus": permits limited, generic advertising about investment company securities*)

- civil liability and antifraud provisions
  - ◆ § 11 Civil Liabilities on Account of False Registration Statement
  - ◆ § 12 Civil Liabilities Arising in Connection With Prospectuses and Communications
  - ◆ Rule 156 Investment Company Sales Literature (*an* ***interpretive rule*** *making the general antifraud provisions of* ***SA §17(a)***, ***SEA §10(b)***, *and* ***Rule 10b-5*** *fully applicable to sales literature used for investment companies*)

Pre-Case Background Note:[Biblio]

Mutual Fund Advertising:
Legal Restraints; Liability; Performance Standardization

Investment company shares may not be sold to the public unless the ***company*** is registered under the Investment Company (IC) Act and its ***shares*** are registered under the Securities Act (SA Act).[1 (p.930)]

Securities Act § 5 Restraints on Sales Literature

Securities Act registration regime restricts the use of investment company "***sales literature***," which, as defined in SA Rule 156, includes "*any communication (whether in writing, by radio, or by television) used by any person to offer to sell or induce the sale of securities of any investment company.*" ***Before filing*** of a registration statement with respect to a security, SA § 5(c) prohibits any "*offer*" to "*sell*" such security as such terms are broadly defined in § 2(a)(3). ***Post-filing but pre-effectiveness*** of the registration statement, § 5(b)(1) prohibits the use of any advertisement to sell the security unless such advertisement meets § 10(b) requirements for a "*prospectus*" as the latter term is defined by § 2(a)(10), which includes "*any ... advertisement ... which offers any security for sale.*" ***After effectiveness*** of the registration statement, under the joint operation of § 5(b)(1) and § 2(a)(10)(a), a supplemental sales literature without meeting § 10(b) requirements for a statutory prospectus may be used if preceded by or accompanied with a § 10(a) final prospectus. Such "supplemental" sales literature—meaning "*supplementing*" the § 10(a) final prospectus[1 (pp.929-30)]—is excepted from the statutory definition of "*prospectus*." Legal restrains on use of sales literature imposed by the Securities Act were intended by Congress to foster rational investment decision-making based on the full disclosures contained in the filed registration statement.[2]

Securities Act Civil Liability and Antifraud Provisions Applicable to Sales Literature

Securities Act also imposes liabilities for the contents of sales literature. SA ***§ 11 liability*** attaches to issuers and a range of other parties for an effective registration statement (which includes the § 10(a) final prospectus) that contained—at the time such registration statement became effective—an *untrue* statement of a material fact or an *omission* of a material fact required to be included in the registration statement or necessary to make the statements in the registration statement not misleading ("***registration statement liability***"). SA ***§ 12(a)(2) liability*** attaches to sellers who offer or sell securities by means of a prospectus or oral communication that includes an *untrue* statement of a material fact, or *omits* to state a material fact necessary in order to make the statements, in the light of the circumstances under which they were made, not misleading ("***prospectus liability***"). SA ***§ 17(a)(2) liability*** attaches to any person who, in the offer or sale of a security, obtains money or property by means of any *untrue* statement of a material fact or any *omission* to state a material fact necessary in order to make the statements made, in light of the circumstances under which they were made, not misleading.[2; 3]

Three Types of Investment Company Sales Literature: Legal Status and Standards of Liability

Subject to SA § 5 restraints on sales literature, mutual fund advertising must either qualify as a "prospectus" under § 10, or qualify for an exception from "prospectus."[1 (pp.932-3)] Mutual fund advertising—in addition to the § 10(a) final prospectus which remains the primary disclosure and sales document for mutual fund shares—includes three types of sales literature:[4 (§14.02)]

- ***Rule 482 omitting prospectus advertisement:*** Rule 482 (initially adopted as Rule 434d in 1979 but redesignated as Rule 482 in 1982)[5b (p.10298 n.1)] permits mutual funds to advertise investment performance data, which is not permitted by Rule 134 governing tombstone advertisements by non-investment company issuers. To balance greater flexibility to investment company issuers with investor protection, while Rule 134 "*tombstone Ad.*" is excepted from "prospectus" pursuant to §

2(a)(10)(b), Rule 482 advertising was adopted as an "***omitting prospectus***" under § 10(b). Thus, Rule 482 omitting prospectus advertisements are subject to civil liability under § 12(a)(2) for false or misleading prospectus. On the other hand, since Rule 482 omitting prospectus is not a § 10(a) full prospectus and thus not part of the registration statement, Rule 482 omitting prospectus advertisements are not subject to civil liability under § 11 for false or misleading registration statement. Importantly, while fund performance advertising complying with Rule 482 standardization and disclosure requirements is deemed to be a § 10(b) "omitting prospectus" for purposes of § 5 of the Securities Act, Rule 482 is not a safe harbor for information contained in the 482 omitting prospectus advertisement from antifraud liability under the federal securities laws.[4 (§§16.01, 16.05, 16.24); 5]

- ***Supplemental sales literature:*** As written communication publicly offering or promoting fund shares, supplemental sales literature would meet the statutory definition of "prospectus" under § 2(a)(10); but it is excepted by § 2(a)(10)(a) from "prospectus" if "*preceded by or accompanied with*" a § 10(a) final prospectus. Not being a prospectus, supplemental sales literature is neither subject to § 11 registration statement liability nor subject to § 12(a)(2) prospectus liability. However, IC Rule 34b-1 applies the standardization and disclosure requirements of Rule 482 omitting prospectus to all investment company "sales literature" including "supplemental sales literature" that contains performance data for an investment company.[4 (§§18.01, 18.04, 18.16)] On the other hand, complying with "the four corners" of Rule 482 is not a safe harbor to shield the supplemental sales literature from the antifraud provisions of the federal securities laws.[5c]
- ***Rule 135a generic advertisement:*** The SEC adopted (pursuant to its rulemaking authority under § 19(a) "Special Powers of Commission") Rule 135a "Generic Advertising" in 1972—prior to its adoption in 1979 of Rule 482 omitting prospectus advertising—as "*a modest step in the direction of liberalizing the rules relating to advertising for investment company securities.*" Rule 135a permits "*generic or institutional advertising*": reference in general terms to investment company securities as a medium of investment and explanatory information relating to different types of funds, without mentioning any particular investment company or any specific security.[6] Importantly, Rule 135a generic Ad. may not include any performance data, as are permitted in Rule 482 omitting prospectus advertising and supplemental sales literature. While a Rule 135a generic Ad. is deemed neither an "offer to sell" a security nor a "prospectus" and thus not subject to §§ 11 and 12 registration statement and prospectus liability, it remains subject to

the antifraud provisions of the federal securities laws.[4 (§§15.01, 15.03, 15.05)]

Standardization of Fund Performance Data

Mutual funds are ***required*** to include in their registration statements their standardized investment performance data based on methods of computation prescribed in the fund registration statement form (Form N-1A). Mutual funds are ***permitted*** to include in their registration statements and supplemental sales literature when preceded or accompanied by a § 10(a) final prospectus additional, non-standardized, non-misleading yield and other performance information. In contrast to registration statements and supplemental sales literature, Rule 482 omitting prospectus ***restricts*** fund performance advertising to standardized yield quotations, standardized total returns, and non-standardized non-misleading total returns when accompanied by standardized total returns. Non-standardized yield quotations are ***prohibited*** in Rule 482 omitting prospectus advertisements.[4 (§16.06); 7; 8; 9]

Money market funds have been subject to standardized yield quotation requirements since 1980, using a ***seven-calendar day base period*** ending on the date of the most recent balance sheet included in the registration statement. The SEC expressed the concern that, money market funds being marketed primarily on the basis of yield to shareholders, yield comparison plays a significant part in investors' investment decisions concerning competing money market funds. Absent the use of a standardized method of yield computation, money market fund yield quotations are not comparable and have a potential for confusing and misleading investors. For example, factors affecting comparability of yield quotations may include the manner of treating unrealized appreciation and depreciation, any weighting factors used with respect to each portfolio security's dollar value and time remaining to maturity, and expenses and charges included in the calculation.[8a] Rule 482 omitting prospectus advertisements ***limit*** a money market fund's yield quotations to "*current yield*" (a simple annualized yield quotation based on the seven-day base period), "*effective yield*" (a compound annualized yield quotation based on the seven-day base period), and "*tax-equivalent current yield*" and "*tax-equivalent effective yield*" where the fund is a tax-exempt money market fund—with the resulting yield figure carried to at least four decimals.[4 (§16.06); 7; 8]

Non-money market mutual funds—funds investing in long-term debt and equities—have been subject to standardized yield quotations and total shareholder return requirements since 1988, based on the SEC's standardization experience in money market funds and its concern over the advertising practices of non-money market funds using different types of performance data and different methods of computation. The standardization sets a ***rolling 30-day base period*** for standardized yield quotations, and ***rolling one, five, and ten year base periods*** for standardized total return computations designed to capture the results of fund operations over one or more business cycles. Since yield and total return are generally inversely related, a fund advertising relatively high yield may in fact be losing shareholder value. Further, while for money market funds "yield" represents the total return, for bond funds "yield" usually does not equal total return; indeed for high risk, high yielding funds, their total returns over time may be lower than their yields due to some loss of principal. Thus, a non-money market fund advertising yield alone without accompanying such yield quotation with total return information may be omitting material information necessary to make the advertisement not misleading.[9] To prevent misleading fund performance advertising and facilitate meaningful comparison and evaluation by investors of fund performance, Rule 482 omitting prospectus advertisements ***must*** include the fund's standardized one, five, and ten year total returns when any such advertisement:[4 (§16.06); 7a; 9]

- contains *any fund performance* information; or
- contains a fund's *standardized yield quotations*; or
- contains a fund's *non-standardized total returns* (*e.g.*, total returns over time periods different from the standardized base periods, using aggregate, average, year-by-year, or other measures of total return).

For **critics** of SEC's regulation of fund performance advertising, see for example, Palmiter & Taha (2012):[10] stating that fund performance advertising is inherently and materially misleading, and that the current SEC-mandated warning does not temper investor enthusiasm for chasing past returns; advocating prohibition of fund performance advertising. For **a different view**, see for example, GAO (2011):[11] finding evidence mixed that investors are harmed by fund performance advertisements; recommending that FINRA develop sufficient mechanisms to effectively communicate across the fund industry new interpretative positions for advertising material that arise during the course of FINRA's regulatory reviews of advertisements, to achieve the important regulatory goal that mutual fund investors receive fair and objective information and are not misled by inappropriate advertising.

Bibliography

1. Kirsch *et al.*, *Mutual Fund and Variable Insurance Products Performance Advertising*, 50 BUS. LAW. 925 (1995)
2. DIV. OF INV. MGMT., SEC. & EXCH. COMM'N, PROTECTING INVESTORS: A HALF CENTURY OF INVESTMENT COMPANY REGULATION, Ch 9 Investment Company Advertising (1992)
3. Securities Offering Reform, 33–8591, IC–26993, 70 FR 44722, IV. Liability Issues (2005)
4. LEMKE, LINS & SMITH, REGULATION OF INVESTMENT COMPANIES, II. Mutual Fund Advertising Requirements (Lexis Advance 2017)
5. Rule 482: **5a.** Advertising by Investment Companies, 33-6116, IC-10852, 44 FR 52816 (1979); **5b.** Advertising by Investment Companies, 33-6454, IC-13049, 48 FR 10297 (1983); **5c.** Amendments to Investment Company Advertising Rules, 33-8294, IC-26195, 68 FR 57760, II.B. Applicability of Antifraud Provisions to Fund Advertising (2003)
6. Rule 135a: Investment Company Advertising and Summary Prospectus for Investment Companies, 33-5248, 37 FR 10071 (1972)
7. Form N-1A: **7a.** Item 26. Calculation of Performance Data, https://www.sec.gov/files/formn-1a.pdf; **7b.** Registration Form Used by Open-End Management Investment Companies; Guidelines, 33-6479, IC-13436, 48 FR 37928 (1982)
8. "Money Market" Funds; Inclusion of a Standardized Yield Computation in Prospectuses: **8a.** 33-6183, IC-11028, 45 FR 7578 (1980); **8b.** 33-6243, IC-11379, 45 FR 67079 (1980); **8c.** Advertising by Investment Companies, 33-6500, IC-13658, 48 FR 55722 (1983)
9. non-money market funds: **9a.** Advertising by Investment Companies; Proposed Rules and Amendments to Rules, Forms, and Guidelines, 33-6660, IC-15315, 151 FR 34384 (1986); **9b.** Advertising by Investment Companies, 33-6753, IC-16245, 53 FR 3868 (1988)
10. Palmiter & Taha, *Mutual Fund Performance Advertising: Inherently and Materially Misleading?*, 46 GA. L. REV. 289 (2012)
11. GAO, MUTUAL FUND ADVERTISING: IMPROVING HOW REGULATORS COMMUNICATE NEW RULE INTERPRETATIONS TO INDUSTRY WOULD FURTHER PROTECT INVESTORS, GAO-11-697 (July 2011), http://www.gao.gov/assets/330/321961.pdf

Case Study: Incubator Fund Performance Reporting

Van Kampen's small asset-base incubator fund reported a "phenomenal" 61.99% one-year total return in its first-year incubation period, when more than 50% of the return was attributable to the fund's investments in hot IPOs. In connection with the fund's public offering, fund investment adviser and principal underwriter advertised the fund's 61.99% one-year return and its #1 Lipper ranking, without disclosing the large impact of hot IPOs on the fund's incubation period return and without disclosing that, given the growth in the fund's total assets, the fund would be unlikely to sustain its incubation period return. Such omissions in the fund advertisements, prospectus, and semi-annual report made the fund performance data materially misleading.

For **empirical literature** studying fund performance and advertising, see for example:

- Evans, *Mutual Fund Incubation*, 65 J. FIN. 1581 (2010) (discussing mutual fund managers' strategy to set up a small group of incubator funds, abandon those performing poorly, and promote those performing well, resulting in an ***upward bias*** in returns data);

- Gaspar *et al.*, *Favoritism in Mutual Fund Families? Evidence on Strategic Cross-Fund Subsidization*, 61 J. FIN. 73 (2006) (finding evidence of in-family ***strategic performance transfer*** in favor of "*high family value*" funds, *i.e.*, funds earning high fees or high past performance thus enhancing the value of the fund management companies, at the expense of "*low family value*" funds thus harming the interests of such funds' shareholders).

In *re* Van Kampen Investment Advisory Corp.

Adm. Proc. 3-10002, IA-1819, IC-23996, 54 S.E.C. 355 (1999)

Research Topic:

Investment fund performance advertising regulation in China.

In *re* Van Kampen Investment Advisory Corp. *et al.*, Respondents

Adm. Proc. 3-10002, IA-1819, IC-23996, 54 S.E.C. 355 (Sept. 8, 1999)

I.

The Securities and Exchange Commission deems it appropriate and in the public interest that public administrative proceedings be instituted against **Van Kampen Investment Advisory Corp.** (*Van Kampen Advisory*) and Alan Sachtleben (collectively, **Respondents**), pursuant to § § 203(e), 203(f) and 203(k) of the Investment Advisers Act of 1940 and § § 9(b) and 9(f) of the Investment Company Act of 1940. In anticipation of the institution of these proceedings, Respondents have submitted an **Offer of Settlement** (*Offer*) which the Commission has determined to accept. Solely for the purpose of these proceedings and any other proceedings brought by or on behalf of the Commission, or to which the Commission is a party, and without admitting or denying the Commission's findings contained herein, except the Commission's findings set forth in Paragraphs III.A through III.D, which are admitted, Respondents consent to the entry of this *Order Instituting Proceedings, Making Findings, Imposing Remedial Sanctions and Ordering Respondents to Cease and Desist pursuant to § § 203(e), 203(f) and 203(k) of the Advisers Act and § § 9(b) and 9(f) of the Investment Company Act* (**Order**).

II.

Accordingly, IT IS HEREBY ORDERED that proceedings pursuant to § § 203(e), 203(f) and 203(k) of the Advisers Act and § § 9(b) and 9(f) of the Investment Company Act be and hereby are instituted.

III.

On the basis of this Order and Respondents' Offer, the Commission makes the following findings.[1]

RESPONDENTS

A. Van Kampen Advisory, a Delaware corporation headquartered in Oakbrook, Illinois, has been incorporated and registered with the Commission as an investment adviser from 1982 through the present. Van Kampen Advisory is a wholly owned subsidiary of **Van**

[1] The findings herein are made pursuant to Respondents' Offer of Settlement and are not binding on any other person or entity in this or any other proceeding.

Kampen Investments Inc. (*Van Kampen Investments*). At all relevant times, Van Kampen Advisory was the investment adviser for, among others, the **Van Kampen Growth Fund** (*Growth Fund*).

B. Sachtleben, age 57 and a resident of Houston, Texas, was, at all relevant times, an associated person of Van Kampen Advisory. He served as the Chief Investment Officer for Equity Investments for Van Kampen Advisory and its predecessor company from October 1987 through approximately June 1998, when he retired. He also served as Vice-President of the Growth Fund during the relevant period. As Chief Investment Officer, Sachtleben supervised, among others, Van Kampen Advisory's portfolio managers, research personnel, and trading staff in Houston.

RELATED ENTITIES

C. Van Kampen Growth Fund was an incubator fund that began operations on December 27, 1995 as a new diversified series of the Van Kampen Equity Trust, an investment company registered with the Commission.[2]

D. **Van Kampen Funds Inc.**, formerly Van Kampen Distributors Inc. (*Van Kampen Distributors*), a broker-dealer registered with the Commission, is the Growth Fund's principal underwriter. In February 1997, Van Kampen Distributors prepared and distributed sales literature on behalf of the Growth Fund concerning its opening to public investors. Van Kampen Distributors is a wholly owned subsidiary of Van Kampen Investments.

FACTS

The Growth Fund's Incubation

E. From its inception on or about December 27, 1995 to on or about February 3, 1997, the Growth Fund was an incubator fund whose shares were generally not available to the public for investment. Van Kampen and persons affiliated with Van Kampen provided seed money for the Growth Fund. During most of 1996, the Growth Fund had net assets of $200,000 to $ 380,000. The portfolio manager, under Sachtleben's supervision, invested the Growth Fund's assets in various securities with, among other things, the goal

---

[2] The term "incubator fund" commonly refers to investment vehicles not generally available to the public created by a sponsor for the purpose of establishing a performance track record and testing investment techniques prior to being offered to the public.

of establishing a performance track record to be used in marketing the fund to the public.

F. During its incubation period, the Growth Fund's Class A shares achieved, without adjusting for the applicable sales load, a 61.99% one-year total return as of December 31, 1996. The Growth Fund was reported to be the best-performing fund in 1996 for its category and a full 20 percentage points ahead of the second-best performing fund based on calculations by Lipper Analytical Services (Lipper). More than 50% of the Growth Fund's 1996 return was attributable to securities it acquired for investment through 31 hot initial public offerings.[3] Although the Growth Fund only purchased 100 to 400 shares in each hot IPO, those IPO shares had a magnified impact on the Growth Fund's return because of its small asset base.

G. During the last quarter of 1996, senior management of Van Kampen Advisory and Van Kampen Distributors decided to market the fund to the general public, in part, as a result of the Growth Fund's performance. The Board of Trustees for the Growth Fund, which was required to approve the opening of any fund for public investment, was scheduled to consider the opening of the Growth Fund at its quarterly board meeting in late January 1997.

The Street Article

H. On or shortly after January 7, 1997, Sachtleben received a copy of a December 31, 1996 article published in THE STREET, an internet publication, which, among other things, questioned the "phenomenal" gains of the Growth Fund and the possible use of hot IPOs to bolster its performance. The article highlighted concerns associated with small funds advertising impressive one-year returns as they go public without disclosing the source of such returns, thus unrealistically raising investor expectations. The article further stated that Van Kampen Advisory could have given "a small fund like Growth a spectacular return by allocating hot initial public offerings to the fund.... Because the fund is so small, any one-shot gains will make a big difference in performance."

The IPO Impact Study

I. In mid-January 1997, shortly after he received the Street Article, Sachtleben directed one of the employees under his supervision to conduct a study to determine the

[3] Hot IPOs generally refer to securities that trade at a premium over their initial public offering price immediately after the initial public offering.

impact of IPOs on the Growth Fund's 1996 performance. The IPO impact study eliminated the effect of the Growth Fund's initial gains from IPOs by assuming that the IPO purchases were made on the secondary market at the higher, post-IPO, price. The results of the study, dated January 21, 1997, showed that the impact of IPOs accounted for approximately one-third of the Growth Fund's 1996 return.[4]

The January 1997 Board of Trustees Meeting

J. Sachtleben and others made presentations regarding the Growth Fund's 1996 performance at the quarterly Board of Trustees meeting on January 23 and 24, 1997, at which the public offering of the Growth Fund was approved. However, Sachtleben did not tell the Trustees that he had initiated a study to determine the impact of IPOs on the Growth Fund's 1996 performance. The results of the study were not discussed at the Board of Trustees Meeting.

Omissions of Material Facts Concerning the Growth Fund's Performance

K. From February 3, 1997 to March 14, 1997, the Growth Fund was open to the public for investment. During that period, the number of shareholders increased from 14 to 14,883 and the Growth Fund raised approximately $109 million from sales of its shares. The Growth Fund's net assets increased from $1.1 million to $110.1 million.

L. While the Growth Fund was open to the public for investment, Van Kampen Distributors disseminated an advertisement to the public called a "Fact Card." The Fact Card prominently displayed the Growth Fund's 61.99% return and its #1 Lipper ranking, but did not disclose that IPOs had a large impact on the Growth Fund's 1996 return. Sachtleben, in his capacity as Chief Investment Officer for Van Kampen Advisory and as an officer of the Growth Fund, was responsible for providing information about the Growth Fund, including the IPO impact, to the Trustees of the Growth Fund and senior officers of Van Kampen Advisory and Van Kampen Distributors. Sachtleben knew that the Growth Fund's performance figures would be used in the Growth Fund's advertising, but he did not tell the Trustees or the senior officers that he had initiated an IPO impact study or the results of the impact study, which reflected that IPOs had a large impact on the Growth

---

[4] However, while the study did not make these calculations, the actual gains from the Growth Fund's IPO shares accounted for more than 50% of the Growth Fund's 1996 return. The actual gains on the IPO shares derived from the difference between the IPO prices paid and the prices at which Van Kampen Advisory sold those shares or the value of the shares it held as of December 31, 1996.

Fund's performance.

M. The Fact Card also contained the following disclaimers: "The Fund's adviser believes the Fund was managed substantially the same as if the Fund had opened for investment to all public investors. No assurance can be given, however, that the Fund's investment performance would have been the same during the period if the Fund had been broadly distributed." These statements were also included in the Growth Fund's December 31, 1996 semi-annual report and in its prospectus. These statements failed to mention that a large portion of the Growth Fund's return was attributable to its investments in IPOs.

N. The Growth Fund's December 31, 1996 semi-annual report, which was filed with the Commission on February 28, 1997, failed to include any information regarding the impact on performance from the hot IPO investments. The Growth Fund's December 31, 1996 semi-annual report, that Sachtleben reviewed and signed, reported, among other things, that the Growth Fund achieved a 61.99% total return for 1996. Despite Sachtleben's having the results of the IPO impact study, the semi-annual report attributed this performance to investment in technology, financial services and health care sectors, which were "some of the best performing [sectors]," and gave examples of four securities that posted large gains during the last six months. None of those securities were IPO securities. In addition, the Growth Fund's semi-annual report included a shareholder letter which discussed the 1996 IPO market generally along with other economic developments. The report gave no indication that the Growth Fund had in any way participated in the IPO market that year. Because information about the impact of IPOs on the Growth Fund's performance would have significantly altered the total mix of information available to investors, this omission made the statements about the Growth Fund's performance in the semi-annual report materially misleading.

O. As a result of the lack of disclosure by Sachtleben to the Trustees of the Growth Fund and senior officers of Van Kampen Advisory and Van Kampen Distributors, none of the fund's communications to potential shareholders or current shareholders (*e.g.*, the Fact Card, prospectus and semi-annual report) at the time of the fund's dissemination of its first year performance returns included information regarding the large impact of IPOs on the Growth Fund's performance.

P. Pursuant to §31(a) of the Investment Company Act, and Rule 31a-2(a)(3) thereunder, Van Kampen Equity Trust maintained the Fact Card in its files as sales literature intended for distribution to prospective investors. In addition, Van Kampen Equity Trust filed the Growth Fund's December 31, 1996 semi-annual report with the Commission on February 28, 1997 without disclosing the large impact that IPOs had on the Growth Fund's 1996 return.

Other Public Statements Attributed to Van Kampen

Q. Statements in the press attributed to representatives of Van Kampen Distributors and Van Kampen Advisory indicated that there were a limited number of IPOs in the Growth Fund during 1996 and they did not greatly affect the fund's performance. These statements included: "It's not as if the Growth Fund has had a bunch of hot IPOs"; and "the performance of the [Growth Fund] last year was not greatly influenced by investments in initial public offerings." Given these statements made in the press and the information available to the public in the Fact Card, prospectus and semi-annual report, investors had no reasonable basis to conclude that the Growth Fund's 1996 performance was largely impacted by investments in IPOs.

VIOLATIONS

R. Under the facts and circumstances of this case, disclosure that a large portion of the Growth Fund's return was attributable to its investments in IPOs would have been material to an investor's decision whether to invest in the Growth Fund, particularly in light of the fact that, given the growth in the fund's total assets, it was questionable whether the fund could continue to experience, by investing in hot IPOs, substantially similar performance as the fund had previously experienced. Based on the foregoing, Van Kampen Advisory willfully violated and Sachtleben caused and willfully aided and abetted Van Kampen Advisory's violation of § 206(2) of the Advisers Act. As part of the conduct described in paragraphs III.E through III.Q above, Van Kampen Advisory and Sachtleben omitted to state material facts to its client, the Growth Fund, Growth Fund shareholders and prospective shareholders concerning the impact of hot IPOs on the Growth Fund's 1996 performance.

S. As part of the conduct described in paragraphs III.K through III.Q above, Van Kampen Advisory and Sachtleben caused and willfully aided and abetted Van Kampen Equity Trust's violations of § 34(b) of the Investment Company Act which prohibits the filing, transmitting or keeping of registration statements, applications, reports, accounts, records, or other documents required to be kept under § 31(a) of the Investment

Company Act that omit to state facts necessary in order to prevent the statements made in those documents, in the light of the circumstances under which they were made, from being materially misleading.

IV.

In view of the foregoing, the Commission deems it appropriate and in the public interest to impose the sanctions that are set forth in the Offer submitted by Van Kampen Advisory and Sachtleben. Accordingly, IT IS ORDERED that:

A. Van Kampen Advisory and Sachtleben are censured;

B. Pursuant to § 203(k) of the Advisers Act and § 9(f) of the Investment Company Act, Van Kampen Advisory and Sachtleben cease and desist from committing or causing any violation and any future violation of § 206(2) of the Advisers Act and § 34(b) of the Investment Company Act.

C. Pursuant to § 203(i) of the Advisers Act and § 9(d) of the Investment Company Act, Van Kampen Advisory shall, within ten days of the entry of this Order, pay a civil penalty in the amount of $100,000 to the United States Treasury....

D. Pursuant to § 203(i) of the Advisers Act and § 9(d) of the Investment Company Act, Sachtleben shall, within ten days of the entry of this Order, pay a civil penalty in the amount of $25,000 to the United States Treasury....

Chapter 5 Certain Pooled Investment Vehicles Beyond Mutual Funds

> "The Commission, by rules and regulations upon its own motion, or by order upon application, may conditionally or unconditionally exempt any person, security, or transaction, or any class or classes of persons, securities, or transactions, from any provision or provisions of this title or of any rule or regulation thereunder, if and to the extent that such exemption is necessary or appropriate in the public interest and consistent with the protection of investors and the purposes fairly intended by the policy and provisions of this title."
>
> ----Investment Company Act of 1940, § 6(c)

Section 5.1 Insurance Company, Separate Accounts, and Variable Contracts

Laws & Rules Highlight:

IC Act (15 USC 80a-1 *et seq.*) & Rules (17 CFR §§ 270.0-1 *et seq.*)
Securities Act (15 USC 77a *et seq.*) & Rules (17 CFR §§ 230.100 *et seq.*)

Investment Company & Securities

- IC Act
  - § 3(a)(1) (*def.* ***"investment company"***); § 2(a)(22) (*def.* ***"issuer"*** *[of a security]*)
    - ✓ § 2(a)(28) (*def. "person"*); § 2(a)(8) (*def. "company"*)
  - § 2(a)(36) (*def.* ***"security"*** *to include* ***"investment contract"***)
- SA Act
  - § 2(a)(4) (*def.* ***"issuer"*** *[of a security]*)
  - § 2(a)(1) (*def.* ***"security"*** *to include* ***"investment contract"***)

Insurance Company & Traditional Insurance Contracts

- IC Act and Rule
  - § 3(c)(3) (***"insurance company" exclusion*** *from IC*); § 2(a)(17) (*def.* ***"insurance company"***)
  - § 2(a)(37) (*def.* ***"separate account"***); Rule 0-1(e)(1) (*def.* ***"separate account,"*** *supplementing statutory definition of "separate account" as condition of relying on specified exemptive IC rules*)

- SA Act and Rule
  - § 3(a)(8) (***insurance exclusion****:* * *"insurance and annuity contracts" are excluded from all provisions of, and are not subject to, the Securities Act*) *[33-6558 n.25]; § 2(a)(13) (*def.* "***insurance company***")
  - Rule 151 Safe Harbor Definition of Certain "Annuity Contracts or Optional Annuity Contracts" Within the Meaning of Section 3(a)(8) (*non-exclusive safe harbor designed to provide a* ***reasonably objective test*** *of "insurance" or "security" status of "guaranteed investment contracts/GICs"; "annuity contracts" and "optional annuity contracts" meeting conditions of the Rule are deemed to be "insurance" under § 3(a)(8) and are excluded from all provisions of SA Act*)
  - § 989J Further Promoting the Adoption of the NAIC Model Regulations That Enhance Protection of Seniors and Other Consumers, DODD-FRANK WALL STREET REFORM AND CONSUMER PROTECTION ACT, PL 111-203, 124 STAT. 1376, 1949 (2010) (*excess interest contracts may rely on SA § 3(a)(8) exemption if satisfying* ***standard nonforfeiture laws*** *of applicable state, as well as meeting other conditions of § 989J*)

Separate Account Issuing Variable Insurance Contracts: Structure of Regulation and Exemptions (IC Act and Rules)

- § 12 Functions and Activities of Investment Companies
  - §§ 12(d)(1)(A)-(B) (***anti-pyramiding*** *provisions, generally imposing fund of funds investment limits*)
  - § 12(d)(1)(E) (*restricts investment by a registered UIT separate account or a sub-account to* ***a single*** *underlying fund or* ***a single*** *series of underlying fund*)
  - § 12(d)(1)(G) (*permits a sub-account to invest in* ***more than one*** *underlying fund or* ***more than one series*** *of underlying fund, if such funds/series and the registered UIT separate account are "part of the same group of investment companies"*)
- § 26 Unit Investment Trusts (*regulates UITs generally*)
  - § 4(2) (*def. "unit investment trust"*)
  - § 26(f) Exemption (***exempts*** *registered variable separate account, sponsoring insurance company, and principal underwriter from § 26(a);* ***imposes*** *reasonable aggregate fees and charges requirement on variable insurance contracts*)
- § 27 Periodic Payment Plans (*regulates UITs issuing "periodic payment plan certificates"*)
  - § 2(a)(27) (*def. "periodic payment plan certificate" to include variable annuity and variable life contracts*)
  - § 27(i) (***exempts*** *registered separate account, sponsoring insurance company, and principal underwriter from § 27;* ***requires*** *variable insurance contract be redeemable security*)
- Rule 0-1(e) Definition of Separate Account and Conditions for Availability of Exemption under [enumerated Investment Company Act rules] (*conditions of exemption from specified IC Act rules for* ***registered "separate account"*** *funding*

*"**variable annuity** contract")*

- Rule 6e-2 Exemptions for Certain Variable Life Insurance Separate Accounts (*conditions of **exemption from IC Act registration** for "**separate account**" funding "**scheduled premium variable life** insurance contract"*)
- Rule 6e-3(T) Temporary Exemptions for Flexible Premium Variable Life Insurance Separate Accounts (*conditions of exemption from specified IC Act provisions for **registered** "**separate account**" funding "**flexible premium variable life** insurance contracts"*)

Topic 1 Ectoplasmic Theory: Insurance Company *vs* Variable Separate Account

Figure 1-1: Contributions and Premium Payments

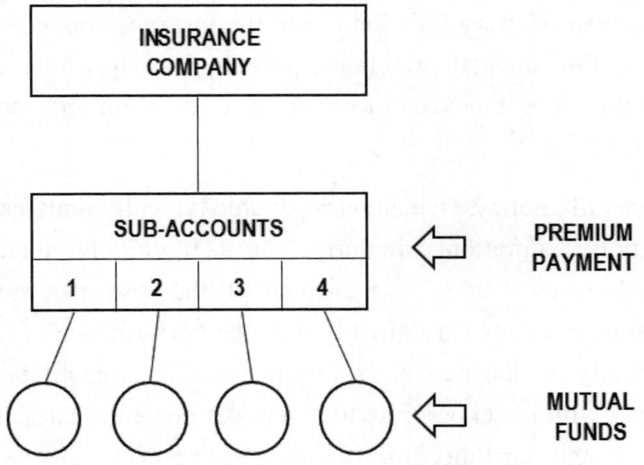

Graph: adapted from VARIABLE ANNUITIES AND VARIABLE LIFE INSURANCE REGULATION Ch.1 § 1:4 Figure 1-1 (Kirsch ed., 2d. 2015)

Pre-Case Background Note:[Biblio]

Structure of Insurance Company Variable Separate Account: Formed as UIT Investing in Mutual Funds and Offering Variable Insurance Contracts

Private insurance business has two branches: life insurance (or insurance on the person), and non-life insurance (or insurance on property). The life branch of insurance includes:

- ***Life insurance***, which pays benefits on a person's ***death***, including:
  - ✓ "*whole life insurance*," which provides coverage for the whole of the insured's life, and makes the face amount payment upon the insured's death regardless of when death occurs;
  - ✓ "*term insurance*," which pays benefits only if the insured dies during the policy term;
  - ✓ "*endowment insurance*," which pays benefits if the insured dies during the policy term but it also pays benefits if the insured survives the policy term; and
- ***Annuities***, which pays benefits on a person's ***living*** a certain length of time.

Thus, the principal purpose of life insurance is the creation of a fund to protect against the loss of income through premature death, while the basic function of annuity is the systematic liquidation of a fund to protect against the possibility of outliving one's income. Despite their contrary functions, both life insurance policies and annuities are based on the same fundamental principles: pooling underlies both; and premiums in each case are computed on the basis of probabilities of death and survival as reflected by mortality tables.[1 (Chs. 1, 5, 8)]

For a traditional life policy, face amount payable typically remains at the same level throughout the policy duration; similarly, for a traditional annuity, benefits are expressed in fixed currency units. In contrast, in the case of a variable life policy, death benefits and cash values vary directly with the performance of a set of earmarked investments; similarly, in the case of a variable annuity, benefit payments and cash values vary directly with the experience of assets designated to back the contract.[1 (Chs. 5, 8)] The total investment portfolio of a life insurance company can be divided into two categories: assets supporting the insurer's general account; and assets supporting its separate accounts. The accounts are classified primarily according to the nature of the liabilities for which the assets are being held and invested:

- ***General Account***: Assets used to support the insurer's contractual obligations providing for guaranteed, fixed benefit payments normally are held in the life insurance company's general account. General account investments are subject to the restrictions of state legal lists of permitted investments and prohibited investments, which are intended to promote insurer solvency and protect safety and security of policy owner claims.
- ***Separate Accounts***: Assets used to support the insurer's liabilities associated with

investment risk pass-through products, such as variable life insurance and variable annuities, are held in special accounts to be separated from all other assets of the insurance company, labeled separate accounts. Separate accounts are not subject to the usual insurer investment restrictions; and the U.S. life insurance industry mix of separate account assets has shown an emphasis on corporate stocks, compared to general account assets. A separate account usually holds the funds of many policy-owners or annuitants in a combined investment arrangement, functioning as a ***pooled investment account***, the investment results of which are passed directly to the variable contract holders participating in such a separate account.[1 (Chs. 21, 33, 34)]

Thus, variable insurance products are both securities and insurance products, and are subject to federal securities laws as well as state insurance laws.[2 (§§17:1 n.1; 17:4)] Under the federal securities regulatory scheme:

- **Variable Insurance Contracts** issued by the separate account (or by a sub-account within the separate account, each sub-account corresponding to one investment portfolio where multiple investment portfolios are offered by the separate account) are regulated as "*securities*" under the Securities Act.[2 (§1:5.2[B1])]
- **Separate Account** issuing variable insurance contracts is regulated as "*investment company*" under the Investment Company Act. Such variable separate account generally is formed as an *unmanaged "unit investment trust"* as defined by IC Act § 4(2) which does not have a board of directors and requires no investment management at the level of the separate account, instead of a "*management company*" as defined by IC Act §§ 4(3) and 5 which would require the account to have its own board of directors separate from the insurance company's board of directors. The "***UIT approach***" thus provides a partial solution to the structural tension and sometimes conflicting requirements, arising from insurance company-variable separate account double-entity treatment under the IC Act on the one hand, and life insurers' conventional separate account operation and single-entity treatment under state insurance laws on the other.[3] The UIT separate account (or a sub-account) must hold *only one* underlying registered fund/series, or *multiple* registered funds/series that are "*part of the same group of investment companies*" with the separate account, to comply with IC Act § 12 "fund of funds" investment restrictions.[2 (§§3A:2.3-2.4)]
- **Registered Fund Underlying** the UIT variable separate account must be *open-end mutual fund* offering *redeemable securities*, instead of "*closed-end fund*" offering *non-redeemable securities*, since the UIT separate account itself must issue

redeemable securities in the form of variable insurance contracts.[2 (§3A:3.1)] The underlying mutual fund may fund a variable annuity separate account *and* a variable life insurance separate account of the same or affiliated insurance companies—a structure called "*mixed funding*"; or fund variable annuity (*or* variable life insurance) separate accounts of *unaffiliated* insurance companies—a structure called "*shared funding*." In any mixed/shared funding structure, the mutual fund board must monitor and remedy any material irreconcilable conflict of interests among the participating separate accounts.[2 (§7:3)]

The two-tier structure of a UIT separate account investing in the underlying mutual fund(s) in effect delegates the portfolio management function from the insurance company to the mutual funds.[2 (§7:1)] To effect integrated registration under both the Securities Act and the IC Act, **Form N-4** is used for UIT-funded variable annuity and **Form N-6** for UIT-funded variable life products; both forms shall be signed by the sponsoring insurance company as depositor of the UIT separate accounts. A **Form N-1A** is used for each of the underlying mutual funds, which are selected by, and may be affiliated or unaffiliated with, the insurance company. *Statutory prospectuses* for variable contracts and those for the underlying funds must both be delivered to the variable contract owners.[2 (Ch.3A §§3A:3.2, 3.4[G-H])]

Commenting on the current framework of regulation of variable separate accounts as registered investment companies "but not equally with registered mutual funds," and the varied exemptions for variable annuities and variable life contracts respectively, a commentator (Jenkins 2014)[2 (§3A:4)] recommends:

> It is time to recognize and classify the variable separate accounts as their own category of investment company under the Investment Company Act; to register the variable products in their own right; and to apply consolidated, consistent, and comprehensive regulation of all variable products, and of all forms of registered separate accounts whether managed separate accounts or separate accounts holding underlying funds—in lieu of the current UIT approach to variable separate account regulation.

Bibliography

1. BLACK, JR. & SKIPPER, JR., LIFE & HEALTH INSURANCE (2000)
2. VARIABLE ANNUITIES AND VARIABLE LIFE INSURANCE REGULATION (Kirsch ed., 2d. 2015)
3. Polikoff, *The Unit Investment Trust Approach to Variable Annuities*, 1968 PROC. OF 61ST ANN. MEETING OF LEGAL SEC. OF AM. LIFE CONVENTION 28 (1968)

Case Study: The *Ectoplasmic* Theory: Variable Separate Account as an IC Existing Within an Exempt Insurance Company

An "insurance company" is excluded from the definition of investment company by IC Act § 3(c)(3), and "insurance and annuity contracts" issued by such insurance company are exempted securities under Securities Act § 3(a)(8). On the other hand, an investment fund created and managed by the insurance company enjoys no exclusion under IC Act § 3(c)(3). Variable annuities issued by such investment fund are securities under the Securities Act, the investment fund being the issuer and an investment company required to register under the IC Act. The case illustrates the ***ectoplasmic theory***:* an exempt entity under the IC Act (the Prudential Insurance Company in this case) creating within itself a nonexempt investment company (the Prudential Insurance variable separate account). The noun form of "ectoplasmic"—"***ectoplasm***,"** literally means the outer layer of a cell which separates the cell from the other cells. The ectoplasmic theory applies the cell separation concept to the treatment of each separate account separately from that of other separate accounts and all other activities of the insurance company, treating each separate account as an individual investment company.

[*Kern, *Variable Annuities*, 1968 INS. L.J. 277 (1968); **ROSENBLUM, INVESTMENT COMPANY DETERMINATION UNDER THE 1940 ACT—EXEMPTIONS AND EXCEPTIONS, Ch.14 n.92 (2nd ed. 2003)].

Prudential Ins. Co. of America v. SEC

326 F.2d 383 (3d Cir. 1964)

[***Procedural history***: In *re* Prudential Ins. Co. of America, IC-3259 (1961); IC-3620, 41 SEC 335 (1963); *aff'd sub nom.* Prudential Ins. Co. of America v. SEC, 326 F.2d 383 (3d Cir. 1964); *cert. denied*, 377 U.S. 953 (1964)]

Topic 2 Issuer of Securities: Insurance Company *vs.* Non-Unitized Separate Account

Pre-Case Background Note:[Biblio]

Insurance, Securities, and Issuer of Securities

I. "***Guaranteed Investment Contract***" (**GIC**): Insurance or Security?

Securities Act § 2(a)(1) defines "*security*" to **include** an "***investment contract***." SA § 3(a)(8) **excludes**[1b (§IV.2 n.25)] from the Act any "*insurance policy*," "*annuity contract*," and "*optional annuity contract*" (collectively, "***insurance contract***") issued by an insurance company. The insurance industry has developed certain types of contracts generally known as "***guaranteed investment contracts***,"[1a] under which the insurer promises to pay interest at a guaranteed rate for the life of the contract and, in some contracts, the insurer may periodically pay discretionary excess interest over and above the guaranteed rate. The "insurance" or "security" status of a "guaranteed investment contract" under the SA Act depends on which party is assuming the ***investment risk*** under the contract—the insurer or the contract owner. To the extent the insurer assumes this risk, the contract is similar to the "traditional annuity contract," which is deemed to be "insurance" and is excluded from the Securities Act by § 3(a)(8). To the extent the insurer does not assume that risk and rather the contract owner assumes the risk, the contract is more like the "variable annuity contract," which case law has held to be a "security" not entitled to rely on § 3(a)(8).[2; 3] To the extent the insurer and the contract owner ***share*** the investment risk to varying degrees—as under a guaranteed investment contract—***guaranteed investment contracts*** cannot always readily be characterized as either "insurance" or a "security" for purposes of § 3(a)(8).[1b]

To provide certainty, in 1986 the SEC adopted SA Rule 151, a non-exclusive safe harbor which treats certain guaranteed investment contracts issued by insurance companies as "annuity contracts" or "optional annuity contracts" (collectively "***annuity contracts***") within the meaning of § 3(a)(8) of the SA Act, if the Rule's conditions are met. Rule 151 provides a ***three-prong objective test*** to determine that such an annuity contract is not a security under the federal securities laws. First, the annuity contract must be *issued by* a state-regulated insurance company ("insurer"). Second, the annuity contract must include *guarantees of principal and interest sufficient for the* *insurer to be deemed to assume the investment risk.* And third, the annuity contract may not be *marketed primarily* as an investment, such as by promoting its particular feature as in competition with certain investment products.[1c]

With respect to investment risk assumption by the insurer under the second test:

- ***Use of non-unitized separate account.*** A non-unitized separate account is a separate account *not* structured as a single unit operating independently of the investment experience of the insurer's general account, and it is supported by the totality of general account assets. To qualify for the safe harbor, the value of the contract ***may not vary*** according to the investment experience of a separate account; but the annuity contract ***may***, for accounting standards, insurance law compliance, and operational reasons, provide for the allocation of contributions to a ***non-unitized separate account*** without being disqualified from relying on Rule 151 safe harbor.[1c; 4a (§2:5.2[B][1]; §2:5.3[B][1])]
- ***Use of MVA features.*** An ***MVA*** (or ***m***arket ***v***alue ***a***djustment) ***feature*** is any feature designed to compensate the insurer for *disintermediation risk* it faces when the prevailing market interest rates rise *vis-à-vis* the insurer's contractually guaranteed rates and the contract owner surrenders a contract or withdraws values from a contract prior to the expiration of a contractually guaranteed period. Depending on the formula used, an MVA feature can invade excess interest only, or guaranteed rates, or even principal. To the extent it protects an insurer from disintermediation risk, the MVA feature effectively transfers investment risk from the insurer to the contract owner. A contract having "*any*"[1c] MVA feature is disqualified from relying on the safe harbor, even if the MVA feature invades excess interest only and may not significantly affect the contract's status under § 3(a)(8). When an MVA can invade principal, the contract is generally viewed as falling outside of § 3(a)(8), and must be registered under the Securities Act.[1c; 4a] (§2:5.2 nn.103-104 & [B][3]; §2:5.3[B][3])
- ***Pegging discretionary excess interest rates to indexes.*** As an appropriate measure of the degree of investment risk borne by the insurer under the safe harbor, the rate of any *discretionary excess interest* guaranteed by the insurer to be credited under the contract may not be modified more frequently than ***once per year***. The insurer may use an ***index*** (such as a composite bond index or Treasury bill rate) in arriving at the excess interest rate, subject to the limitation of no more frequent modification of the rate than once per year. A more frequent pegging of the excess interest rate to an index would cause the contract to operate more like a

security and would shift the investment risk to the contract owner.[1c; 4a(§2:5.2[B][4]; §2:5.3[B][4])]

II. "*Issuer*" of Securities: Insurance Company or Non-Unitized Separate Account?

IC Act § 3(a)(1) defines "***investment company***" as any "***issuer***" which, *inter alia*, "*is ... engaged primarily ... in the business of investing, reinvesting, or trading in securities; ...*" The term "***issuer***" is defined by IC Act § 2(a)(22) to mean "*every person who issues or proposes to issue any security, or has outstanding any security which it has issued.*" The term "***person***" is defined by IC Act § 2(a)(28) to mean "*a natural person or a company.*" The term "***company***" is defined by IC Act § 2(a)(8) to mean

> "*a corporation, a partnership, an association, a joint-stock company, a trust, a fund, or any organized group of persons whether incorporated or not; ...*"

The term "***security***" is defined in IC Act § 2(a)(36) similarly as in Securities Act § 2(a)(1), to include, among other things, an "*investment contract.*" Based on the above statutory analysis, for the purpose of "investment company" status determination, an "issuer" need *not* be an "identifiable legal entity" or a "recognizable business entity."[4b (§3:2.1[A]; §3:4.1[A]; §3:6)]

While an "***insurance company***," as defined in IC Act § 2(a)(17), is **excluded** from the statutory definition of "investment company" by IC Act § 3(c)(3), a ***separate account*** established and maintained by an insurance company in connection with the funding of variable annuities **could be** an "issuer" and an "investment company," under the *ectoplasmic theory* as explained by the *Prudential* court.[5] In the *Prudential* case, although Prudential Insurance Company was the writer and sponsor of the variable annuity contracts, contract owners had participating interests in the ***investment performance of the separate account*** and had no interest in the insurer. The **Prudential Variable Contract Separate Account** was found to be the "*issuer*" of securities in the form of variable annuities, was engaged primarily in the business of investing in securities, and was thus an "*investment company.*"

The *Valley Forge Life (VFL) Insurance Company no-action letter*[6] presents a contrast with the *Prudential* case. In the **VFL Indexed Contract Separate Account** arrangement, the insurer guaranteed to credit S&P 500® index-pegged interest rates to contract owners during a Guarantee Period, subject to an MVA feature; and the insurer registered the indexed contracts under the Securities Act. Critically different from the

Prudential case, in *Valley Forge* while contract owners allocated their premiums to the VFL Indexed Separate Account, the value of contract owners' interests in the separate account was not determined by, and did not reflect, the ***investment performance of assets in the separate account***. Rather, the legally insulated, non-unitized separate account structure was utilized:

- to *permit valuation* of assets in the separate account on a market value basis instead of an amortized cost basis—as required by state insurance laws; and
- to *assure* that, in the event of the insurer's insolvency, the contract owners would have *priority claims* to the portion of the separate account's assets covered by the legal insulation, *i.e.*, an amount equal to the reserves and other contract liabilities of the insurer associated with the separate account and the indexed contracts—a credit-enhancement feature designed to enhance the contracts' competitiveness.

Valley Forge Life argued that it retained the investment interest in the separate account as part of its insurance business. It further argued that the contract owners' interests in the separate account were in the nature of an *interest in collateral* and not in the nature of an *investment interest*, and thus those interests did not constitute "securities." Since the VFL Indexed Separate Account was not an issuer of "*securities*," it was not an "*investment company*."

The SEC granted a no-action request to Valley Forge Life Insurance Company for not registering the VFL Indexed Separate Account under the Investment Company Act.

Bibliography

1. Rule 151-related Rels.: **1a.** Life Insurance Companies—Request for Submission of Views With Respect to the Offer and Sale of Certain Contractual Arrangements, 33-5838, 42 FR 32861 (1977); **1b.** Definition of Annuity Contract or Optional Annuity Contract, 33-6558, 49 FR 46750 (1984); **1c.** 33-6645, 51 FR 20254 (1986)
2. SEC v. Variable Annuity Life Ins. Co., 359 U.S. 65 (1959)
3. SEC v. United Benefit Life Ins. Co., 387 U.S. 202 (1987)
4. VARIABLE ANNUITIES AND VARIABLE LIFE INSURANCE REGULATION (Kirsch ed., 2d. 2014): **4a.** Petito, *Status of Insurance Products Under the Securities Act of 1933* (Ch.2); **4b.** Faria, *Status of Insurance Companies and Insurance Company Separate Accounts Under the Investment Company Act* (Ch.3)
5. Prudential Ins. Co. of America v. SEC, 326 F.2d 383 (3d Cir. 1964), *cert. denied*, 377 U.S. 953 (1964)
6. Valley Forge Life Ins. Co.: VFL Indexed Separate Account, IC Act §§ 2(a)(22) and 3(a) (Jan. 30, 1997)

Case Study: Legally Insulated Non-Unitized Separate Account Not Deemed an Issuer or IC

Valley Forge Life Ins. Co.: VFL Indexed Separate Account

IC Act §§ 2(a)(22) & 3(a), SEC No-Action Letter (Jan. 30, 1997)

[Valley Forge Life Request Letter (Jan 27, 1997); SEC No-Action Reply (Jan 30, 1997)]

Research Topics:

Insurance-security hybrid products; types of insurance company separate accounts; their treatments and regulations under the Chinese insurance law and investment management law.

Prudential Ins. Co. of America, Petitioner v. SEC, Respondent
ICI, Invervenor
Commissioner of Banking and Insurance of the State of N.J., Intervenor
326 F.2d 383 (3d Cir. 1964)

Before STALEY and GANEY, Circuit Judges, and NEALON, District Judge.

OPINION

STALEY, Circuit Judge:

The narrow but provocative question posed by this case is whether the Investment Company Act of 1940 applies to the Investment Fund resulting from the sale of variable annuity contracts to members of the public by The Prudential Insurance Company of America. The Securities and Exchange Commission answered this question in the affirmative, rejecting the view of Prudential that the Act exempts such a program because the contracts are offered and sold by an insurance company. The case is before us on the petition of Prudential for review of the order of the Commission entered pursuant to that determination.

Though there are variations in the form of the variable annuities which Prudential proposes to sell,[1] their salient characteristics are not disputed and their nature has been concisely summarized by the Commission in its opinion in this case:

> "In substance, the variable annuity contracts which Prudential proposes to sell to individuals provide that the purchaser will make monthly purchase payments of fixed amounts over a period of years (the 'pay-in' period), the proceeds of which, after certain deductions, will be invested in a portfolio of securities. The purchaser will be credited monthly with 'units' representing his proportionate interest in this fund. The value of these units will fluctuate, essentially depending upon the investment results of the fund. During the annuity, or 'pay-out' period, Prudential guarantees that the purchaser will receive in cash the varying value of a fixed number of units as monthly annuity payments.
>
> "Specifically the payments made by the purchasers will be placed in a 'Variable

---

[1] Prudential also intends to offer variable group plans in addition to the individual contracts. However, because the Commission is presently dealing with the problems posed by such plans in its administrative capacity, they were excluded from the scope of its opinion. Accordingly, we do likewise.

Contract Account' which will be managed by Prudential and be subdivided into two accounts. The first, the 'Investment Fund' account, will have its assets invested primarily in common stocks and will constitute the fund in which the purchasers hold units; this account will be dedicated solely to the variable annuity contract holders and its assets will not be subject to claims of any other contract or policyholder of the company. The second, the 'Other Assets' account, an administration account, will receive the amounts deducted from the purchase payments to cover administration expenses, sales commissions, and certain taxes, and to provide a surplus or reserve for the obligations to purchasers contained in the contracts. Transfers will be made periodically from the Other Assets account to the Investment Fund account to meet the contractual requirements that the assets of the latter be equal to the company's existing obligations under the variable contracts. Any excess over the amounts estimated to be needed for the foregoing purposes may be declared as so-called 'dividends' which will provide additional fund units or cash payments for the contract holders; it will also be available to support the guarantees on contracts administered by Prudential's other operations. Any deficiency resulting from lower mortality than assumed, for example, will be met out of the general surplus of Prudential.

"During the pay-in period a purchaser will have the right to terminate the contract and receive the value of all units credited to his account, less certain termination charges. If a purchaser should die during the pay-in period, the contract is automatically terminated and his beneficiary is paid the greater of (i) the value of all units credited to the purchaser's account or (ii) an amount equal to the total of all purchase payments made.

"Absent death or redemption, the pay-in period normally runs for at least 15 years. Thereafter, during the pay-out period, the variable annuitant is entitled to receive each month the current value of a fixed number of units determined at the end of the pay-in period. This number of units is calculated on the basis of the number of units accumulated by the purchaser during the pay-in period, an assumed annual investment increment of 2 1/2% From dividend and interest income, and actuarial computations which take into account the length of the pay-out period anticipated in light of the age and sex of the purchaser and any co-annuitant. The value of the variable unit during the pay-in and pay-out periods will be determined at the end of each month and will reflect the changes in the market value of the securities in the Investment Fund account, realized gains and losses, and dividend or interest income. Deductions will be made for investment advisory and other expenses in an amount equal to 0.6% Per annum of the value of the fund's assets and for taxes."

Prudential concedes that such contracts have been held to be "securities" within the meaning of the Securities Act of 1933, *Securities and Exchange Commission v. Variable Annuity Life Insurance Co.* (hereinafter called "**VALIC**"), 359 U.S. 65 (1959), and it is willing to register them under that Act. Prudential argues, however, that the Investment Company Act of 1940 specifically excludes insurance companies from its scope.[2] The Commission acknowledged that Prudential is excluded from the Act, but held that the fund created by the sale of the contracts, which is to be used for investment purposes, gives rise to a separate investment company within the coverage of the statute. The Commission concluded that Prudential is not itself an investment company but is the creator of one, and proposes to be its investment adviser and principal underwriter.[3]

In this court, Prudential, premising its argument on the insurance company exclusion, asserts that this construction of the statute is inordinately complicated, abstruse, and without basis in law. It asserts that the statute is plain and forecloses Commission jurisdiction in this case. However, since it is conceded that Prudential is excluded from the Act, the issue is narrowed to the question of whether the Commission made a permissible interpretation in concluding that the variable annuity program results in the creation of a separate, non-exempt investment company.

Of course, in resolving this issue we start with the premise that securities legislation must be broadly construed in order to insure the investing public a full measure of

---

[2] Insurance companies are excluded from the definition of "investment company" by 15 USC § 80a-3(c)(3). An insurance company is earlier defined as "a company which is organized as an insurance company, whose primary and predominant business activity is the writing of insurance or the reinsuring of risks underwritten by insurance companies, and which is subject to supervision by the insurance commissioner or a similar official or agency of a State ... " 15 USC § 80a-2(a)(17).

[3] The essence of the Commission's reasoning in this regard is contained in the following excerpt from its opinion:

"Thus, Prudential is not itself an investment company, but it is the creator of one—and proposes to be its 'investment adviser' and 'principal underwriter.' That an exempt insurance company performs these functions is irrelevant. The Act's exclusion of insurance companies is to be readily explained: otherwise they would fall within the statute by reason of the investment activities which are a necessary ingredient of their insurance business. Where, however, an insurance company (or any other entity) creates a fund exclusively for investment, and sells equity interests in the fortunes of that fund, the exemption does not carry over to the fund. Furthermore, that Prudential may in the same contract also make, in its own name and backed by its own assets, certain insurance or annuity promises is also irrelevant. VALIC held that such promises do not make the contract as a whole exempt as 'insurance' though made by the same entity and backed by the same assets."

protection. *Securities and Exchange Commission v. Capital Gains Research Bureau, Inc.*, 375 U.S. 180 (1963); *Securities and Exchange Commission v. Ralston Purina Co.*, 346 U.S. 119 (1953); *Securities and Exchange Commission v. W. J. Howey Co.*, 328 U.S. 293 (1946). The parties agree that the statutory definitions contained in the Investment Company Act of 1940 are cast in broad terms. The critical term is "company," which, so far as relevant to our discussion, is defined as "a trust, a fund, or any organized group of persons whether incorporated or not." 15 USC § 80a-2(a)(8).

The Commission determined that the variable annuity contracts constitute the purchasers an "organized group of persons"; that they create a "trust" held by Prudential for these purchasers; and, more importantly, that the separate Investment Fund resulting from the sale of the variable annuity contracts is a "fund" within the statutory definition.

Based upon this last decisive holding, the Commission then concluded that the Investment Fund is the "issuer" of the variable annuity securities, and that it is an "investment company" subject to the Act.[4]

On this score Prudential argues that the Act regulates only identifiable business entities with some sort of internal organization, and that it is the only such entity involved in this program. Thus, it is asserted that the purchasers cannot be described as an "organized group of persons"; that the plan has no elements of a common-law trust; and that the "fund" referred to in the Act means a mutual fund or any other similar entity, but not Prudential's Investment Fund. But, as Mr. Justice Brennan has cogently observed, the regulatory provisions of the Act "are of particular relevance to situations where the investor is committing his funds to the hands of others on an equity basis, with the view that the funds will be invested in securities and his fortunes will depend on the success of the investment." *VALIC, supra* (concurring opinion). Furthermore, a study of the legislative history of the Act shows that Congress intentionally drafted the statutory definitions in general terms in order to control such situations regardless of the legal form or structure of the investment enterprise.

Initially, it must be noted that the Committee reports of both the House and the Senate

---

[4] "Issuer" is defined as "every person (natural person or a company) who issues or proposes to issue any security, or has outstanding any security which it has issued." 15 USC § 80a-2(a)(21). "Investment company" means, inter alia, any issuer which "proposes to engage primarily, in the business of investing, reinvesting, or trading in securities." 15 USC § 80a-3(a)(1).

state that the legislation was drafted principally on the basis of reports submitted by the Securities and Exchange Commission following an extensive study of investment trusts and investment companies undertaken at the direction of Congress. H.R. Rep. No. 2639, 76th Cong., 3rd Sess. 5-6 (1940); S. Rep. No. 1775, 76th Cong., 3rd Sess. 1, 5 (1940). The Act itself contains a similar acknowledgment. 15 USC § 80a-1. The significance of such reports in ascertaining the intent of Congress in enacting securities legislation was recently underscored by the Supreme Court in *Securities and Exchange Commission v. Capital Gains Research Bureau, Inc., supra.*

Among the various types of investment companies referred to in the exhaustive report of the Commission were those involving "an agency relationship between the individual contributors to the fund and the management upon whom they confer substantially a power of attorney to act as agent in the investment of the moneys contributed. The group of individual investors is not a legal entity but rather constitutes in essence a combination of distinct individual interests." H.R. Doc. No. 707, 75th Cong., 3rd Sess. 24 (1939). Additionally, the report made specific reference to an investment company known as the "Alexander Fund" which it described as "merely a descriptive name given to the commingled funds of numerous investors who employed W. Wallace Alexander as their agent to invest such funds." *Id.* at 46. Similarly, in describing the nature of the investment enterprises which Congress was seeking to control, the House Report quotes from the testimony of Commissioner Healy who stated that "Essentially these organizations are large liquid pools of the public's savings entrusted to managements to be invested." H.R. Rep. No. 2639, 76th Cong., 3rd Sess. 6 (1940).

In these circumstances we reject Prudential's argument that the broad statutory phrase "a trust, a fund, or any organized group of persons whether incorporated or not" refers only to recognizable business entities. On the contrary, the legislative history compels the conclusion that Prudential's Investment Fund is a "fund" as that term is used in the statute. As we have previously seen, the Investment Fund is a completely segregated account, devoted to investing in securities. The cash for these investments is derived from payments made by the purchaser of the variable annuity contract. Though the proceeds of the fund are held for the sole benefit of the annuitant, it is this fund, and no other entity, in which he has an interest.[5] Thus, the fund is separable from the

[5] It is true that any deficiency in the variable contract account resulting from lower mortality than assumed would

insurance company which, as the Supreme Court noted in *VALIC*, "guarantee(s) nothing to the annuitant except an interest in a portfolio of common stocks or other equities—an interest that has a ceiling but no floor." The restricted interest of the annuitant is perhaps best expressed in the Court's pithy observation that he "gets only a pro rata share of what the portfolio of equity interests reflects—which may be a lot, a little, or nothing." *Id.*

It follows from this that the Investment Fund, and not Prudential, is the "issuer" of these securities for the purposes of the Investment Company Act of 1940. As the Commission observed, "Prudential would in fact be the writer of the contracts—the insurance and annuity promises and the obligation to set up the investment fund. But the investment fund, the 'company' to which the investment interests relate, is the 'issuer' of those interests."[6]

One of the principal arguments of Prudential in favor of exclusion is that the existence of adequate state regulation was the basis for the exemption of insurance companies. But this line of argument was conclusively rejected by the Supreme Court in *VALIC* for the reason that variable annuities are "securities" and involve considerations of investment not present in the conventional contract of insurance. Prudential attempts to distinguish *VALIC* on the grounds that the company there involved was not, on the basis of the Court's decision, primarily or predominantly engaged in the business of writing insurance. But regardless of the merits of this distinction, that case holds unequivocally that adequate state regulation of insurance is immaterial when variable annuity contracts are being considered under a Federal statute.

Prudential also asserts that the specific exemption provided for the common trust funds of banks shows that regulation under the Act was imposed on an institutional rather than on a functional basis. It is pointed out that this exemption is provided in addition to the general exemption for banks. Prudential declares that such common trust funds are functionally indistinguishable from investment companies, but were excluded from the Act "because they were in fact part of the banking business and intended to be covered by the

---

be met out of the general surplus of Prudential. However, the actuary for Prudential testified that the deductions provided for in the contract would be more than adequate to satisfy the annuity obligations. Hence, the annuitant's interest in the general assets of Prudential is, at best, de minimis.

[6] The mere fact that Prudential is the obligor of certain of the insurance and annuity features of the contract is not significant, for the annuitant's investment participation is measured solely by the Investment Fund.

broad exemption for banks." We think that this specific exemption leads to the opposite conclusion, for as the Commission reasoned:

> "Obviously, if as Prudential argues, the exemption of banks and insurance companies had been intended to include an exemption of funds set up by such companies, there would have been no need to provide for the additional specific exemption of funds set up by banks. Congress thus viewed such funds, even though usually maintained as departments of the bank, as separate from the banking business. It rested this exemption on the special considerations that the funds were used for bona fide fiduciary purposes rather than as a medium for general public investment and had only a limited impact in the investment fund picture."

Considerations of logic and policy provide further support for our conclusion. The Investment Company Act of 1940 contains significant safeguards for the protection of those who, like the purchasers of variable annuities, invest in "securities." These safeguards, characterized by the Commission as insuring "corporate democracy," include disclosure of investment policy and operating practices, and the regulation of fees, trading practices, and changes in investment policy. See *VALIC, supra.* The mere fact that the investment program in the case at bar is under the aegis of an insurance company ought not to negate compliance with these controls in the absence of compelling circumstances. We find no such circumstances here.

We have considered the other contentions advanced by Prudential, but find that they are merely variations on its insurance company exclusion argument and have been fully disposed of by the Commission.

The order of the Commission will be affirmed.

Valley Forge Life Insurance Company

IC Act § § 2(a)(22) & 3(a), SEC No-Action Letter Ref. No. IP-2-97 (Jan. 30, 1997)

Response of the Office of Insurance Products
Division of Investment Management

By letter dated January 27, 1997 (**Request Letter**), you request assurance that the staff would not recommend enforcement action against Valley Forge Life Insurance Company (**Valley Forge**) if the Valley Forge Indexed Separate Account ("**Separate Account**") is not registered as an investment company under the Investment Company Act of 1940 under the circumstances described in the Request letter. The Separate Account is a non-unitized separate account that was established by Valley Forge in connection with certain options ("**Indexed Accounts**") available through annuity contracts that credit interest based in part on changes in a specified market index ("**Contracts**"). The Contracts provide for legal insulation of the Separate Account. As a result of legal insulation of the Separate Account, the Contract owners will, in the event of Valley Forge's liquidation under circumstances where it could not pay all of its insurance obligations, have a priority claim to a portion of Separate Account assets.

I. Operation of the Contracts

I-A. The Indexed Accounts

The Contracts are single premium deferred annuities, providing annuitization, death, and surrender benefits. A Contract owner may allocate all or a portion of the single premium less a premium tax charge ("***Net Single Premium***") and all or a portion of his or her investment in the Contract ("***Account Value***") to an Indexed Account with a specified "Guarantee Period" offered by Valley Forge at the time of allocation.[1] A Guarantee Period is the period of time during which Valley Forge will credit an indexed rate of interest to

[1] A Contract owner also may allocate all or a portion of the Net Single Premium and Account Value to "Interest Accounts." Amounts allocated to an Interest Account earn a stated, guaranteed rate of interest. You state that the Interest Accounts are supported by a legally insulated separate account, the Valley Forge MVA Guaranteed Interest Separate Account (the "VFL Interest Separate Account"). You represent that the VFL Interest Separate Account is similar in all material respects to the legally insulated separate account of The Equitable Life Assurance Society of the United States with respect to which a no-action position under the Investment Company Act was issued. The Equitable Life Assurance Society of the United States (Dec. 22, 1995). Valley Forge is not seeking no-action relief with respect to the VFL Interest Separate Account.

amounts allocated by the Contract owner to that Guarantee Period.[2] Interest is calculated in accordance with a formula that is established and guaranteed in advance and that reflects in part certain positive changes, if any, in the Standard & Poor's 500(R) ("***Index***"). Interest so computed ("***Index Increase***") is determined and credited on each Contract anniversary during a Guarantee Period.

The rate at which the value of an Indexed Account grows depends in part on certain changes in the Index. The value of a Contract owner's interest in the Indexed Accounts ("***Indexed Account Value***"), however, is not determined by, and does not reflect, the investment performance of assets in the Separate Account. Thus, a Contract owner who holds an Indexed Account to the expiration date of a Guarantee Period will receive, without regard to the value of the Separate Account assets, the full amount allocated to the Guarantee Period, plus accumulated interest calculated in accordance with the Index Increase formula, or, if greater, benefits determined based on the Contract's "Reference Value," as described below.

I-B. "Market Value Adjustment"[3]

Any surrender, withdrawal, transfer, or application to an annuity payment option of Indexed Account Value, and the calculation of certain death benefits, are subject to a market value adjustment that may be positive or negative, unless the effective date of the surrender, withdrawal, transfer, application, or calculation is within the last thirty calendar days of a Guarantee Period.

For an Indexed Account, the market value adjustment reflects the relationship between two guaranteed interest rates, the "Credited Rate" and the "Current Rate." The "Credited Rate" is the guaranteed interest rate currently credited by Valley Forge on an Interest Account with the same reset date[4] and Guarantee Period duration as the Indexed

---

[2] The term "Guarantee Period" also is used to describe the period of time during which Valley Forge will credit a guaranteed rate of interest on amounts allocated to an Interest Account.

[3] You state that interests in the Contracts that relate to the Indexed Accounts are registered under the Securities Act of 1933 because the market value adjustment feature imposes on Contract owners certain investment risks. You have not stated your views, nor requested our views, regarding whether registration under the 1933 Act is also required because of other features of the Contracts, particularly the crediting of interest reflecting changes in the Index. It is not necessary to reach this issue for purposes of this letter. Therefore, we express no view on this matter.

[4] Reset date refers to the date of the original allocation of funds to an Interest Account or Indexed Account.

Account from which Account Value is being taken. The "Current Rate" is the guaranteed interest rate that is being offered under the Contracts at the time of the surrender, withdrawal, transfer, annuitization, or death benefit calculation for a new Interest Account with a Guarantee Period of the same duration as the time remaining until the expiration date of the Guarantee Period for the Indexed Account from which Account Value is being taken.

Generally, if the Credited Rate is lower than the Current Rate, then the application of the market value adjustment will result in the payment of an amount less than the Account Value, or portion thereof, being surrendered, withdrawn, transferred, or applied to a death benefit or annuity payment option. It also may result in the payment of an amount less than the Net Single Premium allocated to or the portion of Account Value transferred to the Guarantee Period. Similarly, if the Credited Rate is higher than the Current Rate, then application of the market value adjustment will result in the payment of an amount greater than the Account Value, or portion thereof, being surrendered, withdrawn, transferred, or applied to a death benefit or annuity payment option.

The amount of the adjustment is not determined by the market value of any assets or class of assets, including assets maintained in the Separate Account.

I-C. Reference Value

The Contract provides for surrender and withdrawal, annuity, and death benefits that are based on Indexed Account Value, subject to any applicable market value adjustment and surrender charges. Benefits are also subject to certain minimum values that are based on a Contract's Reference Value. The Reference Value under the Contract is determined pursuant to the following formula:

- (a) 90% of the single premium paid; ***plus***
- (b) any "Excess Interest Credits" (described below); ***less***
- (c) any charges for riders or additional benefits under the Contract, including a rider cost if allocations have been made to Indexed Accounts;[5] ***less***

---

[5] Currently, the only charge for riders or additional benefits under the Contract that reduces the Reference Value is the rider cost imposed if allocations have been made to the Indexed Accounts. The rider cost is an annual charge of 0.85% of the value of any Indexed Account with a five year Guarantee Period, and 1.50% of the value of any Indexed Account with a seven year Guarantee Period. The daily compounded equivalent of this charge is deducted daily from the Reference Value.

- **(d)** the total amount of previous surrenders and withdrawals from the Contract (including market value adjustments); ***plus***
- **(e)** daily interest credited to Reference Value at the "Minimum Interest Rate" specified in the Contract, which will be at least equal to an annual rate of 3%. The Minimum Interest Rate is determined at issue, and fixed for the life of the Contract.

Pursuant to (b) above, as of a reset date, the Reference Value will be increased by an Excess Interest Credit equal to the positive difference, if any, as of such date, between (i) all interest previously credited to Account Value (including, for Indexed Accounts, all previous Index Increases), and (ii) all interest previously credited to Reference Value (including interest at the Minimum Interest Rate, and all previous Excess Interest Credits).

II. Background and Business Purposes of Non-Unitized Separate Accounts

The Request Letter represents that insurers historically have maintained assets supporting modified guaranteed annuity contracts in non-unitized separate accounts primarily to permit such assets to be valued on a market value basis, rather than an amortized cost basis, for purposes of state insurance law requirements. Valley Forge believes that valuation of assets and liabilities associated with modified guaranteed annuity contracts on a market value basis, rather than an amortized cost basis, results in a more timely and direct reflection of the modified guaranteed annuity operations in statutory financial statements. Valley Forge also believes that use of a non-unitized separate account facilitates the establishment and monitoring of specific investment policies appropriate to the assets supporting the Indexed Accounts.

In establishing the Separate Account, Valley Forge was motivated primarily by the foregoing considerations. As a result of legal insulation of the Separate Account, the Contract owners will, in the event of Valley Forge's liquidation under circumstances where it could not pay all of its insurance obligations, have a priority claim to the portion of the Separate Account's assets covered by the insulation provision,[6] while retaining the right to share in the general assets of Valley Forge to the extent of any deficiency in amounts available from the Separate Account. Legal insulation for the Separate Account would therefore serve the additional purpose of providing the Contract owners with enhanced

[6] That is, the portion of the Separate Account's assets equal to the reserves and other contract liabilities of Valley Forge associated with the Indexed Accounts.

assurance that, in the event of Valley Forge's liquidation under circumstance where it could not pay all of its insurance obligations, sufficient assets will be available to satisfy Valley Forge's obligations with respect to the Indexed Accounts. Valley Forge believes that this additional protection may enhance its competitive position with respect to the sale of the Contracts.

III. Account Investment Experience is Not Passed Through to the Contract Owners

Amounts received by the Contract owners upon expiration of a Guarantee Period do not depend upon the investment experience of the Separate Account. As described above, upon the expiration of a Guarantee Period, the Contract owner receives the amount originally allocated to the Guarantee Period, plus accumulated interest calculated in accordance with the Index Increase formula, without regard to the value of the Separate Account assets. Factors guaranteed in the Contract dictate the Index Increase that will be credited; Valley Forge has no discretion in the application of the Index Increase formula.

Nor does the market value adjustment operate to pass through Separate Account gains or losses to Contract owners. The market value adjustment does not correspond to the yield (or any other form of investment performance) with respect to the Separate Account's assets for any period of time. The amount of any market value adjustment results from and depends on the difference between the guaranteed interest rates for a Guarantee Period at the time a Contract owner allocates monies to the Guarantee Period and the time he or she surrenders, withdraws, transfers, or applies amounts in an Indexed Account to an annuity payment option or death benefit.

Amounts received by Contract owners based on a Contract's Reference Value also do not depend on the investment experience of the Separate Account. The minimum values provided by the Contract and based on its Reference Value are determined pursuant to a formula established in advance.

IV. Obligations of Valley Forge

When a Contract owner holds an Indexed Account to the expiration date of a Guarantee Period, Valley Forge is obligated, without regard to the value of Separate Account assets, to pay the full amount allocated to the Guarantee Period, plus accumulated interest calculated in accordance with the Index Increase formula. If, due to negative or flat movements in the Index, no Index Increase is credited, then amounts to be paid upon surrender, withdrawal, transfer, or payment of annuity or death benefits are calculated based on the Contract's Reference Value, which provides minimum values based on the formula set forth above. Valley Forge is also obligated, without regard to the value of the Separate Account assets, to pay the amount specified in the Contract from an Indexed Account upon surrender, withdrawal, transfer, or payment of an annuity or certain death benefits at a time when a market value adjustment, either upward or downward, is made.

So long as Valley Forge is not liquidated under circumstances where it could not pay all of its insurance obligations, Contract owners have no interest in the Separate Account. Moreover, even in the event of Valley Forge's liquidation under circumstances where it could not pay all of its insurance obligations, a Contract owner has a claim against the Separate Account's assets and against Valley Forge that is measured not by the value of the Separate Account's assets or the Separate Account's investment performance over any period of time. Rather, the claim would be for any unpaid amounts guaranteed to the Contract owner by Valley Forge in connection with that owner's Indexed Account and computed in accordance with the terms of the Contract.

State insurance laws require life insurance companies periodically to value their assets and liabilities according to prescribed accounting principles. These laws require that the insurer maintain an excess of such "statutory assets" over "statutory liabilities" of at least a prescribed amount—*i.e.*, a minimum amount of statutory capital and surplus. The minimum capital and surplus required of Valley Forge in its domiciliary state of Pennsylvania is $1.5 million. As a practical matter, Valley Forge has statutory capital and surplus far in excess of that amount—approximately $125 million at September 30, 1996. Under Pennsylvania law, providing legal insulation for a separate account does not affect the computation of (or the required minimum amount of) an insurer's statutory capital and surplus.

Under Pennsylvania law, Valley Forge is required to value the assets and contract liabilities of the Separate Account at least annually. In addition, the law imposes on Valley Forge an ongoing requirement to maintain Separate Account assets at least equal to the accrued amounts guaranteed under the Contracts. If the liabilities exceed the assets, Valley Forge is required immediately to transfer sufficient assets into the Separate Account to remedy the shortfall. On the other hand, whenever the value of the Separate Account's assets exceeds the value of the Separate Account's contract liabilities, state law permits Valley Forge to transfer the surplus to its general account. Contract owners have no claim upon or interest in such transferred assets, except that such assets are part of

Valley Forge's general account. Valley Forge represents that the value of the assets maintained in the Separate Account will at all times at least equal the amount of the Separate Account's contract liabilities.

Providing legal insulation for the Separate Account will not change the Pennsylvania insurance law requirements as to contributing, withdrawing, and maintaining Separate Account assets; nor will it change Valley Forge's practices in these regards.

V. Marketing of the Contracts

Valley Forge will take steps to ensure that its marketing program and materials refer to the Separate Account as a pool of assets that provides an additional measure of assurance that Contract owners allocating Account Value to Indexed Accounts will receive full payment and not as an investment vehicle in whose performance such Contract owners will have any interest.

VI. Conclusion

In *Hartford Life Insurance Company* (pub. avail. Oct. 29, 1984) ("**Hartford**"), we indicated that we would not recommend enforcement action against an insurance company that established a non-unitized separate account to support its liabilities under annuity contracts that contain a "market value adjustment" feature without registration of the account under the Investment Company Act. We have also indicated that we do not believe that legal insulation of the account alone alters the *Hartford* conclusion. *The Equitable Life Assurance Society of the United States* (pub. avail. Dec. 22, 1995) ("**Equitable**"). The facts outlined in the Request Letter are similar to those of *Equitable*, except that Valley Forge guarantees payment of interest calculated in accordance with a formula that is established in advance, rather than a fixed interest rate established in advance. We do not believe that this difference changes the result in *Equitable*. Valley Forge, like Equitable, is obligated to pay the Contract owner an amount that is mathematically determinable and not dependent on the investment experience of a separate account.

Based on the representations in the Request Letter, and without necessarily agreeing with your legal analysis, the staff would not recommend enforcement action against Valley Forge if the Contracts provide for legal insulation of the Separate Account without registration of the Separate Account under the Investment Company Act. Our conclusion is based in particular on the following representations:

(1) A Contract owner allocating Net Single Premium and/or Account Value to an Indexed Account is entitled to Contract benefits (whether based on Indexed Account Value or Reference Value, and whether or not subject to a market value adjustment) that are determined based on a mathematical formula established at the time the Contract is issued, and with respect to subsequent Guarantee Periods, at the beginning of such subsequent Guarantee Period. This mathematical formula is based in part on (i) a market index that is established and guaranteed in advance, and (ii) changes in guaranteed interest rates applicable to Interest Accounts. Neither Index Increases based on a market index nor adjustments based on changes in guaranteed interest rates are affected by the investment experience of the Separate Account.

(2) Valley Forge is obligated to pay all amounts due to a Contract owner allocating Net Single Premium and/or Account Value to an Indexed Account without regard to the value of the Separate Account's assets, and Valley Forge retains the profits and bears the losses from the Separate Account operations.

(3) Valley Forge is obligated under state law to maintain Separate Account assets with a market value at least equal to reserves and other contract liabilities related to the Separate Account and immediately to transfer to the Separate Account sufficient assets to remedy any shortfall, and Valley Forge represents that the value of the assets in the Separate Account will at all times at least equal the amount of that Separate Account's reserves and other contract liabilities.

(4) Whenever the value of the Separate Account's assets exceeds the value of its reserves and other contract liabilities, state law permits Valley Forge to transfer the surplus to its general account, and the Contract owner allocating Net Single Premium and/or Account Value to an Indexed Account has no claim upon or interest in such transferred assets, except that such assets are part of Valley Forge's general account.

(5) Valley Forge established and proposes to provide for legal insulation of the Separate Account for business purposes unrelated to any attempt to pass through investment experience of the Separate Account.

(6) Valley Forge will take steps to ensure that its marketing program and materials refer to the Separate Account as a pool of assets that provides an additional measure of assurance that Contract owners allocating Net Single Premium and/or Account Value to Indexed Accounts will receive full payment and not as an investment vehicle in whose performance such Contract owners will have any interest.

Because our position is based on the facts and representations set forth in the Request Letter, you should note that different facts or representations may require a different conclusion.

Valley Forge Life Insurance Company

IC Act § § 2(a)(22) & 3(a) (Jan. 27, 1997)

Request Letter

From: Sutherland, Asbill & Brennan, L.L.P.

To: Office of Insurance Products, Division of Investment Management

Securities and Exchange Commission

Re: VFL Indexed Separate Account

We are writing on behalf of our client, Valley Forge Life Insurance Company ("**Valley Forge**" or the "**Company**"), a stock life insurance company domiciled in and organized under the laws of the state of Pennsylvania. This letter concerns the status under the Investment Company Act of 1940 of a separate account (the *Valley Forge Life Insurance Company Indexed Separate Account* or "*VFL Indexed Separate Account*" or "*Separate Account*") established by Valley Forge to fund certain options ("**Indexed Accounts**") available through certain single premium deferred annuity contracts[1] that credit interest based in part on certain changes in a specified market index. The VFL Indexed Separate Account is a type of separate account that is commonly described as "non-unitized."

The Contracts that are the subject of this no-action request also include guaranteed interest account options ("**Interest Accounts**"), which provide account values based on the crediting of specified Guaranteed Interest Rates. The Interest Accounts are also supported by a legally insulated separate account (the *Valley Forge Life Insurance Company MVA Guaranteed Interest Separate Account* or "*VFL Interest Separate Account*"). The VFL Interest Separate Account is similar in all material respects to the legally insulated separate account of Equitable Life Assurance Society of the United States ("**Equitable Life**") with respect to which a no-action position under the 1940 Act has previously been issued.[2] Valley Forge is not seeking no-action relief with respect to the VFL Interest Separate Account. The remainder of this no-action request will focus on the

---

[1] In some jurisdictions, the Contract is issued directly to individuals. In other jurisdictions, the Contract is only available as a group contract. Individuals who are part of groups for which a Contract is issued receive a certificate that recites substantially all of the provisions of the group contract. Throughout this letter, the term "Contract" refers both to individual contracts, and to group contracts and individual certificates issued thereunder.

[2] See *The Equitable Life Assurance Soc'y of the U.S.*, SEC No-Action Letter (Dec. 22, 1995).

Indexed Account options.

The Contracts provide that the portion of the VFL Indexed Separate Account's assets equal to the reserves and other contract liabilities under the Indexed Accounts will not be chargeable with liabilities arising from any other business of Valley Forge. Accordingly, the Separate Account's assets will be "legally insulated" from the claims of certain other creditors of Valley Forge.[3] The operation of the VFL Indexed Separate Account is also substantially similar to the operation of Equitable Life's legally insulated separate account with respect to which the Staff issued a no-action position. We are writing this letter to seek assurance that the staff of the Securities and Exchange Commission will not recommend enforcement action to the Commission if the VFL Indexed Separate Account is not registered as an investment company under the 1940 Act.

For the reasons set forth below, the legally insulated Separate Account is not an "issuer" of securities within the meaning of § 2(a)(22)[4] and, therefore, will not be an "investment company" within the meaning of § 3(a). On the contrary, a Contract owner's interest in the Separate Account does not possess the type of investment characteristics that other precedents have relied on for applying the federal securities laws in the context of annuity contracts. Additionally, the precedents and principles applied to pools of securities that serve as collateral in the context of retail repurchase agreements and so-called "defeasance" trusts strongly support our opinion that the Separate Account will not be an investment company.

Moreover, Congress has recognized that owners of traditional annuity contracts generally do not require the protections of the 1940 Act. Legal insulation of the VFL Indexed Separate Account will provide additional protection for Contract owners and will have no adverse consequences for such owners. Legal insulation, therefore, renders 1940 Act regulation of the Separate Account even more unnecessary.

---

[3] Section 40-37-109(a)(5) of the Pennsylvania Insurance Law provides that, to the extent provided in the relevant contracts, "that portion of the assets of any such separate account equal to the reserves and other contract liabilities with respect to such account shall not be chargeable with liabilities arising out of any other business the company may conduct."

[4] Unless stated otherwise, any reference to a particular statutory section in this letter refers to that section of the 1940 Act.

I. THE CONTRACT IN GENERAL

The Contract is a single premium deferred annuity, providing annuitization, death, and surrender benefits, that has been registered under the Securities Act of 1933.[5] * * * *

II. THE INDEXED ACCOUNTS

* * * *

II-A. Market Value Adjustment

. . . Examples of Market Value Adjustment computations are set forth in the Form S-1 registration statement relating to the Contracts on file with the Commission. * * * *

IV. THE VFL INDEXED SEPARATE ACCOUNT

The VFL Indexed Separate Account has been duly established under Pennsylvania insurance law as a separate account of Valley Forge that does not have unit values and thus falls within the category of "non-unitized" separate accounts. Income realized by the Separate Account and other realized and unrealized gains and losses with respect to assets in the Separate Account, pursuant to the requirements of Pennsylvania law, are credited to the Separate Account without regard to any other business conducted by Valley Forge.[6] Nevertheless, the Indexed Accounts are part of Valley Forge's insurance business. Accordingly, the assets in the VFL Indexed Separate Account are the property of Valley Forge and will be managed as a part of Valley Forge's insurance business. That is, like the assets supporting traditional insurance products other than the Indexed Accounts, the Separate Account's assets will be managed with the ultimate objective of generating a return to Valley Forge that, after payment of all of its obligations to owners of Indexed Accounts, covers expenses and provides a profit to Valley Forge. To the extent these efforts are successful, the benefit belongs to Valley Forge. To the extent unsuccessful, the risk belongs to Valley Forge.

---

[5] A registration statement under the 1933 Act on Form S-1 relating to the Contracts became effective on November 8, 1996 (File No. 333-2093).

[6] Pennsylvania Insurance Law § 40-37-109(a)(1). This requirement, however, in no way restricts Valley Forge's right to or access to any assets in a Separate Account that are in excess of the contract liabilities. *Id.* § 40-37-109(a)(5).

V. ANALYSIS

V-A. A Contract owner will not require the protections of the 1940 Act with respect to the legally insulated VFL Indexed Separate Account.

By excluding insurance companies from the 1940 Act definition of an investment company,[7] Congress recognized that, as a general matter, the guarantees of an insurance company, together with the protections afforded by state insurance regulation, make the protection of the 1940 Act unnecessary for purchasers of insurance products. Because, prior to expiration dates, the Market Value Adjustment feature imposes on Contract owners certain investment risks associated with changing interest rates, interests in the Contracts that relate to the Indexed Accounts (and to the Interest Accounts) are registered under the 1933 Act. This 1933 Act registration provides still further protections to Contract owners.

When a Contact owner holds an Indexed Account to its expiration date (the end of the applicable Guarantee Period), the Contract specifically obligates Valley Forge to pay the full amount of the Contract owner's contribution and accumulated interest calculated in accordance with the Index Increase formula, as in the case of fixed insurance products that are excluded from 1933 Act requirements by § 3(a)(8) thereof. If, due to negative or flat movements in the index, no Index Increase is credited, then amounts to be paid upon surrender, withdrawal, transfer, or payment of annuity or death benefits are calculated based on the Contract's Reference Value, which provides minimum values based on the formula set forth above. The Contract also specifically obligates Valley Forge, without regard to the value of Separate Account assets, to pay the amount specified in the Contract from an Indexed Account upon surrender, withdrawal, transfer, or payment of annuity or certain death benefits at a time when a Market Value Adjustment, either upward or downward, is made.[8]

Legal insulation of the Accounts would have relevance for Contract owners allocating Net Single Premium and/or Account Value to Indexed Accounts only in the event of Valley

---

[7] See 1940 Act § 3(c)(3).

[8] The terms of the Contracts do not provide for any "pass through" to Contract owners of any Separate Account investment results in the determination of the amounts owed to such owners upon determination of their Indexed Account Value, either at the expiration dates or prior thereto. Nor will Valley Forge's operation of the Separate Account or administration of the Indexed Accounts effect any such pass through, as explained in V-B below.

Forge's liquidation under circumstances where it could not pay all of its insurance obligations. (This letter refers to such circumstances generally as "insolvency"). Providing legal insulation for the Separate Account, moreover, will not relieve Valley Forge of its obligations referred to in the preceding paragraph, even in the event of the insolvency of Valley Forge.

Section 40-37-109(a)(5) of the Pennsylvania Insurance Law provides "that portion of the assets of any such separate account equal to the reserves and other contract liabilities with respect to such account shall not be chargeable with liabilities arising out of any other business the company may conduct."[9] The effect of this provision is that the Contract owners allocating Net Single Premium and/or Account Value to Indexed Accounts will have a priority claim in the event of the insolvency of Valley Forge to that portion of the assets of the VFL Indexed Separate Account covered by such provision,[10] while retaining the right to share with other insurance policy owners in the general assets of Valley Forge to the extent of any deficiency. On the other hand, to the extent the Separate Account holds more assets than sufficient to discharge the Contract obligations to the Contract owners allocating Account Value to Indexed Accounts, such excess would revert to Valley Forge's estate and not to such owners.

The insurance laws of all states, of course, require life insurance companies periodically to value their assets and liabilities according to accounting principles that are prescribed for these regulatory purposes. These laws uniformly require that the insurer maintain an excess of such statutory assets over statutory liabilities of at least a prescribed amount, *i.e.*, a minimum amount of statutory capital and surplus. These requirements vary from state to state, but the minimum capital and surplus required of Valley Forge in its domiciliary state of Pennsylvania is $1.5 million. As a practical matter, however, this requirement has little relevance to Valley Forge, which has statutory capital and surplus far in excess of that amount—approximately $125 million as of September 30, 1996. Under Pennsylvania law and, so far as Valley Forge is aware, in all other states, providing legal insulation for a separate account currently does not affect the computation of (or the required minimum amount of) the insurer's overall statutory capital and surplus.

---

[9] See *supra* note 3 and accompanying text.

[10] In other words, to assets of the Separate Account, in an amount equal to the reserves and other contract liabilities of Valley Forge associated with the Indexed Accounts.

Pennsylvania, moreover, has published a bulletin that specifically regulates modified guaranteed annuity contracts and the separate accounts that fund them, including the VFL Indexed Separate Account.[11] Among other things, this bulletin prescribes requirements for the terms of the Market Value Adjustment formula, valuation of contract liabilities, and minimum reserve requirements. This bulletin also requires that a Pennsylvania insurer issuing modified guaranteed annuity contracts provide a statement of actuarial opinion regarding the adequacy of separate account reserves based on an asset adequacy analysis that takes into account the market value adjustment formula, the interest guarantees, and the degree to which projected cash flow of separate account assets and liabilities are matched.

The Pennsylvania Insurance law specifically requires Valley Forge to value the assets and contract liabilities of the Separate Account at least annually.[12] However, the law also imposes on Valley Forge an ongoing requirement to maintain separate account assets at least equal to the accrued amounts guaranteed under the contracts funded by the account.[13] If the liabilities exceed the assets, Valley Forge is required immediately to transfer sufficient assets into the separate account from unallocated surplus or contingency reserves not required by law to remedy the shortfall. On the other hand, whenever the value of a separate account's assets exceeds the value of the account's contract liabilities, state law permits Valley Forge to transfer the surplus to its general account. Contract owners will have no claim upon or interest in such transferred assets, except that such assets will become part of Valley Forge's general account.

Valley Forge represents that the value of the assets in the VFL Indexed Separate Account will at all times at least equal the amount of that Separate Account's contract liabilities. Providing legal insulation for the Separate Account will not in any way change the above-described Pennsylvania insurance law requirements as to contributing, withdrawing, and maintaining Separate Account assets; nor will it change Valley Forge's

---

[11] Pennsylvania Insurance Bulletin 94-12.

[12] See *id.* (each insurer authorized to transact the business of separate account modified guaranteed annuities must submit to the Pennsylvania Insurance Commissioner a separate account annual statement which shall include the business of its separate account modified guaranteed annuities). The discussion in this paragraph, although phrased in terms of separate accounts generally, is fully applicable to the VFL Indexed Separate Account, specifically.

[13] *Id.*

practices in these regards.

Under the circumstances, therefore, we respectfully submit that the additional protections afforded by legal insulation will, if anything, make the protections of 1940 Act regulation even less necessary than if the Separate Account was not legally insulated. The Staff recently endorsed this position as a basis for the no-action letter issued to Equitable Life.[14]

V-B. The legally insulated VFL Indexed Separate Account will not closely resemble the types of entities that historically have been subject to 1940 Act regulation.

The principal purposes of the VFL Indexed Separate Account are different from the investment purposes historically associated with investment companies. Historically, insurers have used non-unitized separate accounts to hold the assets supporting modified guaranteed annuity contracts primarily to permit such assets to be valued on a market value basis for purposes of state insurance law requirements that would otherwise require amortized cost valuation.[15] To the extent that an insurer's assets and liabilities associated with modified guaranteed annuity contracts are valued on a market value basis, rather than an amortized cost basis, Valley Forge believes that the insurer's statutory financial statements will reflect the insurer's modified guaranteed annuity operations in a more direct and timely way. Under the insurance laws of many states, including Pennsylvania, the assets can be valued on a market value basis only if they are held in a separate account.[16] Use of a non-unitized separate account facilitates the establishment and monitoring of specific investment policies appropriate to the assets supporting the Indexed Accounts. By segregating such assets in a separate account, Valley Forge is better able to make duration matching calculations and asset/liability management analyses.

Accordingly, in establishing the VFL Indexed Separate Account, Valley Forge was

---

[14] See *The Equitable Life Assurance Soc'y of the U.S.*, SEC No-Action Letter (Dec. 22, 1995).

[15] See, *e.g.*, *Equitable*; *Fortis Benefits Ins. Co.*, SEC No-Action Request Letter (Jan. 17, 1992); *The Travelers T-Mark Annuity*, SEC No-Action Request Letter (March 27, 1992).

[16] See Pennsylvania Insurance Law § 40-37-109(a)(3). The valuation rules for separate account assets differ from the rules generally applicable to an insurer's general account assets, which for the most part do not provide for valuation of those assets at market value. See BLACK, JR. & SKIPPER, JR., LIFE INSURANCE 551-53 (11th ed. 1987); Epsie, *Financial Statements*, in MCGILL, LIFE INSURANCE 860, 864-68 (rev. ed. 1967).

motivated primarily by the above-mentioned accounting, legal, and administrative considerations. Legal insulation for the Separate Account will serve the additional purpose of providing Contract owners with enhanced assurance that, in the unlikely event of Valley Forge's insolvency, sufficient assets will be available to satisfy Valley Forge's obligations with respect to the Indexed Accounts.[17] Valley Forge believes that this additional protection for Contract owners may enhance its competitive position with respect to the offer and sale of the Contracts. For example, because of the credit enhancement inherent in legal insulation, plan fiduciaries may be more likely to make Indexed Accounts available as an investment option under annuity contracts offered pursuant to certain defined contribution employee benefit plans.

In contrast to the above purposes, investment companies customarily are established for the primary purpose of providing investment returns to their security holders.

Income, gains, and losses of the VFL Indexed Separate Account are not passed through to Contract owners making allocations to Indexed Accounts. The formula used to determine the Index Increases applicable to any amount allocated to a Guarantee Period is established at the time of such allocation and does not change for the remainder of the Guarantee Period.

The Index Increases do not operate to "pass through" to Contract owners any future returns, gains, or losses of the VFL Indexed Separate Account. This follows inherently from the fact that Valley Forge, rather than the Contract owners, retains the "spread" (whether positive or negative) between what Valley Forge guarantees to Contract owners (based on the fixed formula) and what it earns in the Separate Account. The Separate Account's portfolio manager's success (or lack thereof) in investing Separate Account assets or in utilizing hedging techniques is irrelevant in determining the amount of interest to be credited to Indexed Accounts. The applicable Index, Floor, Cap, and Index Participation Rate, which are guaranteed in the Contract, dictate the Index Increase that will be credited to Indexed Account Value; Valley Forge has no discretion in the application of the Index Increase formula. The only variable in the formula is the financial performance of the applicable Index, a factor which is unknown at the time a Contract is issued and over which Valley Forge has no control.

---

[17] Other insurers that have proposed legally insulated non-unitized separate accounts in connection with modified guaranteed annuity conflicts have been similarly motivated. See *Equitable*; *Travelers*; *Fortis*.

Moreover, even if Valley Forge wished to establish rates that would pass through to Contract owners future returns, gains, or losses of the related Separate Account, it would not be practical to do so. This results not only from the inherent fallibility of predicting Separate Account investment performance for periods of time that may extend many years into the future, but also from the investment discretion that the Separate Account's portfolio manager is expected to exercise, as discussed below.

As part of its overall investment strategy, Valley Forge intends to maintain assets in the VFL Indexed Separate Account that reflect its obligations to Contract owners that have made allocations to Indexed Accounts. Accordingly, it is anticipated that assets of the VFL Indexed Separate Account will likely consist of fixed income investments, as well as call options or other hedging instruments that relate to movements in the index. The VFL Indexed Separate Account will be managed in such a way that the "duration"[18] of the assets in that Separate Account, taken as a whole, is expected at all times to approximate the duration of the outstanding Guarantee Period liabilities with respect to that Separate Account. This "duration matching" affords the portfolio manager greater flexibility to seek enhanced returns than would be the case if the Separate Account's assets were segmented by Guarantee Period and the assets supporting each Guarantee Period were required to have the same duration as that Guarantee Period. (Exercise of this flexibility, of course, could also affect the Separate Account's investment results adversely.) Other techniques that the portfolio manager is expected to use will likewise cause the Separate Account's investment results to be better (if successful) or worse (if unsuccessful) than could have been predicted at the time Guaranteed Rates are set: *e.g.*, purchase of call options on the S&P 500® to hedge Contract obligations to pay Index Increases, variations in average quality of securities purchased, and other efforts by the portfolio manager to make investment decisions with respect to specific securities that will enhance Valley Forge's return.

Nor does the Market Value Adjustment operate to pass through the VFL Indexed Separate Account gains or losses to Contract owners allocating Account Value to Indexed Accounts. As discussed above, such Market Value Adjustment does not correspond to the

---

[18] "Duration" as used in connection with an Account refers to its dollar-weighted average time of cash flows. Because an Indexed Account is payable at a future date and has no interim cash flow, while most bonds pay periodic interest, an Indexed Account with a given maturity date will have a different duration than, for example, a coupon bond having the same maturity date.

yield (or any other form of investment performance) with respect to the related Separate Account's assets for any period of time, whether before or after the date that any such rate is set. Accordingly, although Contract owners that terminate their Indexed Accounts prematurely are charged, pursuant to the Market Value Adjustment, with certain "losses" and credited with certain "gains" that are associated, respectively, with rising or falling interest rates, such losses or gains bear no precise relationship to losses or gains in the VFL Indexed Separate Account's investment portfolios due to changing interest rates.

Nor does the Market Value Adjustment make any adjustment to reflect any losses or gains that may occur in the VFL Indexed Separate Account's portfolio of investments due to factors other than changing interest rates. Such other factors include changes in creditworthiness of the issuers in which the VFL Indexed Separate Account invests, defaults by such issuers, or the success of the portfolio manager (or lack thereof) in exercising the investment flexibility described above. Moreover, the Indexed Accounts will be guaranteed by Valley Forge, including a guarantee of principal and interest, subject only to the Market Value Adjustment that will apply prior to maturity.[19]

In contrast to the foregoing characteristics of the VFL Indexed Separate Account, most types of investment companies customarily (1) are designed to permit their interest holders to participate directly in the investment results of the securities in which the investment company invests, and (2) do not provide such interest holders a repayment of principal and a specified rate of return that are guaranteed by the investment company's sponsor if the interest is held for a specified period or to a maturity date.

The Commission Staff relied on this distinction in the No-Action Letter issued to Equitable Life in connection with a modified guaranteed annuity legally insulated separate account. The Commission Staffs opinion was based, among other factors, on the representation that "a holder of an MVA Contract receives an amount upon maturity that is mathematically determinable in advance and is not affected by the investment experience of the related Account." Similarly, a Contract owner allocating Account Value to an Indexed Account will receive interest based on a guaranteed mathematical formula regardless of the investment experience of the underlying Separate Account.

[19] Reference Value provides an additional guarantee of minimum Account Value.

V-C. The legally insulated VFL Indexed Separate Account will most clearly resemble pools of collateral that have not historically been regulated as investment companies.

The legal insulation of the VFL Indexed Separate Account will enable it to function as a pool of collateral from which Contract owners allocating Net Single Premium and/or Account Value to Indexed Accounts may receive payment, in the unlikely event that Valley Forge at some future time becomes insolvent. In similar circumstances, other pools of collateral established to secure amounts owed by the primary obligor have not been deemed to be subject to 1940 Act regulation.

Such examples include pools of securities serving as collateral in connection with retail repurchase agreement transactions[20] and "defeasance" trusts established to satisfy the primary obligor's obligation to pay principal and interest on debt obligations.[21] As in traditional collateral arrangements, the amount of the primary obligation under the Indexed Account (*i.e.*, the amount of benefits owed by Valley Forge) does not depend on the value of the collateral (*i.e.*, the VFL Indexed Separate Account's assets).

V-D. The legally insulated VFL Indexed Separate Account is not within the 1940 Act's definition of an "issuer" because the Contract owners' interests in the VFL Indexed Separate Account do not constitute securities.

Section 3(a) includes within the definition of an investment company only "issuers." Section 2(a)(22), in turn, defines an "issuer" to include only persons or entities that issue securities. The only interest of which a VFL Indexed Separate Account could be deemed to be the issuer for this purpose would appear to be the Contract owners' interests in the Separate Account. Thus, if the Contract owners' interests in the legally insulated Separate Account do not constitute securities, the VFL Indexed Separate Account cannot be an investment company.

For this purpose, consistent with the authorities discussed below, the owner's interest under the Contract as a whole is to be distinguished from the owners' interest in the related legally insulated Separate Account. The owner's whole interest under the Contract comprises all of the ownership rights under the Contract. Because of the

---

[20] See *Issuance of "Retail Repurchase Agreements" by Banks and Savings and Loan Associations; Interpretations*, 33-6351, 34-18122, 39-658, IC-11958, 46 FR 48637 (1981).

[21] See *Stephen B. Flood*, SEC No-Action Letter (Feb. 20, 1987); *Centex Corporation*, SEC No-Action Letter (Nov. 20, 1986).

Market Value Adjustment feature, these ownership rights may be deemed to have a significant "investment" character, and, consequently, the Contracts are registered as securities under the 1933 Act. The interest of a Contract owner in a legally-insulated Separate Account, however, is only one of the ownership rights under the Contract as a whole. Moreover, it is a limited and contingent interest that is not in the nature of an investment interest and therefore, in our view, is not itself a security for purposes of § 2(a)(22).

There is considerable relevant precedent for assessing whether the limited interest that the Contract owner has in a Separate Account has sufficient investment characteristics to constitute a security for purposes of § 2(a)(22). One line of precedents essentially analyzes whether an interest in a pool of securities is in the nature of an interest in collateral, as opposed to an investment interest. The former interests are not regarded as securities for purposes of the 1940 Act definition of an issuer, while the latter are. In our view, a Contract owner's interest in the legally insulated Separate Account will not constitute an investment interest for these purposes.

Rather, Valley Forge will retain the investment interest in the Separate Account as part of its insurance business. As noted elsewhere in this letter, the Separate Account is managed with the objective of earning a profit in a manner similar to the profit Valley Forge seeks to earn from investment assets that it owns as other parts of its insurance business. Any such profits belong to Valley Forge, and Contract owners will have no interest in them. Any losses fall on Valley Forge, and Valley Forge will make the VFL Indexed Separate Account whole for any losses. Thus, the Contract owners allocating Account Value to Indexed Accounts have an interest in the VFL Indexed Separate Account that is, in effect, a contingent interest: so long as Valley Forge does not become insolvent, Contract owners will have no interest in the VFL Indexed Separate Account whatsoever. Moreover, even in the unlikely event of Valley Forge's insolvency, the amount of such a Contract owner's claim against the VFL Indexed Separate Account's assets (and against Valley Forge) would not be measured by the value of the VFL Indexed Separate Account's assets or the VFL Indexed Separate Account's investment performance over any period of time. Rather, that claim would be for any unpaid amounts guaranteed to the Contract owner by Valley Forge in connection with that owner's Indexed Account and computed in accordance with the terms of the Contract.

The 1964 *Prudential* case[22] provides the most comprehensive guidance to date as to when an insurance company separate account supporting contracts constitutes an issuer for 1940 Act purposes. In holding that such a separate account constituted an issuer different from the insurance company, the court in that case appears to have placed primary emphasis on the fact that the value of the owners' interest under the relevant contracts was determined solely with reference to the investment performance of the separate account.[23]

The *Prudential* case also established that the interests in a separate account can be distinguished from the other rights under a contract for purposes of determining whether a separate account should be deemed to be a 1940 Act issuer. The *Prudential* court affirmed and essentially adopted the analysis of the Commission Opinion that was before the court on appeal. Under that analysis, "units" of interest in a separate account that are the basis of determining the owner's return are securities of which the separate account is the issuer; and those securities, moreover, are distinct from the owner's other rights under the contracts,[24] of which the insurance company is, in effect, the issuer.[25]

Applying the analysis of the court and the Commission in *Prudential*, the question is whether the limited and contingent interest that Contract owners will have in the legally insulated VFL Indexed Separate Account, as distinct from their other rights under Valley

---

22 *Prudential Ins. Co. of Am. v. SEC*, 326 F.2d 383 (3rd Cir.), *cert. denied*, 377 U.S. 953 (1964) [hereinafter ***Prudential***].

23 The *Prudential* court quoted the Commission's reasoning (set out in the Commission's opinion that precipitated Prudential's appeal before that court) that Prudential would create a separate account "exclusively for investment" and sell "equity interests in the fortunes" of that separate account to holders. *Id.* at 386 n.3 (quoting *The Prudential Ins. Co. of Am.*, SEC Rel. IC-3620 (Jan. 22, 1963) (hereinafter ***Commission Opinion***). The *Prudential* court found that a holder who has an interest in a "completely segregated" separate account that is "devoted to investing" has an interest in that separate account and "no other entity" or, in other words, solely in the separate account. The *Prudential* court characterized this "interest" by quoting the Supreme Court, which observed, in *SEC v. Variable Annuity Life Ins. Co. of Am.*, 359 U.S. 65 (1959) [hereinafter ***VALIC***], that a holder "gets ... a pro rata share of what the portfolio of equity interests reflects—which may be a lot, a little, or nothing" (*Prudential*, quoting *VALIC*) or, in other words, an interest in the investment performance of the separate account.

24 The court, quoting the Commission Opinion being appealed, described such other rights as consisting of "the insurance and annuity promises and the obligation to set up the investment fund." *Prudential*.

25 *Id.* at 386 n.3 (quoting the Commission Opinion).

Forge's contracts,[26] constitutes a security. Unlike *Prudential*'s separate account, the VFL Indexed Separate Account will not have units of interest that measure values under Indexed Accounts by the performance of the VFL Indexed Separate Account. Nor will the VFL Indexed Separate Account have any other outstanding interests that could be viewed as the economic equivalent of such units. Accordingly, we do not believe that, under the reasoning in *Prudential*, the VFL Indexed Separate Account should be construed to be the issuer of securities.

As the Commission staff is aware, a number of precedents bear on the question of whether general account interests under contracts constitute securities for purposes of the federal securities laws.[27] These authorities, generally speaking, evaluate the degree to which such interests have the characteristics of an investment (*i.e.*, a security) or the characteristics of insurance (*i.e.*, not a security). These precedents also have relevance to whether Contract owner interests in the VFL Indexed Separate Account constitute securities because that question also turns on whether such interests are in the nature of an investment interest (rather than primarily an interest in collateral). Such precedents have focused primarily on the following factors:[28]

a. *The degree to which the participant bears the investment risk in connection with the contract.* Providing legal insulation for the VFL Indexed Separate Account, of course, will reduce rather than increase the "credit" risk to which Contract owners allocating Net Single Premium and/or Account Value to Indexed Accounts are exposed and will not affect any other types of investment risk.

b. *The degree to which the insurance company assumes meaningful mortality and*

---

[26] For this purpose, it should not matter whether, as in the *Prudential* case, such other rights do not constitute a security issued by the insurance company or whether, as here, such other rights (because of the Market Value Adjustment feature) do constitute a security issued by the insurance company. Even in the latter case, the security that arises as a result of the Market Value Adjustment feature is a security of which only the insurance company (and not the related Separate Account) is the issuer.

[27] See, *e.g.*, *SEC v. United Benefit Life Ins. Co.*, 387 U.S. 202 (1967); *VALIC, supra*; *Associates in Adolescent Psychiatry, S.C. v. Home Life Ins. Co.*, 941 F.2d 561 (7th Cir. 1991); Rule 151 under the 1933 Act. Certain of the authorities address the status of interests in annuity contracts primarily in terms of the availability of § 3(a)(8) under the 1933 Act. Although § 3(a)(8) by its literal terms exempts annuity contracts from registration under the 1933 Act, the Commission's stated position is that contracts falling within the § 3(a)(8) exemption are not to be regarded as securities for other purposes as well. SEC Rel. 33-6558, n.25 and accompanying text (1984).

[28] As the Commission staff is aware, however, not all of the relevant precedents refer to all of these factors.

investment risks under the contract. Providing legal insulation for the VFL Indexed Separate Account will not in any way affect the mortality or investment risks assumed by Valley Forge under any Contract.[29]

c. *The degree to which the interests are marketed as an investment.* Valley Forge will take steps to ensure that its marketing program and materials refer to the VFL Indexed Separate Account accurately: *i.e.*, as a pool of assets that provides an additional measure of assurance that Contract owners allocating Account Value to Indexed Accounts will receive full payment, and not as investment vehicles in whose performance such Contract owners will have any interest.

Accordingly, regardless of the relative weights given to the above three factors, legal insulation for the Separate Account would not, under the circumstances, tip the scale toward a finding that interests in the VFL Indexed Separate Account are Securities.

VI. CONCLUSION

In summary, we see no basis in public policy, nor anything in the provisions of the 1940 Act, that would require Valley Forge's legally insulated VFL Indexed Separate Account to be deemed to be an "issuer" subject to regulation under the 1940 Act. On behalf of Valley Forge, therefore, we hereby request that the Commission staff provide assurance to Valley Forge that the staff would not recommend that the Commission take enforcement action if the VFL Indexed Separate Account is not registered as an investment company under the 1940 Act. * * * *

---

[29] The Contracts provide annuity payment options that impose significant mortality risks upon Valley Forge that annuitants under those options will live longer than expected. The death benefit provisions impose additional mortality risks on Valley Forge.

Section 5.2 Bank Common Trust Fund and Collective Investment Fund

Laws & Rules Highlight:

IC Act (15 USC 80a-1 *et seq.*); IA Act ((15 USC 80b-1 *et seq.*)
Securities Act (SA) (15 USC 77a *et seq.*); Exchange Act (SEA) (15 USC 78a *et seq.*)

Bank & IC Exclusions

- **IC § 3(c)(3)** (*exclusions from IC: bank and **common trust fund** maintained by the bank **exclusively** in its capacity as a trustee, executor, administrator, or guardian—intended to exclude use of bank common trust fund for direct investment by members of the public*)
  - IC § 2(a)(5) (*def. "bank"*); IC Rule 3c-4 Definition of "Common Trust Fund" as Used in Section 3(c)(3) of the Act
- **IC § 3(c)(11)** (*exclusion from IC: **bank collective investment fund** consisting **solely** of assets of one or more of tax-qualified employee pension/profit-sharing plans*)
- IC § 3(a)(1) (*def. **"investment company"***)
  - IC Rule 3a-4 Status of Investment Advisory Programs (*non-exclusive **safe-harbor** from IC definition for advisory programs meeting Rule 3a-4's requirements*)
- "Exempted Securities"
  - SA § 3(a)(2) (*"exempted securities" include: **interest or participation** in bank common trust fund and collective investment fund excluded from IC by IC Act **§ 3(c)(3) or § 3(c)(11)**; "bank" as defined by IC Act*)
  - SEA § 3(a)(12)(A)(iii) (*"exempted securities" include: **interest or participation** in bank common trust fund and collective investment fund excluded from IC by IC Act **§ 3(c)(3) or § 3(c)(11)***); § 3(a)(6) (*def. "bank"*)

Bank & IA Exclusion

- IA § 202(a)(11)(A) (*def. **"investment adviser"**: bank and bank holding company generally excluded but not excluded if serving as IA to registered IC; bank may register its "separately identifiable department or division" **(SID)** as IA*)
  - § 202(a)(2) (*def. "bank"*); § 202(a)(26) (*def. " 'separately identifiable department or division' of a bank"*)
- IC § 2(a)(20) (*def. **"investment adviser of an investment company"**: bank and bank holding company **not** excluded*)

Banking Law & Regulation

- 12 USC § 92a National Bank Act: Trust Powers
https://www.gpo.gov/fdsys/pkg/USCODE-2011-title12/pdf/USCODE-2011-title12-chap2-subchapIV-sec92a.pdf
    - 12 USC § 92a(a) Authority of Comptroller of the Currency
- 12 CFR Pt 9 OCC Regulation 9: Fiduciary Activities of National Banks
https://www.gpo.gov/fdsys/pkg/CFR-2015-title12-vol1/pdf/CFR-2015-title12-vol1-part9.pdf
    - 12 CFR § 9.2 Definitions (§ 9.2(d) "*fiduciary account*"; § 9.2(e) "*fiduciary capacity*"; § 9.2(g) "*fiduciary powers*")
    - 12 CFR § 9.11 Investment of Fiduciary Funds
    - 12 CFR § 9.18 Collective Investment Funds
        - ✓ § 9.18(a)(1) (*"**(a)(1) funds**" or "**common trust funds**": to commingle assets of personal trust accounts*)
        - ✓ § 9.18(a)(2) (*"**(a)(2) funds**" or "**collective investment funds**": to consist solely of assets of tax-qualified employee benefit plans*)
- Comptroller's Handbook: Asset Management (AM)
https://www.occ.treas.gov/publications/publications-by-type/comptrollers-handbook/index-comptrollers-handbook.html
    - Collective Investment Funds (AM-CIF May 2014)

Topic 1 Fiduciary Trust Services *vs* Investment Management Services

Case Study:* Bank-Sponsored Investment Management Service Creating an Issuer of Securities

The Supreme Court defines the scope of permissible bank collective investment activities: A national bank may, consistently with the banking laws, pool trust assets, act as a managing agent for individual customers, and purchase stock for the account of its customers. But the union of those powers gives birth to an investment fund of commingled managing agency accounts, the "units of participation" wherein constitute "securities." In underwriting the investment fund securities, the bank was selling "investments" rather than selling "fiduciary services," and ran afoul of the Glass-Steagall Act § 16's prohibition of commercial bank participating in investment banking.

The **Glass-Steagall Act of 1933** [PL 66-89, 48 Stat. 184 (1933)]:[1]

- ***prohibited*** *commercial banks* from underwriting or buying and selling equity securities for their own accounts (§ 16), and prohibited *investment banks* from engaging in commercial banking activities (§ 21);

- ***prohibited*** *affiliation* between commercial banks and investment banks (§ 20), and prohibited *interlocking officer or director* between commercial banks and investment banks (§ 32).

The **Gramm-Leach-Bliley Act of 1999 (GLB Act)** [PL 106-102, 113 Stat. 1338 (1999)]:[1]

- ***repealed*** §§ 20 and 32 of Glass-Steagall Act, "to make way for a modern regulatory framework capable of accommodating a consolidated financial services industry"; but
- ***retains*** §§ 16 and 21 prohibitions.

The 1999 GLB Act expands powers of bank holding companies (**BHCs**) under the Bank Holding Company Act, by allowing a BHC to *elect* to become a "***financial holding company***" (**FHC**). An FHC may engage, directly or through a nonbank subsidiary, in any activity that is "financial in nature" and in any activity that is "complementary or incidental" to the financial activity. Thus, an FHC may engage in, for example, investment company management by itself, the bank, or a "*separately identifiable department or division*" of a bank (**SID**), subject to registration of the FHC, the bank, or the SID as an "*investment adviser*" under the Investment Advisers Act.[2]

The **Bank and Savings Association Holding Company and Depository Institution Regulatory Improvements Act of 2010**, **§ 619** "*Prohibitions on Proprietary Trading and Certain Relationships with Hedge Funds and Private Equity Funds*" [Dodd-Frank Wall Street Reform and Consumer Protection Act, PL 111-203, Title VI § 619, 124 Stat. 1376, 1620—1631 (2010)] ***prohibits*** "***banking entities***" from, among others, ***sponsoring*** a ***hedge fund*** or a ***private equity fund***—commonly known as the "**Volcker Rule**."[1; 2; 3; 4] The prohibition has two objectives: (i) to prevent banking entities from circumventing Volcker Rule's restrictions on proprietary trading by shifting their trading activities to banking entity-run hedge funds; and (ii) to limit banking entities' exposure to the risky investing strategies many hedge funds and private equity funds employ.[5]

Under § 619, the term "***banking entity***" is defined to mean any insured depository institution; any company that controls an insured depository institution, or that is treated as a bank holding company for purposes of § 8 of the International Banking Act of 1978; and any affiliate or subsidiary of any such entity. The term to "***sponsor***" a fund means (A) to serve as a general partner, managing member, or trustee of a fund; (B) in any manner to select or to control (or to have employees, officers, or directors, or agents who constitute) a majority of the directors, trustees, or management of a fund; or (C) to share with a fund, for corporate, marketing, promotional, or other purposes, the same name or a variation of the same name. The terms "***hedge fund***" and "***private equity fund***" mean an issuer that would be an investment company as defined in the IC Act but for § 3(c)(1) or § 3(c)(7) of the Act, or such similar funds as the Board of Governors of the Federal Reserve System, the Office of the Comptroller of the Currency of the Department of the Treasury, the Federal Deposit Insurance Corporation, the Securities and Exchange Commission, and the Commodity Futures Trading Commission may by rule determine.

*[**1.** FEIN, SECURITIES ACTIVITIES OF BANKS §§ 4.01-4.03, 7.01, 7.08 (4ed 2014); **2.** FRANKEL & LABY, THE REGULATION OF MONEY MANAGERS—MUTUAL FUNDS AND ADVISERS, §§ 1.05[B][12], [19] (3d. 2017); **3.** FSOC, STUDY & RECOMMENDATIONS ON PROHIBITIONS ON PROPRIETARY TRADING & CERTAIN RELATIONSHIPS WITH HEDGE FUNDS & PRIVATE EQUITY FUNDS (2011); **4.** OCC, Federal Reserve System, FDIC & SEC, *Prohibitions and Restrictions on Proprietary Trading and Certain Interests in, and Relationships with, Hedge Funds and Private Equity Funds*, BHCA-1, 79 FR 5536 (2014); **5.** FED, FDIC & OCC, REPORT TO THE CONGRESS AND THE FINANCIAL STABILITY OVERSIGHT COUNCIL PURSUANT TO SECTION 620 OF THE DODD-FRANK ACT (2016)]

Investment Co. Inst. v. Camp

401 U.S. 617 (1971)

[***Procedural history***: Investment Co. Inst. v. Camp, 274 F. Supp. 624 (D.D.C. 1967), *rev'd sub nom.* National Ass'n of Sec. Dealers v. SEC, 420 F.2d 83 (D.C. Cir. 1969), *rev'd sub nom.* Investment Co. Inst. v. Camp, 401 U.S. 617 (1971)]

Investment Co. Inst. v. Camp, Comptroller of the Currency

401 U.S. 617 (1971)

JUDGES: STEWART, J., delivered the opinion of the Court, in which BLACK, DOUGLAS, BRENNAN, WHITE, and MARSHALL, JJ., joined. HARLAN, J., and BLACKMUN, J., filed dissenting opinions. BURGER, C. J., took no part in the consideration or decision of these cases.

OPINION

Mr. Justice STEWART delivered the opinion of the Court.

These companion cases involve a double-barreled assault upon the efforts of a national bank to go into the business of operating a mutual investment fund. The petitioners in No. 61 are an association of open-end investment companies and several individual such companies. They brought an action in the United States District Court for the District of Columbia, attacking portions of Regulation 9 issued by the Comptroller of the Currency,[1] on the ground that this Regulation, in purporting to authorize banks to establish and operate collective investment funds, sought to permit activities prohibited to national banks or their affiliates by various provisions of the Glass-Steagall Banking Act of 1933, 48 Stat. 162.[2] The petitioners also specifically attacked the Comptroller's approval of the application of First National City Bank of New York for permission to establish and operate a collective investment fund. In No. 59 the National Association of Securities Dealers filed a petition in the United States Court of Appeals for the District of Columbia Circuit seeking review of an order of the Securities and Exchange Commission that partially exempted the collective investment fund of First National City Bank of New York from various provisions of the Investment Company Act of 1940.[3]

In No. 61 the District Court concluded that the challenged provisions of Regulation 9 were invalid under the Glass-Steagall Act.[4] The Comptroller and First National City Bank appealed from this decision, and the appeal was consolidated with the petition for review

---

[1] 12 CFR Pt. 9 (1970).

[2] The provisions of the Glass-Steagall Act are codified in various sections scattered through Title 12 of the United States Code.

[3] The exemption was granted in response to an application filed pursuant to § 6(c) of the Act, 54 Stat. 802, 15 USC § 80a-6(c).

[4] 274 F. Supp. 624 (D. DC 1967).

in No. 59. The Court of Appeals held that the actions taken by the Securities and Exchange Commission and the Comptroller were fully consonant with the statutes committed to their regulatory supervision. Accordingly, it affirmed the order of the Commission and reversed the judgment of the District Court.[5] We granted certiorari to consider important questions presented under federal regulatory statutes.[6] For the reasons that follow, we hold Regulation 9 invalid insofar as it authorizes the sale of interests in an investment fund of the type established by First National City Bank pursuant to the Comptroller's approval. This disposition makes it unnecessary to consider the propriety of the action of the Securities and Exchange Commission in affording this fund exemption from certain of the provisions of the Investment Company Act of 1940.

I.

In No. 61 it is urged at the outset that petitioners lack standing to question whether national banks may legally enter a field in competition with them. This contention is foreclosed by *Data Processing Service v. Camp*, 397 U.S. 150 (1970). There we held that companies that offered data processing services to the general business community had standing to seek judicial review of a ruling by the Comptroller that national banks could make data processing services available to other banks and to bank customers. We held that data processing companies were sufficiently injured by the competition that the Comptroller had authorized to create a case or controversy. The injury to the petitioners in the instant case is indistinguishable. We also concluded that Congress did not intend "to preclude judicial review of administrative rulings by the Comptroller as to the legitimate scope of activities available to national banks under [the National Bank Act]"; *id.* This is precisely the review that the petitioners have sought in this case. Finally, we concluded that Congress had arguably legislated against the competition that the petitioners sought to challenge, and from which flowed their injury. We noted that whether Congress had indeed prohibited such competition was a question for the merits. In the discussion that follows in the balance of this opinion we deal with the merits of the petitioners' contentions and conclude that Congress did legislate against the competition that the petitioners challenge. There can be no real question, therefore, of the

---

5 420 F.2d 83 (DC Cir. 1969).

6 397 U.S. 986 (1970).

petitioners' standing in the light of the Data Processing case. See also *Arnold Tours v. Camp*, 400 U.S. 45 (1970).

II.

The issue before us is whether the Comptroller of the Currency may, consistently with the banking laws, authorize a national bank to offer its customers the opportunity to invest in a stock fund created and maintained by the bank. Before 1963 national banks were prohibited by administrative regulation from offering this service. The Board of Governors of the Federal Reserve System, which until 1962 had regulatory jurisdiction over all the trust activities of national banks, allowed the collective investment of trust assets only for "the investment of funds held for true fiduciary purposes." The applicable regulation, Regulation F, specified that "the operation of such Common Trust Funds as investment trusts for other than strictly fiduciary purposes is hereby prohibited." The Board consistently ruled that it was improper for a bank to use "a Common Trust Fund as an investment trust attracting money seeking investment alone and to embark upon what would be in effect the sale of participations in a Common Trust Fund to the public as investments." 26 Fed. Res. Bull. 393 (1940); see also 42 Fed. Res. Bull. 228 (1956); 41 Fed. Res. Bull. 142 (1955).

In 1962 Congress transferred jurisdiction over most of the trust activities of national banks from the Board of Governors of the Federal Reserve System to the Comptroller of the Currency, without modifying any provision of substantive law. PL. 87-722, 76 Stat. 668, 12 USC § 92a. The Comptroller thereupon solicited suggestions for improving the regulations applicable to trust activities. Subsequently, new regulations were proposed which expressly authorized the collective investment of monies delivered to the bank for investment management, so-called managing agency accounts. These proposed regulations were officially promulgated in 1963 with changes not material here.[7] In 1965 the First National City Bank of New York submitted for the Comptroller's approval a plan for the collective investment of managing agency accounts. The Comptroller promptly approved the plan, and it is now in operation. This plan, which departs in some

---

[7] 12 CFR § 9.18 (a) provides that: "Where not in contravention of local law, funds held by a national bank as fiduciary may be invested collectively: ... (3) In a common trust fund, maintained by the bank exclusively for the collective investment and reinvestment of monies contributed thereto by the bank in its capacity as managing agent under a managing agency agreement expressly providing that such monies are received by the bank in trust ...."

respects from the plan envisaged by the Comptroller's Regulation, is expected, the briefs tell us, to be a model for other banks which decide to offer their customers a collective investment service.[8]

Under the plan the bank customer tenders between $10,000 and $500,000 to the bank, together with an authorization making the bank the customer's managing agent. The customer's investment is added to the fund, and a written evidence of participation is issued which expresses in "units of participation" the customer's proportionate interest in fund assets. Units of participation are freely redeemable, and transferable to anyone who has executed a managing agency agreement with the bank. The fund is registered as an investment company under the Investment Company Act of 1940. The bank is the underwriter of the fund's units of participation within the meaning of that Act. The fund has filed a registration statement pursuant to the Securities Act of 1933. The fund is supervised by a five-member committee elected annually by the participants pursuant to the Investment Company Act of 1940. The Securities and Exchange Commission has exempted the fund from the Investment Company Act to the extent that a majority of this committee may be affiliated with the bank, and it is expected that a majority always will be officers in the bank's trust and investment division.[9] The actual custody and investment of fund assets is carried out by the bank as investment advisor pursuant to a management agreement. Although the Investment Company Act requires that this management agreement be approved annually by the committee, including a majority of the unaffiliated members, or by the participants, it is expected that the bank will continue to be investment advisor.

III.

Section 16 of the Glass-Steagall Act as amended, 12 USC § 24, Seventh, provides that the "business of dealing in securities and stock [by a national bank] shall be limited to purchasing and selling such securities and stock without recourse, solely upon the order, and for the account of, customers, and in no case for its own account .... Except as hereinafter provided or otherwise permitted by law, nothing herein contained shall

---

[8] For example, the investment fund plan as established does not provide that the bank receives the investor's money in trust.

[9] The opinion of the Commission and the dissent of Commissioner Budge are unofficially reported at CCH Fed. Sec. L. Rep., 1964-1966 Decisions, ¶ 77,332.

authorize the purchase by [a national bank] for its own account of any shares of stock of any corporation."[10] The petitioners contend that a purchase of stock by a bank's investment fund is a purchase of stock by a bank for its own account in violation of this section.

Section 16 also provides that a national bank "shall not underwrite any issue of securities or stock." And § 21 of the same Act, 12 USC § 378(a), provides that "it shall be unlawful—(1) For any person, firm, corporation, association, business trust, or other similar organization, engaged in the business of issuing, underwriting, selling, or distributing, at wholesale or retail, or through syndicate participation, stocks, bonds, debentures, notes, or other securities, to engage at the same time to any extent whatever in the business of [deposit banking]." The petitioners contend that the creation and operation of an investment fund by a bank which offers to its customers the opportunity to purchase an interest in the fund's assets constitutes the issuing, underwriting, selling, or distributing of securities or stocks in violation of these sections.

The questions raised by the petitioners are novel and substantial. National banks were granted trust powers in 1913. Federal Reserve Act, § 11, 38 Stat. 261. The first common trust fund was organized in 1927, and such funds were expressly authorized by the Federal Reserve Board by Regulation F promulgated in 1937. REPORT ON COMMINGLED OR COMMON TRUST FUNDS ADMINISTERED BY BANKS AND TRUST COMPANIES, H.R. Doc. No. 476, 76th Cong., 2d Sess., 4-5 (1939). For at least a generation, therefore, there has been no reason to doubt that a national bank can, consistently with the banking laws, commingle trust funds on the one hand, and act as a managing agent on the other. No provision of the banking law suggests that it is improper for a national bank to pool trust assets, or to act as a managing agent for individual customers, or to purchase stock for the account of its customers. But the union of these powers gives birth to an investment fund whose activities are of a different character. The differences between the investment fund that the Comptroller has authorized and a conventional open-end mutual fund are subtle at best, and it is undisputed that this bank investment fund finds itself in direct competition with the mutual fund industry. One would suppose that the business of a mutual fund

---

[10] Section 16, as enacted in 1933, granted no authority to purchase stock for the account of customers and prohibited any purchase of stock by a national bank. The 1935 Amendments to the National Bank Act included a provision intended to make it clear that a national bank may buy stock for the account of customers but not for its own account. S. Rep. No. 1007, 74th Cong., 1st Sess., 17; H.R. Rep. No. 742, 74th Cong., 1st Sess., 18.

consists of buying stock "for its own account" and of "issuing" and "selling" "stock" or "other securities" evidencing an undivided and redeemable interest in the assets of the fund.[11] On their face, § § 16 and 21 of the Glass-Steagall Act appear clearly to prohibit this activity by national banks.[12]

But we cannot come lightly to the conclusion that the Comptroller has authorized activity that violates the banking laws. It is settled that courts should give great weight to

---

[11] A mutual fund is an open-end investment company. The Investment Company Act of 1940 defines an investment company as an "issuer" of "any security" which "is or holds itself out as being engaged primarily ... in the business of investing ... in securities ...." 15 USC § § 80a-2(a)(21), 80a-3(a)(1). An open-end company is one "which is offering for sale or has outstanding any redeemable security of which it is the issuer." 15 USC § 80a-5(a)(1). An investment company also includes a "unit investment trust": an investment company which, among other things, "is organized under a ... contract of ... agency ... and ... issues only redeemable securities, each of which represents an undivided interest in a unit of specified securities ...." 15 USC § 80a-4(2).

[12] Section 20 of the Act, 12 USC § 377, prohibits affiliations between banks that are members of the Federal Reserve System and organizations "engaged principally in the issue, flotation, underwriting, public sale, or distribution at wholesale or retail or through syndicate participation of stocks, bonds, debentures, notes, or other securities ...." And § 32, 12 USC § 78, provides that no officer, director, or employee of a bank in the Federal Reserve System may serve at the same time as officer, director, or employee of an association primarily engaged in the activity described in § 20. The petitioners contend that if a bank's investment fund be conceived as an entity distinct from the bank, then its affiliation with the investment fund is in violation of these sections.

The Board of Governors has had occasion to consider whether an investment fund of the type operated by First National City Bank involves a violation of § 32 of the Glass-Steagall Act. 12 CFR § 218.111 (1970). The Board concluded, based on "general principles that have been developed in respect to the application of Section 32," that it would not violate that section for officers of the bank's trust department to serve at the same time as officers of the investment fund because the fund and the bank "constitute a single entity," and the fund "would be regarded as nothing more than an arm or department of the bank." The Board called attention to § 21 whose provisions it summarized as forbidding "a securities firm or organization to engage in the business of receiving deposits, subject to certain exceptions." The Board, however, declined to express a position concerning the applicability of this section because of its policy not to express views as to the meaning of statutes that carry criminal penalties. Nor has the Board expressed its views on the application of any other provision of the banking law to the creation and operation of a bank investment fund.

We have no doubt but that the Board's construction and application of § 32 is both reasonable and rational. The investment fund service authorized by the Comptroller's regulation and as provided by the First National City Bank is a service available only to customers of the bank. It is held out as a service provided by the bank, and the investment fund bears the bank's name. The bank has effective control over the activities of the investment fund. Moreover, there is no danger that to characterize the bank and its fund as a single entity will disserve the purpose of Congress. The limitations that the banking laws place on the activities of national banks are at least as great as the limitations placed on the activities of their affiliates. For example, § 32 refers to the "public sale" of stocks or securities while § 21 proscribes the "selling" of stocks or securities.

any reasonable construction of a regulatory statute adopted by the agency charged with the enforcement of that statute. The Comptroller of the Currency is charged with the enforcement of the banking laws to an extent that warrants the invocation of this principle with respect to his deliberative conclusions as to the meaning of these laws. See *First Nat'l Bank v. Missouri*, 263 U.S. 640 (1924).

The difficulty here is that the Comptroller adopted no expressly articulated position at the administrative level as to the meaning and impact of the provisions of § § 16 and 21 as they affect bank investment funds. The Comptroller promulgated Regulation 9 without opinion or accompanying statement. His subsequent report to Congress did not advert to the prohibitions of the Glass-Steagall Act. COMPTROLLER OF THE CURRENCY, 101ST ANNUAL REPORT 14-15 (1963).[13] To be sure, counsel for the Comptroller in the course of this litigation, and specifically in his briefs and oral argument in this Court, has rationalized the basis of Regulation 9 with great professional competence. But this is hardly tantamount to an administrative interpretation of § § 16 and 21. In *Burlington Truck Lines v. United States*, 371 U.S. 156 (1962), we said, "The courts may not accept appellate counsel's post hoc rationalizations for agency action .... For the courts to substitute their or counsel's discretion for that of the [agency] is incompatible with the

---

[13] A law review article written by Comptroller Saxon and Deputy Comptroller Miller in 1965 did take the position that the Glass-Steagall Act is inapplicable to bank common trust funds. Saxon & Miller, *Common Trust Funds*, 53 GEO. L.J. 994 (1965). But this view was predicated on the argument that when Congress in 1936 provided a tax exemption for common trust funds maintained by a bank, now 26 USC § 584, it contemplated the exemption of common trust funds created for strictly investment purposes, and that consequently Congress must have assumed that the banking laws, which otherwise appear to proscribe such funds, were not applicable. *Id.*, at 1008-1010. Whatever the merits of this argument, it has no bearing on the instant litigation. It is clear that the collective investment funds authorized by Regulation 9 need not qualify for tax exemption under § 584; the First National City Bank Fund does not so qualify. Moreover, the position advanced in the brief filed on behalf of the Comptroller in this litigation is not that the banking laws are inapplicable to bank investment funds, but rather that the creation and operation of such funds are consistent with the banking laws.

It is noteworthy that the § 584 exemption is available to common trust funds "maintained by a bank ... exclusively for the collective investment and reinvestment of moneys contributed thereto by the bank in its capacity as a ***trustee, executor, administrator, or guardian*** ...." (Emphasis added.) This language, which makes no reference to contributions by the bank in its capacity as managing agent, is identical to that exempting such common trust funds from the Investment Company Act of 1940, 15 USC § 80a-3(c)(3). The Securities and Exchange Commission has taken the position that commingled managing agency accounts do not come within § 80a-3(c)(3). See Statement of Commissioner Cary, Hearings on Common Trust Funds—Overlapping Responsibility and Conflict in Regulation, before a Subcommittee of the House Committee on Government Operations, 88th Cong., 1st Sess., 3 (1963).

orderly functioning of the process of judicial review." Congress has delegated to the administrative official and not to appellate counsel the responsibility for elaborating and enforcing statutory commands. It is the administrative official and not appellate counsel who possesses the expertise that can enlighten and rationalize the search for the meaning and intent of Congress. Quite obviously the Comptroller should not grant new authority to national banks until he is satisfied that the exercise of this authority will not violate the intent of the banking laws. If he faces such questions only after he has acted, there is substantial danger that the momentum generated by initial approval may seriously impair the enforcement of the banking laws that Congress enacted.

IV.

There is no dispute that one of the objectives of the Glass-Steagall Act was to prohibit commercial banks, banks that receive deposits subject to repayment, lend money, discount and negotiate promissory notes and the like, from going into the investment banking business. Many commercial banks were indirectly engaged in the investment banking business when the Act was passed in 1933. Even before the passage of the Act it was generally believed that it was improper for a commercial bank to engage in investment banking directly.[14] But in 1908 banks began the practice of establishing security affiliates that engaged in, inter alia, the business of floating bond issues and, less frequently, underwriting stock issues. The Glass-Steagall Act confirmed that national banks could not engage in investment banking directly, and in addition made affiliation with an organization so engaged illegal. One effect of the Act was to abolish the security affiliates of commercial banks.[15]

It is apparent from the legislative history of the Act why Congress felt that this drastic step was necessary. The failure of the Bank of United States in 1930 was widely attributed to that bank's activities with respect to its numerous securities affiliates.[16] Moreover, Congress was concerned that commercial banks in general and member banks of the Federal Reserve System in particular had both aggravated and been damaged by

---

[14] Hearings Pursuant to S. Res. 71 before a Subcommittee of the Senate Committee on Banking and Currency (hereafter ***1931 Hearings***), 71st Cong., 3d Sess., 40 (1931); 1920 Report of the Comptroller of the Currency. Senator Glass, commenting on earlier banking legislation, said, "We tried to, and thought at the time we had, removed the system as far as possible from the influence of the stock market." *Id.*, at 262.

[15] REPORT ON INVESTMENT TRUSTS AND INVESTMENT COMPANIES, pt.2, H.R. Doc. No. 70, 76th Cong., 1st Sess., 59 (1939).

[16] 1931 Hearings.

stock market decline partly because of their direct and indirect involvement in the trading and ownership of speculative securities.[17] The Glass-Steagall Act reflected a determination that policies of competition, convenience, or expertise which might otherwise support the entry of commercial banks into the investment banking business were outweighed by the "hazards" and "financial dangers" that arise when commercial banks engage in the activities proscribed by the Act.[18]

The hazards that Congress had in mind were not limited to the obvious danger that a bank might invest its own assets in frozen or otherwise imprudent stock or security investments. For often securities affiliates had operated without direct access to the assets of the bank. This was because securities affiliates had frequently been established with capital paid in by the bank's stockholders, or by the public, or through the allocation of a legal dividend on bank stock for this purpose.[19] The legislative history of the Glass-Steagall Act shows that Congress also had in mind and repeatedly focused on the more subtle hazards that arise when a commercial bank goes beyond the business of acting as fiduciary or managing agent and enters the investment banking business either directly or by establishing an affiliate to hold and sell particular investments. This course places new promotional and other pressures on the bank which in turn create new temptations. For example, pressures are created because the bank and the affiliate are closely associated in the public mind, and should the affiliate fare badly, public confidence in the bank might be impaired. And since public confidence is essential to the solvency of a bank, there might exist a natural temptation to shore up the affiliate through unsound loans or other aid.[20] Moreover, the pressure to sell a particular investment and to make the affiliate successful might create a risk that the bank would make its credit facilities more freely available to those companies in whose stock or securities the affiliate has invested or become otherwise involved. Congress feared that banks might even go so far

---

[17] See S. Rep. No. 77, 73d Cong., 1st Sess.

[18] *Id.*; see 1931 Hearings; 75 Cong. Rec. 9911 (remarks of Sen. Bulkley).

[19] 1931 Hearings; 1920 Report of the Comptroller of the Currency.

[20] 1931 Hearings: "Activities of a bank's security affiliate as a holding or finance company or an investment trust are also fraught with the danger of large losses during a deflation period. Bank affiliates of this kind show a much greater tendency to operate with borrowed funds than do organizations of this type which are independent of banks, the reason being that the identity of control and management which prevails between the bank and its affiliate tends to encourage reliance upon the lending facilities of the former."

as to make unsound loans to such companies.[21] In any event, it was thought that the bank's salesman's interest might impair its ability to function as an impartial source of credit.[22]

Congress was also concerned that bank depositors might suffer losses on investments that they purchased in reliance on the relationship between the bank and its affiliate.[23] This loss of customer good will might "become an important handicap to a bank during a major period of security market deflation."[24] More broadly, Congress feared that the promotional needs of investment banking might lead commercial banks to lend their reputation for prudence and restraint to the enterprise of selling particular stocks and securities, and that this could not be done without that reputation being undercut by the risks necessarily incident to the investment banking business.[25] There was also perceived the danger that when commercial banks were subject to the promotional demands of investment banking, they might be tempted to make loans to customers with the expectation that the loan would facilitate the purchase of stocks and securities.[26] There was evidence before Congress that loans for investment written by commercial banks had done much to feed the speculative fever of the late 1920's.[27] Senator Glass made it plain that it was "the fixed purpose of Congress" not to see the facilities of commercial banking diverted into speculative operations by the aggressive and promotional character of the investment banking business.[28]

---

21 75 Cong. Rec. 9912 (remarks of Sen. Bulkley).

22 See 1931 Hearings 87 (remarks of Chairman Glass).

23 See 77 Cong. Rec. 4028 (remarks of Rep. Fish).

24 1931 Hearings.

25 See 75 Cong. Rec. 9912: "And although such a loss would possibly not result in any substantial impairment of the resources of the banking institution owning that affiliate ... there can be no doubt that the whole transaction tends to discredit the bank and impair the confidence of its depositors." (Remarks of Sen. Bulkley)

26 S. Rep. No. 77, 73d Cong., 1st Sess.

27 1931 Hearings; S. Rep. No. 77, 73d Cong., 1st Sess.

28 75 Cong. Rec. 9884. See also S. Rep. No. 77, 73d Cong., 1st Sess., 8: "The outstanding development in the commercial banking system during the pre-panic period was the appearance of excessive security loans, and of overinvestment in securities of all kinds. The effects of this situation in changing the whole character of the banking problem can hardly be overemphasized. National banks were never intended to undertake investment banking business on a large scale, and the whole tenor of legislation and administrative rulings concerning them has been away from recognition of such a growth in the direction of investment banking as legitimate."

Another potential hazard that very much concerned Congress arose from the plain conflict between the promotional interest of the investment banker and the obligation of the commercial banker to render disinterested investment advice. Senator Bulkley stated:

> "Obviously, the banker who has nothing to sell to his depositors is much better qualified to advise disinterestedly and to regard diligently the safety of depositors than the banker who uses the list of depositors in his savings department to distribute circulars concerning the advantages of this, that, or the other investment on which the bank is to receive an originating profit or an underwriting profit or a distribution profit or a trading profit or any combination of such profits."[29]

Congress had before it evidence that security affiliates might be driven to unload excessive holdings through the trust department of the sponsor bank.[30] Some witnesses at the hearings expressed the view that this practice constituted self-dealing in violation of the trustee's obligation of loyalty, and indeed that it would be improper for a bank's trust department to purchase anything from the bank's securities affiliate.

In sum, Congress acted to keep commercial banks out of the investment banking business largely because it believed that the promotional incentives of investment banking and the investment banker's pecuniary stake in the success of particular investment opportunities was destructive of prudent and disinterested commercial banking and of public confidence in the commercial banking system. As Senator Bulkley put it:

> "If we want banking service to be strictly banking service, without the expectation of additional profits in selling something to customers, we must keep the banks out of the investment security business."[31]

V.

The language that Congress chose to achieve this purpose includes the prohibitions of § 16 that a national bank "shall not underwrite any issue of securities or stock" and shall

---

In the same vein Representative Steagall said: "Our great banking system was diverted from its original purposes into investment activities ...." "The purpose of the regulatory provisions of this bill is to call back to the service of agriculture and commerce and industry the bank credit and the bank service designed by the framers of the Federal Reserve Act." 77 Cong. Rec. 3835.

[29] 75 Cong. Rec. 9912.

[30] 1931 Hearings.

[31] 75 Cong. Rec. 9912.

not purchase "for its own account ... any shares of stock of any corporation," and the prohibition of § 21 against engaging in "the business of issuing, underwriting, selling, or distributing ... stocks, bonds, debentures, notes, or other securities." In this litigation the Comptroller takes the position that the operation of a bank investment fund is consistent with these provisions, because participating interests in such a fund are not "securities" within the meaning of the Act. It is argued that a bank investment fund simply makes available to the small investor the benefit of investment management by a bank trust department which would otherwise be available only to large investors, and that the operation of an investment fund creates no problems that are not present whenever a bank invests in securities for the account of customers.

But there is nothing in the phrasing of either § 16 or § 21 that suggests a narrow reading of the word "securities." To the contrary, the breadth of the term is implicit in the fact that the antecedent statutory language encompasses not only equity securities but also securities representing debt. And certainly there is nothing in the language of these provisions to suggest that the sale of an interest in the business of buying, holding, and selling stocks for investment is to be distinguished from the sale of an interest in a commercial or industrial enterprise.

Indeed, there is direct evidence that Congress specifically contemplated that the word "security" includes an interest in an investment fund. The Glass-Steagall Act was the product of hearings conducted pursuant to Senate Resolution 71 which included among the topics to be investigated the impact on the banking system of the formation of investment and security trusts.[32] The subcommittee found that one of the activities in which bank security affiliates engaged was that of an investment trust: "buying and selling securities acquired purely for investment or speculative purposes."[33] Since Congress generally intended to divorce commercial banking from the kinds of activities in which bank security affiliates engaged, there is reason to believe that Congress explicitly intended to prohibit a national bank from operating an investment trust.[34]

But, in any event, we are persuaded that the purposes for which Congress enacted the Glass-Steagall Act leave no room for the conclusion that a participation in a bank

---

[32] S. Res. 71, 71st Cong., 2d Sess., is reprinted in S. Rep. No. 77, 73d Cong., 1st Sess., 1.

[33] 1931 Hearings.

[34] See also *supra*, n. 20.

investment fund is not a "security" within the meaning of the Act. From the perspective of competition, convenience, and expertise, there are arguments to be made in support of allowing commercial banks to enter the investment banking business. But Congress determined that the hazards outlined above made it necessary to prohibit this activity to commercial banks. Those same hazards are clearly present when a bank undertakes to operate an investment fund.

A bank that operates an investment fund has a particular investment to sell. It is not a matter of indifference to the bank whether the customer buys an interest in the fund or makes some other investment. If its customers cannot be persuaded to invest in the bank's investment fund, the bank will lose their investment business and the fee which that business would have brought in. Even as to accounts large enough to qualify for individual investment management, there might be a potential for a greater profit if the investment were placed in the fund rather than in individually selected securities, because of fixed costs and economies of scale. The mechanics of operating an investment fund might also create promotional pressure. When interests in the fund were redeemed, the bank would be effectively faced with the choice of selling stocks from the fund's portfolio or of selling new participations to cover redemptions. The bank might have a pecuniary incentive to choose the latter course in order to avoid the cost of stock transactions undertaken solely for redemption purposes.

Promotional incentives might also be created by the circumstance that the bank's fund would be in direct competition with mutual funds that, from the point of view of the investor, offered an investment opportunity comparable to that offered by the bank. The bank would want to be in a position to show to the prospective customer that its fund was more attractive than the mutual funds offered by others. The bank would have a salesman's stake in the performance of the fund, for if the fund were less successful than the competition the bank would lose business and the resulting fees.

A bank that operated an investment fund would necessarily put its reputation and facilities squarely behind that fund and the investment opportunity that the fund offered. The investments of the fund might be conservative or speculative, but in any event the success or failure of the fund would be a matter of public record. Imprudent or unsuccessful management of the bank's investment fund could bring about a perhaps unjustified loss of public confidence in the bank itself. If imprudent management should place the fund in distress, a bank might find itself under pressure to rescue the fund through measures inconsistent with sound banking.

The promotional and other pressures incidental to the operation of an investment fund, in other words, involve the same kinds of potential abuses that Congress intended to guard against when it legislated against bank security affiliates. It is not the slightest reflection on the integrity of the mutual fund industry to say that the traditions of that industry are not necessarily the conservative traditions of commercial banking. The needs and interests of a mutual fund enterprise more nearly approximate those of securities underwriting, the activity in which bank security affiliates were primarily engaged. When a bank puts itself in competition with mutual funds, the bank must make an accommodation to the kind of ground rules that Congress firmly concluded could not be prudently mixed with the business of commercial banking.

And there are other potential hazards of the kind Congress sought to eliminate with the passage of the Glass-Steagall Act. The bank's stake in the investment fund might distort its credit decisions or lead to unsound loans to the companies in which the fund had invested. The bank might exploit its confidential relationship with its commercial and industrial creditors for the benefit of the fund. The bank might undertake, directly or indirectly, to make its credit facilities available to the fund or to render other aid to the fund inconsistent with the best interests of the bank's depositors. The bank might make loans to facilitate the purchase of interests in the fund. The bank might divert talent and resources from its commercial banking operation to the promotion of the fund. Moreover, because the bank would have a stake in a customer's making a particular investment decision—the decision to invest in the bank's investment fund—the customer might doubt the motivation behind the bank's recommendation that he make such an investment. If the fund investment should turn out badly there would be a danger that the bank would lose the good will of those customers who had invested in the fund. It might be unlikely that disenchantment would go so far as to threaten the solvency of the bank. But because banks are dependent on the confidence of their customers, the risk would not be unreal.

These are all hazards that are not present when a bank undertakes to purchase stock for the account of its individual customers or to commingle assets which it has received for a true fiduciary purpose rather than for investment. These activities, unlike the operation of an investment fund, do not give rise to a promotional or salesman's stake in a particular investment; they do not involve an enterprise in direct competition with aggressively promoted funds offered by other investment companies; they do not entail a threat to public confidence in the bank itself; and they do not impair the bank's ability to give disinterested service as a fiduciary or managing agent. In short, there is a plain difference between the sale of fiduciary services and the sale of investments.[35]

VI.

The Glass-Steagall Act was a prophylactic measure directed against conditions that the experience of the 1920's showed to be great potentials for abuse. The literal terms of that Act clearly prevent what the Comptroller has sought to authorize here. Because the potential hazards and abuses that flow from a bank's entry into the mutual investment business are the same basic hazards and abuses that Congress intended to eliminate almost 40 years ago, we cannot but apply the terms of the federal statute as they were written. We conclude that the operation of an investment fund of the kind approved by the Comptroller involves a bank in the underwriting, issuing, selling, and distributing of securities in violation of § § 16 and 21 of the Glass-Steagall Act. Accordingly, we reverse the judgment in No. 61 and vacate the judgment in No. 59.

It is so ordered.

---

[35] See 26 Fed. Res. Bull. 393 (1940).

Topic 2 Trust Funds and Pension Funds Maintained by Bank

Pre-Case Background Note:[Biblio]

Certain Types of Bank-Sponsored Pooled Investment Vehicles: Status under Investment Company Act and Securities Act

Common trust fund *(commingling personal trust accounts)*

It is a vehicle for the collective investment of the personal trust assets of multiple trusts, as a means of efficient administration of smaller trusts and an alternative to the high-cost, individualized investment management of large trust accounts. IC Act § 3(c)(3) excludes such common trust fund from the definition of "investment company," and Securities Act § 3(a)(2) treats interests in such common trust fund as "exempted securities," where the common trust fund is maintained by a bank ***exclusively*** for bona fide fiduciary purposes in its traditional capacity as trustee, executor, administrator, or guardian.[1; 2 (Pt II); 3; 4; 5]

Managing agent fund *(commingling managing agency accounts)*

Individual "managing agency accounts" are operated by a bank pursuant to powers of attorney conferring investment discretion on the bank as "managing agent" for the customers to hold and manage their respective portfolios of investments.[6] Managing agency account services involve something less than the usual trustee-type relationship, and are functional equivalents of investment advisory services offered by investment advisers.[2 (Pt II); 3] Pooling of managing agency accounts creates an investment company required to register under the IC Act; participation interests in the managing agent fund are securities required to register under the Securities Act.[6]

Collective investment fund for corporate pension plans *(commingling tax code IRC § **401**-qualified "corporate employee" pension plan and "Keogh self-employed person" plan trusts)*

IC Act § 3(c)(11) excludes such collective investment trust fund from the definition of "investment company," and Securities Act § 3(a)(2) and SA Rule 180 "Exemption from Registration of Interests and Participations Issued in Connection with Certain H.R. 10 Plans" treat interests in such trust fund as "exempted securities," where the collective investment trust fund consists "***solely***" of the assets of the qualified corporate pension plans.[2 (Pt II); 4; 5, 7]

Individual retirement account (IRA) collective investment trust fund (*commingling tax code IRC **§ 408**-qualified IRA accounts*)

Individual retirement accounts are a category of pension plans which qualify under the tax code pursuant to the Employee Retirement Income Security Act of 1974 ("ERISA") for employed persons not covered by a corporate employee benefit plan, to encourage retirement savings. Where a bank operates a common trust fund commingling individual trust accounts, or a corporate pension plan collective investment fund commingling qualified corporate pension plans, in a manner incidental to the bank's traditional trust department activities, each such fund is excluded from investment company definition by IC Act § 3(c)(3) or § 3(c)(11).[8]

In contrast, an IRA trust does not establish a fiduciary relationship; a bank operates an IRA fund commingling individual retirement accounts primarily as an investment service for individual members of the public. An IRA collective investment fund thus constitutes an "investment company" required to register under the IC Act, and units of beneficial interest in an IRA fund constitute "securities" required to be registered under the Securities Act.[5; 9]

Small account investment management service (*with no physical pooling of the accounts*)

Computer technology has made it feasible for banks, as well as registered investment advisers, to provide individualized investment advisory services to a large number of investors with relatively small amounts of money to invest. Client accounts are managed on a discretionary basis based on each client's pre-selected investment objectives; clients with similar investment objectives often receive the same investment advice and may hold substantially the same securities in their accounts. On the one hand, such an advisory service can become functionally indistinguishable from an investment company—despite there being no pooling of the accounts in the conventional sense. On the other hand, notwithstanding some overlapping investment advice, the advisory service might be providing individualized service.

There was uncertainty whether a small account investment management service could constitute an "investment company" under the IC Act, and an issuer of "securities" or "investment contracts"—in the form of discretionary accounts—under the Securities Act.[2 (Pt II); 10] Investment Company Act Rule 3a-4, "Status of Investment Advisory Programs," grants such discretionary advisory programs a non-exclusive safe harbor from the definition of investment company, where clients in the program receive individualized management services, and each client retains certain indicia of ownership of all securities and funds in its account. The safe harbor rule is available to both registered investment advisers and banks.[11]

Bibliography

1. Saxon & Miller, *Common Trust Funds*, 53 GEO. L.J. 994 (1965)
2. Lybecker, *Bank-Sponsored Investment Management Services: Consideration of the Regulatory Problems, and Suggested Legislative and Statutory Interpretive Responses*, 1977 DUKE L.J. 983 (1977)
3. Wade, *Bank-Sponsored Collective Investment Funds: An Analysis of Applicable Federal Banking and Securities Laws*, 35 BUS. LAW. 361 (1980)
4. Freeman, *Bank Common Trust Funds and Collective Investment Funds*, 11 INV. LAW. 15 (2004)
5. RIES, REGULATION OF INVESTMENT MANAGEMENT & FIDUCIARY SERVICES, Ch.16 Bank Common and Collective Trust Funds (Regulation 9.18) (2014)
6. **6a.** In the Matter of First National City Bank (Commingled Investment Account), IC-4538, 42 SEC 924 (Mar 9, 1966); **6b.** Investment Co. Inst. v. Camp, 401 U.S. 617 (1971)
7. Exemption From Registration of Interests and Participations Issued in Connection With Certain H.R. 10 Plans, 33-6363, 46 FR 58287 (1981)
8. **8a.** Definition of Terms in and Specific Exemptions for Banks, Savings Associations, and Savings Banks Under Sections 3(a)(4) and 3(a)(5) of the Securities Exchange Act of 1934; Interim final rules with request for comments, 34-44291, 66 FR 27760, 27768 n.82 (2001); **8b.** In the Matter of the Commercial Bank et al., Adm. Proc. 3-8567, 33-7116, IC-20757 (1994)
9. **9a.** Investment Co. Inst. v. Conover, 790 F.2d 925 (DC Cir.1986), *cert. denied*, 479 US 939 (1986); **9b.** Investment Co. Inst. v. Clarke, 789 F.2d 175 (2d Cir.1986), *cert. denied*, 479 US 940 (1986); **9c.** Investment Co. Inst. v. Conover, 593 F. Supp. 846 (ND Ca. 1984), *rev'd sub nom.* Investment Co. Inst. v. Clarke, 793 F.2d 220 (9th Cir. 1986) (Norris, J., concur.; Coughenour, J., dissent.), *cert. denied*, 479 U.S. 939 (1986)
10. **10a.** First National City Bank, SEC Lit. Rel. 4534 (1970); **10b.** REPORT OF THE ADVISORY COMMITTEE ON INVESTMENT MANAGEMENT SERVICES FOR INDIVIDUAL INVESTORS: SMALL ACCOUNT INVESTMENT MANAGEMENT SERVICES, Pts. II-III, VII (1973)
11. Status of Investment Advisory Programs Under the Investment Company Act of 1940, IC-22579, IA-1623, 62 FR 15098, 15101 n.25 (1997)

Case Study 1: § 3(c)(11) Retirement Plan Fund "Maintained" by Bank

The no-action letter interprets the statutory requirement that a § 3(c)(11) fund consisting solely of qualified retirement plan assets be "***maintained***" by a bank in order for the fund to be excluded from the definition of "investment company" under the IC Act; and addresses the implication of a bank's use of an investment adviser for such a § 3(c)(11) fund.

National Bank of Commerce Investment Fund

Securities Act § 3(a)(2), SA Rule 180; Exchange Act § 12(g)(2)(H); IC Act § 3(c)(11)
1986 SEC No-Act. LEXIS 2810 (Oct. 10, 1986)

Case Study 2: Bank Commingling § 3(c)(11) Retirement Plan Fund and § 3(c)(3) Trust Fund

While IC Act § 3(c)(3) excludes a bank common trust fund from the IC definition, and § 3(c)(11) excludes a qualified employee benefit plan fund from the IC definition, a commingling of the two exempt funds gives rise to an "investment company" not excluded from the IC Act.

Santa Barbara Bank & Trust

IC Act § 3(c)(3), 1991 SEC No-Act. LEXIS 1269 (Nov. 1, 1991)

Research Topics:

Bank-sponsored investment management services in China: securities regulation versus banking regulation; fair competition between banking industry and investment management industry; and investor protection.

National Bank of Commerce Investment Fund

Securities Act § 3(a)(2), SA Rule 180; Exchange Act § 12(g)(2)(H); IC Act § 3(c)(11)

SEC No-Action Letter (Oct. 10, 1986)

Letter to SEC:

Securities and Exchange Commission

Office of Chief Counsel

Division of Corporation Finance & Division of Investment Management

(June 5, 1986)

Re: National Bank of Commerce Investment Fund for Qualified Employee Benefit Plans—Employment of Investment Adviser

Gentlemen:

We are writing on behalf of our client, **National Bank of Commerce**, a national banking association with principal place of business in Memphis, Tennessee (the "*Bank*" or the "*Trustee*"). The Trustee has for many years maintained and operated a collective trust fund, named the **National Bank of Commerce Investment Fund for Qualified Employee Benefit Plans** (the "*Trust Fund*"), which has heretofore consisted of three separate investment funds known as the Fixed Income Fund, the Equity Fund and the Special Situation Equity Fund. As of May 8, 1986, the Trustee has amended and restated the trust instrument governing the Trust Fund to, among other things, provide for the creation of two additional investment funds (the "*SAM Funds*") for the Trust Fund, provisionally named the SAM Equity Fund and the SAM Fixed Income Fund. Fractional undivided beneficial interests ("Units") in each of the SAM Funds will be held solely by trusts forming part of pension or profit-sharing plans qualified under § 401(a) and exempt from tax under § 501(a) of the Internal Revenue Code of 1954, as amended (the "Code"). **Southeastern Asset Management, Inc.**, a Tennessee corporation (the "*Adviser*") will be engaged as investment adviser to the Trustee with respect to each of the SAM Funds.

We respectfully request a determination that the Staff will not recommend any enforcement action to the Commission if the Trustee maintains and operates the SAM Funds as part of the Trust Fund:

(i) Without registering the Units in either of the SAM Funds under the Securities Act of 1933, in reliance upon the exemption provided by § 3(a)(2) of such Act and Rule 180;

(ii) Without registering the Units of either SAM Fund under § 12(g) of the Securities Exchange Act of 1934, in reliance upon the exemption provided by § 12(g)(2)(H) of such Act; and

(iii) Without registering the Trust Fund or either of the SAM Funds as an investment company under the Investment Company Act of 1940, in reliance upon the exclusion set forth in § 3(c)(11) of such Act.

I. Description of Proposed Operations

The Bank is a national banking association organized under the laws of the United States and is engaged in all traditional banking activities, including a broad range of fiduciary services through its trust division. These fiduciary services include acting as trustee, co-trustee or investment agent for numerous pension, profit-sharing and other types of retirement plans. In connection with these fiduciary services, the Bank maintains the Trust Fund in accordance with paragraph 9.18(a)(2) of Regulation 9 of the Comptroller of the Currency, as a vehicle for collective investment of assets of corporate retirement plans which are qualified under § 401(a) of the Code. As a means of diversifying the investment opportunities available within the Trust Fund, the Bank now proposes to offer the SAM Funds as additional investment vehicles for assets of retirement plans qualified under § 401(a) of the Code. Initially, the Bank intends to continue to restrict the participating trusts to those which are part of corporate retirement plans, as distinguished from so called "Keogh" plans. However, the Bank may in the future permit participation by Keogh plans, in the manner and to the extent permitted by Rule 180.

The Bank will employ the Adviser to recommend alternative investment strategies and to provide investment advice for the SAM Funds. However, the Bank will continue to act as trustee of the Trust Fund, including the SAM Funds, and as custodian of the assets held by the Trust Fund, including the SAM Funds. The Adviser will present its recommendations to the Trustee; and the Trustee will review the recommendations and may or may not accept the advice offered by the Adviser. It is anticipated that the Trustee will generally accept the Adviser's recommendations; however, the Trustee will expressly retain full, final and complete authority over all transactions of the SAM Funds. It is not proposed that the Adviser have any duties, responsibilities or authority with respect to any part of the Trust Fund other than the SAM Funds.

All investment activities of the Bank's trust division, including investments by the Trust Fund, are supervised by a **Trust Investment Committee** (the "Investment

Committee"), appointed by the Bank's Trust Committee. (The Trust Committee is appointed by the Bank's Board of Directors for general supervision of the trust division). The members appointed to the Investment Committee are selected on the basis of their knowledge and experience in investments.

Initially, the Adviser will recommend to the Investment Committee certain equity securities that the Adviser believes would be appropriate to be held by the SAM Equity Fund and written criteria for fixed income securities and other debt securities that the Adviser believes to be appropriate for securities to be held by the SAM Fixed Income Fund. The Investment Committee will review these recommendations of the Adviser and will have the final authority and responsibility for approving a list of equity securities for investment by the SAM Equity Fund and written criteria for investments by the SAM Fixed Income Fund. With the assistance of the Adviser, the Investment Committee will periodically review the list of approved securities for investment by the SAM Equity Fund, will add or delete securities from the list and will designate which securities on such list are approved to be purchased, sold and/or held by the SAM Equity Fund. With the assistance of the Adviser, the Investment Committee will likewise periodically review the written criteria for investments by the SAM Fixed Income Fund, to determine whether such criteria should be modified. In reviewing all such recommendations of the Adviser, the Investment Committee will assess whether it believes such recommendations are appropriate for the SAM Funds based upon the Investment Committee's independent evaluation of each security recommended for the SAM Equity Fund and of the criteria recommended for investments by the SAM Fixed Income Fund.

The Adviser will monitor the investments held by each of the SAM Funds and will recommend to the Trustee on a day-to-day basis purchases or sales of securities for the account of each SAM Fund. Such recommendations with respect to investments of the SAM Equity Fund will be limited to those securities included in the list approved by the Investment Committee and approved by the Committee as to which securities on the list are approved to be purchased, sold and/or held by the SAM Equity Fund. Recommendations with respect to investments for the SAM Fixed Income Fund will be limited to those securities which conform to the written criteria approved by the Investment Committee. Each such recommendation will be communicated by the Adviser to an officer of the Bank, approved and designated by the Investment Committee. This officer will have authority and responsibility for determining whether the recommended transaction is appropriate for the respective SAM Fund. It is expected that the function of this officer will be primarily to determine whether the recommendation is in accordance with the list and designation of securities approved by the Investment Committee, in the case of transactions for the SAM Equity Fund, and whether the recommendations conform to the written criteria approved by the Investment Committee, in the case of transactions for the SAM Fixed Income Fund. However, this officer will have full authority to reject any such recommendation for any reason. No trade will be effected on behalf of either SAM Fund without the approval of one of the designated officers of the Bank.

In addition to any promotional efforts on the part of the Trustee, the Adviser, as a part of its duties, will be expected to solicit participating accounts on behalf of the Trustee. However, no accounts will be accepted for investment in either SAM Fund unless and until the Bank has first been duly appointed as trustee, co-trustee or investment agent for the relevant retirement plan, by action of the employer or other appropriate plan fiduciary. The Trustee will be under no obligation to the Adviser to accept any account solicited by the Adviser, and the Trustee may reject any such account in its sole discretion.

Mass-Marketing of the SAM Funds and Units therein, if any, will be limited in the following respects: (1) there will be no television or radio advertising; and (2) the SAM Funds and Units will be advertised only by the mailing of written material to retirement plan administrators, representatives of various investment publications and persons requesting such materials and by advertising in selected professional publications and/or investment publications.

No participating trust investing in either SAM Fund will be a part of any plan: (i) contributions under which are held in a single trust fund or separate account maintained by an insurance company for a single employer and under which an amount in excess of the employer's contribution is allocated to the purchase of securities issued by the employer or any company directly or indirectly controlling, controlled by, or under common control with the employer, or (ii) which is a plan funded by an annuity contract described in § 403(b) of the Code.

In accordance with the regulations of the Comptroller of the Currency, employees of the Bank's Trust Division will review each participating trust account annually and report to the Committee that such accounts have been reviewed. The Sam Funds will be under the continuous review of employees of the Bank's Trust Division and will be reviewed formally by the Investment Committee at least monthly.

The Bank will charge an annual fee to each participating account equal to 1.5% of the asset value of the Units held by each such participating account in either of the SAM Funds and of short-term investments awaiting entry into a SAM Fund or proceeds of Unit redemptions awaiting distribution from a participating account. The Bank will retain a portion of this fee equal to $1.50 per $1,000.00 on the first $100,000,000.00, $1.20 per $1,000.00 on the next $50,000,000.00 and $1.00 per $1,000.00 on assets over $150,000,000.00 with a minimum annual fee of $20,000.00. The balance of the annual fee will be paid by the Bank to the Adviser as compensation for the services of the Adviser. In addition to these fees, the Bank may charge participating accounts other fees for other services, should the participating account elect to utilize such services.

II. Statutory Provisions and Analysis

Based upon the facts set forth above, it is our opinion that the proposed SAM Funds and Units comply with statutory provisions which permit the offering of Units (i) without the registration of Units as securities under the 1933 Act or the 1934 Act and (ii) without the registration of the Trust Fund or the SAM Funds as investment companies under the 1940 Act.

Section 3(a)(2) of the 1933 Act exempts, among other things and with certain exceptions not relevant to this request, from the registration provisions of that act "any interest or participation in a ... collective trust fund maintained by a bank ... which interest or participation ... is issued in connection with (A) a stock bonus, pension, or profit-sharing plan which meets the requirements for qualification under § 401 of the Internal Revenue Code of 1954 ... other than any plan described in clause (A) ... of this paragraph ... (ii) which covers employees some or all of whom are employees within the meaning of § 401(c)(1) of such Code...."

Section 12(g)(2)(H) of the 1934 Act exempts, among other things, from the registration provisions of § 12(g) thereof "any interest or participation in any collective trust funds maintained by a bank ... which interest or participation is issued in connection with ... a stock-bonus, pension, or profit-sharing plan which meets the requirements for qualification under § 401 of the Internal Revenue Code of 1954...."[1]

---

[1] Section 3(a)(12) of the 1934 Act also exempts, among other things, from the registration provisions of that act "any interest or participation in a ... collective trust fund maintained by a bank ... which interest or participation is

Section 3(c)(11) of the 1940 Act excludes, among other things, from the definition of an investment company set forth in § 3(a) thereof "any employee's stock bonus, pension, or profit-sharing trust which meets the requirements for qualification under § 401 of the ... Code ...; or any collective trust fund maintained by a bank consisting solely of assets of such trusts...."

We believe that the requirements of the statutory exemptions and exclusion quoted above are all met with respect to the SAM Funds and Units for the following reasons: The SAM Funds will be a collective trust fund, which "may be defined, generally, as funds for the collective investment of assets of employee's stock bonus, pension or profit sharing plans." *Status of Savings and Loan Associations Under the Federal Securities Laws; Advance Notice of Possible Commission Action*, IC-13666 (1983). See also *Employee Benefit Plans; Interpretations of Statute*, 33-6188, Part IV(B)(1)(c) n. 112. Each Unit will be an interest in such a fund, and will be issued in connection with pension or profit-sharing plans meeting the requirements for qualification under § 401 of the Code; therefore, the SAM Funds will consist solely of assets of trusts forming part of such plans, in satisfaction of § 3(a) of the 1940 Act. The ownership of Units by Keogh plans will be permitted, despite the exclusion thereof in § 3(a)(2) of the 1933 Act, because of compliance with Rule 180. Each SAM Fund will be a collective trust fund "***maintained by a bank***," as further discussed below.

The Trustee is a banking institution organized under the laws of the United States. Thus, the Trustee is a "***bank***" within the meaning of § 3(a)(2) of the 1933 Act, § 12(g)(2)(H) of the 1934 Act and § 3(c)(11) of the 1940 Act.[2] The Trustee will make the final decisions to invest in or dispose of investments though it will be assisted by the Adviser in arriving at its investment decisions.

We do not believe that the retention of an investment adviser for the SAM Funds poses new or unique issues. In Release 33-6188 [*supra*], the Commission stated that "[i]n

---

issued in connection with (A) a stock bonus, pension, or profit-sharing plan which meets the requirements for qualification under Section 401 of the Internal Revenue Code of 1954, ... other than any plan described in clause (A) ... of this paragraph ... which covers employees some or all of whom are employees within the meaning of § 401(c)(1) of such Code...."

[2] "Bank" is defined in § 3(a)(6) of the 1934 Act and § 2(a)(5) of the 1940 Act to include "(A) a banking institution organized under the laws of the United States,..." With respect to collective trust funds, § 3(a)(2) of the 1933 Act provides that "the term 'bank' has the same meaning as in the" 1940 Act.

exercising its investment authority over a trust fund, however, a bank may hire an investment adviser to assist it...." [*Id.*], Part IV(A)(3)(a) n. 141. The Commission went on to state, however, that the bank must "exercise substantial investment responsibility over the trust fund administered by it" and "the final decision whether or not to invest must be made by the bank." Both prior to and since the promulgation of Release 33-6188, the Division of Corporate Finance and the Division of Investment Management have taken similar positions in response to requests for no action letters where an investment adviser has been retained to provide investment advice concerning collective trust funds maintained by banks. See *e.g.*; *Bank of Delaware Collective Trust Funds* (April 4, 1986); *National Employee Plan Services, Inc.* (October 16, 1984); *Lincoln First Bank N.A.* (October 24, 1983); *Frank Russell Trust Co.* (July 11, 1980); *Drexel Trust Co.* (September 12, 1983); *Sterling National Bank and Trust Co. of New York* (July 28, 1976); *First Liberty Real Estate Fund* (July 14, 1975). The Bank's discretion in retaining the Adviser, or any other such agent for that matter, is subject to the overriding requirement as stated explicitly in the trust instrument governing the Trust Fund that the investments of the Trust Fund be subject to the Bank's exclusive and overall management and control, and the requirement of the Comptroller of the Currency that a national bank administering such a collective investment fund shall have exclusive management thereof.

The mass-marketing of Units would not detract from the applicability of the aforementioned statutory exemptions and exclusion. The rationale for permitting such exemptions and exclusion from registration applies to many purchases by and sales to qualified plans, of an interest in a collective trust fund maintained by a bank, equally as well as it applies to one purchase or sale. See, *e.g.*, *National Employee Plan Services, Inc.*, *supra.*

Given the proposed operations of the SAM Funds and the protection under the federal securities laws inherent therein, such operations are in the public interest and consistent with the comprehensive regulatory scheme embodied in the federal securities laws.

III. Requested No-Action Position

Based upon the foregoing facts and statutes, we respectfully request that the Staff advise us that it will not recommend to the Commission that any action be taken if the Trustee maintains and operates the SAM Funds as part of the Trust Fund:

(i) Without registering the Units in either SAM Fund under the 1933 Act, in reliance upon the exemption provided by § 3(a)(2) of such Act and Rule 180;

(ii) Without registering the Units under § 12(g) of the 1934 Act, in reliance upon the exemption provided by § 12(g)(2)(H) of such Act; and

(iii) Without registering the Trust Fund or either SAM Fund as an investment company under the 1940 Act, in reliance upon the exclusion set forth in § 3(c)(11) of such Act.

SEC Reply:

Response of the Office of Chief Counsel
Division of Corporation Finance
(Sept. 10, 1986)

Re: National Bank of Commerce Investment Fund for Qualified Employee Benefit Plans

On the basis of the facts presented, the **Division of Corporation Finance** will not recommend any enforcement action to the Commission if, in reliance upon your opinion as counsel that the exemptions provided by § 3(a)(2) of the Securities Act of 1933 and Rule 180 thereunder, and § 12(g)(2)(H) of the Securities Exchange Act of 1934 are available, the Bank maintains and operates the SAM Funds as part of the Trust Fund in the manner you describe without compliance with the registration requirements of the 1933 and 1934 Acts.

The **Division of Investment Management** has asked us to inform you that, on the basis of the facts presented in your letter, it will not recommend any enforcement action to the Commission under the Investment Company Act of 1940 if the Bank maintains and operates the SAM Funds as part of the Trust Fund without registering the Trust Fund or either of the SAM Funds under the 1940 Act, in reliance upon the exclusion in § 3(c)(11) of that Act.

Because this position is based upon the representations made in your letter, it should be noted that any different facts or conditions might require a different conclusion. Further, this response only expresses the Division's position on enforcement action and does not purport to express any legal conclusion on the questions presented.

Santa Barbara Bank & Trust

IC Act § 3(c)(3), SEC No-Action Letter (Nov. 1, 1991)

Incoming Inquiry from:
Santa Barbara Bank & Trust
Trust Division
June 19, 1991

[Santa Barbara Bank & Trust is a state chartered bank and trust company located in Santa Barbara, California. We presently are operating two common trust funds exclusively for our personal trust clients. We would like to be able to commingle funds held in employee benefit accounts, both qualified plans and IRA accounts, into these personal trust funds.]

Response of the Office of Chief Counsel
Division of Investment Management
Securities and Exchange Commission

Your letter of June 19, 1991 asks whether there are any restrictions under the federal securities laws on **Santa Barbara Bank & Trust** (the "Bank") ***commingling*** the assets of qualified employee benefit plan accounts and individual retirement accounts ("IRAs") with the assets of personal trust accounts in its common trust funds.

A pooled securities fund in which interests are offered to the public as investments is an investment company as defined in § 3(a) of the Investment Company Act of 1940. Section 3(c) provides certain exclusions from this definition.

Section 3(c)(3) excludes bank common trust funds from the 1940 Act.[1] The staff has interpreted this exclusion as applying only to a common trust fund, for moneys which a bank has received for bona fide fiduciary purposes, that is not offered to the public.[2] Such a common trust fund serves as an administrative convenience of the bank incidental

---

[1] Section 3(c)(3) excepts from the definition of investment company "any common trust fund or similar fund maintained by a bank exclusively for the collective investment and reinvestment of moneys contributed thereto by the bank in its capacity as a trustee, executor, administrator, or guardian." For a discussion of the legislative and administrative history with respect to common trust funds, see *United Missouri Bank of Kansas City, N.A.* (Dec. 31, 1981).

[2] See, *e.g., Union Bank & Trust* (July 8, 1987); *Owensboro National Bank* (July 29, 1981); *Citytrust* (Mar. 9, 1980); *Howard Savings Bank* (Aug. 13, 1979); *Genessee Merchants Bank & Trust* (Jan. 8, 1979).

to its traditional trust department activities.[3]

The Commission and its staff have stated that this exception is not available for common trust funds holding assets of IRAs.[4] Thus, a common trust fund which pools assets of IRAs, alone or with bona fide trust assets, would be subject to registration and regulation under the 1940 Act and interests in the fund would be subject to the registration provisions of the Securities Act of 1933. A number of banks have organized funds consisting exclusively of IRA assets and have registered them under the 1940 Act.

The staff further takes the position that a common trust fund that ***commingles*** the assets of employee benefit plans meeting the requirements for qualification under §401 of the Internal Revenue Code with §3(c)(3) trust assets must register under the 1940 Act, and interests in that fund must be registered under the 1933 Act.[5] The staff does not believe that the §3(c)(3) exclusion extends to employee benefit plan funds held by a bank as trustee because a separate provision of the 1940 Act, §3(c)(11), already excludes certain employee benefit plans.[6]

Section 3(c)(11) provides that a collective trust fund maintained by a bank consisting solely of the assets of employee benefit plan trusts qualified under §401 of the Internal Revenue Code and government plans is not an investment company. Thus, the Bank could commingle its qualified plan trusts in a collective trust fund consisting solely of assets of such trusts without registering either the fund or interests in the fund.[7]

---

[3] See *Commercial Bank* (Feb. 24, 1988), reconsideration denied (July 13, 1988), Commission review denied (Jan. 11, 1989); *First National Bank of Peoria* (Aug. 4, 1979); *Millikin National Bank of Decatur* (Mar. 31, 1979).

[4] See Testimony of Richard C. Breeden Before the Subcommittee on Telecommunications & Finance of the House Committee on Energy and Commerce, Concerning Proposed Revisions to Rules Governing Bank Common Trust Funds, at n.8 (Oct. 4, 1990) (discussing registration of common trust funds for IRA assets). See also *Commercial Bank, supra* note 3; *Hibernia National Bank of New Orleans* (Sept. 24, 1986); *United Missouri Bank of Kansas City, N.A., supra* note 1; *Owensboro National Bank, supra* note 2; *Citytrust, supra* note 2; *First National Bank of Peoria, supra* note 3; *Millikin National Bank of Decatur, supra* note 3; *Continental Illinois National Bank and Trust Company of Chicago* (Apr. 28, 1975).

[5] See *Millikin National Bank of Decatur, supra* note 3; *First National Bank of Peoria, supra* note 3; *National Boulevard Bank of Chicago* (Mar. 22, 1974), reconsideration denied (Oct. 18, 1974).

[6] See *Millikin National Bank of Decatur, supra* note 3; *First National Bank of Peoria, supra* note 3; *National Boulevard Bank of Chicago, supra* note 5.

[7] A collective trust fund consisting solely of the assets of qualified plans, including assets of Keogh plans, is excepted by §3(c)(11). However, interests in a collective trust fund which includes Keogh plan assets are

However, since IRAs are qualified under § 408 of the Internal Revenue Code, and not § 401, the collective trust fund would not meet the requirements of § 3(c)(11) if it included assets of IRAs and would, therefore, be required to register as an investment company.[8] Finally, the interests in such a fund must be registered under the 1933 Act.

---

securities that must be registered under the 1933 Act unless the plan meets the requirements of Rule 180 thereunder.

[8] See, *e.g.*, *United Missouri Bank of Kansas City, N.A.*, *supra* note 1; *Owensboro National Bank*, *supra* note 2; *Citytrust*, *supra* note 2; *First National Bank of Peoria*, *supra* note 3; *Millikin National Bank of Decatur*, *supra* note 3; *Continental Illinois National Bank and Trust Company of Chicago*, *supra* note 4.

Section 5.3 Pooled Investment Vehicles Funding Pension Plans

Topic 1 Defined Benefit *vs* Defined Contribution

Laws & Rules Highlight:

IC Act (15 USC 80a-1 *et seq.*) & Rules (17 CFR §§ 270.0-1 *et seq.*)
Securities Act (15 USC 77a *et seq.*) & Rules (17 CFR §§ 230.100 *et seq.*)
Employee Retirement Income Security Act of 1974 (ERISA) (29 USC §§ 1001 et seq.)

IC Act

- **§ 3(c)(11)** (***exclusions from IC:*** *IRC § 401-qualified employee pension and profit-sharing* ***plans; bank collective trust fund*** *and* ***insurance company separate account****, consisting* ***solely*** *of assets of one or more of such qualified employee pension/profit-sharing plans*)
- private investment company exclusions
  - **§ 3(c)(1)** (***exclusion from IC:*** *privately offered fund having 100 or fewer beneficial owners*)
    - ✓ § 3(c)(1)(A) (***corporate investor 10% attribution/look through rule:*** *to prevent circumvention of 100-beneficial-owner limitation by use of conduit funds, whether registered or private*)
  - **§ 3(c)(7)** (***exclusion from IC:*** *privately offered fund owned exclusively by unlimited number of "qualified purchasers"*); § 2(a)(51) (*def. "qualified purchaser"*)
    - ✓ Rule 2a51-3 Certain Companies as Qualified Purchasers (***look-through*** *treatment of entity "****formed for the specific purpose****" of acquiring § 3(c)(7) fund securities: to prevent evasion of "qualified purchaser" requirement*)
  - Rule 3c-5 Beneficial Ownership by Knowledgeable Employees and Certain Other Persons (*excluding "knowledgeable employee" from beneficial owner counting under § 3(c)(1) and § 3(c)(7)*)

Securities Act

- § 2(a)(1) (*def. "security" to include "****investment contract****"*)
- **§ 3(a)(2)** (*"****exempted securities****" include: interests or participations in* ***bank collective trust fund*** *and* ***insurance company separate account*** *solely pooling tax-qualified* ***corporate*** *pension/profit-sharing plans, where such trust fund, separate account, and qualified plans are excluded from IC by IC Act § 3(c)(11)*)
  - Rule 405 Definitions of Terms (*"****employee benefit plan****"*)
  - Rule 180 Exemption from Registration of Interests and Participations Issued in Connection with Certain H.R. 10 Plans (***Keogh self-employed person's pension plan****—aka* ***H.R.10 plan:*** *exemption from registration for both participants' interests in*

the H.R. 10 plan, and plan's interests in the funding investment vehicles)

ERISA Act

- § 1002 Definitions
  - § 1002(3) (*def. "employee benefit plan"*); § 1002(7) (*def. "participant"*); § 1002(14) (*def. "party in interest"*); § 1002(16) (*defs. "administrator"; "plan sponsor"*); § 1002(17) (*def. "separate account"*); § 1002(21)(A) (*def. "fiduciary with respect to a plan"*); § 1002(34) (*def. "**defined contribution plan**"*); § 1002(35) (*def. "**defined benefit plan**"*); § 1002(38) (*def. "investment manager"*); § 1002(42) (*def. "plan assets"*)
- Part 4 Fiduciary Responsibility
  - § 1102 Establishment of Plan; § 1103 Establishment of Trust; § 1104 Fiduciary Duties; § 1106 Prohibited Transactions; § 1107 Limitation with Respect to Acquisition and Holding of Employer Securities and Employer Real Property by Certain Plans; § 1109 Liability for Breach of Fiduciary Duty
- Subch. III Plan Termination Insurance
  - § 1302 Pension Benefit Guaranty Corporation; § 1305 Pension Benefit Guaranty Funds

Pre-Case Background Note:[Biblio]

Participation Interests, Corporate Pension Plan, and Private Funding Pools

Based on the types of their sponsors, pension plans may be categorized as corporate pension plans, established by ***corporate employers***; Keogh plans, established by ***self-employed*** individuals for the benefit of themselves and their employees; and IRAs (standing for "**I**ndividual **R**etirement **A**ccounts"), commonly established by ***individual employees*** who are not covered by a corporate or Keogh plan, in order to obtain tax benefits similar to those provided under corporate and Keogh plans.[1a; 1c] This Note uses corporate employee benefit plans (including corporate pension plans) as discussion context.

Benefit Plans: Defined Benefit & Defined Contribution

From the perspective of investment risk bearing as between the employer and the employees, there are two types of pension plans: "defined benefit plans" and "defined contribution plans." In a "**defined benefit plan**," the employer/plan sponsor promises the employees a specific benefit payable upon retirement; chooses the plan's investments; and bears any investment risk associated with the plan. Employers offering defined benefit plans are generally large and sophisticated; and defined benefit plans are generally insured against employer insolvency by the Pension Benefit Guaranty Corporation (PBGC)—a body corporate established within the Department of Labor. Under the Employee Retirement Income Security Act of 1974 (ERISA)—the primary law governing all retirement plans and plan fiduciaries—the plan sponsor for a defined benefit plan has fiduciary duties to choose prudently and monitor the ***plan's investments***.[2 (Ch.3)]

In a "**defined contribution plan**," including its sub-category "***participant-directed*** defined contribution plan," the employer/plan sponsor undertakes to set aside specific contributions to each participant employee's account; the employee participants are themselves responsible for directing the investments of their own individual accounts. The employer promises employee participants a retirement benefit equal to the amounts contributed to their respective accounts, plus investment gains and minus investment losses the accounts experienced—*i.e.*, employee participants bear the investment risks of their own accounts under the plan. Employers offering defined contribution plans are generally small or medium-sized; and there is no PBGC insurance protection for defined contribution plans under ERISA. The plan sponsor for a defined contribution plan has fiduciary duties under ERISA to choose prudently and monitor the ***investment options available to participants***, but has no obligation to ensure that employee participants choose suitable investments from the available investment options.[2 (Ch.3)]

Securities Status: Employee Interests in Plan & Plan Interests in Funding Vehicles

In connection with an "employee benefit plan" (defined by SEC Rule 405 to include pension, profit-sharing and similar plans), the SEC identifies **two types of securities**:[1a-1b; 2 (Ch.3); 3 (Ch.35)]

- ***Employee participation interests in a plan***: If the plan is a non-voluntary, noncontributory defined benefit plan, the employee interests in the plan are *not securities* (*Daniel* 1979).[4] If the plan is a voluntary, contributory defined contribution plan, the employee participation interests in the plan are securities in the form of "*investment contracts*" (*Howey* 1946)[5]: the plan in essence functions as an investment vehicle designed to produce profits, in the form of retirement or other benefits for the employees, through the efforts of the plan manager.
- ***Plan participation interests in underlying investment vehicles***: The interests of a plan—whether defined benefit or defined contribution—in collective investment vehicles are *in all instances* securities, generally in the form of investment

contracts.

Where collective investment vehicles funding the qualified employee benefit plans are bank collective trust funds or insurance company separate accounts consisting solely of the assets of such qualified plans, then both employee interests in the plan (to the extent they are securities) and the plan interests in the funding vehicles are exempt from registration under the Securities Act by § 3(a)(2). The exemptions are based on two rationales: (i) the investment vehicles are subject to regulation under other laws, such as banking law or insurance law, as well as ERISA; (ii) the plan's sponsoring employer (or the plan's professional investment manager) is a sophisticated investor able to fend for itself and for the plan participants. Where a plan permits participating employees' contributions to be invested in the employer stock, then employee participation interests in the plan (*e.g.*, a stock purchase plan) are not exempted from registration: Form S-8 Registration Statement is the principal form used to register both employee interests in the plan and the employer stock—each a distinct security.[1d; 2 (Ch.3)]

IC Status: Benefit Plan & Plan's Funding Vehicles

In connection with a voluntary, contributory benefit plan, there are thus **two levels of issuers**:[1a-1b; 2 (Ch.3)]

- ***plan as issuer***: issuing securities in the form of participation interests or investment contracts to participating employees;
- ***plan's funding investment pools as issuers***: issuing securities in the form of investment contracts to participating plans.

As an issuer of securities investing in other securities, a voluntary, contributory pension plan, as well as its underlying collective investment pools, would thus be an investment company. Tax-qualified corporate pension plans, together with bank collective trust funds and insurance company separate accounts pooling solely the assets of such qualified plans, are excepted by § 3(c)(11) from the definition of IC. Non-qualified pension plans, and collective investment vehicles other than bank collective trust funds and insurance company separate accounts, are generally investment companies unless another exception or exemption applies.[3 (Chs. 20, 35)]

Pension Plan Investing in Private Funds

Pooled investment vehicles funding pension plans may include bank collective trust funds, insurance company separate accounts, registered investment companies, and non-registered private funds (such as private equity funds and hedge funds).[2 (Ch.3); 6] Under the IC Act, there are two private investment company exceptions from IC definition: § 3(c)(1) 100-person fund, and § 3(c)(7) qualified purchaser fund.[7; 3 (Chs. 9, 17); 8 (§§6.04, 6.08); 9]

Under the **§ 3(c)(1) 100-person private fund** exception, the § 3(c)(1) fund is excepted from the IC definition if it satisfies *two conditions*: the fund has not more than 100 holders of its equity and debt securities (other than its commercial paper), and does not make a public offering of its securities—conditions designed to preserve the private nature of an exempt issuer.

To prevent circumvention of the "100-investor limit" through layers of conduit investment companies or private funds, § 3(c)(1) imposes an ***attribution rule***, which, if triggered, will cause investors of a corporate shareholder of a § 3(c)(1) fund to be counted toward, or attributed to, the § 3(c)(1) fund's 100-beneficial owner limit (***look-through approach***).[7b (n.79)] Prior to 1996, § 3(c)(1) adopted a two-part, 10% attribution rule triggered if: (i) the corporate shareholder beneficially owned 10% or more of the voting securities in that § 3(c)(1) issuer (*First 10% Test*); *and* (ii) the corporate shareholder has *more than 10% of its assets* invested in securities of all § 3(c)(1) issuers (*Second 10% Test*).[2 (Ch.2); 3 (§ 9.4)] As amended by the National Securities Markets Improvement Act of 1996,[9] the attribution rule is triggered if: (i) the "*First 10% Test*" is met; *and* (ii) the corporate shareholder is *itself* an investment company or a § 3(c)(1) or § 3(c)(7) private fund.

Thus, the attribution rule would not apply to a corporate shareholder of a § 3(c)(1) issuer that is an "involuntary, noncontributory defined benefit plan"—not being an issuer and thus not an IC. Nor if the corporate shareholder is a "voluntary, contributory defined contribution plan"—being excepted from IC under § 3(c)(11) and not under § 3(c)(1) or § 3(c)(7). On the other hand, if participants in a ***defined contribution plan*** can decide whether or how much to invest in a § 3(c)(1) fund, then such participants are considered beneficial owners of the § 3(c)(1) fund—*independently of the 10%-triggered attribution rule*, on the rationale that the plan may be a conduit created to enable a § 3(c)(1) fund to *indirectly* have more than 100 investors.[3 (§9.5.4); 7b (nn.19, 79)]

Under the **§ 3(c)(7) qualified purchaser fund** exception, the § 3(c)(7) fund is excepted from the IC definition if it satisfies *two conditions*: the fund is owned exclusively by "qualified purchasers" [which, as defined by IC Act § 2(a)(51), include any institutional investor that owns and invests on a discretionary basis not less than $25 million in investments], and does not make a public offering of its securities—conditions based on the theory that highly sophisticated shareholders of such issuer are in a position to appreciate the risks of investing in a § 3(c)(7) fund, and do not need the protection of the IC Act.[2 (Ch.2); 10; 9; 7]

To prevent evasion of the "qualified purchaser" condition, SEC Rule 2a51-3 requires that, in the case of any entity "***formed or operated for the specific purpose***" of investing in a § 3(c)(7) fund, each beneficial owner of such entity must be a "qualified purchaser" of the § 3(c)(7) fund (***look-through approach***).[7b (n.79)] In the case of a ***defined benefit plan***, which owns $25 million of investments in aggregate, whose decision to invest in a § 3(c)(7) fund is made by the plan trustee or other plan fiduciary, and which does not permit participants to direct investment, the "look-through" approach would not apply.[7b (§II.A.8); 3 (Ch.17)]

Bibliography

1. Employee Benefit Plans, interpretive rels.: **1a.** 33-6188, 45 FR 8960 (1980); **1b.** 33-6281, 46 FR 8446 (1981); **1c.** Exemption From Registration of Interests and Participations Issued in Connection With Certain H.R. 10 Plans, 33-6363, 46 FR 58287 (1981); **1d.** Registration and Reporting Requirements for Employee Benefit Plans, 33-6867, 34-28094, 55 FR 23909 (1990)
2. DIV. OF INV. MGMT, SEC. & EXCH. COMM'N, PROTECTING INVESTORS: A HALF CENTURY OF INVESTMENT COMPANY REGULATION (1992)
3. ROSENBLUM, INVESTMENT COMPANY DETERMINATION UNDER THE 1940 ACT—EXEMPTIONS AND EXCEPTIONS (2d ed. 2003)
4. Int'l Bhd. of Teamsters v. Daniel, 439 U.S. 551 (1979)
5. SEC v. W. J. Howey Co., 328 U.S. 293 (1946)
6. DesMarteau, *The Animals in the Employee Benefits Investment Product Zoo*, 29 BENEFITS L.J. 31 (2016)
7. **7a.** Private Investment Companies, IC-22405, IS-1037, 61 FR 68100 (1996); **7b.** Privately Offered Investment Companies, IC-22597, IS-1071, 62 FR 17512 (1997)
8. FRANKEL & LABY, THE REGULATION OF MONEY MANAGERS—MUTUAL FUNDS AND ADVISERS (2017)
9. NATIONAL SECURITIES MARKETS IMPROVEMENT ACT OF 1996 (NSMIA), PL 104-290, 110 Stat. 3416, Title II. Investment Company Act Amendments (1996)
10. ABA Task Force on Hedge Funds, *Report on Section 3(c)(1) of the Investment Company Act of 1940 and Proposals to Create an Exception for Qualified Purchasers*, 51 BUS. LAW. 773 (1996)

Case Study 1: Participation Interests in Defined Benefit Plan

Employees' beneficial interests in a noncontributory, compulsory defined benefit pension plan are not securities within the meaning of the Securities Act and Securities Exchange Act.

Int'l Bhd. of Teamsters v. Daniel

439 U.S. 551 (1979)

[*Procedural history*: Daniel v. Int'l Bhd. of Teamsters, 410 F. Supp. 541 (ND Ill. 1976), *aff'd*, 561 F.2d 1223 (7th Cir. 1977), *rev'd*, Int'l Bhd. of Teamsters v. Daniel, 439 U.S. 551 (1979)]

Case Study 2: Participant-Directed Defined Contribution Plan Investing in Private Funds

Involuntary, noncontributory defined benefit plan. In *Kodak* (1988), based on the reasoning of *Daniel* case, § 3(c)(1) attribution rule does not apply to an involuntary, noncontributory defined benefit plan, and employee participants are not counted as beneficial owners of the § 3(c)(1) fund in which the plan invests.

Participant-directed defined contribution plan. In *Intel Corp.* (1992), ***for purposes of § 3(c)(1)'s attribution rule***, a voluntary, contributory defined contribution plan's ownership of 10% or more of the outstanding voting securities of a § 3(c)(1) fund triggers application of the attribution rule: each employee participant in the plan is counted as a beneficial owner of the § 3(c)(1) fund. Extending *Intel*, *PanAgora* (1994) treats each participant in a participant-directed defined contribution plan as a beneficial owner of the § 3(c)(1) fund securities, ***independently of § 3(c)(1)'s attribution rule***, where the participant ***directs*** investments in the plan to a § 3(c)(1) fund. Limiting *PanAgora*, *Standish Ayer* (1995) allows a participant-directed defined contribution plan to be counted as a single beneficial owner of the § 3(c)(1) fund, where the plan participant ***directs*** the investments into generic investment options and the plan is not managed as a device for facilitating participants' individual decisions to invest in a § 3(c)(1) fund. Extending the *Standish Ayer* rationale **from § 3(c)(1) fund to § 3(c)(7) fund**, *H.E. Butt Grocery Co.* (2001) treats a participant-directed defined contribution plan as a qualified purchaser in a **§ 3(c)(7) fund**: while the plan participants select the investment option with an identified generic investment objective, the plan trustee or other plan fiduciary makes the specific investment decisions for the investment option, operating the defined contribution plan ***resembling a defined benefit plan*** which is treated as a single investor.

H.E. Butt Grocery Co.

IC Act §§ 3(c)(1) & 3(c)(7), 2001 SEC No-Act. LEXIS 578 (May 18, 2001)

[***Cited SEC no-action letters***: Kodak Retirement Income Plan: IC Act § 3(c)(1), (Feb 29, 1988); Intel Corp.: IC Act § 3(c)(1) (Nov 18, 1992); The PanAgora Group Trust: IC Act § 3(c)(1) (April 29, 1994) & (June 30, 1994); The Standish, Ayer & Wood, Inc. Stable Value Group Trust: IC Act § 3(c)(1) (Dec. 28, 1995); H.E. Butt Grocery Co.: IC Act §§ 3(c)(1) & 3(c)(7) (May 18, 2001)]

Research Topic:

Retirement market and funding vehicles in China.

Int'l Bhd. of Teamsters, Petitioner v. Daniel

439 U.S. 551 (1979)

Judges: POWELL, J., delivered the opinion of the Court, in which BRENNAN, STEWART, WHITE, MARSHALL, BLACKMUN, and REHNQUIST, JJ., joined, and in all but the last paragraph of Part III-A of which, BURGER, C. J., joined. BURGER, C. J., filed a concurring opinion. STEVENS, J., took no part in the consideration or decision of the cases.

Opinion

Mr. Justice POWELL delivered the opinion of the Court:

This case presents the question whether a noncontributory, compulsory pension plan constitutes a "security" within the meaning of the Securities Act of 1933 and the Securities Exchange Act of 1934 (Securities Acts).

I.

In 1954 multiemployer collective bargaining between Local 705 of the International Brotherhood of Teamsters, Chauffeurs, Warehousemen, and Helpers of America and Chicago trucking firms produced a pension plan for employees represented by the Local. The plan was compulsory and noncontributory. Employees had no choice as to participation in the plan, and did not have the option of demanding that the employer's contribution be paid directly to them as a substitute for pension eligibility. The employees paid nothing to the plan themselves.[1]

The collective-bargaining agreement initially set employer contributions to the Pension Trust Fund at $2 a week for each man-week of covered employment.[2] The Board of Trustees of the Fund, a body composed of an equal number of employer and union representatives, was given sole authority to set the level of benefits but had no control over the amount of required employer contributions. Initially, eligible employees received $75 a month in benefits upon retirement. Subsequent collective-bargaining

---

[1] For examples of other noncontributory, compulsory pension plans, see *Allied Structural Steel Co. v. Spannaus*, 438 U.S. 234 (1978); *Malone v. White Motor Corp.*, 435 U.S. 497 (1978); *Alabama Power Co. v. Davis*, 431 U.S. 581 (1977).

[2] Contributions were tied to the number of employees rather than the amount of work performed. For example, payments had to be made even for weeks where an employee was on leave of absence, disabled, or working for only a fraction of the week. Conversely, employers did not have to increase their contribution for weeks in which an employee worked overtime or on a holiday. Trust Agreement, Art. 3, § 1, App. 62a.

agreements called for greater employer contributions, which in turn led to higher benefit payments for retirees. At the time respondent brought suit, employers contributed $21.50 per employee man-week and pension payments ranged from $425 to $525 a month depending on age at retirement.[3] In order to receive a pension an employee was required to have 20 years of continuous service, including time worked before the start of the plan.

The meaning of "continuous service" is at the center of this dispute. Respondent began working as a truck driver in the Chicago area in 1950, and joined Local 705 the following year. When the plan first went into effect, respondent automatically received 5 years' credit toward the 20-year service requirement because of his earlier work experience. He retired in 1973 and applied to the plan's administrator for a pension. The administrator determined that respondent was ineligible because of a break in service between December 1960 and July 1961.[4] Respondent appealed the decision to the trustees, who affirmed. Respondent then asked the trustees to waive the continuous-service rule as it applied to him. After the trustees refused to waive the rule, respondent brought suit in federal court against the International Union (Teamsters), Local 705 (Local), and Louis Peick, a trustee of the Fund.

Respondent's complaint alleged that the Teamsters, the Local, and Peick misrepresented and omitted to state material facts with respect to the value of a covered employee's interest in the pension plan. Count I of the complaint charged that these misstatements and omissions constituted a fraud in connection with the sale of a security in violation of § 10(b) of the Securities Exchange Act of 1934, and the Securities and Exchange Commission's Rule 10b-5. Count II charged that the same conduct amounted to a violation of § 17(a) of the Securities Act of 1933. Other counts alleged violations of

---

[3] Because the Fund made the same payments to each employee who qualified for a pension and retired at the same age, rather than establishing an individual account for each employee tied to the amount of employer contributions attributable to his period of service, the plan provided a "defined benefit." See 29 USC § 1002(35); *Alabama Power Co. v. Davis, supra.*

[4] Respondent was laid off from December 1960 until April 1961. In addition, no contributions were paid on his behalf between April and July 1961, because of embezzlement by his employer's bookkeeper. During this 7-month period respondent could have preserved his eligibility by making the contributions himself, but he failed to do so.

various labor-law and common-law duties.[5] Respondent sought to proceed on behalf of all prospective beneficiaries of Teamsters pension plans and against all Teamsters pension funds.[6]

The petitioners moved to dismiss the first two counts of the complaint on the ground that respondent had no cause of action under the Securities Acts. The District Court denied the motion. 410 F. Supp. 541 (ND Ill. 1976). It held that respondent's interest in the Pension Fund constituted a security within the meaning of § 2(1) of the Securities Act, and § 3(a)(10) of the Securities Exchange Act,[7] because the plan created an "investment contract" as that term had been interpreted in *SEC v. W.J. Howey Co.*, 328 U.S. 293 (1946). It also determined that there had been a "sale" of this interest to respondent within the meaning of § 2(3) of the Securities Act, and § 3(a)(14) of the Securities Exchange Act,[8] It believed respondent voluntarily gave value for his interest in the plan, because he had

---

[5] Count III charged the Teamsters and the Local with violating their duty of fair representation under § 9(a) of the National Labor Relations Act, 29 USC § 159 (a), and Count V (later amended as Count VI) charged the Teamsters, the Local, Peick, and all other Teamsters Pension Fund trustees with violating their obligations under § 302(c)(5) of the Labor Management Relations Act, 29 USC § 186(c)(5). Count IV accused all defendants of common-law fraud and deceit.

[6] As of the time of appeal to the Seventh Circuit the District Court had not yet ruled on any class-certification issues.

[7] Section 2 (1) of the Securities Act defines a "security" as "any note, stock, treasury stock, bond, debenture, evidence of indebtedness, certificate of interest or participation in any profit-sharing agreement, collateral-trust certificate, preorganization certificate or subscription, transferable share, investment contract, voting-trust certificate, certificate of deposit for a security, fractional undivided interest in oil, gas, or other mineral rights, or, in general, any interest or instrument commonly known as a 'security,' or any certificate of interest or participation in, temporary or interim certificate for, receipt for, guarantee of, or warrant or right to subscribe to or purchase, any of the foregoing."

The definition of a "security" in § 3(a)(10) of the Securities Exchange Act is virtually identical and, for the purposes of this case, the coverage of the two Acts may be regarded as the same. *United Housing Foundation, Inc. v. Forman*, 421 U.S. 837 (1975); *Tcherepnin v. Knight*, 389 U.S. 332 (1967).

[8] Section 2(3) of the Securities Act provides, in pertinent part, that "[the] term 'sale' or 'sell' shall include every contract of sale or disposition of a security or interest in a security, for value." Section 3(a)(14) of the Securities Exchange Act states that "[the] terms 'sale' and 'sell' each include any contract to sell or otherwise dispose of." Although the latter definition does not refer expressly to a disposition for value, the court below did not decide whether the Securities Exchange Act nevertheless impliedly incorporated the Securities Act definition, cf. n.7, *supra*, as in its view respondent did give value for his interest in the pension plan. In light of our disposition of the question whether respondent's interest was a "security," we need not decide whether the meaning of "sale" under the Securities Exchange Act is any different from its meaning under the Securities Act.

voted on collective-bargaining agreements that chose employer contributions to the Fund instead of other wages or benefits.

The order denying the motion to dismiss was certified for appeal pursuant to 28 USC § 1292(b), and the Court of Appeals for the Seventh Circuit affirmed. 561 F.2d 1223 (1977). Relying on its perception of the economic realities of pension plans and various actions of Congress and the SEC with respect to such plans, the court ruled that respondent's interest in the Pension Fund was a "security." According to the court, a "sale" took place either when respondent ratified a collective-bargaining agreement embodying the Fund or when he accepted or retained covered employment instead of seeking other work.[9] The court did not believe the subsequent enactment of the Employee Retirement Income Security Act of 1974 (ERISA), 88 Stat. 829, 29 USC § 1001 *et seq.*, affected the application of the Securities Acts to pension plans, as the requirements and purposes of ERISA were perceived to be different from those of the Securities Acts.[10] We granted certiorari, 434 U.S. 1061 (1978), and now reverse.

II.

"The starting point in every case involving construction of a statute is the language itself." *Blue Chip Stamps v. Manor Drug Stores*, 421 U.S. 723 (1975) (POWELL, J., concurring); see *Ernst & Ernst v. Hochfelder*, 425 U.S. 185 (1976). In spite of the substantial use of employee pension plans at the time they were enacted, neither § 2(1) of the Securities Act nor § 3(a)(10) of the Securities Exchange Act, which define the term "security" in considerable detail and with numerous examples, refers to pension plans of any type. Acknowledging this omission in the statutes, respondent contends that an employee's interest in a pension plan is an "investment contract," an instrument which is included in the statutory definitions of a security.[11]

---

[9] The Court of Appeals and the District Court also held that § 17(a) of the Securities Act provides private parties with an implied cause of action for damages. In light of our disposition of this case, we express no views on this issue.

[10] Respondent did not have any cause of action under ERISA itself, as that Act took effect after he had retired.

[11] Respondent also argues that his interest constitutes a "certificate of interest or participation in any profit-sharing agreement." The court below did not consider this claim, as respondent had not seriously pressed the argument and the disposition of the "investment contract" issue made it unnecessary to decide the question. 561 F.2d 1223 (CA7 1977). Similarly, respondent here does not seriously contend that a "certificate of interest ... in any profit-sharing agreement" has any broader meaning under the Securities Acts than an "investment contract."

To determine whether a particular financial relationship constitutes an investment contract, "[the] test is whether the scheme involves an investment of money in a common enterprise with profits to come solely from the efforts of others." *Howey, supra.* This test is to be applied in light of "the substance—the economic realities of the transaction—rather than the names that may have been employed by the parties." *United Housing Foundation, Inc. v. Forman*, 421 U.S. 837 (1975). Accord, *Tcherepnin v. Knight*, 389 U.S. 332 (1967); *Howey, supra.* Cf. *SEC v. Variable Annuity Life Ins. Co.*, 359 U.S. 65 (1959) (BRENNAN, J., concurring) ("[One] must apply a test in terms of the purposes of the Federal Acts ...."). Looking separately at each element of the *Howey* test, it is apparent that an employee's participation in a noncontributory, compulsory pension plan such as the Teamsters' does not comport with the commonly held understanding of an investment contract.

II-A. Investment of Money

An employee who participates in a noncontributory, compulsory pension plan by definition makes no payment into the pension fund. He only accepts employment, one of the conditions of which is eligibility for a possible benefit on retirement. Respondent contends, however, that he has "invested" in the Pension Fund by permitting part of his compensation from his employer to take the form of a deferred pension benefit. By allowing his employer to pay money into the Fund, and by contributing his labor to his employer in return for these payments, respondent asserts he has made the kind of investment which the Securities Acts were intended to regulate.

In order to determine whether respondent invested in the Fund by accepting and remaining in covered employment, it is necessary to look at the entire transaction through which he obtained a chance to receive pension benefits. In every decision of this Court recognizing the presence of a "security" under the Securities Acts, the person found to have been an investor chose to give up a specific consideration in return for a separable financial interest with the characteristics of a security. See *Tcherepnin, supra* (money paid for bank capital stock); *SEC v. United Benefit Life Ins. Co.*, 387 U.S. 202 (1967) (portion of premium paid for variable component of mixed variable- and fixed-annuity contract); *Variable Annuity Life Ins. Co., supra* (premium paid for variable-annuity

---

In *Forman, supra,* we observed that the *Howey* test, which has been used to determine the presence of an investment contract, "embodies the essential attributes that run through all of the Court's decisions defining a security."

contract); *Howey, supra* (money paid for purchase, maintenance, and harvesting of orange grove); *SEC v. C.M. Joiner Leasing Corp.*, 320 U.S. 344 (1943) (money paid for land and oil exploration). Even in those cases where the interest acquired had intermingled security and nonsecurity aspects, the interest obtained had "to a very substantial degree elements of investment contracts...." *Variable Annuity Life Ins. Co., supra* (BRENNAN, J., concurring). In every case the purchaser gave up some tangible and definable consideration in return for an interest that had substantially the characteristics of a security.

In a pension plan such as this one, by contrast, the purported investment is a relatively insignificant part of an employee's total and indivisible compensation package. No portion of an employee's compensation other than the potential pension benefits has any of the characteristics of a security, yet these noninvestment interests cannot be segregated from the possible pension benefits. Only in the most abstract sense may it be said that an employee "exchanges" some portion of his labor in return for these possible benefits.[12] He surrenders his labor as a whole, and in return receives a compensation package that is substantially devoid of aspects resembling a security. His decision to accept and retain covered employment may have only an attenuated relationship, if any, to perceived investment possibilities of a future pension. Looking at the economic realities, it seems clear that an employee is selling his labor primarily to obtain a livelihood, not making an investment.

Respondent also argues that employer contributions on his behalf constituted his investment into the Fund. But it is inaccurate to describe these payments as having been "on behalf" of any employee. The trust agreement used employee man-weeks as a convenient way to measure an employer's overall obligation to the Fund, not as a means of measuring the employer's obligation to any particular employee. Indeed, there was no fixed relationship between contributions to the Fund and an employee's potential benefits. A pension plan with "defined benefits," such as the Local's, does not tie a qualifying employee's benefits to the time he has worked. See n.3, *supra*. One who has engaged in covered employment for 20 years will receive the same benefits as a person who has worked for 40, even though the latter has worked twice as long and induced a

---

[12] This is not to say that a person's "investment," in order to meet the definition of an investment contract, must take the form of cash only, rather than of goods and services. See *Forman, supra*.

substantially larger employer contribution.[13] Again, it ignores the economic realities to equate employer contributions with an investment by the employee.

II-B. Expectation of Profits from a Common Enterprise

As we observed in *Forman*, the "touchstone" of the *Howey* test "is the presence of an investment in a common venture premised on a reasonable expectation of profits to be derived from the entrepreneurial or managerial efforts of others." The Court of Appeals believed that Daniel's expectation of profit derived from the Fund's successful management and investment of its assets. To the extent pension benefits exceeded employer contributions and depended on earnings from the assets, it was thought they contained a profit element. The Fund's trustees provided the managerial efforts which produced this profit element.

As in other parts of its analysis, the court below found an expectation of profit in the pension plan only by focusing on one of its less important aspects to the exclusion of its more significant elements. It is true that the Fund, like other holders of large assets, depends to some extent on earnings from its assets. In the case of a pension fund, however, a far larger portion of its income comes from employer contributions, a source in no way dependent on the efforts of the Fund's managers. The Local 705 Fund, for example, earned a total of $31 million through investment of its assets between February 1955 and January 1977. During this same period employer contributions totaled $153 million.[14] Not only does the greater share of a pension plan's income ordinarily come from new contributions, but unlike most entrepreneurs who manage other people's money, a plan usually can count on increased employer contributions, over which the plan itself has no control, to cover shortfalls in earnings.[15]

The importance of asset earnings in relation to the other benefits received from employment is diminished further by the fact that where a plan has substantial preconditions to vesting, the principal barrier to an individual employee's realization of pension benefits is not the financial health of the fund. Rather, it is his own ability to

---

13 Under the terms of the Local's pension plan, for example, respondent received credit for the five years he worked before the Fund was created, even though no employer contributions had been made during that period.

14 In addition, the Fund received $7,500,000 from smaller pension funds with which it merged over the years.

15 See Note, *The Application of the Antifraud Provisions of the Securities Laws to Compulsory, Noncontributory Pension Plans After Daniel v. International Brotherhood of Teamsters*, 64 VA. L. REV. 305 (1978).

meet the fund's eligibility requirements. Thus, even if it were proper to describe the benefits as a "profit" returned on some hypothetical investment by the employee, this profit would depend primarily on the employee's efforts to meet the vesting requirements, rather than the fund's investment success.[16] When viewed in light of the total compensation package an employee must receive in order to be eligible for pension benefits, it becomes clear that the possibility of participating in a plan's asset earnings "is far too speculative and insubstantial to bring the entire transaction within the Securities Acts," *Forman, supra.*

III.

The court below believed that its construction of the term "security" was compelled not only by the perceived resemblance of a pension plan to an investment contract but also by various actions of Congress and the SEC with regard to the Securities Acts. In reaching this conclusion, the court gave great weight to the SEC's explanation of these events, an explanation which for the most part the SEC repeats here. Our own review of the record leads us to believe that this reliance on the SEC's interpretation of these legislative and administrative actions was not justified.

III-A. Actions of Congress

The SEC in its *amicus curiae* brief refers to several actions of Congress said to evidence an understanding that pension plans are securities. A close look at each instance, however, reveals only that Congress might have believed certain kinds of pension plans, radically different from the one at issue here, came within the coverage of the Securities Acts. There is no evidence that Congress at any time thought noncontributory plans similar to the one before us were subject to federal regulation as securities.

The first action cited was the rejection by Congress in 1934 of an amendment to the Securities Act that would have exempted employee stock investment and stock option plans from the Act's registration requirements.[17] The amendment passed the Senate but

---

[16] See Note, *Interest in Pension Plans as Securities: Daniel v. International Brotherhood of Teamsters*, 78 COLUM. L. REV. 184 (1978).

[17] The amendment would have added the following language to § 4(1) of the Securities Act: "As used in this paragraph, the term 'public offering' shall not be deemed to include an offering made solely to employees by an issuer or by its affiliates in connection with a bona fide plan for the payment of extra compensation or stock investment plan for the exclusive benefit of such employees." 78 Cong. Rec. 8708 (1934).

was eliminated in conference. The legislative history of the defeated proposal indicates it was intended to cover plans under which employees contributed their own funds to a segregated investment account on which a return was realized. See H.R. Conf. Rep. No. 1838, 73d Cong., 2d Sess., 41 (1934); Hearings before the House Committee on Interstate and Foreign Commerce on Proposed Amendments to the Securities Act of 1933 and to the Securities Exchange Act of 1934, 77th Cong., 1st Sess., pt.1 (1941). In rejecting the amendment, Congress revealed a concern that certain interests having the characteristics of a security not be excluded from Securities Act protection simply because investors realized their return in the form of retirement benefits. At no time, however, did Congress indicate that pension benefits in and of themselves gave a transaction the characteristics of a security.

The SEC also relies on a 1970 amendment of the Securities Act which extended § 3's exemption from registration to include "any interest or participation in a single or collective trust fund maintained by a bank ... which interest or participation is issued in connection with ... a stock bonus, pension, or profit-sharing plan which meets the requirements for qualification under section 401 of title 26,..." § 3(a)(2) of the Securities Act. It argues that in creating a registration exemption, the amendment manifested Congress' understanding that the interests covered by the amendment otherwise were subject to the Securities Acts.[18] It interprets "interest or participation in a single ... trust fund ... issued in connection with ... a stock bonus, pension, or profit-sharing plan" as referring to a prospective beneficiary's interest in a pension fund. But this construction of the 1970 amendment ignores that measure's central purpose, which was to relieve banks and insurance companies of certain registration obligations. The amendment recognized only that a pension plan had "an interest or participation" in the fund in which its assets were held, not that prospective beneficiaries of a plan had any interest in either the plan's bank-maintained assets or the plan itself.[19]

---

[18] Section 17(c) of the Securities Act and § 10(b) of the Securities Exchange Act (when read with § § 3(a)(10) and (12) of that Act) indicate that the antifraud provisions of the respective Acts continue to apply to interests that come within the exemptions created by § 3(a)(2) of the Securities Act and § 3(a)(12) of the Securities Exchange Act.

[19] See S. Rep. No. 91-184, p. 27 (1969); Hearings before the Senate Committee on Banking and Currency on Mutual Fund Legislation of 1967, 90th Cong., 1st Sess., pt. 3, pp. 1341-1342 (1967); Mundheim & Henderson, *Applicability of the Federal Securities Laws to Pension and Profit-Sharing Plans*, 29 L. & CONTEMP. PROBS. 795 (1964); Saxon & Miller, *Common Trust Funds*, 53 GEO. L.J. 994 (1965). The SEC argues that the addition by the

III-B. SEC Interpretation

The court below believed, and it now is argued to us, that almost from its inception the SEC has regarded pension plans as falling within the scope of the Securities Acts. We are asked to defer to what is seen as a longstanding interpretation of these statutes by the agency responsible for their administration. But there are limits, grounded in the language, purpose, and history of the particular statute, on how far an agency properly may go in its interpretative role. Although these limits are not always easy to discern, it is clear here that the SEC's position is neither longstanding nor even arguably within the outer limits of its authority to interpret these Acts.[20]

As we have demonstrated above, the type of pension plan at issue in this case bears no resemblance to the kind of financial interests the Securities Acts were designed to regulate. Further, the SEC's present position is flatly contradicted by its past actions. Until the instant litigation arose, the public record reveals no evidence that the SEC had ever considered the Securities Acts to be applicable to noncontributory pension plans. In

---

House of the language "single or" before "common trust fund" indicated an intent to cover the underlying plans that invested in bank-maintained funds. The legislative history, however, indicates that the change was meant only to eliminate the negative inference suggested by the unrevised language that banks would have to register the segregated investment funds they administered for particular plans. Because the provision as a whole dealt only with the relationship between a plan and its bank, the revision did not affect the registration status of the underlying pension plan. See 116 Cong. Rec. 33287 (1970). This was consistent with the SEC's interpretation of the provision. Hearings, *supra*. The subsequent addition of another provision excepting from the exemption funds "under which an amount in excess of the employer's contribution is allocated to the purchase of securities ... issued by the employer or by any company directly or indirectly controlling, controlled by or under common control with the employer" appears to have been simply an additional safeguard to confirm the SEC's authority to require such plans, and only such plans, to register. See H.R. Conf. Rep. No. 91-1631 (1970).

[20] It is a commonplace in our jurisprudence that an administrative agency's consistent, longstanding interpretation of the statute under which it operates is entitled to considerable weight. *United States v. National Assn. of Securities Dealers*, 422 U.S. 694 (1975); *Saxbe v. Bustos*, 419 U.S. 65 (1974); *Investment Company Institute v. Camp*, 401 U.S. 617 (1971); *Udall v. Tallman*, 380 U.S. 1 (1965). This deference is a product both of an awareness of the practical expertise which an agency normally develops, and of a willingness to accord some measure of flexibility to such an agency as it encounters new and unforeseen problems over time. But this deference is constrained by our obligation to honor the clear meaning of a statute, as revealed by its language, purpose, and history. On a number of occasions in recent years this Court has found it necessary to reject the SEC's interpretation of various provisions of the Securities Acts. See *SEC v. Sloan*, 436 U.S. 103 (1978); *Piper v. Chris-Craft Industries, Inc.*, 430 U.S. 1 (1977); *Ernst & Ernst v. Hochfelder*, *supra*; *Forman*, *supra*; *Blue Chip Stamps v. Manor Drug Stores*, *supra*; (POWELL, J., concurring); *Reliance Electric Co. v. Emerson Electric Co.*, 404 U.S. 418 (1972).

1941, the SEC first articulated the position that voluntary, contributory plans had investment characteristics that rendered them "securities" under the Acts. At the same time, however, the SEC recognized that noncontributory plans were not covered by the Securities Acts because such plans did not involve a "sale" within the meaning of the statutes. *Opinions of Assistant General Counsel*, CCH Fed. Sec. L. Serv. ¶ 75,195 (1941); Hearings before the House Committee on Interstate and Foreign Commerce on Proposed Amendments to the Securities Act of 1933 and to the Securities Exchange Act of 1934, 77th Cong., 1st Sess. (1941) (testimony of Commissioner Purcell).[21]

In an attempt to reconcile these interpretations of the Securities Acts with its present stand, the SEC now augments its past position with two additional propositions. First, it is argued, noncontributory plans are "securities" even where a "sale" is not involved. Second, the previous concession that noncontributory plans do not involve a "sale" was meant to apply only to the registration and reporting requirements of the Securities Acts; for purposes of the antifraud provisions, a "sale" is involved. As for the first proposition, we observe that none of the SEC opinions, reports, or testimony cited to us address the question. As for the second, the record is unambiguously to the contrary.[22] Both in its

---

[21] Subsequent to 1941, the SEC made no further efforts to regulate even contributory, voluntary pension plans except where the employees' contributions were invested in the employer's securities. Cf. n.19, *supra*. It also continued to disavow any authority to regulate noncontributory, compulsory plans. See Letter from Assistant Director, Division of Corporate Finance, May 12, 1953, CCH Fed. Sec. L. Rep. ¶ 2105.51 [1978]; Letter from Chief Counsel, Division of Corporate Finance, Aug. 1, 1962, CCH Fed. Sec. L. Rep. ¶ 2105.52 [1978]; Hearings before the Senate Committee on Banking and Currency, supra n.19; 1 LOSS, SECURITIES REGULATION 510-511 (2d ed. 1961); 4 *id.*, at 2553-2554 (2d ed. 1969); Hyde, *Employee Stock Plans and the Securities Act of 1933*, 16 W. RES. L. REV. 75 (1964); Mundheim & Henderson, *supra* n.19; Note, *Pension Plans as Securities*, 96 U. PA. L. REV. 549 (1948).

[22] On occasion the SEC has contended that because § 2 of the Securities Act and § 2 the Securities Exchange Act apply the qualifying phrase "unless the context otherwise requires" to the Acts' general definitions, it is permissible to regard a particular transaction as involving a sale or not depending on the form of regulation involved. See 1 LOSS, SECURITIES REGULATION 524-528 (2d ed. 1961); 4 *id.*, at 2562-2565 (2d ed. 1969). The Court noted the contention in *SEC v. National Securities, Inc.*, 393 U.S. 453 (1969). On previous occasions the SEC appears to have taken a different position: In 1943 it submitted an amicus brief in the Ninth Circuit arguing that a transaction must be a sale for all purposes of the Securities Act or for none, and it did not begin to rely on its "regulatory context" theory until 1951. See Brief for the SEC in *National Supply Co. v. Leland Stanford Junior University*, No. 10270 (CA9 1943); 1 LOSS, *supra*, at 524 n.211; Cohen, *Rule 133 of the Securities and Exchange Commission*, 14 RECORD OF N.Y.C.B.A. 162 (1959). We also note that, with respect to statutory mergers, the area in which the SEC originally developed its theory as to the bifurcated definition of a sale, the SEC since has abandoned its position and finds the presence of a "sale" for all purposes in the case of such mergers. See 17 CFR

1941 statements and repeatedly since then, the SEC has declared that its "no sale" position applied to the Securities Acts as a whole. See opinions of Assistant General Counsel, CCH Fed. Sec. L. Serv. ¶ 75,195 (1941); Hearings before the House Committee on Interstate and Foreign Commerce, supra; Institutional Investor Study Report of the Securities and Exchange Commission, H.R. Doc. No. 92-64, pt.3 (1971) ("[The] Securities Act does not apply ...."); Hearings before the Subcommittee on Welfare and Pension Funds of the Senate Committee on Labor and Public Welfare on Welfare and Pension Plans Investigation, 84th Cong., 1st Sess., pt.3 (1955). Congress acted on this understanding when it proceeded to develop the legislation that became ERISA. See, *e.g.*, Interim Report of Activities of the Private Welfare and Pension Plan Study, 1971, S. Rep. No.92-634 (1972) ("Pension and profit-sharing plans are ***exempt from coverage*** under the Securities Act of 1933 ... unless the plan is a voluntary contributory pension plan and invests in the securities of the employer company an amount greater than that paid into the plan by the employer") (emphasis added). As far as we are aware, at no time before this case arose did the SEC intimate that the antifraud provisions of the Securities Acts nevertheless applied to noncontributory pension plans.

IV.

If any further evidence were needed to demonstrate that pension plans of the type involved are not subject to the Securities Acts, the enactment of ERISA in 1974, 88 Stat., 829, would put the matter to rest. Unlike the Securities Acts, ERISA deals expressly and in detail with pension plans. ERISA requires pension plans to disclose specified information to employees in a specified manner, see 29 USC § § 1021-1030, in contrast to the indefinite and uncertain disclosure obligations imposed by the antifraud provisions of the Securities Acts, see *Santa Fe Industries, Inc. v. Green*, 430 U.S. 462 (1977); *TSC Industries, Inc. v. Northway, Inc.*, 426 U.S. 438 (1976). Further, ERISA regulates the substantive terms of pension plans, setting standards for plan funding and limits on the eligibility requirements an employee must meet. For example, with respect to the underlying issue in this case—whether respondent served long enough to receive a pension— § 203(a) of ERISA, 29 USC § 1053(a), now sets the minimum level of benefits an employee must receive after accruing specified years of service, and § 203 (b), 29 USC § 1053(b), governs continuous-service requirements. Thus, if respondent had retired

§ 230.145 (1978). In view of our disposition of this case, we express no opinion as to the correct resolution of the divergent views on this issue.

after § 1053 took effect, the Fund would have been required to pay him at least a partial pension. The Securities Acts, on the other hand, do not purport to set the substantive terms of financial transactions.

The existence of this comprehensive legislation governing the use and terms of employee pension plans severely undercuts all arguments for extending the Securities Acts to noncontributory, compulsory pension plans. Congress believed that it was filling a regulatory void when it enacted ERISA, a belief which the SEC actively encouraged. Not only is the extension of the Securities Acts by the court below unsupported by the language and history of those Acts, but in light of ERISA it serves no general purpose. See *California v. Sanders*, 430 U.S. 99 (1977). Cf. *Boys Markets, Inc. v. Retail Clerks*, 398 U.S. 235 (1970). Whatever benefits employees might derive from the effect of the Securities Acts are now provided in more definite form through ERISA.

V.

We hold that the Securities Acts do not apply to a noncontributory, compulsory pension plan. Because the first two counts of respondent's complaint do not provide grounds for relief in federal court, the District Court should have granted the motion to dismiss them. The judgment below is therefore

Reversed.

H.E. Butt Grocery Co.

IC Act § § 3(c)(1) & 3(c)(7), SEC No-Action Letter (May 18, 2001)

Response of the Office of Chief Counsel
Division of Investment Management

H.E.B. Investment and Retirement Plan
File No. 132-3

Your letter dated April 10, 2001, requests our assurance that we would not recommend enforcement action to the Commission under § 7(a) of the Investment Company Act of 1940 against funds that are excepted from the definition of "investment company" by § 3(c)(7) of the Investment Company Act ("**§ 3(c)(7) Funds**") if the **H.E.B. Investment and Retirement Plan** ("Plan") invests in such funds.

FACTS

You state that the Plan is a qualified defined contribution plan that provides retirement benefits for the participating employees and beneficiaries ("**Plan participants**") of the **H.E. Butt Grocery Company** ("Company"). You also state that the aggregate amount of investments owned by the Plan as of March 30, 2001, was approximately $800,000,000. You represent that the Company and the Plan participants contribute to the Plan, and the Plan qualifies under § 401(k) of the Internal Revenue Code of 1986, as amended, with respect to the Plan participant contributions. You state that Plan participants may allocate their account value as they elect among six investment options that are managed and invested by the eight trustees of the Plan. The investment options are the Aggressive Fund, the General Fund, the Conservative Fund, the Stocks-only Fund, the Bonds-only Fund, and the Money Market Fund (collectively, "**Investment Options**"). You state that investment decisions for the Investment Options are made by the Plan trustees, through an investment committee consisting of five of the trustees.

You state that the Plan trustees have invested portions of the Aggressive Fund and the General Fund in investments that are excepted from the definition of "investment company" by § 3(c)(1) of the Investment Company Act ("**§ 3(c)(1) Funds**").[1] You also

[1] Section 3(c)(1) of the Investment Company Act generally excepts from the definition of investment company "any issuer whose outstanding securities (other than short-term paper) are beneficially owned by not more than one hundred persons and which is not making and does not presently propose to make a public offering of its securities." Section 3(c)(1) is intended to except from regulation under the Investment Company Act private

state that the Plan trustees are responsible for making the initial decision to invest Plan assets in a § 3(c)(1) Fund and subsequent decisions regarding the amount and the duration of the investment. You represent that the Plan participants' investment discretion is limited to allocating their accounts among the Investment Options. You represent that the Plan trustees have managed the Plan according to the representations set forth in *The Standish, Ayer & Wood, Inc. Stable Value Group Trust* (Dec. 28, 1995) ("*Standish Ayer*") in order to ensure that a § 3(c)(1) Fund may treat the Plan as a single beneficial owner for purposes of the one hundred-person limit of § 3(c)(1).[2]

You state that the Plan trustees now propose to invest a portion of the Aggressive and General Funds in § 3(c)(7) Funds. You ask us to conclude, analogous to our § 3(c)(1) position in *Standish Ayer*, that a § 3(c)(7) Fund in which an Investment Option of the Plan invests may treat the Plan, and is not required to treat each Plan participant, as a qualified purchaser for § 3(c)(7) purposes.

ANALYSIS

The NATIONAL SECURITIES MARKETS IMPROVEMENT ACT OF 1996[3] ("NSMIA") added § 3(c)(7) to the Investment Company Act. Section 3(c)(7) excepts from the definition of "investment company" any issuer whose outstanding securities are owned exclusively by persons who, at the time of the acquisition of the securities, are qualified purchasers, and which is not making and does not propose to make a public offering of its securities. Section 2(a)(51)(A)(iv) defines "qualified purchaser" to include "any person, acting for its own account or the accounts of other qualified purchasers, who in the aggregate owns and invests on a discretionary basis, not less than $25,000,000 in investments."[4] You assert that the Plan will meet the definition of "qualified purchaser," as defined in § 2(a)(51) and

---

companies in which there is no significant public interest and which are therefore not appropriate subjects of federal regulation. See SMALL BUSINESS INVESTMENT INCENTIVE ACT OF 1980, H. Rep. No. 1341, 96th Cong., 2nd Sess. (1980).

[2] See *infra* note 13 (setting forth the *Standish Ayer representations*).

[3] PL No. 104-290 (1996) (codified in various sections of the United States Code).

[4] Section 2(a)(51)(A) of the Investment Company Act also generally defines "*qualified purchaser*" to include: (1) any natural person who owns not less than $5 million in investments; (2) certain family-owned companies that own not less than $5 million in investments; and (3) any trust that does not meet the definition of family-owned company in § 2(a)(51)(A)(ii) and that was not formed for the specific purpose of acquiring the securities offered by the § 3(c)(7) Fund, and the trustees and settlors of which are qualified purchasers.

required by § 3(c)(7), because the Plan owns and invests on a discretionary basis not less than $25 million in investments and will be acting for its own account. You state that most of the Plan participants will not meet the "qualified purchaser" definition.

The Commission, when adopting rules to implement § 3(c)(7), discussed the circumstances under which a pension or other type of employee benefit plan that owns and invests on a discretionary basis not less than $25 million of investments in the aggregate could be considered to be a qualified purchaser.[5] The Commission stated that a defined benefit retirement plan would be a qualified purchaser with respect to investments made by plan trustees if (1) plan participants are not permitted to decide whether or how much to invest in particular investment alternatives, and (2) the decision to invest in a § 3(c)(7) Fund is made by the plan trustee or other plan fiduciary that makes investment decisions for the plan. The Commission indicated, however, that a § 3(c)(7) Fund should treat § 401(k) plans differently from such defined benefit plans when a § 401(k) plan allows an employee to direct the investment of his or her account balance to specified investment alternatives that are made available through the plan (a "**participant-directed plan**"). In that case, a § 3(c)(7) Fund should "*look through*" the participant-directed plan to the plan's participants for purposes of determining whether each investor in the § 3(c)(7) Fund is a qualified purchaser. The Commission also noted in the Adopting Release the staff's positions in *The PanAgora Group Trust* (Apr. 29, 1994) ("*PanAgora*") and *Standish Ayer* that, taken together, provide guidance regarding the circumstances under which a participant-directed plan that operates in a manner resembling a defined benefit plan may, for certain purposes, be treated like a defined benefit plan.

Briefly, in ***PanAgora***, the staff looked through a participant-directed plan and concluded that each participant in the plan who allocates a portion of his or her account to a particular § 3(c)(1) Fund should be treated by the fund as a single beneficial owner for purposes of the one hundred-person limit of § 3(c)(1). In *PanAgora*, each plan participant could attain individualized levels of potential risk and return and make individual investment decisions by allocating his or her plan account assets among various investment alternatives, including by investing entirely or partially in a § 3(c)(1) Fund. We took the position that, for purposes of determining compliance with the one

---

[5] See *Privately Offered Investment Companies*, IC-22597, 62 FR 17512 (1997) ("*Adopting Release*").

hundred-person limit of § 3(c)(1), each plan participant in a participant-directed plan who invests through the plan in a generic investment option consisting of a § 3(c)(1) Fund, and who decides whether or how much to invest in the § 3(c)(1) Fund, should be treated as a single beneficial owner of the § 3(c)(1) Fund's securities.[6]

In ***Standish Ayer***, we took the position that a participant-directed plan that offers its plan participants generic investment options that, in turn, may invest a portion of their assets in a § 3(c)(1) Fund, could be treated as a single beneficial owner of the § 3(c)(1) Fund's securities when, among other things, the decision as to whether and how much to invest in a § 3(c)(1) Fund would be made solely by a plan fiduciary, and no representation would be made to plan participants that any specific portion of the relevant generic investment option would be invested in any particular § 3(c)(1) Fund. In *Standish Ayer*, the plan was managed so that plan participants would be unaware of how much an investment option invested in any particular § 3(c)(1) Fund. Our position in Standish Ayer recognized that a participant-directed plan may operate in a manner resembling a defined benefit plan under certain circumstances.

In the ***Adopting Release***, the Commission affirmed our position in *PanAgora* but stated that it was not endorsing the analysis set forth in *Standish Ayer* for purposes of § 3(c)(7).[7] The Commission did not reject the staff's analysis in *Standish Ayer*. Instead, the Commission requested that we reconsider whether the position taken in *Standish Ayer* is consistent with the position reflected in *PanAgora* for purposes of § 3(c)(1) and consider whether the position taken in *Standish Ayer* is appropriate in the context of § 3(c)(7). As a result, before considering your specific request, we must first reconsider the application of *Standish Ayer* in the context of § 3(c)(1), including its consistency with *PanAgora*.

Standish Ayer* is Consistent with *PanAgora

The staff has taken the position that, for purposes of the one hundred-person limit of § 3(c)(1) of the Investment Company Act, a partnership will constitute only one beneficial owner (provided that the attribution provision does not apply)[8] when the

---

[6] In contrast, a § 3(c)(1) Fund could treat a defined benefit plan as a single beneficial owner of the fund's securities under certain circumstances. See *Owens-Illinois, Inc.* (June 24, 1994).

[7] See *Adopting Release, supra* note 5, at § II.A.8.

[8] Under the § 3(c)(1)(A) attribution provision, as amended by NSMIA, a "*company*" is treated as a single beneficial

partnership is managed as a common investment vehicle, rather than as a device for facilitating individual investment decisions.[9] In contrast, the staff also has taken the position that for § 3(c)(1) purposes it will look through a partnership and treat each individual partner as a beneficial owner of a § 3(c)(1) Fund's securities, regardless of the applicability of the attribution provision, when the partnership is managed as a device for facilitating individual investment decisions of the partners, instead of as a common investment vehicle.[10] Consequently, when a partnership holds a § 3(c)(1) Fund's securities, the beneficial owner of those securities for § 3(c)(1) purposes will be deemed to be the partnership if the partnership decides whether and how much to invest in the § 3(c)(1) Fund; when the individual partners, however, have the ability to determine whether or how much of a partnership's capital will be invested in a § 3(c)(1) Fund, the § 3(c)(1) Fund should "look through" the partnership, and treat the individual partners as the beneficial owners of the § 3(c)(1) Fund's securities for purposes of § 3(c)(1).

In both *PanAgora* and *Standish Ayer*, we considered the prior no-action positions

---

owner unless the company owns ten percent or more of the outstanding voting securities of the § 3(c)(1) Fund, and the company is, or but for the exceptions in § 3(c)(1) or § 3(c)(7) would be, an investment company. Under § 2(a)(8) of the Investment Company Act, a "*company*" is defined as "a corporation, a partnership, an association, a joint-stock company, a trust, a fund, or any organized group of persons whether incorporated or not." The purpose of the attribution provision is to "ensure that an investment company issuer cannot evade the requirements of the [Investment Company Act] simply by using one or more other companies to purchase blocks of its securities and, in turn, sell those companies' securities to investors." See H. Rep. No. 1341, *supra* note 1. NSMIA amended the attribution provision to simplify the way in which a § 3(c)(1) Fund may count the number of its beneficial owners for purposes of the one hundred-person limit.

[9] See *Merrill Lynch & Co., Inc.* (Apr. 23, 1992), in which the staff took the position that a general partnership should be treated as a single beneficial owner for § 3(c)(1) purposes when, among other things, the affairs of the partnership, including its proposed holdings in § 3(c)(1) Funds, would be administered solely by its managing general partner, and the individual partners would neither make decisions regarding the allocation of the partnership's capital among the § 3(c)(1) Funds nor have discretion or input with respect to the allocation of their capital contributions among the § 3(c)(1) Funds. See also *Handy Place Investment Partnership* (July 19, 1989).

[10] See *Six Pack* (Nov. 13, 1989), in which, despite the representation of Six Pack (the general partnership) that it would at all times own less than ten percent of the outstanding interests of any § 3(c)(1) Fund (and thus the attribution provision would not apply), the staff concluded that Six Pack was not managed as a common investment vehicle, but rather as a device for facilitating the individual investment decisions of the five general partners, because each partner was permitted to determine the amount of his or her contribution to each particular investment made by the general partnership based upon his or her specific investment objectives. See also *WR Investment Partners Diversified Strategies Fund, L.P.* (Apr. 15, 1992) ("*WR Investment Partners*"); *Tyler Capital Fund, L.P./South Market Capital* (Sept. 28, 1987) ("*Tyler Capital Fund*").

issued in the context of partnership investments in § 3(c)(1) Funds, and we applied a similar analysis.[11] In *PanAgora*, we concluded that the individualized nature of the plan participant's investment decisions required each plan participant to be treated as a beneficial owner for § 3(c)(1) purposes; plan participants could elect to invest all or a portion of their assets in certain investment alternatives that could consist entirely of a particular § 3(c)(1) Fund.[12] In *Standish Ayer*, in contrast, the participant-directed plan was not managed to facilitate a participant's decision to invest in any particular § 3(c)(1) Fund, and we viewed the plan as a single beneficial owner of a § 3(c)(1) Fund for § 3(c)(1) purposes.[13] Each plan participant in *Standish Ayer* made a decision to invest in generic investment options that, in turn, could invest in unspecified § 3(c)(1) Funds. Because of these distinctions, we continue to believe that *Standish Ayer* is consistent with *PanAgora*, as well as consistent with the prior no-action positions issued in the context of partnership investments in § 3(c)(1) Funds.

The *Standish Ayer* Position is Appropriate for Purposes of § 3(c)(7)

The Commission has adopted the analysis set forth in *PanAgora* for purposes of § 3(c)(7).[14] Consequently, a § 3(c)(7) Fund should "look through" a participant-directed

---

[11] In *PanAgora*, we considered *Merrill Lynch & Co., Inc., supra* note 9, *WR Investment Partners, supra* note 10, and *Tyler Capital Fund, supra* note 10. In *Standish Ayer*, in addition to *WR Investment Partners* and *Tyler Capital Fund*, we also considered *Six Pack, supra* note 10.

[12] The positions in both *PanAgora* and *Standish Ayer* were taken independent of the applicability of the attribution provision (*i.e.*, among other things, it was assumed that the plans would not own ten percent or more of the outstanding voting securities of a § 3(c)(1) Fund). See *supra* note 9.

[13] Our position in ***Standish Ayer*** was based upon a number of **representations** made by Standish Ayer, including, among other things, that: (1) a plan's investment in a § 3(c)(1) Fund would be made with assets directed by plan participants to a generic investment option (*i.e.*, an account with an identified generic investment objective); (2) the decision to invest (both initially and subsequently) and to withdraw assets from a § 3(c)(1) Fund would be made solely by a plan fiduciary, without direction from or consultation with any plan participant; (3) immediately following each purchase of securities of a § 3(c)(1) Fund by a generic investment option, at least 50% of the assets of the generic investment option would consist of securities or property other than units of the § 3(c)(1) Fund; (4) no representation would be made to plan participants that any specific portion of their contributions or account balances, or any specific portion of the generic investment option, would be invested in a § 3(c)(1) Fund; and (5) if a plan delivers any information to the plan participants mentioning an investment in a § 3(c)(1) Fund, it would be accompanied by a disclaimer that no assurance can be given that the generic investment option would continue to invest in the § 3(c)(1) Fund.

[14] See *Adopting Release, supra* note 5, at § II.A.8.

plan in which each plan participant may invest through the plan in a generic investment option consisting of a § 3(c)(7) Fund and may determine whether or how much to invest in the § 3(c)(7) Fund.[15] Under such circumstances, each plan participant investing in the § 3(c)(7) Fund is acting for his or her own account and must meet the definition of qualified purchaser.[16] As noted above, however, with respect to a participant-directed plan operated in a manner resembling that of a defined benefit plan, the Commission directed us to consider whether the position taken in *Standish Ayer* is appropriate in the context of § 3(c)(7).[17] We believe that it is.

Specifically, we believe that applying the *Standish Ayer* analysis in the § 3(c)(7) context is consistent with the Commission's statements regarding the treatment of defined benefit plans as qualified purchasers. In the Adopting Release, the Commission stated that a retirement plan that owns and invests on a discretionary basis not less than $25 million of investments in the aggregate should be treated as a qualified purchaser if (1) plan participants are not permitted to decide whether or how much to invest in particular investment alternatives, and (2) the decision to invest in a § 3(c)(7) Fund is made by the plan trustee or other plan fiduciary that makes investment decisions for the plan. In our view, a participant-directed plan that can make all of the representations made in *Standish Ayer* meets those factors. Accordingly, we believe that such a plan that owns and invests on a discretionary basis not less than $25 million of investments in the aggregate would, like a defined benefit plan, meet the definition of qualified purchaser because it is acting for its own account. We also note that our position is consistent with Congress's treatment of certain operating companies as qualified purchasers.[18]

We also believe that applying the *Standish Ayer* analysis in the context of § 3(c)(7) is consistent with the purpose of § 3(c)(7). The exception provided by § 3(c)(7) reflects

---

[15] In particular, such a participant-directed plan would not be a qualified purchaser as defined in § 2(a)(51)(A)(iv) of the Investment Company Act because it would not be acting for its own account.

[16] A § 3(c)(7) Fund or a person acting on its behalf must have a reasonable belief that a person purchasing the § 3(c)(7) Fund's securities meets the definition of qualified purchaser in § 2(a)(51)(A) of the Investment Company Act. See Rule 2a51-1(h) under the Investment Company Act.

[17] See *Adopting Release, supra* note 5, at § II.A.8.

[18] See § 2(a)(51)(A)(iv) of the Investment Company Act (the definition of qualified purchaser includes a company, acting for its own account, that owns and invests on a discretionary basis not less than $25 million in investments, regardless of whether the company's shareholders qualify as qualified purchasers).

Congress's recognition that financially sophisticated investors are in a position to appreciate the risks associated with certain investment pools and do not need the protections of the Investment Company Act.[19] Under a plan operated in accordance with *Standish Ayer*, a plan trustee or other fiduciary would make specific investment decisions for an investment option on behalf of all of the plan participants who had selected the investment option, and such a plan would not facilitate the individual investment decisions of the individual plan participants. As previously noted, the Commission has acknowledged that a defined benefit plan would be a qualified purchaser with respect to investments made by plan trustees when, among other things, the decision to invest in a § 3(c)(7) Fund is made by the plan trustee or other plan fiduciary. The Commission's approach ensures that, in the context of a defined benefit plan, the person or persons making the investment decision would be in a position to appreciate the risks of investing in a § 3(c)(7) Fund. We believe that it is appropriate to apply a similar approach to a participant-directed plan operated in a manner resembling a defined benefit plan.[20]

---

[19] See S. Rep. No. 293, 104th Cong., 2d Sess. 10 (1996) ("Generally, these investors can evaluate on their own behalf matters such as the level of a fund's management fees, governance provisions, transactions with affiliates, investment risk, leverage, and redemption rights.").

[20] See *Adopting Release, supra* note 5, at § II.A.8. We note that the Commission indicated in the Adopting Release that, under Rule 2a51-1(g) under the Investment Company Act, a "qualified institutional buyer" ("QIB") as defined in Rule 144A under the Securities Act of 1933, generally will be deemed to be a qualified purchaser for purposes of § 3(c)(7). Rule 144A generally defines a QIB as, among other things, (1) certain institutions that own and invest on a discretionary basis $100 million of securities of issuers that are not affiliated with the institution, and (2) certain employee benefit plans and trusts that hold assets of employee benefit plans. See Rule 144A under the Securities Act of 1933. The Commission also stated in the *Adopting Release* that, despite the inclusion of employee benefit plans as QIBs, "a self-directed employee benefit plan (such as a "401(k)" plan) generally would not be considered to be a qualified purchaser for purposes of rule 2a51-1; rather, an employee could invest in a § 3(c)(7) Fund through a self-directed plan only if the employee is a qualified purchaser. [Rule 2a51-1(g)] therefore is not available to a self-directed plan." See *Adopting Release, supra* note 5, at § II.A.1. The Commission further stated in the *Adopting Release* that "Rule 2a51-1(g)(1)(ii) provides that a plan will not be deemed to be acting for its own account if investment decisions with respect to the plan are made by the beneficiaries of the plan. In other words, the investment decision must be made by a qualified purchaser." *Id.* at § II.A.1. n.33. We note that these statements by the Commission address situations in which a benefit plan that meets the QIB definition permits plan participants to make investment decisions to invest directly in § 3(c)(7) Funds, or in investment options that are § 3(c)(7) Funds. We believe that, consistent with the wording of Rule 2a51-1(g), when "investment decisions [are] made solely by the fiduciary, trustee or sponsor of such plan," as in the present case, a plan can qualify as a qualified purchaser under Rule 2a51-1(g).

Accordingly, based on the facts and representations set forth in your letter, we would not recommend enforcement action to the Commission under § 7(a) of the Investment Company Act against the § 3(c)(7) Funds in which the Plan invests a portion of its assets if those § 3(c)(7) Funds treat the Plan as a qualified purchaser for § 3(c)(7) purposes. We rely upon your representation that the Plan will own and invest on a discretionary basis not less than $25 million in investments and was not formed for the specific purpose of acquiring the securities offered by any § 3(c)(7) Fund.[21] We also rely upon your representation that the Plan is a § 401(k) plan, subject to the provisions of the Employee Retirement Income Security Act of 1974 ("ERISA"), and the Plan trustees, who are fiduciaries subject to the fiduciary provisions of ERISA,[22] make all of the investment decisions for the Plan. We further rely upon your representations which, we believe, ensure that the Investment Options are not used to facilitate the individual investment decisions of Plan participants into any § 3(c)(7) Fund. These representations include:

- other than the Plan trustees acting in their capacity as Plan fiduciaries,[23] a Plan participant's investment discretion will be limited to allocating his or her account among a number of Investment Options, each of which has an identified generic investment objective;
- the decision to invest the assets of an Investment Option in a § 3(c)(7) Fund (both initially and subsequent to the initial investment), and to withdraw the assets from

---

[21] Among other things, Rule 2a51-3 under the Investment Company Act provides that a company shall not be deemed to be a qualified purchaser under § 2(a)(51)(A)(iv) of the Investment Company Act if the company was formed for the specific purpose of acquiring the securities offered by a § 3(c)(7) Fund.

[22] The fiduciary standards under ERISA generally require that a fiduciary discharge his or her duties with respect to a plan solely in the interest of the participants and beneficiaries and (1) for the exclusive purpose of "providing benefits to participants and their beneficiaries" and "defraying reasonable expenses of administering the plan," (2) "with the care, skill, prudence, and diligence under the circumstances then prevailing that a prudent man acting in a like capacity and familiar with such matters would use in the conduct of an enterprise of a like character and with like aims," (3) "by diversifying the investments of the plan so as to minimize the risk of large losses, unless under the circumstances it is clearly prudent not to do so," and (4) "in accordance with the documents and instruments governing the plan...." See 29 USC § 1104. You represent that, in meeting their fiduciary duties, the Plan trustees, when making investment decisions, will, among other things, consider the cash flow requirements of the Plan. See, *e.g.*, *GIW Indus., Inc. v. Trevor, Stewart, Burton & Jacobsen, Inc.*, 895 F.2d 729 (11ths Cir. 1990).

[23] You state that certain Plan trustees may also be Plan participants (per a telephone conversation between Brent J. Fields of the staff and William G. Lee of Vinson & Elkins L.L.P. on April 25, 2001).

the § 3(c)(7) Fund, and the amount of assets invested, will be made solely by one or more Plan fiduciaries, without direction from or consultation with any Plan participant other than the Plan trustees acting in their capacity as Plan fiduciaries;

- immediately following each purchase of any § 3(c)(7) Fund's securities by an Investment Option, at least 50% of the assets of the option will consist of securities or property other than securities of the § 3(c)(7) Fund;[24]
- no representation will be made to Plan participants that any specific portion of their contributions to or account balances under the Plan, or any specific portion of the relevant Investment Option, will be invested in the § 3(c)(7) Fund. If the Plan delivers any information to Plan participants that mentions an investment in a § 3(c)(7) Fund, it will be accompanied by a disclaimer to the effect that no assurances can be given that the Investment Option will continue to invest its assets, or the same portion of its assets, in the § 3(c)(7) Fund.

Our position is based upon the facts and representations set forth in your letter. Any different facts or representations may require a different conclusion.

[24] Similar to *Standish Ayer*, the 50% limitation is intended to ensure that a Plan participant's decision to allocate assets to an Investment Option is not the substantial equivalent of an investment in a § 3(c)(7) Fund. As we noted in *Standish Ayer*, by incorporating the 50% representation into our response, we do not suggest that a higher percentage investment necessarily would mean that a Plan's participants must be treated as the owners of the securities of an underlying § 3(c)(7) Fund. Further, consistent with our statements in the § 3(c)(1) context in *Standish Ayer*, we will not respond to no-action requests that involve a plan's generic investment option seeking to invest more than 50% of its assets in a § 3(c)(7) Fund if the request does not otherwise differ materially from the facts described in *Standish Ayer* or your incoming letter.

Section 5.4 Structured Financing Vehicles

Topic 1 Mortgage-Related Pools

Laws & Rules Highlight:

IC Act (15 USC 80a-1 *et seq.*) & Rules (17 CFR §§ 270.0-1 *et seq.*)
IA Act (15 USC 80b-1 *et seq.*); Securities Act (15 USC 77a *et seq.*)

SPV and IC status (IC Act)

- § 3(a)(1) (*def. "investment company"*); § 2(a)(36) (*def. "**security**" to include bond and evidence of indebtedness*); § 3(a)(2) (*def. "investment securities"*); § 2(a)(32) (*def. "redeemable security"*)
- § 3(c)(5)(C) (*mortgage banking issuer exclusion from IC: entity **primarily engaged** in purchasing mortgages and other liens on or interests in real estate, and not issuing redeemable securities—an **active lender** exclusion*)
- IC Rule 3a-7 Issuers of Asset-Backed Securities (***safe harbor** from IC for: issuer that pools income-producing "eligible assets" and issues non-redeemable, "fixed-income securities" backed by such assets—a **passive investment pool** exclusion; independent trustee requirement*)

SPV Sponsor and IA status (IA Act)

- § 202(a)(11) (*def. "investment adviser"*); § 202(a)(18) (*def. "**security**" to include bond and evidence of indebtedness*)
- § 202(a)(11)(A) (*IA exclusion for bank, and bank holding company which is not an IC, unless serving as IA to registered IC; if advisory services are performed through a "separately identifiable department or division of a bank" (SID), such an SID and not the bank shall be deemed IA*)
- § 202(a)(11)(C) (*IA exclusion for broker-dealer, subject to "solely incidental" and "no special compensation" conditions*)
- § 202(a)(11)(E) (*IA exclusion for advice solely relating to U.S. government or agency securities*)

ABS/MBS under Securities Act

- § 2(a)(1) (*def. "**security**" to include bond and evidence of indebtedness*)

- Regulation AB—Asset-Backed Securities
    - § 229.1101(b) (*def. "**asset-backed issuer**"*); § 229.1101(c) (*def. and additional conditions of "**asset-backed security**"*); § 229.1101(e) (*def. "**depositor**"*); § 229.1101(f) (*def. "**issuing entity**"*); § 229.1101(i) (*def. "**obligor**"*); § 229.1101(j) (*def. "**servicer**"*); § 229.1101(l) (*def. "**sponsor**"*)
    - § 229.1109 Trustees and Other Transaction Parties; § 229.1110 Originators; § 229.1111 Pool Assets
- Rule 144A Private Resales of Securities to Institutions (*safe harbor permits unlimited resales of certain unregistered securities to "**QIBs**"*)
    - Rule 144A(a)(1) (*def. "qualified institutional buyer" QIB*)
- Regulation D Rule 506 Exemption for Limited Offers and Sales Without Regard to Dollar Amount of Offering (*safe harbor permits unregistered sales solely to "**accredited investors**" if general solicitation or general advertising is used in offering*)
    - 501(a) (*def. "accredited investor"*)

Mortgage Securitization Structure—An Illustration:
Customized Loans-to-Standardized Securities Conversion

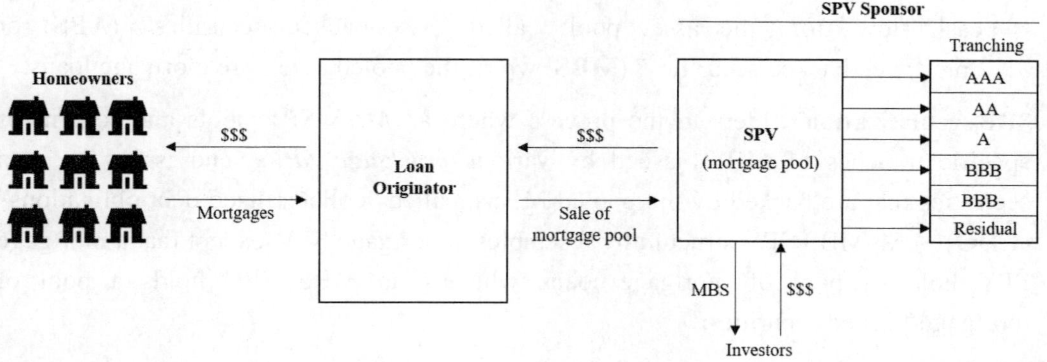

Re-Securitization Structure—An Illustration:
MBS-CDO-CDO^2 Conversion

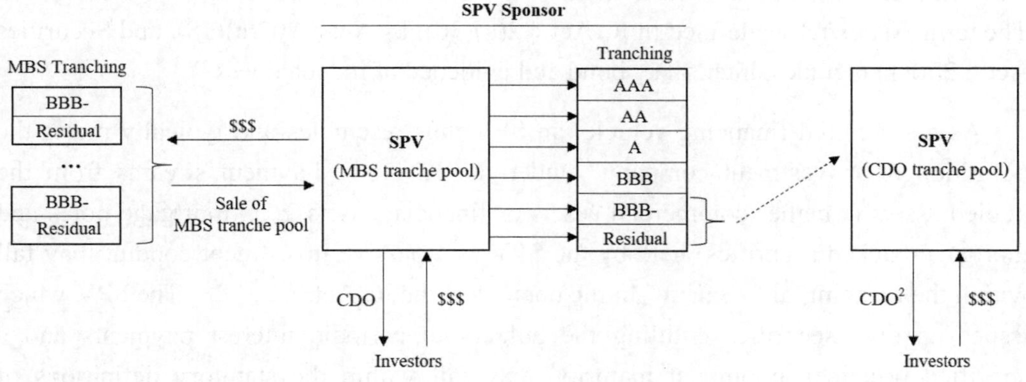

Pre-Case Background Note:[Biblio]

Mortgage-Related SPV *versus* Conventional IC

"**Securitization**" is also referred to as "**structured finance**." Securitization involves:[1; 2 (Ch.1); 3 (Chs.1, 6); 4]

- ***pooling*** of income-producing financial assets (whether mortgage assets or non-mortgage assets), which are typically customized and illiquid;

- ***sale*** of the asset pool to an entity: a "special purpose vehicle" (SPV) or interchangeably a "special purpose entity" (**SPE**); and
- ***issuance*** by the SPV of standardized and liquid securities that are backed by the cash flow from the asset pool: called "asset-backed securities" (**ABS**) or "mortgage-backed securities" (**MBS**) where the pooled assets are mortgage loans.

"**Re-securitization**" refers to the process where an ***MBS SPV*** pools and securitizes specific tranches of MBSs issued by various ***mortgage SPVs***, and issues its own securities that are backed by the pooled MBSs, called "collateralized debt obligations" (**CDO**). An MBS SPV structurally resembles a mortgage SPV, except that a mortgage SPV holds a pool of mortgage loans whereas an MBS SPV holds a pool of mortgage-backed securities.[5]

An "**investment company**," as defined in IC Act, means an "***issuer***" of securities that is "engaged primarily ... in the business of investing, reinvesting, or trading in securities" [§ 3(a)(1)(A)]; or "owns or proposes to acquire investment securities having a value exceeding 40 per centum of the value of such issuer's total assets (exclusive of Government securities and cash items) on an unconsolidated basis" [§ 3(a)(1)(C)]. The term "***security***" as defined in IC Act § 2(a)(36), IA Act § 202(a)(18), and Securities Act § 2(a)(1) includes, inter alia, "bond and evidence of indebtedness."

As a structured financing vehicle, an SPV thus resembles and typically meets the definition of "investment company" under the IC Act. Payment streams from the pooled assets (whether commercial assets or financial assets, *e.g.*, mortgage notes and mortgage-backed securities) held by the SPV as a passive investment conduit may fall within the meaning of "security" in the context of the IC Act.[1 (n.339); 6e] The SPV, which issues its own securities entitling the holders to periodic interest payments and a specified principal amount at maturity, may fall within the statutory definitions of "issuer" and "investment company" under the IC Act.[1; 2 (Ch.6); 3 (Ch.11); 4] While IC Act **§ 3(c)(5)(C)** excludes from the IC definition companies which are ***primarily engaged in the mortgage banking business***—in contrast to issuers in the investment company business, an SPV whose sole purpose is to ***passively*** hold a pool of mortgages and mortgage-related instruments ("***mortgage-related pool***")[6d (n.1)] may not be able to rely on a statutory exclusion from IC regulation intended for active mortgage banking companies.[6a; 6d] On the other hand, subjecting the mortgage-related SPVs to the regulatory regime of the IC Act would make the SPV operations non-feasible.[1 (n.253); 6]

Noting the "broad economic implications" resulting from IC Act's application to structured financings, and the need to remove "an unnecessary and unintended barrier" to the use of structured financings in all sectors of the economy to address their capital needs, the SEC adopted **Rule 3a-7 safe harbor** to conditionally exclude "***structured financing issuers***" or "**SPVs**" from the definition of IC. The safe harbor conditions, highlighted below, serve to ***distinguish*** **SPVs**—which are intended as a financing technique to generate capital by integrating the capital markets with borrowers, ***from regulated*** **ICs**—which are intended to provide investment diversification, economies of scale, and professional management to investors:[1; 6b; 6c]

- ***SPV the issuer***—the issuer must be engaged in the business of *acquiring and holding* eligible financial assets, and may engage in activities *related or incidental* thereto; the issuer may not issue *redeemable* securities, as registered mutual fund and UIT do.
- ***The SPV securities***—securities issued by the SPV must be "*fixed-income securities*" or other securities *primarily backed by* the cash flows from eligible assets; securities sold to the public must be rated as *investment grade* or better by at least one NRSRO at the time of their initial sale; *non-conforming securities* may only be sold to "qualified institutional buyers" or "accredited investors."
- ***SPV asset pool operation***—any *addition to or removal from* the SPV asset pool of any eligible assets during the operation of the financing must be effected only in compliance with the financing's organizational documents, to prevent self-dealing and overreaching by the SPV sponsor or other insiders, and avoid activities resembling mutual fund portfolio management.
- ***Independent trustee for SPV assets***—who must be a *bank* meeting the requirements of § 26(a) of the IC Act; may *not be affiliated* with the issuer or any person involved in the organization or operation of the issuer; and must obtain a perfected security interest or ownership interest in the *eligible assets that principally* generate the cash flows needed for payment on the fixed-income securities.

More generally on the IC status and exclusions of a **structured financing vehicle** *aka* an "**asset-backed issuer**" (*i.e.*, issuer of fixed income securities the payments on which depend primarily on the cash flows generated by a specified pool of underlying financial assets):[6e (n.1)] An asset-backed issuer typically meets the definition of "investment company" under § 3(a)(1) of the IC Act, since it issues securities and is engaged in the business of investing in, owning, or holding financial assets that are securities under the IC Act.[6e] Two types of exclusions from the IC definition are available to an asset-backed issuer: an issuer asset or activity-based exclusion, and an investor-based exclusion.[7] An asset-backed issuer that is ***primarily*** engaged in ***commercial finance or mortgage banking businesses*** is excluded from IC definition by §§ 3(c)(5)(A), (B) or (C) of the IC Act.[1; 6d] An asset-backed issuer complying with ***Rule 3a-7 conditions*** may publicly offer, pursuant to Regulation AB,[8] their securities without having to register itself as "investment company" under the IC Act.[6c] An asset-backed issuer may rely on ***§ 3(c)(1) "private investment company" exclusion*** if it does not make any public offering of its securities and its outstanding securities are beneficially owned by not more than one hundred investors.[6e (n.30)] An asset-backed issuer may rely on ***§ 3(c)(7) "private investment company" exclusion*** if it does not make any public offering of its securities and its outstanding securities are exclusively owned by "qualified purchasers."[6e (n.30)]

In a twenty-year review of Rule 3a-7 operations since its adoption in 1992 to conditionally exclude structured financing vehicles from IC status, and noting the role mortgage-backed securities issuers played in the 2008 financial crisis, the SEC in 2011 sought public comments on, *inter alia*, whether:

> Along the line of anti-pyramiding of investment companies under the IC Act, the restriction should similarly be applied to the embedded leverage upon embedded leverage structures inherent in CDO and CDO^2?[6e; 9; 10]

Bibliography:

1. SEC DIV. INV. MGMT., PROTECTING INVESTORS: A HALF CENTURY OF INVESTMENT COMPANY REGULATION, Ch.1 The Treatment of Structured Finance under the Investment Company Act (1992)
2. SCHWARCZ ET AL., SECURITIZATION, STRUCTURED FINANCE AND CAPITAL MARKETS (2004)
3. FRANKEL, SECURITIZATION—STRUCTURED FINANCING, FINANCIAL ASSETS POOLS, AND ASSET-BACKED SECURITIES (2005)
4. LEMKE ET AL, MORTGAGE-BACKED SECURITIES, Ch.6 § XIII Investment Company Act of 1940 Requirements (2013-2014 ed.)
5. Rosen, *The Role of Securitization in Mortgage Lending*, CHICAGO FED LETTER NO. 244 (2007)
6. § 3(c)(5)(C) & Rule 3a-7 releases: **6a.** Statement of the Commission as to the Applicability of the Federal Securities Laws to Real Estate Investment Trusts, IC-3140, 25 FR 12177 (1960); **6b.** Exclusion from the Definition of Investment Company for Structured Financings, IC-18736, 57 FR 23980 (1992); **6c.** IC-19105, 57 FR 56248 (1992); **6d.** Companies Engaged in the Business of Acquiring Mortgages and Mortgage-Related Instruments; Concept Release, IC-29778, 76 FR 55300 (2011); **6e.** Treatment of Asset-Backed Issuers Under the Investment Company Act, IC-29779, 76 FR 55308 (2011)
7. KRAVITT, SECURITIZATION OF FINANCIAL ASSETS, § 12.03 Exceptions from the Definitions of Investment Company (2nd ed. 2010)
8. Regulation AB releases: **8a.** Asset-Backed Securities, 33-8518, 34-50905, 70 FR 1506, § III.A.2.c (2005); **8b.** Asset-Backed Securities Disclosure and Registration, 33-9638, 34-72982, 79 FR 57184, § I.C n.41 (2014)

9. THE REPORT OF THE COUNTERPARTY RISK MANAGEMENT POLICY GROUP III, CONTAINING SYSTEMIC RISK: THE ROAD TO REFORM, III. High-Risk Complex Financial Instruments (2008)
10. THE FINANCIAL CRISIS INQUIRY COMMISSION, THE FINANCIAL CRISIS INQUIRY REPORT, Ch.8 The CDO Machine (2011)

Case Study 1: Mortgage Banking Issuer Exclusion from IC

Great Ajax Funding LLC

IC Act § 3(c)(5)(C), 2018 SEC No-Act. LEXIS 82 (Feb. 12, 2018)

Case Study 2: SPV Safe Harbor from IC: ABS Trustee Independence

Wells Fargo Bank, N.A., *et al.*

IC-32218, 81 FR 55510 (Aug. 19, 2016) (Application)

IC-32253 (Sept. 7, 2016) (Order)

Case Study 3: Conflict of Interest of CDO Underwriter

Goldman, Sachs & Co., the principal United States broker-dealer of The Goldman Sachs Group, Inc., a global investment banking and investment management firm, underwrote a synthetic collateralized debt obligation (CDO) named *ABACUS*. The performance of the ABACUS CDO was tied to the performance of referenced subprime residential mortgage-backed securities (RMBS) portfolio. **Paulson & Co. Inc.**, one of the world's largest hedge funds, paid Goldman Sachs $15 million to structure a transaction in which Paulson could both select the RMBS portfolio underlying ABACUS CDO and at the same time short the RMBS securities via credit default swap (CDS) transactions, giving Paulson every economic incentive to choose what it viewed as the poorest-quality RMBS securities and enabling Paulson poised to gain from defaulting RMBS securities.

In its marketing materials, Goldman misrepresented that the RMBS portfolio underlying ABACUS CDO was selected by an **independent third party collateral manager**, the ACA Management LLC. Even sophisticated institutional investors such as U.S. and foreign financial institutions were misled and induced into purchasing ABACUS, unaware of Paulson's role in the selection, and its simultaneous shorting, of the RMBS portfolio. The investors in ABACUS lost over $1 billion. Goldman settled the SEC's civil fraud enforcement action, paying $15 million in disgorgement and $535 million in penalty; of the total $550 million, $250 million was used to compensate investors, and $300 million went to the United States Treasury.

SEC v. Goldman Sachs & Co. and Fabrice Tourre

10 CV. 3229 (SEC Compl., SDNY 2010)

[***Related proceedings & materials***: Lit. Rel. 21489, *The SEC Charges Goldman Sachs with Fraud in Connection with the Structuring and Marketing of a Synthetic CDO* (April 16, 2010); SEC v. Goldman, Sachs & Co. and Fabrice Tourre, 10 CV. 3229 (SEC Comp. SDNY April 16, 2010); Lit. Rel. 21592, *Goldman Sachs to Pay Record $550 Million to Settle SEC Charges Related to Subprime Mortgage CDO* (July 15, 2010); SEC v. Goldman Sachs & Co., 790 F. Supp. 2d 147 (SDNY 2011); SEC v. Tourre, 4 F. Supp.3d 579 (SDNY 2014); Prohibition Against Conflicts of Interest in Certain Securitizations, 34-65355, 76 FR 60320 (2011)]

Research Topic:

Financial assets securitization in China: types of assets and conflicts of interest regulation.

Great Ajax Funding LLC

IC Act § 3(c)(5)(C), SEC No-Action Letter (Feb. 12, 2018)

Response of the Chief Counsel's Office
Division of Investment Management

In your letter, dated February 1, 2018, you request assurance that the staff of the Division of Investment Management will not recommend that the U.S. Securities and Exchange Commission take enforcement action under § 7 of the Investment Company Act of 1940 against **Great Ajax Funding LLC**, a Delaware limited liability company that is the depositor for, and sponsor of, multiple securitization trusts that hold whole mortgage loans (**Depositor**), in reliance on § 3(c)(5)(C) of the 1940 Act, if the Depositor operates in the manner described in your letter and summarized below without registering as an investment company under the 1940 Act.

FACTS

You state the following: **Great Ajax Corp.** (*the Company*), a Maryland corporation and publicly traded real estate investment trust (**REIT**), is engaged in the business of acquiring, investing in and managing a portfolio of whole mortgage loans and, to a lesser extent, real property. The Company conducts substantially all of its business through its operating partnership, **Great Ajax Operating Partnership LP**, a Delaware limited partnership (*the Operating Partnership*) and its wholly-owned subsidiaries.

As a means of obtaining debt financing for the Company, the **Depositor**, a wholly-owned subsidiary of the Operating Partnership, was formed to establish and sponsor trusts that securitize pools of whole mortgage loans (each a **Trust**). The officers of the Depositor, which are the same officers as the Operating Partnership,[1] periodically select whole mortgage loans from the Operating Partnership (or one of the Operating Partnership's wholly-owned subsidiaries) that are then transferred to the Depositor. The Depositor subsequently transfers the mortgage loans to a Trust. Despite being transferred to the Trust, however, the mortgage loans continue to remain on the Company's consolidated balance sheet and be serviced by **Gregory Funding LLC**, an affiliated entity.

The Trust issues **Class A notes** and one or more series of **Class B notes** (or

---

[1] You state that the Depositor has no employees.

similar subordinated notes) which are secured solely by the underlying mortgage loans held by the Trust, and payments on which are dependent on the cash flows from such loans. The Class A notes, which are senior, sequential pay, fixed-rate notes, are sold to institutional investors in private offerings. The Class B notes, which are sequential pay, fixed-rate notes that are subordinate to the Class A notes, are held by the Depositor as consideration for the whole mortgage loans. The proceeds received from the notes issued by the Trust are primarily used by the Operating Partnership to acquire additional mortgages.

The Depositor also holds the Trust's equity interests, evidenced by trust certificates representing the residual interests in the Trust's assets (**Trust Certificates**). As the holder of the Trust Certificates, the Depositor is entitled to receive its share of any remaining amounts held by the Trust after the Class A notes and Class B notes are paid in full. In addition, as the Trust Certificate holder, the Depositor exercises significant control over the operations and management of the Trust.[2] The only assets held by the Depositor are the Class B notes and the Trust Certificates acquired from each Trust, and the Depositor's income is derived exclusively from its ownership of such assets.

LEGAL BACKGROUND

Section 3(c)(5)(C) of the Act

Section 3(a)(1) of the Act, in relevant part, defines an investment company as any issuer that: is, or holds itself out as being engaged primarily, or proposes to engage primarily, in the business of investing, reinvesting or trading in securities; or is engaged or proposes to engage in the business of investing, reinvesting, owning, holding or trading in securities, and owns or proposes to acquire "investment securities" having a value exceeding 40% of the value of its total assets (exclusive of Government securities and cash items) on an unconsolidated basis.[3] Section 7(a) of the 1940 Act prohibits an investment

---

[2] You state that as the Trust Certificate holder, the Depositor has the right to: (i) redeem the Trust's outstanding notes without the consent of the note holders following a specified period; (ii) direct the owner trustee in the operation of the Trust, including the removal and/or substitution of mortgage loans; (iii) acquire defaulted mortgage loans from the Trust and foreclose on the real estate underlying such loans; and (iv) dissolve and wind up the Trust following a specified period.

[3] Section 3(a)(2) defines "investment securities" to include all securities except (A) Government securities, (B) securities issued by employees' securities companies, and (C) securities issued by majority-owned subsidiaries that are not themselves investment companies and are not relying on the exclusion from the definition of investment

company organized or otherwise created under the laws of the United States or of a state and having a board of directors from, among other things, offering or selling any security (or engaging in certain other activities) by use of the mails or any means or instrumentality of interstate commerce unless the company is registered under the 1940 Act.

Section 3(c)(5)(C) of the Act, in relevant part, provides an exclusion from the definition of investment company for any person that is "primarily engaged in ... [the business of] purchasing or otherwise acquiring mortgages and other liens on and interests in real estate, ..." We have taken the position that the exclusion in § 3(c)(5)(C) may be available to an issuer if: at least **55%** of its assets consist of "mortgages and other liens on and interests in real estate" (***qualifying interests***) and the remaining **45%** of its assets consist primarily of real estate-type interests (***55%/45% asset test***); at least **80%** of its total assets consist of qualifying interests and real estate-type interests; and no more than **20%** of its total assets consist of assets that have no relationship to real estate (***miscellaneous assets***).[4]

We generally have taken the position that qualifying interests are assets that represent an actual interest in real estate or are loans or liens fully secured by real estate. Thus, we have not objected if an issuer treated as qualifying interests, among other assets, mortgage loans fully secured by real estate, fee interests in real estate, second mortgages secured by real property, deeds of trust on real property, installment land contracts and leasehold interests secured solely by real property.[5] In contrast, we generally have taken

---

company under § 3(c)(1) or § 3(c)(7) of the Act.

[4] See, *e.g.*, *Salomon Brothers, Inc.*, SEC Staff No-Action Letter (June 17, 1985); *Citytrust*, SEC Staff No-Action Letter (Dec. 19, 1990); *Greenwich Capital Acceptance Inc.*, SEC Staff No-Action Letter (Aug. 8, 1991).

[5] See, *e.g.*, *United States Property Investment N.V.*, SEC Staff No-Action Letter (May 1, 1989) (mortgage loan secured exclusively by real estate in which the value of the real estate was equal or greater than the note evidencing the loan); DIV. INV. MGMT., SEC, THE TREATMENT OF STRUCTURED FINANCE UNDER THE INVESTMENT COMPANY ACT, PROTECTING INVESTORS: A HALF CENTURY OF INVESTMENT COMPANY REGULATION (1992), Ch.1 n. 345 and accompanying text (mortgage loan in which 100% of the principal amount of each loan was fully secured by real estate at the time of origination and 100% of the market value of the loan was fully secured by real estate at the time of acquisition); *United Bankers*, SEC Staff No-Action Letter (Mar. 23, 1988) (fee interests in real estate); *The State Street Mortgage Co.*, SEC Staff No-Action Letter (July 17, 1986) (second mortgages); *First National Bank of Fremont*, SEC Staff No-Action Letter (Nov. 18, 1985) (deeds of trust on real property); *American Housing Trust I*, SEC Staff No-Action Letter (May 21, 1988) (installment land contracts); *Health Facility Credit Corp.*, SEC Staff No-Action Letter (Feb. 6, 1985) (leasehold interests).

the position that an asset is not a qualifying interest for purposes of § 3(c)(5)(C) if it is an interest in the nature of a security in another issuer engaged in the real estate business.[6]

Analysis

You argue that the Depositor should be able to rely on § 3(c)(5)(C)[7] because the Depositor is primarily engaged in the mortgage loan business, and thus is an issuer that is primarily engaged in a type of business that § 3(c)(5)(C) intended to exclude from regulation under the Act. You state that the Depositor's assets consist solely of, and its income is derived exclusively from, the Class B Notes and the Trust Certificates issued by Trusts.[8]

---

[6] See *Urban Land Investments Inc.*, SEC Staff No-Action Letter (Nov. 4, 1971); *The Realex Capital*, SEC Staff No-Action Letter (Mar. 19, 1984); *M.D.C. Holdings*, SEC Staff No-Action Letter (May 5, 1987). This position is consistent with the position taken by the Commission in a 1960 release that discussed the applicability of the federal securities laws to the then newly enacted Internal Revenue Code REIT provisions. In that release, the Commission stated that a REIT might not be able to rely on § 3(c)(5)(C) if it invests "to a substantial extent in other [REITs] ... or in companies engaged in the real estate business or in other securities." See *Real Estate Investment Trusts*, IC-3140 (Nov. 18, 1960).

We have, however, made exceptions to these two positions. See, *e.g.*, *Capital Trust Inc.*, SEC Staff No-Action Letter (May 24, 2007) (certain Tier 1 mezzanine loans); *Capital Trust Inc.*, SEC Staff No-Action Letter (Feb. 3, 2009) (certain B Notes); *American Home Finance Corp.*, SEC Staff No-Action Letter (Apr. 9, 1981) (agency whole pool certificates).

[7] We note that the exclusion in § 3(c)(5)(C) is not available to an issuer that is in the business of issuing redeemable securities, face-amount certificates of the installment type or periodic payment plan certificates. You represent that the Depositor does not engage in such a business.

[8] You note that a possible alternative basis for the Depositor's exclusion from investment company status may exist if the Depositor is not an investment company under § 3(a)(1). In particular, you note that the Depositor would not meet the third prong of the investment company definition, in § 3(a)(1)(C), if it does not own or propose to acquire "investment securities," as defined in § 3(a)(2), that have a value exceeding 40% of the value of its total assets. As noted above, the definition of "investment securities" excludes securities issued by majority-owned subsidiaries that are not themselves investment companies and that do not rely on the exclusions in § 3(c)(1) or § 3(c)(7). See *supra* note 3 and accompanying text. Section 2(a)(24) generally defines a majority-owned subsidiary of a person as a company 50% or more of the outstanding voting securities of which are owned by such person, or by another company which is a majority-owned subsidiary of such person; and § 2(a)(42) defines "voting security" as any security presently entitling the owner to vote for the election of directors of a company. You state that although the Trusts are passive entities that do not have boards of directors, the Trust Certificates are the functional equivalent of voting securities under the 1940 Act. If that is the case, the Trusts arguably would be majority-owned subsidiaries of the Depositor under § 2(a)(24), such that the Trust Certificates held by the Depositor would be excluded from the definition of "investment security." However, because of the availability of relief for the Depositor under § 3(c)(5)(C), you do not ask for our views on this possible alternative

You further state that the Depositor acquired these assets as a direct result of the Depositor being in the business of acquiring and securitizing whole mortgage loans. You explain that the Depositor acquires whole mortgage loans from the Operating Partnership and then transfers these mortgage loans into a Trust which the Depositor establishes and for which it acts as sponsor. You further state that proceeds from the sale of the Class A notes are used by the Operating Partnership to acquire additional whole mortgage loans, some of which are eventually transferred to the Depositor which, in turn, transfers them to a Trust. You conclude that the Class B notes and the Trust Certificates retained by the Depositor are indicative of the Depositor's engagement in the mortgage loan business for purposes of § 3(c)(5)(C) because the Depositor acquires these assets as a direct result of being in the business of acquiring and securitizing whole mortgage loans.

We agree.

THE REAL ESTATE FINANCE BUSINESS

Section 3(c)(5)(C) generally was intended to exclude from regulation under the Act issuers that were primarily engaged in the mortgage banking and real estate businesses and that did not resemble, or were not considered to be, issuers that were in the investment company business (together, ***real estate finance business***).[9] Section 3(c)(5)(C) refers to an issuer in this business, in relevant part, as being in the business of purchasing or otherwise acquiring "mortgages and other liens on and interests in real estate." As discussed above, and with some exceptions, we have generally interpreted the assets listed in § 3(c)(5)(C) as assets that represent an actual interest in real estate or are loans or liens fully secured by real estate.[10]

The real estate finance business, however, has evolved substantially since the enactment of the Act, with the creation and use of new debt financing techniques and mortgage-related products. Thus, an issuer that is engaged in the real estate finance business might hold assets, acquired in the course of engaging in the operation of its business, that are not the assets specified in § 3(c)(5)(C). Nevertheless, the issuer's assets,

---

basis for exclusion, nor do we opine on your analysis.

[9] See, *e.g.*, H.R. Rep. No. 2639, 76th Cong., 3d Sess. 12 (1940); H.R. Rep, No. 1382, 91st Cong., 2d Sess. 17 (1970). See also SEC, REPORT ON THE PUBLIC POLICY IMPLICATIONS OF INVESTMENT COMPANY GROWTH, H.R. Rep. No. 2337, 89th Cong. 2d Sess. 328 (1966); *Exclusion from the Definition of Investment Company for Certain Structured Financings*, IC-18736, text following n.5 (1992).

[10] See *supra* notes 5-6 and accompanying text.

sources of income, historical development, public representations of its policy, and the activities of its officers, directors and employees (and other relevant factors) may indicate that the issuer is primarily engaged in the real estate finance business, and therefore should be able to rely on the § 3(c)(5)(C) exclusion.[11]

THE ISSUER'S BUSINESS ACTIVITIES

We believe that, consistent with the plain wording of § 3(c)(5)(C), an issuer that purchases or otherwise acquires whole mortgage loans is engaged in an activity consistent with being in the real estate finance business. We also recognize that such an issuer may also acquire certain other assets as a direct result of being engaged in the business of purchasing or otherwise acquiring whole mortgage loans and, under certain facts and circumstances, those assets might also be indicative of the issuer being in the business of acquiring whole mortgage loans. In these instances, such assets could potentially be treated as qualifying interests for purposes of § 3(c)(5)(C).

Thus, we agree that an issuer, such as the Depositor, that acquires whole mortgage loans, which it then transfers into a securitization trust which it sponsors for the purpose of obtaining financing to acquire additional whole mortgage loans, may treat as qualifying interests for purposes of § 3(c)(5)(C) any securities issued by that trust that it retains because such securities are acquired as a direct result of the issuer being engaged in the business of purchasing or otherwise acquiring whole mortgage loans.[12] We note, however, that our position focuses on the business activities of the issuer and not on the assets themselves;[13] thus, our position does not encompass securities issued by a securitization trust that are acquired in a different manner (*e.g.*, from an unaffiliated third

---

[11] These or similar factors have been considered when determining an issuer's primary business engagement in various contexts under the Act. See, *e.g.*, *Tonopah Mining Company of Nevada*, 26 SEC 426, 427 (1947) (§ 3(b)(2)); *Dan River Inc. v. Ichan*, 701 F.2d 278, 291 n.14 (4th Cir. 1983) (§ 3(a)(1)(A)); *Moses v. Black*, Fed. Sec, L. Rep. (CCH) P97,866 (SDNY 1981) (§ 3(b)(1)); Rule 3a-1 under the 1940 Act; Rule 3a-8 under the 1940 Act.

[12] We would be willing to entertain other no-action requests to treat as qualifying interests certain other mortgage-related assets if they are acquired by an issuer as a direct result of the issuer being engaged in the business of purchasing or otherwise acquiring whole mortgage loans (*e.g.*, certain A-Notes and servicing rights).

[13] Similarly, rather than focusing solely on an issuer's assets when determining whether the issuer is primarily engaged in the real estate finance business and thus can rely on § 3(c)(5)(C), we would be willing to entertain no-action requests that would broaden the "primarily engagement" test to include other factors that would indicate whether the issuer is primarily engaged in the real estate finance business. See, *e.g.*, *supra* note 11 and accompanying text.

party) because acquiring such assets in this manner could be more consistent with the issuer being engaged in an investment activity rather than a financing activity.

CONCLUSION

Based on the facts and representations in your letter, we would not recommend enforcement action to the Commission under § 7 of the 1940 Act against the Depositor if the Depositor relies § 3(c)(5)(C) of the 1940 Act.[14] Any different facts or representations may require a different conclusion.

---

[14] See *supra* note 7.

Wells Fargo Bank, N.A., *et al.*

Notice of Application, IC-32218, 81 FR 55510 (Aug. 19, 2016)

Applicants' Representations

1. Each applicant is a wholly-owned indirect subsidiary of **Wells Fargo & Company**. Each applicant is frequently selected to act as trustee in connection with ABS issued by Issuers. * * * *

Applicant's Legal Analysis

1. **Rule 3a-7** excludes from the definition of investment company under § 3(a) of the Act an Issuer that meets the conditions of the rule. One of rule 3a-7's conditions, set forth in paragraph (a)(4)(i), requires that the Issuer appoint a trustee that is not affiliated with the Issuer or with any person involved in the organization or operation of the Issuer (the "**Independent Trustee Requirement**"). Rule 3a-7(a)(4)(i) therefore prohibits an Issuer from appointing a trustee that is affiliated with an underwriter. * * * *

3. Applicants request ***exemptive relief*** under § 6(c) of the Act from rule 3a-7(a)(4)(i) under the Act to the extent necessary to permit an Issuer to appoint an applicant as a trustee to the Issuer when such applicant is affiliated with an underwriter involved in the organization of the Issuer....

4. Applicants note that when rule 3a-7 was proposed in 1992, virtually all trustees were unaffiliated with the other parties involved in an ABS Transaction. Applicants state that ***consolidation within the banking industry***, as well as economic and other business factors, has resulted in a significant decrease in the number of bank trustees providing services to Issuers. Applicants also state that bank consolidation has been accompanied by the expansion of banks into investment banking, including the underwriting of ABS Transactions. Applicants further state that due to these banking industry changes, most trustees that provide services to Issuers, including an applicant, have affiliations with underwriters to Issuers. Applicants state that, as a result, when an affiliate of an applicant is selected to underwrite ABS in an ABS Transaction, rule 3a-7(a)(4)(i)'s Independent Trustee Requirement generally prevents applicant from serving as trustee for the Issuer. Applicants state that the Independent Trustee Requirement imposes an unnecessary regulatory limitation on trustee selection and causes market distortions by leading to the selection of trustees for reasons other than customary market considerations of pricing and expertise. This result is disadvantageous to the ABS market

and to ABS investors.

5. Applicants submit that due to the ***nature and timing of the roles*** of the trustee and the underwriter, an applicant's affiliation with an underwriter would not result in a conflict of interest or possibility of overreaching that could harm investors. Applicants state that the trustee's role begins with the Issuer's issuance of its securities, and the trustee performs its role over the life of the Issuer. Applicants state that, in contrast, the underwriter is chosen early in the ABS Transaction process, may help to structure the ABS Transaction, distributes the Issuer's securities to investors, and generally have no role subsequent to the distribution of the Issuer's securities. Applicants further state that an ABS trustee does not monitor the distribution of securities or any other activity performed by underwriters and there is no opportunity for a trustee and an affiliated underwriter to act in concert to benefit themselves at the expense of holders of the ABS either prior to or after the closing of the ABS Transaction. * * * *

7. Applicants submit that the ***concerns underlying the Independent Trustee Requirement*** are not implicated if the trustee for an Issuer is *independent of* the sponsor, servicer, and credit enhancer for the Issuer, but is *affiliated with* an underwriter for the Issuer, because in that situation no single entity would act in all capacities in the issuance of the ABS and the operation of an Issuer. Applicants state that each applicant would continue to act as an independent party safeguarding the assets of any Issuer regardless of an affiliation with an underwriter of the ABS. Applicants submit that the concern that affiliation could lead to a trustee monitoring the activities of an affiliate also is not implicated by a trustee's affiliation with an underwriter, because, in practice, a trustee for an Issuer does not monitor the distribution of securities or any other activity performed by underwriters. Applicants further state that the requested relief would be consistent with the broader purpose of rule 3a-7 of not hampering the growth and development of the ABS market, to the extent consistent with investor protection. * * * *

Applicants' Conditions

Each applicant agrees that any order granting the requested relief will be subject to the following conditions:

1. The applicant will not be affiliated with any person involved in the organization or operation of the Issuer in an ABS Transaction ***other than the underwriter***.

2. The applicant's relationship to an affiliated underwriter will be ***disclosed in writing***

to all parties involved in an ABS Transaction, including the rating agencies and the ABS holders.

3. An underwriter affiliated with the applicant will not be involved in the ***operation*** of an Issuer, and its involvement in the ***organization*** of an Issuer will extend only to determining the assets to be pooled, assisting in establishing the terms of the ABS to be underwritten, and providing the sponsor with a warehouse line of credit for the assets to be transferred to the Issuer in connection with, and prior to, the related securitization.

4. An affiliated person of the applicant, including an affiliated underwriter, will not provide ***credit or credit enhancement*** to an Issuer if the applicant serves as trustee to the Issuer.

5. An underwriter affiliated with the applicant will not engage in any ***remarketing agent activities***, including involvement in any auction process in which ABS interest rates, yields, or dividends are reset at designated intervals in any ABS Transaction for which the applicant serves as trustee to the Issuer.

6. All of an ***affiliated underwriter's contractual obligations*** pursuant to the underwriting agreement will be enforceable by the sponsor.

7. Consistent with the requirements of rule 3a-7(a)(4)(i), the applicant will ***resign as trustee*** for the Issuer if the applicant becomes obligated to enforce any of an affiliated underwriter's obligations to the Issuer.

8. The applicant ***will not price*** its services as trustee in a manner designed to facilitate its affiliate being named underwriter.

In *re* Wells Fargo Bank, N.A.,
Wells Fargo Bank Northwest, N.A., Wells Fargo Delaware Trust Company, N.A.
Order, IC-32253 (Sept. 7, 2016)

* * * *

IT IS ORDERED, under § 6(c) of the Act, that the requested exemption from certain requirements of rule 3a-7(a)(4)(i) under the Act is granted, effective immediately, subject to the conditions contained in the application, as amended.

SEC v. Goldman Sachs & Co. and Fabrice Tourre

10 CV. 3229 (SEC Compl., SDNY 2010)

OVERVIEW

1. The Commission brings this securities fraud action against **Goldman, Sachs & Co.** (GS&Co) and a GS&Co employee, Fabrice Tourre (**Tourre**), for making materially misleading statements and omissions in connection with a synthetic **collateralized debt obligation** (CDO) GS&Co structured and marketed to investors. This synthetic CDO, ABACUS 2007-AC1 (**ABACUS**), was tied to the performance of subprime **residential mortgage-backed securities** (RMBS) and was structured and marketed by GS&Co in early 2007 when the United States housing market and related securities were beginning to show signs of distress....

2. GS&Co marketing materials for ABACUS—including the term sheet, flip book and offering memorandum for the CDO—all represented that the reference portfolio of RMBS underlying the CDO was selected by **ACA Management LLC** (ACA), a third-party with experience analyzing credit risk in RMBS. Undisclosed in the marketing materials and unbeknownst to investors, a large hedge fund, **Paulson & Co. Inc.** (Paulson), with economic interests directly adverse to investors in the ABACUS CDO, played a significant role in the portfolio selection process. After participating in the selection of the reference portfolio, Paulson effectively shorted the RMBS portfolio it helped select by entering into **credit default swaps** (CDS) with GS&Co to buy protection on specific layers of the ABACUS capital structure. Given its financial short interest, Paulson had an economic incentive to choose RMBS that it expected to experience credit events in the near future. GS&Co did not disclose Paulson's adverse economic interests or its role in the portfolio selection process in the term sheet, flip book, offering memorandum or other marketing materials provided to investors....

5. The deal closed on April 26, 2007. Paulson paid GS&Co approximately $15 million for structuring and marketing ABACUS. By October 24, 2007, 83% of the RMBS in the ABACUS portfolio had been downgraded. By January 29, 2008, 99% of the portfolio had been downgraded. As a result, investors in the ABACUS CDO lost over $1 billion. Paulson's opposite CDS positions yielded a profit of approximately $1 billion for Paulson.

6. By engaging in the misconduct described herein, GS&Co and Tourre directly or

indirectly engaged in transactions, acts, practices and a course of business that violated § 17(a) of the Securities Act of 1933, § 10(b) of the Securities Exchange Act of 1934, and Exchange Act Rule 10b-5....

DEFENDANTS

8. Goldman, Sachs & Co. is the principal United States broker-dealer of **The Goldman Sachs Group**, Inc., a global investment banking, securities and investment management firm headquartered in New York City. GS&Co structured and marketed ABACUS.

9. Fabrice Tourre, age 31, is a registered representative with GS&Co. Tourre was the GS&Co employee principally responsible for the structuring and marketing of ABACUS....

FACTS

A. GS&Co's Correlation Trading Desk

10. GS&Co's structured product correlation trading desk was created in and around late 2004/early 2005. Among the services it provided was the structuring and marketing of a series of synthetic CDOs called "ABACUS" whose performance was tied to RMBS.... According to an internal GS&Co memorandum to the **Goldman Sachs Mortgage Capital Committee** (MCC) dated March 12, 2007, "[e]xecuting this transaction [ABACUS] and others like it helps position Goldman to compete more aggressively in the growing market for synthetics written on structured products."

B. Paulson's Investment Strategy

11. Paulson & Co. Inc. is a hedge fund founded in 1994. Beginning in 2006, Paulson created two funds, known as the Paulson Credit Opportunity Funds, which took a bearish view on subprime mortgage loans by buying protection through CDS on various debt securities. A **CDS** is an over-the-counter derivative contract under which a protection buyer makes periodic premium payments and the protection seller makes a contingent payment if a reference obligation experiences a credit event.

12. **RMBS** are securities backed by residential mortgages. Investors receive payments out of the interest and principal on the underlying mortgages. Paulson developed an investment strategy based upon the belief that, for a variety of reasons, certain mid-and-subprime RMBS rated "Triple B," meaning bonds rated "BBB" by S&P or "Baa2" by Moody's, would experience credit events. **The Triple B tranche** is the lowest investment grade RMBS and, after equity, the first part of the capital structure to

experience losses associated with a deterioration of the underlying mortgage loan portfolio.

13. **CDOs** are debt securities collateralized by debt obligations including RMBS. These securities are packaged and generally held by a special purpose vehicle (**SPV**) that issues notes entitling their holders to payments derived from the underlying assets. In a **synthetic CDO**, the SPV does not actually own a portfolio of fixed income assets, but rather enters into CDSs that reference the performance of a portfolio (the SPV does hold some collateral securities separate from the reference portfolio that it uses to make payment obligations).

14. Paulson came to believe that synthetic CDOs whose reference assets consisted of certain Triple B-rated mid-and-subprime RMBS would experience significant losses and, under certain circumstances, even the more senior AAA-rated tranches of these so-called "mezzanine" CDOs would become worthless.

C. GS&Co and Paulson Discuss a Proposed Transaction

* * * *

16. Paulson discussed with GS&Co possible transactions in which counterparties to its short positions might be found. Among the transactions considered were synthetic CDOs whose performance was tied to Triple B-rated RMBS. Paulson discussed with GS&Co the creation of a CDO that would allow Paulson to participate in selecting a portfolio of reference obligations and then effectively short the RMBS portfolio it helped select by entering into CDS with GS&Co to buy protection on specific layers of the synthetic CDO's capital structure....

18. At the same time, GS&Co recognized that market conditions were presenting challenges to the successful marketing of CDO transactions backed by mortgage-related securities....

D. Introduction of ACA to the Proposed Transaction

19. GS&Co and Tourre knew that it would be difficult, if not impossible, to place the liabilities of a synthetic CDO if they disclosed to investors that a short investor, such as Paulson, played a significant role in the collateral selection process. By contrast, they knew that the identification of an experienced and independent third-party collateral manager as having selected the portfolio would facilitate the placement of the CDO

liabilities in a market that was beginning to show signs of distress.

20. GS&Co also knew that at least one significant potential investor, **IKB Deutsche Industriebank AG** (IKB), was unlikely to invest in the liabilities of a CDO that did not utilize a collateral manager to analyze and select the reference portfolio.

21. GS&Co therefore sought a collateral manager to play a role in the transaction proposed by Paulson. Contemporaneous internal correspondence reflects that GS&Co recognized that not every collateral manager would "agree to the type of names [of RMBS] Paulson want[s] to use" and put its "name at risk ... on a weak quality portfolio."

22. In or about January 2007, GS&Co approached **ACA** and proposed that it serve as the "**Portfolio Selection Agent**" for a CDO transaction sponsored by Paulson. ACA previously had constructed and managed numerous CDOs for a fee. As of December 31, 2006, ACA had closed on 22 CDO transactions with underlying portfolios consisting of $15.7 billion of assets.

23. Internal GS&Co communications emphasized the advantages from a marketing perspective of having ACA associated with the transaction....

24. Likewise, an internal GS&Co memorandum to the Goldman Sachs MCC dated March 12, 2007 described the marketing advantages of ACA's "brand-name" and "credibility" ...

E. Paulson's Participation in the Collateral Selection Process

25. In late 2006 and early 2007, Paulson performed an analysis of recent-vintage Triple B RMBS and identified over 100 bonds it expected to experience credit events in the near future. Paulson's selection criteria favored RMBS that included a high percentage of adjustable rate mortgages, relatively low borrower FICO scores, and a high concentration of mortgages in states like Arizona, California, Florida and Nevada that had recently experienced high rates of home price appreciation. Paulson informed GS&Co that it wanted the reference portfolio for the contemplated transaction to include the RMBS it identified or bonds with similar characteristics....

27. On January 9, 2007, GS&Co sent an email to ACA with the subject line, "*Paulson Portfolio.*" Attached to the email was a list of 123 2006 RMBS rated Baa2. On January 9, 2007, ACA performed an "overlap analysis" and determined that it previously had purchased 62 of the 123 RMBS on Paulson's list at the same or lower ratings....

29. On January 10, 2007, Tourre sent an email to ACA with the subject line, "*Transaction Summary.*" The text of Tourre's email began, "we wanted to summarize ACA's proposed role as '*Portfolio Selection Agent*' for the transaction that would be sponsored by Paulson (the '*Transaction Sponsor*')." The email continued in relevant part, "[s]tarting portfolio would be ideally what the Transaction Sponsor shared, but there is flexibility around the names."

30. On January 22, 2007, ACA sent an email to Tourre and others at GS&Co with the subject line, "*Paulson Portfolio 1-22-10.xls.*" The text of the email began, "Attached please find a worksheet with 86 sub-prime mortgage positions that we would recommend taking exposure to synthetically. Of the 123 names that were originally submitted to us for review, we have included only 55." * * * *

32. On February 2, 2007, Paulson, Tourre and ACA met at ACA's offices in New York City to discuss the reference portfolio. Unbeknownst to ACA at the time, Paulson intended to effectively short the RMBS portfolio it helped select by entering into CDS with GS&Co to buy protection on specific layers of the synthetic CDO's capital structure. Tourre and GS&Co, of course, were fully aware that Paulson's economic interests with respect to the quality of the reference portfolio were directly adverse to CDO investors.... Later the same day, ACA emailed Paulson, Tourre, and others at GS&Co a list of 82 RMBS on which Paulson and ACA concurred, plus a list of 21 "replacement" RMBS. ACA sought Paulson's approval of the revised list, asking, "Let me know if these work for you at the Baa2 level."

33. On February 5, 2007, Paulson sent an email to ACA, with a copy to Tourre, deleting eight RMBS recommended by ACA, leaving the rest, and stating that Tourre agreed that 92 bonds were a sufficient portfolio.

34. On February 5, 2007, an internal ACA email asked, "Attached is the revised portfolio that Paulson would like us to commit to—all names are at the Baa2 level. The final portfolio will have between 80 and these 92 names. Are 'we' ok to say yes on this portfolio?" The response was, "Looks good to me. Did [Paulson] give a reason why they kicked out all the Wells [Fargo] deals?" Wells Fargo was generally perceived as one of the higher-quality subprime loan originators.

35. On or about February 26, 2007, after further discussion, Paulson and ACA came to an agreement on a reference portfolio of 90 RMBS for ABACUS 2007-AC1.

F. GS&Co Misled Investors by Representing That ACA Selected the Portfolio Without Disclosing Paulson's Significant Role in Determining the Portfolio and Its Adverse Economic Interests

* * * *

37. [A] 9-page **term sheet** for ABACUS finalized by GS&Co on or about February 26, 2007 described ACA as the "*Portfolio Selection Agent*" and stated in bold print at the top of the first page that the reference portfolio of RMBS had been "*selected by ACA*." This document contained no mention of Paulson, its economic interests in the transaction, or its role in selecting the reference portfolio.

38. [A] 65-page **flip book** for ABACUS finalized by GS&Co on or about February 26, 2007 represented on its cover page that the reference portfolio of RMBS had been "*Selected by ACA Management, LLC*." The flip book included a 28-page overview of ACA describing its business strategy, senior management team, investment philosophy, expertise, track record and credit selection process, together with a 7-page section of biographical information on ACA officers and employees. Investors were assured that the party selecting the portfolio had an "alignment of economic interest" with investors. This document contained no mention of Paulson, its economic interests in the transaction, or its role in selecting the reference portfolio....

40. The Goldman Sachs MCC, which included senior-level management of GS&Co, approved ABACUS on or about March 12, 2007. GS&Co expected to earn between $15-and-$20 million for structuring and marketing ABACUS.

41. On or about April 26, 2007, GS&Co finalized a 178-page **offering memorandum** for ABACUS. The cover page of the offering memorandum included a description of ACA as "Portfolio Selection Agent." The Transaction Overview, Summary and Portfolio Selection Agent sections of the memorandum all represented that the reference portfolio of RMBS had been selected by ACA. This document contained no mention of Paulson, its economic interests in the transaction, or its role in selecting the reference portfolio....

G. GS&Co Misled ACA into Believing Paulson Was Long Equity

44. GS&Co also misled ACA into believing that Paulson was investing in the equity of ABACUS and therefore shared a long interest with CDO investors. The equity tranche is at the bottom of the capital structure and the first to experience losses associated with deterioration in the performance of the underlying RMBS. Equity investors therefore

have an economic interest in the successful performance of a reference RMBS portfolio. As of early 2007, ACA had participated in a number of CDO transactions involving hedge funds that invested in the equity tranche.

45. Had ACA been aware that Paulson was taking a short position against the CDO, ACA would have been reluctant to allow Paulson to occupy an influential role in the selection of the reference portfolio because it would present serious reputational risk to ACA, which was in effect endorsing the reference portfolio. In fact, it is unlikely that ACA would have served as portfolio selection agent had it known that Paulson was taking a significant short position instead of a long equity stake in ABACUS. Tourre and GS&Co were responsible for ACA's misimpression that Paulson had a long position, rather than a short position, with respect to the CDO....

51. On February 12, 2007, ACA's Commitments Committee approved the firm's participation in ABACUS as portfolio selection agent. The written approval memorandum described Paulson's role as follows: "*the hedge fund equity investor* wanted to invest in the 09% tranche of a static mezzanine ABS CDO backed 100% by subprime residential mortgage securities." Handwritten notes from the meeting reflect discussion of "*portfolio selection work with the equity investor*."

H. ABACUS Investors

1. IKB

52. IKB is a commercial bank headquartered in Dusseldorf, Germany....

53. The identity and experience of those involved in the selection of CDO portfolios was an important investment factor for IKB. In late 2006 IKB informed a GS&Co sales representative and Tourre that it was no longer comfortable investing in the liabilities of CDOs that did not utilize a collateral manager, meaning an independent third-party with knowledge of the U.S. housing market and expertise in analyzing RMBS. Tourre and GS&Co knew that ACA was a collateral manager likely to be acceptable to IKB.

54. In February, March and April 2007, GS&Co sent IKB copies of the ABACUS term sheet, flip book and offering memorandum, all of which represented that the RMBS portfolio had been selected by ACA and omitted any reference to Paulson, its role in selecting the reference portfolio and its adverse economic interests. Those representations and omissions were materially false and misleading because, unbeknownst to IKB, Paulson played a significant role in the collateral selection process

and had financial interests in the transaction directly adverse to IKB. Neither GS&Co nor Tourre informed IKB of Paulson's participation in the collateral selection process and its adverse economic interests....

58. ABACUS closed on or about April 26, 2007. IKB bought $50 million worth of Class A-1 notes at face value. The Class A-1 Notes paid a variable interest rate equal to LIBOR plus 85 basis points and were rated Aaa by Moody's Investors Services, Inc. ("Moody's") and AAA by Standard & Poor's Ratings & Services (S&P). IKB bought $100 million worth of Class A-2 Notes at face value. The Class A-2 Notes paid a variable interest rate equal to LIBOR plus 110 basis points and were rated Aaa by Moody's and AAA by S&P.

59. The fact that the portfolio had been selected by an independent third-party with experience and economic interests aligned with CDO investors was important to IKB. IKB would not have invested in the transaction had it known that Paulson played a significant role in the collateral selection process while intending to take a short position in ABACUS. Among other things, knowledge of Paulson's role would have seriously undermined IKB's confidence in the portfolio selection process and led senior IKB personnel to oppose the transaction.

60. Within months of closing, ABACUS's Class A-1 and A-2 Notes were nearly worthless. IKB lost almost all of its $150 million investment. Most of this money was ultimately paid to Paulson in a series of transactions between GS&Co and Paulson.

2. ACA Capital; ABN AMRO

61. ACA's parent company, **ACA Capital Holdings, Inc.** (ACA Capital), provided financial guaranty insurance on a variety of structured finance products including RMBS CDOs, through its wholly-owned subsidiary, **ACA Financial Guaranty Corporation**. On or about May 31, 2007, ACA Capital sold protection or "wrapped" the $909 million super senior tranche of ABACUS, meaning that it assumed the credit risk associated with that portion of the capital structure via a CDS in exchange for premium payments of approximately 50 basis points per year.

62. ACA Capital was unaware of Paulson's short position in the transaction. It is unlikely that ACA Capital would have written protection on the super senior tranche if it had known that Paulson, which played an influential role in selecting the reference portfolio, had taken a significant short position instead of a long equity stake in ABACUS.

63. The super senior transaction with ACA Capital was intermediated by **ABN AMRO Bank N.V.** ("ABN"), which was one of the largest banks in Europe during the relevant period. This meant that, through a series of CDS between ABN and Goldman and between ABN and ACA that netted ABN premium payments of approximately 17 basis points per year, ABN assumed the credit risk associated with the super senior portion of ABACUS's capital structure in the event ACA Capital was unable to pay.

64. GS&Co sent ABN copies of the ABACUS term sheet, flip book and offering memorandum, all of which represented that the RMBS portfolio had been selected by ACA and omitted any reference to Paulson's role in the collateral selection process and its adverse economic interest. Tourre also told ABN in emails that ACA had selected the portfolio. These representations and omissions were materially false and misleading because, unbeknownst to ABN, Paulson played a significant role in the collateral selection process and had a financial interest in the transaction that was adverse to ACA Capital and ABN.

65. At the end of 2007, ACA Capital was experiencing severe financial difficulties. In early 2008, ACA Capital entered into a global settlement agreement with its counterparties to effectively unwind approximately $69 billion worth of CDSs, approximately $26 billion of which were related to 2005-06 vintage subprime RMBS. ACA Capital is currently operating as a run-off financial guaranty insurance company.

66. In late 2007, ABN was acquired by a consortium of banks that included the **Royal Bank of Scotland** (RBS). On or about August 7, 2008, RBS unwound ABN's super senior position in ABACUS by paying GS&Co $840,909,090. Most of this money was subsequently paid by GS&Co to Paulson.

CLAIMS FOR RELIEF

FIRST CLAIM: § 17(a) of the Securities Act

* * * *

68. GS&Co and Tourre each violated § § 17(a)(1), (2) and (3) of the Securities Act....

69. Goldman and Tourre, in the offer or sale of securities or securities-based swap agreements, by the use of means or instruments of interstate commerce or by the mails, directly or indirectly (a) employed devices, schemes or artifices to defraud; (b) obtained money or property by means of untrue statements of material facts or omissions of

material facts necessary in order to make the statements made, in the light of the circumstances under which they were made, not misleading; or (c) engaged in transactions, practices or courses of business which operated or would operate as a fraud or deceit upon purchasers of securities....

SECOND CLAIM: § 10(b) and Rule 10-b(5) of the Exchange Act

72. GS&Co and Tourre each violated § 10(b) of the Exchange Act and Rule 10b-5....

73. GS&Co and Tourre, in connection with the purchase or sale of securities or securities-based swap agreements, by the use of means or instrumentalities of interstate commerce or of the mails, directly or indirectly (a) employed devices, schemes or artifices to defraud; (b) made untrue statements of material facts or omissions of material facts necessary in order to make the statements made, in the light of the circumstances under which they were made, not misleading; or (c) engaged in transactions, practices or courses of business which operated or would operate as a fraud or deceit upon persons....

PRAYER FOR RELIEF

WHEREFORE, the Commission respectfully requests that this Court enter a judgment:

* * * *

C. Ordering GS&Co and Tourre to disgorge all illegal profits that they obtained as a result of their fraudulent misconduct, acts or courses of conduct described in this Complaint, and to pay prejudgment interest thereon;

D. Imposing civil monetary penalties on GS&Co and Tourre pursuant to § 20(d)(2) of the Securities Act and § 21(d)(3) of the Exchange Act; and

E. Granting such equitable relief as may be appropriate or necessary for the benefit of investors pursuant to § 21(d)(5) of the Exchange Act.

Section 5.5 Private Investment Companies

Topic 1 Hedge Fund

Laws & Rules Highlight:

IC Act (15 USC 80a-1 *et seq.*)
Securities Act (SA); Securities Exchange Act (SEA)

Private Funds

- **§ 3(c)(1)** (*exclusion from § 3(a) IC status: privately offered fund having 100 or fewer beneficial owners—**100-person fund***)
  - § 3(c)(1)(A) (***corporate investor 10% attribution rule:** to prevent circumvention of 100-beneficial-owner limitation by use of conduit funds, whether registered or private*)
  - § 3(c)(1) & § 12(d)(1)(A)(i) & § 12(d)(1)(B)(i) (***3(c)(1) fund's purchase limit** of any single registered fund: **3%** of voting securities*)
- **§ 3(c)(7)** (*exclusion from § 3(a) IC status: privately offered fund owned exclusively by unlimited number of "qualified purchasers"—**qualified purchaser fund***)
  - § 2(a)(51) (*def. "qualified purchaser"*); Rule 2a51-3 Certain Companies as Qualified Purchasers (***"formed for the specific purpose" attribution rule***)
  - § 3(c)(7)(D) & § 12(d)(1)(A)(i) & § 12(d)(1)(B)(i) (***3(c)(7) fund's purchase limit** of any single registered fund: **3%** of voting securities*)
  - § SEA 12(g)(1)(A) (*exempts equity securities of 3(c)(7) private fund from § 12(g) registration if holders of record are **fewer than 2,000 persons***)
- **§ 12(d)(1)** (*anti-pyramiding provision*)
  - § 12(d)(1)(A)-(B) (*anti-pyramiding provision **not applicable** to a private fund's investments in other private funds*)
  - § 12(d)(1)(F) (***conditional exemption:** unaffiliated "fund of funds"*); Rule 12d1-1 Exemptions for Investments in Money Market Funds (*permits **unregistered** fund to invest in **registered** MMFs in excess of 12(d)(1) limits, designed to permit "cash sweep" arrangements*)
- SA § 4(a)(2) (*non-public offering exemption*)
- SA Regulation D Rule 506 Exemption for Limited Offers and Sales Without Regard to Dollar Amount of Offering (*offering meeting SA Act Rule 506 deemed "non-public" for purposes of IC Act §§ 3(c)(1) and 3(c)(7)*)

- Rule 506(c) (*as amended pursuant to JOBS Act: permits* ***general solicitation/general advertising*** *in private offerings; but interests in the private offering may only be sold to "****accredited investors****"*)
- Rule 501(a) (*def. "accredited investor"*)

Typical Hedge Fund Structure and Prime Brokerage Arrangement*

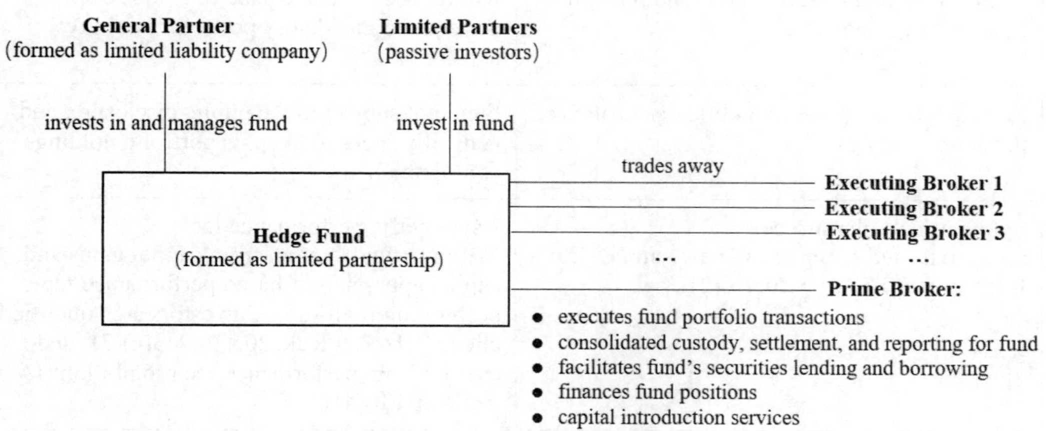

**Ref.* [LEMKE ET AL., HEDGE FUNDS AND OTHER PRIVATE FUNDS: REGULATION AND COMPLIANCE, Ch.2, § 5.11 (2015); STAFF REPORT TO THE UNITED STATES SEC. & EXCH. COMM'N, IMPLICATIONS OF THE GROWTH OF HEDGE FUNDS § IV.E.2 (2003); Prime Broker Committee, SEC No-Act Letter (Jan 25, 1994)]

Research Note:[Biblio]

Mutual Fund and Hedge Fund: A Comparison of Certain Regulatory Features	
Registered Fund: Mutual Fund	**Private Fund: Hedge Fund**
Fund to register under Investment Company Act (§ 8); offering of fund shares to register under Securities Act (§ 5); fund investments open to the general public.	Fund to meet IC Act § 3(c)(1) or § 3(c)(7) exemption; offering of fund interests to meet SA § 4(a)(2) or Reg. D exemption; fund investments restricted to sophisticated investors.
Fund board and independent directors oversee fund operations and address conflicts of interest; fund advisory contract subject to § 15(c) annual re-approval by fund board.	Fund generally structured as limited partnership or limited liability company, with no board of directors; advisory contract not subject to annual re-approval process.

Fund subject to § 17 affiliated transaction restrictions.	Fund allowed to engage in transactions with affiliates, subject to disclosure.
Fund subject to §§ 12, 13 & 18 restrictions on investments, change of fundamental policies, and use of leverage; § 5(b)(1) diversification requirement.	Fund has flexibility in investments and use of leverage; not subject to mandatory diversification.
Fund subject to IC Act § 2(a)(41) and Rule 2a-4 "fair value," Rule 22c-1 daily valuation, § 22(e) redeemable share, and fund portfolio liquidity requirements.	Fund has flexibility in valuation method and valuation intervals; shareholders limited withdrawal right and subject to "lock-up" periods; no mandatory portfolio liquidity constraint.
Fund subject to quarterly public disclosures of portfolio holdings.	Fund not subject to the public disclosure, and generally seeks to keep its portfolio holdings confidential.
Symmetrical fulcrum fee: registered fund permitted to pay symmetrical fulcrum fee (IA Act § 205(b)(2)).	Asymmetric performance fee: § 3(c)(1) fund exempt from capital gains and capital appreciation-based performance fee prohibition if all fund's investors are "qualified clients" (IA Act Rule 205-3); § 3(c)(7) fund exempt from performance fee prohibition (IA Act § 205(b)(4)).

Bibliography

1. LEMKE ET AL., HEDGE FUNDS AND OTHER PRIVATE FUNDS: REGULATION AND COMPLIANCE, §§ 4:18-4:19 (2015)
2. Stulz, *Hedge Funds: Past, Present, and Future*, 21 J. ECON. PERSP. 175 (2007)
3. STAFF REPORT TO THE UNITED STATES SEC. & EXCH. COMM'N, IMPLICATIONS OF THE GROWTH OF HEDGE FUNDS (2003)

Research Note:[Biblio]

Fund of Hedge Funds and Retailization of Hedge Funds

Hedge funds generally would fall within the statutory definitions of "investment company" under § 3(a)(1)(A) "orthodox IC" and under § 3(a)(1)(C) "prima facie IC" standards. Hedge funds typically are structured and operated to be exempt from the IC Act regulation: as ***§ 3(c)(1) "100-beneficial owner" private fund***, or as ***§ 3(c)(7) "exclusively qualified purchaser" private fund***. The offerings of securities by either § 3(c)(1) private funds or § 3(c)(7) private funds must be limited to private placement, typically pursuant to Securities Act § 4(a)(2) non-public offering exemption, or SA Act

Regulation D Rule 506 safe harbor for offerings sold exclusively to "*accredited investors*." A § 3(c)(7) private fund's "***qualified purchaser***" concept is similar to Reg. D private offering's "***accredited investor***" concept, except that the former has higher net worth requirements.[1 (§III.A)] Investments in individual hedge funds require high investment thresholds, and expensive due diligence and monitoring costs; diversification across hedge funds for a single investor requires a very large commitment of investable wealth.[2]

A "***fund of hedge funds***," or **FOHF**, is a hedge fund that utilizes a multi-manager, multi-strategy (*e.g.*, long-short equity strategy, event-driven strategy, global macro strategy, and fixed-income arbitrage strategy) approach, by investing all, or a significant portion, of its assets in other hedge funds.[1 (§IV.J); 2] An FOHF provides investors a diversified portfolio of hedge funds and a way to share the due diligence costs with other investors; FOHF investors rely on the FOHF manager to monitor the underlying hedge funds.[2] The anti-pyramiding provision of IC Act § 12(d)(1), which governs a registered IC's purchase or sale of other ICs (whether registered or unregistered), does not apply to § 3(c)(1) and § 3(c)(7) private funds' investments in other § 3(c)(1) or § 3(c)(7) private funds.[3 (§§4:31, 4:41)] Thus, the hedge funds underlying an FOHF (first level FOHF) could also be FOHFs themselves (second level FOHFs). Investors in an FOHF are charged at least two layers of fees and expenses: directly at the FOHF level, and indirectly by the underlying hedge funds. If the underlying hedge funds are themselves FOHFs, the investors in the top-level FOHF could be paying three layers of fees and expenses.[1 (§IV.J., n.241); 4] In addition, since an FOHF provides after-fee returns to its investors, the FOHF effectively passes on to investors any incentive fees paid to the underlying fund managers. Thus FHOF investors may end up paying incentive fees even though the overall FOHF loses money. The inability of investors to hedge underlying incentive fees due to lack of information has been described as "a deadweight cost."[5]

Most FOHFs are ***not registered*** as investment companies under the IC Act, and are regulated similar to individual hedge funds.[1 (§IV.J)] Of the ***registered*** FOHFs, which are structured as closed-end funds or interval funds,[3 (Ch.11)] there are two types: "**40 Act only Registered FOHFs**," which do not register their funds' securities offerings under the Securities Act, and which must thus only privately place their securities; and "**Dual Registered FOHFs**," which both register the funds under the IC Act and register the funds' securities offerings under the Securities Act, and which may thus offer and sell their securities to the public. Dual Registered FOHFs, although self-imposing certain minimum investment thresholds and investor eligibility criteria, nevertheless result in "***retailization***" of hedge funds—public investors' indirect investments in or exposure to the very hedge funds in which they may not invest directly.[1 (§§IV.J, VI.C); 6]

In addition to registered FOHFs, other forms of retailization of hedge funds include:

- ***IPOs of hedge fund advisers***, which offer an alternative for retail investors to derivatively invest in hedge funds (Davidoff 2008);[7]
- "***hedged mutual funds***" (Shadab 2008),[8] or mutual funds implementing "***hedge fund 'lite' strategies***" (Stulz 2007),[2] or "***alternative mutual funds***" (Frankle 2017),[9] which are registered mutual funds but which mimic hedge fund strategies, thus exposing retail investors to the same kinds of risks and complicated strategies as hedge funds;
- investments in hedge funds, or in FOHFs, by ***institutional investors with fiduciary duties*** (such as private sector defined benefit pension plans) (Stulz 2007),[2] and (GAO 2008).[10]

Bibliography

1. STAFF REPORT TO THE UNITED STATES SEC. & EXCH. COMM'N, IMPLICATIONS OF THE GROWTH OF HEDGE FUNDS (2003)
2. Stulz, *Hedge Funds: Past, Present, and Future*, 21 J. ECON. PERSP. 175 (2007)
3. LEMKE ET AL., HEDGE FUNDS AND OTHER PRIVATE FUNDS: REGULATION AND COMPLIANCE (2015)
4. Judge, *Intermediary Influence*, 82 U. CHI. L. REV. 573, § II.C.2 Fund of Funds (2015)
5. Brown *et al.*, *Fees on Fees in Funds of Funds*, 2 J. INV. MGMT. 39 (2004)
6. William H. Donaldson, Chairman, U.S. Sec. & Exch. Comm'n: *Investor Protection and the Regulation of Hedge Funds Advisers*, Testimony Before the U.S. Sen. Comm. on Banking, Housing, and Urban Affairs (July 15, 2004)
7. Davidoff, *Paradigm Shift: Federal Securities Regulation in the New Millennium*, 2 BROOK. J. CORP. FIN. & COM. L. 339 (2008)
8. Shadab, *Fending for Themselves: Creating a U.S. Hedge Fund Market for Retail Investors*, 11 N.Y.U.J. LEGIS. & PUB. POL'Y 251 (2008)
9. FRANKEL & LABY, THE REGULATION OF MONEY MANAGERS—MUTUAL FUNDS AND ADVISERS, § 31.02[K] (3d. 2017)
10. GAO, DEFINED BENEFIT PENSION PLANS: GUIDANCE NEEDED TO BETTER INFORM PLANS OF THE CHALLENGES AND RISKS OF INVESTING IN HEDGE FUNDS AND PRIVATE EQUITY, GAO-08-692 (2008)

Topic 2 Performance Fee

Laws & Rules Highlight:

IA Act ((15 USC 80b-1 *et seq.*) & Rules (17 CFR §§ 275.0-2 *et seq.*)

Performance-Based Management Fee: Prohibition and Exemptions

- **§ 205(a)(1)** (*generally **prohibits** registered IA from charging **performance fees** based on capital gains or capital appreciation*)
  - Rule 205-3 Exemption from the Compensation Prohibition of Section 205(a)(1) for Investment Advisers (*exempts **§ 3(c)(1) private fund** from performance fee prohibition if **all equity owners** of the fund are "**qualified clients**"; def. "qualified client"*)
  - § 205(b)(4) (*exempts **§ 3(c)(7) private fund** from performance fee prohibition*)
  - § 202(a)(29) (*def. "**private fund**," referring to IC Act §§ 3(c)(1) & 3(c)(7) funds*)
- **§ 205(b)(2)** (*permits **registered IC** to pay symmetrical **fulcrum fee***)
  - Rule 203A-1 Eligibility for SEC Registration; Switching to or from SEC Registration (*requires IAs to registered ICs to register with the SEC*)
  - Rule 205-1 Definition of "Investment Performance" of an Investment Company and "Investment Record" of an Appropriate Index of Securities Prices
  - Rule 205-2 Definition of "Specified Period" Over Which the Asset Value of the Company or Fund Under Management Is Averaged
- **§ 205(e)** (*gives authority to SEC to grant exemptions from performance fee prohibition based on certain **factors***)

Pre-Case Background Note:[Biblio]

Adviser Performance Fee: Types, Regulation, and Impact on Performance

Investment Advisers Act **§ 205(a)(1)** generally prohibits any registered IA from receiving compensation based on capital gains or capital appreciation of a client's account—commonly referred to as "***performance fee***."[1; 2] The performance fee prohibition reflected Congressional concern that performance fees created a "*heads I win, tails you lose*"[3a] incentive for advisers to take inappropriate risks and to speculate unduly in managing a client's account: earning a bonus for good performance without suffering proportionate penalty for poor performance. To promote competition among advisers and to provide more flexibility for investors without sacrificing investor protections,[3b] **§ 205(e)** authorizes the SEC to grant exemptions from the performance fee proscription, based on factors such as *financial sophistication*, *net worth*, *knowledge of and experience in financial matters*, *amount of assets under management*, *relationship with the registered IA*, and other factors which the SEC determines to be consistent with § 205.

Private funds (*i.e.*, § 3(c)(7) funds and § 3(c)(1) funds) are ***exempt***, by IA Act § 205(b)(4) and IA Rule 205-3 respectively, from performance fee proscription where each equity owner of the private fund is a "*qualified purchaser*" as defined by IC Rule 2(a)(51) in the case of a § 3(c)(7) fund, or is a "*qualified client*" as defined by IA Rule 205-3 in the case of a § 3(c)(1) fund. In a **§ 3(c)(1) private fund-of-funds**, the adviser must "***look through***" each tier of funds: if the first tier private fund seeking a performance fee arrangement is owned by a second tier private fund, the adviser must look to the ultimate client of the second (and any further) tier to determine that such ultimate client is a "qualified client." On the other hand, any "equity owners" of a private fund who are not charged a performance fee need not meet the "qualified client" criteria.[3c; 3d] The incentive allocation or performance fee arrangement between a hedge fund adviser and hedge fund investors often contain provisions designed to protect investors from paying incentive allocations for poor performance, such as hurdle rates and high water marks. A ***hurdle rate*** establishes a performance floor that the investment adviser must exceed in order to obtain an incentive allocation. ***High water marks*** are an adviser's previous high points that the adviser must achieve before an incentive allocation can be assessed, so as to disallow an adviser from collecting an incentive allocation twice for the same performance.[4]

Registered ICs are permitted by § 205(b)(2) to pay adviser incentive compensation which *increases and decreases proportionately* with the investment performance of the IC, over a specified period, and in relation to the investment record of an appropriate index of securities prices or such other benchmarks as the SEC may specify—commonly referred to as "***fulcrum fee***." The key concern with a fulcrum fee is fairness. The point, *i.e.*, the *fulcrum* from which the increases and decreases are measured, is the fee paid when the investment performance of the IC is *equivalent* to that of the appropriate index. ***Fairness*** of performance fee thus critically depends on the selection of an appropriate index; the determination of a fair fulcrum fee; a sufficiently long period on a rolling basis to evaluate the adviser's performance; and avoidance of basing significant fee adjustments upon random fluctuations rather than upon the adviser's skill or lack of skill.[5]

Finance and economics literature is inconclusive on whether performance fees lead to improved management:

- Admati & Pfleiderer (1997)[6] (theoretical study, finding: ***Managed portfolio total return-based compensation scheme*** is potentially valuable for aligning the manager's preferences with those of the investor, and for motivating the adviser to expend effort. However, ***benchmark-adjusted compensation scheme*** plays no role in aligning the manager's preferences with the investor's, due to the manager's risk tolerance constraint on his portfolio choice; and is irrelevant to the manager's incentives to expend effort because it does not enhance the investor's ability to assess the manager's skill. Concluding: Benchmark-adjusted compensation schemes are not useful in screening out uninformed managers.).
- Elton *et al.* (2003)[7] (empirical study examining the ***effect of incentive fees on the behavior of mutual fund managers***, finding: (1) Funds with incentive fees exhibit better stock picking ability and lower expenses, but they do not on average earn positive or negative incentive fees; this is because incentive fee funds have on average a beta less than one, causing their underperformance relative to the benchmark. (2) Compared with non-incentive fee funds, on average incentive-fee funds take on more risk, and they increase risk after a period of poor performance and decrease risk after a period of good performance. (3) Cash flows into incentive fee funds are greater than cash flows into non-incentive fee funds, *ceteris paribus*; however, evidence is inconclusive whether this is due to ***motivation*** supplied by incentive fees, or due to incentive fees being useful ***marketing tools***.).
- Goetzmann *et al.* (2003)[8] (empirical study on the ***value of high-water mark contracts to hedge fund managers***, showing: High-water mark compensation contracts used by hedge funds have option-like features particularly suited to the types of investment strategies employed by hedge funds. Mutual funds pursuing long asset portfolio strategies compensate their managers for past superior performance with a fixed percentage fee on increased assets attracted by good performance. In contrast, hedge fund managers are made up of event arbitrageurs, global macro market and debt market speculators, pairs traders, and opportunistic managers exploiting undervalued securities. By their very nature, such arbitrages in expectations are not infinitely exploitable, and hedge funds may not be able to scale these arbitrage returns. Thus the high-water mark compensation contract between the hedge fund manager and the investor is more ***a way of financing the firm***, than ***an incentive contract for the manager***.).

Bibliography

1. SEC DIV. INVEST. MGMT., PROTECTING INVESTORS: A HALF CENTURY OF INVESTMENT COMPANY REGULATION, Ch.6 Performance Based Advisory Compensation (1992)
2. BINES & THEL, INVESTMENT MANAGEMENT LAW AND REGULATION, § 5.03[B] Performance and Incentive Fees (3d. 2014)
3. Performance Fee Rels.: **3a.** Contingent Advisory Compensation Arrangements (Statement of Staff Interpretive Position), IA-721, 45 FR 34876 (1980); **3b.** Exemption to Allow Registered Investment Advisers to Charge Fees Based Upon a Share of Capital Gains Upon or Capital Appreciation of a Client's Account, IA-996, 50 FR 48556 (1985); **3c.** Exemption to Allow Investment Advisers to Charge Fees Based Upon a Share of Capital Gains Upon or Capital Appreciation of a Client's Account, IA-1731, 63 FR 39022, § II-C. Identification of the Client n.31 (1998); **3d.** Investment Adviser Performance Compensation, IA-3372, 77 FR 10358, 10364 n.65 (2012)
4. STAFF REPORT TO THE UNITED STATES SEC. & EXCH. COMM'N, IMPLICATIONS OF THE GROWTH OF HEDGE FUNDS, § IV-F. Hedge Fund Advisory Fees (2003)
5. Fulcrum Fee Rels.: **5a.** Factors to be Considered in Connection with Investment Company Advisory Contracts Containing Incentive Arrangements (Interpretive Release), IC-7113, IA-315, 37 FR 7690 (1972); **5b.** Adoption of Rule 205-1 Under the Investment Advisers Act of 1940 Defining "Investment Performance" of an Investment Company and "Investment Record" of an Appropriate Index of Securities Prices, IA-327, 37 FR 17467 (1972); **5c.** Adoption of Rule 205-2 Under the Investment Advisers Act of 1940, as Amended, Defining "Specified Period" Over Which the Asset Value of the Company or Fund Under Management Is Averaged, IC-7484, IA-347 (1972)
6. Admati & Pfleiderer, *Does It All Add Up? Benchmarks and the Compensation of Active Portfolio Managers*, 70 J. BUS. 323 (1997)
7. Elton *et al.*, *Incentive Fees and Mutual Funds*, 58 J. FIN. 779 (2003)
8. Goetzmann *et al.*, *High-Water Marks and Hedge Fund Management Contracts*, 58 J. FIN. 1685 (2003)

Case Study 1: Performance Fee in Private Fund of Funds Structure

EBF & Assocs., L.P.

IA Act § 205(a)(1) & Rule 205-3, 1993 SEC No-Act. LEXIS 1234 (Dec. 22, 1993)

Case Study 2: Contingent Fee: Opposite of "Heads I Win, Tails You Lose"

Amerivest Invest. Mgmt., LLC

IA Act § 205(a)(1), 2014 SEC No-Act. LEXIS 335 (Aug 19, 2014)

EBF & Assocs., L.P.

IA Act § 205(a)(1) & Rule 205-3, SEC No-Action Letter

Ref. No. 93-573, File No. 132-3 (Dec. 22, 1993)

Response of the Office of Chief Counsel

Division of Investment Management

By letter dated September 10, 1993, you request assurances that the staff would not recommend that the Commission take enforcement action against **EBF & Associates, L.P.** (EBF) under § 205(a)(1) of the Investment Advisers Act of 1940, if EBF registers under the Advisers Act and accepts compensation on the basis of a share of capital gains upon or capital appreciation of the funds or any portion of the funds of the client ("***performance fees***") under the circumstances described in your letter.

EBF is an investment adviser within the meaning of § 202(a)(11), but is exempt from registration under § 203(b)(3).[1] EBF serves as general partner or investment adviser to several "private investment companies" ("***PICs***"), as defined in Rule 205-3(g)(2),[2] from whom it accepts performance fees ("***first-tier PICs***"). EBF permits other PICs ("***second-tier PICs***") to invest in the first-tier PICs. The second-tier PICs that are the subject of this no-action request will not be organized or controlled by EBF or any of its affiliates. In addition, neither EBF nor any of its affiliates has performed or performs, directly or indirectly, any capital raising function for these second-tier PICs, and neither EBF nor any of its affiliates has served or serves as investment adviser to these second-tier PICs. Both the first- and second-tier PICs satisfy the eligibility requirements contained in Rule 205-3(b)(1).[3] The equity owners of the second-tier PICs, however, may not satisfy these eligibility requirements. This is currently permissible because EBF is not a registered adviser. EBF would like to register as an investment adviser, however, and

---

[1] Section 203(b)(3) generally exempts from the registration requirements of the Advisers Act any investment adviser who during the course of the preceding twelve months has had fewer than fifteen clients and who neither holds himself out generally to the public as an investment adviser nor acts as an investment adviser to any registered investment company.

[2] A "private investment company" is a company that would be an investment company under § 3(a) of the Investment Company Act of 1940 but for § 3(c)(1) of the Investment Company Act.

[3] Rule 205-3(b)(1) provides that clients entering into a performance fee contract must have, immediately after entering into the contract, at least $500,000 under the management of the adviser, or have (or be reasonably believed to have), at the time the contract is entered into, a net worth exceeding $1,000,000.

continue to receive performance fees from the first-tier PICs, notwithstanding the fact that the equity owners of the second-tier PICs may not all satisfy the eligibility requirements of Rule 205-3(b)(1).

Rule 205-3(b) permits a registered investment adviser to accept performance fees from a PIC if the PIC, and all equity owners of the PIC, satisfy the eligibility requirements contained in Rule 205-3(b)(1). Where a second-tier PIC is itself the equity owner of a first-tier PIC seeking to enter into a performance fee advisory contract, the equity owners of the second-tier PIC must themselves satisfy the eligibility requirements of Rule 205-3(b)(1). In proposing Rule 205-3, the Commission stated that:

> A question may arise as to the requirements of the proposal where a private investment company is itself the equity owner of another private investment company, registered investment company or business development company seeking to enter into a performance fee contract under the proposal. In such a case, the same rule applicable to the first level private investment company, *i.e.*, that each of its equity owners must satisfy one of the alternate tests of paragraph (b)(1) of the rule, applies to the second (and any other) level private investment company. This result is required by paragraph (b)(2) which excludes any private investment company from the companies referred to in paragraph (b)(1) of the rule unless each equity owner satisfies the eligibility standards of paragraph (b).[4]

Rule 205-3 and the Proposing Release clearly state the Commission's intent that equity owners of second-tier (and any other tier) PICs investing in first-tier PICs must satisfy the eligibility requirements of the Rule before the adviser to the first-tier PICs may receive performance fees. Although one of the policy reasons for this requirement is to ensure that an adviser does not pool small client accounts to circumvent the objective eligibility standards of the Rule,[5] the Commission did not so qualify the Rule, but adopted it without regard to whether the PICs were organized by the adviser. In view of the clear language of the Rule and the Proposing Release, we decline to grant EBF the requested relief by no-action or interpretive response.

* * * *

---

[4] See *Conditional Exemption to Allow Registered Investment Advisers to Charge Fees Based upon a Share of Capital Gains or upon Capital Appreciation of a Client's Account*, IA-961, 50 FR 11718, 11721-22 n.21 (1985) ("***Proposing Release***").

[5] *Id.*, at 11721.

Amerivest Invest. Mgmt., LLC

IA Act § 205(a)(1), SEC No-Action Letter Ref. No. 20144101037 (Aug 19, 2014)

Response of the Chief Counsel's Office

Division of Investment Management

Your letter dated August 18, 2014 requests our assurance that we would not recommend enforcement action to the Securities and Exchange Commission under § 205(a)(1) of the Investment Advisers Act of 1940 against **Amerivest Investment Management, LLC** (*Amerivest*), an investment adviser that is an affiliate of **TD Ameritrade, Inc.** (*TD Ameritrade*) and is registered with the Commission under the Advisers Act, if Amerivest offers to certain clients an advisory fee rebate (the "***Proposed Fee Arrangement***") in the manner described in your letter and summarized below.

Background

You state the following:

Amerivest currently offers a discretionary advisory service known as **Amerivest Portfolios**, which is made available to retail brokerage clients of TD Ameritrade (the "***Service***"). Under the Service, Amerivest serves as the investment adviser to the clients and is responsible for implementing the asset allocation models and corresponding mutual fund and exchange-traded fund investment recommendations provided by **Morningstar Associates, LLC** (Morningstar Associates). Morningstar Associates serves as an investment adviser and independent consultant to Amerivest with respect to the Service, but does not enter into an investment advisory agreement with Amerivest's clients. Amerivest vets and implements Morningstar Associates' investment recommendations in their entirety, subject to non-investment related factors such as tax considerations and any reasonable restrictions a client may impose.[1] Morningstar Associates is compensated by Amerivest based on a fee schedule that includes an asset-based fee component and a

[1] You state that Amerivest's vetting process is designed to consider whether the asset allocations and securities recommendations provided by Morningstar Associates are reasonable in relation to the investment mandate and risk/return characteristics of each model portfolio and the overall operation of the Service. You state further that Amerivest may choose not to implement a recommendation provided by Morningstar Associates based on non-investment related considerations that might adversely impact client accounts (*e.g.*, the tax ramifications of substituting one ETF for another). You represent that the mere fact that Amerivest has deviated from or declined to implement a recommendation of Morningstar Associates will not—in and of itself—cause a client to be ineligible for the rebate.

licensing fee component. Accordingly, Morningstar Associates does not receive performance-based compensation.

Under the Proposed Fee Arrangement, Amerivest would continue to charge a quarterly asset-based advisory fee in advance. However, Amerivest would rebate investment advisory fees for eligible clients who are invested in a model portfolio that experiences two consecutive discrete calendar quarters of negative performance (before advisory fees) during a twelve-month period (a "***Term***"). The amount of the rebate would be equal to 100% of the advisory fees paid by each eligible client for the two calendar quarters in which the performance composite for the model portfolio corresponding to the client's account experienced negative performance. To determine whether performance was negative, each calendar quarter would be measured independently; the performance for multiple quarters would not be aggregated. Amerivest will fully and clearly disclose the rules governing eligibility for the Proposed Fee Arrangement and the methodology for calculating the composite performance (together, the "***Rebate Terms***") to all clients participating in the Service. Amerivest will follow the Rebate Terms and apply them fairly and consistently. In the event that Amerivest decides to change the Rebate Terms in a manner that would disadvantage participating clients, Amerivest will notify participating clients of the change, and no such change will become effective prior to the commencement of the next subsequent Term.

The Proposed Fee Arrangement will not contain any "catch up" or other provision that would allow Amerivest to recapture foregone fees through future appreciation. Amerivest will not deviate from or otherwise seek to influence Morningstar Associates' investment recommendations for the purpose of avoiding payment of any fee rebate under the Proposed Fee Arrangement. Amerivest may deviate from Morningstar Associates' recommendations solely: (i) for non-investment and non-performance related reasons such as tax considerations or reasonable client restrictions; or (ii) to the extent so required to fulfill its fiduciary duty to clients. Amerivest will make and keep true, accurate and current records detailing any such deviation and explaining why such deviation was necessary. There will be no contract, arrangement, or other understanding, explicit or tacit, by and between Amerivest and Morningstar Associates or any principals thereof, such that Morningstar Associates' compensation or continued engagement would be affected by the payment or non-payment by Amerivest of any fee rebate pursuant to the Proposed Fee Arrangement.

The Proposed Fee Arrangement would be implemented for (i) all new discretionary client accounts, and (ii) all existing discretionary client accounts with a new deposit of $25,000 or higher, provided that the new deposit represents net new assets to Amerivest. Clients would not have to elect to participate in the Proposed Fee Arrangement or request a fee rebate. The fee rebate would automatically apply in the event of two consecutive calendar quarters of negative performance. To be eligible for the Proposed Fee Arrangement, an account must participate in the Service for a minimum of two consecutive calendar quarters during the Term, and during such participation the client must not withdraw more than the required deposit of $25,000 to remain eligible for subsequent quarters. Amerivest would reserve the right to extend the Term for additional twelve-month periods or to discontinue the Proposed Fee Arrangement upon ninety days advance written notice to clients.

Subject to enforcing the requirements set forth in the preceding paragraph, Amerivest will not take any action for the purpose of negating or compromising a client's eligibility for the rebate, including, without limitation, any action that would result in a client no longer participating in the Service.

Analysis

Section 205(a)(1) of the Advisers Act generally prohibits registered investment advisers from entering into, extending, renewing or performing any investment advisory contract that provides for compensation to the investment adviser on the basis of a share of capital gains or capital appreciation in a client's account or any portion thereof. Section 205(a)(1) is designed, among other things, to eliminate "profit sharing contracts [that] are nothing more than 'heads I win, tails you lose' arrangements," and that "encourage advisers to take undue risks with the funds of clients," to speculate, or to overtrade.[2]

You argue that § 205(a)(1) does not, on its face, extend to fee waivers or rebates that are contingent on negative performance. You acknowledge, however, that the SEC staff in [*Contingent Advisory Compensation Arrangements*, IA-721, 45 FR 34876 (1980)]

---

[2] *Trainer, Wortham & Co., et al.*, SEC Staff No-Action Letter (Dec. 6, 2004) (***Trainer***), *citing* S. Rep. No. 1775, 76th Cong., 3d Sess. 22 (1940), H.R. Rep. No. 2639, 76th Cong., 3d Sess. 29 (1940), and Securities and Exchange Commission, *Investment Counsel, Investment Management, Investment Supervisor and Investment Advisory Services*, H.R. Doc. 477, 76th Cong., 2nd Sess. at 30 (1939).

(**Release 721**) stated that the concerns animating the performance fee ban "are as apposite to advisory fees which are contingent upon an advisory account obtaining a certain level of performance as they are to fees which vary directly with capital gains or appreciation."

You note that the SEC staff has nonetheless provided no-action assurances in situations where fees are contingent on performance, but the conflicts of interest associated with performance fees are not present or are substantially mitigated.[3] In particular, you state that in ***Trainer*** the SEC staff took the position that although a general satisfaction guarantee supported by the offer of a full refund was a contingent fee arrangement squarely within the scope of Release 721, it was "structured in a manner that would greatly reduce any incentive on the part of the advisers to take undue risks, speculate, or overtrade" and "could serve to encourage the advisers to develop a strong culture of client service and responsiveness."[4]

While you acknowledge that the Proposed Fee Arrangement represents a contingent fee arrangement of the kind prohibited by §205(a)(1) for the reasons discussed in Release 721, you argue that several aspects of the Proposed Fee Arrangement make it highly unlikely that Amerivest would attempt to avoid the rebate by taking undue risks, timing transactions in a client's account or over-trading. In particular, you argue that Amerivest would not be in a position to directly affect the value of a client's account because Morningstar Associates, an investment adviser that is independent from Amerivest, would be responsible for security selection and asset allocation recommendations with respect to the model portfolios. Moreover, you believe that any incentive that Amerivest might have to override Morningstar Associates' asset allocation recommendations in order to invest in more speculative investments is mitigated by the inability to recapture waived or rebated fees. You argue that the Proposed Fee Arrangement is designed to further align Amerivest's interests with those of its clients because Amerivest does not make money if an eligible client does not make money. You contend that the Proposed Fee Arrangement is the opposite of the "heads I win, tails you

---

[3] In addition, the SEC staff has stated that §205(a)(1) does not prohibit a voluntary refund of advisory fees by an investment adviser, provided that there is no contractual provision or other understanding between the adviser and the client regarding a fee refund or waiver related to investment performance. *Investment Advisers, Interpretive Matters (George Coleman)*, SEC Staff No-Action Letter (Jul. 18, 1995).

[4] *Trainer.*

lose" approach that § 205(a)(1) was designed to prevent.

[no action recommendation]

We believe that certain aspects of the Proposed Fee Arrangement—particularly the role of Morningstar Associates in selecting securities and making asset allocation recommendations and the limited discretion Amerivest would have to deviate from such recommendations—help to alleviate the concerns that form the basis of § 205(a)(1). Based on the facts and representations in your letter, we would not recommend enforcement action to the Commission under § 205(a)(1) of the Advisers Act against Amerivest if Amerivest enters into the Proposed Fee Arrangement as described in your letter and summarized above.

Our position is based particularly on your representations that:

(1) Amerivest will fully and clearly disclose the Rebate Terms to all clients participating in the Service, and will follow the Rebate Terms and apply them fairly and consistently;

(2) In the event that Amerivest decides to change the Rebate Terms in a manner that may disadvantage participating clients, Amerivest will notify participating clients of the change, and no such change will become effective prior to the commencement of the next subsequent Term;

(3) The Proposed Fee Arrangement will not contain any "catch up" or other provision that would allow Amerivest to recapture foregone fees through future appreciation;

(4) Amerivest will not deviate from or otherwise seek to influence Morningstar Associates' investment recommendations for the purpose of avoiding payment of any fee rebate under the Proposed Fee Arrangement;

(5) Amerivest may deviate from Morningstar Associates' recommendations solely: (i) for non-investment and non-performance related reasons such as tax considerations or reasonable client restrictions; or (ii) to the extent so required to fulfill its fiduciary duty to clients;

(6) Amerivest will make and keep true, accurate and current records detailing any such deviation and explaining why such deviation was necessary;

(7) The mere fact that Amerivest has deviated from or declined to implement a recommendation of Morningstar Associates will not—in and of itself—result in a loss of eligibility for the rebate;

(8) There will be no contract, arrangement, or other understanding, explicit or tacit, by and between Amerivest and Morningstar Associates or any principals thereof, such that Morningstar Associates' compensation or continued engagement would be affected by the payment or non-payment by Amerivest of any fee rebate pursuant to the Proposed Fee Arrangement; and

(9) Subject to enforcing certain eligibility requirements, Amerivest will not take any action for the purpose of negating or compromising a client's eligibility for the rebate including, without limitation, any action that would result in a client no longer participating in the Service.

Because our position is based on the facts and representations made in your letter, you should note that any different facts or circumstances might require a different conclusion.